An Outlet For A Creative Mind.........

ThinkQuest~2010

ThinkQuest~2010

International Conference on Contours of Computing Technology

Chairperson
Dr. H. B. Kekre
(Senior Professor, MPSTME, NMIMS, Mumbai, India)

Review Panelists

Dr. B. K. Lande
(Deputy Director, VJTI, Mumbai, India)

Dr. B. Krishan Mohan
(Principal Research Engineer, CSRE , IIT Bombay, Mumbai, India)

Dr. U. B. Desai
(Director, IIT Hyderabad, India)

Dr. Chelpa lingam
(Principal, MGM College of Engg. & Technology, Kamothe, Navi Mumbai, India)

Dr. S. N. Merchant
(Professor, IIT Bombay, Mumbai, India)

Dr. M. G. Phadnis
(M.D., CoreTech, Ex HOD, BARC, India)

Dr. Sanjay Moghe
(CEO, RFIC Solution, USA)

Dr. Vijay Wadhai
(Professor and Dean Research, MITSOT, MAE, Pune, India)

Dr. Sunita Sane
(Professor and Head, Computer Technology Dept. VJTI, Mumbai, India)

Dr. Avinash Keskar
(Professor, Dept. of Electronics & Comp Science, Dean (R&D),Visvesaraya Regional college of Engineering, Nagpur, India)

Dr. S. C. Sahastrabuddhe
(Director, Dhirubhai Ambani Institute of Information & Communication Technology, Mumbai, India)

Dr. Vamsi Gondi
(Associate Researcher, LRSN University, France)

Dr. S. Dasgupta
(Asst. Professor, Semiconductor Device and VLSI Technology, IIT Roorkee, India)

Dr. A. K. Saxena
(Professor, Semiconductor Device and VLSI Technology, IIT Roorkee, India)

Dr. Meena Panse
(Professor, Electrical Dept., VJTI, Mumbai, India)

Dr. M. U. Kharat
(Head Computer Dept., MET, Nashik, India)

Dr. S. G. Bhirud
(Professor, Dept. of Computer, VJTI, Mumbai, India)

Dr. Sanjay Sarang
(Director, Kynetia & cons, SUN Microsystems, USA)

Dr. Kamlan Fathulla
(University of Northampton, UK)

Dr. Kamsetty Rao
(Professor, Texas University, USA)

Dr. N. M. Singh
(Professor, Electrical Dept., VJTI, Mumbai, India)

Dr. S.A. Bhosale
(Business Head, Growel Softech Ltd., Mumbai, India)

Prof. D. R. Mehta
(Asst. Professor, Electrical Dept., VJTI, Mumbai, India)

Prof. M. M. Shah
(Technical Activity Chair, IEEE Bombay Section, Mumbai, India)

Prof. Amudha JayKumar
(Asst. Professor, Electrical Dept., VJTI, Mumbai, India)

Mr. Ashok Jagtia
(Secretary, EEE Bombay Section, Mumbai, India)

Convener
Principal S. J. Pise, BGIT, Mumbai, India

Event-Chief Coordinator
Prof. Ajit B. Parab, BGIT, Mumbai, India

Event Coordinators
Prof. Prasad Kulkarni   Prof. Surabhi Crasto
Prof. Sachin Kadam   Prof. Harshal Dalvi
Mr.Yogesh Sawant

Support Team
BGIT STAFF

An Outlet For A Creative Mind.........

ThinkQuest~2010

International Conference on Contours of Computing Technology

On

13th and 14th March, 2010

In
Association with

 Springer

Organised By

Maratha Mandir's

BABASAHEB GAWDE INSTITUTE OF TECHNOLOGY
MUMBAI

Editor
S. J. Pise
Babasaheb Gawde Institute of Technology
Mumbai
India
principal@mmbgit.org

ISBN 978-81-322-1707-7   ISBN 978-81-8489-989-4 (eBook)
DOI 10.1007/978-81-8489-989-4
Springer New Delhi Dordrecht Heidelberg London New York

Printed on acid-free paper

Springer is part of Springer Science+Business Media (www.springer.com)

From the Trustee's Desk

The world around us is witnessing a rapid development in technology and communication. In order to be ready for the future challenges in technical education, we at BGIT offer courses in Diploma Engineering at a level comparable to the very best in the world.

The challenge before us is to create and develop a system that prepares each individual student in our institute to work in a global environment with ease and comfort. The mission of BGIT is to anticipate the technological needs for India and to plan and prepare a system to cater to men.

BGIT is renowned for cutting edge training program and for imparting state of the art education to the students. Through rigorous and transparent admission process we attract some of the brightest students. Those selected go through one of the toughest under graduate program which emphasize on innovative thinking, effective expression, ability to lead and determination to achieve one's goal.

We organize programs for faculty development both for our own staff and for professors from other engineering institutions. At the same time we develop close collaboration with industry by organizing various industrial visits and expert lectures from eminent professionals from reputed organizations.

Our institute is proud to play an active role in the creation and nurturing of future engineers of this country and maintains a symbiotic relationship with the industry and this year we would like to take this opportunity to reinforce it even further thank you.

Mr. R.P. Gawde
Hon. Secretary, Maratha Mandir

From the Principal's Desk

It has been an encouraging experience to organize **Thinkquest – 2010** International Conference on Contours of Computing Technology in association with Springer Publication and technical sponsor IEEE Bombay section and industry Giants PCS & Siemens technology.

All the concerned dignitaries extended full co-operation for which we are grateful to them. We are to state that the response is so over-whelming that it indicates the urge for basic research in this field which is the need of the time for our national development. We are thankful to all who exhibited their initiative.

Thanks are due to all the members of Organizing Committee who have very successfully completed their tasks in addition to their day to day duties.

We are extremely happy to present this issue containing meaningful papers in the field of Computing Technology.

Principal S.J. Pise
Babasaheb Gawde Institute of Technology

Contents

Access networks aided network selection procedure for heterogeneous wireless and cellular networks

Dr. Vamsi Krishna Gondi[1] · **Mr. Nazim Agoulmine[2]** · **Dr. Vijay Wadhai[3]**

[1]Networks and Multimedia Systems Group, University of Evry-Val d'Essonne, Evry Courcouronnes, France
[2]Networks and Multimedia Systems Group, University of Evry-Val d'Essonne, Evry Courcouronnes, France
[3]Prof and Dean Maharashtra Institute of Technology, Pune, India

I. Introduction

Advances in wireless communication technologies are driving the evolution toward B3G networks to provide rich services at low cost for the end users. These networks consists of wide range coverage with 3G networks, medium range high bandwidth WIMAX network and low range high bandwidth low cost WLAN networks. These networks provide different services in different access networks which are likely operated by different service providers. These networks are intended to provide users different IP based services at any time any where independent of the operating scenarios. Wireless technologies provide extensible service coverage by using adjacent cells, each one containing a radio transceiver known as point of attachment (PoA) in order to serve the mobile nodes (MN) in their coverage areas. MNs may need to change their PoA while moving in order to maintain a suitable radio link quality; this process is called handover. When this mobility is achieved in the same technologies with the same operator, it is called horizontal handover and when it is between different technologies and operators, it is called vertical handover. In order to achieve seamless handovers and hide it to users at the application level, there is a need for changes in the communications management mechanisms on the access networks and the terminals. For example, link layer protocols will need to implement discovery, selection, and link reestablishment mechanisms. Furthermore, IP implements similar ones to allow the MNs acquire new IP configuration and update the location information whenever an IP handover occurs.

After the adaptation of the IEEE 802.11 in the early 2000, operators have planned to provide services through the WLAN hot spots, but due to its limited range (about 200 meters), a single operator cannot provide the access in all places however different operators can establish agreements amount them to provide a global connectivity. WI-FI alliance [1] has been launched o facilitate the inter-network and inter-operator roaming among different WISPs (Wifi Internet Service

Providers) and vendors. IEEE 802.16 [2] is a technology that provides broadband wireless access. WiMax the commercial name given to the IEEE 802.16 standard is a wireless technology designed to cover wide geographical areas serving large numbers of users at low cost. Initial study has been done by the WiMax forum to define inter working mechanisms with cellular networks as defined by the 3GPP system [3]. At the same time the 3GPP standardization has also issued documents 3GPP 23.234, 3GPP 23.934 [4–7] to specify the inter working mechanisms across WLAN and 3GPP networks. WLAN and PLMN (Public Land Mobile Network) are classified into two different mechanisms; loosely coupled inter working and tightly coupled inter working [8]. To provide inter working across heterogeneous networks security authentication, mobility management must be maintained across the access networks [5]. According to [9] roaming involves the network selection, authentication, authorization, and billing settlements between operators. The current network selection procedures are limited and provide seamless roaming mechanisms with little efficiency operating passively with very limited resources. The proposed mechanisms in the above mentioned solutions are not suitable for real time data applications. Also the proposed mechanisms don't have any clarifications on issues of QoS, SLAs using for network selection which place an important role during authentication and service adaptation for data after network selection procedures. The issues of user mobile node mobility are not discussed efficiently in the previously proposed network selections procedure. There

S.J. Pise (ed.), *ThinkQuest 2010*, DOI 10.1007/978-81-8489-989-4_1,

is a need for new network selection procedures to adapt for heterogeneous networks using WLAN, WIMAX and 3G networks, where a user move across these networks using services efficiently. From the network operator's perspective, network selection for different services adapted for the users is the biggest challenge, as it involves the resource management, proper network planning involved existing networks and new technologies adding onto existing one. Involvement of multiple operator networks in the areas of operation complicates NS for heterogeneous networks. The ultimate goal of providing low cost efficient services for users is compromised without network selection procedures. In this process there is a need for mechanisms where the user mobility and access mechanisms has to be controlled from the network side as the amount of resources available at operator network are far superior than in the mobile terminals and also the knowledge of operation involves high technical expertise where most subscribers lacks. Taking all the above mentioned problems we are proposing a network selection procedures involved mobile terminal with the network assistance. Using network assistance the several issues such as coverage of multiple access technologies can be determined precisely, future location of mobile terminal before disconnecting the current connected network, allocation of resources even before mobile terminal roam/handover to future network, SLAs with visiting networks as well as current user profiles. In this paper we are proposing enhanced as well as novel mechanisms at various levels of access networks, to develop a network assisted or aided network selection i.e. user terminal during mobility in heterogeneous networks will be assisted by the networks to achieve in an efficient manner their handover so that it is transparent to the user. In this process we have identified two scenarios; one is user accessing initially, and the other is when the user is performing handover or roaming. In the initial method with the available profile of access network the mobile terminal performs network selection; the profiles are update regularly by access network. In the second process mobile terminal is assisted by access network i.e. the access network does the network selection and ask mobile terminal to trigger handover on the selected network. The mobile terminal communicates regularly with home access network providing information of required bandwidth, current location from GPS, battery status, available interfaces and scanned networks with corresponding SNR. In this process we have identified different mechanisms to assists for context transfers from access networks and mobile terminal. The most suitable is EAP coupled with AAA as a solution. EAP is generally widely used in wireless networks, and due to its pass through behavior for accessing networks at layer 2, no modifications is required at access points level in access networks. In this paper we are proposing to extend EAP with a new method called handover with NS as subtype to provide communication channel between access network and user terminal. This new method collects data

available in the user terminal including available networks in the vicinity and sends them to the network using the proposed extension of EAP to be assisted in the mobility. While in the case of cellular networks there is no need for context transfer mechanisms as this is been achieved using special dedicated GTP sessions by access networks and mobile terminals. On the other side the operator access networks are widely supported by AAA to provide authentication and access support such as billing, profile maintenance of users etc.. The AAA server can be modified adding new modules with the existing support to provide seamless mobility support. In our architecture we are proposing to add new modules such as network selection, security, mobility, QoS and presence in AAA to support handover management. These modules can be used as add-ons so that the operator can use according to their convenience. Also using these modules we are enabled to provide context management for access networks to provision the information of users for low latency handover. In network selection procedure the home AAA server of mobile terminal receives a request through EAP NS, AAA provides the support for its request and chooses best available network by negotiating with the future visiting network of mobile terminal. The proposed mechanism also evaluates at each time the position of mobile terminal and its mobility pattern to estimate the future location of user at any given instance. We propose to use a GIS (Geographic Information Server) system to identify the available networks in the vicinity of the user terminal. Based on the information in the context, the mobility pattern and a set of information provided by the user terminal and future visiting networks, the network selection mechanisms on access network AAA server determine the best target network for handover for mobile terminal.

The remaining paper is organized as follows; issues of network selection for heterogeneous networks are discussed in section 2 of this paper. Section 3 provides localization mobile terminal including mobile terminal location identification procedures, Geo-information system models and mobility prediction models. Section 4 defines mechanisms for network selection; section 5 provides message exchange between different components involved in network selection procedures. Section 6 provides information on new methods that are included in EAP and AAA for supporting network selection procedures and final section concludes our work and future work.

2. Network selection issues

At any given instance a mobile terminal/card is capable to scan the available networks in its vicinity. This capability exists in any wireless or cellular networks. With multiple network interfaces, terminals are able to collect information on potentially heterogeneous networks belonging to one or several operators. In case of virtual operators, access network infrastructure including e.g. the access points can be shared by multiple operators [10]. In this case, the user needs to have a set of credentials to be able to access to these networks. Sometime this process is made easier if the virtual operation have roaming agreement between them. This functionality is largely used in cellular networks to provide users with a universal cellular access worldwide. This is possible because operators have established among them specific roaming service level agreements (SLA) to allow their customers to roam and handover in other visiting networks. When a user of a network operator wants to access different operator networks, issues of SLAs (roaming agreements) arrive between the user and the network operator and between operators. The network selection procedure should take into consideration the right of the user to access the network as well as their right to use some specific service, authorization policies and privacy policies for the access networks

3. Localization and mobility prediction

3.1 Location identification

The User Location identification aims to locate the user terminal in the ecosystem. If the user is connected to an UMTS network, the Cell ID and Observed time difference can be used. The cell ID based positioning method is the most trivial indication of the user location, and does not require specific functionality in the UMTS network. It is however not very accurate, because the average size of radio cells in UMTS can vary from 800 meters radius in dense urban areas to about 6 kilometers in rural areas. With additional measurements it is sometimes possible to achieve a higher accuracy [11]. The Observed Time Difference Of Arrival (OTDOA) method uses the observed time differences between the mobile terminal and nearest base stations. The measurements of different base stations are used to triangulate the location. The accuracy of the OTDOA positioning method varies depending on the actual location of the terminal within the cell. Especially if a terminal is close to one of the base stations, it may be difficult to "hear" the two other base stations needed for the triangulation. The accuracy is approximately between 50 and 200 meters. The GPS method requires the mobile terminal is equipped with a GPS receiver. The accuracy is approximately of 50 meters in a dense urban environment and a few meters in an open environment. Determining the location of an end-user in a WLAN network can be achieved using a triangulation method similar to UMTS triangulation method described above. A common method is based on signal strengths to multiple (more than three) Access Points, which can be obtained from both the AP itself and the client device

3.2 GIS Information model

A Geographic Information Server maintains information about the coverage of operators' networks The geographical area of the location is divided into different cells covering the operators' networks range. In this process the location

of BS (Base Station) or AP and their ranges are mapped to these cells.

This server can therefore identify at any given time the available access networks at a particular location. The GIS is also capable to predict the location of the mobile terminal during mobility. For that it is necessary to provide it with information such as user terminal mobility, speed of the terminal, present location and previous locations within the stipulated time constant using Gauss-Markov model [8]. The defined prediction model is presented in the following section.

The GIS is used whenever a mobile terminal is requesting support for network selection during mobility. The mobile terminal sends a request with the current data available from its GPS to the network. The network forward the request to GIS server to (1) predict the future location of mobile terminals, (2) map this geographic location to available networks database in the vicinity; (3) select the available networks that conforms to the selection criteria (user right, QoS, cost, etc) (4) sends as a reply to the mobile terminal.

3.3 User Mobility prediction

Several Mobility models [12] have been proposed in the literature. Among them, the Random Walk Mobility Model and the Random Waypoint Mobility Model are the two most common mobility model used by researchers. The current speed and direction of a mobile station is independent of its past speed and direction. This characteristic can generate unrealistic movements such as sudden stops and sharp turns. To fix this discrepancy, we use in this work the Gauss-Markov Mobility Model [12]. This model is designed to adapt various levels of randomness using one tuning parameter.

4. Network selection algorithm

During the handover procedure, the user terminal needs to select the most appropriate access network of the same or different access technologies to continue ongoing session seamlessly. However, as the terminal is blind of the global situation in its neighborhood, we propose that in any situation the terminal collaborate with the network to be assisted in this procedure. The network selection service in the network assists the mobile terminal in its hand over ensuring it to select the best target network depending on the available bandwidth, QoS as well as the cost, for instance when the user is browsing (low bit rate), VoIP and video on demand services (high bit rate).

Once the localization of the mobile terminal evaluated and the set of networks that are operated in the vicinity of that localization, the home access network of mobile terminal performs the network selection with the help of visiting networks. The local database on the mobile terminal is stored with the required information from home network. These details contain available access networks, SLAs, roaming agreements between other operators, cost of communication for using different access technologies. At any given instance the mobile terminal can access this information for decision making. The mobile terminal has capability to access and initiate different interfaces available such as WLAN, WIMAX and 3G to collect details of networks availability its RSS and SNR.

Initial network selection procedure involves scanning all the network interfaces available on the mobile terminal. Once the wireless interfaces are identified, interfaces are probed for available access networks in the vicinity of mobile terminal.

We have identified two working scenarios for network selection procedure one is when the mobile terminal does initial access and other is when performing handover or roaming. In the initial access information is collected from interfaces and previous connected networks. The current location of mobile terminal identified by GPS is provided in the extension of the EAP request to the access network.

The new extension for EAP to supporting HO [13] allows the mobile terminal to request assistance during mobility to its home network. In this method the handover method is subdivided in several methods, NS is one such sub method. On the other side the AAA [14] is also extended so that it recognizes handover and NS as sub methods. When required, the mobile terminal sends a request to the home network, to identify access networks in its future localization. It provides the current and previous GPS locations info and available access networks at that moment. Due to pass through behavior and already existing support for EAP and AAA in wireless networks we use new extensions instead of creating new protocols for context transfer. On the cellular networks the mobile terminal uses GTP session dedicated to the mobile terminal to send the information request to the server in the access networks. When the

AAA server receives the request, it communicates first with the GIS to identify the following location of the mobile terminal as well as the available networks at that location (and therefore their corresponding AAA). Then, it communicates with the other access networks AAA using radius roaming extensions [15] to retrieve information relates to the QoS in the target network, access policy and cost.

4.1 Network selection procedure in mobile terminal

Network selection engine in the mobile terminal is the core of the procedure, where it collects details from different entities of mobile terminal. It collects required QoS, expected cost of communication, available networks and their respective SNRs, location of mobile terminal and previous associated networks at that location and networks availability from the database provided by home operator network, SLAs and profiles. With the scanned networks and high value SNR networks are prioritized, from the previous connected networks are again prioritized with the context transferred information of networks availability from home network with the new protocols, later the networks belongs to home operators are given more priority than the visiting operator networks. These prioritized networks are sent to next procedures such as handover or authentication use. If ever the access networks are not available are out of range the NS procedure is performed again. The flow charts are mentioned in Figs. 1 and 2.

Network Selection during Initial Access: In this process the mobile terminal initiates the network selection procedure, after initiation the mobile terminal starts the network scan. During the network scan the device probes the different devices available and scans the available networks. The client terminal process the information from devices and process the SSID of the networks. And the terminal initi-

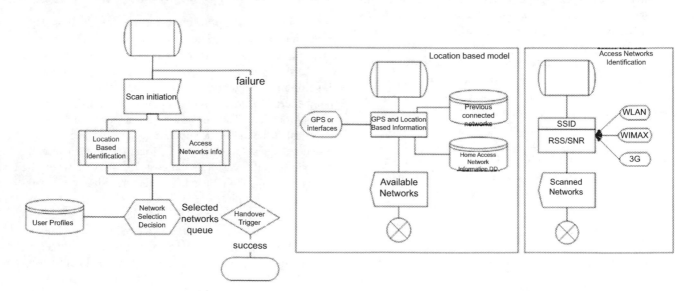

Fig. 1 Network selection procedure during initial access in mobile terminal

ates the location based process such as GPS, and available home network from the local database. With all the available networks gathered from different processes, policy of the user, client selects best suitable network. The client can initiates the NAI of the home network or depending on the selected network it can initiates the mediating network. The whole process is shown in Fig. 1. Network Selection during Handover or Roaming: In this process the mobile terminal constantly monitor the SNR and availability of bandwidth of the connected network. When the threshold of the required SNR and bandwidth are below the required par for services, the mobile terminal initiates network selection procedure. As in the initial process in this procedure GPS is triggered and current location between different time intervals are identified and sent to home access network through EAP extensions. Mobile terminal also probes the available network interfaces for scanned SSIDs and their respective SNRs, these information is also passed to home access network. Once the data sent is processed on the home network, after selecting best available network, home AAA server sends a response with best suitable network. The process mechanism is shown in Fig. 2.

5. Message exchanges between different components

This section provides information on message exchange between different components of the architecture proposed in this paper. Figure 5 provides the detailed message sequence diagram. As mentioned earlier mobile terminal does the initial network selection with the available resources and perform authentication and access the networks. Once the mobile terminal is provided access NS procedure on terminal does communicates for context transfer with home access network.During an ongoing communication, mobile terminal initiates EAP HO NS and sends a request to AP or BS, then AP forwards the request to AAA of the access network. Checking the realm of the user with NS request, AAA server forwards the request to home AAA erver of the user or process locally. When the local network has a indirect SLA with the operator of user it forwards request through RII mediating network. Once the home AAA server receives the request for NS it process data inside the request, check GPS locations and scanned SSIDs. The AAA server sends a request to GIS server with the available information; GIS server does the mobility prediction of the user and maps the location collects the available networks information and forwards to home AAA server. After checking the available access networks belongs to local or visiting networks (direct or indirect SLA), AAA sends a radius NS request to that access networks AAA.

After receiving request, visiting networks check available resources of the AP or BS and responds with available networks as a response to home network. If ever the operators doesn't have direct SLAs they use RII mediating network for network selection. Once the network selection is performed the home access networks AAA sends EAP response to mobile terminal with the available access networks suitable at current and predicted location. Once NS is performed in the access networks, they initiate next steps

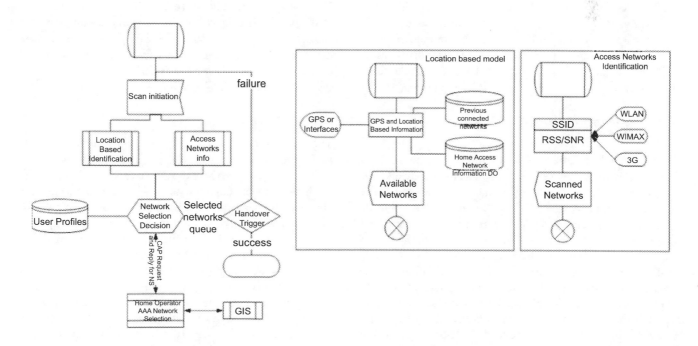

Fig. 2 Network selection procedure during handover or roaming in mobile terminal

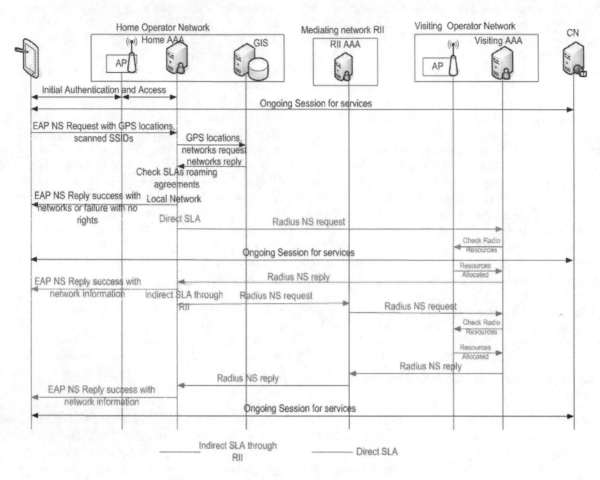

Fig. 3 Message sequence exchange between components using proposed mechanism

such as security and mobility context for the mobile terminal and visiting networks. Once NS, security and mobility context are initiated, mobile terminal does initiate handover, using this procedure latency for handover is reduced drastically and whole process is controlled at every single step of handover making this architecture robust and secured.

5.1   Network selection procedure in access networks

As shown in Fig. 3 the EAP NS on the client communicates with the home AAA server with the target network IDs, home AAA differentiates with the Local networks, networks which have direct SLA agreement or have with the RII mediating network [16]. According to the type of network home AAA process the information in different manner. If the home network have a indirect SLA, through the RII server home AAA server sends a radius NS extensions request to the RII server, RII server process the information and adds the request to the database with the stripped user ID and the access network. With the available target lists the AAA of RII sends a NS request to AAA of the visiting network. Visiting network process the available information and sends the available target ID as a reply to the RII.

If ever the request failed it sends NS failure as code value of the packet. If ever the visiting network has a direct SLA the home network communicates with the visiting network directly. In this case it sends a user without any stripped ID of the user, after checking the available resources the visiting network sends a reply with a NS extension of AAA.

6.   Conclusions

The paper proposes new network selection procedure using access networks consent. The proposed mechanism supports WLAN, WIMAX and 3G networks. Using mobility prediction model coupled with GIS information system the access networks at future location of mobile terminal. Using pre handover mechanisms with EAP HO NS and AAA extensions proposed in this paper the home access networks negotiate with visiting access networks and networks entities to allocate and reserve resources for accommodating mobile terminals enabling the solution proposed is efficient. Using these mechanisms the mobile terminal mobility can be handled efficiently in any access networks. The proposed solution addresses all the issues that are raised by network selection procedures. As a part of our future work we are coupling this mechanism with security, mobility and handover management procedures to control and provide seamless handover during roaming

References

1. WI-FI Alliance WISP Roaming www.wi- fi.org
2. IEEE 802.16-2001, "IEEE Standard for Local and Metropolitan Area Networks Part 16: Air Interface for Fixed Broadband Wireless Access Systems," Apr. 8, 2002
3. http://www.wimaxforum.org/technology/documents
4. 3GPP 23.234 3GPP system to Wireless Local Area Network (WLAN) interworking; System description.
5. 3GPP 33.234 3G security; Wireless Local Area Network (WLAN) interworking security.
6. 3GPP 22.934 Feasibility study on 3GPP system to Wireless Local Area Network (WLAN) interworking
7. 3GPP 23.934 3GPP system to Wireless Local Area Network (WLAN) interworking; Functional and architectural definition
8. M. Buddhikot, G. Chandranmenon, S. Han, Y. W. Lee, S. Miller, L. Salgarelli, "Integration of 802.11 and Third-Generation Wireless Data Networks", Infocom 2003, San Francisco, USA, March 30 - April 3, 2002.
9. Wireless Hotspots and Network Interworking Initiative, Research and Development INTEL.
10. J. Arkko et all "Network Discovery and Selection Problem", IETF RFC draft-ietf-eap-netsel-problem-04 May 25, 2006
11. Yilin Zhao, "Standardization of Mobile Phone Positioning for 3G Systems", IEEE Communications Magazine, July 2002;
12. B. Liang and Z. Haas,"Predictive distance-based mobility management for PCS networks", In Proceedings of the Joint Conference of the IEEE Computer and Communications ocieties(INFOCOM),March 1999.
13. Aboba, B., Blunk, L., Vollbrecht, J., Carlson, J., and H. Levkowetz, "Extensible Authentication Protocol (EAP)",RFC 3748, June 2004.
14. Rigney, C., Willens, S., Rubens, A., and W. Simpson, "Remote Authentication Dial In User Service (RADIUS)", RFC 2865, June 2000.
15. Vamsi Krishna Gondi and Nazim Agoulmine "Radius Roaming Extensions", IETF RFC proposal draft-gondi-radext-radius-roaming-01, march 2008.
16. Vamsi Krishna Gondi and Nazim Agoulmine "Secured Roaming Over WLAN and WIMAX Networks using RII architecture", IEEE IM BCN 2007, munich, march 2007

ECG beat detection using wavelet denoising

Shilpa S. Joshi · Prerana Shrivastava

L.T.C.O.E, Navi Mumbai, India

1. Introduction

In the framework of biomedical engineering the analysis of Electrocardiogram (ECG) is one of the most wildly studied topics. The easy recording and visual interpretation of the non invasive Electrocardiogram signal is a powerful way for medical professional to extract important information about the clinical condition of their patients. The ECG is a measure of electrical activity associated with the heart. It is characterize by a time variant cyclic occurrence of patterns with different frequency contentment (QRS complex, P & T wave).The P wave corresponds to the contraction of the atria, the QRS complex to the contraction of the ventricles and the T wave to their depolarization. Because the ventricles contains more muscle mass than the atria the QRS complex is more intensive than the P wave. The QRS wave is therefore the most representative feature of the ECG. Further more, once the QRS complex has been identified other features of interest can be more easily detected. Accurate determination of the QRS complex in particular, accurate detection of the R peak is essential in computer based ECG signal analysis for a correct measurement of Heart Rate and Heart Rate variability. Automatic ECG processing consists essential in the detection and location of these signal characteristics points and is an important tool in the management of cardiac diseases. The most relevant task is the detection of the QRS complex, namely the R-peak after which analysis of each beat can be obtained.

The objective to analyze accurately an ECG signal is especially important where the features extraction of the ECG signal is to locate the interested characteristics points that can be used to detect possible cardio vascular abnormalities.

The topic is further complicated, since most of the times the desire ECG signal are either corrupted or embedded in noises. Since various sources of existing noise contraction are frequently such as Baseline drifts, Power line interference, motion artifacts and muscular activities. So obtaining the true ECG signa from the noisy observation

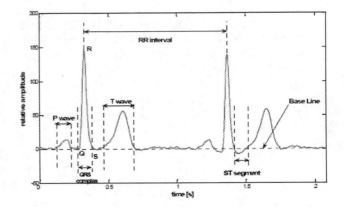

Fig. 1 Schematic of an ECG signal

can be formulated as problem of signal estimation or signal denoising [1, 10]. To clarify the process for automatic arrhythmia diagnosing the whole process is divided to three parts viz.

1.1 Wavelet denoising

Noise reduction in ECG signal is one of the main problems, which appear during the analysis of electrical activity of the heart. The various sources of the noises are difficult to remove using typical filtering procedures. Efficient analytical tool which allows to increase signal to noise ratio is a technique of averaging of cardiac cycles. Effectiveness of this method strictly depends on stable sinus rhythm that requirement is however not fulfilled in the case of Arrhythmia or the presence of man extra systoles. In such signals noise reduction is only possible with using more advanced signal processing method as wavelet denoising technique [3, 13].

1.2 R Peak detection

Many QRS detection algorithms [2, 9, 12, 15] were proposed in succession. In this paper algorithm based on first derivative only is applied for R peak detection.

S.J. Pise (ed.), *ThinkQuest 2010*, DOI 10.1007/978-81-8489-989-4_2,

The detection of the R peaks in an ECG signals provides information on Heart Rate, the conduction velocity, the conduction of tissues within the heart as well as various other abnormalities and thus it supplies evidence to support the diagnosis of cardiac diseases.

1.3 Calculation of heart rate

To predicts abnormalities through R-R interval.

2. Methods and materials

2.1 Wavelet denoising

The wavelets transform is widely used pre filtering step for subsequent R spike detection by thresholding of the coefficients. The time frequency decomposition is indeed a powerful tool to analyze a non stationery signals. Wavelets denoising procedures involves three steps and are developed in MATLAB.

• **Decomposition**

Choose a Wavelet; choose a level N.
Compute the wavelet decomposition of the signals at level N.

• **Thresholding details coefficients**

For each level from 1 to N select a threshold & apply soft thresholding to the detail coefficients.

• **Reconstruction**

Compute wavelet reconstruction using the original approximation coefficients of level N & the modified detail coefficients of levels from 1 to N [4].

As for thresholding, we can settle either a level dependent threshold vector of length N or a global threshold of a constant value for all levels. According to D. Donoho's method, the threshold estimate _ for denoising with an orthonormal basis is given by [5].

$$\delta = \sigma \sqrt{2 \log L} \tag{1}$$

Where the noise is Gaussian with standard Deviation σ of the DWT coefficient and L is the number of samples of the processed signal. This estimation concept is used by MATLAB. From another point of view, thresholding can be either soft or hard [5]. Soft thresholding is used for denoising which cause no discontinuation in the resetting signal. Denoising of ECG signal is displayed in Fig. 3. The removing of noise is carried out is carried out by thresholding of the DWT up to level 3. As a wavelet function we choose the sym 4 since in this application it performs better than db4. As a thresholding method we use soft global threshold δ of an estimated value given by equation (1).

2.2 R peak detection

In derivative based algorithm the high pass filter is often, in particular in the older algorithms, released as a differentiator. This method makes use of the characteristics steep slope of the QRS complex for its duration. On the contrary to the algorithms based on amplitude and the first derivatives, only the first derivative is considered and the amplitude information is rejected. According to algorithm proposed by Menard [8] the first derivative is calculated.

$$Y(n) = -2f(n-2) - f(n-1) + f(n+1) + 2f(n+2) \tag{2}$$

The slope threshold h is calculated as fraction of max slope for the first derivative.

$$h = \alpha \max \{Y(n)\} \tag{3}$$

The first derivative is searched, for points, which exceed the slope threshold. Then first point that exceeds the slope is taken as the onset of a QRS candidate (R Peak).

2.3 Calculation of heart rate

R peak detection is important in all kinds of ECG signal processing. The R wave is most often used in calculation of heart period (because of its relatively large size). The term "heart rate" normally refers to the rate of ventricular contractions. Ventricular rate can be determined by measuring the time intervals between the QRS complexes, which is done by looking at the R-R intervals.

$$\text{Heart rate} = 60 / \text{R-R interval} \tag{4}$$

The first thing to examine while analyzing an ECG signal is sinus rhythm. The criterion for a Normal Sinus Rhythms is:

• A QRS width should be of 0.04 to 0.12 seconds and be preceded by a P-wave.
• The rate for a normal sinus rhythm is 60 to 100 beats a minute. If the rate is below 60 beats a minute but the rest is the same it is a Sinus Bradycardia. If the rate is between 100 to 150 beats a minute with the same intervals it is a Sinus Tachycardia. When the pattern becomes irregular with normal intervals it is a Sinus Arrhythmia.

3. Results

The evaluation of detection methodology is carried out using records available online from the MIT-BIH arrhythmia database [16]. As presented in the table the results are analogous to the once obtained by wavelet denoising and derivative based methodologies. In this work we pointed out the noise reduction using wavelet transform associated with noise thresholding strategy. The advantage of wavelet method is possibility to receive good quality signal for bit to bit analysis. Further the possibility of detecting positions of R peaks in ECG signals is tested on the MIT-BIH arrhythmia database.

4. Conclusion

A set of recordings from MIT-BIH arrhythmia database is used to measure the accuracy of the algorithm and its

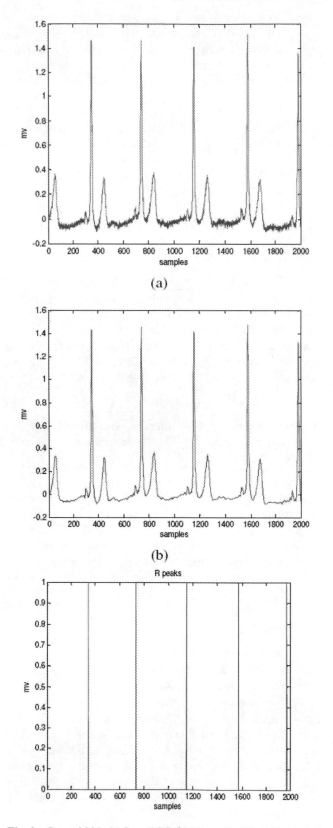

Fig. 2   Record 202: (a) Raw ECG (b) Filtered ECG (c) Estimated R peak locations

Table 1   Performance of this algorithm

S. N.	Data	Actual beast (N1)	Detected beast (N2)	Rate of detection = (N2/N1)* 100%
1	100	74	74	100
2	103	70	70	100
3	105	83	83	100
4	106	67	66	98.50
5	108	58	52	89.65
6	109	91	92	101.09
7	112	85	84	98.82
8	113	58	56	96.55
9	115	63	63	100
10	116	78	79	101.28
11	119	65	65	100
12	121	60	60	100
13	122	87	87	100
14	124	49	49	100
15	201	90	90	100
16	202	53	53	100
17	203	102	96	94.11
18	205	89	88	98.47
19	208	106	104	98.11
20	209	93	88	94.62
21	210	92	88	95.65
22	212	90	88	97.77
23	213	111	111	100
24	217	72	69	95.83
25	219	74	74	100
26	220	72	70	97.22
27	221	78	78	100
28	223	80	80	100
29	231	63	59	93.65
30	234	92	92	100

describing the steps consisting of pre processing stage dealing with noise reduction, feature extraction and the decision stage involved in R peak detection. The evaluation of the performance of the proposed algorithm is dealt in table. But for an advanced application, more information hidden in ECG signals should also be detected. The further information includes P-R interval, S-T interval, Q-T interval and distribution of Pwaves and T-waves. In this study, the goal was narrowed down for detecting two common illconditions of arrhythmia.

References

1. Wu YF and Rangayyan RM (2007) An algorithm for evaluating the performance of adaptive filters for the removal of artifacts in ECG signals. In Proc. 20th Canadian

reliability is evident by the results obtained. Section II deals with the main core of the paper and is focused on

Conf. Electrical and Computer Engineering (CCECE'07), Vancouver, BC, Canda

2. Meyer C, Gavela JF and Harris (2006) Combining algorithms in automatic detection of QRS complexes in ECG signals. IEEE Trans. Information Technology in Biomedicine 10 (3):468–475

3. Mahmoodabadi SZ, Ahmadian A, Abolhasani MD (2005) ECG Feature Extraction Using Daubechis Wavelets. Proceedings of the Fifth IASTED International Conference, Visualization, Imaging and Image processing, Benidorm, Spain

4. Nguyen T, Strang G (1996) Wavelets and Filter Banks. Wellesley-Cambridge Press

5. Oppenheim G, Poggi JM, Misiti M, Misiti Y (2001) Wavelet Toolbox. The Math Works , Inc., Natick, Massachusetts 01760

6. Haykin S (2002) Adaptive Filter Theory, 4th ed. Englewood Cliffs, N J: Prentice Hall PTR

7. Moody GB, Mark RG and Goldberger AL (2001) Physionet: A web-based resource for the study of physiologic signals. IEEE Engineering in Medicine and Biology Magazine 20(3):70–75

8. Menrad A et al. Dual microprocessor system for cardiovascular data acquisition, processing and recording. Proc. 1981 IEEE Int. Conf. Elect. Contr. Instrument, pp. 64–69

9. Afonso VX, Tompkins WJ, Nguyen TQ, Michler K and Luo S (1996) Comparing stress ECG enhancement algorithms. IEEE Engineering in Medicine and Biology Magazine 15(3): 37–44

10. Thakor NV and Zhu YS (1991) Applications of adaptive filtering to ECG analysis: Noise cancellation and arrhythmia detection. IEEE Trans. Biomedical Engineering 38(8): 785–794

11. Skordalakis E (1986) Syntactic ECG processing: A review. Pattern Recognition 977–985, 1979. 19:305–313

12. Tompkins WJ, Pan J (1985) A real time QRS detection algorithm. IEEE Trans. on Biomedical Engg BME-32, No. 3: 230–235

13. Polikar R (1998) Wavelet tutorial. eBook, http://users.rowan.edu

14. Rissam HS, Kishore S, Srivastava S, Bhatia ML, Trehan N (1998) Evaluation of cardiac symptoms by trans-telephonic electrocardiographic (TTEM)monitoring: preliminary experience. IndianHeart J 50(1):55–58

15. Friesen GM, Jannett TC, Jadallash MA, Yates SL, Ouint SR and Nagle HT A Comparison of the Noise Sensitivity of Nine QRS Detection Algorithms. IEEE Trans on Biomedical Engg 371:85–98

16. http://www.physionet.org./physiobank/database/mitdb

Remote monitoring and controlling of agriculture systems through wireless embedded system

Mrs. Shinde Sunita Sunil[1] · **Prof. Patil Ravindra Tanaji[2]**

[1]A. D. C. E. T. Ashta, India
[2]T. K. I. E. T. Warananagar, India

1. Introduction

As we know today everyone is facing electric load-shedding problem. This effect is more serious to industrial and agricultural sector. This tends to financial loss. We know our country is an agriculture-oriented country. About 70 percent of the people of India are still rooted in agriculture and related Sectors. According to the Central Statistical Organization (CSO) estimates, annual Economic surveys of the Union Government is that the decline in public investment in the Agricultural sector had arisen mainly because of the diversion of resources from creation of assets (Irrigation capacity, water management, rural infrastructure) into subsidies of various kinds-foods, fertilizers, water, power and so forth. Along with this, the person works day and night for our country, and us who is he? He is a farmer. The farmer works in his field facing with electricity problems (Load Shedding), Water management problem, etc that directly affects on the farm production and economy. Due to load shedding, farmers has to go at mid-night also. They are unable to take rest and so many financially bad things. These are harmful to his life. Now, what can we do for him? It is our responsibility to help the farmers by providing some technical facilities, which will be very helpful for farmer as well as changing lifestyle of farmers.

Taking into consideration all adverse situations related to electricity and water management we developed an electronic system which can be operated from remote place with help of mobile. They will help the farmer in saving water and electricity

2. Theory

Now a day's people facing the difficulties are:

2.1 Load shedding

Due to load shedding there is a big loss in agriculture area. In addition to this irregular supply failure creates the problems and loss of electricity and water.

2.2 Pump related problems

Like over load, dry run, single phase, etc.

2.3 Unpredictable rain conditions

Due to unpredictable raining and climates many times waste of water and electricity takes place or many times we keep pump off and there is no rain. It is waste of time if supply is there.

2.4 Moisture contents of Soil

Many times we use to give water without requirement and necessity. OR soil becomes total dry.

All above and other problems can be solved using electronic agro-control system and the hectic work of controlling pump at far distance from home can be controlled using wireless techniques. The agro-control system based on mobile technology is

- Cost effective to farmer.
- Provides Safety and relief.
- Reduces working time of farmer.

Here implies that an electronic Mobile unit is used to remotely Monitor and Control agro-parameters through GSM SMS.

Figure 1 shows the flow of SMS first farmer (user) sends a SMS to the GSM terminal, then our agro-control system reads it and do the monitoring and controlling actions and

S.J. Pise (ed.), *ThinkQuest 2010*, DOI 10.1007/978-81-8489-989-4_3,
© Springer India Pvt. Ltd. 2011

builds the reply SMS and sends it to the farmer (user) via the GSM terminal.

3. Block schematic of Agro-controller system

The Agro-Control system consists of different sensors, analog to digital converter (A/D), a microcontroller, and a GSM terminal, starter unit as it is shown in Fig. 2. When

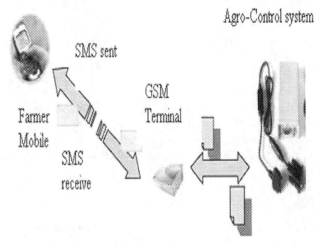

Fig. 1 The SMS flow in the agrocontrol system

the GSM terminal receives a message (SMS), the Micro-controller reads it via the serial port. The Microcontroller analyses this SMS and do the particular monitoring / controlling action. After a particular action the Microcontroller constructs the SMS. The SMS is sent to the GSM terminal via the serial port and then to the farmer (user) via the GSM network. This system is capable to control the many pump and agriculture parameters. The system consists of following control and monitoring parameters.

3.1 Motor/pump parameters

- Mains Supply
- Over Load
- Single Phase
- Dry Run
- Thermal Shutdown
- Auto/man start-stop

Time controlling and recording (ON-OFF)

3.2 Other parameters: (required in green house)

- Water level in Tank/Well
- Moisture in soil
- Temperature in the Farm (For green house)

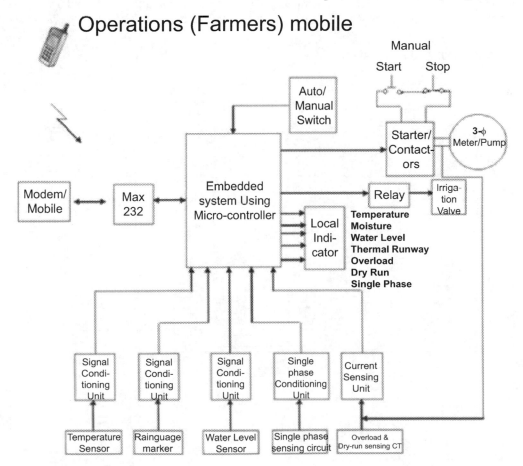

Fig. 2 Block diagram of agro-control system

3.3 Indicators

- Over Load
- Single Phase
- Dry Run
- Thermal Shutdown

3.4 Two way communication

- Status of all parameters indication to master mobile

4. Agro-control system design

4.1 H/W design and development

The system design basically consists of the Microcontroller unit along with the ADC, the LCD module, and the wireless module. Various signal conditioning circuits of the sensors, the controlling relay.

The microcontroller has four 8-bit I/O ports, port 0 to port 3. The output current of the microcontroller is about 150 µA that is very insufficient to drive certain modules and devices. Hence external pull up resistor banks of 4.7 KΩ are used. The clock to the microcontroller is given by 11.0592MHz crystal, as various standard baud rates for serial communication, can be derived from that frequency. Two capacitors of 33Pf are connected between each of the

pins of the crystal and ground to reduce the noise content of the crystal's output. The reset circuit consists of a 10µF capacitor between the Vcc and the reset pin (pin no. 9) and a resistor of 10K between ground and reset pin of the controller AT89S52. The reset time is given by $T = 0.693 \times 10K \times 10\mu F = 0.0693$ SecThis is sufficient time for the Microcontroller to be reset.

Interfacing

The microcontroller is interfaced with an ADC, a LCD display.

Port 0 – LCD Module

Port 1 – ADC data

Port 2 – Gives control signals to ADC, motor drive pin, overload and dry run sensing pin, water level1 sensing pin, LCD control pin.

Port 3 – RXD serial input port; TXD serial output port to modem.

4.2 Temperature sensing unit

LM35 is a linear device that converts temperature into voltage with slope of 10 mV/°C. So for 100°C the output of LM35 will be 100°C X10mV/°C = 1V. The signal conditioning circuit is used to adjust the gain as 8 required for ADC. Gain = 1+RV1/R1= 1+7/1= 8 Output of signal

Mini Microcontroller System

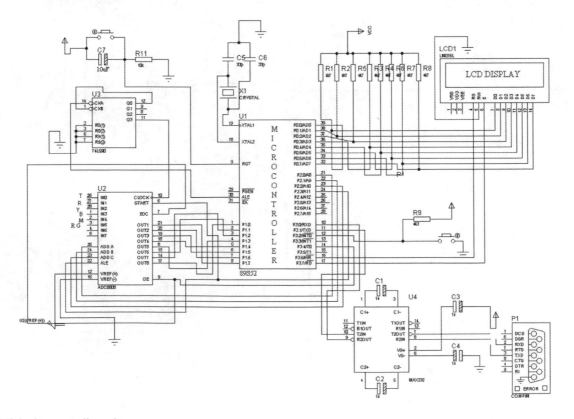

Fig. 3 Mini microcontroller unit

conditioner =0.5V X 8= 4V The signal conditioning circuit is used to adjust the gain as 8 required for ADC. Gain = 1+RV1/R1= 1+7/1= 8 Output of signal conditioner =0.5V X 8= 4V

4.3 Single phasing circuit

The circuit described in Fig. 5 is quite cheap and electrically isolated. D1, R1, D2 and C1 provide a 9V supply which is further reduced by R2 and connected to pins 1 and 2 of the Optocoupler MCT2E. Opto-coupler IL206 or CNY17 can also be used in place of MCT2E. The continuity between the outputs pins 4 and 5 remains as such, unless that particular phase voltage fails. When voltage 5V is applied to the circuit through resistor R3.The output of the Opto-coupler is adjusted by using potentiometer and applied to particular channel.(As channel 1, channel 2, channel 3).

4.4 Moisture sensing circuit

Different moisture sensors are available today but having high price.Due to high price, in this circuit only related output signal is used. (For 0 to 1V – Nominal 0 to 60% volume).

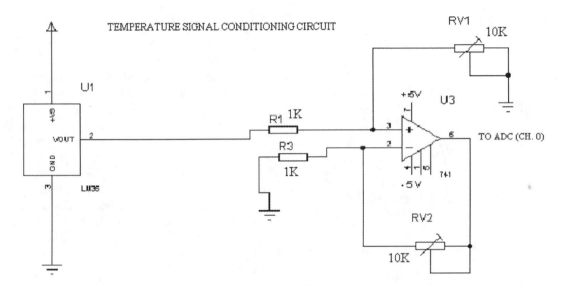

Fig. 4 Temperature signal conditioning circuit

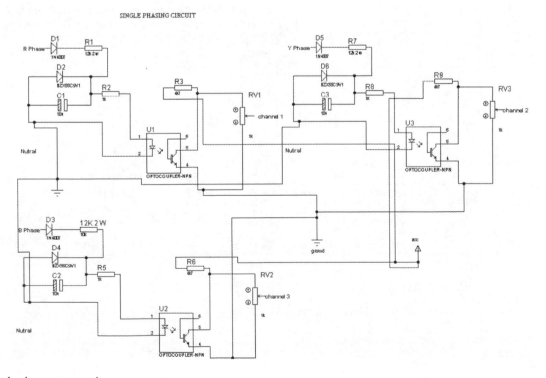

Fig. 5 Single phase sensor unit

4.5   Rain-gauge sensing circuit

A variable resistor float, which is used in normal two wheelers, is used as a water level sensor for rain gauge measurement. The resistance of the float varies from 5 Ω to 100 Ω.This is the input to the instrumentation

amplifier. Hence as R4 varies from 100 Ω to 5 Ω the input to instrumentation amplifier varies from 0V to 0.1V. But the input to ADC varies from 0V to 4.0V. For this the gain of the instrumentation amplifier is chosen to be A = 40.

Gain = (1+2R4/RV1) × (Rf/R1)

40.82 = (1+2 x10k)/RV1) × (1K/1K)

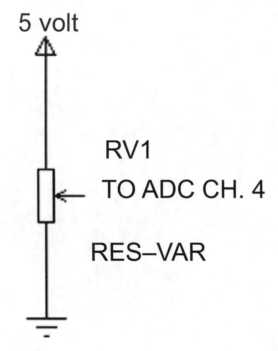

Fig. 6   Moisture sensor unit

40.82-1 = 20K/RV1

39.82/20K = 1/RV1

RV1=502.26 Ω; RV1 502 Ω

4.6   Water level sensing circuit

The input to pin no 2 and 6 is 2.5 V. The voltage at the reference copper rod is zero. So when there is water at level 1 the voltage at pin 5 becomes zero volt from 5v. The output at pin 7 becomes zero from 5 volt. The same thing happens for water level 2. Output of pin 1 and 7 are given to microcontroller I/O pins.

4.7   Over-load dry-run sensing circuit

Figure 9 shows Over-Load and Dry-Run sensing along with signal conditioning circuit. The motor current is taken as the input of the current sensing circuit. It is applied to a current transformer turn ratio 1:1000. So when 30A current is applied to the primary the secondary gives a current of 30mA. This current is then converted into 9 Vrms voltage. For this the current is made to pass through a resistance of 9 V/30 mA = 300Ω.

The maximum output of CT is converted into 9 Vrms. This voltage then has to be converted into a DC voltage between 0 to 5V. For this secondary voltage of transformer is given to attenuator circuit. The attenuator circuit is used to bring the secondary voltage into the range of 0–5V, and it takes care that it does not go beyond it. It is a voltage divider circuit using a 4.3K resistance in series with a 10K preset.

This is then applied to a precision rectifier circuit of unity gain. Precision rectifier then converts this AC voltage into pulsating DC voltage of approximately 4 Vrms. The ripples in this signal are smoothened using a filter circuit. This converts the pulsating DC to pure DC. Then this volt-

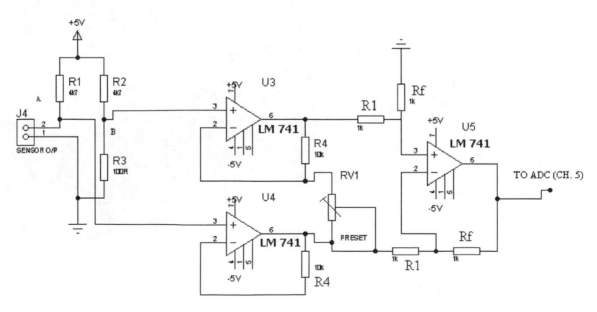

Fig. 7   Rain-guage sensing circuit

age is compared with motor dry-run voltage as well as over-load voltage. The change in output of respective comparator gives the indication.

4.8 Relay circuit

Figure 10 relates to relay driver which consists of two transistors (BC 547) connected in a Darlington pair configuration. A freewheeling diode IN4007 is connected across the relay which operates at current rating of 35–50 mA. Gain of BC547 = 200. Current to base of 1st transistor = 0.25mA Current to base of 2nd transistor = 1.25mA The value of the base resistance can thus be calculated by using the following formulae VOH –VBE1 –VBE2 / 1.25mA =R 4–1.4 / 0.25mA =R So we get approximately R=2 M Ω. Any resistance < 2M Ω will serve. So, we have selected $R = 10K$ for our circuit.

S/W development

The software tools used to develop this application are PROTEUS 7.2, PINNACLE, TM2 GSM/ GPRS Module, Assembler.

5. Results

The system is tested for various values of parameters and the performance is found satisfactory.Parameter monitoring and controlling

5.1 On/Off

Action of pump is carried out by the relays.

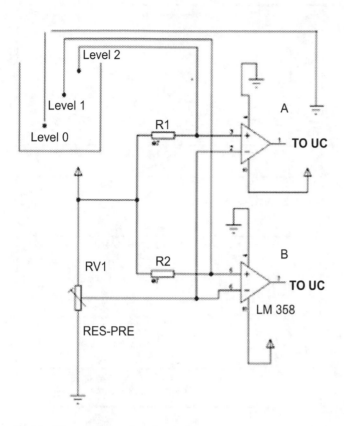

Fig. 8 Water level sensing circuit

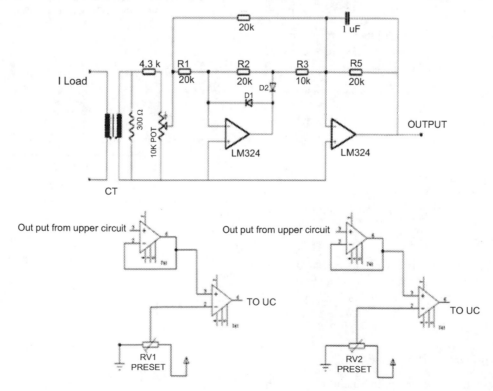

Fig. 9 Over-Load and dry-run sensing circuit

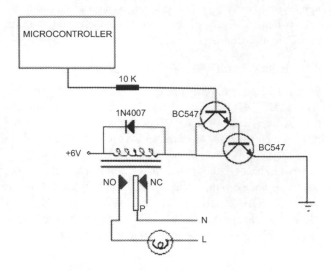

Fig. 10   Relay driver circuit

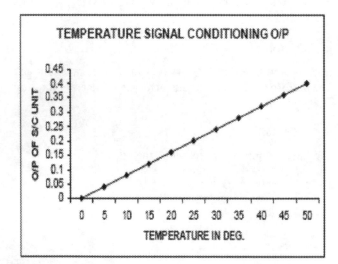

Graph 1   Temperature signal conditioning with gain Av=8

5.2   Temperature

The system displays the temperature on field display. If temperature exceeds the set point then µC trips the pump and gives message to the user as "Thermal Runway".

5.3   Phase protection

If any phase is failed or there is any problem related to any phase, then µC trips the motor and gives related messages to the user as "Single Phase problem 'R' Phase"; or *"Single Phase problem 'Y' Phase"; or "Single Phase problem 'B' Phase"* .

5.4   Dry run and overload protection

If voltage is less than the set point then µC trips the pump and gives message to the user as "dry run motor off". Also If voltage is greater than the set point then µC trips

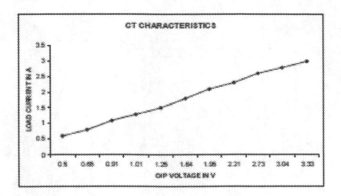

Graph 2   VI characteristics of CT

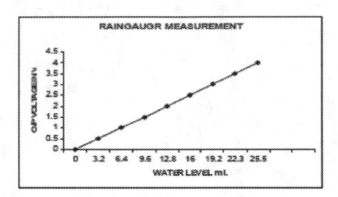

Graph 3   Rain gauge measurement

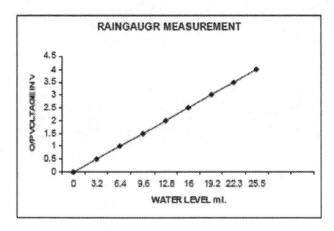

Graph 4   Moisture sensor

the pump and gives message to the user as "over voltage motor off"

5.5   Rain gauge measurement

With the help of float, water level of rain Gauge measurement is done and displays on field display.

5.6   Water level detection

Two discrete water levels are measured as High Level and Low Level and displays on field display.

5.7 Moisture sensing

Related Moisture displays on field display. Following are the different results which we getting along with this.

6. Conclusion

The agro-system should be operated through a remote mobile and controls the agro-pump (ON/OFF) action. It gives information about few parameters of agro-system like Temperature, Water Level of the tank, Rain gauge measurement, Single phasing problem, Dry run and Overload condition of the Pump.

References

1. Control and Data Transfer via SMS" by Dr.Nizar Zarka, Mr. Iyad Al-Houshi (HIAST) Damascus-Syria
2. "Remote Mobile Control of Home Appliances" by Mariana Nikolova, Frans Meijs and peter Voorwinden, IEEE transactions on consumer Electronics, Vol.49, N0.1, Feb 2003
3. "Design and development of web based D.A.S." by B. Rajesh, K. Shridharan and K. Srinivasan, IEEE transactions on Instrumentations and Measurement, Vol.51, No.3, June 2002
4. "Agricultural Remote Sensing Basics" by John Nowatzki, Robert Andres and Karry Kyllo, April 2004
5. "Real Time Wireless eCommerce for Agricultural and Forestry Operations" by Per Bjarne Bro, Narciso Cerpa, Samuel Ortega- Farías.
6. "An event chain notification and management
7. System using SMS" by A.B.Mnaour, A. Aendenernoomer, Lisa Hismanto, IEEE, CIRA2003, Intl. Symp. on Computational Intelligence in Robotics and automation, Kobe Japan, July 2003
8. "Mobile and Personal Communication Systems and Services," by Raj Pandya, Prentice – Hall of India Pvt. Ltd, New Delhi, 2004. Page No. 27–49, 73–86

Primary user emulation (PUE) attacks and mitigation for cognitive radio (CR) network security

Shweta K. Kanhere[1] · Amol D. Potgantwar[2] · Vijay M. Wadhai[3]

[1]PG Student, Department of Electornics, MITSOT, MAE, Pune, India.
[2]Lecturer Department of Comp. Engg, SITRC Nashik (MS) India.
[3]Prof & Dean Research MITSOT, MAE, Pune India.

1. Introduction

The need to meet the ever-increasing spectrum demands of emerging wireless applications and the need to better utilize spectrum have led the Federal Communications Commission (FCC) to revisit the problem of spectrum management. In the conventional spectrum management paradigm, most of the spectrum is allocated to licensed users for exclusive use. Recognizing the significance of the spectrum shortage problem, the FCC is considering opening up licensed bands to unlicensed operations on a non-interference basis to licensed users. In this new paradigm, unlicensed users (a.k.a. secondary users) "opportunistically" operate in fallow licensed spectrum bands without interfering with licensed users (a.k.a. primary or incumbent users), thereby increasing the efficiency of spectrum utilization. This method of sharing is often called Dynamic Spectrum Access (DSA).

Cognitive Radios (CRs) [1, 2] are seen as the enabling technology for DSA. Unlike a conventional radio, a CR has the capability to sense and understand its environment and proactively change its mode of operation as needed. CRs are able to carry out spectrum sensing for the purpose of identifying fallow licensed spectrum—i.e., spectrum "white spaces". Once white spaces are identified, CRs opportunistically utilize these white spaces by operating in them without causing interference to primary users. The successful deployment of CR networks and the realization of their benefits will depend on the placement of essential security mechanisms in sufficiently robust form to resist misuse of the system. Ensuring the trustworthiness of the spectrum sensing process is a particularly important problem that needs to be addressed. The key to addressing this problem is being able to distinguish primary user signals from secondary user signals in a robust way. Recall that, in a CR network, secondary users are permitted to operate in licensed bands only on a non-interference basis to primary users. Because the primary users' usage of licensed spectrum bands may be sporadic, a CR must constantly monitor for the presence of primary user signals in the current operating band and candidate bands. If a secondary user (with a CR) detects the presence of primary user signals in the current band, it must immediately switch to one of the fallow candidate bands. On the other hand, if the secondary user detects the presence of an unlicensed user, it invokes a coexistence mechanism to share spectrum resources. The above scenarios highlight the importance of a CR's ability to distinguish between primary user signals and secondary user signals. Distinguishing the two signals is non-trivial, but it becomes especially difficult when the CRs are operating in hostile environments. In a hostile environment, an attacker may modify the air interface of a CR to mimic a primary user signal's characteristics, thereby causing legitimate secondary users to erroneously identify the attacker as a primary user. We coin the term primary user emulation (PUE) attack to refer to this attack. There is a realistic possibility of PUE attacks since CRs are highly reconfigurable due to their software based air interface [1]. To thwart such attacks, a scheme that can reliably distinguish between legitimate primary signal transmitters and secondary signal transmitters masquerading as primary users is needed. In hostile environments, such a scheme should be integrated into the spectrum sensing mechanism to enhance the trustworthiness of the sensing result. Some researchers have reported a transmitter verification procedure that employs a *non-interactive location verification* scheme to exploit the fact that the incumbent signal transmitters are placed at fixed locations [3]. Because the location verification

S.J. Pise (ed.), *ThinkQuest 2010*, DOI 10.1007/978-81-8489-989-4_4,

scheme is non-interactive, no modification to the incumbent signal transmitters is needed. In the proposed location verification scheme, designated verifiers cooperatively verify the legitimacy of an incumbent signal transmitter's location by passively listening to its signal without interacting with the transmitter. The main contribution of this work is threefold: identification of the PUE attack, demonstration of its harmful effects on a CR network, and the proposal of a transmitter verification procedure to detect such an attack. The proposed procedure can be integrated into existing spectrum sensing schemes to enhance their trustworthiness.

We summarized the paper in different section, where section I describes introduction and section II describe a CR overview, key features and its evolution. The section III discuss about PUE attack and its significance. However, sections IV discuss the migitation of PUE attack by using different algorithms. Further, section V mention the results of analysis and simulation in detail and section VI discuss the conclusions from the study.

2. Cognitive radio (CR)

2.1 Overview

A cognitive radio (CR) employs software to measure unused portions of the existing wireless spectrum (so-called white space) and adapts the radio's operating characteristics to operate in these unused portions in a manner that limits interference with other devices [1]. Spectrum regulators such as the Federal Communications Commission (FCC) in the United States (US), recognize that CRs can be applied to dynamically reuse white spaces in licensed spectrum bands, thereby efficiently utilizing under-utilized spectrum [FCC02]. The technological advances in CRs are of such a magnitude that the FCC is of the view that none of the other advances "holds greater potential for literally transforming the use of spectrum in the years to come than the development of software-defined and cognitive or "smart" radios" [1, 2].

2.2 Cognitive radio (CR) cycle

The cognitive capability of a cognitive radio enables real time interaction with its environment to determine appropriate communication parameters and adapt to the dynamic radio environment. The tasks required for adaptive operation in open spectrum are shown in Fig. 1, which is referred to as the cognitive cycle. In this section, we provide an overview of the three main steps of the cognitive cycle: spectrum sensing, spectrum analysis, and spectrum decision. The steps of the cognitive cycle as shown in Fig. 1 are as follows:

1. *Spectrum sensing:* A cognitive radio monitors the available spectrum bands, captures their information, and then detects the spectrum holes.

2. *Spectrum analysis:* The characteristics of the spectrum holes that are detected through spectrum sensing are estimated.

3. *Spectrum decision:* A cognitive radio determines the data rate, the transmission mode, and the bandwidth of the transmission. Then, the appropriate spectrum band is chosen according to the spectrum characteristics and user requirements.

Some of the key features that are typically associated with CR includes [5]:

- *Maintains awareness* of surrounding environment and internal state
- *Adapts* to its environment to meet requirements and goals
- *Reasons* on observations to adjust adaptation goals
- *Learns* from previous experiences to recognize conditions and enable faster reaction times
- *Anticipates* events in support of future decisions
- *Collaborates* with other devices to make decisions based on collective observations and knowledge.

However, once the operating spectrum band is determined, the communication can be performed over this spectrum band. However, since the radio environment changes over time and space, the cognitive radio should keep track of the changes of the radio environment.

2.3 Attacks in CR

A denial-of-service (DoS) attack is an act of preventing authorized access to a system resource or the delaying of system operations and functions. In this paper, it is a denial of communication to legitimate users the CR seven when the system resources such as unused frequencies are available. Another DoS attack relevant to CRs is when a CR is induced to communicate so that This attack, is also a form of DoS if it leads to a, perceived failure of CR that forestalls the widespread deployment of CR technology, preventing

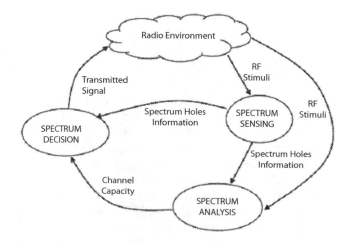

Fig. 1 Cognitive radio (CR) cycle

Table 1 The features of CR from the perspective of the attacker

CR Feature	What this means to the CR	What this means to the Attacker	Potential attack/ Malicious Tactic	Potential Goal/ Desired Effect	Implication for attacker and attacker capability
Maintains awareness	CR is performing functions such as spectrum censing (what spectrum is being used, who/ what is using it)	Opportunity for spoofing	Create a signal environment to cause erroneously perceived environment by cognitive network member (s)	Cause CR to sense an environment defined and controlled by malicious attacker	Must known what victim is sensing, and have capability to cerate the desired signal environment (occupy spectrum and pretend to be certain device/ signal types)
Adapts	CR adapts its behavior based on perceived environment	Opportunity to force desired changes in behavior in victim	N/A -attack influences this through awareness spoofing	Cause radio to adapt in a way controllable by malicious attacker	Must have insight into methods/ algorithms and objective/ goals that govern CR adaptation
Reasons	CR adapts its a adaptation methods based on awareness to accommodate changing goals	Opportunity to influences fundamental behavior of CR	N/A attack influences this through awareness spoofing	Introduce basis into CR decision -making process by shaping goals in a way advantageous to attacker	Need to fine-tune attack strategy for desired behaviors. Need insight into reasoning algorithms. Need insight into changing goals.
Leams	CR adapts its a adaptation methods based on awareness to improve adaption methods	Opportunity to affect long -lasting impact on CR behavior	N/A attack influences this through awareness spoofing	Introduce basis into CR decision making process by introducing basis into CR adaptation rules/algorithms	Need to observe long - term effect to adapt attack as necessary Need insight into learning algorithms. Need ability for long -term awareness spoofing
Anticipates	CR uses awareness to predict future environment to proactively adapt/ reason/leam	Opportunity for long-lasting impact	N/A attack influences this through awareness spoofing	Control/influence future actions of CR by sustained awareness spoofing	Need to observe long - term effect to adapt attack as necessary. Need ability for long- term awareness spoofing
Collaborates	CRs share information and use that information in adaptation/ reasoning/leaming /anticipation process	Opportunity for propagate attack through network	N/A- attack influences this through awareness spoofing. collaborative attack could influences from multiple network points	Control/influence actions and future action of CR (s) outside the physical reach of attacker	Can observe neighboring nodes to assess effectiveness

the anticipated benefits to spectrum management from being realized.

- Traditional Jamming Attack
- Traditional vs CR Avenues of Attack

However, there is no mechanism to know that the signal that is observed is an authentic TV signal. As such, a jammer could generate a signal that resembles a TV signal and then broadcast that into the 802.22 WRAN. The jammer can then adjust its signal level until it observes an adaptation by the WRAN. This immediately gives the jammer knowledge of the required signal power to induce an adaptation, and it can then begin 'chasing' the signal targets across spectrum, causing continual adaptation and outage of service. This could present an opportunity for a jammer to disrupt service at power levels far less than otherwise required, increasing

the ease of operation and/or reach of the jammer. This is illustrated in Fig. 2.

2.4 Failures in CR

The CR has some failures in operation at six different avenues of attack, the relative effectiveness of each and the respective protection countermeasures.

- Spectrum Occupancy Failures
- Policy Failures
- Location failures
- Sensor Failures

Transmitter/Receiver Failures

- Compromised Cooperative CR
- Common Control Channel Attacks

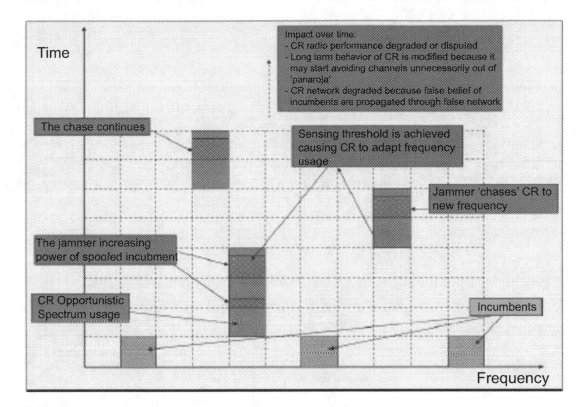

Fig. 2 Incumbent-spoofing chaser Jammer' Threat to a cognitive radio network

3. Primary user emulation (PUE) attack

One of the major technical challenges in spectrum sensing is the problem of precisely distinguishing incumbent signals from secondary user signals. To distinguish the two signals, existing spectrum sensing schemes based on energy detectors [3] implicitly assume a "naive" trust model. When energy detection is used, a secondary user can recognize the signal of other secondary users but cannot recognize primary users' signal. When a secondary user detects a signal that it recognizes, it assumes that the signal is that of a secondary user; otherwise it concludes that the signal is that of a primary user. Under such an overly simplistic trust model, a selfish or malicious secondary user (i.e., an attacker) can easily exploit the spectrum sensing process. For instance, an attacker may "masquerade" as an incumbent transmitter by transmitting unrecognizable signals in one of the licensed bands, thus preventing other secondary users from accessing that band.

There exist alternative techniques for spectrum sensing, such as matched filter and cyclostationary feature detection [3]. Nodes that are capable of such detection techniques are able to recognize the intrinsic characteristics of primary user signals, thus enabling them to distinguish those signals from those of secondary users. However, such detection techniques are still not robust enough to counter PUE attacks. For instance, to defeat cyclostationary detectors, an attacker may make its transmissions indistinguishable from incumbent signals by transmitting signals that have the same cyclic spectral characteristics as incumbent signals. Depending on the motivation behind the attack, a PUE attack can be classified as either a selfish PUE attack or a malicious PUE attack.

3.1 Selfish PUE attacks

In this attack, an attacker's objective is to maximize its own usage of spectrum resources. When selfish PUE attackers detect a fallow spectrum band, they prevent other secondary users from competing for that band by transmitting signals that emulate the signal characteristics of incumbent signals [3]. This attack is most likely to be carried out by two selfish secondary users whose intention is to establish a dedicated link.

3.2 Malicious PUE attacks

The objective of this attack is to obstruct the OSS process of legitimate secondary users—i.e., prevent legitimate secondary users from detecting and using fallow licensed spectrum bands. Unlike a selfish attacker, a malicious attacker does not necessarily use fallow spectrum bands for its own communication purposes. It is quite possible for an attacker to obstruct OSS in multiple bands simultaneously by exploiting two OSS mechanisms implemented by every legitimate secondary user. The first mechanism requires a secondary user to wait for a certain amount of time before using the identified fallow band to make certain that the band is indeed unoccupied. Existing research shows that this time delay is non-negligible [1,2]. second mechanism requires a CR to periodically sense the current operating band to detect primary user signals and to immediately switch to another band when such signals are detected. By launching a PUE attack in multiple bands in a round-robin fashion, an attacker can effectively limit the legitimate secondary users from identifying and using fallow spectrum bands. Both attacks could have disruptive effects on CR networks. (Their disruptive effects will be studied using simulation in Section IV.) To thwart PUE attacks, one needs to first detect the attack. In the next section, we describe a transmitter verification scheme that can be integrated into a spectrum sensing scheme to detect PUE attacks under certain conditions.

3.3 PUE attack detection schemes

3.3.1 *Transmitter verification scheme for spectrum sensing*

Before describing the transmitter verification scheme for spectrum sensing, we state some of the assumptions that form the foundation of the scheme. The primary user is assumed to be a network composed of TV signal transmitters (i.e., TV broadcast towers) and receivers. A TV tower's transmitter output power is typically hundreds of thousands of Watts, which corresponds to a transmission range from several miles to tens of miles. secondary users, each equipped with a hand-held CR device, form a mobile ad-hoc network. Each CR is assumed to have self-localization capability and have a maximum transmission output power that is within the range from a few hundred milliwatts to a few watts—this typically corresponds to a transmission range of a few hundred meters. An attacker, equipped with a CR, is capable of changing its modulation mode, frequency, and transmission output power.

Based on the above assumptions, we propose a transmitter verification scheme for spectrum sensing that is appropriate for hostile environments; the transmitter verification scheme is illustrated in Fig. 3. In the network model under consideration, the primary signal transmitters are TV broadcast towers placed at fixed locations. Hence, if a signal source's estimated location deviates from the known location of the TV towers and the signal characteristics resemble those of primary user signals, then it is likely that the signal source is launching a PUE attack. An attacker, however, can attempt to circumvent this location-based detection approach by transmitting in the vicinity of one of the TV towers. In this case, the signal's energy level in combination with the signal source's location is used to detect PUE attacks.

It would be infeasible for an attacker to mimic both the primary user signal's transmission location and energy level since the transmission power of the attacker's CR is several orders of magnitude smaller than that of a typical TV tower.Once an instance of a PUE attack has been detected,

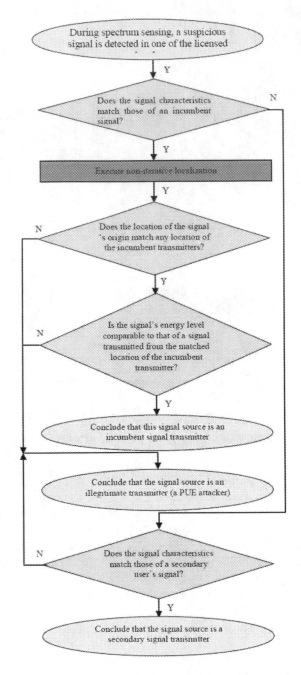

Fig. 3 Flowchart of transmitter verification scheme

the estimated signal location can be further used to pinpoint the attacker. As Fig. 1 shows, the transmitter verification scheme includes three steps: verification of signal characteristics, measurement of received signal energy level, and localization of the signal source. To date, the technical problems related to the first two steps, in the context of CR networks, have attracted a lot of attention [16].

In contrast, there is very little existing research that directly addresses the third step. Therefore, in the following discussions, we focus on the problem of transmitter localization. This problem—called by various names such as location estimation, location identification, localization, positioning etc.—has been studied extensively in the past. The primary signal transmitter localization problem (which is referred to as the PST localization problem hereafter), however, is more challenging for two reasons. First, the following requirement must be met: no modification should be made to primary users to accommodate the DSA of licensed spectrum. Because of this requirement, including location information in a primary user's signal is not a viable solution. The requirement also excludes the possibility of using a localization protocol that involves interaction between a primary user and the localization device(s).Thus, the PST localization problem becomes a non-interactive localization problem. Second, it is the transmitter but not the receiver that needs to be localized. When a receiver is localized,one does not need to consider the existence of other receivers. However, the existence of multiple transmitters may add difficulty to transmitter localization. In the next section, we describe the proposed solution to the non-interactive PST localization problem in detail.

3.3.2 *Non-interactive localization of primary signal transmitters*

3.3.2.1 Conventional localization techniques

Before introducing the proposed localization system, in this subsection, we first summarize conventional localization techniques in wireless networks and then discuss how these techniques should be improved to address the PST localization problem in CR networks. The conventional localization approaches are based on one or several of the following techniques: Time of Arrival (TOA) & Angle Of Arrival (AOA). Using the same principle, angle of arrival information to multiple receivers can be used to determine the transmitter's location. RSS-based localization techniques arise from the fact that there is a strong correlation between the distance of a wireless link and RSS. Specifically, given a transmitter receiver pair, RSS can be modeled as a function of transmitted power and transmitter-receiver distance. Therefore, if a correct model is used and there are multiple observers taking RSS measurements from a transmitter, then the transmitter location can be estimated using the model. In contrast, RSS-based techniques are more practical for most consumer premise devices in a CR network. However, for the PST localization problem in CR networks, one should also consider the issues of possible manipulation of a malicious transmitter or multiple transmitters and the innate inaccuracy of RSS measurement. In the following subsections, the issues can be addressed by taking many RSS measurement and properly processing the measured RSS data

3.3.2.2 Architecture of localization system

The basic idea of the proposed localization system uses the fact that the magnitude of an RSS value typically decreases as the distance between the signal transmitter and the re-

ceiver increases. A PUE attacker may constantly change its location or vary its transmission power to evade localization, thus causing RSS measurements to fluctuate drastically within a short period of time. This problem cannot be mitigated by taking the average of measurements taken at different times, since the RSS values measured at a given position at different times have different distributions.

A possible solution to this problem is to take a "snapshot" of the RSS distribution in a given network, i.e., requiring the sensors of a WSN to take synchronized RSS measurements in a given band. The second problem arises from the fact that RSS usually varies by a large magnitude (30dB to 40dB) [3] over short distances. This makes it very challenging to decide the location of primary users just by reading the raw data in a snapshot of RSS distribution. We conducted a simulation experiment to illustrate this problem

A 2000 m × 2000 m network with two transmitters located at (800m, 1800m) and (1300m, 550m) was simulated. Each transmitter's transmission power was 500mW, working at the UHF frequency of 617MHz. The phase shift between the two transmitters was randomly chosen. A statistical log-loss signal propagation model, which was shown to be appropriate for modeling signal propagation behavior in many situations [3], was employed in the simulation. In this model, the expected RSS in decibels is given by Eq. 1:

$$\mu = p + \beta_0 + \beta_1 \ln s \qquad 1$$

where s is the transmitter-receiver distance, p is the transmitted power in decibels, and $\beta0$, $\beta1$ are constant parameters that need to be calibrated for a specific environment. Note that this is offsite calibration, and no onsite calibration is required [3].

However, if the variance can be reduced to a sufficiently low level, the snapshot would clearly indicate the RSS peaks as illustrated in Fig. 4(b). It is therefore reasonable to conjecture that if one is able to decrease the variance using an appropriate data smoothing technique; it may be possible to solve the PST localization problem by using the aforementioned localization approach. In the next subsection, we focus on the design of such a data smoothing technique. In the offsite calibration, one needs to tune the parameters related to the channel environment (e.g., rural, urban, etc.). Using the model, the distribution of RSS is characterized as a Gaussian random variable with a mean of μ and a variance of σ^2. In [3], a set of parameters approximating real world results was used, where $(\beta0, \beta1) = (-30.00, -10.00, 10.0)$. We used the same set of parameters for our simulation. Fig. 4(a) shows a snapshot of the RSS in dBm. It can be seen that because of the large variance of the RSS, the snapshot does not reveal obvious RSS peaks (which can be used as approximations for the transmitter locations)

3.3.3 RSS smoothing procedure

Data smoothing techniques [3] aim to capture important patterns in raw data, while leaving out noise. By smooth-

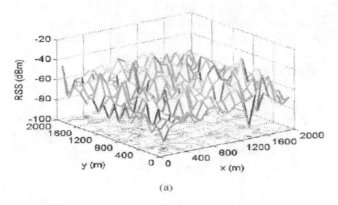

Fig. 4a   Snapshot of RSS raw-data distribution

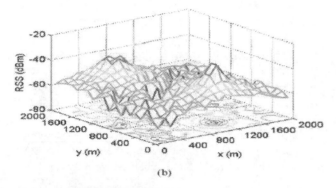

Fig. 4b   The RSS distribution in the network when σ = 0

ing a snapshot of an RSS distribution in a network, one can decrease the variance in the raw RSS measurements, thus making it possible to identify the RSS peaks.

There are three data smoothing techniques that are usually used to eliminate noise: local averaging, Fourier filters, and loess fitting. In our RSS smoothing problem, robustness against outliers is an important requirement for two reasons. First, the large variance in RSS measurements may result in a large number of outliers. Second, when an adversarial environment is considered, compromise of sensor nodes may lead to false data injection. Among the three data smoothing techniques, Fourier filters is known to be vulnerable to large variation. Loess fitting requires a large, densely sampled dataset and its robustness against outliers depends on careful design of the weight mechanism used for computing least squares. In contrast, local averaging, especially when the median value is taken, provides the best robustness against outliers. Therefore, we use local averaging, using median values, to smooth RSS measurement data. The details of the smoothing technique are described below. Without loss of generality, we assume that the coverage area of the WSN is identical to that of a CR network under consideration, which covers an area of $D_x \times D_y$ (m²). Suppose we sample a group of "pivot" points that are placed at the intersections of the vertical and horizontal lines of a two dimensional grid, where each element on the grid is a square with a side of length d. For each pivot point we calculate a "smoothed" RSS value by calculating the median value from the set of RSS measure-

ments collected by neighboring sensor nodes that are located inside an area enclosed by a circle of radius r centered at the pivot point. See Fig. 5 for an illustration of how the pivot points are positioned. Once data smoothing is applied to RSS measurements, one can estimate the positions of the primary signal transmitters by identifying the positions of the pivot points that generate "peak" median values.

4. Results and discussions

The results are simulated on the effects of PUE attacks & localization system are discussed in the detail in the following section

4.1 Effects of PUE attacks

We carried out simulation experiments to showcase the disruptive effects of PUE attacks. In the simulated network, 300 secondary users (which include both legitimate users and attackers) are randomly located inside a 2000 m × 2000 m square area, each with a transmission range of 250m and an interference range of 550m. These range values are consistent with the protocol interference model used in [3]. Two TV broadcast towers act as primary signal transmitters. Each TV tower has ten 6MHz channels, and the duty cycle of all the channels is fixed at 0.2. One tower is located 8000m east of the square area and has a transmission radius of 9000m; the other tower is located 5000m south of the square area with a transmission radius of 7000m. The layout of the simulated network is shown in Fig. 6(a). Each secondary user node is randomly placed in the network area and moves according to a random waypoint model by repeatedly executing the following four steps: 1) It randomly chooses a destination in the square area with a uniform distribution; 2) It chooses a velocity v that is uniformly distributed over $[v_{min}, v_{max}]$; 3) It moves along a straight line from its current position to the destination with velocity v; and 4) It pauses in the destination for a random period that is uniformly distributed over $[0, t_{p-max}]$. We chose the values $v_{min} = 5$m/s, $v_{max} = 10$m/s, and $t_{p-max} = 60$s. Each simulation instance spans a period of 24 hours.

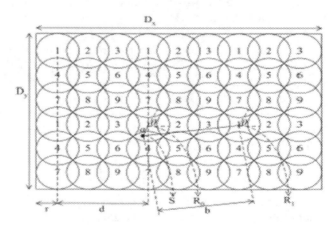

Fig. 5   Using local averaging to smooth RSS measurement [3]

Another one hour before the 24 hours was simulated to ensure that the random waypoint model entered steady state. The number of malicious PUE attackers was varied from 1 to 30 and that of selfish PUE attackers was varied from 1 to 30 pairs. Fig. 6(b) and 6(c) show the simulation results for the selfish PUE attack and the malicious PUE attack, respectively. The y-axis in the figures represents the amount of link bandwidth each secondary user is able to

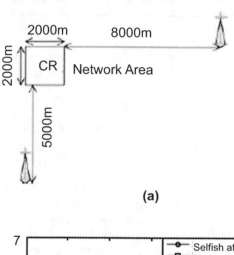

(a)

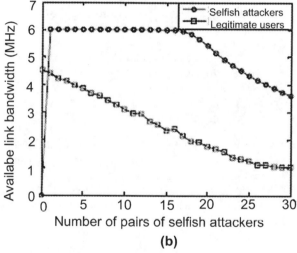

(b)

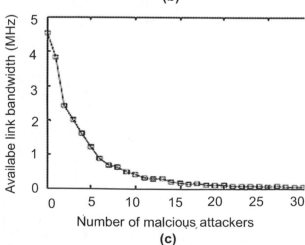

(c)

Fig. 6 Simulation showing effect of PUE attacks

detect. The results show that a selfish PUE attack can effectively steal bandwidth from legitimate secondary users while a malicious PUE attack can drastically decrease the link bandwidth available to legitimate secondary users.

4.2 Effects of localization system

The proposed transmitter localization scheme was simulated. However, the verification of signal characteristics and measurement of signal energy level are not included in this simulation study. The value of Dh (Transmitter location) was used to compare the likelihood that a primary signal transmitter is on the border of the WSN (Wireless Sensor Network) and in out-of-range locations. A PUE attacker is fixed at location (1950m, 1000m) and set a primary user at location $((1950 + \delta_x)$m, 1000m), where δ_x is a variable in the simulation. The PUE attacker is transmitting while the primary user is not transmitting. The result in Fig. 8 shows that when the distance between the PUE attacker and the out-of-range primary user is large, the D_h value induced by the attacker is much smaller than that induced by the primary user, showing that the attacker's location will be correctly output by Eqn.2. [3].

$$h_0 = \arg{}_h \min D_h \qquad\qquad 2$$

However, when the distance between the PUE attacker and the primary user is relatively small, due to the modeling error and the localization error, D_h cannot be used for distinguishing the attacker from the primary user. In this case, as the flowchart in Fig. 7 shows, the signal energy level will be further examined to judge the legitimacy of the transmitter.

5. Mitigation in networks

In this paper, the focus is primarily on the physical (PHY) layer, and further to provide a general analysis of threats to different types of cognitive radio (including both policy and learning radios). We then present a rough sketch at how such attacks can be mitigated in cognitive radio implemen-

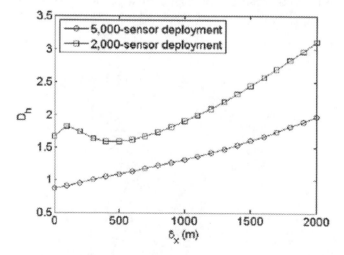

Fig. 7 D_h vs δ_x [3]

tations, and provide a road-map for extending this analysis to the medium access control (MAC) layers and higher. An ideal cognitive engine would provide optimization across all layers, and the threat model fundamentals would apply to those higher layers as well; however, most of the current cognitive radio technologies focus on the PHY, so we use attacks against the cognitive radio PHY as exemplars. In a network of cognitive radios, where we assume there is some sort of control-channel connectivity between cognitive engines, mitigating possible threats becomes a very interesting space. We now have a group of independent AI agents each seeking to maximize their own performance, and possibly global performance, depending on their level of cooperation with the devices around them.

This new-found connectivity at the cognitive-engine level between peers allows us to use various techniques from *swarm intelligence* [4]. One technique of specific applicability to security is particle swarm optimization (PSO). Each cognitive radio in a network represents a particle, each with it's own hypothesis about what the best behavior is in a particular situation. The behavior it selects, however, is not wholly dependent on its own hypothesis, but is actually a weighted average of all hypotheses in the network. This approach could also be used in adaptive radio. For example, in the scenarios we described earlier, radios used various learning algorithms to determine how their inputs affected their objective function. An attacker could manipulate that process to cause altered behavior in the radio.

6. Conclusions

Cognitive Radio is to permeate the entire network stack to allow intelligent control and security to an entire system. LocDef detects and pinpoint PUE attacks in modest way as compared to other techniques in hostile environments. The alternative approach that uses the intrinsic characteristics of RF signals distinguishes and identifies emitters—i.e. RF fingerprinting resulted in thwarting PUE attacks where the primary transmitters are mobile and have low power, localization-based approaches for do not work. Cognitive radios

had control over and sensory input from PHY-level components, such as energy detectors, signal classifiers, modem components, and error correcting codes. Cognitive Radio capabilities can be extended to the MAC, routing, transport, or even application layers.

References

1. I.F. Akyildiz, W. Y.l Lee, M. C. Vuran, Shantidev Mohanty, NeXt generation/dynamic spectrum access/cognitive radio wireless networks: A survey", Computer Networks, 50, pp. 2127-2159, 2006
2. T. X. Brown, "Potential Cognitive Radio Denial-of-Service Vulnerabilities and Protection Countermeasures: A Multi-dimensional Analysis and Assessment", Mobile Networks and Applications, Vol.(5), Oct. 2008, pp. 516-532
3. R. Chen, Jung-Min Park, and J. H. Reed, "Defense against Primary User Emulation Attacks in Cognitive Radio Networks", Bradley Department of Electrical and Computer Engineering, Virginia Polytechnic Institute and State University Blacksburg, VA 24061
4. T. C. Clancy & N. Goergen, "Security Cognitive Radio in Networks: Threats and Mitigation", Laboratory for Telecommunication Sciences,US Department of Defense
5. J. L. Burbank, "Security in Cognitive Radio Networks: The Required Evolution in Approaches to Wireless Network Security" Johns Hopkins University, Laurel, MD 2072
6. Cabric, D.; Mishra, S; Willkomm, D.; Broderson, R; Wolisz, A.;—*A cognitive radio approach for usage of virtual unlicensed spectrum*, White paper 2004
7. The Federal Communications and Commissions, *Spectrum Policy Task Force Report,* ET Docket No. 02-155, November 2002
8. J. Mitola III and G. Q. Maguire Jr., Cognitive Radio: Making Software Radios More Personal, *IEEE Personal Communication.* vol. 6, no. 4, Aug. 1999, pp. 13–18
9. J. Mitola, Cognitive Radio: An Integrated Agent Architecture for Software Defined Radio, Ph.D. dissertation Royal Institute of Technology (KTH), 2000
10. Mathworks Inc. (2005) MATLAB and Simulink Release 14 user's guide. [Online]. Available: http://www.mathworks.com

Kernel based object tracking with enhanced localization

Shilpa Wakode[1] · Krithiga A.[1] · K. K. Warhade[2] · V. M. Wadhai[3]

[1]Lecturer, LTCE, Navi-Mumbai, India
[2]Assistant Professor LTCE, Navi-Mumbai, India
[3]Professor, MITSOT, MAE Pune, India

1. Introduction

The large number of high-powered computers, the availability of high quality and inexpensive video cameras, and the increasing need for automated video analysis has generated a great deal of interest in object tracking algorithms. Real time object tracking has many practical applications, both commercial and military, such as visual surveillance, traffic monitoring, vehicle navigation, precision targeting, perceptual user interfaces and artificial intelligence.

In real time applications kernel based object tracking (KBOT) [1] is a robust and efficient tracking technique. First of all Comaniciu in [1, 2] used kernel based mean shift algorithm to track moving object. He used Bhattacharyya coefficient as a tool to compare between object models and object candidate and used mean shift algorithm to search the optimum object candidate. His method was good for object tracking and hence many researchers use this as a base for advance tracking algorithms. Peng [3] and Comaniciu [4] respectively proposed the automatic selection of bandwidth for mean shift-based object tracking; Peng [5] also propose an updating method of object model in mean shift algorithm. However mean shift algorithm has many flaws like the tracking errors or object lost. Background pixels in object model increase localization error of object tracking. Little background pixels in object model, give good result of object tracking. But in order to let the object contained in object model, some background pixels will certainly get introduced in object model. To reduce the localization errors of object tracking, it is required to omit the background pixels from object model when the color kernel histogram is being computed. Collins [6] used a "center surround" approach to sample pixels from object and background. To represent the object pixels a rectangular set of pixels cover-ing the object is chosen, while a larger surrounding ring of pixels is chosen for background. For both object and background the normalized histograms are created. Then mean shift is used to track object. This approach is effective for overcoming the errors produced by background pixels in object model. But in case of localization error or occlusion, the object may be incomplete in object model and it will give larger tracking error. In [7], the problem due to background pixels in object model affecting tracking accuracy is principally studied. A weight parameter integrating background feature and object feature is used in object model to reduce the localization error of object tracking. The weighted histogram provides proper discrimination between object and background. This reduces the localization error of object tracking. However, there are other factors which have an effect on localization, such as Taylor approximate expansion formula which is applied in mean shift, and color histogram [13]. Also color and grey level histograms were successfully applied in KBOT algorithms and observed to be robust. Still in complex tracking applications it does not represent the best nonparametric density estimate [8, 11]. Therefore, it is not enough to use histogram for feature description alone. In case of target tracking this insufficiency would often cause false convergence especially when similar color modes exist in the target neighborhood [9]. The initialization point for mean shift tracker plays an important role for its convergence to true local maxima. The similarity coefficient surface obtained tends to be flat due to target-shift invariance of the compact histogram. It would make the mean-shift algorithm converge to false local maxima and result in inaccurate target localization.

To make the original KBOT more robust, for the mean-shift necessary post processing using some structural features is applied. Updating the model estimated

S.J. Pise (ed.), *ThinkQuest 2010*, DOI 10.1007/978-81-8489-989-4_5,

by mean shift algorithm along with calculating the edge based centroid [10, 12], tends to converge on the target true center. This method handles the problem of localization by a similar post processing step, which is carried out using tracked object structure. Edge based information is used to determine object structure. It helps in updating the mean shift estimated centroid to new position. The centre of track window is then shifted to this new centroid position, ensuring real search point for next iteration.

The paper is organized as follows: In Section II, we give an overview of the original KBOT algorithm. In Section III, the KBOT with centroid based technique is described. Section IV contains the comparative results. Section V contains the drawn conclusions and discussion of future development.

2. Kernel based approach

The KBOT is broadly classified into two components viz. target model representation and target localization. The target model is represented in its feature space by its probability density function (PDF), which is calculated using kernel density estimation [31] given by

$$f(x) = \frac{1}{nh^d} \sum_{i=1}^{n} K(\frac{x - x_i}{h})$$ (1)

where h is the bandwidth of the kernel and is the center of the d dimensional kernel while n is total number of points in the kernel. Kernel density can be determined with the application of Epanechnikov kernel [1] which is defined as

$$K_E = \begin{cases} \frac{1}{2} C_d^{-1}(d+2)(1 - \|x\|^2) & if \ \|x\| \leq 1 \\ 0 & otherwise \end{cases}$$ (2)

where C_d is the volume of the d-dimensional space. The target is selected manually in the first frame and its PDF is calculated by considering its location centered at y_0. To track target in the next frame its PDF in the next frame is calculated at the same location as

$$\hat{p}_u(y) = C_h \sum_{i=1}^{n} K\left[\left\|\frac{y - x_i}{h}\right\|^2\right] \delta[b(x_i) - u]$$ (3)

where $$C_h = \frac{1}{\sum_{i=1}^{n_h} K\left[\left\|\frac{y - x_i}{h}\right\|^2\right]}$$

and u = 1 ... m. Here m is the number of bins used for the calculation of PDF for target representation which is centered at 0. h is the bandwidth of the kernel and x_i is the center of the d dimensional kernel. While n is total number of points in the kernel and $\delta\left[b\left(x_i\right) - u\right]$ is Kroneckor delta function $b(x_i)$ is image feature value at spatial location x_i and h is bandwidth of the kernel used. C is the normaliza-

tion constant. Bhattacharya coefficient is used to derive the similarity or correlation between the target model and target candidate. It is specified in the form of a distance given by

$$d = \sqrt{1 - \hat{\rho}(y)}$$ (4)

where

$$\hat{\rho}(y) = \hat{\rho}[\hat{p}(y), \hat{q}] = \sum_{u=1}^{m} \sqrt{\hat{p}_u(y), \hat{q}_u}$$

and term $\hat{\rho}(y)$ is referred as Bhattacharya coefficient. New target location y_1 in current frame is found by iteratively proceeding towards the maxima in the neighborhood. The new target location y_1 is obtained by recursively traveling from its initial location y_0, using the relation where w_i are the respective weights

$$y_1 = \frac{\sum_{i=1}^{n_h} x_i w_i}{\sum_{i=1}^{n_h} w_i}$$ (5)

3. Kbot with centroid based approach

The basic KBOT rely only on image spectral features which results in poor localization to avoid that in this approach object structure information is integrated into image histogram to get combine effect of both spectral and gray level features. The accuracy of mean shift depends upon a many things like target surroundings, noise, shape and size modifications etc. Because of this the track window around the target fails to be at the location it is supposed to be. This problem is overcome by the edge based centroid estimation of the target object and relocation of the track window on the middle of the target object [10]. This post processing step makes tracking robust even for convex shaped objects. Following approach is used to relocate the track window on the centre of the target object:

1. A window whose center is proposed by mean shift must be taken from the video and the window size should be made twice the size of the original target window. Here increasing window size will also compensate fast object motion and scaling.
2. Canny edge detector should be used for edge detection of that image.
3. Appropriate threshold should be used to binarize the image.
4. The centroid of a finite set of points $x_1 + x_2 + ... + x_k$ in R^n should be calculated as

$$C = \frac{x_1 + x_2 + ... + x_k}{k}$$ (6)

For calculating edge based centroid:

a) Along the horizontal axis, the position of edge on the right and left of the center point provided by mean shift should be observed and the column number of center of the video must be adjusted by applying above formula.

b) Using the new column number as the center, the same step for the edges above and below the center point must be repeated with adjusting the row number.

5. The track window must be placed on the new center point calculated by edge based centroid estimation.

The application of centroid estimation mode is linked with the result of Bhattacharya coefficient between target model and candidate. This similarity measure is divided into three stages.

- High localization (HLoc) similarity range which states that KBOT algorithm is working well and proper localization of object is being achieved. So no post processing is required.
- Low localization (LLoc) similarity range states that KBOT algorithm has poor localization still it can be used for application of centroid estimation technique.
- Worst localization similarity range states that object being tracked is facing full occlusion. So edge detection or centroid estimation at this stage is not reliable.

The complete algorithmic flow chart is shown in Fig. 1.

4. Results

Both KBOT and extended KBOT with centroid based approach are tested on different video data with variety of targets and found satisfactory results. The comparison of experimental results between proposed method and KBOT [1] is showed in Figure 1. In order to show the comparison of results in more details, the following formula is used to compute error of tracking location in i^{th} frame:

$$error_i = |T_i - C_i| \tag{7}$$

where Ti is the tracking location in ith frame, Ci is the accurate location of object in ith frame.

In addition, the average error of object tracking is measured using following formula:

$$Average\, error = \sum_{i=1}^{N} (error / N) \tag{8}$$

where, N is total number of frames. Equation (7) and (8) are used to compute the errors of object location in each frame and the average error along x and y direction. Here Ci *is* decided by man-manipulation. This method is subjective for object localization and it gives some errors for each location. But the average error is less as compared to original KBOT [1]. A quantitative evaluation of test results between the two methods is given in Table 1.

As shown in Table 1 the average Bhattacharyya coefficient value vary little in edge based method comparing

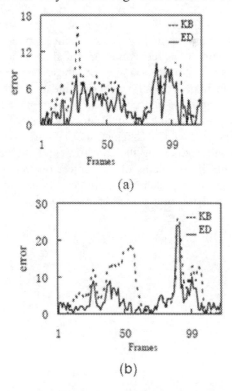

(a)

(b)

Fig. 2 The error of object location in each frame along (a) x direction (b) y direction, where ED denotes edge based centroid method, and KB denotes original KBOT method.

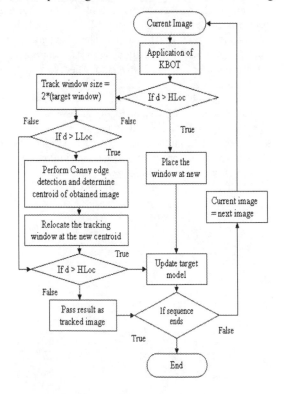

Fig. 1 Flow chart for complete object tracking algorithm

Table 1   Comparative results

Comparison for tracking	KBOT	Edge based centroid approach
Avg. error in x direction	5.0	3.21
Avg. error in y direction	7.08	3.62
Avg. iterations	27.55	22.49
Avg. Bhattacharya coefficient value	0.947	0.948

to original KBOT, but when occlusion occur, the Bhattacharyya coefficient value in edge based method is larger than that in KBOT. The original KBOT was having localization issues while handling the same video with improved centroid estimated KBOT implementation the algorithm was successful in tracking the target with improved localization.

5. Conclusion and future direction

The problem of weak localization in target tracking is addressed by using the extended centroid based KBOT. The experimental results have shown that it works fine even in the difficult situations such as partial occlusions, noisy background and scaling, where the original KBOT fails. This technique is more robust as compare to the original KBOT and do not need fine tuning to adapt to various scenarios.

Many robust trackers have been developed which can track objects in real time in simple scenarios. To simplify the tracking problem they use to make various assumptions like simple object motion, minimal amount of occlusion, constant illumination, etc. But these assumptions are violated in many realistic scenarios and therefore limit a tracker's usefulness in applications like automated surveillance, human computer interaction, video retrieval, traffic monitoring, and vehicle navigation. In future work can be done towards enhancing the capabilities of the tracker by eliminating the problems of full object obstruction, complex object motion, changing light conditions and application of KBOT for multiple target tracking.

References

1. D. Comaniciu, V. Ramesh, and P. Meer, "Kernel-Based Object Tracking", IEEE Trans Pattern Analysis and Machine Intelligence, Vol. 25, No. 5, 2003 pp 564–575
2. D. Comaniciu, V. Ramesh, and P. Meer, "Real-Time Tracking of Non-Rigid Objects Using Mean Shift," Proc. of IEEE Conf.on Comp. Vision and Pattern Recog., 2000, pp 142–149
3. N. Peng, S,Yang J,Liu Z, et al.,"Automatic Selection of Kernel-Bandwidth for Mean-Shift Object Tracking", Journal of Software, Vol. 16, No.9, 2005, pp.1542–1550
4. D. Comaniciu, "An Algorithm for Data-Driven Bandwidth Selection", in IEEE Trans.On pattern analysis and machine intelligence. Vol. .25, No.2, 2003, pp.281–288
5. N. Peng, S,Yang J, Liu Z., "Mean Shift BlobTracking With Kernel Histogram Filtering and Hypothesis Testing", Pattern Recognition Letters, Vol. 26, No.5, 2005, pp. 605–614
6. R T Collins, Y Liu, and M Leordeanu, "Online Selection Of Discriminative Tracking Features", IEEE Trans. on pattern analysis and machine intelligence, Vol. 27, No.10, 2005, pp 1631–1643
7. Z. Wen, Z. Cai, "A Robust Object TrackingApproach using Mean Shift", Third International Conference on Natural Computation (ICNC 2007), Sep 2007
8. M. Shah "Object Tracking: A Survey" ACM Computing Survey, Vol. 38, No 4, Article 13, Dec 2006
9. Xu Dong, Y. Wang, and Jinwen "Applying a New Spatial Color Histogram in Mean- Shift Based Tracking Algorithm", Image and Vision Comp., Univ. of Otago, New Zealand, 2005
10. R. Mehmood, M. Ali, I. Taj "Applying Centroid Based Adjustment to Kerne Based Object Tracking for ImprovingL ocalization", IEEE, 2009
11. K. Fukanaga and L. Hostetler, "The Estimation of the Gradient of a Density Function, with Applications in Pattern Recognition," IEEE Trans. Info. Theory Vol.21, 1975, pp 32–40
12. C. Yunqiang and R. Yong, "Real Time Object Tracking in Video Sequences", Signals and Communications Technologies, Interactive Video, Part II: 2006, pp. 67–88
13. A. Lehuger, P. Lechat and P. Perez, "An Adaptive Mixture Color Model for Robust Visual Tracking", in Proc. IEEE Int. Conf. on Image Process, Oct 2006, pp. 573–576

Computation and economics of nodal price in a restructured electricity market

S. B. Warkad[1] · Dr. M. K. Khedkar[2] · Dr. G. M. Dhole[3]

[1]Department of Electrical Engg, Disha Institute of Management & Technology, Raipur, India
[2]Department of Electrical Engg, Visvesvaraya National Institute of Technology, Nagpur, India
[3]Department of Electrical Engg, Shri Sant Gajanan Maharaj College of Engineering, Shegaon, India

1. Introduction

Since last century, the electrical power industry world wide has been continuously restructured from a centralized monopoly to a competitive market. Under it, competitive market is one of the effective mechanism for energy supply to free the customer's choices and improve overall social welfare. The aim of this restructuring is to promote competition and to make the electricity market more efficient. Recently, the electric power industry has entered in an increasingly competitive environment under which it becomes more realistic to improve economics and reliability of power systems by enlisting market forces [1]. In developing countries, the trend of electricity market is heading towards Transmission Open Access (TOA) whereby transmission providers will be required to offer the basic transmission service (operational and/or ancillary services) and pricing [2]. Electricity nodal pricing in this context is an effective scheme for providing techno-economic benefits to the market participants. Nodal prices contain valuable information useful for Poolco operation and, hence the scheme is to accurately determine them, continue to be an active area of research. Recent application of Nodal prices is to develop Financial Transmission Rights instrument used to hedge congestion and to reduce nodal price volatility in a competitive market. In coming years, power consumption in developing countries have expected to more than double compared to 35 to 40% increase in developed countries. Besides, many developing countries are facing the problems of transmission congestions, infrastructure investment in transmission and distribution segment. To reduce the gap between transmission capacity and power demand, trend is to adopt HVDC transmission system to gain advantages of the investment. This trend has therefore needed to address

in formulating nodal pricing scheme. The electricity nodal pricing literature studies have reviewed as a background of the present work but with no intention to cover all the published work [2] developed spot price model by describing the meaning and numerical properties of the generation and transmission components of spot price based on "slack bus" and "system lambda" [3] introduced an OPF based decomposition of spot prices to perform the operation of the Poolco model. Results have derived using the decomposition of the Lagrangian multipliers corresponding to power balance equations into components that represented the sum of generation, losses and system congestion [4] introduced the concept of spot price into power systems and provided the foundation and starting point for most successive research [6] presented an integrated spot pricing model by modifying existing Newton OPF by Interior Point algorithms. It included derivation of optimal nodal specific real-time prices for active and reactive powers and the method to decompose it into generation, loss, and ancillary services such as spinning reserve, voltage control and security control [7] investigated pricing behavior at New Zealand spot market, called "Price Inversion" by DC power flow and a full AC power flow. It was shown dependent on the physical characteristics of the power system [8] provided a detailed description and components of nodal prices i.e. generation, transmission congestion, voltage limitations and other constraints [9] presented a model for efficient calculation of spot prices, animation and visualization of spot prices based on the quadratized power flow approach [10] discussed the pricing of marginal transmission network losses in the Locational Marginal Pricing (LMP) deployed in the ISO New England standard market design. Study achieved market-clearing results by introducing loss distribution factors to balance explicitly the consumed losses in the lossless

S.J. Pise (ed.), *ThinkQuest 2010*, DOI 10.1007/978-81-8489-989-4_6,

DC power system. The distributed market slack references have discussed [11] provided explicit formulas to calculate components of LMPs i.e. reference price, congestion price, and loss price based on the single-slack power-flow formulation [12] presented an approach for the allocation of transmission network costs by controlling the electricity nodal prices. It introduced generation and nodal injection penalties into the economic dispatch to create nodal price differences that recover the required transmission revenue from the resulting congestion rent. The prices reflect both the marginal costs and the capital costs of the network [13] presented electricity price forecasting techniques, can be useful at different time horizons for electricity price forecasting in LMP spot markets. Fuzzy inference system, least-squares estimation, and the combination of both have proposed to improve the short-term forecasting performance [14] provided an iterative DCOPF-based algorithm to calculate LMPs and to analyze the sensitivity of LMP with respect to the system load. After this introduction, section 2 provides the need of modeling electricity nodal prices. Section 3 formulates AC-DC OPF based nodal pricing methodology. In section 4, nodal prices have simulated for IEEE-118 Bus system computed prices for real system of India. The impacts of HVDC transmission, Generation addition and Transmission Loading on electricity nodal prices have also evaluated. Finally, the conclusion is presented in section 5.

2. Need of modeling electricity prices

Restructuring within electricity markets worldwide have resulted in competition in generation, Transmission and distribution segments. In addition, the reductions in regulation and government price setting in the market have led to wholesale electricity market prices became much more volatile. This resulted market participants facing increased risk in terms of volumes of electricity they can produce and sell, and the prices they will receive for it. To facilitate market participants in terms of operations, risk management and investments, need is to model accurately nodal price behaviour. Aside from generators, investors and regulators, customers also require models of nodal prices in order to study market behaviour. Also often forecast and models of nodal prices serve various applications in the operation of electricity markets. For example, in short-run, generating companies have to make decisions regarding unit commitment. They will only want their generators is to be dispatched if it is profitable, and as these decisions are often required hours or days in advance, so they require forecast of future nodal prices in order to determine profitability. In the medium term, scheduled maintenance of generating plants have to be decided based on nodal price forecast to manage offline period that will have the least impact on profitability. In the longer term, potential investors need forecasts of nodal prices in order to determine the potential profitability of their investment. Many industries use and pay for electricity as an important input in their operations, they

also require forecasts of nodal prices to determine their own profitability. In many markets around the world, users are able to purchase contracts for electricity at a fixed price over a specified time. The valuation of such financial derivatives requires estimation of both the likely levels and volatility of nodal prices in order to determine what that fixed price should be, as well as fair price for the contract itself. Thus Nodal prices provided information about locational pricing, value of locating new generation, transmission upgradation etc. This enhances functions and efficiency of wholesale electricity market and improves the systems' ability to meet electricity demand.

3. Electricity nodal price formulation

To induce efficient use of the transmission grid and generation resources by providing correct economic signals, a nodal price theory for the restructured electricity markets is developed [4]. It is a method to determine market-clearing prices for several locations on the transmission grid (node). The price at each node reflects cost of the energy and the cost of delivering it.

3.1 Problem formulation:

3.1.1 *AC system equations*

Let $P = (p1,.....,pn)$ and $Q = (q1,.....,qn)$ for n bus system, where pi and qi be active and reactive power demands of bus-i respectively. The variables in power system operation to be $X = (x1,....,xm)$, i.e. real and imaginary bus voltages. Then the operational problem of a power system for given load (P, Q) can be formulated as OPF problem,

Minimize $f(X, P, Q)$ for X (1)

Subject to $S(X, P, Q) = 0$ (2)

$T(X, P, Q) 0$ (3)

where $S(X) = (s1(X, P, Q),.......,sn1(X, P, Q))^T$ and $T(X) = (t1(X, P, Q),......., tn2(X, P, Q))T$ have n1 and n2 equations respectively, and are column vectors. Here A^T represents the transpose of vector A.

$f(X, P, Q)$ is a scalar, short term operating cost, such as fuel cost. The generator cost function $fi(P_{Gi})$ in \$/MWh is considered to have cost characteristics represented by,

$$f = \sum_{i=1}^{NG} a_i P_{Gi}^2 + b_i P_{Gi} + c_i \qquad (4)$$

where, P_{Gi} is the real power output; a_i, b_i and ci represents the cost coefficient of the ith generator, NG represents the generation buses, The constraints to be satisfied during optimization are, (1) Vector of equality constraint such as power flow balance (i.e. Kirchoff's laws) has represented as:

$S(X, P, Q) = 0$ or

$$P_G = P_D + P_{DC} + P_L \text{ and } Q_G = Q_D + Q_{DC} + Q_L \qquad (5)$$

where suffix D represents the demand, G is the generation, DC represents dc terminal and L is the transmission loss. (2) The vector of inequality constraints includes all variables and function limits, such as upper and lower bounds of transmission lines, generation outputs, stability and security limits may be represented as,

$$T(X, P, Q) \, 0 \text{ or} \qquad (6)$$

(i) The maximum and minimum real and reactive power outputs of the generating sources have given by,

$$P_{Gi}^{min} \le P_{Gi} \le P_{Gi}^{max} \text{ and } Q_{Gi}^{min} \le Q_{Gi} \le Q_{Gi}^{max} \quad (i \in G_B) \qquad (7)$$

where P_{Gi}^{min}, P_{Gi}^{max} are the minimum and maximum real power outputs of the generators Q_{Gi}^{min}, Q_{Gi}^{max} and are the minimum and maximum reactive power outputs.

(ii) Voltage limits (Min/Max) signals the system bus voltages to remain within a narrow range. It is denoted by the following constraints,

$$\left| V_i^{min} \right| \le |V_i| \le \left| V_i^{max} \right| \quad (i = 1, \ldots, N_B) \qquad (8)$$

where, N_B represents number of buses.

(iii) Power flow limits is the transmission line's thermal or stability limits capable of transmitting maximum power (MVA) flow through the lines and it is expressed by the following constraints,

$$P_f^{min} \le P_f \le P_f^{max} \quad (f = 1, \ldots, Noele) \qquad (9)$$

where, $Noele$ represents number of transmission lines connected to grid. Then, operating conditions of a combined ac-dc electric power system may described by the vector,

$$X - [\delta, V, x_c, x_d]^t \qquad (10)$$

where, δ and V are the vectors of the phases and magnitude of the phas or bus voltages; x_c is the vector of control variables and x_d is the vector of dc variables.

3.1.2 DC system equations

The following relationship is for the dc variables. Using the per unit system [5], the average value of the dc voltage of a converter connected to bus 'i' is

$$V_{di} = G_i V_i \cos \alpha_i = r_{ci} I_{di} \qquad (11)$$

where, α_i is the gating delay angle for rectifier operation or the extinction advance angle for inverter operation; r_{ci} is the commutation resistance, and a_i is the converter transformer tap setting. By assuming a lossless converter, the equation of the dc voltage written as,

$$V_{di} = a_i V_i \cos \varphi_i \qquad (12)$$

where, $\varphi_i = \delta_i - \xi_i$, and φ is the angle by which the fundamental line current lags the line-to-neutral source voltage. The real power flowing in or out of the dc network at terminal 'i' may expressed as,

$$P_{di} = V_i I_i \cos \varphi_i \text{ or } P_{di} = V_{di} I_{di} \qquad (13)$$

The reactive power flow into the dc terminal is

$$Q_{di} = V_i I_i \sin \varphi_i \text{ or } Q_{di} = V_i a I_i \sin \varphi_i \qquad (14)$$

The equations (13)–(14) can substituted into the equation (5) to form part of the equality constraints. Based on these relationships, the operating condition of the dc system can describe by the vector

$$X_d = [V_d, I_d, a \cos \alpha \, \varphi]^t \qquad (15)$$

The dc currents and voltages have related by the dc network equations. In ac case, a reference bus is specified for each separate dc system; usually the bus of the voltage controlling dc terminal operating under constant voltage (or constant angle) control is chosen as the reference bus for that dc network equation. Here equations (1)–(3) are an OPF problem for the demand (P, Q). There are many approaches that can be used to get an optimal solution such as linear programming, Newton method, quadratic programming, nonlinear programming, interior point method, artificial intelligence (i.e. artificial neural network, fuzzy logic, genetic algorithm, evolutionary programming, ant colony and particle swarn optimization etc.) methods [8, 15].

3.1.3 Electricity nodal price

The real and reactive power prices at bus 'i' is the Lagrangian multiplier value of the equality and in-equality constraints. These values have calculated by solving the first order condition of the Lagrangian, partial derivatives of the Lagrangian with respect to every variable concerned. Therefore the Lagrangian function (or system cost) of equation defined as,

$$
\begin{aligned}
L = & \sum_{i=1}^{NG} a_i P_{Gi}^2 + b_i P_{Gi} + c_i + \sum_{i \in LB} \lambda p_i (P_{Di} - P_{Gi} + P_{DCi} + P_{Li}) + \\
& \sum_{i \in LB} \lambda q_i (Q_{Di} - Q_{Gi} + Q_{DCi} + Q_{Li}) + \sum_{i \in GB} \rho p_{Li} (P_{Gi}^{min} - P_{Gi}) \\
& + \sum_{i \in GB} \rho p_{ui} (P_{Gi} - P_{Gi}^{max}) + \sum_{i \in GB} \rho q_{Li} (Q_{Gi}^{min} - Q_{Gi}) \\
& + \sum_{i \in GB} \rho q_{ui} (Q_{Gi} - Q_{Gi}^{max}) + \sum_{i=1}^{NB} \rho V_{Li} \left(\left| V_i^{min} \right| - |V_i| \right) \\
& + \sum_{i=1}^{NB} \rho V_{ui} \left(|V_i| - \left| V_i^{max} \right| \right) + \sum_{i=1}^{NB} \rho \theta_{Li} (\theta_i^{min} - \theta_i) + \\
& \sum_{i=1}^{NB} \rho \theta_{ui} (\theta_i - \theta_i^{max}) + \sum_{i=1}^{Noele} \rho p_{Li} (P_{fi}^{min} - P_{fi}) \\
& + \sum_{i=1}^{Noele} \rho p_{ui} (P_{fi} - P_{fi}^{max})
\end{aligned}
\qquad (16)
$$

where, '*l*' and '*u*' are the lower and upper limits; $\lambda = (\lambda 1,$ ....,$\lambda n)$ is the vector of Lagrange multipliers concerning the equality constraints; $\rho = (\rho 1, ...,\rho n)$ are the Lagrange multipliers concerning to the inequality constraints. Then at an optimal solution (X, λ, ρ) and for a set of given (P,Q), the nodal price of real and reactive power for each bus is expressed below for

$i = 1,.........,n.$

$$\pi_{p,i} = \frac{\partial L(X, \lambda, \rho, P, Q)}{\partial p_i} = \frac{\partial f}{\partial p_i} + \lambda \frac{\partial S}{\partial p_i} + \rho \frac{\partial T}{\partial p_i} \qquad (17)$$

$$\pi_{q,i} = \frac{\partial L(X, \lambda, \rho, P, Q)}{\partial q_i} = \frac{\partial f}{\partial q_i} + \lambda \frac{\partial S}{\partial q_i} + \rho \frac{\partial T}{\partial q_i} \qquad (18)$$

Here π_p,i and π_q,i are active and reactive nodal prices at bus '*i*', respectively. The difference i.e. $\pi_{p,}i - \pi_{p,}j$ and $(\pi_{q,}i - \pi_{q,}j)$ represents active and reactive power transmission charges from bus-j to bus-i. Equation (17) can be view as the system

marginal cost created by an increment of real power load at bus *i*. The above formulations have simulated in MATLAB programming using the '*fmincon*' function available in the optimization toolbox based on interior point algorithms. An advantage of it is that the constraints can be directly evaluated as functions of the state variables which can be separate modules reducing programming complexity.

4. Problems, simulations and example

4.1 Modified IEEE-118 bus system

The given scheme has simulated on a large-scale power system i.e. IEEE-118-Bus system [16]. The system consists of 54 generators and 186 branches (Fig. 1 Appendix). A HVDC link has connected between bus 12 and bus 44. The ratings of the converter at these buses are 1.0 Per Unit (PU). The voltage values for all buses have bounded between 0.95 and 1.05. All of the values have indicated by PU. The nodal prices of real power with and without HVDC links have simulated and compared shown in the Table 1. The

Table 1 IEEE 118-Bus test system: simulated results for bus voltage and nodal price

Bus No	Bus Voltage (PU)		Nodal Price (S/MWh)		Bus No	Bus Voltage (PU)		Nodal Price (S/MWh	
	With Out HV DC	With HV DC	With out HV DC	WITH HV DC		With Out HV DC	With HV DC	With Out HV DC	With HV DC
1	0.96	0.95	136	101	60	0.98	0.96	96	91
2	0.98	0.97	98	98	61	0.95	0.97	94	92
3	0.95	0.96	115	100	62	0.95	0.97	95	88
4	0.97	0.98	101	100	63	0.95	0.96	101	95
5	0.97	0.99	109	100	64	0.97	0.99	114	96
6	0.96	0.99	96	98	65	0.97	0.99	72	66
7	0.98	0.99	100	97	66	1.05	1.01	73	73
8	1.03	1.01	62	54	67	1.01	1.00	82	80
9	1.01	1.03	74	54	68	1.02	1.00	69	67
10	0.98	1.01	53	53	69	1.04	1.02	67	68
11	0.97	0.98	93	97	70	1.05	1.04	62	67
12	0.97	0.99	99	95	71	1.05	1.01	55	59
13	1.05	0.98	101	93	72	1.05	1.01	65	60
14	1.03	1.00	114	90	73	1.05	1.02	70	59
15	1.02	1.04	65	74	74	1.03	1.01	64	68
16	1.03	1.00	90	88	75	1.03	1.01	77	69
17	1.01	1.05	117	70	76	1.04	1.02	72	69
18	1.02	1.05	83	71	77	1.04	1.02	62	68
19	0.98	1.05	92	73	78	1.02	1.01	83	69
20	1.05	1.04	84	72	79	1.05	1.01	78	69
21	1.04	1.03	69	71	80	1.04	1.02	77	68
22	1.05	1.04	68	69	81	1.02	1.01	79	67
23	0.95	1.05	76	66	82	1.03	1.03	68	66
24	1.03	1.05	70	64	83	1.01	1.03	76	66
25	1.01	1.05	68	65	84	1.02	1.04	86	65

Table 1   *Continued*

26	0.95	1.05	75	65	85	1.01	1.05	71	64
27	1.01	1.05	87	68	86	0.99	1.04	63	62
28	1.05	1.04	67	69	87	1.05	1.05	60	60
29	0.97	1.05	87	69	88	1.01	1.04	66	64
30	0.95	1.05	82	65	89	0.98	1.05	69	64
31	1.03	1.01	87	69	90	1.05	1.04	62	64
32	1.05	1.02	88	68	91	1.05	1.02	66	61
33	1.03	1.03	91	73	92	1.04	1.01	70	64
34	1.05	1.01	91	69	93	1.03	1.00	63	65
35	1.05	1.05	92	69	94	1.03	1.01	69	66
36	1.05	1.02	91	69	95	0.98	1.01	67	67
37	1.05	1.02	88	69	96	0.97	1.02	66	67
38	1.04	1.05	89	67	97	1.04	1.01	59	68
39	1.05	1.04	68	70	98	1.05	1.02	77	67
40	1.03	1.02	63	70	99	1.05	1.01	99	64
41	1.02	1.01	96	71	100	1.04	1.02	88	64
42	1.03	1.02	98	72	101	1.03	1.00	68	64
43	1.02	1.00	82	72	102	1.04	1.00	66	64
44	1.01	1.01	78	76	103	1.05	1.01	69	62
45	1.01	1.01	82	76	104	1.05	1.01	60	62
46	0.98	1.02	74	74	105	1.05	1.05	62	62
47	1.05	1.03	77	75	106	1.02	1.04	60	63
48	1.04	1.02	79	76	107	1.02	1.05	59	61
49	1.05	1.03	79	76	108	1.05	1.01	60	61
50	1.05	1.01	72	78	109	1.05	1.01	60	61
51	1.02	0.99	83	82	110	1.05	1.03	64	60
52	1.03	0.98	82	83	111	1.05	1.01	54	59
53	0.97	0.98	88	85	112	1.05	1.02	72	59
54	0.98	0.99	89	85	113	1.05	1.03	79	69
55	0.98	1.01	86	85	114	1.04	1.04	68	68
56	0.98	0.99	87	85	115	1.04	0.99	67	68
57	0.97	0.99	83	83	116	1.03	1.00	63	67
58	0.96	0.98	84	84	117	1.03	0.97	98	97
59	0.95	0.98	90	91	118	1.05	1.02	66	69

result indicates that with the incorporation of HVDC link in existing AC transmission system, electricity nodal prices at several buses have reduced.

4.2 Indian electricity market and real transmission network

4.2.1 *Indian electricity market*

India's electricity sector has grown to 143,061 MW as on 31st March 2008 with a compound annual growth rate of 8-9%. This sector is been characterized by shortage of supply vis-avis demand. In order to improve its performances, GoI initiated electricity sector restructuring in 1991. The

EA 2003 is been brought to facilitate private investments and to help cash strapped State Electricity Boards to meet electricity demand. On the electricity transmission front, the Indian grid is divided into five sub grids namely, Northern, Western, Southern, Eastern and North-Eastern called regional grids. Each one has number of constituent sub grids formed by state and private utility networks. All these sub grids and networks have connected to form a 400 kV national grid. The constituent systems have their own generation in additional to generation by central government undertakings in different parts of the country and feeds power in the grid at different locations. The Central and State Transmission Utility is responsible for the national and regional transmission system development and is also providing *Open Access* on it's inter and intra-state transmission system. The Power Grid Corporation of India Limited is set up for establishment and operation of regional and national power grids to ease transfer of power within and across the regions with reliability, security and economy, on sound commercial principles. Power Trading Corporation is helping market participants to find counterparts. To increase efficiency and competition in the sector, Central Electricity Regulatory Commission (CERC) allowed open access to market participants, *National Grid* formation and development of inter-regional electricity transmission linkages and implemented Availability Based Tariff for real time balancing market. To promote power trading in a free power market, CERC recenty setup Indian Energy Exchange (IEX). It has developed as market based institution for providing price discovery and price risk management to the electricity generators, distribution licensees, electricity traders, consumers and other stakeholders. At present, IEX offers day-ahead contracts whose time line is set in accordance with the operations of Regional Load Dispatch Centers (RLDCs). IEX coordinates with the National Load Dispatch Centers/RLDCs and State LDCs for scheduling of traded contracts.

4.2.2 Real transmission Network of India

Maharashtra State Electricity Board is the largest installed capacity of 15,580 MW in India. In 2005, it was unbundled into Generation, Transmission and Distribution Company. Maharashtra State Electricity Transmission Company Limited (MSETCL) infrastructure consists of ± 500 kV HVDC, 400 kV, 220 kV, 132 kV, 110 kV, 486 EHV sub-stations, and 35626 circuit km lines. Due to inadequate investment, transmission sector is also feeling the strain. The current transformation capacity is of 22,168 MVA, which have proposed to enhance to 68,182 MVA to bring down line loading with an investment of over Rs. 200 Billion. It has also proposed to offer most of the new evacuation lines and substations to private sectors on tariff-based bidding.

Present study considered a real network of 400 kV MSETCL shown in Fig.2-Appendix. It consists of 19 intra-state buses (i.e. Bus No. 1 to 19) and 8 inter-state buses. Additional power to fulfill real power demands has imported from inter-state generators namely BHILY, KHANDWA, SDSRV, BOISR, BDRVT, TARAPUR, and SATPR. The generator installed capacity, upper and lower bounds for generators, fuel cost function for intra and inter-state generators expressed as

$$(f_i = a_i P_{Gi}^2 + b_i P_{Gi} + c_i)$$

in ($/MWh) and real power demand is shown in Table 2-Appendix. The voltages at all buses have bounded between 0.96 and 1.04 PU. The operating data for HVDC link has shown in Table 3-Appendix. The transmission line loading capacity expressed in MVA has shown in Table 4- Appen-

dix. CHDPUR selected as a reference bus. This system have 2×16 equalities constraints of S of their respective real and reactive power balances of the buses without a generator, and 48 inequalities constraints of T of 27 pairs of voltage, 2×11 pairs of generation output and one pair of line flow upper and lower bounds.

4.2.3 Case-1: system simulation without HVDC link

Electricity nodal prices obtained at various buses are high for 400 kV MSETCL system without considering HVDC link as shown in Table 5. It is due to huge active power deficit at KOYNA-4, CHDPUR and KORDY, congestions in the transmission lines namely, CHDPUR-KORDY, BHSWL2-ARGBD4 and CHDPUR-PARLY2, rising power demand and costly power imported to fulfill present demand. The

Table 2 Generation capacity and costs characteristics and real peak demand

Bus/ Generator	Gen. Cap (PU)	PG (PU)		Generation cost (S/MWh)			Real Load (PU)
		Max	Min	Ai	Bi	Ci	
Intra-State Buses/Generators							
CHDPUR	2.3	1.72	0.2	0.20	20.4	10.2	0.3
KORDY	1.06	0.54	0.2	0.20	22.4	10.2	0.3
BHSWL2							0.2
ARGBD4							0.5
BBLSR2							0.5
DHULE							0.2
KALWA							0.3
KARGAR							0.3
LONKAND							0.6
NGOTNE							0.3
DABHOL	1.50	1.44	0.2	1.02	71.4	10.2	0.0
KOYNA-N							0.4
KOYNA-4	1.50	0.19	0.1	0.20	20.4	10.2	0.0
KLHPR3							0.4
JEJURY							0.3
KARD2							0.5
SOLPR3							0.3
PARLY2							0.05
PADGE							0.4
Intra-State Buses/Generators							
BHILY		0.6	0.1	0.20	36.9	10.2	
KHANDWA		0.7	0.2	1.02	36.9	10.2	
SDSRV		0.5	0.1	1.02	77.6	10.2	
BOISR		0.2	0.1	1.02	55.7	10.2	
BDRVT		1.7	0.2	0.20	22.5	10.2	
TARAPUR		0.4	0.1	1.02	58.6	10.2	
SATPR		0.2	0.1	1.02	55.7	10.2	

Table 3 Data: ±500kV CHDPUR-PADGE HVDC Link

Particulars	Data	Particulars	Data
Power Flow Rating	1500 MW	**Thyristor Valves**	
		Max.Voltage	7 KV
		Rated current	1700 Adc
Converter X'mer	500 KV 298.6 MVA	**Resistance** (1-Pole) (2-Pole) Metallic Return	7.5 Ohms 7.5 Ohms 15 Ohms
Voltage of each pole Rated power of unit			
HVDC Line Length of line Number of poles Nominal DC voltage	753 Km 2 =500 Kv	**Operation** CHDPUR Converter/ Rectifie R PADGE-Inverter	12.5 to 15 Degree 17 to 22 Degree

Table 4 Transmission line loading (MVA) of 400 kV MSETCL system

Name of Xn. Line	Design MVA	ATL	Name of Xn. Line	Design MVA	ATL
CHDPR-KORDY	500	403	LNKND-JYNA4	500	352
KORDY-BHILY	1000	636	KYNA4-KYNAN	1000	900
KORDY-SATPR	500	436	NGTNE-DABHOL	1000	900
KORDY-BSWL2	1200	1022	KYNAN-DBHOL	1000	900
BSWL2-ARGD3	500	352	KYNAN-KARD2	1000	900
BSWL2-BBLSR2	500	416	KLPR3-MAPUSA	1000	900
ARGD3-BBLSR2	500	142	KLPR3-KARAD2	1000	900
BBLSR2-DHULE	1000	522	KYNA4-JEJURY	500	450
DULE-KHDWA	2000	1040	LNKND-JEJURY	500	450
DULE-SDSRV	1000	226	LNKND-KARD2	500	310
BBLSR2-PADGE	1000	542	KARAD2-SOLPR3	500	340
PADGE-BOISR	1000	900	LNKND-PARLY2	1400	1060
PADGE-KNKND	500	274	SOLPR3-PARLY2	1000	544
PADGE-KAGAR	500	198	PARLY2-CHDPR	2100	1716
PADGE-KALWA	1000	573	BDRVT-CHDPR	4000	2188
PADGE-NGTNE	1000	900	PADGE-TARAPR	1000	450
KALWA-KAGAR	500	177	CHDPUR-PADGE	3000	2800
KALWA-LNKND	500	420			

#ATL Average Transmission Line Loading (MVA)

state of Maharashtra has been facing severe power shortages at peak hours. The state utility is making all efforts to fulfill demand by power purchases and load shedding. To make wholesale electricity market more competitive, need is to pour large value of active power in the state. Similarly new investment in transmission segment in above transmission lines are needed to remove congestions.

4.2.4 *Case-2: system simulation with HVDC link*

The electricity demand in the Maharashtra state is concentrated in the western region and the major generation in the eastern gion. The state's share is of 1,700 MW from central generating station is received at CHDPUR. The AC transmission network comprising of three 400 kV circuits between CHDPUR and Mumbai, can safely transmit around 1200 MW of power without any contingency outage. Therefore, it was necessary to provide additional transmission capacity of around 1,500 MW. Expansion of 400 kV lines was not feasible due to sever constraints of right-of-way and cost considerations. The option of ± 500 kV HVDC bipole has found most viable. The electricity nodal prices have simulated with HVDC link shown in Table 6. The obtained nodal prices are lower as compared to previous case. Moreover, congestions in the above mentioned transmission lines reduced. Bus voltages are improved and it is possible to transmit sufficient and cheaper power available at BDRVT to fulfill the demand. This link is vital in peak load condition to maintain the prices within limit.

4.2.5 *Case-3: system simulation with HVDC link and generation addition*

The nodal prices can reduce with addition of hydro generation KOYNA-4 at its full extent. The prices obtained are the lowest and uniform at several buses shown in Table 7. At peak load, hydro generation plays a key role to reduce the prices and avoids costly inter-state power purchases. This move can promotes competition in the wholesale electricity market from strategically located lower-cost units and demand response can benefit to MSETCL, as the transmission grid can utilize more efficiently. Fig. 3 shows improved bus voltages at several buses with the addition of HVDC link and Hydro Generation at peak load.

4.2.6 *Case-4: system simulation with HVDC link and transmission line loading*

Figure 4 shows the comparison of nodal price behavior in transmission line loading environment. Higher

Table 5 Electricity nodal price ($/MWh) and bus voltages without HVDC link at peak load condition

Bus No	Bus Name	PG(PU)	Nodal Price	Bus No	Bus Name	PG(PU)	Nodal Price
1	CHDPUR	1.44	24	10	LONKED	-	168
2	KORDY	0.54	46	11	NGOTNE	-	105
3	BHSWL2	-	90	12	DABHOL	1.44	60
4	ARGBDA	-	104	13	KONA.N	-	288
5	BBLSR2	-	118	14	KONA-4	0.19	279
6	DHULE	-	116	15	KLHPR3	-	309
7	PADGE	-	140	16	JEJURY	-	223
8	KALWA	-	142	17	KARD2	-	309
9	KARGAR	-	142	18	SOLPR3	-	526
				19	PARLY2	-	20

Inter state Power Purchase - PG(PU): BHILY: 0.6: KHNDWA:0.89: SDSRV:0.3: BOISR:0.12: BDRVT:0.1:TARAPR:0.49:SATPR: 0.09

Table 6 Electricity nodal price ($/MWh) with HVDC link for peak load

Bus No	Bus Name	PG(PU)	Nodal Price	Bus No	Bus Name	PG(PU)	Nodal Price
1	CHDPUR	1.72	23.55	10	LONKED	-	58.99
2	KORDY	0.54	30.18	11	NGOTNE	-	64.24
3	BHSWL2	-	43.67	12	DABHOL	1.10	70.19
4	ARGBDA	-	48.01	13	KONA.N	-	73.62
5	BBLSR2	-	52.13	14	KONA-4	0.19	72.70
6	DHULE	-	50.99	15	KLHPR3	-	82.54
7	PADGE	-	58.99	16	JEJURY	-	66.07
8	KALWA	-	58.99	17	KARD2	-	82.30
9	KARGAR	-	58.99	18	SOLPR3	-	137.86
				19	PARLY2	-	11.89

Inter state Power Import Purchase - PG(PU): BHILY: 0.4: KHNDWA:0.89: SDSRV:0.27: BOISR:0.12: BDRVT:0.84:TARAPR:0.29: SATPR:0.01

Table 7 Electricity nodal price ($/MWh) with HVDC link and generation addition

Bus No	Bus Name	PG(PU)	Nodal Price	Bus No	Bus Name	PG(PU)	Nodal Price
1	CHDPUR	2.00	23.78	10	LONKED	-	25.92
2	KORDY	0.64	24.30	11	NGOTNE	-	26.00
3	BHSWL2	-	25.67	12	DABHOL	0.1	25.83
4	ARGBDA	-	26.12	13	KONA.N	-	25.77
5	BBLSR2	-	26.14	14	KONA-4	1.5	25.71
6	DHULE	-	26.19	15	KLHPR3	-	25.93
7	PADGE	-	25.98	16	JEJURY	-	25.94
8	KALWA	-	26.02	17	KARD2	-	25.89
9	KARGAR	-	26.05	18	SOLPR3	-	25.62
				19	PARLY2	-	25.02

Inter state Power Purchase - PG(PU): BHILY: 0.5: KHNDWA:0.10: SDSRV:0.01: BOISR:0.01: BDRVT:1.7:TRAPR:0.05:SATPR: 0.01

prices obtained at several buses at average transmission line loading. MSETCL at present reviewing the investments in transmission segment to reduced transmission loading. The present transmission infrastructure is inadequate to encourage competition in this segment and to create wholesale electricity market. Huge investments have needed to reduce price volatility and to encourage competition.

5. Conclusion

In several developing countries, due to electricity transmission congestions and lack of investments further reduces the consumer benefits. To overcome these barriers and to meet consumer benefits, developing countries now adopting HVDC transmission in the existing systems to gain techno-economical advantages of it. In addition, a common element of restructuring in transmission has opened for use by all eligible market participants under open access regime. Under it, economic analysis of investments and its impact on electricity nodal prices can play a vital role to motivate investors and the utility to develop wholesale power market. This study which is demonstrated for

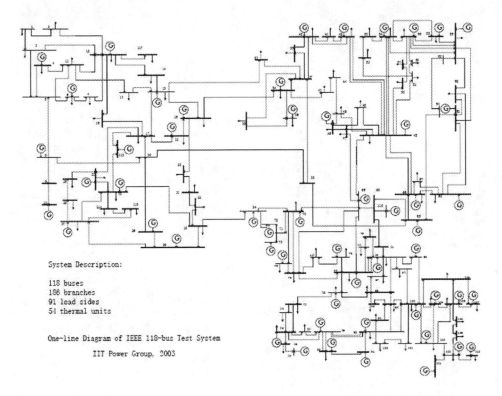

System Description:

118 buses
186 branches
91 load sides
54 thermal units

One-line Diagram of IEEE 118-bus Test System

IIT Power Group, 2003

Fig. 1 IEEE-118 bus test system

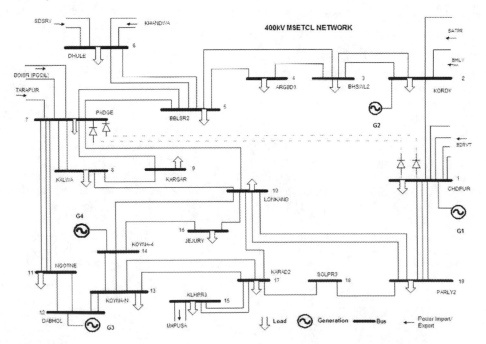

Fig. 2 400 KV MSETCL, India

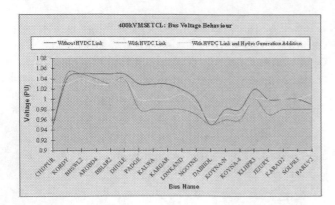

Fig. 3 Impact of addition of HVDC link and hydro generation on bus voltage behaviour

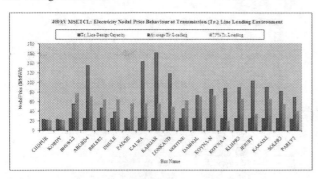

Fig. 4 Nodal price behaviour in transmission loading environment

Indian electricity market, gives valuable information about electricity nodal prices, transmission investments, and power quality to the system operator, regulatory commissions and utilities to develop efficient wholesale electricity markets.

References

1. D. Ray and F. Alvarado, *"Use of an engineering model for economic analysis in the electric utility industry,"* presented at the Advanced Workshop on Regulation and Public Utility Economics, The State University of New Jersey, Rutgers University, May 25-27, pp. 23–29, 1988
2. M. Rivier and I. J. Perez-Ariaga, *"Computation and decomposition of spot price far transmission pricing,"* in 11th PSC conference, Avignon, Francia. Agosto, pp 39–46, 1993
3. D. Finney, H. A. Othman, and W. L. Rutz, *"Evaluating transmission congestion constraints in system planning,"* IEEE Trans. Power Sys., vol. 12, No. 3, pp. 1143–1150, Aug. 1997
4. F. C. Schweppe, M. C. Caramis, R. D. Tabors, R. E. Bohn, *Spot Pricing of Electricity*, Kluwer Academic Publishers, Boston, 384 p. 1988
5. C. N. Lu, S. S. Chen, C. M. Ong, *"The Incorporation of HVDC Equations in Optimal Power Flow Methods using Sequential Quadratic Sequential Quadratic Programming Techniques"*, IEEE Trans. Power Sys., Vol. 3, No.3, pp. 1005–1011, August 1988
6. Kai Xie, Yong-Hua Song, John Stonham, Erkeng Yu, and Guangyi Liu, *"Decomposition Model and Interior Point Methods for Optimal Spot Pricing of Electricity in Deregulation Environments"*, IEEE Trans. Power Sys., Vol. I, No. 1, pp. 39–50, February 2000
7. G. Ward, N. R. Watson, C. P. Arnold, A. J. Turner, and B. J. Ring, *"Inversion of Real Time Spot Prices in the Direction of Real Power Flow in a Transmission Line"*, IEEE Trans. Power Sys., Vol. 15, No. 4, pp 1197–1203, November 2000
8. Luonan Chen, Hideki Suzuki, Tsunehisa Wachi, and Yukihiro Shimura, *"Components of Nodal Prices for Electric Power Systems"*, IEEE Trans. Power Sys., Vol. 17, No. 1, pp. 41–49, 2002
9. P. Meliopoulos, S. Kang, G. Cokkinides, R. Dougal, *"Animation and Visualization of Spot Prices via Quadratized Power Flow Analysis"*, Proceedings of 36th Hawaii International conference on System Sciences (HICSS'03) - Track 2, Vol. 2, pp.49b, January 06–January 09, 2003
10. Eugene Litvinov, Tongxin Zheng, Gary Rosenwald, and Payman Shamsollahi, *"Marginal Loss Modeling in LMP Calculation"*, IEEE Trans. Power Sys., Vol. 19, No. 2, pp. 880–888, May 2004
11. Tong Wu, Ziad Alaywan, and Alex D. Papalexopoulos, *"Locational Marginal Price Calculations Using the Distributed-Slack Power-Flow Formulation"*, IEEE Trans. Power Sys., Vol. 20, No. 2, pp. 1188–1190, May 2005
12. Hugo A. Gil, Francisco D. Galiana, and Edson L. da Silva, *"Nodal Price Control: A Mechanism for Transmission Network Cost Allocation"*, IEEE Trans. Power Sys., Vol. 21, No. 1, pp. 3–10, February 2006
13. Guang Li, Chen-Ching Liu, Chris Mattson, and Jacques Lawarree, *Day- Ahead Electricity Price Forecasting in a Grid Environment"*, IEEE Trans. Power Sys., Vol. 22, No. 1, pp. 266–274, February 2007
14. Fangxing Li, and Rui Bo, *"DCOPF-Based LMP Simulation: Algorithm, Comparison with ACOPF, and Sensitivity"*, IEEE Trans. Power Sys.,Vol. 22, No. 4, pp. 1475–1485, November 2007
15. Pandya K.S., Joshi S. K., *"A survey of Optimal Power Flow Methods"*, Journal of Theoretical and Applied Information Technology, Vol. 4 No. 5, pp. 450–458, 31st May 2008
16. H. You, V. Vittal, and X. Wang, *"Slow coherency based islanding,"* IEEE Trans. Power Sys., Vol. 19, No. 1, pp. 183–491, February, 2004

Ontology based expert systems – replication of human learning

Rahul Matkar[1] · **Ajit Parab[2]**

[1]Vidyalankar School of Information Technology, Mumbai, India
[2]H.O.D. Computer Technology Department, Babasaheb Gawde Institute of Technology, Mumbai, India

1. Introduction

This paper mainly focuses of the learning ability of the Expert Systems. This paper presents an elite system well known as Expert Systems, which tries to replicate the behavior of a 'Human Expert'. The expert systems work on the concept of 'Knowledge Base'. This knowledge base is developed by a 'Knowledge Engineer' after conducting a series of interviews with the 'Human Expert'. The 'Inference Engine' uses the facts from the 'Knowledge Base' in order to derive a solution to a problem. The performance of the Expert System fully depends on the quality of the Knowledge Base and the Inference Engine. The major issue to be considered under the development of theExpert systems is the ability to learn things by themselves. Expert Systems 'Replicate' the approach of human experts towards solving a problem, similarly the expert systems can also 'Replicate the behavior of Human Learning'. While learning a new fact humans use their existing knowledge and try to respond to the new fact accordingly. Similarly, an Expert System, if given a 'Baseline – A strict set Rules to follow' and the 'Ability to Derive a Relation between various Facts (An Ontology)' while learning, they can also 'derive' or 'learn' new facts the same way Human Experts learn or Expand their knowledge.

2. Expert systems

Expert Systems are special kind of software systems which aim to solve the problems to which human experts give better solutions.

Expert Systems try to replicate the behavior of a human expert. Expert Systems work on the concept of special kind of databases known as Knowledge base. These Knowledge bases store facts about the domain of the expert system.

This Knowledge Base is designed by a Knowledge Engineer. The Knowledge base is designed by the knowledge engineer after detailed interview sessions with the human expert. A Knowledge Acquisition System is built to keep the Knowledge Base Complete Consistent and Correct.

2.1 Development of an expert system

First of all the Developer should understand the system should achieve. Initially the Knowledge Engineer conducts a series of interviews with the human expert in that particular domain and understands his ways of solving expert level problems.

Although the expert might give solution to a problem easily, he or she may find it difficult to explain how he or she gave the solution. It is the job of the Knowledge Engineer to extract all the essential details about the domain to build a proper Knowledge Base also it is his job to represent the knowledge in a proper format in the Knowledge Base for convenience of writing code. This task is extremely important because the performance of the expert system depends a lot on the quality of the Knowledge Base. This series of interviews goes on until the Knowledge Engineer feels he has acquired all the appropriate facts about the Domain. A major requirement of the end user is getting an explanation for the decisions taken by an Expert System. An Explanation System was introduced for an Expert System to give explanation of the decisions taken by it. To extract this kind of explanation, the Knowledge in the Knowledge Base is written in the form of rules i.e. in he form of it-then rules like "IF you want to score good marks then you have to study hard". Changing the Knowledge into rules is not a simple task because of the ambiguity and duplications of facts in the Knowledge Base; it is needed to be managed as

S.J. Pise (ed.), *ThinkQuest 2010*, DOI 10.1007/978-81-8489-989-4_7,

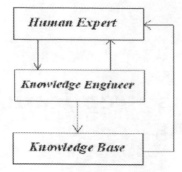

Fig. 1 Development of a simple expert system

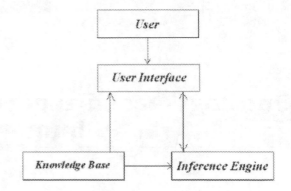

Fig. 2 Architecture of a simple expert system

accurately as possible. Fig. 1 shows the development of an Expert System [1]

2.2 Architecture of an expert system

The Architecture of the Expert System reflects the Knowledge Engineers' understanding of the methods of representing knowledge and of how to perform intelligent decision making on basis of the Knowledge. The software architecture of the expert system is hardware independent. The end user communicates with the system with the help of a user interface which allows the user to enter facts about a particular situation and ask questions of the system. The system intern responds to the request via the user interface. The user interface is further connected to the Knowledge base and the inference engine. The user interface acquires a set of facts from the inference engine and the Knowledge Base. Like the Knowledge Base the Inference engine also contains a set of rules and facts. However the rules and facts in a knowledge base are restricted to a domain of particular expertise, while those of an inference engine contain the general control and search strategy employed by the expert system to arrive on a solution. The inference engine uses facts provided by the user and the knowledge base to generate new facts. This architecture replicates the thinking process of a human expert. Fig. 2 shows the architecture of an Expert System.

2.3 Knowledge base

The Knowledge base is the core part of the Expert System and for this reason the expert system is also known as a rule based system. If the expert system is considered as a production system, then the knowledge base is the set of production rules. The expertise concerning the problem area is represented by productions. In a rule based system he data is kept in the format if – a given condition is true then – perform the action corresponding to a given situation. The Expert System knowledge isrepresented in the form of a tree. It consists of a root frame and a number of sub-frames. The frame structure is organized in a hierarchical structure such that each frame has its respective rules, characteristics and parameters.

2.4 The inference engine

An inference Engine serves as the inference (the creation of knowledge from the existing fact) and control mechanism. The design of the inference engine determines the effectiveness and efficiency of the system. For a problem to be solved the inference engine loads only the required context about the problem and works for a solution for the problem. The inference engine extracts the required facts from the knowledge base about the given domain and also receives the facts to be worked on from the user through the user interface. When the inference engine extracts the solution it gives it to the user through the user interface. As the inference engine follows a systematic approach, it is able to deliver the most important explanation to the user for attaining a given solution.

2.5 Role of the knowledge engineer

The Knowledge Engineer plays the most important role in the development of the knowledge base. It is the responsibility of the knowledge engineer to accurately estimate the requirement of the user. The Knowledge Engineer conducts a series of interviews with the Human Expert to attain the accurate, complete, correct and consistent knowledge about the domain.

The knowledge engineer has to build small prototypes of the system to ensure proper functioning by testing it under various situations. There are a number of faults like semantic errors, experts' knowledge errors, syntax errors, inference engine errors, chain errors and so on. These errors are needed to be avoided by the Knowledge Engineer to ensure the creation of an ideal Knowledge Base.

3. Ontology

3.1 Creation of 'ontology'

Ontology is the "study of the kinds of things that exist" [7, 8].Ontologism are a shared and common understanding of a domain that can be communicated between people and application systems [12]. In the artificial intelligence community, ontology refers to the *representation vocabulary*, typically a body of knowledge describing some domain. This representation vocabulary includes the conceptualizations that the terms in the vocabulary desire to capture. There is a relationship described between these conceptual elements included in the representation vocabulary. This relationship described between conceptual elements allow the production of rules governing how these elements are 'related' to each other or 'wired together' [6]. The use of ontology for the creation of the knowledge base gives birth to the advantage of replicating the real world objects in the knowledge base at ease [8, 9].

In this scenario the final information product contains the information captured from datasets, methods and the human expert, Fig. 3. In the case of datasets, domain *ontology* describes salient properties such as location, scale, date, format, etc., as currently captured in meta-data descriptions.

In the case of methods, *domain ontology* describes the services a method provides in terms of a transformation from one semantic state to another. In the case of human experts the simplest representation is again a *domain ontology* that shows the contribution that a human can provide in terms of steering or configuring methods and data. The synthesis of a specific information product is specified via a *task ontology* that must fuse together elements of the domain and application ontologies to attain its goal. An innovation of this framework is the dynamic construction of the solution network, similar to the *application ontology*. In order for resources to be useful in solving a problem, their ontologies must also overlap. Ontology is a useful metaphor for describing the genesis of the information product. A body of knowledge described using the domain ontology is utilized in the initial phase of setting up the expert system. Task ontology is created at the conclusion of the automated process specifically defining the concepts that are available. An information product is derived from the use of data extracted from databases and knowledge from human experts in methods [6]. Figure 3 exhibits the same.

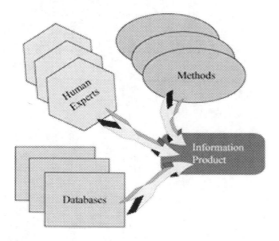

Fig. 3 Information products derived from the interaction of entities

Ontology is used at 'design time'. In some cases, it is required to check if a given term confirms to the ontology and if so, what version. In this case Ontology is used at 'run time'.

4. Model for learning in expert systems

Learning of new concepts has always been an issue for the development of expert systems. Once the knowledge has been entered in the knowledge base, relating new facts to it is a very difficult task. Defining the appropriate boundary for knowledge itself is a very difficult task. If the Expert Systems store the facts (knowledge) in the knowledge base in the form of 'Ontology', then adding new facts which are related to the knowledge domain becomes much easier. Ontology is a sort of data model, so we would like to adopt an existing representation language derived from different modeling traditions. Some systems come from Information Engineering and some from System Engineering.

4.1 Learning

Learning for an expert system is the process of improving a knowledge system by extending and rearranging its knowledge. This is one of the most interesting problems artificial intelligence has ever faced and is still under development. In early days of AI research, a simple parametric method was used for learning. There could be several different levels at which learning could be achieved.

Weak learning is improving problem solving capabilities with the use of examples. *Strong learning* requires an additional capability to represent the newly learnt knowledge explicitly in the form understood by a third party other than the learner and the tutor. *Very strong learning* comprises the requirements of strong learning with the requirement that the acquired knowledge is operational for the third party [2].

4.2 Role of 'Ontology' in the creation of the knowledge base

'Ontology' is a system of interrelated concepts used for representing the knowledge in some knowledge domain [2]. The basic idea behind creating ontologies is to represent the real world objects in the Knowledge Base by categorizing them under various classes. Ontology together with a set of individual instances of classes constitutes a knowledge base. In reality, there is a fine line where the ontology ends and the knowledge base begins. Whenever a knowledge base is to be filled by knowledge, a language is used for defining knowledge objects and an interpretation which will give meaning for those objects. However some initial knowledge is required to begin with. This knowledge constitutes an ontology that is used for writing meaningful texts in the language of the knowledge system. In other words ontology is a set of concepts and basic relationship between those concepts: being a sub concept (inherited), being a part of, being a property of or being a value of a property. A good point is ontologies developed for a specific restricted application domain, the relations may be more specific. Its use also facilitates better analysis of data [5].

4.3 Creation of layered knowledge base using ontology

In order to achieve learning in expert systems, the proposed system suggests a layered architecture as shown in Fig. 4. The first layer consists of Permanent facts that are the baseline for the knowledge base. The facts in this part of the knowledge base are never to be overruled while deriving a new fact or during the inference process. The next layer of the knowledge base comprises of the core knowledge base. This is the part of the knowledge base where the actual knowledge required for the system to function is stored. This knowledge base is structured using' Ontology'. The knowledge in this part of the knowledge base is stored in the form of classes which will are described by attributes. The third layer of the knowledge base consists of the newly derived facts encountered by the expert system which might be added to the second layer of the knowledge base later.

4.4 Expert systems replicating human learning

Whenever humans come across a new fact, they first try to figure how true the fact is according to their previous knowledge. Next they try to map it with the facts stored in their memory which they confidently consider to be true. If the newly derived fact is true in context of the previously acquired knowledge then it is stored in human memory. Next the humans try to apply this fact somewhere and observe the outcome. If the outcome is convincing enough then the humans confidently store the fact and as the number of successful events increase the confidence on the fact increases. Similar idea can be used by the expert systems. Expert systems have a special ability of giving an explanation about its decision about a particular domain. At the end of every decision, the expert systems give a weight value which decides the reliability of the decision made. Now, when the infer-

ence engine derives a new fact during its operation, firstly the weight value of the fact is checked. Depending on this weight value the decision of adding the fact to the knowledge base will be taken. The other half of the decision will be taken on basis of the relation of the fact with the domain knowledge base considering the ontological structure.

- The knowledge base should be created using an ontology following the layered architecture, Fig. 5.
- The minimum value to be possessed by the derived fact to be added to the newly derived facts section of the knowledge base.
- The number of successful and unsuccessful applications of the newly derived facts in order to be added to the core knowledge base is also set according to the nature of the domain.
- If the fact is the outcome of the inference process, then, after comparing its weight value with the limit set and after considering the relation of the newly derived fact with the existing knowledge (ontology) the fact should be added to the newly derived facts section of the knowledge base.
- Next, the fact is now applied in practical (except for critical cases).
- If the newly derived fact yields success for the number of successful attempts set, then the fact is added to the knowledge base considering the ontology. But if it fails for the number of times the limit set, then the fact is discarded.

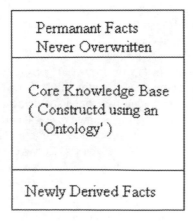

Fig. 4   Layered architecture of the knowledge base

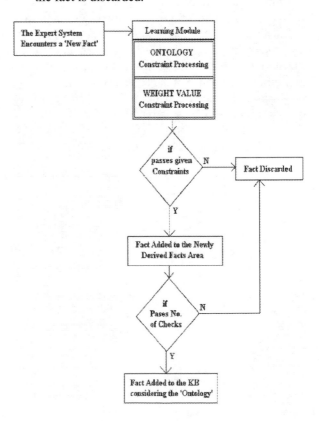

Fig. 5   Architecture of a self learning expert system

4.6 Application of learning in robots

Robotics has always been a field where the need for decision making, learning has always been felt. Any automated robot consists of a sensor and actuator mechanism. With the use of artificial intelligence efforts are being made to automate the behavior of robots. The AI approach proposes the robot with

a few successive layers [3]:
  i. Sensors get data in.
  ii. The interpreter interprets data.
  iii. The modeler builds a model.
  iv. The planner makes a movements plan in order to take the robot to its goal.
  v. The robot sends orders to actuators.

Lately Expert Systems have been used by robots to learn to walk just by observing the surrounding. The learning model of the Expert System could also be well applied in a Robot. Using the proposed architecture the Robots could replicate the learning techniques of the human beings. The information acquired by the sensors can filtered i.e. the information to be stored in the knowledge base can be refined. The decisions made by the robots can be also updated into their Knowledge Base considering ontological structure of the knowledge base. This technique would prove to be very useful for robots to acquire knowledge as they work.

5. Conclusion

Learning capabilities of an expert system play a very vital role under the development of an expert system. The research under Ontology is moving fully towards web development, which should also focus on creation of Knowledge Base for Expert Systems. Expert systems have been under research for a considerable amount of time but they are even today a topic under research and are needed to be explored much further.

References

1. N.P. Padhy, Artificial Innelligence and Inteligent Systems.
2. Enn Tyugu, Algorithms and Architechtures of Artificial Intelligence.
3. Marco Morales, Jesus Savage, "Motion control of a Robot using Expert Systems And Artificial Neural networks"
4. Ekaine Rich and Kevin Knight, Artificial Intelligence.
5. Natalya F. Noy and Deborah L. McGuinness, "Ontology Development101: A guide to create your first ontology.
6. Pundt, H. and Bishr, Y., 2002, Domai ontologies for data sharing–an example from environmental monitoring using field GIS. *Computers &Geosciences*, 28: 95-102.
7. Chandrasekaran, B. Josephson, J.R. and Benjamins, V.R., 1997. Ontologies of Tasks and Methods, AAAI Spring Symposium.
8. Guarino, N., 1997b. Understanding, building and using ontologies. *International Journal of Human-Computer Studies*, 46: 293-310.
9. Kokla, M. and Kavouras, M., 2002. Theories of Concepts in ResolvingSemantic Heterogeneities, 5th AGILE Conference on Geographic Information Science, Palma, Spain, pp. 2.
10. Robert M. Colomb, Ontology and the Symantic web.
11. Martin Hepp, Alo De Moor, Pieter De Leenheer and York Sure,Ontology Management.
12. John Davies, Dieter Fensel and Frank Van Harmelen, Towards the Symantic Web – Ontology Driven Knowledge Management

Case-based reasoning for adaptive content delivery in e-learning systems using mobile agents

S. R. Mangalwede[1] · Dr. D. H. Rao[2]

[1]Research Scholar, Department of Computer Science and Engg, Gogte Institute of Technology, Belgaum, India
[2]Director, MATS School of Business, Belgaum, India

1. Introduction

With the advent of information and communication technology and acceptance of Internet, e-Learning coupled with multimedia and network technology provides new methods and ideas for traditional teaching. e-Learning can be defined as a learning environment supported by continually evolving, collaborative processes focused on increasing individual and organizational performance [1]. e-Learning has become the unifying term to describe the fields of online learning, web-based training, and technology-delivered instruction. However, the emphasis of eLearning has shifted from static content delivery to personalized, context-aware knowledge service based on learner profile and modern pedagogy.

A Mobile Agent (MA) can be defined as autonomous, problem solving computational entity capable of effectively performing operations in dynamic unpredictable environments. Such environments are known as multi-agent systems [2]. Agents interact and cooperate with other agents. They are capable of exercising control over their actions and interactions and do not always have to wait for commands. An agent adapts its behavior in response to the changing environment. It can migrate from server to server in heterogeneous networks. A mobile agent consists of two different parts: the code itself, which is composed of instructions that define the behavior of the agent and its intelligence, and the current state of execution of the agent. On each server, the agent interacts with stationary services and other resources to accomplish its mission. It can communicate to anticipate, adapt and plan tasks. Its behavior consists of beliefs, desires, and interaction depending on the place function of an entity within an agent-based system. The traditional educational system architecture has three main components: domain knowledge, pedagogical expertise and learner model. But such systems have shown to be too rigid to deal with the quick evolution of knowledge and diversity of human culture, learning behavior and cognitive styles. The multi-agent approach applies very well to domains where distance, cooperation among different entities, and integration of different components of software are critical issues. Figure 1 shows the elements of e-Learning. A trainer is responsible for developing the content. The content can be of different media types that are pertinent to the course for which the content is being authored. The e-Learning system is expected to capture the learner characteristics - in the form of educational, personal and technological background and create a learner profile. The learner profile is an important element of eLearning that aids the system to personalize the content based on the traits of the learner. The learner assessment is done to decide on the progress of the learner that leads to the learner profile being dynamically updated to reflect the learner's progress in order to adapt the content needed to be delivered. Also, based on the feedback obtained at the end of the course, the course content can be updated to reflect the learning behavior. The profiles maintained by the eLearning system are used to dynamically decide the nature of content to be delivered to a future learner sharing a similar profile.

Any e-Learning system development involves a complete analysis of the learning domain. The learners are different in age level, sex, and social role. Their culture, education background, attention, interests, hobby etc. also have a great impact. Giving corresponding learning contents and tactics to realize teaching according to learners' needs is very difficult. Other issues include weak interaction, uneven geographic distribution of teaching resources, different structures of different kinds of networks and learning groups, that make e-Learning more difficult. Interdependence and independence in learning environment, implementation technology, scalability and accessibility are also challenges. To overcome all these limitations and constraints, the proposed approach uses intelligent collaborative multiagent systems in e-Learning [3]. The proposed framework is generic and it can be employed not only for the development of e-Learning system within a local network of workstations, but also for the development of the system accessible to the public on the Internet.

2. Mobile agents in e-Learning system

As distributed computing became widespread, more flexibility and functionality was required than Remote Procedure Calls (RPC) could provide. RPC proved suitable for two-tier client/server architectures where the application logic is either in the user application or within the actual database or file server. As three-tier client/server architectures gained ground, where the application is split into client application (usually a GUI – Graphical User Interface or browser), application logic and data store (usually a database server), the advantages started becoming obvious in the form of reusable, modular, easily deployable components. The current generations of e-Learning systems predominantly make use http (hypertext transfer protocol) where an http client connects to a http server to download web documents (containing e-Learning content). The client needs to be connected for the entire learning session with the server. Few implementations of e-Learning systems make use of applet-servlet communication model as well as Java RMI (Remote Method Invocation). Some of the characteristics of these technologies that impact their decision are Support for Objects, Statefulness of components, Blocking versus non-blocking calls, Communication Protocol, Speed, and Robustness [4]. To justify the use of mobile agents as a technology for implementation of e-Learning system, we considered these different Java-based approaches viz., RMI, Servlets and MA.

For performing a comparative study of the three approaches, we developed a demonstrative application that generates requests for certain service available remotely. The experimental setup is shown in Fig. 2.
We define a metric *Elapsed Time (ET) as,*

$$ET = L1 + PT + L2 + TT$$

where, L1 is the latency at the client, L2 is the latency at the server (or at both hosts in case of Content Authoring Trainer Content Learner Learner Profiling Profile Content Delivery Learner Assessment Feedback Aglets),PT is the Processing Time for service, and TT is the trip time for the request and response.

From the results obtained, we observed that both RMI and MA perform similarly with reference to the ET.

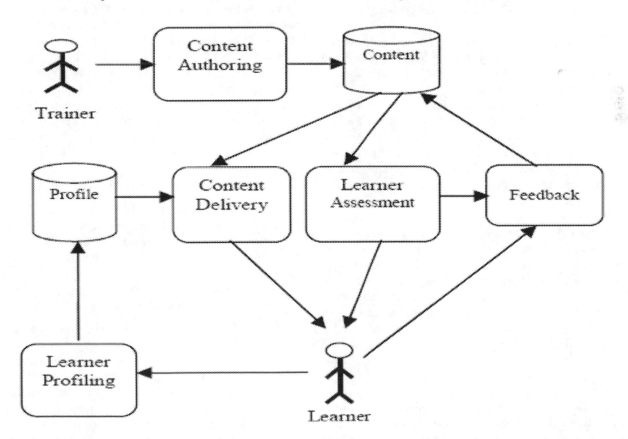

Fig. 1 Elements of e-learning system

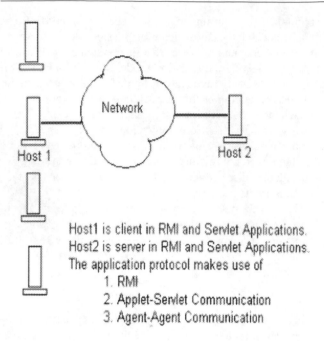

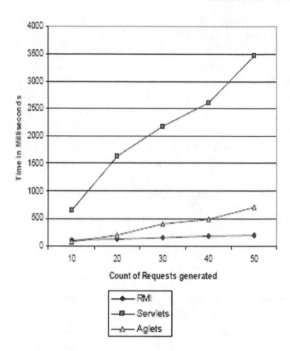

Fig. 2   Experimental setup

The size of the MA has minimal effect on the network latency and the round trip time, though the object serialization mechanism of the agent has a significant effect on the performance. Also, that the agent has to be instantiated at the context to which it migrates contributes to the ET that is slightly larger than that of RMI. RMI does not suffer from this overhead. However, the important characteristic of MA is its autonomy and ability to work even in disconnected environment as it doesn't use synchronous communication.

On the other hand, when we compare the performance of applet-servlet communication for distributed computing applications with that of RMI and MA-based approach, we can observe that the need for http request and http response formation, as well as the connection management contribute to the large amount of time required for the appletservlet communication. Figure 3 shows the results of the experiment on a network.

Comparison of different Approaches to Distributed computing (Experiments conducted on LAN)

All the three approaches make use of transport layer virtual circuit for the purpose of communication. However, only RMI and MA are fully object oriented. Applet-Servlet approach does not have object-oriented interface. Both RMI and Applet-Servlet approaches have added security for client and server by means of employing SSL (Secure Sockets Layer). Security in MA approach is an area of active research. However, a secure protocol doesn't necessarily translate into a secure system as most of the security breaches take place by exploiting the defects in implementation and not through protocol weaknesses. The authors and others have addressed various security related issues in MA design. [5–10].

Fig. 3   Experimental Results

Each of the approach has its relative advantages and disadvantages. However, MA approach may be considered over others as the advantages of MA outweigh the disadvantages [11]. The autonomy, ability to operate in volatile, disconnected network environments, and ability to collaborate proactively with other MAs are striking features of MA that are not available with other approaches considered. In applications such as adaptive e-Learning where remotely available content should be delivered after processing the learner profile and learning characteristics, autonomy becomes an important issue and MA technology seems a feasible approach as compared to other approaches that we considered.

3.   Proposed model for content delivery

The various design entities that we considered in an e-Learning system include Learning entity (the Student), Teaching authority (the Teacher), Formative assessment (to help implement adaptive learning), Summative assessment engine.

Figure 4 shows the architecture of the proposed model. The model deals with following agents.

1.   Student Agent performs two functions:
   i.   If registered learner, then presents the content information from content database to read.
   ii. If new learner, then asks for registration to collect information to prepare learner profile and uploads this information in student database.
2.   Teacher Agent performs two functions:
   i.   if registered teacher, then provides authority to upload the new contents in different file formats

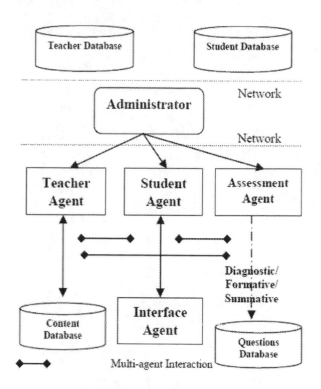

Fig. 4 Proposed architecture

including audio and videos. Also provides for content authoring to implement adaptive learning.

ii. If new teacher, then presents registration form to collect teacher specific information and course offerings.

3. Administrator agent deals with teacher, student, content, case-base and assessment databases.

4. Interface Agent accepts student requests and takes care of displaying content after fetching from the content database.

5. Assessment Agent helps in displaying assessment questions, depending on type selected from student, self or final. Teacher can provide the assessment questionnaires. The assessment is both diagnostic (used to identify the current knowledge and skill level), formative (possible development activities required in order to improve the level of understanding) as well as summative (to grade and judge a learner's level of understanding).

Student database will profile the personal information about each student, as well as information about their motivations, knowledge and skills, experience, cultural background, necessity for considering the course, preferences towards certain media for representation of the learning material, learning performance, etc. When a learner finishes a certain course/learning session, he/she will undergo self-assessment test in order to check the understanding of his/her knowledge in that module. At that point, a mechanism for

extracting the questions from learning materials and generating tests is activated. The results of those tests are used for updating the student profile database. As previously stated the questions will be formative with each question being marked either as answered definitely, answered with hint or answer was prompted. The learner's responses will be recorded and this will be used for generating and delivering appropriate learning content next.

The student agent implements Case-Based Reasoning (CBR) technique for personalized content delivery, access and interaction. CBR was described by Aamodt and Plaza [12] as combination of the following four processes:

- Retrieve previously experienced case or cases related to the current problem.
- Reuse this or these case(s) in one way or another.
- Revise the solution based on previous cases.
- Retain the new solution(as a new case) by adding it into the existing case-based database The degree of similarity in CBR is assessed by means of a matching function such as the Nearest Neighbor (NN) matching function:

$$\text{Similarity } (N, P) = \frac{\sum_{i=1}^{n} f(N_a, P_a) * w_a}{\sum_{i=1}^{n} w_a}$$

where N is the new case (new learner), P is the previous case (past learner history), n is the number of features in each case, i is an individual feature from 1 to n, f is the match function for attribute a in cases N and P, and wn is the weight of the ath attribute which reflects the relative importance of that attribute.

We have developed the learner profile taking into account different parameters like, technological. (bandwidth supported at the client, round-trip time an agent takes to reach the learner), cultural (vernacular medium of instruction that learner comes from, whether the learner is from urban or rural background) and educational (whether the learner is a graduate from science, arts or computer background). This profile is stored into the casebase. The case-base developed takes different combination of the learner traits and has around 30 entries in it. New learner information is captured and is passed through a CBR engine to decide the best suited learning content to be delivered to him/her. In case the learner profile doesn't match with the case-base, we add the profile as a new case as also the profile is added into the student database.

The e-Learning content is organized as a knowledge grid that caters to different types of content viz., plaintext based content, media-rich content (like word or pdf documents) and audio/video content. These different content repositories could be located at different servers geographically. For the purpose of our research, we have developed different

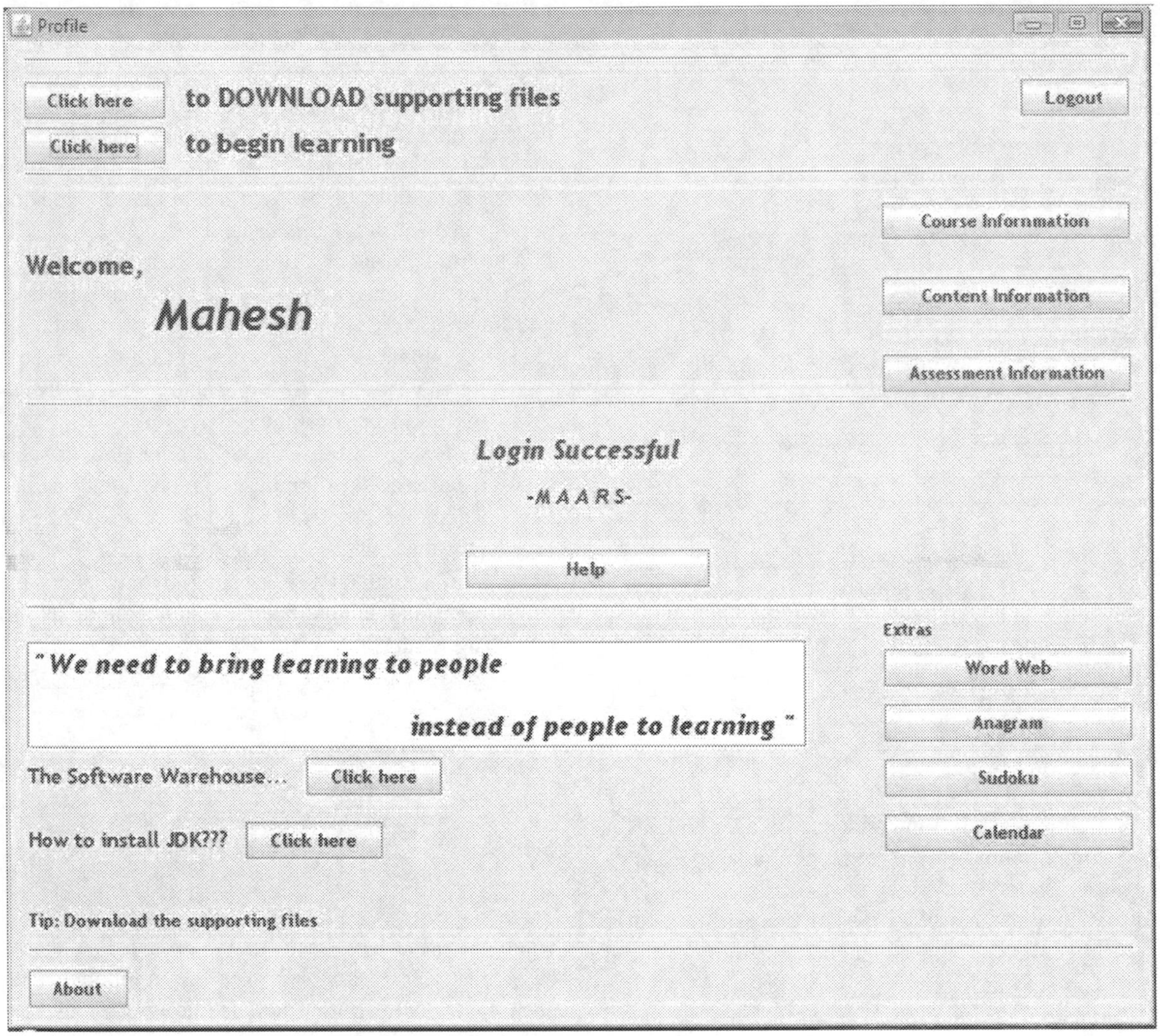

Fig. 5   Screenshot after capturing profile

types of content hosted on different content servers, for a course in Java programming.

Along with the CBR engine, the student agent conducts a diagnostic assessment of the learner to ascertain the level of understanding of the programming languages. The diagnostic assessment poses questions based on computers, programming in languages like C, C++ that are assumed to be a prerequisite for the course being offered. CBR engine generates the screenshot shown in Fig. 5 after capturing the learner profile and performing nearest match function.

At the end of each module of the course, a formative assessment of the progress of the learner is made. This assessment will be in the form of multiple choice questions. Along with the profile, the performance of the learner is used as the basis for delivering the content for the next module.

4.   Future work

It is envisaged to take a random sample of learners with closely matching profiles and make a subset of them undergo the course content using the e-Learning system

implemented in this work. Remaining subset of the learners will undergo the traditional e-Learning content (usually a set of static web documents that do not take the learner profile into account to personalize the content). After going through the course content in both the cases, it is planned to make the two sets of learners to undergo a summative assessment to evaluate the learner's understanding of the course. This may give us an idea about the efficacy of the proposed model.

5.   Conclusion

Maintaining an active connection to the server is a major limitation of traditional e-Learning systems. With mobile agents this drawback is overcome as the communication in MA is asynchronous and can happen in any direction. Multi-agent technology coupled with Case-Based Reasoning may be considered as a viable approach for developing an adaptive e-Learning system that personalizes the content delivery and assesses the learner progress intelligently.

References

1. K.A. Papanikolaoui, M. Grigoriadou et.al, Towards new forms of knowledge communication: the adaptive dimension of a web-based learning environment, *Computers and Education* 39, 4 (2002), 333-360

2. Danny B. Lange, "*Mobile Objects and Mobile Agents: The Future of Distributed Computing?*," Ju (Ed.): ECOOP'98, LNCS 1445, pp.1 -12, 1998

3. S.R. Mangalwede, D.H. Rao, "Context-Aware Intelligent Multi-Agent Technology in Knowledge Grid Environments for E-Learning Systems," in Proc. of *International Conference on Advances in Computing, Communication and Control*, 2009. ICAC3'09. ACM SIGART, pp. 257 – 263. *ISBN: 978-1-60558-351-8*

4. Distributed Computing Technologies – Selecting an Appropriate Approach, Philip Maechling, *Web Services Workshop, UNAVCO/IRIS Joint Workshop*, 8 June 2006

5. Stefan Pleisch, Andre Schiper, "Modeling Fault- Tolerant Mobile Agent Execution as a sequence of Agreement Problems", in *Proc. of the 19th IEEE Symposium on Reliable Distributed Systems*(SRDS'00), 2000

6. Michael R. Lyu, Xinyu Chen and Tsz Yeung Wong, "Design and Evolution of a Fault-Tolerant Mobile- Agent System", *IEEE Computer Society* 2004

7. S.R. Mangalwede, et.al, "A Reliable Agent Tracking Mechanism", in *Proc. of 3rd International Conference ObCom-2006, Mobile, Ubiquitous & Pervasive Computing*, December 16-19, 2006, Vellore Institute of Technology, Vellore, TN, India

8. S.R. Mangalwede, et.al, "Hierarchical Domain-based Authentication Framework for Mobile Agent Applications", in *Proc. of 3rd International Conference ObCom-2006, Mobile, Ubiquitous & Pervasive Computing*, December 16-19, 2006, Vellore Institute of Technology, Vellore, TN, India

9. S.R. Mangalwede, D.H. Rao, "A Review of Agent Tracking Mechanism and Security Issues in Mobile Agent-based Distributed Computing Systems", in *Proc. of National Conference on Advanced Technologies in Electrical and Electronic Systems, ATEES-07*, October 30, 2007, Gogte Institute of Technology, Belgaum. India

10. Carine G. Webber, et.al., "Towards Secure ELearning Applications: a Multiagent Platform", ournal of Software, Vol 2, No.1, February 2007

11. S.R.Mangalwede,et.al., Effectiveness and Suitability of Mobile Agents for Distributed Computing Applications, in *Proc. of 2nd International Conference on Autonomous Robots and Agents*, December 13-15, 2004, Palmerston North, New Zealand

12. Aamodt and E. Plaza (1994),CaseBased Reasoning: Foundational Issues. Methodological Variations, and System Approaches, Artificial Intelligence Communications, 10s Press, Vol. 7: I, pp. 39-59

Dynamically adjusted flooding scheme for vehicular ad-hoc networks

Nischal S. Puri · P. Kulkarni · S. Akojwar

Department of Computer Science & Engg. RGCE Research & Technology, Chandrapur, India

1. Introduction

In this article there is detailed discussion on MANET's & Broadcast problem and how it helps to solve the Broadcast storm problem in VANET's. First about the Mobile ad hoc networks i.e. (MANETs) they are self-organizing mobile wireless networks that do not rely on a preexisting infrastructure to communicate. Nodes of such networks have limited transmission range, and packets may need to traverse multiple other nodes. Although straightforward, flooding is far from optimal and generates a high number of redundant messages, wasting valuable limited resources such as bandwidth and energy supplies to network; such a scenario has often been referred to as the broadcast storm problem [2], and has generated many challenging research issues.

Same problem arises in VANET's i.e. although Vehicular ad hoc networks are different from usual mobile ad hoc networks (MANETs) in many aspects. First, VANETs consist of mostly highly mobile nodes moving in the same or opposite directions. Second, the network shape can be best described by a one-dimensional line (for a single-lane road) or a strip (for a multilane road) rather than a square or torus shape. Third, Last but not least, most applications targeting VANETs rely heavily on broadcast transmission to provide traffic related information to all reachable nodes within a certain geographical area. Because of the shared wireless medium, blindly broadcasting packets may lead to frequent contention and collisions in transmission among neighboring nodes. This problem is sometimes referred to as the broadcast storm problem. While multiple solutions exist to alleviate the broadcast storm in the usual MANET environment, only a few solutions have been proposed to resolve this issue in the VANET context.

The remainder of this article is organized as follows. First, we provide the necessary background and related work in MANET's context in which firstly we have discuss about broadcasting the packets using phase transition to reduce the redundancy of packets this was one of the first flooding scheme which supports probabilistic approach .Then in next discussion probabilistic approach is used on basis of dense & sparse networks. In sparse networks there is much less shared coverage; thus some nodes will not receive all the Broadcast packets unless the probability parameter is high. So if the rebroadcast probability p is set to a far smaller value, reach ability will be poor. On the other hand, if p is set for large, many redundant rebroadcasts will be generated. The need for dynamic adjustment, thus, rises. However above discussions are under the context of MANET's.

On the basis of above discussion we have proposed our schemes based on the dynamic adjustment. Then we quantify the impact of the broadcast storm Problem in MANETs and co relates with VANET's which is discuss in details. Next, we present a proposed broadcast mitigation algorithm, and briefly explain the network model and assumptions.

2. Related work under Manet's

This section analyses the related work which directly or indirectly aims at reducing the number of broadcast packets generated by the flooding algorithm. The high number of redundant broadcast packets due to flooding in MANETs has been referred to as the "Broadcast Storm Problem" [2]. There are five proposed flooding schemes [1] in MANETs called probabilistic, counter-based, distance-based, location based [1] and cluster based [1, 2]. In the probabilistic scheme, when receiving a broadcast message for the first time, a host rebroadcasts the message with a fixed probability P. To the best of our knowledge, besides [3], previous publications having studied probabilistic broadcast for flooding in MANETs [1, 4] have not done so within the context of phase transition. This paper contributes in a first stage to a better understanding of the various factors that influence phase transition in ideal MANET environments.

2.1 The phase transition phenomenon

In this paper [5] Yoav, David and Andre discussed about phase transition is a phenomenon where a system undergoes a sudden change of state: small changes of a given parameter in the system induce a great shift in the system's global behavior. This abrupt transition occurs at a specific value P_c called the critical point or critical threshold. Below pc the system is said to be in a subcritical phase — the global behavior is non-existent. Above P_c the system is in a supercritical phase and the global property may be almost surely observed. Figure 1 illustrates the phase transition probability Θ given the probability P of a problem specific parameter λ. L denotes the size of the system considered. It would be extremely cost-efficient to observe phase transition in a probabilistic flooding algorithm within all or known subsets of MANET topologies. The implication within such cases would be that there exists a certain probability threshold P_c < 1 at which the flooded message will almost surely reach all nodes within multihop broadcast reach. Broadcasting with a probability p > P_c will not provide any significant improvement.

They define the square grid model such as each node communicates with is direct vertical and horizontal neighbors, such that each node has exactly four neighbors. We broadcast one message from a single source positioned at the center of the grid. Using the regular algorithm for flooding in order to achieve our broadcast, a total of $m2$ messages will be transmitted (Algorithm 1). Algorithm 1 flood (m)

1. upon reception of message m at node n
2. if message m received for the first time then

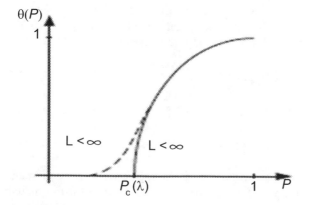

Fig. 1 Phase transition

3. broadcast(m) {This is the basic local broadcast primitive to nodes within range only}
4. end if

Algorithm 2 p-flood (m,p)

1. upon reception of message m at node n:
2. if message m received for the first time then
3. broadcast(m) with probability p {This is the basic local broadcast primitive to nodes within range only}
4. end if

Although phase transition is not observed, probabilistic flooding nonetheless greatly enhances the successful delivery of packets in dense networks. For future work, it would be interesting to explore algorithms in which nodes would dynamically adjust the probability p for probabilistic flooding based on local graph topology information. Another potential area for study would be to understand within probabilistic flooding the combined effects on MANET's performance of modifying the nodes' transmission range r with regard to p.

2.2. Adjusted probabilistic flooding

In this paper [6] discussed about the adjusted probabilistic flooding. In dense networks, multiple nodes share similar transmission range. Therefore, these probabilities control the frequency of rebroadcasts and thus might save network resources without affecting delivery ratios. Note that in sparse networks there is much less shared coverage; thus some nodes will not receive all the broadcast packets unless the probability parameter is high.

So if the rebroadcast probability p is set to a far smaller value, reachability will be poor. On he other hand, if p is set far large, many redundant rebroadcasts will be generated. The need for dynamic adjustment, thus, rises.

The rebroadcast probability should be set high at the hosts in sparser areas and low at the hosts in denser areas. It was simple method for density estimation requires mobile hosts to periodically exchange HELLO messages between neighbors to construct a 1-hop neighbour list at each host. A high a number of neighbours implies that the hosts in denser areas, a low number of neighbors imply that the host is in sparser areas. We increase the rebroadcast probability if the value of the number of neighbours is too low (or similarly if the current node is located in a sparse neighborhood), which indirectly causes the probability at neighbouring hosts to be incremented. Similarly, we decrease the rebroadcast probabilities if the value of number of neighbours is too high.

On hearing a broadcast message m at node X, the node rebroadcast a message according to a high probability if the message is received for the first time, and the number of neighbours of node X is less than average number of neighbours typical of its surrounding environment. Hence, if node X has a low degree (in terms of the number of neighbours), retransmission should be likely. Otherwise, if X has a high degree its rebroadcast probability is set low.

Receiving protocol ()

On hearing a broadcast packet m at node X Get the Broadcast ID from the message; n verage number of neighbor (threshold value);

 Get degree n of a node X (number of neighbors);
 If packet m received for the first time then
 If n < $\bar{n}$ then
   Node X has a low degree: set high rebroadcast probability p= p1;
 Else n =
  Node X has a high degree:
  set low rebroadcast probability p= p2;
 End if
 End if
 Generate a random number RN over [0, 1]
 If RN = p rebroadcast message; otherwise, drop.

This algorithm is a combination of probabilistic and knowledge based approaches. It dynamically adjusts the rebroadcast probability p at each mobile host according to the value of the local number of neighbours. The value of p changes when the host moves to a different neighborhood. In a sparser area, the rebroadcast probability is larger and in denser area, the probability is lower. Compared with the probabilistic approach where p is fixed, our algorithm achieves higher saved rebroadcast.

Average no. of neighbours

$\bar{n} = $ (N–1) 0.8*Π^2/A

Let A be the area of an ad hoc network,
N be the number of mobile hosts in the network, and
R be the transmutation range.
$\bar{n}$ average number of neighbors can be obtained

2.3 Another probabilistic approach

In this paper, we propose a dynamic probabilistic approach for broadcast based on previous work on MANET's context. We set the rebroadcast probability of a host according to number of neighbor nodes information. The rebroadcast probability would be low when the number of neighbor nodes is high which means host is in dense area and the probability would be high when the numbers of neighbor nodes are low which means host is in sparse area. Simulation results show that broadcast redundancy can be significantly reduced through the proposed approach.

3. Proposed system model

3.1 System overview

A wide spectrum of services in VANETs include, but are not limited to, public safety, traffic management, freight/cargo transport, transit, and traveler information. It is anticipated that vehicles in the future will be equipped with DSRC devices capable of communicating with nearby vehicles in one-hop or multihop fashion in order to extend the drivers' range of awareness to beyond what they can directly see. Emergency information such as collision or emergency braking can be propagated along the road to notify drivers ahead of time so that necessary action can be taken to avoid accidents. In addition to an emergency warning, drivers can also plan a trip in accordance with traffic conditions received from other vehicles or roadside units in order to save time on the road. The scope of applications can also be expanded to cover other services, which are of private business or automotive industry interests, such as on- oad entertainment streaming/downloading and Internet access.

3.2 Introduction

The basic broadcast techniques follow either a 1- persistence or p-persistence rule. Despite the excessive overhead, most routing protocols designed for multihop ad hoc wireless networks follow the brute force 1-persistence flooding rule, which requires that all nodes rebroadcast the packet with probability 1 because of the low complexity and high packet penetration rate. A gossip-based approach, on the other hand, follows the ppersistence rule, which requires that each node reforward with a predetermined probability p. This approach is sometimes referred to as probabilistic flooding [7]. In both schemes repeated reception of the same message or any expired messages should be ignored by broadcasting nodes in order to avoid inevitable service disruptions due to network saturation. In the following we propose broadcast scheme that allow each node to calculate its own reforwarding probability based only on its local information.

3.3 Dynamically adjusted flooding scheme

Rule - Upon receiving a packet from node i, node j checks the packet ID and rebroadcasts with probability Pij if it receives the packet for the first time; otherwise, it discards the packet. Also it checks the no. of neighbouring nodes and if they are high in numbers it means network is Denser probability is less else for Sparse network probability is high Denoting the relative distance between nodes i and j by Dij and the average transmission range by R, the forwarding probability, Pij, can be calculated on a per packet basis using the following simple expression:

$$P_{ij} = \frac{D_{ij}}{R}$$

Average no. of neighbours

$$\bar{n} = (N-1)0.8\frac{\pi^2}{A}$$

Let A be the area of an ad hoc network, N be the number of mobile hosts in the network, and **R** be the transmutation range.
Average number of neighbors can be obtained.

3.4 Network model and assumptions

Although most MANET studies typically assume a two-dimensional network with random topology, in this work we claim that a one-dimensional line network can best capture the topology of a vehicle based ad hoc network on a highway or in an urban area where mobile nodes are more likely to be on a well defined path and road. Therefore, we consider two types of network topologies in this article: a one-dimensional line or single-lane network and a multi-lane network. In the former case adjacent nodes are separated by a distance D that is exponentially distributed with mean. A multilane network is modeled with multiple singlelane networks. In order to understand the fundamental impact each of the broadcast schemes has on network performance, we developed a network simulator to create a broadcast scenario on a straight road, similar to that shown in Fig. 2, where each vehicle can perform the basic broadcast operations proposed earlier without the complication of the MAC and MANET routing protocol. For each simulation run, a new topology is created and one broadcast message is propagated for 100 hops; the time to live (TTL) of the packet is set to 100. Given the type of VANET applications considered earlier, we assume that there is only one active source in the network, and all the nodes within the broadcast range of the transmitter can correctly receive the packet. Upon receiving the broadcast message, each node keeps track of the number of packets it receives and immediately retransmits the packet according to the rules described earlier. Other statistics such as packet loss ratio and propagation delay are presented later; we also include the effect of 802.11a MAC and the routing protocol.

3.5 Expected result

In this section we will compare the performance of the proposed broadcast schemes with conventional 1-persistence and p-persistence flooding schemes. Each node has a broadcast range of 500 m. The reforwarding probability is assumed to be 0.5 in the sparse area which is away from the sending node. Following are the parameters on which we will analyze the performance on simulation such as Packet Loss Ratio, Latency etc.

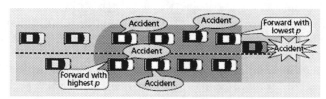

Fig. 2

4. Conclusion

Since most applications in VANETs favor broadcast transmission as opposed to point-to-point routing, routing protocols should be designed to address the broadcast storm problem to avoid unnecessary loss of important safety related packets during a broadcast storm. In this article we have proposed three techniques that depend only on the local positions of the receiver and transmitter nodes. The algorithms are completely distributed and computationally efficient in that they require only minor computations. In the absence of the GPS signal, the proposed algorithms can also be modified to use. The packet received to determine whether or not the packet should be retransmitted, although this approach is not as efficient as the GPS approach. It is worth mentioning here that while the broadcast storm problem can also be tackled at the MAC layer, this article takes the viewpoint that the current DSRC employs a fixed MAC protocol for VANETs specified by the standard [2], and therefore focuses on solving the broadcast storm problem at the network layer via intelligent routing strategies. We consider both of these approaches viable and interesting (and different) ways of solving the same problem. In addition, given that currently active safety applications mainly concern car manufacturers, solving the broadcast storm problem

References

1. B. Williams, T. Camp, Comparison of broadcasting techniques for mobile ad hoc networks. Proc. *ACM Symposium* on Mobile Ad HocNetworking & Computing (MOBIHOC 2002), pp.194– 205, 2002.
2. Y.-C. Tseng, S.-Y. Ni, Y.-S. Chen, and J.-P. Sheu. The broadcast storm problem in a mobile ad hoc network. Wireless Networks, 8(2/3):153– 167, 2002
3. Zygmunt J. Haas, Joseph Y. Halpern, and Li Li. Gossip-based ad hoc routing. In IEEE INFOCOM, Jun 2002.
4. Sze-Yao Ni, Yu-Chee Tseng, Yuh-Shyan Chen, and Jang-Ping Sheu. The broadcast storm problem in a mobile ad hoc network. In Proceedings of the Fifth Annual ACM/IEEE International Conference on Mobile Computing and Networking, pages 151–162, Aug 1999.
5. Y. Sasson, D. Cavin, A. Schiper, Probabilistic broadcast for flooding in wireless mobile ad hoc networks, EPFL Technical Report IC/2002/54,Swiss Federal Institute of Technology(EPFL), 2002.
6. M. Torrent-Moreno, D. Jiang, and H. Hartenstein, "Broadcast Reception Rates and Effects of Priority Access in 802.11-Based Vehicular Ad Hoc Networks,"Proceeding in ACM. Vehicular Ad hoc Networks, Philadelphia, PA, Oct. 2004.
7. Z. Haas, J. Halpern, and L. Li, "Gossip-Based Ad Hoc Routing," Proc. IEEE INFOCOM, vol. 3, New York, NY, June 2002, pp. 1707–1716

Reconfigurable cognitive radio technology for next generation networks

Mr. D. D. Chaudhary[1] · **Mrs. V. V. Joshi**[1] · **Dr. V. M. Wadhai**[2] · **Dr. L. M. Waghmare**[3]

[1]Sinhgad Institute Of Technology, Lonavala, Dist Pune, India
[2]Maharashtra Acadamy of Engineering, Alandi, Pune, India
[3]Shri Guru Govind singh Institute of Tecnology, Nanded, India

1. Introduction

Basically Radio is Wireless transmission of signals, by modulation of EM waves with frequencies below those of visible light. And Software Radio (SR) is an ideal radio directly samples the antenna output. On this line Cognitive Radio (CR) can be define as a radio combines an SR with a Personal Digital Assistant (PDA).

1.1 Advantages of SDR

Reduced content of expensive custom silicon reduce parts inventory Ride declining prices in computing A Software Defined Radio (SDR) system is a radio communication system which can potentially tune to any frequency band and receive any modulation across a large frequency spectrum by means of as little hardware as possible and processing the signals through software. It accepts fully programmable traffic & control information. It supports broad range of frequencies, air interfaces, and application software. Also it changes its initial configuration to satisfy user requirements. DSP can compensate for imperfections in RF components, allowing cheaper components to be used. Open architecture allows multiple vendors.[6] Basic cognitive radio componants are as shown in Fig. 1.

1.2 Drawbacks of SDR

- Owner consumption
- Security
- Cost
- Software reliability
- Keeping up with higher data rates
- Fear of the unknown

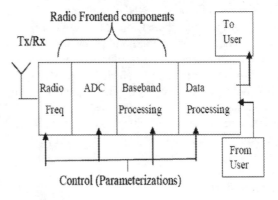

Fig. 1 Basic radio components

- Both subscriber and base units should be SDR for maximum benefit [6].

1.3 Introduction to cognitive radio

Cognitive radio term is coined by Mitola in 1999. Mitola's definition is that "Software radio that is aware of its environment and its capabilities. It Alters its physical layer behavior & also capable of following complex adaptation strategies." A radio or system that senses, and is aware of, it's operational environment and can dynamically and autonomously adjust its radio operating parameters accordingly" Learns from previous experiences and deals with situations not planned at the initial time of design [8].

1.4 Goal driven operation

1. Processes for learning about environmental parameters
2. Awareness of its environment
3. Signals transmission

S.J. Pise (ed.), *ThinkQuest 2010*, DOI 10.1007/978-81-8489-989-4_10,

4. Channels utilization
5. Awareness of capabilities of the radio
6. An ability to negotiate waveforms with other radios

1.5 Cognitive cycle

1. Sensing its environment
2. Tracking changes
3. Reacting upon its findings
4. Needing the feedback channel
5. Dynamically and automatically changing its parameters.

As per Table 1, it shows nine level of Functionality.

2. Why cognitive radio?

Cognitive radios are a powerful tool for solving two major problems:

1. Access to spectrum (finding an open frequency and using it) as shown in Fig. 2.
2. Interoperability (talking to legacy radios using a variety of incompatible waveforms) Existing spectrum policy has full allocation but poor utilization [3, 5].

3. What is a cognitive radio?

Cognitive means "Smart" & "Alert". It knows where it is. It knows what services are available, for example, it can identify then use empty spectrum to communicate more efficiently It knows what services interest the user, and knows how to find them. It knows the current degree of needs and future likelihood of needs of its user. Learns and recog-

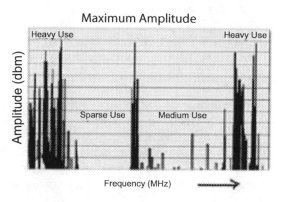

Fig. 2 Spectrum availability

nizes usage patterns from the user Applies "Model Based Reasoning" about user needs, local content, environmental context. A radio frequency transmitter/receiver that is designed to intelligently detect whether a particular segment of the radio spectrum is currently in use, and to jump into (and out of, as necessary) the temporarily-unused spectrum very rapidly, without interfering with the transmissions of other authorized users."Two primary objectives in mind highly reliable communications whenever and wherever needed; and efficient utilization of the radio spectrum. Design point of view Cognitive radio is different from other radios. Conventional Radio is having traditional RF design & traditional base band design. Software Radio is having conventional radio along with software architecture. Also it is having reconfigurability & provisions for easy upgrades. Cognitive Radio is having SDR along with intelligence, awareness learning observations. How cognitive radio is different from other radios? - (Application point of view).

Conventional Radio supports a fixed number of systems. In it, reconfigurability decided at the time of design & it may support multiple services, but chosen at the time of design. Software Radio dynamically support multiple variable systems, protocols and interfaces & interface with diverse systems. Also it provides a wide range of services with variable QoS. Cognitive Radio can create new waveforms on its own. It can negotiate new interfaces & adjusts operations to meet the QoS required by the application for the signal environment. [5].

4. Main features of cognitive radio

1. Observation of spectrum utilization.
2. Deciding about spectrum allocation.
3. Learning from past spectrum utilization
4. Acting in specifying current spectrum usage

CR is an autonomous unit in a communications environment. In order to use the spectral resource most efficiently, it has to be aware of its location be interference sensitive comply with some communications etiquette be fair against other users CR should:

Table 1 Nine level of functionality

Level	Capability	Comments
0	Preprogrammed	A Software Radio
1	Goal Driven	Chooses Waveform According to Goal Requires Environment Awareness
2	Context Awareness	Knowledge of what the user is trying to Do
3	Radio Aware	Knowledge of Radio and Network Components Environment model
4	Capable Planning	Analyze situation (level2&3) to determine Goals(Q0s,power)Follows prescribed plans
5	Conducts Negotiation	Settle on plan with Another Radio
6	Learns Environment	Autonomously Determines Structure of Environment
7	Adapts Plan	Generates New Goal
8	Adapts protocols	Proposes and Negotiates New protocols

1. Sense the spectral environment over a wide bandwidth
2. Detect presence/absence of primary users.
3. Transmit in a primary user band only if detected as unused.
4. Adapt power levels and transmission bandwidths to avoid interference to any primary user. Basic Idea of Cognitive Radio is that Software radios permit network or user to control the operation of a software radio. It enhances the control process by adding intelligent, autonomous control of the radio and it has an ability to sense the environment [4].

5. CR capabilities

1. Frequency Ability – ability of a radio to change its operating frequency, combined with ability to dynamically select appropriate operating frequency based on, for example, sensing of signals from other transmitters (DFS)
2. Transmit Power Control –transmission at allowable limits when necessary but reducing transmit power to allow greater sharing of spectrum when higher power operation is not necessary.
3. Spectrum Sharing Mechanism – enabling sharing of spectrum under terms of an agreement between licensee and a third party.
4. Adaptive Modulation – modifying transmission characteristics and waveforms to exploit opportunities to use spectrum.
5. Location Determination – ability to determine its location and location of other transmitters, and then select the appropriate operating parameters (e.g. power, frequency) allowed at its location.
6. Security Features - incorporated to permit only authorized use and prevent unauthorized modifications [5].

6. CR characteristics

1. Improve Access to Spectrum without causing interference to other spectrum.
2. Exploit frequency and geography (frequency reuse) now.
3. Exploit Time in the near future.
4. Exploit Spatial (e.g., Smart Antennas) in the future.
5. Can Assess Signal Environment.
6. Spectrum estimation and Beacon processing.
7. ID Signal Formats.
8. Location Awareness.
9. Reconfigurability.
10. Adapt Modulation/Coding.
11. Power Control.
12. Frequency Agility.

6.1 How can CR improve spectrum utilization?

1. Cognitive radio is basically used to improve the spectrum utilization. Following steps have to be followed for it:
2. Allocate the frequency usage in a network.
3. Assist secondary markets with frequency use, implemented by mutual agreements.
4. Negotiate frequency use between users.
5. Provide automated frequency coordination.
6. Enable unlicensed users when spectrum not in use.
7. Overcome incompatibilities among existing communication services.

7. CR advantages

Cognitive radios are expected to be powerful tools for mitigating and solving general and selective spectrum access issues.

- Improves current spectrum utilization (Fill in unused spectrum and move away from occupied spectrum).
- Improves wireless data network performance through increased user throughput and system reliability.
- More adaptability and less coordination required between wireless networks.

7.1 Cognitive radio drawbacks

Significant research to realize

- Information collection and modeling
- Decision processes
- Learning processes
- Hardware support
- Regulatory concerns
- Loss of control
- Fear of undesirable adaptations
- Need some way to ensure that adaptationsyield

8. Applications of CR technology

Application of cognitive radio technologies are in field of Dynamically coordinating spectrum sharing, Facilitating interoperability between communication systems, Use in systems such as mesh networking and Third party access in licensed networks for TV bands (400-800 MHz) are more predominant. In addition to this following are some main applications,

8.1 Potential applications of CR are in

Mobile service providers, manufacturers, academics, radar operators, and regulators (MoD, Ofcom). The main *Issues which may arises are,* CR systems need to coexist with primary systems without guaranteed access to spectrum may get data delays, dropped signals, acquisition delay, Nontime sensitive services, such as downloading could be most appropriate.

8.2 Some most promising applications are

In Multimedia downloads, Emergency communications, Broadband wireless services and Multimedia wireless networking.

8.3 Example of CR in cellular environment

- Cognitive radio is aware of areas with a bad signal.
- Can learn the location of the bad signal.
- Radio takes action to compensate for loss of sign
- Actions available.
- Power, bandwidth, coding, channel
- Radio learns best course of action from situation

9. What are the challenges of CR?

- Economics
- Cost of CR devices over simpler delivery mechanism likely to be higher
- Non-real time services for CR not as valuable.
- Depends on spectrum congestion and demand.
- Sharing issues.
- Ensure CRs do not interfere with each other.
- Making sure that they can exist with legacy users and other CR devices.
- Controlling CRs to ensure they have the same spectrum picture.
- How will groups of CRs know what's going on?
- Security and malicious use
- Licensed User Emulation Attack[10]

10. Future directions

- Cognitive radio system defined and research continuing in critical areas
- Sensing with multiple antennas
- System implementation of protocols
- Wideband, high dynamic range frontends
- Investigation of co-existence strategies of conventional radios -in particular UWB and WiMAX
- High level programming support for BEE2
- Radio metrics must be redefined to better analyze frequency availability (spectrum sensing) and radio sensitivity (transmission power).
- Federal Regulations and Incumbent Frequency Band Licensees pose a valid threat to CR advancement [10].

11. Conclusions

In parallel with the development of 4G, specific activities have also been started in the context of the introduction of cognitive radio systems and enabling interoperation between different technologies. As per the Study Group 8 of ITU-R who has adopted a question entitled "Cognitive Radio systems in the mobile service". According to that, a lot of research and development has been carried out on cognitive radio and related topics, and it is observe that cognitive radio may facilitate a more efficient use of spectrum in mobile radio system.

Following issues are on the top priority of ITU-R

1. What is the ITU definition of cognitive radio systems?
2. What is the closely related radio Technologies e.g. smart radio, reconfigurable radio, policy defined adaptive radio and their associated control mechanisms and their functionalities that may be a part of cognitive radio systems?
3. What key technical characteristics, requirements, performance and benefits are associated with the implementation of cognitive radio systems?

This line of thought process of ITU and other researchers explores that cognitive Radio has very significant role in the era of implementation of 3G and 4G wireless communications Technology. This is quit possible because Cognitive Radio Technology is enabled by the special features like General Purpose RF Sections, High Powered Digital Computation Engines, Reconfigurability, Artificial Intelligence, Multiple Applications, Smart Spectrum Access and Utility, Authentication, Geolocation and Networking. With all this advantages reconfigurable cognitive radio will be the road map for next generation wireless communication technology.

References

1. *A Statistical Method for Reconfiguration of Cognitive Radios,* Weingart, T.; Sicker, D.C.;Grunwald,D.; Wireless Communications, IEEE[see also IEEE Personal Communications] Volume 14, Issue4, August 2007 Page(s):34 – 40 DigitalObjectIdentifier10.1109/MWC.07
2. *Game Theory to Analyze Physical Layer Cognitive Radio Algorithms,* James Neel, Rekha Menon, Jeffrey H. Reed, Allen B. MacKenzie
3. Overview of Cognitive Radio: Patricia MARTIGNE
4. Cognitive Radio: From Utopia to Reality Freeband Ambient Communication Event, Enschede
5. '*Cognitive Radio Architecture: The Engineering Foundations of Radio XML*", J. Mitola, Wiley, 2006
6. J. Mitola, "*Software Radio Architecture Evolution: Foundations, Technology Tradeoffs, and Architecture Implications (Invited Paper)*" IEICE Transactions on Communications, Special Issue on Software Radio Technology
7. S. Haykin, "*Cognitive Radio: Brain-empowered Wireless Communications*, IEEE J. Selected Areas in Communications, vol. 23, pp. 201-220, February
8. V. Bhargavaand E. Hussain, ed.," *Cognitive Radio Networks*", Springer-Verlag, 2007
9. J. Mitola, "*Cognitive Radio: Model-Based Competence for Software Radio Licentiate Thesis*" (Stockholm: KTH) 1999
10. J. Mitola III, "*Cognitive Radio*", Doctoral Dissertation (Stockholm: KTH) March 2000
11. Didier Bourse (Motorola Labs), Rahim Tafazolli (*University of Surrey, CCSR) BeyondZ3G/ 4G Radio Access Technologies (RATs),and Standards Roadmaps,* eMobility Technology Platform Whitepaper Version 1.0 – December 07

Adaptive coded modulation in physical layer of WiMAX

Winnie Thomas · Rizwan Ahmed Ansari · R. D. Daruwala

Department of Electrical Engineering, V. J. T. I., Mumbai, India

1. Introduction

The Institute of Electrical and Electronics Engineers (IEEE) 802.16 standard is a real revolution in wireless metropolitan area networks (Wireless MANs) that enables high speed access to data, video, and voice services. Worldwide Interoperability for Microwave Access (WiMAX) is the industry name given to the 802.16-2004 amendment by the vendor interoperability organization. IEEE 802.16 is mainly aimed at providing broadband wireless access (BWA) and thus it may be considered as an attractive alternative solution to wired broadband technologies like digital subscriber line (xDSL) and cable modem access. It's main advantage is fast deployment which results in cost savings. Such installation can be beneficial in very crowded geographical areas like cities and in rural areas where there is no wired infrastructure. The IEEE 802.16 standard provides network access to buildings through external antennas connected to radio BSs. The frequency band supported by the standard covers 2 to 66 GHz. In theory, the IEEE 802.16 standard, known also as WiMAX, is capable of covering a range of 50 km with a bit rate of 75 Mb/s. However, in the real world, the rate obtained from WiMAX is about 12 Mb/s with a range of 20 km. The Intel WiMAX solution for fixed access operates in the licensed 2.5 GHz and 3.5 GHz bands and the license-exempt 5.8 GHz band. This standard addresses the connections in wireless metropolitan area networks (WMANs). It focuses on the efficient use of bandwidth and defines the medium access control (MAC) layer protocols that support multiple physical (PHY) layer specifications. These can easily be customized for the frequency band of use.

2. Physical layer

The physical layer (PHY) is the lowest layer of the model of open systems interconnection (OSI). It includes tools for signal transfer on the level of individual bits. In the WiMAX system this layer provides functions for a higher layer which controls access to the medium (MAC). The IEEE 802.16 standard defines three specifications of the physical layer optimized for different operations and operating conditions. The PHY layer service is provided to the MAC entity at both the BS (Base Station) and SS (Subscriber Station) through the PHY layer SAP (Service Access Point), and PHY layer service is described using a set of primitives. The primitives associated with communication between the MAC and PHY layers fall into three basic categories: (a) Service primitives that support the data transfer, (b) Service primitives that have local significance and support sub-layer-to-sub-layer interactions related to layer control. (c) Service primitives that support management functions. For transmission from the SS to the BS, demand assignment multiple access time division multiple access (DAMA-TDMA) is used. DAMA is a capacity assignment technique that adapts as needed to respond to demand change, among multiple stations. TDMA is the technique of dividing time as a channel into a sequence of frames. Each one of the frames has slots, allocating one or more slots per frame to form a logical channel [1]. Figure 1 shows the typical frame for the TDD. As we can see, the frames are divided into three basic parts: the downstream time slots, the guard time, and the upstream time slots. The downstream traffic is mapped onto the time slots by the BS. However, the upstream traffic is more complex and depends on the QoS-level requirement of the network implementation [1]. In this paper, only the WirelessMAN OFDM PHY specification will be described, which uses the OFDM modulation with 256 subcarrier tones. This specification is designed for application in frequency bands from 2 to 11 GHz without the necessity of line of sight (LOS). Both frequency duplex (FDD) and time duplex (TDD) can

S.J. Pise (ed.), *ThinkQuest 2010*, DOI 10.1007/978-81-8489-989-4_11,
© Springer India Pvt. Ltd. 2011

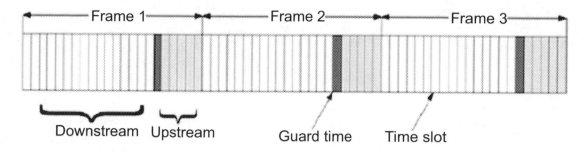

Fig. 1 Example of TDD frame

be used. Other optional mechanisms are also admissible such as the adaptive antenna system (AAS).

2.1 802.16 specifications

This PHY layer specification, targeted for operation in the 10–66-GHz frequency band, is designed with a high degree of flexibility in order to allow service providers the ability to optimize system deployments with respect to cell planning, cost, radio capabilities, services, and capacity. In order to allow for flexible spectrum usage, both TDD and FDD configurations are supported. Both cases use a burst transmission format whose framing mechanism supports adaptive burst profiling in which transmission parameters, including the modulation and coding schemes, may be adjusted individually to each SS on a frame-by-frame basis. The FDD case supports full-duplex SSs as well as half-duplex SSs, which do not transmit and receive simultaneously. The uplink PHY layer is based on a combination of TDMA and DAMA. In particular, the uplink channel is divided into a number of time slots. The number of slots assigned for various uses (registration, contention, guard, or user traffic) is controlled by the MAC layer in the BS and may vary over time for optimal performance. The downlink channel is time division multiplexed, with the information for each SS multiplexed onto a single stream of data and received by all SSs within the same sector. To support half-duplex FDD SSs, provision is also made for a TDMA portion of the downlink [1].

2.2 Physical layer frames

Within each frame there are a downlink subframe and an uplink subframe. The downlink subframe begins with information necessary for frame synchronization and control. In the TDD case, the downlink subframe comes first, followed by the uplink subframe. In the FDD case, uplink transmissions occur concurrently with the downlink frame. A network that utilizes a shared medium should provide an efficient sharing mechanism. Two way point-to-multipoint and mesh topology wireless networks are examples for sharing wireless media. Here the medium is the space through which the radio waves propagate [5].

Though the MAC specification invokes the Internet protocols, they are required only as a standard basis for element management rather than MAC operation, since, in all practicality, element management is necessary in this type of network [5]. Each SS should attempt to receive all portions of the downlink except for those bursts whose burst profile either is not implemented by the SS or is less robust than the SS's current operational downlink burst profile. Half-duplex SSs should not attempt to listen to portions of the downlink coincident with their allocated uplink transmission, if any, adjusted by their TX time advance [1]. The receipt of the primitive causes the MAC entity to process the MAC SDU through the MAC sublayer and pass the appropriately formatted PDUs to the PHY layer for transfer to the peer MAC sublayer entity using the node ID specified [5]. Elements within this PHY layer include TDD and FDD support, TDMA UL, TDM DL, block adaptive modulation and FEC coding for both UL and DL, framing elements that enable improved equalization and channel estimation performance over the non-line-of-sight (NLOS) and extended-delay spread environments, symbol unit granularity in packet sizes, concatenated forward error correction (FEC) using Reed–Solomon and pragmatic TCM with optional interleaving, FEC options using block turbo code (BTC) and convolutional turbo code (CTC), no-FEC options using automatic repeat request (ARQ) for error control, STC (Space Time Coding) transmit diversity option, and parameter settings and MAC/ PHY layer messages that facilitate optional AAS implementations [5]. This layer also specifies that there must be frequency band, a modulation scheme, error correction techniques, synchronization bandwidth TX and RX data rates, and TDM architecture.

2.3 OFDM symbol

Orthogonal frequency-division multiplexing (OFDM) is a discrete Fourier transform (DFT) based multicarrier modulation (MCM) scheme. The basic idea of OFDM is to transform a frequency-selective fading channel into several parallel frequency flat fading subchannels on which modulated symbols are transmitted. In the time domain, the total time of the OFDM symbol is formed by the useful time of the symbol and the protection time of the symbol. The length of the protection time may range between 3 and 25% of the total symbol time. By using a longer protection time, the system can better cope with multipath signal propagation. If a shorter protection time is used with a lower multipath occurrence, the receiver can receive a stronger signal, which will reduce the number of errors during transfer and the data can be transferred more quickly, using the multistate modulation. In the frequency domain, the OFDM symbol is made up of subcarrier tones, whose number determines the size of the FFT used. Three kinds of tones are used. Data subcarriers are used to transfer data, pilot subcarriers serve various estimation processes and main subcarriers form the protection tones, non-active tones and the DC component.

3. Signal flow diagram

The block diagram of the physical layer of the system is shown in Fig. 2. First the input data are randomized and then the signal protection against errors during transfer (FEC) is performed. In the WiMAX system the concatenated Reed-Solomon convolution coding (RS-CC) and interleaving are used. The standard specifies further optional coding — block turbo-coding and convolution turbo coding. The signal is then modulated via a suitable digital modulation. Phase shift keying (PSK) and quadrature amplitude modulation (QAM) are used in different modifications (BPSK, QPSK, 16-QAM and 64-QAM). The series-to-parallel conversion, the inverse fast Fourier transform, and the reverse conversion to the series form arc performed. Subsequently, the data are split into symbols and the symbol protection time is inserted. A signal processed in this way is ready for transfer via a communication channel. At the receiver end, the inverse operations are performed. After processing, the signal is converted from the series into the parallel form transformed by the fast Fourier transform and then demodulated. Interleaving is suppressed and a check is made with possible corrections of errors arising during the transfer through the communication channel. By this procedure the data are converted back into the original form and, in the ideal case, the original data signal will be obtained on the output.

4. Channel coding

All Channel coding consists in three steps: randomization, forward error correction (FEC) and interleaving. At the receiving end, channel decoding takes place, with the operations being performed in reverse order.

4.1 Randomization

The data signal is randomized for the sake of spreading the sequences of ones and zeros in order to obtain easier decoding and tune synchronization at the receiver end. It is performed on each data cluster in both the downlink and the uplink.

A generator of pseudo-random sequences with the (1+X14+X15) polynomial is used for the randomization.

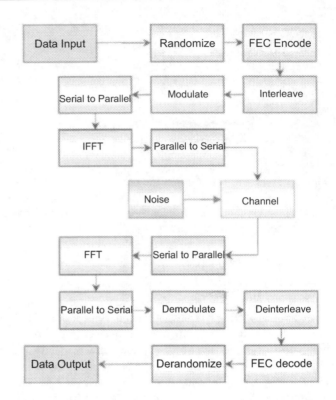

Fig. 2   Signal processing steps in WiMAX

The randomization sequence is applied to the information bits only. In the downlink, the randomizer is initialized at the beginning of each frame by the sequence 100101010000000. At the beginning of cluster #1 the randomizer is not reset. It is reinitialized only at the beginning of each subsequent cluster by a vector that consists of three important four-bit parameters. The first of them (BSID) serves the identification of the base station (BS), with which the subscriber (SS) communicates. The second parameter is the Downlink Interval Usage Code (DIUC). It is a code that identifies the burst profile which is a set of parameters describing the transfer properties, e.g. the FEC type used, modulation, length of the introductory parts of the OFDM symbol, and the protection bands. The third parameter is the Frame number, i.e. the number of the frame in which communication with the subscriber proceeds.

4.2 RS-CC FEC coding

Protecting the signal against errors (FEC), takes the form of concatenating the Reed-Solomon external coding and the internal convolution coding (RS-CC). It is done in both the uplink and the downlink. The arithmetic with Galois fields is used in the WiMAX system, the RS codes use the GF(28) field, where the word length in the code used corresponds to bytes. To calculate the code, the status or the trellis diagram is used. After coding the so-called code narrowing, or puncturing, is performed. The code-narrowing procedure is such that bits are left out in the output sequence, which results in increased code ratio and, simultaneously, reduced output bit rate of the signal compared to the basic code with R=1/2. The mandatory parameters of RSCC coding differ depending on the type of modulation used. The prescribed values are given in Table 1.

4.3 Interleaving

Interleaving is used to protect the signal against group errors and it is a complement to channel coding. If a group error appears in the signal, then as a result of signal storage and signal read-out the group error is "spread" at the receiving end and only individual errors appear in its place. The memory parameters depend on the external code frame and the depth of interleaving. These parameters determine the size of the group error that the interleaver is able to spread out. The interleaving process itself is realized with the aid of the memory. At the transferring end the signal is stored in the memory line by line, and it is read column by column. In this way the individual signal bits get mixed up at the transferring end. After passing through the transfer channel the bits at the receiving end are stored in a similar memory but this time column by column, and they are read line by line. If in the transfer channel a group error is superposed on the signal, then at the receiving end the above operation will spread the group error into individual erroneous bits, which can be corrected by the codes used. The size of the block with which the bit interleaver works corresponds to the number of coded bits of the OFDM symbol.

4.4 Modulation

The WIMAX system allows changing the modulation scheme: Adaptive Coded Modulation (ACM). If the radio medium is of good quality, a higher-grade modulation scheme can be used that enables achieving a higher data transfer rate. In the case where the quality of radio medium decreases (due to increased noise and interference), the WiMAX system can switch over to a lower-grade modulation scheme such that sufficient quality and stability of communication can be assured. The above options make it possible for time system to respond even to the time-variant size of interference. The WiMAX system employs the phase and quadrature-amplitude modulations BPSK, QPSK, 16-QAM, and 64-QAM. In Fig. 3 the application of individual modulations is indicated. The BPSK and QPSK modulations are used for communication over longer distances or in impaired conditions since they are less demanding as regards the SNR. The required SNR is 9 dB for QPSK and 6 dB for BPSK. Their disadvantage lies in the low data signaling rate, with QPSK 2 bits/symbol are transferred, with BPSK only 1bit/symbol. The QAM modulations provide a better utilization of the status diagram. The 16-QAM modulation can be applied also in unfavorable conditions but the required SNR is 16 dB at least. The 64-QAM modulation is practically used only for line-of-sight communication and over shorter distances. The required SNR is 22 dB. An advantage of the QAM modulations is their higher data signaling rate. With the 16 QAM modulation 4 bits/symbol, and with the 64-QAM modulation as many as 6 bits/symbol are transferred.

5. BER

The mathematical model of the AWGN (Additive White Gaussian Noise) yields a relatively good simulation of tile interference appearing in the real environment. The resistance of a system to interference is evaluated using BER (Bit Error Rate), which is defined as the ratio of erroneous received bits to the total number of bits sent in a certain time interval. A parameter of BER is the signal-to-noise ratio.

6. Simulation & analysis

The above processes of digital signal processing in the WiMAX system are simulated in the Mat lab environment. The AWGN transmission channel is considered with different SNR values. For the simulation all modulation

Table 1 Mandatory channel coding per modulation

Modulation	Uncoded block size (bytes)	Coded block size (bytes)	Rs code	CC code rate
BPSK	12	24	(12,12,0)	1/2
QPSK	24	48	(32,24,4)	2/3
QPSK	36	48	(40,36,2)	5/6
16-QAM	48	64	(64,48,8)	2/3
16-QAM	72	96	(80,72,4)	5/6
16-QAM	96	144	(108,96,6)	3/4

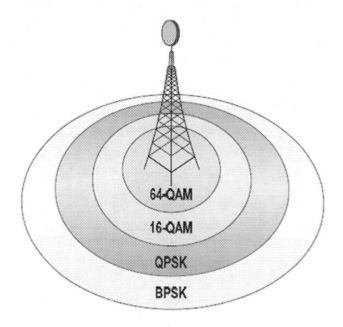

Fig. 3 Adaptive coded modulation

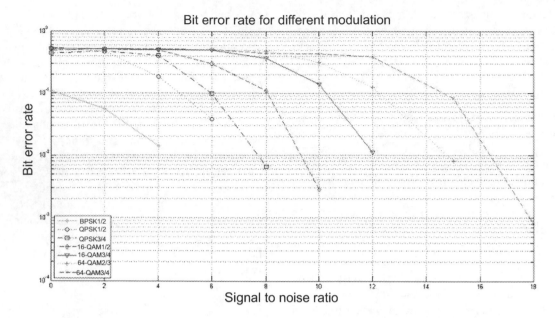

Fig. 4 Comparison of different modulation schemes

schemes are used to compare the performance of the system under different dynamic channel conditions, i.e. different SNR values, BER is calculated. From experimental results we find that for 64 QAM BER is of the order of 10-3, 16 QAM: BER is of the order of 10-2, QPSK: BER is in the range of 10-2 to 10-1 & for BPSK, it is in the range of 1 to 10-1.

7.   Conclusion

In this paper, we presented the proof of concept (POC) for Adaptive Coded Modulation in WiMAX system. From experimental results we conclude that if the channel conditions are good enough then we can use more robust modulation technique to improve BER, and as mobile station moves away from base station, received signal level decreases (SNR decreases) then under these conditions less complex modulation schemes are used, and BER is compromised, as channel link is more important than BER, so as to maintain the communication link.

References

1. Yang Xiao and Yi Pan, Emerging Wireless LANs, Wireless PANs, and Wireless MANs, A John Wiley & Sons, Inc., Publication, Newjersey, 2009
2. David Tung and Peng-Yong, Wireless Broadband Networks, A John Wiley & Sons, Inc., Publication, Newjersey, 2009
3. Vincent Poor and G. Wornell, Wireless Communications: Signal Processing Perspectives, Prentice Hall Publication, Newjersey, 1998
4. Yan Zhang and H. Chen, Mobile WiMAX, Auerbach Publication, New York, 2008
5. LAN/MAN Standards Committee of the IEEE Computer Society, "802.16a IEEE standard for local and metropolitan area networks, Part 16: Air interface for fixed broadband wireless access systems—Amendment 2: Medium access control modifications and additional physical layer specifications for 2–11 GHz," IEEE Computer Society, Apr. 1, 2003
6. LAN/MAN Standards Committee of the IEEE Computer Society, 802.16, "IEEE standard for local and metropolitan area networks, Part 16: Air interface for fixed broadband wireless access systems," IEEE Computer Society, Apr. 8, 2002

Dynamic signature pre-processing by modified digital difference analyzer algorithm

H. B. Kekre · **V. A. Bharadi**

MPSTME, NMIMS University, Mumbai, India

1. Introduction

Dynamic Signature Recognition is one of the highly accurate biometric traits. We capture live signature of the person hence it is possible to have dynamic characteristics of signature for matching purpose. The signature captured by digitizer hardware is in the form of discreet points; we have observed that because of speed limitations of the hardware we get signature points with small time gap causing loss of information in between two points. Here we propose a system to suppress the loss of point and calculate intermediate point location. We have proposed use of Digital Difference Analyzer (DDA) algorithm with certain modifications for the interpolation of points. This method gives fair reconstruction of dynamic signature with captured multidimensional features.

2. Biometrics

A problem of personal verification and identification is an actively growing area of research. The methods are numerous, and are based on different personal characteristics. Voice, lip movements, hand geometry, face, odor, gait, iris, retina, fingerprint are the most commonly used authentication methods. All of these and behavioral characteristics are called biometrics. The biometrics is most commonly defined as measurable psychological or behavioral characteristic of the individual that can be used in personal identification and verification. The driving force of the progress in this field is, above all, the growing role of the Internet and the requirements of society. Therefore, considerable applications are concentrated in the area of electronic commerce and electronic banking systems and security applications of vital installations. The biometrics has a significant advantage over traditional authentication techniques (namely passwords, PIN numbers, smartcards etc.) due to the fact that biometric characteristics of the individual are not easily transferable, are unique of every person, and cannot be lost, stolen or broken. The choice of one of the biometric solutions depends on several factors [2]: • User acceptance • Level of security required • Accuracy • Cost and implementation time. Biometric and biomedical informatics are the fast developing scientific direction, studying the processes of creation, transmission, reception, storage, processing, displaying and interpretation of information in all the channels of functional and signal systems of living objects which are known to biological and medical science and practice. Modern natural sciences at present sharply need in the updating of scientific picture of the world, and the essential contribution in this process can be made by the biometric and biomedical methods. Only some more simple (statistical) forms of biometric and biomedical information have found their application when person identification, and raised interest for these methods of identification can be caused by new possibilities of information technologies.

2.1 Handwritten signature recognition

Handwritten signature verification has been extensively studied & implemented. Its many applications include banking, credit card validation, security systems etc. In general, handwritten signature verification can be categorized into two kinds – online verification and off–line verification [3–5]. On–line verification requires a stylus and an electronic tablet connected to a computer to grab dynamic signature information [5]. Off–line verification, on the other hand, deals with signature information which is in a static format. In On–line approach we can acquire more information about the signature which includes the dynamic

S.J. Pise (ed.), *ThinkQuest 2010*, DOI 10.1007/978-81-8489-989-4_12,

properties of signature. We can extract information about the writing speed, pressure points, strokes, acceleration as well as the static characteristics of signatures [6]. This leads to better accuracy because the dynamic characteristics are very difficult to imitate, but the system requires user co-operation and complex hardware. Digitizer tablets or pressure sensitive pads are used to scan signature dynamically, one such tablet is shown in Fig. 1.

In off–line signature recognition we are having the signature template coming from an imaging device, hence we have only static characteristic of the signatures. The person need not be present at the time of verification. Hence off-line signature verification is convenient in various situations like document verification, banking transactions etc. [1, 7–9]. As we have a limited set of features for verification purpose, off-line signature recognition systems need to be designed very carefully to achieve the desired accuracy.

3. Signature recognition systems

A popular means of authentication historically has been the handwritten signature. Though such signatures are never the same for the same person at different times, there appears to be no practical problem for human beings to discriminate visually the real signature from the forged one. It will be extremely useful when an electronic device can display at least the same virtuosity. The development of computer–aided handwritten signature verification systems has been ongoing for decades. Different approaches are developed to deal with the handwritten signature recognition problem.

3.1 Hardware approach

The hardware approach is faster and convenient, Texas instruments has come up with a DSP chip TMS320.

Fig. 1   Digitizer tablet for on-line signature scan (Wacom Intuos4)

This is a family of digital signal processors which is capable of handling neural clustering techniques to enhance the discriminating power and arrive at a very simple and low-cost solution that can be embedded in existing pen-based systems, such as handheld computers and transaction units. Dullink and Dallen [10] have reported FRR up to 1% and FAR up to 0.01% using TMS320 family.

3.2 On-line approach

On-line signature recognition considers the dynamic characteristics of signatures. In [2] Jain & Ross have used critical points, speed curvature angle as features and they have reported FRR 2.8% and FAR 1.6 %. They used common as well as writer dependent thresholds but it was observed that the writer dependent thresholds give better accuracy. Considering another approach Lei, Palla and Govindarajalu [11] have proposed a technique for finding correlation between two signature sequences for online recognition, they mapped the occurrence of different critical points on signature and the time scale and the correlation between these sequences was evaluated using a new parameter called Extended Regression Square (ER2) coefficient the results were compared with an existing technique based on Dynamic Time Wrapping (DTW). They reported Equal Error rate (EER) 7.2% where the EER reported by DTW was 20.9 % with user dependent thresholds. In [12] Rhee and Cho used Model guided segmentation approach for segment-to-segment comparison to obtain consistent segmentation. They used discriminative feature selection for skilled as well as random forgeries. They reported EER 3.4 %. Nalwa [13] used a moment and torque base approach for on-line signature recognition. His work is based parameterizing each on-line curve over its normalized arc-length. These parameters are then represented along the length of the curve, in a moving coordinate frame. The measures of the curve within a sliding window that are analogous to the position of the center of mass, the torque exerted by a force, and the moments of inertia of a mass distribution about its center of mass. Further, He suggested the weighted and biased harmonic mean as a graceful mechanism of combining errors from multiple models of which at least one model is applicable but not necessarily more than one model is applicable. He recommended that each signature be represented by multiple models, these models, perhaps, local and global, shape based and dynamics based. The reported FRR was 7% and FAR was 1%. One thing that should be noted is that all these approaches need signature data with dynamic information. When the data comes from the hardware it is raw and we have to pre-process it to normalize the errors due to sampling, quantization, speed of hardware, signing position etc. We are using Wacom Intuos 4 for our experiments and we have also experienced the need of pre-processing the data. Doroz and Wrobel [14] have discussed this issue and proposed a technique of sampling the point uniformly to have equal number of points per unit time. They have used Signature verification Competition database [15]. As we are using hardware as discussed above to capture the signature, we have observed issues in captured signature. The problem and the proposed solution are discussed in the next section.

4. Need for signature pre-processing

In the experiment carried we are using Digitizer Tablet Wacom Intuos 4, Typical features of the tablets is as follows 1. Active Area (W x D) 157.5 x 98.4 mm 2. Connectivity-USB connectivity 3. Pressure levels-2048 4. Sensor pen without battery 5. Minimum ON weight (Minimum weight sensed by the pen tip) – 1 Gram. 6. Report rate-197 Points per second 7. LPI - lines per inch-5080 lpi 8. Maximum Data Rate: 200 packets/Second. The digitizer tablet is interfaced [16] to the application using an ActiveX COM component VBTablet [17]. In the application development we have observed that the interface could deliver only 100 Packets/ Second. As the digitizer has finite rate of sampling and data transfer, it cannot capture all the points on a curve but captures finite points as per the sampling rate. This gives the results as follows, shown in Fig. 2.

There is loss of continuity in the captured points, we have a static scanned signature as shown in Fig. 2(a), same persons dynamic signatures are shown in Fig. 2(b, c, d), different colours indicate different pressure levels. We can clearly see the points that are sampled. If the signing speed is high then the captured points are less. One such situation is shown in Fig. 3. This causes loss of precision in the input data and may result in decreased accuracy of the matching algorithm.

To solve this problem a method to calculate missing point's information and reduce the sampling error has been proposed by the authors. This method interpolates the captured points and calculates the missing information without loss of consistency. The method proposed is not same as normal interpolation as the missing points are on a curve and accuracy should be preserved in calculation as these points are on a biometric signature of a human being which can be used for authentication or authorization

5. Proposed technique for pre-processing

Here we propose a technique that can be applied to any digitizer to calculate maximum possible points on the signature curve. Here we make use of the points in hand in order to calculate the parameters of points which are missing. Each captured points has multi-dimensional information. Each point contains information about X, Y, Z-Coordinates, Pressure, Azimuth and Altitude of the pen tip. Hence i[th] point Pi can be considered as:

$$Pi = \{Xi,\ Yi,\ Zi,\ Pri,\ Azi,\ Alti\} \tag{1}$$

We have to calculate the points between Pi & Pi+1 if any points exist between them. To calculate the parameters we consider one fact that the points are consistent as they come from human behavior; and the consequent points tend to have values near to their neighbors' value. If we estimate X,Y & Z co-ordinates of missing points the remaining values can be taken as average between the Pi & Pi+1 parameters. Proposed algorithm is divided into two steps.

1. Calculate X,Y Coordinates of missing points between Pi & Pi+1 using Modified Digital Difference Analyzer (MDDA) Algorithm.
2. Estimate Z, Pressure, Azimuth, Altitude Values from the given interval points Pi & Pi+1. by averaging. We first discuss the proposed modified DDA Algorithm and then the averaging

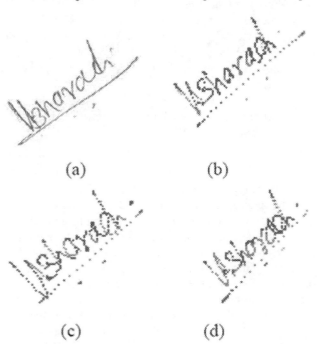

(a)   (b)

(c)   (d)

Fig. 2 Signature samples of a person (a) Static scanned signature, (b), (c) & (d) dynamic signature scanned by Wacom Intuos 4

Fig. 3 Poorly sampled signature due to high signing speed

5.1 Modified digital difference analyzer algorithm (MDDA)

Digital Difference Analyzer Algorithm (DDA) is mainly used in computer graphics [18] for Line drawing on the raster. It calculates points on the line defined by two end points (X1,Y1) & (X2,Y2). It uses differential equation of a straight line.

$$\frac{dy}{dx} = m \tag{2}$$

$$\frac{\Delta y}{\Delta x} = \frac{Y2 - y1}{X2 - X1} \tag{3}$$

The intermediate points can be calculated as

$$Xi + 1 = Xi + \Delta x \tag{4}$$

$$yi + 1 = yi + \frac{Y2 - Y1}{X2 - Xq} \Delta y \tag{5}$$

In the literature we can see that this algorithm is weidely used for the scan conversion of a line. In our application we have different domain, we use this algorithm for finding missing points between the two interval points, these points are actually on a curve but as the distance between two points is very small (generally 0 to 4 Pixels maximum), hence the points can be assumed on a line and DDA can be used for calculation of points which lie one a line between two given points Pi & Pi+1. We have made the following changes in the algorithm.

1. In case of X2 < X1 of the two points (X1, Y1) & (X2,Y2), the two points are interchanged for calculation, we use a flag here to mark the condition as we do not want interchange of the points as they lie on a signature curve.
2. In DDA the points are calculated and plotted on the screen, we use one two-dimensional array to store (X,Y) co-ordinates calculated.
3. If at the start of calculations the two points are interchanged, we check the flag and reverse the array content order to have actual sequence of the point on the signature.

The proposed MDDA Algorithm as follows :

1. read the interval points (x1, y1) & (x2, y2) if (x1 > x2) then exchange the points;
Set the flag reverse = true.
2. Calculate the difference
dx = x2–x1;
dy = y2–y1;
3. If Abs(dx) > Abs(dy) then
m = dy / dx;
y = y1;
Calculate the points between X1 & X2 by
for (x = x1; x < x2; x++)
{

Xi = Round(x);
Yi = Round(y);
Store Xi,Yi to array Points[][];
y = y + m;
}
else Go to step 4;
Go to Step 6.
4. If Abs(dx) < Abs(dy) then
m = dx / dy;
x = x1;
if (y1 < y2) then
Calculate the points between Y1 & Y2 by
for (y = y1; y < y2; y++)
{
Xi = Round(x);
Yi = Round(y);
Store Xi, Yi to array Points[][];
x = x + m;
}
else Go to Step 5;
Go to Step 6.
5. If (y1 > y2) then
Calculate the points between Y1 & Y2 by
for (y = y1; y > y2; y--)
{
Xi = Round(x);
Yi = Round(y);
Store Xi, Yi to array Points[][];
x = x - m;
}
6. If reverse flag is set then
Rearrange the Points[][] array in reverse order.
7. Insert the points (Xi, Yi) from Points[][] array into the main signature features array between Pi & Pi+1.

In the next section we discuss the calculation of other parameters.

5.2 Calculating Z co-ordinate, pressure, azimuth, and altitude

In the previous section we have discussed Modified DDA algorithm to calculate X & Y co-ordinates of points between two signature points Pi & Pi+1, still we have to calculate the other parameters of the interpolated points. We have to calculate Z Co-ordinate, Pressure, Azimuth, and Altitude of the points given by previous step. The signature points have temporal locality; means the consecutive points tend to have similar value as their neighbors'. The maximum packet rate is 200packets /seconds; it has been observed that the time difference between two sampled points varies from 5ms to 10 ms. Hence we use this fact to interpolate the other parameters. We calculate the Z co-ordinate (Distance of pen tip from the digitizer surface), Pressure, Azimuth, Altitude (Azimuth & Altitude give information about pen tip angle whine signing). We calculate the values by taking Average of the parameters of Pi & Pi+1.

To find the parameter of nth point between Pi & Pi+1, we use following equations.

$$Zn = \frac{Zi+Zi+1}{2} \qquad (6)$$

$$Prn = \frac{Pri+Pri+1}{2} \qquad (7)$$

$$Azn = \frac{Azi+Azi+1}{2} \qquad (8)$$

$$Aln = \frac{Ali+Ali+1}{2} \qquad (9)$$

Thus we get complete set of information between the sampled points Pi & Pi+1. Each point has the format as follows,

$$Pn = \{Xn,\ Yn,\ Zn,\ Prn,\ Azn,\ Altn\} \qquad (10)$$

In Fig. 4 we can see the captured signature which has errors due to sampling of points, we calculate the missing points using proposed scheme and the interpolated set of points give the signature as shown in Fig. 4(b), we can clearly see that the Signature is fairly continuous. In the next section we discuss the results

Table 1 Interpolation results for different signatures with their parameters and calculation time

Sampled Signature	Packet Count	Center of Mass of Signature (Cx,Cy)	Slope Angle	Pixel Count	Signature Arch Length in Pixels	Calculation Timing milliseconds	Signature Timing milliseconds
Sampled Signature 1	157	103, 95	12.8	132	842	31.25	1140
Interpolated Signature 1		122, 100	11.18	246	907		
Sampled Signature 2	227	132, 96	30.69	255	637	15.625	1500
Interpolated Signature 2		119, 92	29.38	349	649		
Sampled Signature 3	709	123, 96	38.66	473	995	46.875	2500
Interpolated Signature 3		153, 66	38.02	530	999		

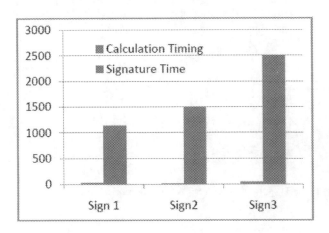

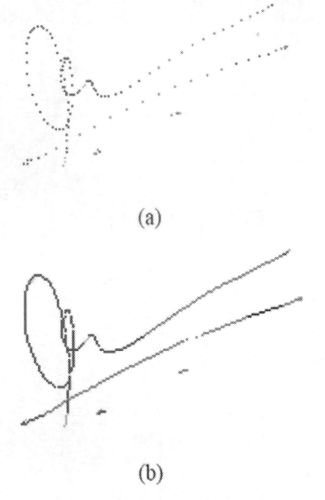

(a)

(b)

Fig. 4 Results of MDDA based Interpolation of dynamic signature (a) Captured signature (b) Interpolated signature

6. Results

The proposed algorithm was tested on 30 different signatures at different speeds. We show some of the signatures and their interpolated form in Table 1. We can see that because of interpolation the pixel count has drastic change as the missing pixels are calculated but the global features like the Signature Arc length; Slope Angle and the center of mass have less change in sampled and interpolated version. The interpolated signatures are continuous and can be further used for testing any dynamic signature recognition algorithm. In Fig. 5 we plot the graph of signature time (signing time of signature) and the time required for the calculation of missing points; i.e. interpolation time. The interpolation time is very less and was observed between 10ms to 50ms. This makes the algorithm very attractive for real time implementation. The program was tested on AMD Athlon 64 Processor running at 1.8 GHz, 1.5 GB ram and Windows XP SP3 Operating System. Application programming platform is Visual C# 2005,. NET Framework version 2.0.

Fig. 5 Signature time & interpolation timing comparison (X-axis-signature no., Y axis-calculation time in milliseconds)

7. Conclusion

In this paper a novel dynamic signature pre-processing algorithm. This algorithm is based on proposed Modified Digital Difference Analyzer (MDDA) technique. The proposed algorithm is hardware independent and can be used with any type of digitizer tablet. This algorithm gives missing point because of finite data transfer & sampling rate of the hardware. The algorithm is fast and required maximum 50 milliseconds under testing hence it is very attractive for real time use. The signature templates generated are continuous and any existing Dynamic Signature recognition technique can use this method as their preprocessing step for better accuracy.

References

1. A. K. Jain, A. Ross, S. Prabhakar, "An Introduction to Biometric Recognition", IEEE Transactions on Circuits and Systems for Video Technology, Vol. 14, No. 1, January 2004
2. A. K. Jain, A. Ross, and S. Prabhakar, "On Line Signature Verification", Pattern Recognition, vol. 35, no. 12, Dec 2002. pp. 2963-2972
3. A. Zimmer and L.L. Ling, "A Hybrid On/Off Line Handwritten Signature Verification System", Seventh International Conference on Document Analysis and Recognition, vol.1, pp.424-428, Aug.2003
4. D. Hamilton, J. Whelan, A. McLaren, "Low cost dynamic signature verification system", Security and Detection, 1995. IEEE CNF European Convention, 16-18 May 1995. pp 202–206
5. R. Plamondon, G. Lorette, "Automatic Signature Verification and Writer Identification – The State of the Art", Pattern Recognition, vol. 4, no. 2, pp. 107–131, 1989
6. R. Plamondon, "The design of an On-line signature verification system", Theory to practice, International journal of Pattern Recognition and Artificial Intelligence, (1994). pp 795–811
7. H B kekre, V A Bharadi, "Specialized Global Features for Off-line Signature Recognition", 7th Annual National

Conference on Biometrics RFID and Emerging Technologies for Automatic Identification, VPM Polytechnic, Thane, January 2009

8. H B Kekre, V A Bharadi, "Signature Recognition using Cluster Based Global Features", IEEE International Conference (IACC 2009), Thapar University, Patiala- Punjab, India. March 2009

9. H. Baltzakis, N. Papamarkos, "A new signature verification technique based on a two-stage neural network classifier", Engineering Applications of Artificial Intelligence 14 (2001)

10. H. Dullink, B. van Daalen, J. Nijhuis, L. Spaanenburg, H. Zuidhof, "Implementing a DSP Kernel for Online Dynamic Handwritten Signature Verification using the TMS320 DSP Family", EFRIE, France December 1995 SPRA304

11. H. lei, S. Palla and V Govindraju, "ER2: an Intuitive Similarity measure for On-line Signature Verification", Proceedings of CUBS 2005

12. T. Rhee, S. Cho, "On line Signature Recognition Using Model Guided Segmentation and Discriminative feature selection for skilled forgeries", IEEE Transaction on pattern recognition, Jan 2001

13. V. Nalwa, "Automatic On-Line Signature Verification", proceedings of the IEEE Transactions on Biometrics, vol. 85, No. 2, February 1997

14. R. Doroz, K. Wrobel "Method of Signature Recognition with the Use of the Mean Differences", Proceedings of the ITI 2009 31st Int. Conf. on Information Technology Interfaces, June 22-25, 2009

15. SVC (Signature Verification Competition) database available at the website: http://www.cse.ust.hk/svc2004/index.html

16. H. B. Kekre, V A Bharadi, "Using Component Object Model for Interfacing Biometrics Sensors to Capture Multidimensional Features", IJJCCT 2009, Shanghai, China, Dec 2009

17. http://sourceforge.net/projects/vbtablet/

18. A. P. Godse, "Computer Graphics", Technical publication. 2002

Image stitching techniques

Jalpa D. Mehta · **S. G. Bhirud**

Department of Computer Technology, VJTI, Mumbai, India

1. Introduction

Image stitching or photo stitching is the process of combining multiple photographic images with overlapping fields of view to produce a segmented panorama or high-resolution image. Commonly performed through the use of computer software, most approaches to image stitching require nearly exact overlaps between images and identical exposures to produce seamless results. It is also known as mosaicing. "Stitching" refers to the technique of using a computer to merge images together to create a large image, preferably without it being at all noticeable that the generated image has been created by computer. Algorithms for aligning images and stitching them into seamless photo-mosaics are among the oldest and most widely used in computer vision. Frame-rate image alignment is used in every camcorder that has an "image stabilization" feature. Image stitching algorithms create the high resolution photo-mosaics used to produce today's digital maps and satellite photos. They also come bundled with most digital cameras currently being sold, and can be used to create beautiful ultra wide-angle panoramas.

We describe various Image Stitching phases in section 1. In section 2, We give details of Image Acquisition phase. Image remapping is an essential process of Image Stitching described in section3. Finally aligned images are blended together t avoid seams in the stitched image this procedure is known as Image Blending specified in Section 4.

1.1 Different kinds of image stitching

- Mosaic – stitch multiple rows of pictures that were taken without rotating the camera around a single point, but with the camera kept perpendicular with the subject.

- Panorama (single-row) – stitch a single row of pictures (created by rotating the camera around a single point in a flat plane, which is normally parallel with the horizon).
- Panorama (multi-row) – stitch multiple rows of pictures (created by rotating the camera around a single point in a flat plane but tilting or pitching the camera up and/or down so that for each row of pictures the lens is not necessarily parallel with the plane of rotation).
- Panorama (pano-camera) – just stitch together the ends of panoramic picture created with a panoramic camera.

1.2 Stages of the image stitching process

Image Acquisition – This stage of Image stitching is to do calibration of Images. It requires selection of the position and acquisition of images. In this step, a decision needs to be made on the type of resultant panoramic images. According to the required panoramic images, different image acquisition methods are used to acquire the series of images.

Image Remapping (Image Warping) – Remapping is the process of changing the image geometry in order to fit to the adjacent images that should contribute to a panorama. This remapping process "warps" the images in such a way so that they can be aligned perfectly. Without this remapping process, the images will not join together correctly. It includes conversion of camera image to sphere, Image alignment, setting screen projection.

Image Blending – Once the source pixels have been remapped onto the final composite surface, we must still decide how to blend them in order to create an attractive looking panorama. Blending is used to remove visible

S.J. Pise (ed.), *ThinkQuest 2010*, DOI 10.1007/978-81-8489-989-4_13,

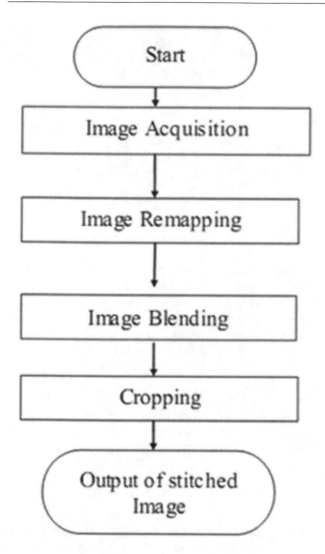

Fig. 1 Flowchart of producing panoramic image

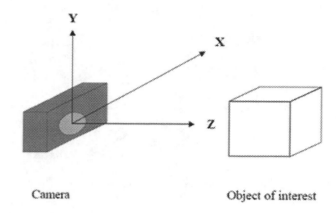

Fig. 2 Camera co-ordinate system

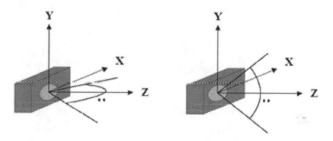

Fig. 3 The horizontal and vertical angles of view

The camera's angles of view in the horizontal and vertical directions decide each image's coverage in the horizontal and vertical directions. The angles of view are defined in Fig. 3, where the angles and respectively represent the camera's angles of view in the horizontal and the vertical directions.

2.1 Acquisition by camera rotations

In the first set-up, the camera is set upon a tripod and the images are obtained by rotating the camera. In this acquisition method, the tripod is set levelly at a chosen position and stays in the same position throughout the acquisition of the images. After securing the camera on the tripod, the camera is focused on the objects of interest and rotated with respect to the vertical axis in one chosen direction. One image is taken with each rotation of the camera until the desired range has been covered. Fig. 4. shows the set-up of the tripod and the camera for image acquisition by camera rotations. In an ideal set-up, the Y-axis should pass the optical centre of the camera and there should not be any camera rotations except for the rotation about the Y-axis between successive images.

Each image in the series acquired for panoramic image stitching partially overlaps the previous and the following images. The size of the overlapping region is an important factor in image stitching. it is desirable to have 50% of the image overlap with the previous image and the other 50% of the image overlaps with the following image. A larger overlapping region allows adjacent images to be merged

seams (due to exposure differences), blurring (due to miss-registration), or ghosting (due to moving objects).

Cropping – Image cropping refers to removing unwanted areas from a photographic or illustrated image. One of the most basic Image manipulation processes, it is performed in order to remove an unwanted subject or change its aspect ratio, or to improve the overall composition.

2. Image acquisition

Different image acquisition methods can be used to acquire input images that produce different types of panoramic images, depending on the type of panoramic images required and the availability of equipment. Three set-up's to acquire images for panoramic image generation are described and discussed in this section. In all three set-up's, a still image camera has been used to take the images. The camera co-ordinate system is shown in Fig. 2 where the Z-axis points towards the object of interest and the Y-axis passes through the optical axis of the camera.

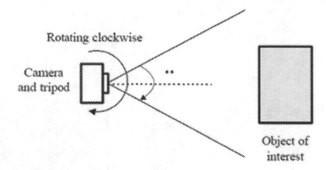

Fig. 4 Camera and tripod for acquisition by camera rotations

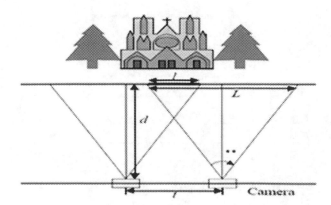

Fig. 6 Geometry for image acquisition by camera translations

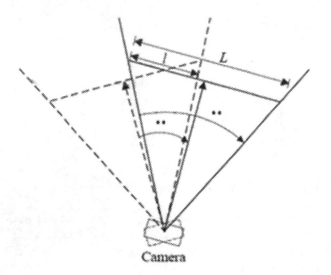

Fig. 5 Geometry of overlapping images

more easily in the image merging step of image stitching. Fig. 5. illustrates the geometry of two overlapping images as viewed from above. In Fig. 5, L represents the width of the acquired image and l represents the width overlapping region between adjacent images. The ratio of l to L is dependent upon the angle of rotation between successive images, and the horizontal angle of view

The ratio of the width of the overlapping region to the width of the image can be estimated by Eqn 1.

$$l / L = \frac{L/2[1-(\tan(-1/2)/\tan(1/2))]---}{L}$$
$$= 1/2[1 - [(\tan(-1/2) / \tan(1/2)]] \tag{1}$$

However, the actual size of the overlapping region might differ from the calculated if the camera is tilted, i.e., there is camera rotation other than the required rotation about the Y-axis. Rotations other than in the specified direction cause problems in the image stitching and affect the quality of the resultant panoramic image. Therefore, in the acquisition of images by camera rotation, it is undesirable to have rotations in directions other than about the specified axis. Another factor which needs to be taken into consideration is the fact that the objects in the real world are projected onto a 2D plane.

Hence, by rotating the camera during image acquisition, the distances between points might not be preserved. Since the camera is rotated between successive images, the orientation of each imaging plane is different in this acquisition method. Therefore, images acquired by this method need to be projected onto the same surface, such as the surface of a cylinder or a sphere, before image registration can be performed.

One advantage with acquiring images by rotation is that the camera can stay in one place during the acquisition of the series of images. Rotation of the camera does not require a large amount of measurement and can be performed easily.

2.2 Acquisition by camera translations

The second set-up places the camera on a sliding plate and the images are obtained by shifting the camera on the sliding plate In this acquisition method, the camera is shifted in a direction parallel to the imaging plane. On a smaller scale, the camera can be mounted onto a sliding plate to achieve the translations. The camera and the sliding plate are placed directly in front of the objects of interest and an image is taken with each translation of the camera until the series of images cover the desired range. Fig. 6. Shows the setup of this method, where the camera is aligned with the sliding plate so that the imaging plane parallel to the orientation of the sliding plate.

Given the camera translation, t, the distance between camera and object of interest, d, and the camera's horizontal angle of view, $**$, the ratio of the overlapping region to the whole image can be estimated by Eqn. 2,

$$l/L = 1 - t/2d \tan (1/2) \tag{2}$$

Nevertheless, the actual size of the overlapping region between successive images is determined by the accuracy in setting up the camera. In acquiring images by translation, it is important to ensure that the image planes are parallel to the direction of camera translations. Otherwise, the size of the objects in the images varies as the camera is shifted, causing problems in image stitching.One disadvantage of this method is that the required translation, t, increases as the distance between the camera and the object of interest, d, increases, if the acquired images are to have the same sized overlapping region.

2.3 Acquisition by a hand held camera

This acquisition method is comparatively easy to perform; the user simply holds the camera and takes images of his/her surroundings by either rotating on the same spot or moving in a predefined direction roughly parallel to the image plane. However, images acquired by this method can be difficult to stitch, due to the amount of unwanted camera rotation or translation during the acquisition of images.

In the case of the user turning with the camera to obtain the images, the user acts as the tripod of the camera in Section 2.1. However, rather than rotating about, or approximately about the vertical axis of the camera, there are inaccuracies in the alignment of the rotating axis with the vertical axis. It is also difficult to control the angles rotated between successive images. Therefore, the sizes of the overlapping regions between adjacent images have a greater variation than for images acquired by a camera mounted on a tripod.

When the user holds up the camera and moves in one direction to acquire the images, the user acts as the sliding plate in acquisition by translation in Section 2.2. However, in this situation, it is even more difficult to control the distance shifted between each image and keep each image on the same imaging plane. Therefore, apart from the difference in the size of the overlapping regions, the image planes of the acquired images have different orientations and cause problems in image stitching.

3. Image remapping (Image Warping)

Remapping is the process of changing the image geometry in order to fit to the adjacent images that should contribute to a panorama. This remapping process "warps" the images in such a way so that they can be aligned perfectly. Without this remapping process, the images will not join together correctly. It highly depends on aligning, since any alignment change of an image requires a different remapping. Remapping is an inherent part of the stitching process. Remapping includes the following steps

3.1 Conversion of camera image to sphere

The camera image has to be transformed into angle space, which here is visualized as projecting the image from a virtual camera, reversing the light path, onto a sphere

3.2 Image alignment (Image Registration)

Generally, one is free to choose any orientation of the virtual camera/projector. But for panoramic images, one wants to align these images. The usual software approach is to mark a set of same features in image pairs, and have the distance between such markers pairs minimized in an overall optimization process. In this section we describe different image alignment techniques.

3.2.1 *Feature based registration*

A feature (key point) is a significant piece of information extracted from an image which provides more detailed understanding of the image. In other words, features are objects, which should be distinct, salient and preferable frequently spread over the image and easy to detect. The objects can be for example landmarks or segmented areas and even intensity can be seen as a feature. The number of common detected objects (seen in both images) must be sufficiently high to be able to perform a good estimation of the transformation model.

The features can then be seen as points, lines, and regions. The first task of the registration is to decide what kind of feature we search for, and how to represent them. Most of the feature based registrations techniques can be divided into three steps.

Feature detection The salient and distinctive features are detected. After deciding what kind of features we are looking after we apply suitable detector method on the images. The method could be either worked interactively with an expert or automatically. The choice is depending on the situation. Automatically methods usually applied when extrinsic methods are used, or when geometrically landmarks are used. For region features we can use segmentation methods. Line features are usually detected by means of a edge detector like the Canny detector. When we are looking for point features corner detectors e.g. the Harris corner detector is suitable.

Feature matching where the feature correspondences between the images are established. The goal of feature

Fig. 7 Conversion of camera image to sphere

Fig. 8 Image alignment by matching features

matching is to establish correspondences between two sets of features. The problems that can occur here can be caused by incorrect feature detection, or by image distortion. Here we described two methods of feature matching.

Scale-invariant feature transform (SIFT) is an algorithm to detect and describe local features in images The SIFT features are local and based on the appearance of the object at particular interest points, and are invariant to image scale and rotation. They are also robust to changes in illumination, noise, and minor changes in viewpoint. In addition to these properties, they are highly distinctive, relatively easy to extract, allow for correct object identification with low probability of mismatch and are easy to match against a (large) database of local features. Object description by set of SIFT features is also robust to partial occlusion; as few as 3 SIFT features from an object are enough to compute its location and pose.

3.3 Selection of projection

The first choice to be made is how to represent the final image. If only a few images are stitched together, a natural approach is to select one of the images as the *reference* and to then warp all of the other images into the reference coordinate system. The resulting composite is sometimes called a *flat* panorama, since the projection onto the final surface is still a perspective projection

For larger fields of view, however, we cannot maintain a flat representation without excessively stretching pixels near the border of the image. (In practice, flat panoramas start to look severely distorted once the field of view exceeds 90° or so.) The usual choice for compositing larger panoramas is to use a cylindrical (Szeliski 1994, Chen 1995) or spherical (Szeliski and Shum 1997) projection. In fact, any surface used for *environment mapping* in computer graphics can be used, including a *cube map* that represents the full viewing sphere with the six square faces of a cube (Greene 1986, Szeliski and Shum 1997). Images in the computer environment are flat, hence one has to remap the spherical geometry. This can be a general mathematical mapping function. Some mappings, as the rectilinear projection below, can be visualized as an optical projection, using a point light source in the centre of the sphere.

3.4 Selection of view

Once we have chosen the output parameterization, we still need to determine which part of the scene will be *centered* in the final view. As mentioned above, for a flat composite, we can choose one of the images as a reference. Often, a reasonable choice is the one that is geometrically most central. For example, for rotational panoramas represented as a collection of 3D rotation matrices, we can choose the image whose z-axis is closest to the average z-axis (assuming a reasonable field of view). Alternatively, we can use the average zaxis (or quaternion, but this is trickier) to define the reference rotation matrix. For larger (e.g., cylindrical or spherical) panoramas, we can still use the same heuristic if a subset of the viewing sphere has been imaged. If the case of full 360° panoramas, a better choice might be to choose the middle image from the sequence of inputs, or sometimes the first image, assuming this contains the object of greatest interest. In all of these cases, having the user control the final view is often highly desirable.

3.5 Exposure setting

Input images need not have the same exposure, or white balance. Together with vignetting (images are darker in the corners than in the middle) the required corrections can be derived from images with a suitably large overlap area.

4. Image blending

Once we have registered all of the input images with respect to each other, we need to decide how to produce the final stitched (mosaic) image. This involves selecting a final compositing surface (flat, cylindrical, spherical, etc.) and view (reference image). It also involves selecting which pixels contribute to the final composite and how to optimally blend these pixels to minimize visible seams, blur, and ghosting.

Once the source pixels have been mapped onto the final composite surface, we must still decide how to blend them in order to create an attractive looking panorama. If all of the images are in perfect registration and identically exposed, this is an easy problem (any pixel or combination will do). However, for real images, visible seams (due to

Fig. 9 Projection of sphere image to screen

Fig. 10 Exposure setting

exposure differences), blurring (due to mis-registration), or ghosting (due to moving objects) can occur.

Creating clean, pleasing looking panoramas involves both deciding which pixels to use and how to weight or blend them. In this section we describe different image blending techniques.

4.1 Average blending

The simplest way to create a final composite is to simply take an *average* value at each pixel,

$$c(x) = \sum_{k} Wk(x) * Ik(x) \div \sum_{k} Wk(x),$$

where *Ik(x)* are the warped (re-sampled) images and *Wk(x)* is 1 at valid pixels and 0 elsewhere.

Simple averaging usually does not work very well, since exposure differences, miss-registrations, and scene movement are all very visible (Fig. 12a). If rapidly moving objects are the only problem, taking a *median* filter (which is a kind of pixel selection operator) can often be used to remove them (Irani and Anandan 1998) (Fig. 12b).

4.2 Alpha blending

4.2.1 *RGBA color space*

RGBA stands for Red Green Blue Alpha. While it is sometimes described as a color space, it is actually simply a use of the RGB color model, with extra information. The color is RGB, and may belong to any RGB color space, but an integral alpha value as invented by Catmull and Smith between 1971 and 1972 enables alpha blending and alpha compositing. The inventors named *alpha* after the Greek letter in the classic linear interpolation formula $\alpha A + (1-\alpha)B$.

4.2.2 *Alpha channel*

The alpha channel is normally used as an opacity channel. If a pixel has a value of 0% in its alpha channel, it is fully transparent (and, thus, invisible), whereas a value of 100% in the alpha channel gives a fully opaque pixel (traditional digital images). Values between 0% and 100% make it possible for pixels to show through a background like a glass, an effect not possible with simple binary (transparent or opaque) transparency. It allows easy image compositing. Alpha channel values can be expressed as a percentage, integer, or real number between 0 and 1 like RGB parameters. In graphics, a portion of each pixel's data that is reserved for transparency information. 32-bit graphics systems contain four channels -- three 8-bit channels for red, green, and blue RGB and one 8-bit alpha channel. The alpha channel is really a *mask* -- it specifies how the pixel's colors should be merged with another pixel when the two are overlaid, one on top of the other. Linear interpolation is often used to blend two images. Blend fractions (alpha) and (1 - alpha)

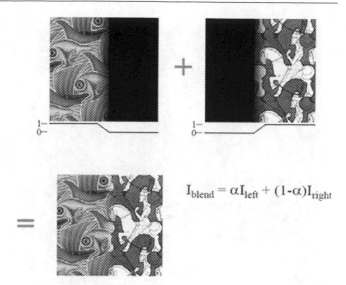

Fig. 11 Alpha blending

are used in a weighted average of each component of each pixel:

$$I(blend) = \alpha * I(Left) + (1-\alpha) * I (right)$$

Typically alpha is a number in the range 0.0 to 1.0. This is commonly used to linearly interpolate two images. What is less often considered is that alpha may range beyond the interval 0.0 to 1.0.

4.3 Feathering

A better approach to averaging is to weight pixels near the center of the image more heavily and to downweight pixels near the edges. When an image has some cutout regions, down-weighting pixels near the edges of both cutouts and edges is preferable. This can be done by computing a *distance map* or *grassfire transform*. Weighted averaging with a distance map is often called *feathering* and does a reasonable job of blending over exposure differences however, blurring and ghosting can still be problems

4.4 Pyramidal blending

Once the seams have been placed and unwanted objects removed, we still need to blend the images to compensate for exposure differences and other misalignments. An attractive solution to this problem was developed by Burt and Adelson Instead of using a single transition width, a frequency adaptive width is used by creating a band-pass (Laplacian) pyramid and making the transition widths a function of the pyramid level. First, each warped image is converted into a band-pass (Laplacian) pyramid. Next, the masks associated with each source image are converted into a lowpass (Gaussian) pyramid and used to perform a per-level feathered blend of the band-pass images. Finally, the composite image is reconstructed by interpolating and summing all of the pyramid levels (band-pass images).

(a)

(b)

(c)

Fig. 12 Blending computed by a variety of algorithms:
(a) average, (b) median, (c) feathered

5. Conclusion

In this paper, We have described basics of image alignment and stitching. We basically concentrated on techniques for registering partially overlapping images and blending them to create seamless panoramas. A large number of additional techniques have been developed for solving related problems such as increasing the resolution of images by taking multiple displaced pictures (super resolution), stitching videos together to create dynamic panoramas, and stitching videos and images in the presence of large amounts of parallax. While image stitching is by now a fairly mature field with a variety of commercial products, there remain a large number of challenges and open extensions. One of these is to increase the reliability of fully automated stitching algorithms

References

1. P.J.Burt, E.H. Andelson, "A multiresolution spline with application to image mosaics", ACM transactions on Graphics 2 (4) (1983)
2. M. Brown and D. G. Lowe, "Recognizing Panorama" IEEE transaction on Image Processing-2003
3. Richard Szeliski, "Image Alignment and Stitching"- Microsoft Reasearch lab 2005
4. Jiaya jia, Chi-keung Tang, "Image Stitching using Structure Deformation"-IEEE transaction on pattern analysis and machine intelligence, vol 30, 2008
5. E. H. Adelson, C. H. Anderson, J. R. Bergen "Pyramid methods in image processing", 1984
6. J.-Y. Guillemaut, J. Kilner, J. Starck, A. Hilton, "Dynamic Feathering: Minimising Blending Artefacts in View-Dependent Rendering" – IEEE transaction on Image processing 2008
7. Jiaya Jia, Chi-Keung Tang, "Eliminating Structure and Intensity Misalignment in Image Stitching" Research Grant Council of Hong Kong Special Administration Region, China (AOE/E-1999)
8. H.-Y. Shum and R. Szeliski. "Construction of panoramic mosaics with global and local alignment". International Journal of Computer Vision, 36(2):101–130, February 2000. Erratum published July 2002, 48(2):151–152

Cross layer QOS routing for various traffic patterns in mobile ADHOC network through bandwidth estimation

Rekha Patil[1] · A. Damodaram[2] · Rupam Das[3]

[1]Assistant Professor, Computer Science and Engg Department, P D A College of Engineering, Gulbarga, India
[2]Professor, Computer Science and Engg Department, JNTU College of Engineering, JNT, University, Hyderabad, India
[3]Team Member, Intergrated Ideas, Gulbarga, India

1. Introduction

1.1 MANET

A mobile ad-hoc network (MANET) is a self configuring network of mobile routers (and associated hosts) connected by wireless links—the union of which form an arbitrary topology. The routers are free to move randomly and organize themselves arbitrarily; thus, the network's wireless topology may change rapidly and unpredictably. MANETs are usually set upin situations of emergency for temporary operations or simply if there are no resources to set up elaborate networks. These types of networks operate in the absence of any fixed infrastructure, which makes them easy to deploy, at the same time however, due to the absence of any fixed infrastructure, it becomes difficult to make use of the existing routing techniques for network services, and this poses a number of challenges in ensuring the security of the communication, something that is not easily done as many of the demands of network security conflict with the demands of mobile networks, mainly due to the nature of the mobile devices (e.g. low power consumption, low processing load). Many of the ad hoc routing protocols that address security issues rely on implicit trust relationships to route packets among participating nodes. Besides the general security objectives like authentication, confidentiality, integrity, availability and non repudiation, the ad hoc routing protocols should also address location confidentiality, cooperation fairness and absence of traffic diversion. In this paper we attempt to analyze threats faced by the ad hoc network environment and provide a classification of the various security mechanisms. We analyzed the respective strengths and vulnerabilities of the existing routing protocols and suggest a broad and comprehensive framework that can provide a tangible solution. Ad-hoc networks are a new paradigm of wireless communication for mobile hosts. There is no fixed infrastructure such as base stations for mobile switching.

Nodes within each other's radio range communicate directly via wireless links while those which are far apart rely on other nodes to relay messages. Routing and session, route maintenance technique are very important challenges in such network due to probability of constant change of topology in such networks. In more dynamic networks a reactive routing is adopted where by A route is discovered on the fly when a source wants to communicate with a destination, and the route is removed once the communication is over. Working of MANET is depicted in Fig. 1.

1.2 Quality of services

Quality of Service is a method of providing better service for selected traffic types over various types of packet-switched networks. The network medium used could be any one of several types of technology ranging from Ethernet to Wireless and Frame Relay networks to ADHOC Network. QoS provides a method for determining which traffic should be given priority on a network segment.

As the topology of MANET is dynamic in nature, the link characteristics between the nodes changes very often. It therefore presents a great deal of challenge for the network to provide quality of services to different nodes. In short QOS can be said as a standard by means of which nodes in MANET forward the packets with minimum and acceptable delay, with high throughput, minimum jitter, minimum BER and maximum power possible. The level of acceptable noise or power loss varies from application to application. Thus we can say that QOS is a set of acceptable constraints for a particular traffic type by the network.

S.J. Pise (ed.), *ThinkQuest 2010*, DOI 10.1007/978-81-8489-989-4_14,

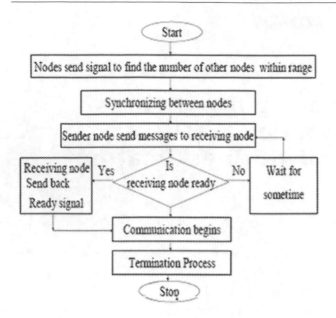

Fig. 1 Working of a general ad-hoc network

A QOS is guaranteed in mainly two ways. I) at the time of route discovery itself a path is determined in such a way that the best QOS is provided along the path. This is known as Discovery level QOS. II) QOS is provided at the time of data transmission by analyzing the QOS constraints amongst the layers. Second technique is also known as cross layer QOS mechanism. Data communication is virtually divided into layers. Each layer plays a significant role in packet transmission. Hence while discussing about QOS, it is equally important that we discuss about the layers and their demands for type of quality and constraints. In the following section, we will discuss about Cross layer QOS support.

1.3 Layers in QOS

Network layer

The role of Network layer in MANET like other networks is to find out a suitable route from a source node to a destination node. In QOS routings, the routes need to be selected in such a manner that it meets the qos requirements. Hence in qos aware routing, network layer must be notified by the application layer about the type of services it expects. Hence they are also called service discovery protocol. Network layer finds out a path and puts the incoming packets in a queue. Then it suitably forwards the packets by checking the constraints and the way they are met. As it is already being discussed the routing protocols are either pre established or on demand paths. Generally QOS requires an on demand path establishment where the links in the paths meets the qos requirements. It is quite understandable that decision making of the network layer depends upon application layer demands.

During route establishment when network layer tries to find out network characteristics, it has to rely on another low layer i.e. MAC layer.

MAC layer

MAC layer is responsible for channel sharing and allocation to the nodes. It allows transmission between two nodes based on set of control packets(for example RTS and CTS) packets. MAC layer also monitors the link facilities. It can calculate the power levels, energy of the nodes, collision and hence BER in the network. Where as situations like congestions can be directly measured in the network layer itself. Traffic volume send by application layer, collision and delays caused due to congestion all results in significant delay and data loss in the network. In the context of the QOS aware routing, it is important that MAC layer permits a transmission based on service requirement asked by the network layer which interns is asked by application layer. For example if for a certain type of traffic Xbps bandwidth is required, then MAC calculates the bandwidth and notifies the network layer if the bandwidth is available or not. Based on this information the routing decision can be made.

Cross layer

From the above discussion it is apparent that if qos constraints are to be made a collaboration between the layers is very important. A cross layer solution is one where a layer can bypass another layer and communicate directly to it's next layer. For example if the application layer notifies the MAC layer about the bandwidth requirement and if MAC directly sends the information to the application layer, then both are said to bypass the network layer. Therefore it can be termed as a cross layer solution. A cross layer can also be a communication scenario when a lower layer can directly send an information to it's upper layer even when there is no payload. As it is been discussed that QOS is a qualitative measure of layers or nodes provided to a specific type of traffic, it is essential to know about the traffic patterns. In following section we will discuss about the traffic patterns and their role in QOS protocols.

1.4 Traffic types in MANET

Traffic in MANET is generally categorized as either CBR (Constant bit rate traffic) or Burst Traffic. A constant Bit rate traffic is one where data rate in the network is consistent. Chatting or text messaging falls into this category. Burst traffic is one where the packet density suddenly increases and then decreases. Sudden surge in packet density is caused by specifically multimedia traffic. CBR are difficult to provide qos because the overall required bandwidth is unpredictable. Hence MANET generally adopts routing protocols where bandwidth is a constraint for such traffics. In elaborated terms, to serve burst traffic MANET nodes tries to find out a path which comprises of links which have sufficient bandwidth to handle the burst. Such traffics also requires traffic shaping and scheduling algorithms. Traffic shapings are the means of transmitting the traffic via many different paths so that they can be reached at thereceiver node with the requirement of very high bandwidth at any node. Burst traffic causes a great deal of congestion in the network which in terms results into data loss or latency. CBR on the other hand doesn't require any sophisticated mechanisms as the load or the required bandwidth can be easily predicted by the nodes. Based on delay sensitivity the traffic is divided into 1) Real time traffic and 2) non real time traffic. A real time traffic is one where the packets must reach to the destination without significant latency. Voice and video communications falls in this category. Such traffics may interns be either CBR or BT. To handle such traffic delay sensitive routings are adopted. Nodes here find out the links where the traffic is minimum o that the packets can be transmitted through those paths. Throughput is not considered as a major issue here. This is because of advance digital recovery algorithms which can predict the loss frames and generate the frames. For example in video transmission, some of the video frames are interleaved. Decoder can generate such frames by motion detection algorithm. Suppose during communication, one frame is lost then also it can be generated at the receiver. No such delay constraints exists for non real time traffics.

These traffics are mostly text data and files. They demand more accuracy in delivery than the delay. Here the contents of the documents are more important than the latency. Therefore throughput aware routings are adopted for delivery of such traffics.

2. Problem formation

2.1 Related work

[1] States that the, available bandwidth estimation is a vital component of admission control for wireless networks. The available bandwidth undergoes fast time-scale variations due to channel fading and error from physical obstacles [2] does not require any centralized entity to co-ordinate users' transmissions. The MAC layer uses a CSMA/CA algorithm for shared use of the medium. The design scheme of [1] does not modify the CSMA/CA MAC protocol in any manner, but gauges the effect of phenomena such as medium contention, channel fading and interference, which influence the available bandwidth, on it. Based on the effect of the phenomena on the working of the medium-access scheme, it has estimated the available bandwidth of a wireless host to each of its neighbors [3] propose a QoS-aware routing protocol, which is based on residual bandwidth estimation during route set up. Soft QoS or better and best-effort service, and guaranteed hard QoS are compared in [4]. This reveals that, if the topology changes too frequently, the source host cannot detect the network status changes and cannot make the corresponding adjustment to meet the specific QoS requirements, rendering the QoS meaningless. Therefore, combinatorial stability1 must first be met before any design can consider providing QoS to real-time applications. Estimating the end-to-end throughput can be simpli-

fied into finding the minimal residual bandwidth available among the hosts in that route [6, 7]. Reveals about various techniques for QOS and compares their performances in MANET. It also provides guidelines for selection criteria for the protocols.

2.2 Proposed work

When a path is established from a source to a destination, data communication takes place. Once data communication begins link quality varies amongst the links of the routes. Therefore it is quite difficult to device a packet rate in such situations. It is overcome by a collaboration of MAC and Network layer. Generally the bandwidth available to any node in MANET is affected by the neighbors of the node and the traffic that the node is currently handling. In MANET (MAC standard of 802.11) channel is shared between the nodes in a contention basis. Hence bandwidth measurement must take into account of the contention amongst the nodes and also the traffic pattern. It is important as merely estimating bandwidth and based on available bandwidth determining the packet rate may not provide suitable QOS. This is due to the fact that for burst traffic, it is essential to, predict the probability of next burst to arrive. Scheduling or queuing or other corrective measure can be taken based on that.

3. Methodology

For providing best QOS technique, accurate bandwidth estimation is very important. Generally bandwidth measurement technique concentrate towards estimating used bandwidth between all neighboring links of a node. But in case of Burst traffic it is equally important that we take into consideration of self generated traffic by a node. A typical bandwidth consumption by Neighbors of A is depicted in Fig. 2.

(1) gives the bandwidth consummation at any node X where $B_{self}(X)$ is the self traffic generated at Node X.

$$B_{cons}(X) = \sum_{i \in N_X} B_{self}(i).$$

(1)

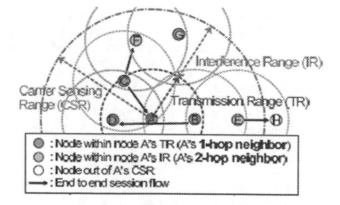

Fig. 2 Bandwidth consumption on node A

We assume that the channel capacity in a network is C(channel capacity here is assumed as the Ideal available bandwidth in ideal time at any node). For simplicity we consider one way link here.

We express bandwidth at any node I is

$$\sum_N B_i <= C/a. \tag{2}$$

Where N is the number of nodes that shares the channel and 1/a is termed as channel utilization rate. It is quite obvious that as number of nodes in an area increases(node density) channel will be shared by that much more number of nodes or in other terms utilization par node will decrease. Hence we can device a theory that a α Node_Density.

We choose a=Node_Density by optimizing the proportionality constant to 1 as it will not have direct effect on the performance. Based on this we can say that bandwidth at any node I is

$$B_i = C/a * 1/ni - U_i. \tag{3}$$

where ni is the total neighbours of I and Ui is the used bandwidth by node i. This bandwidth measurement is very significant as a node only needs to know about it's neighbours and can still estimate the available bandwidth. From (1) and (2) we can device a new bandwidth estimation (Bandwidth consumed at a node).

$$B_{cons}(X) = \sum_{i \in N_X} B_{self}(i) + C/a \tag{4}$$

From (4) and (3), Total available bandwidth can be calculated by

$$Ba(x) = C/a * 1/nx + \sum_{i \in N_x} B_{self}(i) - U(x) \tag{5}$$

where Ba(x) is the total available bandwidth at node x. from 5 it is very clear that if Traffic generation at each node is controlled by the node, QOS can be provided to overall network.

4. Simulation

Algorithm for proposed technique is given bellow.

Let traffic rate be P packets/second for fixed traffic and ex where x is random Gaussian distribution with probability density function 5. (We have selected Gaussian distribution for our traffic generation, because of it's bursty nature).

Let L=P/2 be the queue length at any node.

Total available bandwidth C = 11.2 MBPS
Total area of simulation be A m2
Let total Number of Nodes be N
a=N/A

Let P be total Number of paths selected and S={s1,s2..sp} be the set of source node and D={d1,d2...dp} be the set of destination node

For each source in S
Generate RREQ

do
At every node I that has received RREQ
Calculate available bandwidth at i.
If(Bi< L)
           Drop RREQ
        End
         End
Till i=destination
//Now we have QOS path, formed based on CBR traffic pattern.

For every path p in P
  Select traffic pattern
For every node I in p
do
If(Bi<L)
  // Bi measured by MAC layer and
information is passed to application layer.
  Store L traffic in queue
Restrict self traffic so that L
  Is minimum // by application layer
  End
Till i=destination of p
End

End

5. Results

5.1 The performance of the system for burst traffic is given bellow

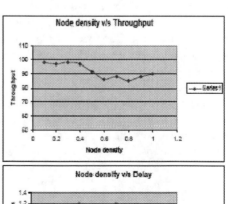

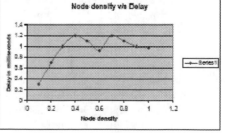

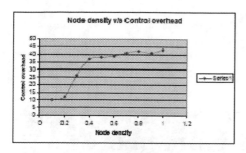

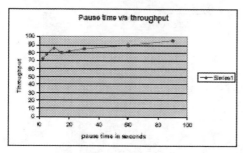

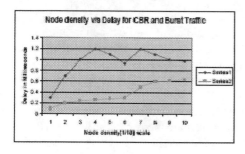

Series 1 Burst traffic
Series 2 CBR

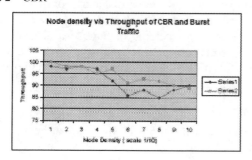

Series 1 Burst traffic
Series 2 CBR

6. Conclusion

Various bandwidth estimation and scheduling techniques have been proposed for qos routing in MANET. In this paper we have proposed a unique technique of QOS mechanism by a cross layer collaboration of Network layer, MAC layer and application layer. We have proposed a mechanism for traffic limiting and scheduling inorder to get a good QOS. The simulation gives satisfactory result in terms of QOS , delay, and control overhead. Simulation also shows that performance of CBR is optimum. But the behavior of the system is consistent for both types of traffics. Result can be further improved by integrating congestion control techniques by adopting feedback mechanism where not only will the traffic limiting will improve the QOS but also nodes can device qos strategies based on other nodes' traffic patterns.

References

1. Samarth H. Shah, Kai Chen, Klara Nahrstedt, Available Bandwidth Estimation in IEEE 802.11-based Wireless Networks Department of Computer Science University of Illinois at Urbana-Champaign
2. IEEE standard for wireless LAN MediumAccess Control (MAC) and Physical Layer(PHY) specification, June 1997
3. Lei Chen, and Wendi B. Heinzelman,QoS-Aware Routing Based on BandwidthEstimation for Mobile Ad Hoc Networks, IEEE JOURNAL ON SELECTED AREAS IN COMMUNICATIONS, VOL. 23, NO. 3, MARCH 2005
4. S. Chen and K. Nahrstedt, "Distributed quality-of-service in ad hoc networks,"*IEEE J. Sel. Areas Commun.*, vol. 17, no 8, Aug. 1999
5. S. Chen, "Routing support for providing guaranteed end-to-end quality-of-service," Ph.D. dissertation, Univ. Illinois at Urbana–Champaign, Urbana–Champaign, IL, 1999
6. P. Mohapatra, J. Li, and C. Gui, "QoS in mobile ad hoc networks," *IEEE Wireless Commun. Mag. (Special Issue on QoS in Next-GenerationWireless Multimedia.Communications Systems)*
7. Fethi Filali," QoS Issues and Solutions in Wireless Networks", CNRS- GDR – ARP – QoS Day :Paris, June 4, 2004
8. R. S. Prasad M. Murray_ C. Dovrolis_ K.Claffy,"Bandwidth estimation: metrics, measurement techniques, and tools"
9. Toshaki Osada, Gen Kitagata, A new QOS routing scheme for MANET

A new bimodal identification based on hand-geometry and palm-print

M. P. Dale · Hiren Galiyawala · M. A. Joshi

MES's College of Engineering, Pune, India

1. Introduction

Recently, biometric based personal identification is emerging as a powerful means for automatically recognizing a person's identity with a higher confidence. It concerns with identifying people by their physiological characteristics such as fingerprint, iris, retina, palm print, hand geometry and face or some behavioral aspects such as voice, signature and gesture. Currently, hand-based biometric technologies such as fingerprint verification and hand geometry verification most appeal to the biometric identification market. Automatic fingerprint verification is the most mature biometric technology, having been studied for more than 25 years. Currently, fingerprint authentication handles clear fingerprints very well but, because of skin problems or the nature of their work, around 2% of the population are unable to provide clear fingerprint images Another popular, hand-based biometric technology is hand geometry. Hand geometry uses geometric information from our hands for personal verification. Simple hand features, however, provide limited information, with the result that hand geometry is not highly accurate. To overcome problems in the hand-based biometric technologies, another hand-based biometric for use in personal identification/verification, the palmprint. The palmprint, the large inner surface of a hand, contains many line features such as principal lines, wrinkles, and ridges. Because of the large surface and the abundance of line features, we expect palm prints to be robust to noise and to be highly individual.

In this paper, palm-print and hand-geometry are combined for person identity verification. Unlike other multimodal biometric systems, two biometrics can be taken from the same image. This method attempts to improve the performance of palm-print-based verification system by integrating hand geometry feature. The proposed system consists of four major blocks: Image acquisition module, image pre-processing block, feature extraction and identification. The detailed system block diagram is shown in the Fig. 1. The entire system diagram is briefly described as follows.

First, the palm print and hand geometry image acquisition module uses a digital camera to capture the hand images. The preprocessing module employs image processing algorithms to separate the region of interest (ROI) from an input image. This module performs three major tasks: palm print and hand geometry preprocessing, noise reduction and smoothening of boundary. Next, the feature extraction module extracts the features of hand geometry and palm print. Finally, recognition module employs a minimum distance classifier according to Euclidean distance metric to recognize the hand pattern by comparing the feature vector with the enrolled data in the database. Hand geometry features includes length of four fingers and three widths of each one of them plus palm width. Total 17 hand features are calculated. Palm print features are extracted using Discrete Cosine Transform. The frequency distribution of DCT coefficient are arranged in particular manner and standard deviation is calculated as feature vector. The detailed technique will be explained later in section II. Total 36 features are taken from palm print. Database used consist of 84 person and 8 images of hand for each person. Volunteers given their hand image are from the institute in the age group of 18 to 50. We have used k images (where k is 2, 4, 6) for training and remaining 8-k for testing as given in table 1.

Table 1 Number of palm print images for training and testing set

K	Training	Testing Set
2	2×84 = 168	6×84 = 504
4	4×84 = 336	4×84 = 336
6	6×84 = 504	2×84 = 168

S.J. Pise (ed.), *ThinkQuest 2010*, DOI 10.1007/978-81-8489-989-4_15,
© Springer India Pvt. Ltd. 2011

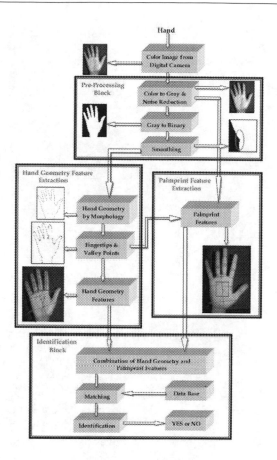

Fig. 1   System block diagram

Table 2

Method	TR=2 TS=6	TR=4 TS=4	TR=6 TS=2
Hand Geometry	83.92	80.95	83.92
Palm	95.03	95.03	97.81
Hand Geometry + Palm	97.8	100	100

When more than one image is used for training to create database feature vector the average value of respective feature is taken as final feature vector. The algorithm is checked in identification mode, by comparing remaining images from the database against feature vector created for all. Testing is carried out using only hand geometry features, only palm print features and then decision level fusion of both the features.

Euclidean distance is used to find out the minimum distance match between feature vectors of database image and query(test) image. Recognition rate for each one of them is presented here.

As can be seen from the Table 2, recognition rate remains more or less same even if training set has been increased for hand geometry. For palm using DCT features, recognition rate increases as the training set is increased. Finally when hand geometry and palm features are combined we get the highest recognition rate even at lower training set. Also

imposter analysis is carried out by taking 70 images as genuine and 14 images as imposter. By plotting threshold vs False Acceptance Rate and False Rejection Rate, Equal Error Rate (EER) point is found. The distribution of FAR and FRR for hand geometry, palm print and both combined are as shown in Fig. 2 (a), (b) and (c). As training set is increased at fusion level EER becomes low as shown in Fig. 2(c). Important feature of the proposed algorithm is that it does not use any kind of reprocessing(enhancement etc.) on extracted ROI and does not use any classification or mapping technique after applying the transform to resized ROI.

2.   System architecture

The proposed hand-geometry and palmprint recognition system expects to provide a simple, low-cost, non contact, comfortable and user-friendly acquisition mechanism. The mechanism for hand image is shown in Fig. 3. The peg-free mechanism is arranged to make the system suitable for any applications and environments. Unlike other bimodal biometric systems in which the different modalities may be acquired using different sensors, undergoing the inconvenience to the users and more system cost, the proposed mechanism can acquire the hand-shape and palmprint features from the same image simultaneously using a digital camera. The images are taken in natural indoor en-

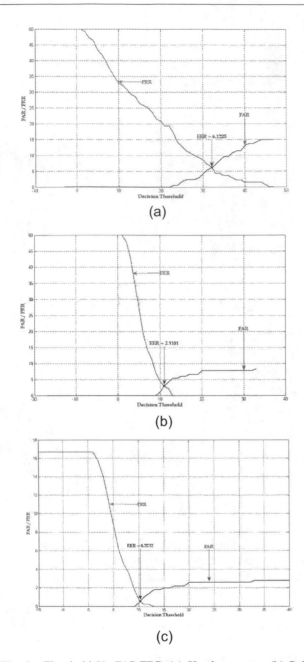

(a)

(b)

(c)

Fig. 2 Threshold Vs FAR/FRR (**a**) Hand geometry (**b**) Palm print (**c**) Hand geometry and palmprint combined

vironment without any extra illumination except flash light of digital camera. The users were only requested to make sure that their fingers do not touch each other. The KODAK Z740 digital camera was used to acquire the hand images. Images taken from digital camera are of resolution 1164 x 1552 pixels with flash light.

2.1 Preprocessing module

Preprocessing for hand geometry:

Step 1: Color to gray transformation – Since gray level image is adequate for hand shape segmentation process, we need to convert color image to gray-level image.

Fig. 3 Image acquisition module

Step 2: Noise reduction and gray-to-binary *transformation* – Averaging filter is applied to remove the noise pixels from the gray level image. Furthermore, the gray level image is binarized.

Step 3: Edge smoothing – Because the binarization possibly generates notch edges, as shown in Fig. 4 (a), we have used morphological opening operation to smooth the edges.

Step 4: Boundary extraction by morphology – The boundary of the hand is extracted by first "eroding" output image of step-3 with the structuring element (disk type) and then performing the image difference between output image of step-3 and its erosion (see Fig. 4(b)).

$$\beta(A) = A - (A \ominus B)$$

where, $\beta(A)$ = Boundary of A
$\quad\quad B$ = Structuring element

By taking negative image of Fig. 4 (b), we have obtained the contour of hand (see Fig. 3 (c)).

Step 5: Locating peak and valley points – This step has much importance for the further processing and algorithm, because the output image from this step has all reference points i.e. fingertips and valley points, which are useful to extract the Region of Interest (ROI) of palm. To locate the peak and valley points on the hand boundary, the basic steps are as follows:

- Find the lower left most point on the boundary (see Fig. 4 (d)) and consider this point as reference point for further processing.
- Next, trace the boundary of the hand starting from reference point to accumulate all the boundary pixels.
- Find the Euclidean distance of all boundary pixels with respect to the starting reference point and plot these all distance with respect to index of all points (see Fig. 4 (g)).

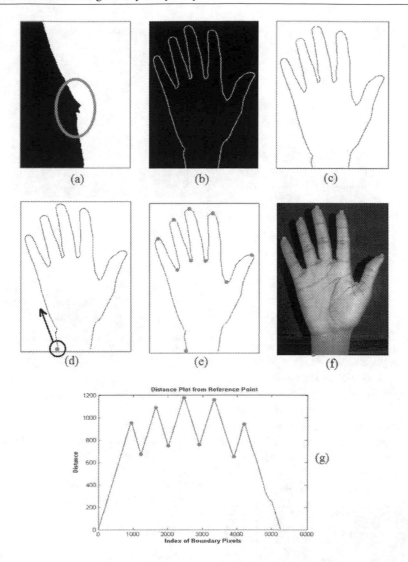

Fig. 4 (**a**) Notch edges, (**b**) and (**c**) Boundary of hand, (**d**) Reference point, (**e**) and (**f**) Location of points on hand contour and gray image, (**g**) Distance plot

- Plot all these peak and valley points on hand boundary as well as on the gray image (see Fig. 4 (e) & (f)).

Preprocessing for Palmprint: In this preprocessing first three steps are same as pre-processing steps of the hand geometry.Peak and valley points of the geometry are used for the extraction of palm ROI.

2.2 Feature extraction module

In this module we extract hand geometry features (finger lengths, finger widths, palm width) and palmprint features. All the features of the hand geometry are in the form of the Euclidian distance between two points i.e. between two pixels. Palmprint features are extracted by applying Discrete Cosine Transform (DCT). The Euclidian Distance between two points (X1, Y1) and (X2, Y2) is given by,

$$ED = \sqrt{(X_1 - X_2)^2 + (Y_1 - Y_2)^2}$$

Hand Geometry Feature Extraction Illustrated in Fig. 4, four valley points are located in between the fingers on the hand boundary. Because the middle-finger is the only finger which does not have large spatial variations of its valley points for different placement of the hands, the middle-finger baseline is formed by connecting the second and third (count from the left) valley points. For remaining finger baseline, we have assumed that two end points of each baseline have the same distance from the respective fingertip point. Using one of the respective valley points as one of the end points we locate the other end point by searching for the point which has the same distance from the fingertip at the another side of the boundary of the finger.

Steps involve in extraction of geometrical features are described as follows:

- Locate the base lines for all the fingers
- Locate middle points of all the base lines.

The middle point between two points (X1, Y1) and (X2, Y2) is given by equation,

$$Middle\ Point = \left(\frac{X_1 + X_2}{2}, \frac{Y_1 + Y_2}{2}\right).$$

Finger lengths are calculated by ED between respective fingertip points and middle points of the respective base lines.

For all the fingers, three widths (*W1, W2 and W3* in Fig. 5) are taken at different places. These three widths are measured at fix Euclidian distance of 1/4, 2/4 and 3/4 respectively, with respect to the fingertips. Along with this palm width is also calculated. Thus, total 17 geometrical features (4 finger lengths, 12 finger widths and palm width) are taken in to consideration.

Palmprint Feature Extraction Region of interest of palm of size 256×256 is cropped as shown in Fig. 6(a) and cropped portion of palm is shown in Fig. 6(b).

The size of cropped palm is too big to process hence it is further resized to size of 128×128 hereafter called as resized ROI. The resized ROI image undergoes no further preprocessing. The algorithm first divides the image into four non overlapping parts around center point as shown in Fig. 7(a). The 2-D transform is applied on each sub-image separately. The DCT transformed coefficients are now grouped into different nine frequency bands (blocks) as shown in Fig. 7(b). For each numbered block the standard deviation is calculated. Such features are calculated from four sub images and hence form a feature vector of 36 (4×9=36) which is used in enrollment as well as matching phase. These are

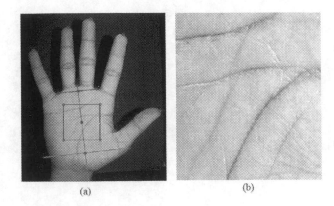

Fig. 6 (a) ROI from palm (b) Cropped palm

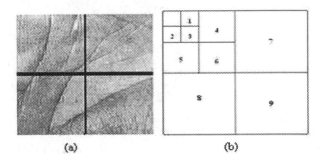

Fig. 7 (a) Resized ROI in 4 parts. (b) Arrangement of sub-image DCT coefficient

stored as float values so take 144 bytes (36x4) to store the feature vector for one person.

3. Identification scheme

The experimental scheme is designed to follow k images for training and 8-k images for testing. Euclidean distance is used as distance measure to find the identity between query image and images in the database. As seen in Fig. 2 and Table 2 in abstract, we can see clearly that the results of the person authentication experiences are acceptable. The performance is greatly better than uni-modal biometric authentication. The time required for training and testing equal images(336) at fusion level is around 70 sec. Time calculations are done on machine Pentium® D CPU 2.8 GHz. The experiments discussed in this paper re realized using Matlab language.

4. Conclusion

The objective of this work was to investigate the integration of simplest palm print features and hand geometry features and to achieve higher performance that may not be possible with single biometric indicator alone. The algorithm is based on pure 1-D human hand print features. The experimental results indicate that the proposed method is robust with respect to translation and small rotation. Main feature of algorithm is, it is tested in identification mode and achieved

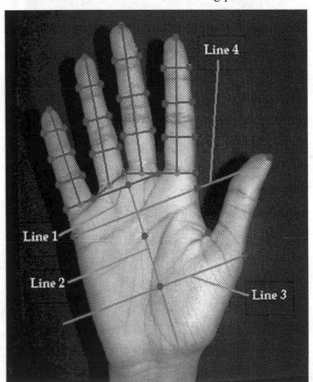

Fig. 5   Hand geometry features

recognition rate of 100%. Proposed method also presents less computational complexity and time complexity.

References

1. A. Jain, R. Bolle and S. Pankanti (eds.), Biometrics: Personal Identification In Networked Society, Boston, Mass: Kluwer Academic Publishers, 1999
2. D. Zhang,W. Kong, J. You, and M.Wong, "Online palmprint identification," IEEE Transactions on Pattern Analysis and Machine Intelligence, vol. 25, no. 9, pp. 1041–1050, 2003
3. W. Li, D. Zhang, and Z. Xu, "Palmprint Identification by Fourier Transform", International Journal of Pattern Recognition and Artificial Intelligence, vol.16, no. 4, pp. 417-432, 2002
4. Kei Yih Edward Wong, G. Sainarayanan, Ali Chekima, "Palmprint Identification Using Wavelet Energy", Proceedings of Int.Conf. on Intelligent and Advanced Systems, Malaysia, Nov. 2007
5. A. K. Jain, Fundamentals of Digital Image Processing, Englewood Cliffs, NJ: Prentice-Hall, 1989
6. Xiao-Yuan Jing and David Zhang, "A Face and Palmprint Recognition Approach Based on Discriminant DCT Feature Extraction", IEEE Transaction on Systems, Man and Cybernetics-Part B: Cybernetics, Vol. 34, No. 6, December 2004
7. T. Amornraksa and S. Tachaphetpiboon, "Fingeprint Recognition using DCT Feature," Electronic Letters, Vol. 42, No. 9, 2006
8. Hui Yan, Duo Long, "A Novel Bimodal Identification Approach Based on Hand-print", 2008 congress on Image and Signal Processing
9. Fan Yang, Baofeng Ma, "A New Mixes-Mode Biometrics Information Fusion Based-on Fingerprint, Hand-geometry and Palm-print", IEEE, 2000

Optimization in virtualization

Sonali Ajankar · **Ashish Mohta** · **S. S. Sane**

Department of Computer Technology, Veermata Jeejabai Technological Institute Mumbai, India

1. Introduction

Virtualization is becoming a core business strategy from desktop to data centre. It can provide an isolated execution environment to applications, support share and reuse of hardware resources. The cost reduction and simplicity of management are the prominent advantages. It can help to deliver high priority business services more quickly. Enhance energy efficiency. Optimizing the various resources with virtualization helps to improve organization efficiency. Here, the various optimization methods like desktop, server, network and storage are included. Optimization is the process of making something more efficient or optimal. Optimization is about virtualization of storage, servers and move towards on demand computing.

Desktop optimization enables organizations to centrally define virtual machines (VMs) and assign these VMs to authenticated users to run on their PCs. It offers temporary access to a corporate desktop, and provides higher security for corporate applications and data.

The major part of overhead in Xen's network performance degradation was caused by the long data transfer path as well as the repeated VM EXIT that leads to trap in Xen hypervisor in a HVM domain. By shorten the data transfer path and optimize the interrupt deliver route, the network virtualization performance was improved.

After that, evaluate three techniques for optimizing network performance. First, redefine the virtual network interfaces of guest domains to incorporate high-level network offload features available in most modern network cards. Second, optimize the implementation of the data transfer path between guest and driver domains. The optimization avoids expensive data remapping operations on the transmit path, and replaces page remapping by data copying on the receive path. Finally, provide support for guest operating systems to effectively utilize advanced virtual memory features such as super pages and global page mappings. The overall impact of these optimizations is an improvement in transmit performance of guest domains by a factor of 4.4. The receive performance in guest domains improves by 18%.

Storage Optimization can help to identify storage inefficiencies and areas for improvement and help design and build a virtualized storage solution that can increase storage capacity utilization, enable interoperability between heterogeneous storage devices and support non disruptive hardware change.

Server Optimization becomes necessary because there is need for fully realizing the benefits of sever virtualization, also organizations require expert planning, design and implementation for their virtualization projects

The following figures show a simple comparison of three applications running in a regular computer versus a virtualized computer. In Non-virtualizes computer operating system directly run on the hardware as shown in Fig. 1.

In virtualizes computer a VMM layer placed between hardware and operating system as shown in Fig. 2. Here the guest operating systems may be the same or different.

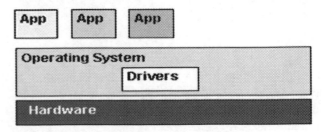

Fig. 1 The non-virtualized computer

S.J. Pise (ed.), *ThinkQuest 2010*, DOI 10.1007/978-81-8489-989-4_16,
© Springer India Pvt. Ltd. 2011

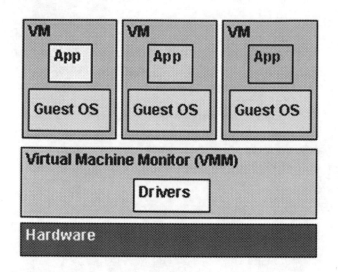

Fig. 2 The virtualized computer

In virtualization number of operating system can be run on the same computer at the same time. It provides the security as applications running on different VMs do not interfere with each other.

This paper first gives the overview of virtualization. The section 2 deals with the desktop virtualization optimization then in section 3 describe the different methods of optimization of network virtualization then storage virtualization optimization is cover in section 4 and server virtualization optimization describe in section 5.

2. Desktop virtualization optimization

Desktop virtualization is a server-centric computing model that borrows from the traditional thin-client model but is designed to give system administrators and end-users the best of both worlds: the ability to host and centrally manage desktop virtual machines in the data center while giving end users a full PC desktop experience.

Desktop optimization is intended to deploy legacy applications to users running a newer desktop OS, such as Vista or Windows 7, or for restricted or temporary use by users such as contract workers [8].

2.1 Working

Desktop optimization management tools enable administrators to deliver and manage VMs centrally, and control when users can access them, while a technology called Trim Transfer makes VM distribution and patching practical over corporate networks. Its client can make virtualization transparent to PC users.

2.1.1. Managing Desktop VMs: Administrators use a management console to assign VMs stored in the central repository to authenticated users by defining workspaces using Active Directory. A workspace is a VM configured to run in Virtual PC along with a usage policy, such as who is authorized to use the VM, when they may use it, when the

authorization expires. Desktop optimization applications do not require installation or configuration by the end user and workspaces can be deployed via its server; by using automated tools, such as System Centre Configuration Manager; by downloading over the Internet. These clients then manage the execution of the VM on the local computer, in compliance with the policy defined by the administrator. Once provisioned on a client PC, VMs can run disconnected from the corporate network.

Applications are protected by authentication and policy, and their use may be revoked either when the client agent contacts the server for updates to the workspace or after a specified, resettable expiry period. The latter is useful when a PC is used remotely with only occasional connection to the corporate network.

The Desktop Optimization Management Server also aggregates clients events, such as who has used an application and what errors might have occurred, and stores them in a centralized SQL Server database for monitoring and reporting.

2.1.2. Trim Transfer for Fast Deployment: Because VHDs (Virtual hard disk) are large, desktop optimization uses incremental data transfer technology called Trim Transfer for distribution of VM images, cutting down on network traffic for both the initial deployment and updates. Transfers run in the background, when network and CPU resources are not needed by other applications.

Trim Transfer uses existing local files to build the VM image, some resources required by the VM (e.g., system and application files) already exist on the client computer. Trim Transfer scans the local hard drive, compares the result with what is needed in the VM, and uses the network to transfer only those files that are different. Microsoft says this delivers significant savings for many applications; for example, approximately 40% of the files needed for office installations on Windows XP are also needed for Office on Vista, so in the case of a VM that runs Office on XP that is transferred to a computer running Office on Vista, Desktop optimization transfers only the differences and uses files already on the client for installation.

When updating to a new image version, only the blocks of the VHD that has changed are downloaded, not the entire VHD, significantly reducing the required network bandwidth and delivery time. The client guarantees the integrity of the final image by ensuring that the local blocks to be used are bit-by-bit identical to those in the desired VM image.

2.1.3. Hiding the Virtual PC and the OS: Desktop optimization application is more transparent and simpler for the end user than Virtual PC 2007. Although it provides a complete computer as a VM running in Virtual PC, administrators can configure to hide the Virtual PC and the VM's guest OS desktop so that end users see applications as if they were running natively on the PC; they do not have to manage the Virtual PC or install VMs. Desktop optimization applications can be started from the Windows Start menu or from an icon on the host desktop, and users are only aware that the application is running in a VM.

2.2 Advantages

Desktop optimization simplifies desktop management, but it confers some unique advantages. The technology removes a barrier to OS upgrades, strengthens centralized management of applications, offers temporary access to a corporate desktop, and provides higher security for corporate applications and data.

3. Network virtualization optimization

3.1 Xen network I/O architecture

Xen is a virtual machine monitor for IA-32 (x86, x86-64), IA-64 and PowerPC 970 architectures. It allows several guest operating systems to be executed on the same computer hardware concurrently. Xen uses a spit driver model, among all domains running on Xen, only domain0 has direct access to physical I/O devices. It performs I/O operations on behalf of the other domain. In order to access device, guest OS sends request to the Frontend and Frontend will transfer request to the corresponding Backend. In this way, each data transmit or receive operation must go through domain0, which makes the network I/O virtualization architecture in Xen a bottleneck for networking performance.

3.1.1 Data Transfer: The performance is even worse for a HVM (Hardware virtual machine) domain without Front driver like windows. Fig. 3 shows the network send packet flow in a HVM domain:

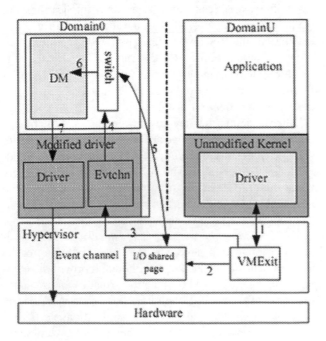

Fig. 3   Xen network virtualization I/O process flow

- When a guest domain (domain), sends data packet, the In/Out instruction will trigger VM Exit, control will transmit from guest domain to Xen. A function will be called to handle VM Exit. If this function can handle it directly, the process will be finished immediately.
- Xen writes the detail information of the In/Out instruction to a shared page between Domain0 and DomainU, and then notifies domain0 via event-channel. After this, Xen will block DomainU and schedule other domains to run.
- Xen restores domain0 and transfers control to domain.
- The first function on domain0 to be called is the callback function hypervisor_callback, which will call evtchn_do_upcall to collects I/O request from domainU.
- gevtchn_do_upcall will trigger the select system call in switch and then call I/O request handle function cpu_handle_ioreq. The latter will call cpu_get_ioreq to get the I/O request information in the shared page.
- DM figures out what kind device the request wants to access, and calls the corresponding callback function registered when the device was initialized to process the request.
- Those call back function were executed to send/ receive data through the physical driver in domain0.
- When the data transfer finished, DM will notify Xen that the data transfer has been completed. Xen will unblock domainU when it gets the notification, and then domainU can run again.

3.2 Overview of optimized network architecture

Shared I/O page data structure in Ioreq.h is used to store the information of I/O requests and the process results of those requests. Both Xen and domain0 have direct access to this shared I/O page. The following optimizations algorithmic steps were based on this feature:

- Move Ne200State to the shared I/O page. So that both Xen hypervisor and Domain0 can access it directly.
- Change the original way to access the Ne2000 virtual NIC.
- Move the functions that read registers and write state registers to Xen hypervisor.
- Add a simple switch in Xen hypervisor.

For judging whether this optimization driver can handle the requests from a HVM guest domain.

The overall optimization model changes only a little part of Ne2000 virtual NIC and adds a small patch to the Xen hypervisor. It does not affect the reliability and performance of Xen hypervisor. By moving the state information of Ne2000 virtual NIC to I/O shared page, a lot of register read operations and state register I/O requests can be processed in Xen directly. This model reduces the switches between Xen and domain, shortens the data transfer path, and improves the Ne2000 virtual NIC performance.

3.2.1. Data Transfer Flow: Fig. 5 describes the work flow of the optimization model. Taking data transfer as an example, the optimization model works in the following way:

- When the HVM guest domain sends data packet to other machine, it will write the control register or state register of Ne2000 virtual NIC. IN/OUT instruction will cause VM Exit and traps in Xen.
- Xen gets control of CPU and calls function vmx_vmexit_handle, which will read reasons of VM Exit from VMCS structure. The hypervisor will get the detail information about the I/O operation, such as I/O type, I/O port address, data length, etc. vmx_vmexit_handle will call vmx_io_ instruction to handle I/O operations, which will invoke send_pio_req function later.
- Send_pio_req will analyze the I/O request information and call the new switch to judge whether this request can be handled by this model.
- Described as the dashed line in Fig. 5, if the request can be handled in Xen, the request will be sent to the modified Ne2000 I/O functions immediately, and the results will be written to the shared I/O page. As soon

as this process finished, it will notify Xen hypervisor. It is observed in Fig. 5 that the data will flow in the dashed line. Hence the data transfer path is greatly shortened compared with the original model.

- If this request cannot be handled by Xen alone, the switch places the I/O request in the shared I/O page and notifies domain0 to handle it by the original way shown in Fig. 3. Compared Fig. 3 with Fig. 5, this optimization model greatly shortens the data transfer path by intercepting I/O requests and handling it immediately. In this way here reduced the switch between the Xen hypervisor and domain0, which is the major reason for the high performance degradation, and thus improved the performance of Xen network virtualization.

3.3 Experimental results and evaluation

The optimization model improved the throughput with the average of 1.56. The experiment shows that when sending small records, the latency of the optimized virtual NIC is also improved. TLB misses does not concentrate on several functions but scatters in domain [5]. Due to the increase of throughput, the data transfer time is greatly reduced. The CPU overheads are reduced by 73%. The reasons of CPU overheads improvements lie in the shortening of I/O transfer path and the reduction of cache miss. These result shows that modification made to the previous architecture are very advantages. As it improve overall network performance.

3.4 Another methods of network optimization

This paper presents another three optimizations to the Xen network virtualization architecture to address network performance problems identified in guest domains namely

1. Virtual interface optimization
2. I/O channel optimization
3. Virtual memory optimization

These optimizations fall into the following three categories:

First optimization is to redefine the virtual network interfaces of guest domains to incorporate high-level network offload features available in most modern network cards. For that add three capabilities to the virtualized network interface: scatter/gather I/O, TCP/IP checksum offload, and TCP segmentation offload (TSO). Scatter/gather I/O and checksum offload improve performance in the guest domain. Scatter/gather I/O eliminates the need for data copying by the Linux implementation of sendfile (). TSO improves performance throughout the system. In addition to its well-known effects on TCP performance benefiting the guest domain, it improves performance in the Xen VMM and driver domain by reducing the number of network packets that they must handle. These capabilities also improve the efficiency of the virtualization path connecting the virtual and physical network interfaces.

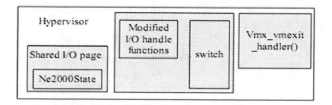

Fig. 4 Optimization architecture overview

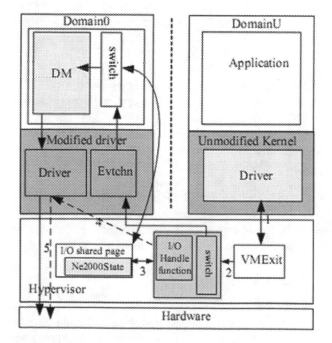

Fig. 5 Data transfer flow in the optimized model

Second, optimize the implementation of the data transfer path between guest and driver domains. For that introduce a faster I/O channel for transferring network packets between the guest and driver domains. The optimization avoids expensive data remapping operations on the transmit path, and replaces page remapping by data copying on the receive path.

Finally, provide a new memory allocator in the VMM which tries to allocate physically contiguous memory to the guest OS. These mechanisms allow guest OSes to make use of superpage and global page mappings on the Intel x86 architecture, which significantly reduce the number of TLB misses by guest domains. Overall impact of these optimizations is an improvement in transmit performance of guest domains and the receive performance of the driver domain of native Linux performance. Emulating TSO in software in the driver domain results in higher network performance than performing TCP segmentation in the guest domain. The receive performance of guest domains remains a significant bottleneck which remains to be solved.

4. Storage virtualization optimization

Storage virtualization is the pooling of physical storage from multiple network storage devices into a single storage device that is managed from a central console. Storage virtualization is commonly used in a SAN. The management of storage devices can be tedious and time-consuming. Storage virtualization helps the storage administrator perform the tasks of backup, archiving, and recovery more easily, and in less time.

With Storage Optimization gain access to trained consultants and architects who can help identify storage inefficiencies and areas for improvement and help design and build a virtualized storage solution that can increase storage capacity utilization, enable interoperability between heterogeneous storage devices and support non disruptive hardware change [9].

4.1 Optimizing storage utilization

In a optimization reallocate storage space dynamically to support fluctuating workload conditions and develop a storage architecture governance model so implement changes to existing storage management processes such as capacity planning and provisioning, helping to dramatically improve overall storage capacity utilization. It also improves device utilization levels, reduces storage management complexity and overall costs, facilitates interoperability and more "open" storage systems, enable resource consolidation.

5. Server virtualization optimization

Server virtualization means the partitioning of a physical server into smaller virtual servers. In server virtualization the resources of the server itself are hidden, or masked, from users, and software is used to divide the physical server into multiple virtual environments, called virtual or private servers for example Web servers. Instead of requiring a separate computer for each server, dozens of virtual servers can co-reside on the same computer.

Server virtualization can facilitate the alignment of IT to business objectives. It can play a major role in IT optimization. It can act as a key building block in a SOA environment; also contribute to the greening of data centre. Helping to lower the TCO including costs associated with hardware purchases, maintenance and facilities [10].

While it's clear that x86 server virtualization can deliver many benefits, there's a catch. To fully realize these benefits, organizations require expert planning, design and implementation for their virtualization projects and that's where Server Optimization and Integration Services come in.

5.1 Building a virtualization business case

Server Optimization and Integration Services starts with a solution framing step that can help answer a key question: What can x86 server virtualization accomplish in the IT environment? The solution looks at business readiness and recommends strategies for supporting a shared service model. Working with the business and technology managers and IT architect documents current business processes surrounding server purchasing, provisioning and management. This review details budget allocation and how budgets are currently assigned to projects and to the common infrastructure. The architect also documents current operational and support model for change management, help desk and support staff roles, along with training needs and any internal service level agreements.

Next, the architect assesses backend infrastructure components—for example, storage, network, backup, systems management, security and time synchronization—to help ensure that they can support virtualization. The architect also reviews and documents current environment and makes recommendations for essential changes. The architect can gain a clear understanding of the environment and the various systems' configuration and utilization. The architect also analyzes business, infrastructure and workload constraints in order to accurately calculate the size of a potential virtualization platform.

Finally, the architect assesses the virtualization host server to determine if it is large enough to deliver acceptable levels of services to all guests. The architect also performs a detailed hardware inventory and performance utilization analysis for suitability within a virtualized environment.

5.2 Detailed design

To produce a virtual infrastructure design that meets specific requirements, the IT architect performs a second step, plan and design, which produces a detailed design document that sets naming and security standards, defines the disk and network structure, and documents any required system tuning elements. This document includes the security and administration model backup methodology host physical and virtual disk layout, specifically file system structure and dedication of disks to guests, where applicable virtual network topology structure and format, plus interconnection with the physical network, host server hardware specification, virtual machine distribution among hosts, processes and procedures for ongoing management, implementation tables and configuration settings.

5.3 Services

Server optimization offers the optional custom services for post implementation support includes operational support which provides services like monthly "health checks", thirty hours of engineering support per month, optional four-hour emergency response service and provide full remote management services like new guest provisioning, host hardware support, virtualization software support, status monitoring, performance and capacity management, documentation, security management, system software support, system backup and recovery, infrastructure resilience and operational processes.

6. Conclusion

Many organizations want to increase the performance and reduce the cost and complexity of their application-hosting infrastructures. This efforts increase virtualization optimization and decrease power consumption while having capability to increase their overall system utilization.

Along with providing industry-leading expertise and using good methodologies and tools to speed design and implementation processes, paper presents worldwide various optimization methods, as well as proven reference architectures and best practices to accelerate the installation of new Extended and Optimized Deployment of software.

Hence, this area of virtualization is one of the interesting areas which introduce the industry and application oriented work in academic environment.

References

1. *Virtualization*, from Wikipedia, the free encyclopedia
2. R.P. Goldberg, *"Survey of Virtual Machine Research,"* Computer, June 1974, pp. 34–45
3. *Virtualization and virtual Machine* by Silpa Jain
4. *The Optimization of Xen Network Virtualization,&* by Zhand Jian, Li Xiaoyong, Guan Haibing
5. *Diagnosing Performance Overheads in the Xen Virtual Machine Environment,&* by Menon, J. R. Santos, Y. Turner, G. J.Janakiraman, and W. Zwaenepoel. In First ACM/USENIX Conference on Virtual Execution Environments (VEE'05), June 2005
6. *Optimizing Network Virtualization in Xen,&* by Aravind Menon, Alan L. Cox, Willy Zwaenepoel. In Proceedings of the 2006
7. C. Waldspurger. *Memory resource management in VMware ESX server.* In Operating Systems Design and Implementation (OSDI), Dec 2002
8. *Enterprise Desktop virtualization Joins Optimization Pack&*, publish on Monday, 18 May 2009
9. *IBM Storage Optimization and Integration Services – storage virtualization,* Produced in the United States of America 11-07
10. *IBM Server Optimization and Integration Services – VMware server virtualization,* Produced in the United States of America 05-08

Analysis of linear multiuser detection for DS CDMA

Srihari D. · Mrs. Y. M. Vaidya

College of Engineering, Pune, India

1. Introduction

Spread spectrum techniques originated in answer to the needs of military communications. They are based on signaling schemes which greatly expand the transmitted spectrum relative to the data rate. A transmission technique in which a pseudorandom code, independent of the data, is employed as a modulation wave form to spread the signal energy over a band width much greater than the information signal band width is called SSM. The modulated output signals occupy a much greater band width than the signals base band information band width. To qualify has a spread spectrum signal, two criteria should be met.

1. The transmitted signal band width is much greater than the information band width.
2. Some function other than the information being transmitted is employed to determine the resultant transmitted band width.

2. PN sequences

The PN sequence is produced by the pseudo-random noise generator that is simply a binary linear feedback shift register, consisting of XOR gates and a shift register. This PN generator has the ability to generate an identical sequence for both the transmitter and the receiver, and yet retaining the desirable properties of a noise-like randomness bit sequence. A PN sequence has many characteristics such as having a nearly equal number of zeros and ones, very low correlation between shifted versions of the sequence and very low cross correlation with any other signals such as interference and noise. However, it is able to correlate very well with itself and its inverse. Another important aspect is the autocorrelation of the sequence as it decides the ability to synchronize and lock the spreading code to the received signal. This effectively combats the effects of multipath interference and improves the SNR.

Gold sequences

The m-sequences have excellent autocorrelation properties but their cross-correlation properties do not follow any particular rules and typically exhibit undesirably high values Furthermore, the number of msequences for a given number of registers in an LFSR is limited. Gold sequences address these problems, and are derived by combining the m sequences from two LFSRs In comparisons to m-sequences; Gold sequences provide larger sets of sequences and exhibit better cross correlation properties Gold sequences are generated from two equal length m-sequences that form a so called preferred pair. The cross-correlation of two m-sequences that form a preferred pair is tri-valued and it takes the values from the set $\{1, -t(m), t(m) -2\}$, where, $t(m) = 1 + 2^{\frac{m+2}{2}}$ and m is the number of binary shift registers in the LFSR. A requirement for the generation of Gold sequences is that m should be equal to 2 modulo 4.

3. Multiuser detection

Synchronous DS-CDMA system transmitter model

$$r_k(t) = A_k b_k s_k(t - iT_b) iT_b \le t < (i+1)T_b$$

$$s_k(t) = \frac{1}{\sqrt{N}} \sum_{n=1}^{N} s_{kn} rect(t - (n-1)Tc)$$

$$rect(t) = u(t) - u(t - Tc)$$

u(t) is the unit step function, and b_k (i) 2 $\{-1, +1\}$. Tb is the bit duration, Tc is the chip duration and N = Tb/Tc is the spreading gain. S_k (N × 1) vector is the chip spreading

S.J. Pise (ed.), *ThinkQuest 2010*, DOI 10.1007/978-81-8489-989-4_17,

sequence for the kth user. Definition of the time-correlation between the signature waveforms of users i and j as

$$R_{ij} = \int_0^{T_b} s_{i(t)}\, s_j(t)\, dt$$

Since more than one user can transmit at the same time, we assume all K users to be simultaneously active. Assuming a synchronous AWGN channel (i.e. the data from all users arrives at the receiver at the same instant of time), It can write the received signal at the receiver as follows.

$$r(t) = \sum_{i=1}^{K} r_k(t) + n(t)$$

$$r(t) = \sum_{i=1}^{k} A_k b_k s_k (t - iT_b) + n(t)$$

$$iT_b \leq t < (i+1)T_b$$

Synchronous DS-CDMA system Receiver model To simplify the discussion, we make assumptions that all carrier phases are equal to zero. This enables us to use baseband notation while working only with real signals. We also assume that each transmitted signal arrives at the receiver over a single path. The bank of matched filters consists of K filters matched to the individual spreading codes. This detector is a matched filter to the desired signal. Other users' signals are treated as noise (self noise). These self noise limit the system's capacity and can jam out all communications in the presence of a strong nearby signal (Near-Far Problem). The out of the kth user matched filter is

$$y_j = \int_0^{T_b} r(t) s_j(t)\, dt$$

$$A_j b_j + \sum_{\substack{k=1 \\ k \neq j}}^{k} A_k b_k(i) R_{kj} + n_j$$

The first term is desired information. The second term is interference from other users.

3.1 Decorrelating detector

The Decorrelating receiver applies the inverse of the correlation matrix to the output of the matched filter in order to decouple the data.

Decorrelating detector in the synchronous channel

Consider the output of the bank of K matched filters $y = RAb + n$; Where n is a Gaussian random vector with zero mean and covariance matrix. If we process the output

vector as

$$R^{-1}y = Ab + R^{-1}n$$

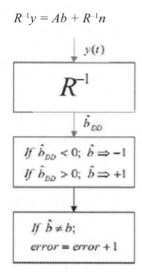

Clearly the kth component of vector R^{-1} y is free from interference caused by any other users for any k (since A is diagonal). Note that the cross correlation matrix R is invertible if signature sequences are linear independent. If the background noise is vanishing, that is, = 0, then

$$\hat{b}_k = \mathrm{sgn}(R^{-1}y)_k = \mathrm{sgn}((Ab)_k)$$

Hence, in absence of background noise, we get error free performance. In the presence of the background noise, decision is affected only by the background noise, that is,

$$\hat{b}_k = \mathrm{sgn}(R^{-1}y)_k = \mathrm{sgn}((Ab + R^{-1})_k)$$

This is why the detector is called the decorrelating detector. Decorrelating detector can achieve any given performance level in the multiuser environment regardless of the multiuser interference, provided that the desired user is supplied enough power. Thus, it provides a substantial performance or capacity gains over the conventional detector under most conditions. For the case of 2 users, the correlation matrix is

$$R^{-1} = \frac{1}{1-\rho^2}\begin{bmatrix} 1 & -\rho \\ -\rho & 1 \end{bmatrix}$$

The output of decorrelator given by

$$R^{-1}\underline{y} = \begin{bmatrix} A_1 b_1 + \dfrac{n_1 - \rho n_2}{1-\rho^2} \\ A_2 b_2 + \dfrac{n_2 - \rho n_1}{1-\rho^2} \end{bmatrix}$$

This detector,

1. Completely eliminates the MAI, hence is near-far resistant
2. Does not require estimates of the channel parameters

3. Enhances the noise,(in two user case noise is enhanced by more significant disadvantage of this detector is that the computations needed to invert the matrix R are difficult to perform in real time. For synchronous systems, the problem is somewhat simplified. We can decorrelate one bit at a time. In other words we can apply the inverse of a K*K correlation Matrix

3.2 Minimum mean-squared error (MMSE) detector

Algorithm

The MMSE detector implements a linear mapping L which minimizes the mean squared error. $E[|(b_k - Ly)|]^2$ The detection scheme can be written as

$$\hat{b} = sign(Ly)$$

$$R = \begin{bmatrix} 1 & \rho \\ \rho & .1 \end{bmatrix}$$

The approach here is to turn linear multi-user detection problem into a linear estimation problem.

It Require MSE between the kth user bit b_k and the output of the linear transformation $m_k^T yk$ to be minimized For the kth user solve

$$MER^{\underset{K*K}{min}} \left[E(b_k - m_k^T y)^2 \right]$$

k=1.........K; $m_k \in R^K$

Combining the K equations

$$MER^{\underset{K*K}{min}} E \left[\|b - Ly\|^2 \right]$$

where the expectation is with respect to bits and noise. Since, $\|x\|$ trace$\{xx^T\}$ the above problem is equivalently represented by

$$J_{opt}(L) = E[(b - Ly)^T (b - Ly)]$$
$$= E[b^T b] - 2E[b^T Ly] + E[y^T L^T Ly]$$

$$\frac{dj_{opt}(L)}{dL} = 0 - 2E[b^T y] + 2E[Ly^T y]$$

To get minimum value $\frac{dj_{opt}(L)}{dL} = 0$ then

$$-2E[b^T y] + 2E[Ly^T y] = 0$$
$$-2E[b^T y] = 2E[Ly^T y]$$
$$L = E[b^T y]E[y^T y]^{-1}$$
$$y = RAb + n;$$

$$E[b^T y] = A^T R^T$$

$$E[y^T y] = RAA^T R^T + \sigma^2 I$$

$$L = [R + \sigma^2 A^{-2}]^{-1} \quad (37)$$

It was shown that $L = [R + \sigma A^{-2}]^{-1}$ is the optimum transformation and hence the MMSE linear detector output decision is

$$\hat{b}_k = sgn\left(\frac{1}{A_k} ([R + \sigma^2 A^{-2}]y)_k \right)$$
$$= sgn(([R + \sigma^2 A^{-2}]y)_k)$$

where the scaling factor A^{-1} can be dropped without affecting the decision rule. Hence the linear transformation is

$$L = [R + \sigma^2 A^{-2}]^{-1}$$

MMSE detector is a compromise between the conventional receivers (optimizes to fight only background noise) and the decorrelator (optimizes to fight only interference). It takes into account both the interfering user and the background noise.

In the limiting case, A2, A3....Ak → 0 with A1 being fixed, and then the first row of

$$[R + \sigma^2 A^{-2}]^{-1} \rightarrow \left[\frac{A_1^2}{A_1^2 + \sigma^2}, 0, \ldots, 0 \right]$$

This is the same as a conventional receiver (matched filter) for user 1. As $\sigma \rightarrow 0$

$$[R + \sigma^2 A^{-2}]^{-1} \rightarrow R^{-1}$$

Therefore, the MMSE linear detector converges to the Decorrelating detector.

4 Results

Simulations are carried out considering Conventional detector, Decorrelating detector and MMSE (Minimum Mean Square Error) detector. AWGN channel is considered and there is perfect power control.

Case 1: Gold sequence of length 31 and 2 users

Two users synchronously transmitting the 5000 bits through an AWGN channel. For spreading gold sequence of length Lc=31 is used.SNR is varying from 1dB to 8 dB.

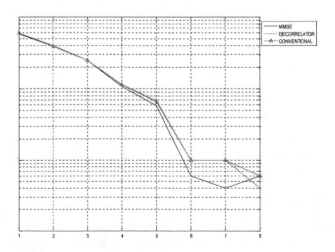

BER performance of the three detectors for K = 2, Lc = 31

Case 2: Gold sequence of length 31 and 4 users

Four users synchronously transmitting the 5000 bits through a AWGN channel. For preading gold sequence of length Lc=31 ia used.SNR is varying from 1dB to 8 dB

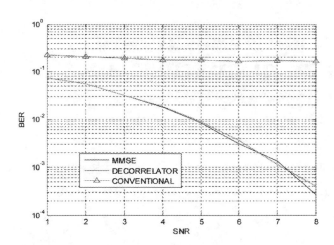

BER performance of the three detectors for K = 4, Lc = 31

5 Conclusion

The number of interfering users increases, the amount of MAI becomes greater as well. Thus there is a trade of between the performance measures (BER vs. SNR) and the practicality measure (complexity and detection delay).

Depending on the situations, a suboptimum receiver satisfying the implementation constrains can be chosen. Multiuser detection holds promise for improving DS-CDMA performance and capacity.

References

1. Jinfang Zhang, Zbigniew Dziong, "Multiuser Detection Based Mac Design for Ad Hoc Networks"IEEE Transactions on Wireless Communications, Vol. 8, No. 4, April 2009
2. Girish Manglani and A. K. Chaturvedi "Application of Computational Geometry to Multiuser Detection in CDMA, IEEE Transactions on Communications, VOL. 54, NO. 2, February 2006
3. H. S. Lim, M. V. C. Rao, Alan W. C. Tan, and H. T. Chuah "Multiuser Detection for DSCDMA Systems Using Evolutionary Programming". IEEE Communications Letters, Vol. 7, No. 3, March 2003
4. R Lupas and S. Verdu "Linear Multiuser Detectors for Synchronous Code Division Multiple Access Channels "IEEE Transactions on Information Theory, Vol. 35, pp. 23-136, Jan 1989
5. S. Moshavi, and Bellcore (1996)," Multiuser detection for DS-CDMA communications" IEEE Communications Magazine, pp.124-135, October 1996
6. S. Verdu "Minimum Probability of Error for Asynchronous Gaussian Multiple Access Channel". IEEE Transactions on Information Theory, Vol. IT-32, pp.85-96, Jan 1986
7. AnderaGoldsmith, "wireless communications" Cambridge University press

Kekre's fast codebook generation in VQ with various color spaces for colorization of grayscale images

Dr. H. B. Kekre · Tanuja K. Sarode · Sudeep D. Thepade · Pallavi N. Halarnkar

Mukesh Patel School of Technology Management and Engineering, SVKM's NMIMS, Mumbai, India

1. Introduction

Colorization is the term which means to color any gray scale image. In digital image processing terms colorization of grayscale image is nothing but assigning the red, green and blue color component values to each gray value of grayscale image [1, 2]. Colorization is very difficult because it involves assigning three-dimensional (RGB) pixel values to an image which varies along only one dimension (luminance or intensity) [3]. Since different colors may have the same luminance value but vary in hue or saturation, the problem of colorizing grayscale images has no inherently 'unique' solution [4]. So user intervention becomes trivial in colorization process to select the 'better' match (red, green and blue values) for every grayscale pixel. In [1, 2] authors have proposed some of the simple approaches for colorization of grayscale images, where user intervention is needed only to select the source color image to be used to generate color palette. In [1, 5] different color spaces and pixel window sizes are worked out for coloring grayscale images. All these techniques gives the results subjective to the source color image considered for coloring are very heavy with respect to time complexity. To speed up the process different search algorithms are proposed in [1, 4]. But everywhere the size of source color image is assumed to be equal to or more than to be colored target grayscale image. The paper presents novel colorization technique where this size dependency of source color image and target grayscale image are taken out. The proposed technique generates color palette using vector quantization codebook generation approach. Here Kekre's fast codebook generation (KFCG) [16, 20, 21] algorithm is used.

The vector quantization basics and KFCG are discussed in section 2. Section 3 deals with the color spaces considered and gives the YCbCr to RGB and Kekre's LUV to RGB inter-conversion matrices. Section 4 gives the proposed colorization technique. Results are given in section 5 with the discussions and observations. Concluding remarks are mentioned in section 6.

2. Vector quantization

Vector Quantization (VQ) [14–31] is an efficient technique for data compression and has been successfully used in variety of research fields such as video-based event detection and anomaly intrusion detection systems, image segmentation [16–19], speech data compression [15], CBIR [21, 22] and face recognition [20]. VQ [14-31] can be defined as the mapping function that maps k-dimensional vector space to the finite set CB = { C1, C2, C3, ..., CN}. The set CB is called codebook consisting of N number of codevectors and each codevector Ci = {ci1, ci2, ci3, ……, cik} is of dimension k. The key to VQ is the good codebook.

2.1 Kekre's fast codebook generation (KFCG)

Here the Kekre's Fast Codebook Generation algorithm given in [16, 20, 21] for image data compression is used. This algorithm reduces the time of code book generation. Initially we have one cluster with the entire training vectors and the code vector C1 which is centroid. In the first iteration of the algorithm, the clusters are formed by comparing first element of training vector with first element of code vector C1. The vector Xi is grouped into the cluster 1 if $xi1 < c11$ otherwise vector Xi is grouped into cluster 2 as shown in Fig. 1a. where code vector dimension space is 2. In second iteration, the cluster 1 is split into two by comparing second element $xi2$ of vector Xi belonging to cluster 1 with that of the second element of the code vector. Cluster 2 is

S.J. Pise (ed.), *ThinkQuest 2010*, DOI 10.1007/978-81-8489-989-4_18,

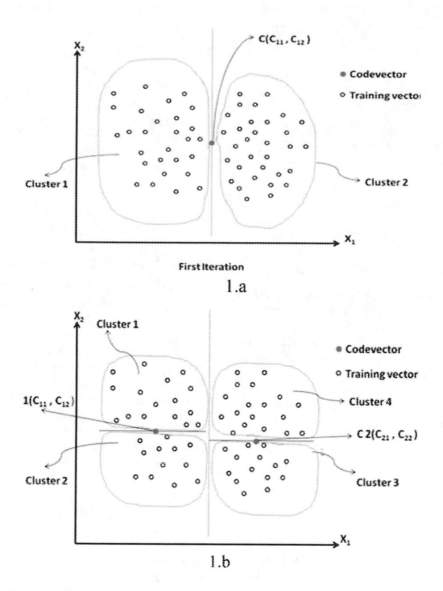

Fig. 1 KFCG algorithm for 2 dimensional case

split into two by comparing the second element xi2 of vector Xi belonging to cluster 2 with that of the second element of the code vector as shown in Fig. 1b. This procedure is repeated till the codebook size is reached to the size specified by user. It is observed that this algorithm gives less error as compared to LBG and requires least time to generate codebook as compared to other algorithms, as it does not require any computation of Euclidean distance. The algorithm shown in Fig. 1a and Fig. 1b for two dimensional case it is easily extended to higher dimensions.

3. Color spaces

A color model is an abstract mathematical model describing the way colors can be represented as tuples of numbers, typically as three or four values or color components. Color space is set of colors where the color model is associated

with a precise description of how the components are to be interpreted.

3.1 RGB color space

RGB uses additive color mixing, because it describes what kind of light needs to be emitted to produce a given color. Light is added together to create form from out of the darkness. RGB stores individual values for red, green and blue.

3.2 YCbCr color space [5, 9, 13]

Here we have used YCbCr color Space. Where Y gives luminance and Cb and Cr gives chromaticity values of color image. To get YCbCr components we need the conversion of RGB to YCbCr components. The RGB to YCbCr conversion matrix given in equation 1 gives the Y, Cb, Cr components of color image for respective R, G, B components.

$$\begin{vmatrix} Y \\ Cb \\ Cr \end{vmatrix} = \begin{vmatrix} 0.2989 & 0.5866 & 0.1145 \\ -0.1688 & -0.3312 & 0.5000 \\ 0.5000 & -0.4184 & -0.0816 \end{vmatrix} \begin{vmatrix} R \\ G \\ B \end{vmatrix} \qquad (1)$$

The YCbCr to RGB conversion matrix given in equation 2 gives the R, G, B components of color image for respective Y, Cb, Cr components.

$$\begin{vmatrix} R \\ G \\ B \end{vmatrix} = \begin{vmatrix} 1 & -0.0010 & 1.4020 \\ 1 & -0.3441 & -0.7140 \\ 1 & 1.7718 & -0.0010 \end{vmatrix} \begin{vmatrix} Y \\ Cb \\ Cr \end{vmatrix} \qquad (2)$$

3.3 Kekre's LUV color space [5–8, 10–12]

Here we have used Kekre's LUV color Space, which is special case of Kekre Transform [10]. Where L gives luminance and U and V gives chromaticity values of color image. Positive value of U indicates prominence of red component in color image and negative value of V indicates prominence of green component. This needs the conversion of RGB to LUV components. The RGB to LUV conversion matrix given in equation 1 gives the L, U, V components of color image for respective R, G, B components.

$$\begin{vmatrix} L \\ U \\ V \end{vmatrix} = \begin{vmatrix} 1 & 1 & 1 \\ -2 & 1 & 1 \\ 0 & -1 & 1 \end{vmatrix} \begin{vmatrix} R \\ G \\ B \end{vmatrix} \qquad (3)$$

The LUV to RGB conversion matrix given in equation 4 gives the R, G, B components of color image for respective L, U, V components.

$$\begin{vmatrix} R \\ G \\ B \end{vmatrix} = \begin{vmatrix} 1 & -2 & 0 \\ 1 & 1 & -1 \\ 1 & 1 & 1 \end{vmatrix} \begin{vmatrix} L/3 \\ U/6 \\ V/2 \end{vmatrix} \qquad (4)$$

4. Proposed colorization technique

The colorization technique can be divided into main steps [1–5] as preparing color palette from source image and colorization of grayscale image using this color palette.

4.1 Color palette generation using KFCG

The steps generates color palette as the VQ codebook of source color image.

    i.   In case of YCbCr color space convert source color image to YCbCr using equation 1. In case of LUV domain convert source color image to LUV using equation 3.

    ii.   This source color image is divided into pixel windows of size 2×2 (each pixel consisting of red, green and blue components).

    iii.   These are put in a row to get 12 values per vector (as 4 sets of Y, Cb and Cr values in YCbCr color space or 4 sets of L, U and V values in LUV color space or 4 sets of red, green and blue values in RGB color space). Collection of these vectors is a training set (initial cluster).

    iv.   The Kekre's Fast codebook generation algorithm is applied on this initial training set to obtain the codebook of specific size (here four sizes are considered 64, 128, 256, 512).

4.2 Grayscale image colorization

The target grayscale image is divided into pixel windows of size 2×2. These 4 values are put into the row and are compared with L component of all the code-vectors in LUV color space, with Y component of the all the code-vectors in YCbCr color space and with average of RGB for each of the four pixels of the code-vector in RGB color space. The closest match in the color palette is determined by calculating the Euclidean distance between L/Y/Average RGB of four values in color palette (Codebook) and grayscale pixel window values from the gray image. The direct Euclidian distance between pixel window row P and the color palette row Q of added columns can be given as below.

$$ED = \sqrt{\sum_{i=1}^{4}(Vpi - Vqi)^2} \qquad (5)$$

where, Vpi and Vqi be the considered pixels pixel window row P and color palette row of added columns Q respectively with size '4'. The respective red, green and blue component values for the gray pixels in considered pixel window of target image. Thus the target image could be colored using these red, green and blue planes generated by finding the best match for all non-overlapping gray target pixel windows from the color palette.

5. Results and discussion

Quality of grayscale image colorization technique is subjective to the source color image selected for coloring and also to the grayscale image to be colored. There are no objective criteria to check the performance of colorization method. At most one may take a source grayscale of source color image and try to recolor it using the colors from source color image. The mean squared error (MSE) difference between the original color and recolored images may serve as performance measure to see the quality of colorization method. So to compare the proposed colorization techniques here 5 color test images are recolored and the MSE differences are computed as shown in Table 1. From the table one could observe that improved colorization quality (reducing MSE) can be achieved by increasing the codebook size. Also

Table 1 MSE differences of original color image and recolored images

Color	MSE			
	64	128	256	512
	Sushmita			
RGB	241.3630	229.3784	219.7638	206.0178
YCbCr	594.6414	572.8771	556.8272	541.6201
Kekre's LUV	135.9109	114.5147	97.7301	81.8014
	Puppy			
RGB	275.8037	281.9594	296.3886	290.4889
YCbCr	460.9490	452.9316	441.8076	433.5560
Kekre's LUV	140.9780	132.9780	122.3735	114.4820
	Rose			
RGB	1162.7	1176.3	1127.2	1098.0
YCbCr	582.3125	553.5746	529.0433	515.7344
Kekre's LUV	537.3980	516.5762	491.3699	476.4875
	Micky			
RGB	1430.3	1422.9	1351.5	1184.2
YCbCr	1064.2	1005.7	963.8284	952.4351
Kekre's LUV	230.3013	175.0219	148.5717	125.3959
	Pepper			
RGB	2148.9	2027.8	1968.8	1909.5
YCbCr	1401.8	1354.7	1292.5	1226.9
Kekre's LUV	975.3824	917.1943	874.2084	824.7130

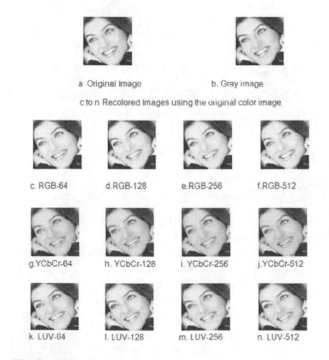

Fig. 2 Original color Sushmita image and recolored Sushmita images using proposed colorization techniques

a. Original Image   b. Gary Image

c to e. Recolored Images using the original color image.

c. RGB- 64   d. YCbCr-512   e. LUV- 512

Fig. 3 Original color Puppy image and recolored Puppy images (Here the best recolored images per color space are only shown)

Kekre's LUV color space outperforms other color spaces in quality of colorization. Kekre's LUV color space with codebook size 64 gives lesser MSE even than RGB and YCbCr color spaces with codebook size 512. In RGB and YCbCr, the colorization methods using RGB color space are better

a. Original Image   b. Gray Image

c to e Recolored Images using the original color image.

c.RGB-512   d.YCbCr-512   e.LUV-512

Fig. 4 Original color Rose image and recolored Rose images (Here the best recolored images per color space are only shown)

a. Original Image   b. Gray Image

c to e Recolored Images using the original color image

c.RGB-512   d.YCbCr-512   e. LUV-512

Fig. 5 Original color Mickey image and recolored Mickey images (Here the best recolored images per color space are only shown)

Figures 5–10 show the colorization results of proposed techniques where the source color image is selected by user and target grayscale images are colorized.

Figure 1 shows original color sushmita image and recolored sushmita images using proposed colorization techniques. The perceptibility of LUV-512 result is better in all the results shown in Figs. 2–5 shows the results of best recolored images in respective color spaces. In all Kekre's LUV color space is giving better coloring. In codebook sizes 512 is giving better recolored images which is also obvious, as the codebook size increases the color palette entries become more and hence more accurate options are available for colorization (better matches for gray pixel windows).

6. Conclusion

Colorization improves the perceptibility of grayscale image to great extent. The novel technique of grayscale image

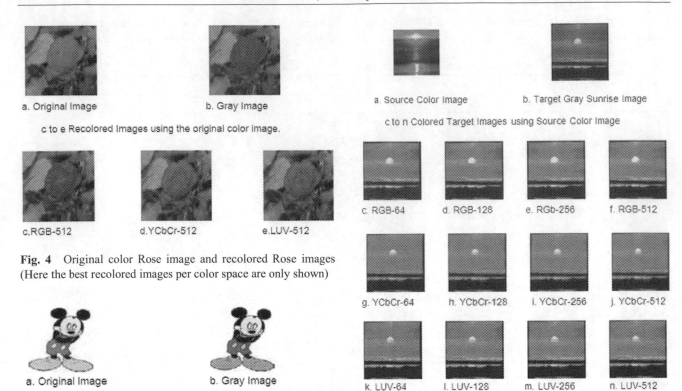

a. Source Color Image   b. Target Gray Sunrise Image

c to n Colored Target Images using Source Color Image

c. RGB-64   d. RGB-128   e. RGb-256   f. RGB-512

g. YCbCr-64   h. YCbCr-128   i. YCbCr-256   j. YCbCr-512

k. LUV-64   l. LUV-128   m. LUV-256   n. LUV-512

Fig. 6 Colorization of gray Sunrise image using proposed techniques

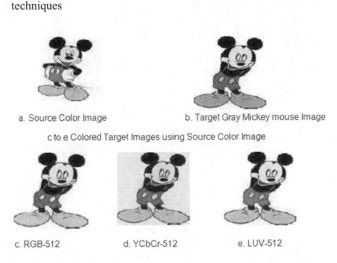

a. Source Color Image   b. Target Gray Mickey mouse Image

c to e Colored Target Images using Source Color Image

c. RGB-512   d. YCbCr-512   e. LUV-512

Fig. 7 Colorization of Gray Mickey mouse image using proposed technique (here LUV gives better colorization)

colorization is presented in the paper with help of VQ codebbok generation algorithm KFCG. The technique helps to overcome the assumption of having source color image size bigger than the target grayscale for coloring considered in earlier approaches. In all 12 versions of proposed technique for 4 codebook sizes (64, 128, 256, 512) with 3 color spaces RGB, YCbCr and Kekre's LUV are proposed and compared in the paper. From the results one can conclude that, increasing codebook size improves the quality of coloring. In all Kekre's LUV color space gives better colorization even at minimum codebook size.

a. Source Color Image   b. Target Gray Dog Image

c to e. Color Target Images using Source Color Image

c. RGB-512   d. YCbCr-512   e. LUV-512

Fig. 8 Colorization of Gray Dog image using proposed techniques (Here LUV gives better colorization)

a. Source Color Image   b. Target Gray Kajol Image

c to e. Colored Target Images using Source Color Image

c. RGB-512   d. YCbCr-512   e.LUV-512

Fig. 9 Colorization of Gray Kajol Image using proposed technique (Here LUV gives better colorization)

a. Source Color Images   b. Target Gray Houseboat Image

c to e. Colored Target images using Source Color Image

c. RGB-512   d. YCbCr-512   e.LUV-512

Fig. 10 Colorization of Gray Houseboat Image using proposed techniques (here LUV gives better colorization)

References

1. H. B. Kekre, Sudeep D. Thepade, "Color Traits Transfer to Grayscale Images", In Proc. of IEEE –International Conference on Emerging Trends in Engineering and Technology, ICETET-2008, 16-18 July 2008, Raisoni College of Engg., Nagpur. is uploaded and available online at IEEE Xplore CSDL, ACM Portal

2. H.B.Kekre, Sudeep D. Thepade, "Colorization of Grayscale Images using Kekre's LUV Color Space", In Proc. of National Level Technical Paper presentation Competition THINKQUEST-2009, 14 Mar 2009, Babasaheb Gawde Institute of Technology, Mumbai

3. H.B.Kekre, Sudeep D. Thepade, "Algorithm for Fusion of Color and Grayscale Partial Images in Seascape Formation", In Proc. of National Conference on Algorithms-2008, FCRCE, Bandstand, Bandra (W), Mumbai

4. H.B.Kekre, Sudeep D. Thepade, Adib Parkar, "A Comparison of Kekre's Fast Search and Exhaustive Search for various Grid Sizes used for Colouring a Grayscale Image", In Proc. of 2nd IEEE International Conference on Signal Acquisition and Processing (ICSAP 2010), IACSIT, Bangalore, pp. 53-57, 9-10 Feb 2010

5. H.B.Kekre, Sudeep D. Thepade, Archana Athawale, Adib Parkar, "Using Assorted Color Spaces and Pixel Window Sizes for Colorization of Grayscale Images", (Selected), ACM-International Conference and Workshop on Emerging Trends in Technology (ICWET 2010), TCET, Mumbai, 26-27 Feb 2010

6. H.B.Kekre, Sudeep D. Thepade, "Image Blending in Vista Creation using Kekre's LUV color Space" , Proceedings of SPIT -IEEE Colloquium and International conference. SPIT, Mumbai, 4, 5 Feb 2008

7. H.B.Kekre, Sudeep D. Thepade, "Rotation Invariant Fusion of Partial Image Parts in Vista Creation using Missing View Regeneration", WASET International Journal of Electrical Computer and Systems Engineering (IJECSE), Volume 2, Number 2, pp 94-101, 2008. http://www.waset.org/ijecse

8. H.B.Kekre, Sudeep D. Thepade, "Boosting Block Truncation Coding with Kekre's LUV Color Space for Image Retrieval" WASET International Journal of Electrical Computer and Systems Engineering (IJECSE), Volume 2, Number 3, pp. 172-180, Spring 2008. http://www.waset.org/ijecse

9. H.B.Kekre, Sudeep D. Thepade, "Improving 'Color to Gray and Back' using Kekre's LUV Color Space", In Proc. of IEEE International Advanced Computing Conference 2009 (IACC'09), Thapar University, Patiala, INDIA, 6-7 March 2009. Is uploaded and available online at IEEE Xplore

10. H.B.Kekre, Sudeep D. Thepade, "Image Retrieval using Non-Involutional Orthogonal Kekre's Transform", International Journal of Multidisciplinary Research and Advances in Engineering (IJMRAE), Ascent Publication House, 2009, Volume 1, No. I, pp 189-203, 2009. Abstract available online at www.ascent-journals.com

11. H. B. Kekre, Sudeep D. Thepade, "Improving the Performance of Image Retrieval using Partial Coefficients of Transformed Image", International Journal of Information Retrieval, Serials Publications, Volume 2, Issue 1, 2009, pp. 72–79

12. H.B.Kekre, Sudeep D. Thepade, "Creating the Color Panoramic View using Medley of Grayscale and Color Partial Images ", WASET International Journal of Electrical, Computer and System Engineering (IJECSE), Volume 2, No. 3, Summer 2008. Available online at www.waset.org/ijecse/v2/v2-3-26.pdf

13. H.B.Kekre, Sudeep D. Thepade, "Color Based Image Retrieval using Amendment Block Truncation Coding with YCbCr Color Space", International Journal on Imaging (IJI), Volume 2, Number A09, Autumn 2009, pp. 2-14. Available online at www.ceser.res.in/iji.html (ISSN: 0974-0627)

14. R. M. Gray, "Vector quantization", IEEE ASSP Mag., pp.: 4-29, Apr. 1984

15. H. B. Kekre, Tanuja K. Sarode, "Speech Data Compression using Vector Quantization", WASET International Journal of Computer and Information Science and Engineering (IJCISE), vol. 2, No. 4, pp.: 251-254, Fall 2008. available: http://www.waset.org/ijcise

16. H. B. Kekre, Tanuja K. Sarode, Bhakti Raul, "Color Image Segmentation using Kekre's Fast Codebook Generation Algorithm Based on Energy Ordering Concept", ACM International Conference on Advances in Computing, Communication and Control (ICAC3-2009), pp.: 357-362, 23-24 Jan 2009, Fr. Conceicao Rodrigous College of Engg., Mumbai. Available on ACM portal

17. H. B. Kekre, Tanuja K. Sarode, Bhakti Raul, "Color Image Segmentation using Kekre's Algorithm for Vector Quantization", International Journal of Computer Science (IJCS), Vol. 3, No. 4, pp.: 287-292, Fall 2008. Available: http://www.waset.org/ijcs

18. H. B. Kekre, Tanuja K. Sarode, Bhakti Raul, "Color Image Segmentation using Vector Quantization Techniques Based on Energy Ordering Concept" International Journal of Computing Science and Communication Technologies (IJCSCT) Volume 1, Issue 2, pp: 164-171, January 2009

19. H. B. Kekre, Tanuja K. Sarode, Bhakti Raul, "Color Image Segmentation Using Vector Quantization Techniques", Advances in Engineering Science Sect. C (3), pp.: 35-42, July-September 2008

20. H. B. Kekre, Kamal Shah, Tanuja K. Sarode, Sudeep D. Thepade, "Performance Comparison of Vector Quantization Technique – KFCG with LBG, Existing Transforms and PCA for Face Recognition", International Journal of Information Retrieval (IJIR), Vol. 02, Issue 1, pp.: 64-71, 2009

21. H. B. Kekre, Tanuja K. Sarode, Sudeep D. Thepade, "Image Retrieval using Color-Texture Features from DCT on VQ Codevectors obtained by Kekre's Fast Codebook Generation", ICGST-International Journal on Graphics, Vision and Image Processing (GVIP), Volume 9, Issue 5, pp.: 1-8, September 2009. Available online at http://www.icgst.com/gvip/Volume9/Issue5/P1150921752.html

22. H. B. Kekre, Tanuja K. Sarode, Sudeep D. Thepade, "Color-Texture Based Feature Based Image Retrieval using DCT applied on Kekre's Median Codebook", International Journal of Imaging (IJI), Volume 2, No. A09, Autumn 2009, ISSN 0974-0627. Available online at. http://www.ceser.res.in/ceserp/index.php/iji/issue/view/72

23. H. B. Kekre, Tanuja K. Sarode, "New Fast Improved Codebook Generation Algorithm for Color Images using Vector Quantization," International Journal of Engineering and Technology, vol.1, No.1, pp.: 67-77, September 2008

24. H. B. Kekre, Tanuja K. Sarode, "Fast Codebook Generation Algorithm for Color Images using Vector Quantization," International Journal of Computer Science and Information Technology, Vol. 1, No. 1, pp.: 7-12, Jan 2009

25. H. B. Kekre, Tanuja K. Sarode, "An Efficient Fast Algorithm to Generate Codebook for Vector Quantization," First International Conference on Emerging Trends in Engineering and Technology, ICETET-2008, held at Raisoni College of Engineering, Nagpur, India, pp.: 62- 67, 16-18 July 2008. Avaliable at IEEE Xplore

26. H. B. Kekre, Tanuja K. Sarode, "Centroid Based Fast Search Algorithm for Vector Quantization", International Journal of Imaging (IJI), Vol 1, No. A08, pp.: 73-83, Autumn 2008, Available at http://www.ceser.res.in/iji.html

27. H. B. Kekre, Tanuja K. Sarode, "Fast Code-vector Search Algorithm for 3-D Vector Quantized Codebook", WASET International Journal of cal Computer Information Science and Engineering (IJCISE), Volume 2, No. 4, pp.: 235-239, Fall 2008. Available: http://www.waset.org/ijcise

28. H. B. Kekre, Tanuja K. Sarode, "Fast Codebook Search Algorithm for Vector Quantization using Sorting Technique", ACM International Conference on Advances in computing, Communication and Control (ICAC3-2009), pp: 317–325, 23–24 Jan 2009, CRCE, Mumbai. Available on ACM portal

29. H. B. Kekre, Tanuja K. Sarode, "2-level Vector Quantization Method for Codebook Design using Kekre's Median Codebook Generation Algorithm", Advances in Computational Sciences and Technology (ACST), ISSN 0973-6107, Volume 2 Number 2, 2009, pp. 167–178. Available online at. http://www.ripublication.com/Volume/acstv2n2.htm

30. H. B. Kekre, Tanuja K. Sarode, "Multilevel Vector Quantization Method for Codebook Generation", International Journal of Engineering Research and Industrial Applications (IJERIA), Volume 2, No. V, 2009, ISSN 0974-1518, pp.: 217-235. Available online at. http://www.ascent-journals.com/ijeria_contents_Vol2No5.htm

31. H. B. Kekre, Tanuja K. Sarode "Vector Quantized Codebook Optimization using K-Means", International Journal on Computer Science and Engineering (IJCSE) Vol.1, No. 3, 2009, pp.: 283-290, Available online at: http://journals.indexcopernicus.com/abstracted.php?level=4&id_issue=839392

Performance evaluation of MB-OFDM UWB WPAN system based on channel estimation technique using realistic channel models

Susmita Das · Bikramaditya Das · Atul Gupta

Department of Electrical Engineering, National Institute of Technology, Rourkela, India

1. Introduction

Under the condition of indoor short-range wireless transmission, the UWB systems can provide very high data rate whereas the power consumption is very low, which makes it a promising candidate for wireless personal area networks (WPAN) where the data rate is greater than 110Mbps and the range is shorter than 10 meters in general. Moreover, UWB is also introduced into the underlying transport mechanism of wireless USB and wireless 1394 for even higher throughput up to 480Mbps within 2 meters [1]. The UWB systems based on MB-OFDM divide the whole assigned spectrum into several smaller sub-bands and each sub-band into a few subcarriers to transmit the information, which leads to lower design complexity as well as better spectral efficiency and flexibility than the DS-UWB systems [1–3].

In particular, for highly dispersive channels in the dense multi-path environment, an MB-OFDM UWB receiver is more efficient at capturing multi-path energy and more robust against inter-symbol interference (ISI) than an equivalent single carrier system using the same total bandwidth. Channel estimation is a very important issue for coherent OFDM systems. Generally, the MB-OFDM UWB systems adopt continuous modulation rather than differential modulation in considering of saving transmission power and providing relatively high data rates. Hence, coherent detection is required in receiver, which needs an estimation and compensation of the channel impulse response (CIR) before the demodulation. Channel estimation can be avoided by using differential modulation, but there is a 3dB loss in signal-to-noise ratio (SNR) approximately [4]. The channel model for UWB OFDM [5–7] communication is different from plain UWB channels because of different multipath resolution and operating frequencies. The result of channel estimation is also used in diversity combination and optimization of the receiver performance. Due to the time frequency two-dimension grid structure of OFDM signal, the channel estimator is allowed to use both time and frequency correlation [5]. However, such an estimator structure is generally too complex for a practical implementation. The channel estimation techniques based on block type and comb type pilot arrangement are analyzed in [6]. In [7], the performance of comb-type estimator and block-type estimator is compared for indoor channels that have low frequency selectivity relatively. The performance of least square (LS) and minimum mean-square error (MMSE) estimators is analyzed in [4, 6, 8].

The rest of the paper is organized as follows. In Section II we study the structure of UWB MB-OFDM and system model. We introduce the approaches of modified UWB (IEEE 802.15.3a) channel model in Section III .In section IV we study performance analysis UWB channel estimation techniques that based on training sequence and pilot tones, combined with two kinds of linear estimation criterion: LS and MMSE under different UWB channel conditions. Simulation results are discussed in Section V. Section VI concludes the paper.

2. MB-OFDM UWB system description

The multi-band OFDM system is an OFDM solution proposed for the UWB WPAN physical layer standard [6]. In that proposal, the whole available ultra wideband spectrum between 3.1–10.6 GHz is divided into several sub-bands with smaller bandwidth. The bandwidth of each sub-band is larger than 500 MHz in compliance with the FCC rules for UWB transmission [2]. Specifically, the proposal uses 528 MHz sub-bands. Figure 1 shows the band planning for

S.J. Pise (ed.), *ThinkQuest 2010*, DOI 10.1007/978-81-8489-989-4_19,

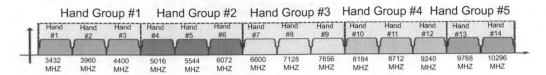

Fig. 1   Band planning for the multi-band OFDM system

the multi-band OFDM system. In each sub-band a normal. OFDM modulated signal with N=128 sub-carriers and QPSK modulation is used. In the current proposal, there are four groups of 3-band systems to support 4 independent piconets. The main difference between the multi-band OFDM system and other narrowband OFDM systems is the way that different sub-bands are used in the system. The transmission is not done continually on all sub-bands. Rather, it is time multiplexed between different bands in order to use a single hardware for communications over different sub-bands continually on all sub-bands. Rather, it is time multiplexed between different bands in order to use a single hardware for communications over different sub-bands. The baseband and modulation structure of OFDM based UWB transmitter is shown in Fig. 2. The transmitted RF signal is described as

$$S_{RF}(t) = \text{Re}\left\{ \sum_{k=0}^{K-1} S_k(t - kT_{SYM}) \exp(j2\pi f_{(k \bmod s)}t) \right\}$$ (1)

where

$TSYM$ is the OFDM symbol interval, and k is the number of OFDM symbols transmitted. The 7.5GHz UWB spectrum is divided into 14 sub-bands that are 528MHz wide each and the data is transmitted across these sub-bands using a time-frequency code (TFCs).

3. Modified UWB channel model

The amplitude statistics in S–V model are based on Rayleigh distribution, the power of which is controlled by the cluster and ray decay factor. However recent measurements in UWB channel show that amplitudes do not follow Rayleigh distribution rather it follows lognormal distribution. The impulse response of UWB channel can be written as

$$h(t) = X_i \sum_{l=0}^{L-1} \sum_{k=0}^{K-1} \alpha_{k,l} \delta(t - T_l - \tau_{k,l})$$ (2)

where $\alpha_{k,l}$ is the multipath gain coefficient of kth ray related to l^{th} cluster. T_l is the delay or arrival time of first path of lth cluster. $\tau_{k,l}$ is he delay of kth path within the lth cluster relative to T_l. X is the lognormal shadowing term.

The above channel model is quite general, and it is described for 167 ps multipath resolution or 7.5 GHz bandwidth. In IEEE 802.15.3a wireless personal area networks, the entire UWB spectrum is divided into 'NT' band each with a bandwidth of 'B'. The multipath resolution and center frequency for each band is different. So the above multipath UWB channel model is no longer applicable and it has to be resampled with respect to specific UWB pulse shape. An arbitrary realization of the channel can be represented with a finite impulse response filter as [18],

$$h(t) = \sum_{r=0}^{N-1} \alpha_r \delta(t - r\Delta)$$ (3)

where α_r is the path gain, D = 167 ps is the multipath resolution and N is the maximum delay spread. Assume that UWB pulse within the 2–8 GHz band is x(t); $0 < t < T_p$. T_p is the pulse width. The minimum multipath resolution T_p is needed in the receiver to match the received signal. The tapped delay line channel model for a multipath resolution T_p is given as

$$h_m(t) = \sum_{i=0}^{M-1} \beta_i \delta(t - iT_p)$$ (4)

where βi is the path gain and MT_p is the maximum delay spread. When x(t) is passed through the multipath channel in (3), the received signal is

$$r(t) = x(t) * h(t) = \sum_{r=0}^{N-1} \alpha_r X(t - r\Delta)$$ (5)

If $T_p \gg$ D , the overlapping lapping between multipath component will occur which leads to pulse distortion. To construct an optimum receiver a local reference signal should be constructed as in Eq. (3). But this is not possible practically and the strength of the received signal is very poor. However, the receiver performance can be improved

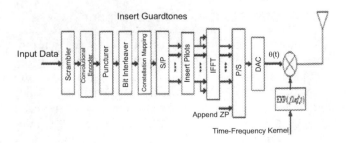

Fig. 2   TX architecture for MB-OFDM UWB system

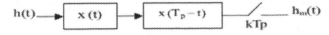

Fig. 3   Channel modification method

by modifying the realistic multipath channel model into tapped delay line model. For the particular waveform x(t), the UWB channel model is modified and it is shown in Figure 3.From the above figure, the realization of UWB channel model are filtered with a filter x(t) and its matched filter $x(Tp\ t)$. A switch is adopted to sample the matched filter signal with a time spacing Tp. To compare the difference between modified channel model and the original channel, Eq. (5) can be decomposed as

$$r(t) = \sum_{r=0}^{N-1} \alpha_r x(t - r\Delta) = \sum_{i=0}^{M-1} \beta_i x(t - iT_p) + err\ (t) \qquad (6)$$

where err(t) is the modification error. It can be easily deduced such that err(t) is orthogonal with Eq. (4).

4. Channel estimation techniques

At the receiver, the demodulated MB-OFDM signal after FFT can be expressed in matrix notation

$$Y = XFh + I + W \qquad (7)$$

where X is the matrix of transmitted signal, h is time domain channel impulse response, I is ISI and ICI, W is Additive White Gaussian Noise (AWGN) through zero-meanvand variance N 0 , F is the DFT matrix, $H = F.h$ is the channel frequency response. Here

$$X = diag\ \{X\ (0),\ X\ (1),\ldots\ X\ (N-1)\} \qquad (8)$$

$$Y = [Y\ (0),\ Y\ (1),\ldots\ Y\ (N-1)]^T \qquad (9)$$

$$W = [W\ (0),\ W\ (1),\ldots\ W\ (N-1)]^T \qquad (10)$$

$$H = [H\ (0),\ H\ (1),\ldots\ H\ (N-1)]^T \qquad (11)$$

$$F = \begin{bmatrix} W_N^{00} & \cdots & W_N^{00} \\ \vdots & & \\ W_N^{(N-1)0} & \cdots & W_N^{(N-1)(N-1)} \end{bmatrix} \qquad (12)$$

$$W_N^{nK} = \frac{1}{N} e^{-j2\pi(n/N)k} \qquad (13)$$

Considering the length of ZP is larger than the maximum delay spread of the UWB channel [3], the ISI is effectively suppressed. At the same time, assuming perfect frequency synchronization, the ICI is negligible. Then, the received signal can be written as

$$Y = XFh + W \qquad (14)$$

The expression of frequency domain LS estimation is

$$H_{LS} = X^{-1}\ Y \qquad (15)$$

which minimizes $(Y - XFh)\ H\ (Y - XFh)$.

Assuming the vector h is Gaussian and uncorrelated with the channel noise W . The frequency domain MMSE estimate can be represented by

$$H_{MMSE} = FR_{hY}\ R_{YY}^{-1} Y \qquad (16)$$

Where $\qquad R_{hY} = E[hY] = R_{hh}\ F^H\ X^H \qquad (17)$

is the cross covariance matrix between h and Y ,

$$R_{YY} = E[YY] = XFR_{hh}\ F^H\ X^H + \sigma^2 I_N \qquad (18)$$

R_{YY} is the auto-covariance matrix of Y. R_{hh} is the auto variance matrix. σ^2 is the noise variance. The MMSE estimation has better performance than LS estimation for exploiting the prior information on channel statistics, however the computational complexity is higher consequently [4]. In every packet with a sequence of OFDM symbols multiplexed onto, training symbols are added in the preamble part and a few pilot symbols are inserted in each OFDM symbol. The channel estimation of OFDM based UWB systems can be performed by, either adopting preamble training sequence or inserting pilots into each OFDM symbol. In the training sequence assisted channel estimation, the channel should be regarded as slow fading and not time variant over the packet period [6]. The CES is constructed by successively appending six periods of known OFDM symbols at best. The estimation can be based on LS or MMSE and used for the channel state information (CSI) at all sub-carriers. The estimations remain available for the rest data of the packet so long as the channels are not changed.

The pilots assisted channel estimation has been introduced when the channel changes even in one OFDM block. To this purpose, known pilots are often multiplexed into the OFDM symbols. This approach consists of algorithms to estimate the channel at pilot sub-carriers and to interpolate the channel at data sub-carriers then M-pilots are inserted in the transmitted signal we can get

$$X(P_i) = X_p(i), \qquad i = 0,1,2\ldots.\ M{-}1 \qquad (19)$$

where the pilots can be expressed as

$$X_P = [X_P(0),\ X_P(1),\ldots\ldots \qquad ..X_P = (M{-}1)]^T \qquad (20)$$

5. Simulation results and discussion

The performance of four different UWB channel model is analyzed based on the parameters of modified IEEE 802.15.3a standard. The entire UWB operating bandwidth is considered as 7.5 GHz and it is divided into 13 bands of 528 MHz each . The UWB modified channel model CM1, CM 2, CM 3 and CM 4 are considered with a multipath resolution of 1.8938ns[15]. Table I provides system parameter.

The 528MHz bandwidth is divided into 128 tones and cyclic prefix of 32 carriers. So the subcarrier frequency spacing is 4.125MHz and OFDM symbol duration is 312.5 ns. Here 10 of 128 subcarrier are used as guard carrier and 12 as pilot carriers. Table II. provides Statistics of original channel realizations and modified ones. We assumed perfect synchronization between transmitter and receiver and that perfect channel knowledge is available at the transmitter unless specified. In the receiver, channel equalization is done by LS and MMSE based channel estimation method.

The performance analysis of modified channel realization for all channel model based on LS and MMSE method are shown in Figures 4 and 5. From the MMSE estimate, it can be seen that 10–15 dB gain in signal-to-noise ratio (SNR) exists for the same mean square error of channel estimation over LS estimate.

In the training sequence assisted approach of channel estimation, the performance of BER has been compared according to LS and MMSE under the LOS (0-4m) and NLOS (0–4m) channel environments respectively. From

Figure 6 we can see that MMSE shows better performance than LS. Given the same SNR, the BER under NLOS channel is higher than that under LOS channel because the impact of multi-path propagation in NLOS channel is more significant.

In the pilots assisted approach of channel estimation, the performance of BER has been compared when adopting linear interpolations under LOS channel. Figure 7 shows that the performance of linear interpolation for both LS and MMSE. The BER performance of MMSE is better than that of LS, since LS estimation is susceptible to noise and ICI.

In Figure 8, the performance of BER has been compared between estimation approaches of training sequence and

Table 1 MB-OFDM system parameter

Bandwidth	528 MHz
No. of subcarriers	128
Information length	242.5
OFDM Symbol length	312.5ns
Coding Rate	1/2
Subcarrier frequency spacing	4.125 MHz
Data Transmission rate	200 Mbps
Pilot carrier	500
FFT size	128
No. of data tones	100
No.of pilot tones	12
No. of guard tones	10
Constellation	QPSK

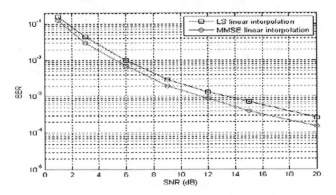

Fig. 6 Training sequence assisted channel estimation

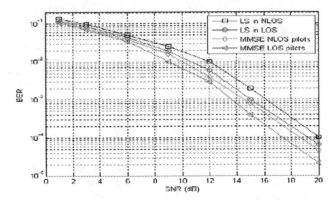

Fig. 7 Pilots assisted channel estimation

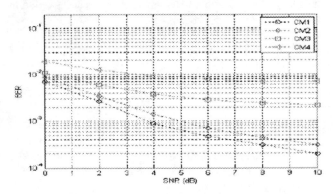

Fig. 4 LS method

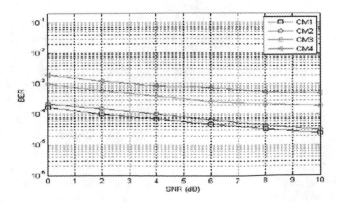

Fig. 5 MMSE method

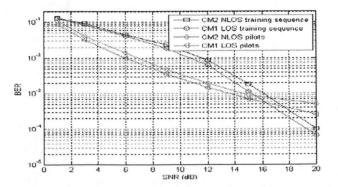

Fig. 8 Performance comparison for training sequence and pilots

Table 2 Statistics of original channel realizations and modified ones

Statistics	Channel Model			
	CM 1 LOS Original/modified	CM 2 NLOS Original/modified	CM 3 NLOS Original/modified	CM4 NLOS Original/modified
Mean excess delay (nsec)	5.4627/5.9854	9.7628/10.4428	15.4725/16.2088	27.3022/29.1430
RMS delay (nsec)	5.6879/5.6847	8.3800/8.6050	14.2170/14.7270	25.4445/25.9955
NP(85% energy)	14/4.25	16.53/6.77	25.9/9.39	63.71/15.77
NP(10 db peak)	22.91/4.5	35.36/6.94	63.71/8.59	116.490/12.88

pilots assisted (linear interpolation) according to LS under the CM1 LOS (0-4m) and CM2 NLOS (0-4m) channel environments. The time delay spread under NLOS (0-4m) channel is larger than that of LOS (0-4m) channel; therefore the frequency selectivity between sub-carriers of NLOS is more serious than that of LOS.

6 Conclusions

A novel modification method is proposed which modifies the multipath UWB channel model into a tapped delay line channel model with specific center frequency and multipath resolution. The modified channel model matches the simulation capabilities of the particular UWB waveform. The modified example shows that the mean delay, RMS delay spread and the average multipath power delay profile of the modified channel are similar to the original but the number of dominant paths decreases greatly. The modified channel model is statistically analyzed using LS and MMSE method. In MMSE method, 10 dB better performances is achieved compared to the other. The BER performance of MMSE is better than that of LS, since LS estimation is susceptible to noise and ICI. The time delay spread under CM2 NLOS (0-4m) channel is larger than that of CM1 LOS (0-4m) channel. The performance of CM1 LOS pilot assisted sequence performs better than that of CM1 LOS training sequence .These results are of great importance both in design and analysis of UWB design.

References

1. M.Z. Win and R.A. Scholtz, "Characterization of Ultra-Wide Bandwidth Wireless Indoor Communication Channel: A Communication Theoretical View", IEEE JSAC, Vol. 20, No. 9, pp. 1613–1627

2. M.Z. Win and R.A. Scholtz, "On Robustness of Ultra-Wide Bandwidth Signal in Dense Multipath Environments", IEEE Communication Letters, Vol. 2, pp. 51–53, February 1998

3. Porcino and W. Hirt, "Ultra-Wide Band Radio Technology: Potential and Challenges Ahead", IEEE Communication Magazine, July 2003

4. A.F. Molisch, "Channel Models for Ultra-Wide Band Personal Area Networks", IEEE Wireless Communication, December 2003., "High speed digital-to-RF converter," U.S. Patent 5 668 842, Sept. 16, 1997

5. A.F. Molisch, I. Ramachandran, and P. Orlik, "Low-Complexity Ultra-Wide Band Transceiver with Compatibility to Multiband OFDM", Technical Report, Mitsubishi Electric Research Laboratories

6. A.H. Tewfik and E. Sabernia, "High Bit Rate Ultra-Wideband OFDM", IEEE GLOBECOM, 2002

7. E. Sabernia and A.H. Tewfik, "Single and Multi-Carrier UWB Communications", IEEE Symposium on Signal Processing and Application, Vol. 2, pp. 343–346, 2003

8. A. Saleh and R. Valenzuela, "A Statistical Model for Indoor Wireless Multipath Propagation", IEEE JSAC, Vol. SAC-5, No. 2, pp. 128–137, February 1987

9. L. Yang and G.B. Giannaki, "Ultra-Wide Band Communication: An Idea Whose Time Has Come", IEEE Signal Processing Magazine, pp. 26–54, November 2004

10. http://grouper.ieee.org/groups/802/15/pub/2002/Jul02.

11. Multiband OFDM Physical Layer Proposal for IEEE 802.15 Task Group 3a. www.ieee802.org/15/

12. J.F. Robert, "Recent Applications of Ultra Wideband Radar and Communication Systems", Multi Spectral Solution Inc.(http://www.multispectral.com)

13. L.J. Cimini, Jr., "Analysis and Simulation of Digital Mobile Channel Using "Orthogonal Frequency Division Multiplexing", IEEE Trans. Comm., Vol. 33., No. 7, pp. 665–675, July 1985

14. S. Coleri, M. Ergen, A. Puri, "A Study of Channel Estimation in OFDM Systems", IEEE GLOBECOM, 2002

15. C. Ramesh and V. Vaidehi, "Performance analysis of UWB channels for UWB Wireless Personal area Network", In Proceedings of the Wireless Personal Communication, pp. 169-178, 2007

16. J.-J. van de Beek, O. Edfors, and P.O. Borjesson, "On Channel Estimation in OFDM Systems", In Proceedings of IEEE Vehicular Technology Conference (VTC'95), Vol. 2, pp. 815–819, Chicago, USA, July 1995

17. P. Schramm and R. Muller, "Pilot Symbol Assisted BPSK on Rayleigh Fading Channels with Diversity: Performance Analysis and Parameter Optimization", IEEE Transaction on Communication, Vol. 46, No. 12, pp. 1560–1563, 1998

18. R. Negi and J. Cioffi, "Pilot Tone Selection for Channel Estimation in a Mobile OFDM System", IEEE Trans. Consumer Electron., Vol. 44, No. 3, pp. 1122–1128, 1998

Codebook optimization using genetic algorithm and simulated annealing

Dr. H. B. Kekre[1] · **Chetan Agarwal[2]**

[1]Senior Professor, Professor, MPSTME, NMIMS University, Mumbai, India
[2]Lecturer, Dept. of Information Technology, Thadomal Shahani Engg. College, Mumbai, India

1. Introduction

The demand for handling images in digital form has increased dramatically in recent years. The use of computer graphics in scientific visualization and engineering applications is growing at a rapid pace. Despite the advantages, there is one potential problem with digital images, namely, large number of bits required to represent them. Fortunately, digital images, in their canonical representation, generally contain a significant amount of redundancy. Image compression, is the art / science of efficient coding of picture data that aims at taking advantage of this redundancy to reduce the number of bits required to represent an image.

Vector quantization, popularly known as VQ plays a fundamental role in compressing data. VQ is an efficient approach, which breaks a sequence of symbols into blocks of uniform size, called vectors, and maps these vectors onto a small set of similar vectors. The set is called the codebook and each individual vector in it is called a codevector or codeword. The codebook is the heart to vector quantization's effectiveness and several algorithms have been proposed to design a codebook from a training set of typical vectors. Given an adequate statistical specification of the source image and a prescribed codebook size, the most challenging task is to design a codebook that contains the best, or nearly the best, collection of codevectors which effectively represent the variety of source vectors to be encoded.

Codebook design and codevector search are the two basic steps in the VQ coding. Generally, codebook design is carried out in two steps: (i) initialization: i.e. what codevectors should be included in the codebook and (ii) optimization, i.e. improving these codevectors in an iterative learning process to find a (local / global) optimal set of codevectors. Lot of methods to design the codebook have been developed, such as Linde Buzo and Gray algorithm (LBG) [1–4], Kekre Fast Codebook Generation algorithm (KFCG) [7], Kekre Proportionate Error Algorithm (KPE) [31, 32], Kekre Mean Codebook Generation Algorithm (KMCG) [6], etc. Based on their nature of selecting codevectors from the training set, these algorithms tend to develop different codebooks. An efficient codebook results in minimum distortion i.e. Mean Square Error (MSE).

Moreover, once a codebook is generated from an algorithm, the distortion (MSE) resulting from that codebook remains constant for that codebook. It can be further reduced by increasing the number of codevectors in the codebook. Our goal in this paper is to find alternative solutions by which the quality of the codebook can be optimized without altering the size of the codebook.

Moreover, once a codebook is generated from an algorithm, the distortion (MSE) resulting from that codebook remains constant for that codebook. It can be further reduced by increasing the number of codevectors in the codebook. Our goal in this paper is to find alternative solutions by which the quality of the codebook can be optimized without altering the size of the codebook.

2. Vector quantization

In Vector Quantization (VQ), the original image is first decomposed into n-dimensional image vectors. The vectors can be generated in a number of different ways. For example, $n = 1 \times m$ block of pixel values can be ordered to form an n-dimensional vector, or a 3-dimensional vector can be formed from the RGB color components of an individual pixel.

S.J. Pise (ed.), *ThinkQuest 2010*, DOI 10.1007/978-81-8489-989-4_20,
© Springer India Pvt. Ltd. 2011

Each image vector, X, is then compared with a collection of representative templates or codevectors, $\hat{X}_i$, $i = 1, \ldots, N$, taken from the previously generated codebook. The codevectors are also of dimension n. The best match codevector is chosen using the minimum distortion rule; i.e. choose $\hat{X}_k$ such that $d(X, \hat{X}_k) \leq d(X, \hat{X}_j)$ for all $j = 1 \ldots N$, where $d(X, \hat{X})$ denotes the distortion incurred in replacing the original vector x with the codevector $\hat{X}$.

The most common distortion measure used in image VQ is mean squared error (MSE), which corresponds to the square of the Euclidean distance between the two vectors; i.e.

$$d(X, \hat{X}) = \frac{1}{n} \sum_{i=1}^{n} (x_i - \hat{x}_i)^2 \tag{1}$$

After a minimum distortion codevector has been selected, its index k is transmitted. At the receiver, this index is used to find the associated codeword. A block diagram of a basic VQ structure is shown in Fig. 1.

3. Codebook generation algorithms

3.1 Linde buzo gray algorithm

The LBG VQ design algorithm [1–4] is an iterative algorithm; the algorithm iteratively minimizes the total distortion by representing the training vectors by their corresponding code vectors. The algorithm prepares an initial codebook which consists of a code vector C1. This code vector C1 is obtained by taking the centroid of entire training sequence. The code vector is then split into two, by adding constant error in both positive and negative direction. The training vectors are split in two clusters using Euclidean Distance as a criterion. The two code vectors are obtained by finding centroids of each of them. Then they are splitted into four and the process is repeated until the desired number of code vectors is obtained.

3.2 Kekre's fast codebook generation algorithm

The LBG algorithm has the following drawbacks:

1. This algorithm heavily depends on calculation of Euclidean distances which requires multiplications and additions, which has a very high computational complexity.
2. Since ±1 error is added to generate two codevectors from a single vector. This tends to form the clusters which are at 135° in the two-dimensional case. Otherwise for higher dimensions, they are elongated which results in inefficient clustering.
3. In many cases the voids are generated leading to poor utilization of codebook.

To avoid these drawbacks, a new algorithm has been suggested by Kekre et. al. where Euclidean Distance calculations are replaced by comparisons and no addition of error is required to split the cluster in two parts. It has been observed that this algorithm is computationally less complex and takes far less time as compared to LBG. It also gives less MSE.

The KFCG algorithm [7] first calculates the average of the given cluster along the first dimension and then splits the cluster by keeping all the vectors which are less than or equal in one cluster and the remaining in another cluster. It then continues to split the resulting clusters by computing their averages with respect to the next dimension. The process is repeated till the desired number of codevectors is obtained.

The result containing the MSE values for codebooks of different images prepared by using the LBG and KFCG algorithms can be summarized as given in Table 1 below:

4. Codebook optimization algorithms

From Table 1 in can be observed that for the same image size and different codebook size, KFCG gives less MSE than LBG. This indicates that by properly selecting the codevectors from the image domain, the MSE can be further reduced keeping the codebook size same. In this section, we describe three optimization algorithms that try to search for better codevectors, to further optimize the quality of codebook and try to reach for minimal MSE value. The codebooks that is generated from the above two algorithms are applied as input to each of the optimization algorithms and their effect on codebook design and ability to converge towards a minimal MSE is studied.

4.1 K-means clustering algorithm

The k-means algorithm [12, 18] is a simplest unsupervised learning algorithm that solves the well known clustering

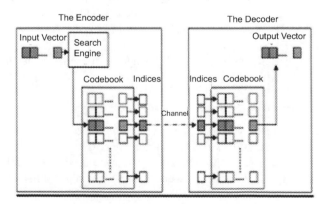

Fig. 1 Block diagram of a basic VQ structure

Table 1 Comparison of MSE values for LBG and KFCG algorithms

Images	LBG	KFCG
Bird (Codebook Size:64)	63.60	45.14
Pepper (Codebook Size:128)	44.24	33.21
Winter-leaves (Codebook Size:256)	39.29	30.50

problem. The procedure follows a simple and easy way to classify a given data set through a certain number of clusters (assume k clusters) fixed a priori. The main idea is to define k arbitrary points, one for each cluster. These arbitrary points should be placed in a cunning way because different location causes different result. So, the better choice is to place them as far away as possible from each other. The next step is to take each training point belonging to a given data set and associate it to the nearest pre-selected points. At this point we need to re-calculate k new centroids of the clusters resulting from the previous step. After we have these k new centroids, a new binding has to be done between the same data set points and the nearest new centroids. As a result, we may notice that the k centroids change their location step by step until no more changes are done.

4.2   Genetic algorithm

The genetic algorithm (GA) [5, 8–11, 13–16, 17, 19, 20, 31] is a search procedure inspired by the mechanisms of biological evolution. First proposed by Holland, the genetic algorithm is effective for solving various kinds of heuristic and optimization problems. The principal idea of GA is based on Darwin's natural selection theory: survival of fittest. Thus, we regard a codeword as a chromosome and a codebook as an individual. To improve the quality of the codebook, we utilize the genetic operations of selection, crossover and mutation to sieve out the fittest chromosomes. The proposed genetic algorithm is summarized as follows:

Step 1 (Initialization) The initial codebook for the given image is constructed using either LBG algorithm or Kekre Fast Codebook Generation algorithm. Each codevector in the initial codebook represents a chromosome in the population.

Step 2 (Evaluation) Calculate the mean square error of each cluster corresponding to each codevector. All the codevectors are then arranged in the ascending order of the mean square error. The net MSE of the image is calculated.

Step 3 (Survival of the fittest chromosome) The MSE value of a codevector is considered as the fitness criteria. Codevector having less MSE is considered to be more fit than codevector having more MSE. Thus, half of the codevectors pertaining to the least mean square errors from the ascending order calculated in Step 2 are considered as fit codevectors and carried to the next generation.

Step 4 (Crossover) After the best codevectors are selected for the next generation the remaining codevectors are generated by performing crossover operation. The first codevector and the last codevector are paired using single point crossover technique. The procedure continues till the remaining codevectors are generated to complete the new codebook.

Step 5 (Termination) the new codebook is evaluated as given in Step 2. If the net MSE from the resultant new codebook is more than the net MSE of the previous iteration,

the algorithm stops, else it continues to search for better codevectors by repeating steps 3 & 4.

4.3   Simulated annealing

Simulated Annealing (SA) [21–30] is a stochastic optimization technique introduced in 1983 by Kirkpatrick et. al. [21]. The term 'annealing' comes from analogies to the cooling of a liquid or solid. In optimization the analogy to a minimum energy state for a system is the minimizing value of the function. The technique of simulated annealing attempts to capture the process of controlled cooling associated with physical processes, the aim being to reach the lowest value of the function in the phase of possible local minima. The essential idea is to add randomness to the optimization in order to allow the algorithm to escape local minima in its search for the state which has a global minimum of the energy. The SA algorithm can be summarized as follows:

1. Place K codevectors into the space represented by the pixels that are being clustered. These codevectors represent the cluster centroids formed using the LBG or KFCG algorithm.
2. Calculate the mean square error of each cluster and the overall net MSE of the configuration.
3. Select a cluster (Cluster A) containing highest MSE.
4. Repeat the following until a new configuration is accepted.
   a. Select 4 neighboring clusters for the above selected worst cluster and sort them in ascending order of MSE values.
   b. From the 4 clusters, select a cluster (Cluster B) having the least MSE value.
   c. Merge clusters A and B and form two new clusters using either LBG or KFCG algorithm.
   d. Replace the old codevectors of clusters A and B with the centroids of these new clusters.
   e. Calculate the overall net MSE of the configuration.
   f. If the net MSE of the new configuration is less than the old configuration, accept the new configuration, else repeat steps 4 b to 4f.
5. Replace the current codebook with the new codebook.
6. Repeat step 2 to 5 till change in the MSE values is within the acceptable error range.

5.   Results and discussion

Experiments were conducted to evaluate the performance of K-means, GA and SA. Three images Bird, Pepper and Idol of size 128 × 128 and 256 × 256 were used. Codebook size of 64, 128 and 256 were created. The algorithms are evaluated using the MSE values. Initial codebook is generated using one of the two codebook generation algorithms viz. LBG & KFCG. The generated codebook is then passed as input to each of the three optimization algorithms. Results are presented in the form of tables as well as images to get pictorial overview. Figures 2 and 3 represents the relative performance of the optimized codebooks in coding the images. Tables 2 and 3 compares the MSE values obtained by running the optimization algorithms on the three images of size 128 × 128 and using LBG and KFCG initialization algorithms. It can be observed that Kmeans, GA & SA consistently performed better by optimizing the codebook generated using the LBG & KFCG algorithms, thereby proving that the MSE can be reduced further keeping the codebook size constant. Thus evolutionary algorithms can help to further improve the quality of codebook by finding the sub-optimal codebook that minimizes MSE

Depending on the nature of the images, K-means algorithm sometimes gives better result than SA & GA and for some other images GA performs better. Irrespective of the initial error generated while preparing the codebook, the optimization algorithms converge towards the same optimal value. Mostly due to its nature, GA always takes long time to converge towards optimality. The number of iterations taken by these optimization algorithms to optimize the codebook in case of KFCG is less as compared to that of LBG, because KFCG already generates a better codebook which is closer to the optimal value.

6. Conclusion

In this paper, we have used three algorithms K-Means, SA and GA to optimize codebook design. Comparison from K-Means and SA as shown in Tables 2 and 3 concludes that GA performs better in compressing images and producing better quality of codebooks than other algorithms for most of the images. GA improves the quality of codebook for a particular image to a considerable extent and reduces the

Table 2 Comparison of MSE values with 128 × 128 image size and codebook initialization using LBG

	Bird (Codebook size:64)	Pepper (Codebook size:128)	Idol (Codebook size:256)
Initial MSE	63.60	44.24	31.69
K-means	38.12	27.80	20.79
GA	37.05	28.11	17.31
SA	39.31	28.52	16.95

Table 3 Comparison of MSE values with 128 × 128 image size and codebook initialization using KFCG

	Bird (Codebook size:64)	Pepper (Codebook size:128)	Idol (Codebook size:256)
Initial MSE	45.14	33.21	25.77
K-means	36.63	27.50	20.66
GA	35.74	27.64	20.42
SA	36.15	27.51	20.65

Fig. 2 Output images for Idol using LBG for 128 × 128 image size and codebook size 256

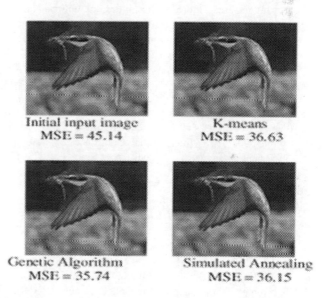

MSE values. GA can well be applied to image compression systems to achieve better compression ratios. Although GA takes a longer time to converge, this is a secondary concern since the codebook is designed only once and the complexity of the actual coding operations is unaffected. In summary, the paper demonstrates that a useful improvement on the design of codebook can be achieved with the help of evolutionary algorithms like GA. It may be observed that the minimized MSE in all three cases is close by suggesting that they are close to optimal point.

References

1. Y. Linde, A. Buzo and R.M. Gray, "An algorithm for vector quantizer design," IEEE Transactions on Communications, Vol. 28, No. 1, pp. 84-95, January 1980

2. R. M. Gray, "Vector Quantization", IEEE ASSP Magazine, Vol. 1, pp. 4–29, April 1984

3. A. Gersho, "Principles of Quantization", IEEE Transactions on Circuits and Systems, Vol. 25, No. 7, pp. 427–436, July 1978

4. A. Gersho, " On the structure of Vector Quantizers", IEEE Transactions on Information Theory, Vol. 28, No. 2, pp. 157–166, March 1982

5. D. Goldberg, "Genetic Algorithms in Search, Optimization and Machine Learning", Addison- Wesley Reading, MA, 1989

6. H. B. Kekre, Tanuja K. Sarode, "New Fast Improved Codebook Generation Algorithm for Color Images using Vector Quantization" International Journal of Engineering and Technology, vol. 1, Sept. 2008,pp.67-77

7. H. B. Kekre, Tanuja K. Sarode, "Fast Codebook Generation Algorithm for Color Images using Vector Quantization" International Journal of Computer Science and Information Technology (IJCSIT), Volume 1, Number 1, pp.7-12, Jan-June 2008

8. Mohammed A.F. Al-Husainy, "A Tool for Compressing Images Based on genetic Algorithm", Information Technology Journal 6(3), 2007, pp. 457–462

9. Wei Lu and Issa Traore, "Determining the optimal Number of Clusters Using a New Evolutionary Algorithm", Proceedings of the 17th IEEE International Conference on Tools with Artificial Intelligence (ICTAI'05), IEEE, 2005

10. V. Delport and M. Koschorreck, "Genetic Algorithm for Codebook Design in Vector Quantization", Electronics Letters, Volume 31, No. 2, 1995

11. Liu Ying, Zhou Hui and Yu Wen-Fang, "Image Vector Quantization Coding Based on Genetic Algorithm", Proceedings of the 2003 IEEE International Conference on Robotics, Intelligent Systems and Signal Processing, pp. 773–777, October 2003

12. K Krishna and M. Narasimha Murty, "Genetic K-means Algorithm", IEEE Transactions on Systems, Man and Cybernetics–Part B, Volume 29, No. 3, pp -433–439, June 1999

13. J.S.Pan , F.R.McInnes and M.A.Jack , "VQ codebook design using genetic algorithms", Electronic Letters, vol. 31, no.17,17th August 1995

14. Xiaowei Zheng, Bryant A. Julstrom, and Weidong Cheng, "Design of Vector Quantization Codebooks using a Genetic Algorithm", IEEE 1997

15. Jianmin Jiang and Darren Butler, "A Genetic Algorithm Design for Vector Quantization", Genetic Algorithms in Engineering Systems: Innovations and Applications, 12–14 September 1995, Conference Publication No. 414, IEE, 1995, pp. 331–336

16. Gao Li'ai, Zhang Shuguang, ZhouYongjie and Li Lihua, "A New Codebook Design Method Based on Genetic Programming", The Eight International Conference on Electronic Measurement and Instruments, ICEMI'2007, pp. 3-250–3-253

17. Wee-Keong Ng, Sunghyun Choi, Chinya V. Ravishankar, "An Evolutionary Approach to Vector Quantizer Design", IEEE International Conference on Evolutionary Computation, Volume 1, pp. 406–411, 29 Nov.–1 Dec. 1995

18. K Krishna, K R Ramakrishnan and M A L Thathachar, "Vector Quantization using Genetic K-Means Algorithm for Image Compression", International Conference on Information, Communications and Signal Processing, ICICS'97, pp. 1585–1587, 9–12 September 1997

19. N. M. Nasrabadi and R. A. King, "Image Coding using Vector Quantization: A Review", IEEE Transactions on Communications, Vol. 36, pp 957–971, August 1988

20. Yoshitaka Takeda, Sinya Watanabe and Yukinori Suzuki, "Code Book Optimization with a Genetic Algorithm for Vector Quantization", IEEE Conference on Soft Computing in Industrial Applications (SMCia/08), pp. 411–414, June 25-27, 2008

21. S. Kirkpatrick, C.D. Gelatt, and M. P. Vecchi, "Optimization by Simulated Annealing", Science, Vol. 220, pp. 671– 680, May 1983

22. Jacques Vaisey and Allen Gersho, "Simulated Annealing and Codebook Design", IEEE, 1998

23. G. Phanendra Babu and M. Narasimha Murty, "Simulated Annealing for Selecting Optimal Initial Seeds in the K-Means Algorithm", Indian Journal of Applied Mathematics, January & February 1994, pp. 85–94

24. J. K. Flanagan, D.R. Morrell, R.L. Frost, C.J. Read and B.E. Nelson, "Vector Quantization Codebook Generation Using Simulated Annealing", IEEE, 1989

25. Peter W.M. Tsang and W.T. Lee, "Enhanced Hit Rate Simulated Annealing in codebook Training", International Symposium on Signal Processing and its Applications, pp. 152 -154, August 1996

26. Abbas A. EL Gamal, L.A. Hemachandra, I. Shperling and V.K. Wei, "Using Simulated Annealing to Design Codebooks", IEEE Transactions on Information Theory, volume IT-33, no. 1, pp. 116–123, January 1987

27. Zhenya He, Chenwu Wu, Jun Wang and Ce Zhu, "A New Vector Quantization Algorithm Based on Simulated Annealing", 1994 International Symposium on Speech, Image Processing and Neural Networks, Hong Kong, pp. 654–657, 13–16 April 1994

28. A. E. Cetin and V. Weerackody, "Design of Vector Quantizers using Simulated Annealing", IEEE Transactions on Circuits and Systems, Vol. 35, pp.1550, December 1988

29. Ngoc-Ai Lu and Darryl R. Morrell, " VQ Codebook Design Using Improved Simulated Annealing Algorithms"

30. WEI Yanna and WAN G. Sheguo, "An Optimized Method of VQ Codebook Based on Genetic Algorithm", Modern Electronics Technique, Beijing, No. 13, pp. 151– 153, 2006

31. H. B. Kekre, Tanuja K. Sarode, "Fast Improved Clustering Algorithms for Vector Quantization", National Conference on Image Processing, TSEC, India, Feb 2005

32. H. B. Kekre, Tanuja K. Sarode, "Fast Improved Clustering Algorithms for Vector Quantization", NCSPA 2007, Padmashree Dr. D. Y. Patil Institute of Engineering and Technology, Pune, India, September 2007

PDSRS: An attribute based approach for multimedia data storage and retrieval

Najibullah Shaikh[1] · **Sanjay Nalbalwar[2]** · **Z. A. Usmani[3]**

[1]M. H. Saboo Siddik College of Engg, Mumbai (M.S), India
[2]Dr. Babasaheb Ambedkar Technological University, Raigad (M.S), India
[3]M. H. S. S. College of Engg, Mumbai (M.S), India

1. Introduction

Multimedia information and its databases are becoming an essential element for computer and telecommunication consideration in today's world. Application areas in which attribute-based storage and retrieval is becoming a principal activity are among others, TV productions, video on demand, home entertainment, art galleries and museum management, architectural and engineering design, geographic information systems, finger print and image matching, find out citizenship by election card detail and so on. Other applications are related to the development of information superhighways. When the bandwidth needed for interactive multimedia will be available at home, each user could access a remote server containing very large image and video databases. In this scenario attribute-based storage and retrieval assumes a fundamental role. Also Multimedia Information Systems [7] can benefit of attribute-based retrieval technology; although they will mainly provide techniques to manage and distribute large amounts of multi-source multimedia information, automatic storage by attributes of images and data.

Previous approaches to image storage by indexing and content-based retrieval are mainly based on features and manually described by an operator. Retrieval is performed within the framework of conventional DBMS. During a database storage a new video or image is added to the DB, its content is adequately coded based on the data model used. This step should be as automatic as possible due to the large amount of data to be inserted. However it should be noted that some manual annotation is still essential if the application requires retrieval is related also to traditional features, e.g., object names, dates, and so on. Depending on the used data model direct queries may be based [7] on sketch, objects-shape, color, motion, and so on.

This paper completely describes automatically multimedia data storage and retrieval based on data attributes. We are suggested in this paper to use RDBMS with DB2 i.e. the concept of Data-ware housing and mining for large multimedia data in their database to increase retrieval efficiency and avoid wastage of memory and time to store.

In Section 2, we address recent related work. In Section 3, we describe the general architecture and algorithm of the proposed system i.e. PDSRS, the data storage and retrieval flowchart, algorithms and the features used to characterize the videos frame by change frame in sequence and no. of frame. In the section 4, includes concluding remarks, future direction, acknowledgment and references.

2. Related work

In the previous research and paper last years several attribute-based multimedia data storage and retrieval systems have been developed. These systems differ in terms of features extracted, degree of automation reached for feature extraction and level of domain independence.

The QBIC system [5, 6, 10, 11] is a system treating both images and video. The data model has scenes (full images) that contain objects (subsets of an image), and video shots that consist of sets of contiguous frames and contain moving objects. Representative frames (r-frames) are generated for each shot. R-frames are treated as still images but further processing of shots generates motion objects. Scenes and objects are described in terms of color, texture, shape and motion.

S.J. Pise (ed.), *ThinkQuest 2010*, DOI 10.1007/978-81-8489-989-4_21,

An integrated solution for video parsing and attribute-based video retrieval and browsing has been presented in [17]. Video parsing consists in temporal segmentation of a video into single camera shots, abstraction of each shot into key-frames, and content extraction from key-frames, driven by visual features like color and texture. Temporal shot characteristics, such as camera operations and temporal variations of brightness and colors, are also extracted. Retrieval and browsing are based on key-frame features, temporal shot features, or a combination of the two. The system can also operate on compressed (MPEG) video.

The OVID [14] system uses an original data model called Video Object Data Model. A video object is an arbitrary frame sequence (a meaningful scene). Each video object has attributes and attributes values describing its content. Moreover the video [1] object data model is schema less and inheritance based on interval inclusion relationship is introduced to share description data among

video objects. The video characterization takes place at high level and is done manually. Visual See [15] is a content-based query system allowing for querying by color and spatial layout of color regions. Visual Seek represents the global color information using color histograms and provides histogram similarity measures for comparing the image color features. Tools for annotating images and for searching archives using text are also provided. CHABOT [13] allows for the storage and retrieval of a vast collection of digitized images. One of the goals in the CHABOT system is to integrate image analysis techniques into text-based retrieval systems.

The CANDID system [8, 9] is a content- based storage and retrieval system of digital images. For each image a global signature comprising texture, color and shape information is automatically computed. Queries are specified by example. The VISION system [12] is devoted to efficient creation and exploration of digital video libraries. A two-step algorithm, based on first the video and then the audio contents, is used to segment videos into a number of logically meaningful clips. Video-based segmentation is achieved using the absolute difference of the color histogram between successive frames. Audio-based post processing allows for the correction of falsely detected shot boundaries, even in presence of editing effects. Also the CMU approach to digital video libraries [2] is based on the collaborative interaction of image content and speech and natural language understanding. Browsing and retrieval in large digital video libraries are the main goal of some approaches based on non-linear descriptions of video content. In [16, 17] clustering of similar shots is proposed. Compressed video sequences are initially analyzed to identify both abrupt and gradual shot transitions. Similarity measures of images, based on color and luminance information, are then used to build shot clusters with an adjustable tolerance degree.

A shot cluster is considered a scene. A hierarchical [2]scene transition graph, i.e., a collection of directed graphs, is then used to model the video structure, with no a priori knowledge of the story. Each node of the graph at the lowest level of the hierarchy represents a scene, and edges represent the progress of the story from a scene to the next. Thus browsing is based on both visual content (and temporal variations) of shots and video structure A structured conceptual schema for movie data based on a graph-like model is proposed also in [3, 4]. This hypermedia system exploits both a feature extraction engine, able to automatically detect some of the production characteristics of a movie, such as editing operations, and a user-guided iconic interface, that enables complex queries to be formulated, even without the knowledge of any formal query language.

3. PDSRS

PDSRS stands for Proficient Data Storage Retrieval System. PDSRS mainly work on attribute based but intelligently since retrieval is not only based on attribute but some time based on knowledge.

3.1 The general architecture and algorithm of the proposed system

There are two ways to store and retrieve data to or from multimedia database. First, image match, captured by digital video camera or by scanner and second, by physical or subjective information. The indexing of multimedia data take place by color shape and motion attributes. Our suggested algorithm will work in such a way that first it will distinguish data based on attributes using digital signal and image processing technique. And then retrieve or store per the matched attribute. The multimedia data are segmented into different frames especially video based on color resolution, motion and audio. We have to store only the changes frame in the frame sequence to change DB2 and total number of frames in Tolfram DB2. The videos are crack in short sequences called shots by the shot extractor. A few representative frames (said r-frames) are therefore selected from each shot and described in terms of color, shape and motion attributes.

3.2 Algorithm for data store

1. Input data to store.
2. Find out the types of data to store and retrieve based on attributes.
3. Is video or still image or text to store?
4. Compressed video by MPEG, still image by JPEG and text by CCITT Group 3 2D.
5. After compression according to data type store in specified database as per data contents.

The system operation is explained in Fig. 1.

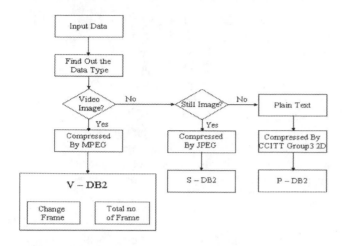

Fig. 1 System operation

3.3 Retrieving data from database

When a query, direct or by example, is put to the system, the query processor module interprets it and arranges the query parameters for the operation of the match engine module worked on data attribute and knowledge. as shown in Fig. 2.

The match engine searches for the best similar frame (requested Data) by analyzing the data stored in the different DB based on data attributes and knowledge. In initial search many frames or data extracted but on the next level only the best match will retrieve and display in the output. On search level there is pointer pointing to various database and pointer point only on the given data condition.

3.4 Simulated algorithm and results

For simulating the above algorithm for data store and retrieval, we consider four balls with different color i.e. Red, Green, Blue and Yellow. The four balls represent different data types. We are going to store and retrieve based on the attributes of the balls (where color represents one of the attributes). The red ball will be stored in the red location, green ball in the green location and so on. And we can retrieve any one of the balls based on the attributes from their respective locations easily and efficiently. In other example if we want to find out the detail of any citizen as per nation wise then we can match the photo on the citizen card or by any unique physical information mention on the card. That kind of extraction is under image and text.

Each type of data is inputted through system operation as shown in Fig. 1. Using the suggested algorithm, the multimedia data can be retrieved from multimedia data base as per the query. An example, for retrieval of flowers, fruits and vegetables by matching on color and shape in multimedia Image database using search and match engine (Fig. 2). The select options are shown in Fig. 3.

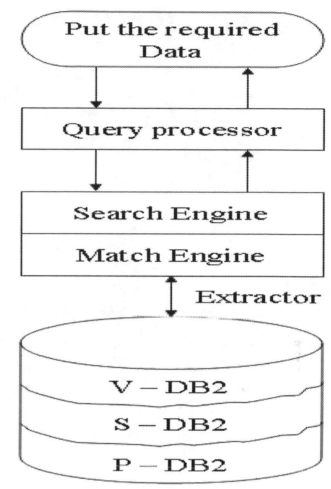

Fig. 2 Retrieving data from database

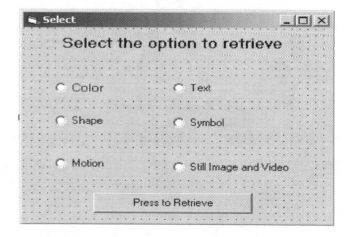

Fig. 3 Simulation of multimedia data retrieval

The performance of suggested algorithm is shown below as a graph in Fig. 4. Performance is measured based on the retrieved data in GB and the total time required in retrieving data from multimedia data base.

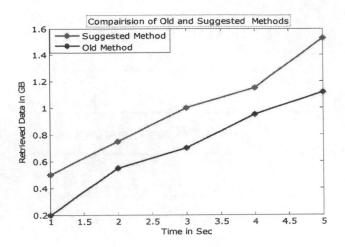

Fig. 4   Simulated result

4.   Concluding remarks

In this paper we described a system using multimedia data storage and retrieval based on attributes. The major characteristics of the system are the automatic capability to store data. No human interaction is required during the storage of data in the data base level for small applications.

The system uses color, shape and motion attributes as well as knowledge. These attributes and knowledge are currently related to entire images to retrieve different product in super market, details of any citizen etc… either by matching image or by unique physical information. This paper completely describes how proficiently multimedia data storage and retrieval take place based on data attributes and knowledge. Suggested method can increase the efficiency to store, retrieve and transmit data. It also minimizes the wastage of memory during data storage. It is complicated for large applications, but works very accurately for any applications. Also it is less expensive as compare to the old suggested methods software and hardware wise.

References

1. E. Ardizzone, M. La Cascia, and D. Molinelli, "Motion and color based video indexing and retrieval," in Proc. of Int. Conf. on Pattern Recognition, ICPR, Wien, Austria, 1996
2. M.G. Christel, "Addressing the contents of video in a digital library," in Proc. of ACM Workshop on Effective Abstractions in Multimedia: Layout, Presentation and Interaction, San Francisco, 1995
3. J.M. Corridoni and A. DelBimbo, "Film semantic analysis," in Proc. of Computer Architecture for Machine Perception, CAMP, Como, Italy, 1995
4. J.M. Corridoni, A. DelBimbo, and D. Lucarella, "Navigation and visualization of movies content," in Proc. Int. Conf. on Visual Languages, VL'95, Darmstadt, Germany, 1995

Performance issues of real time Kernels

Gajendra Bamnote · Jyoti Sawant · Sujata Deshmukh

Department of Computer Engg., Lokmanya Tilak College of Engineering, Navi Mumbai, India

1. Introduction

Real-time systems by definition are systems in which the correctness of the computed results not only depends on the results themselves, but also on the time frame in which they have been obtained. Real Time Operating Systems (RTOS) are responsible for the allocation of processors and computing resources to the collection of co-operating tasks in a way which will enable them to execute according to their timing constraints [7]. In general, real time systems are classified into hard real-time systems and soft real-time systems according to the degree of criticality in timing requirement. In hard real-time systems, time constraints as well as logical correctness must be satisfied to guarantee their correct behavior. Examples include most of the mission oriented systems for control purposes where timing errors would cause catastrophic results. On the other hand, in soft real-time systems like OLTP systems it is not always necessary to execute the transactions within time constraints. Furthermore, the hard real-time system often has distributed architecture as its inherent property. Real-time operating systems can be characterized by two requirements which are essential within its application area: timeliness and dependability [1, 2, 5]. These requirements are implemented within the current technology using the following principles:

- Multitasking, efficient task communication and synchronization.
- Efficient time and event handling.
- Transparent distribution in a local area network.

The previous list gives a guideline for planning a set of measures of the real-time system performance. In general, RTOS should support following features:

- Fast process or thread switch.
- Small size.
- Ability to respond to the external interrupts quickly.
- Multitasking with inter-process communication tools such as semaphores, signals and events.
- Use of special sequential files that can accumulate data at a fast rate
- Preemptive scheduling based on priority, Special alarms and timeouts
- Minimization of intervals during which interrupts are disabled
- Primitives to delay tasks for fixed amount of time and to resume tasks

2. Performance evaluation for real-time operating systems

There is a growing need for performance measures, specifically intended for real-time computer systems. The most vital characteristic of a real-time operating system is how responsive the operating system is in servicing internal and external events. These events include external hardware interrupts, internal software signals, and internal timer interrupts. One measure of responsiveness is latency, the time between the occurrence of an event and the execution of the first instruction in the interrupt code. A second measure is jitter, the variation in the period of nominally constant-period events. To be able to offer low latency and low jitter, the operating system must ensure that any kernel task will be preempted by the real-time task. The real-time Linux-Researchers have attempted to gain insight in the RTOSs performance by the means of two main approaches:

S.J. Pise (ed.), *ThinkQuest 2010*, DOI 10.1007/978-81-8489-989-4_22,
© Springer India Pvt. Ltd. 2011

Fine-grained benchmarks

These benchmarks investigate a RTOS at a low level, evaluating the efficiency of the hardware and software interaction for the most frequently used services. The Rhealstone metric is used to obtain a figure of merit from six quantitative measurements: task switching time, task preemption time, interrupt latency time, semaphore shuffling time, deadlock breaking time and datagram throughput time.

Application-oriented benchmarks

These benchmarks take a much higher level look at a RTOS, usually in terms of the number of deadlines kept or missed and the utilization point at which the system begins to break down. They are often implemented as synthetic applications running on top of the real-time plug-in. Hartstone metric consists of five series of tests that mix periodic and aperiodic tasks, with increasing frequency requirements. The results are based on the number of deadlines.

Rhealstone is not complete. There are situations not considered in its metrics (e.g., time for priority inversion management for a given resource) that can be of special relevance for many present-day real-time applications. It is not focused on providing accurate worst-case measures.

Hartstone is excessively generic, but lacks details such as response to external events, inter-task data transferring, etc. It seems to be a useful test for a very specific type of applications, but not for a broadly oriented benchmark. Hartstone is not satisfactory in predicting the behavior of a RTOS.

2.1   Features of modern RTOS kernels

- Response to external events (interrupts)
- Inter-task synchronization and resource sharing (object synchronization)
- Inter-task data transferring (message passing).

2.1.1   Response to external events

Response to external events by means of hardware interrupt handling has been deemed as a foremost issue for real-time systems. Not only fast and predictable response is required; a RTOS must also optimize the interaction between application processes and external events, acting in a timely manner and reducing the time consumed to a minimum [2, 6].

▪ Interrupt processing

Whenever an external device wants to inform of an event's occurrence, it sends a signal to the CPU. The signal received is only transformed into an interrupt. The interval in which interrupts cannot be acknowledged is frequently known as

Interrupt Disable Time. The time elapsed until the processor sends an acknowledge signal to the device that caused the interrupt is called Interrupt Latency Time.

Once the interrupt is accepted, the processor has to complete the instruction currently in process. This time can be considerably long for complex CISC instructions. After the instruction has been processed, the processor's state has to be preserved in order to continue with the execution of the application code after the completion of the interrupt service. The processor's state will be restored after the interrupt code fetches the return instruction. Then, a start-up time must be considered, involving the refilling of the pipeline. This interval is normally short and occurs in a noncritical timeframe. The RTOS ordinarily requires the provision of a sufficient context for the execution of the Interrupt Service Routine (ISR), and the preservation of the state of the task that was running when the interrupt arrived. The Interrupt Service Time should be kept as small as possible, in order not to interfere with the service of other interrupts and with the scheduling of real-time processes that are handled at a lower scheduling priority. Thus, maintaining the interrupts disabled for a long time, due to an incorrect kernel design or excessively long ISRs should be avoided. The synchronization between normal flow application tasks and external events should be kept simple. Tasks may want to be aware of the occurrence of an event and perhaps perform kernel-mode operations (accessing to the hardware or memory, executing processor's privileged instructions). Although in simple RTOSs, this relation can be established using semaphores. Sometimes, the communication between interrupt level code and schedulable code is restricted. In this case, a valuable parameter is the User Task Dispatch Latency Time that accounts for the time span from the activation of the external event to the execution of the first instruction within the responding task. For systems in which user tasks do not possess the same privileges as kernel tasks, drivers are the only means for the user level to request the kernel features. Driver-related metrics are relevant in order to characterize the operating system's behavior, when dealing with the control issues. One metric that should be considered is the Driver Dispatch Latency Time, defined as the time interval from the instant when the interruption was raised until the first instruction of the driver's code waiting for the occurrence of the event is executed. The synchronization with the interrupt thread should be accomplished in the fastest possible way (usually by means of semaphores). The User Task Dispatch Latency Time (the driver may activate user task code) takes into account the overhead included in the driver facility. Some RTOSs offer kernel level threads that gather thread benefits with kernel-level features for the driver code. Additional delays can be found in special situations. Some operations, without being so restrictive to require interrupt disabling, may demand certain degree of privacy that is usually obtained by applying mutual exclusion for the access to the common data structures. If an ISR asks for a service that must be accessed in a mutual exclusion fashion, and the task interrupted was making use of the shared resource, the ISR will be forced to stop until the task exits the critical section. Two context switches will be added. This situation will only happen if the operating system provides the ISR with an appropriate context to allow blocking. If the RTOS does not allow blocking operations, some calls like the ones related to object creation (tasks, semaphores, and queues) or memory allocation will be forbidden [1, 2].

2.1.2 Inter-task synchronization and resource sharing

Synchronization objects are RTOSs services used to control access to the shared resources and to signal synchronous events among tasks. Since these objects are frequently used in real-time programming, the impact of its execution times may be determinant for the achievement of the performance required.

▪ **Synchronization objects**

A semaphore is the lower level mechanism that a RTOS provides for synchronization purposes between several tasks. The actions carried out by the kernel whenever a semaphore primitive is called are summarized in the following two tables:

A mutex is a variation of the semaphore scheme, modified to address the particular problem of serialization, in accessing the shared resources. Its main characteristic resides in the concept of ownership: the task that acquires the mutex is the only task allowed to release it.

This feature allows the implementation of protection and error recovering mechanisms, while providing additional services (implementation of control algorithms, e.g. Basic Priority Inheritance) in order to prevent priority inversion. Condition variables are useful to solve a problem frequently found in inter-task synchronization in a neat and efficient way: the access to a shared resource only when a given condition is satisfied. Condition variables are closely related to mutexes. [1, 2, 6, 7].

Table 1 Possible actions when request is invoked

Primitive	State>0	State<=0
Request	Decrement state (request-decr)	Decrement state and block task (request-block)

Table 2 Possible actions when relinquish is invoked

Primitive	State>=0	State<0
Relinquish	Increment state (relinquish -incr)	Increment state and unblock blocked tasks (relinquish-unblock)

3. Overview of available real-time operating systems

In this section top four RTOS are discussed in terms of Latency numbers provided in the corresponding performance sections are derived from a report generated by the Dedicated Systems Encyclopedia.

3.1 VxWorks

Wind River's VxWorks has been widely used in robotics, process control, avionics, CNC equipment, and fight simulation control applications. The wind micro-kernel core of VxWorks provides multitasking, interrupt support and both preemptive and round robin scheduling. The intertask communications mechanisms supported by VxWorks includes shared memory, message queues, semaphores (binary, counting, mutual exclusion with priority inheritance), events and pipes, sockets and remote procedure calls, and signals. VxWorks is POSIX compliant, implements the POSIX pThreads and adheres to the POSIX Real Time Extension, including asynchronous I/O, counting semaphores, message queues, signals, memory management (page locking), and scheduling control.

3.1.1 Performance

Average latency 1.7 microseconds, maximum latency 6.8 microseconds on a 200MHz Pentium machine [13, 14].

3.2 Windows CE.NET

Microsoft's Windows CE. NET is a real-time operating system designed for mobile applications and applications requiring a small footprint. It supports wireless technologies such as Bluetooth, 802.1x, IPv6, Object Exchange Protocol (OBEX), Media Sense, and Real Time Communication (RTC) / Session Initiation Protocol (SIP). Windows CE. NET supports the Kerberos Security Protocol and the Secure Sockets Layer (SSL). It provides 256 levels of thread priority, nested interrupts, priority inversion and can be configured to be 200 Kb with limited kernel functions. The New Platform Wizard helps in starting designs for devices such as Cell phones / Smart phones, Digital imaging devices, industrial automation devices, Internet/media appliances and Personal digital assistant (PDA)/Mobile handhelds. The POSIX API is not supported by Windows CE. NET. Windows CE. NET, as a real-time version of Windows, is not POSIX compliant since Windows is not a Unix-like operating system. [15]

3.2.1 Performance

Average latency 2.4 microseconds, maximum latency 5.6 microseconds on a 200MHz Pentium Machine [13].

3.3 QNX neutrino RTOS

This RTOS has been deployed in embedded systems for over 20 years in mission and life-critical systems, medical instruments, aviation and space systems, process-control systems, and in-car devices. QNX Neutrino complies with the IEEE 1003.1b real-time standard. The QNX micro-kernel provides services such as thread scheduling, inter-process communication, and uses synchronous message passing to communicate with other OS modules. All OS modules run in their own memory protected address space. QNX Neutrino also provides conventional synchronization services like semaphores, conditional variables, and spin locks. Qnet, the QNX transparent distributed processing mechanism facilitates individual nodes in the network to access and use resources from any other node on the network. File system support is provided for QNX, Linux, DOS, Flash, CD-ROM/DVD, CIFS and NFS. QNX Neutrino provides networking support with QNX Neutrino distributed processing (Qnet), Tiny TCP/IP stack, and NetBSD 1.5 IPv4 or IPv6 stack. Devices supported include USB, audio, PCI, serial, parallel, and IDE and SCSI disks.

3.3.1 Performance

Average latency 1.6 microseconds, maximum latency 4.1 microseconds on a 200 MHz Pentium machine [13].

3.4 pSOSystem 3

Wind River's pSOSystem 3 is a multitasking environment designed for use in embedded system development for both simple and complex networked applications. The pSOSystem 3 multitasking device independent kernel manages/allocates resources and coordinates multiple asynchronous activities. It's priority based task scheduler supports task specific, time-based preemptive scheduling and handles interrupts externally. pSOS+ services include task management, semaphores, events, timers, fixed/variable length queues, and asynchronous signals. Other features include User and Supervisor modes, and an Event logger. POSIX style signals (timers, semaphores and messages) and extensions for pThreads are supported. Event driven operations are facilitated by allowing tasks to simultaneously wait for events, timers, queues and semaphores. pSOSystem 3 provides QBIND(quick bindings) mode which result in speed improvements for selected system calls. Networking support provided by the pSOSystem 3 includes TCP/IP stacks, LAN/WAN protocol, RPC, NFS client/server protocols, STREAMS, SNMP and HTTP.

3.4.1 Performance

Average latency 1.9 microseconds, maximum latency 3.8 microseconds on a 200MHz Pentium machine [13].

4. Conclusions

In this paper, the requirements of real time operating system are discussed based on the time constraints of real time tasks, such requirement analysis can be applied to the design of the future real time operating system environment such as process control for factory automation. To remain highly reliable as compared to general operating system, RTOS should be realized based on reliable task model, characterized by redundancies of resources including active resources, passive resources, and time resources. The specifications of top four RTOS provides memory efficiency, rapid and deterministic event response and well supported industrial-grade software products, which can be useful for designing future generation embedded RTOS.

References

1. William Stallings, operating SystemsInternals and design principles, Reading,Pearson Prentice Hall, fifth edition, 2006
2. Man Sang Chung and Heonshik Shin, "Requirements Specification of Distributed Hard Real-time Operating Systems", IECON'9, 1991
3. Alberto Garcia-Martincez, Jesus F. Conde and Angel Vina, "A Comprehensive Approach in Performance Evaluation for Modern Realtime Operating Systems", IEEE Proceedings of EUROMICRO-22, 1996
4. Krzyszt of M. Sacha, "Measuring the Realtime Operating System Performance", IEEE, 1995
5. Matti A. Hiltunen, Richard D. Schlichting, Xiaonan Han, Melvin M. Cardozo, and Rajsekhar Das, "Real-time Dependable Channels: Customizing Q0s Attibutes for Distributed Systems", IEEE, 1999
6. Shourong Lu, Wolfgmg A. Halang, Roman Gumzej' "Towards Platform Independent Models of Real Time Operating Systems", IEEE, 1999
7. Sindhwani, M and Srikanthan, T," Framework for Automated Application-Specific Optimization of Embedded Real-Time Operating Systems", IEEE, 2005
8. Sang H. Son, Stravros Yannapaulos, Young Kuk-Kim and Carmen C. Iannacone, "Integration of Database system with real-time kernel for Time- critical applications", IEEE Proceedings of EUROMICRO-22, 1992
9. Clifford W. Mercer and Hideyuki Tokuda, "Premptability in Real-Time Operating Systems", IEEE Proceedings of EUROMICRO-22, 1992
10. Sindhwani, M and Srikanthan. T, "Framework for Automated Application-Specific Optimization of Embedded Real-Time Operating Systems", IEEE, ICICS 2005
11. She Kairui, Bai Shuwei, Zhou, Nicholas, Li Lian, "Analyzing RTLinux/ GPL Source code for education"
12. Daniel P.Bovert & Marco Cesati, 2005, "Understanding the Linux Kernel", O'Reilly & Associates
13. Frederick & Simon, "Introduction to Linux for Real-Time Control", National Institute of Standards and Technology
14. IEEE. Information technology—Portable Operating System Interface (POSIX)-Part1: System Application: Program Interface (API) [C Language], ANSI/IEEE Std 1003.1,1996 edition
15. C.Muench and R.Kath, "The Windows CE Technology Tutorial: Windows Powered Solutions for the Developer's, First edition, Addison-Wesley, 2000

A switched capacitor based universal filter for IVRS

Ajay Lahane[1] · Swapnali G. Gharat[2] · Uday Pandit Khot[3]

[1]U.M.I.T, S.N.D.T. University, Mumbai, India
[2]I.I.T. Bombay, Mumbai, India
[3]Thadomal Shahani Engineering College, Mumbai, India

1. Introduction

Interactive voice response systems (IVRS, IVR System) are currently used in abundance as interfaces at a wide variety of support centers, call centers and other information retrieval centers. When a support center with IVRS is contacted by a caller, the caller is typically first presented with voice information from an interactive voice response unit (IVRU). The caller responses to the voice queries by providing input through the phone keypad. Each key input provided by the caller from the keypad is assigned with specific information in the database of the IVRS [1].

A caller who contacts in IVRS equipped support centers can choose to have the voice information contained in the IVRS menus displayed graphically on the caller's communication terminal. The graphical display allows a caller to navigate up and down in the IVRS menus, skipping intermediate steps that would be required making responses to voice queries. Graphical display of IVRS menus also saves support costs since a caller may find desired information without interaction with support center personnel [2].

The existing IVRS requires many modules in the detection of input key from the caller. The active filters with resistive network require more chip area in IC fabrication. The presence of many modules is not suitable in the VLSI design technology.

The proposed IVR system requires less modules compared to the existing IVRS. The DTMF switching network in the proposed IVRS consist of low-pass filter and high-pass filter section. The details about DTMF tone detection is given in [3]. The separated frequencies from lowpass and high-pass section are converted into square wave using limiter. The Micro-controller is used to measure the converted square wave from the lowpass and high-pass

filter section. The Microcontroller sends the detected key to the IVRS database. The information assigned with the keys received is sent to the caller. The band-pass filters and detectors required in the exiting IVRS are replaced by the Micro-controller and the comparator in the proposed IVRS. Proposed IVRS requires less modules compared to the existing IVRS. The DTMF switching networks of the proposed IVRS, resistors are realized by the MOS switches and a capacitor. The simulation of a resistor using MOS switches and a capacitor required less chip area in IC fabrication. The resistance is inversely proportional to the capacitor and the switching clock frequency [4], [5]. The resistance realizes using MOS switches and capacitor can be varied by changing external switching clock frequency. The high resistances are difficult in the IC fabrication. The switched capacitor filter allows for very accurate and tunable analog circuits to be manufactured without using resistors compared to the conventional RC circuits.

2. The proposed interactive voice response system

The proposed IVRS requires fewer modules as the various filters and detectors required in existing system are replaced by the universal filter and Micro-controller. The MOS technology is relatively easy to implement capacitors and switches.

The proposed IVR systems are included DTMF detector, IVRS clients, IVRS server and data base as shown in Fig. 1.

The pair frequency of low-pass group & high-pass group are assigned to each key of the telephone keypad. For every input from the caller, the DTMF detector at the IVRS received the DTMF pair frequency. In the SC based IVRS,

S.J. Pise (ed.), *ThinkQuest 2010*, DOI 10.1007/978-81-8489-989-4_23,

the DTMF tones frequency is connected to the DTMF preamplifier which amplify the signal level. The DTMF demodulator is used to generate the original DTMF tone pair of frequency.

3. Universal SC filter

The functional block diagram of the SC based universal filter is shown in Fig. 2. The universal SC filters consist of low-pass and high-pass filters are controlled by the Micro-controller. The Microcontroller is used to measure the converted frequencies from the low-pass and high-pass filter section. The outputs of the comparators are connected to the input of the multiplexer. The multiplexer output is connected to the input port of the Micro-controller as shown in Fig. 2.

The frequency of band-pass is measured by the Micro-controller. The resistors in the low-pass and high-pass filter realized using SC. The low-pass and high-pass filter can be defined to new cutoff frequency by varying the input clock frequency without changing the components. The low-pass and high-pass filter together acts like a band-pass filter. So the low-pass and high-pass filter based on SC along with the Micro-controller is operating as universal filter.

3.1 The switched capacitor based low-pass Butterworth filter

In a SC based filter all SCs are connected on one side in phase 1 and change over simultaneously to the other side in phase 2. The non overlapping switching frequency is generated with offset compensation [6]. Figure 3 shows

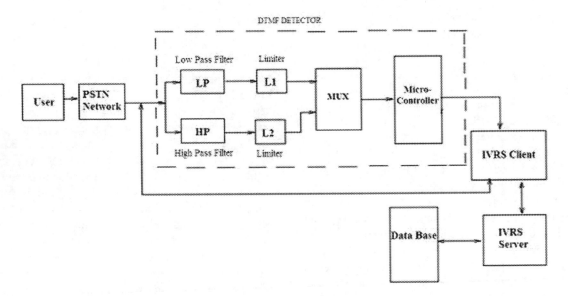

Fig. 1   A block diagram of SC based IVR system

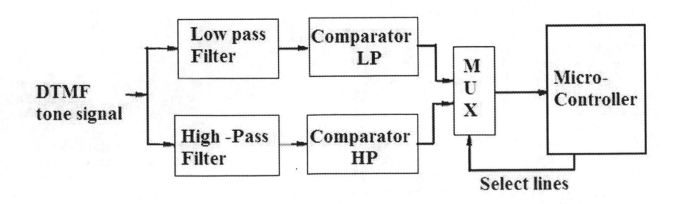

Fig. 2   A block diagram of universal SC filters

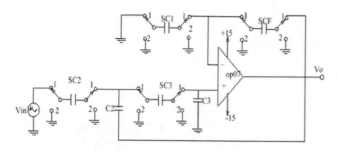

Fig. 3 A low-pass SCs based Butterworth filter

a second-order low-pass SCs based Butterworth filter [7, 8]. The value of this resistance decreases with increasing switching frequency or increasing capacitance and vice versa.

The low-pass second-order filter designed for high cutoff frequency f_H. The magnitude gain is nearly equal to A_F for low frequency. At $f = f_H$, the voltage magnitude gain is –3 dB. The low-pass filter passed the low frequency up to f_H without attenuation. The input frequency higher than f_H are attenuated with 40 dB/decade rolls off [10].

3.2 The SC based second-order Butterworth high-pass filter

The high-pass filters are often formed simply by interchanging frequency-determining SC and capacitors in low-pass filters [9]. A second-order high-pass filter is obtained from a second-order SC based low-pass filter. The lower cutoff frequency f_L is the frequency at which the magnitude of the gain is 0.707 times its pass-band value. All frequencies higher than f_L are pass-band frequencies, with the highest frequency determined by the closed-loop bandwidth of the op-amp. The resistors are replaced by MOS switches and equivalent capacitor. The value of the equivalent resistors is inversely proportional to the phase clock frequency and the capacitance [8]. The circuit diagram for switched capacitor based high-pass filter is as shown in Fig. 3. The cutoff frequency of the high-pass filter can be varied by changing the clock frequency [11]. The voltage gain magnitude equation of the second-order high-pass filter is as follows

$$\left| V_o / V_{in} \right| = \frac{A_F}{\sqrt{1 + \left(\frac{f_L}{f} \right)^4}}$$

At very low frequencies, that is, $f < f_L$, the voltage magnitude gain is very less than A_F. At $f = f_L$, the voltage magnitude gain is 0.707 A_F. At frequencies higher than f_L, the voltage gain is nearly equal to A_F [10].

3.3 The DTMF detection using micro-controller

The IVR system respond to the caller based on the key input received. The IVR systems consist of DTMF receiver,

DTMF decoder, IVRS client, and database server. The input signal frequency is applied to both low-pass filter and high-pass filter section. The separated tones from the low-pass and high-pass filter section are then converted to square waves of fixed amplitude using limiter. This conversion is done so that input signal frequency measured by the Micro-controller [12]. This dc switching signals are connected to the input port of the Micro-controller. The frequency is measured by the Micro-controller which identifies the key assigned to the measured frequency. The Micro-controller provides the signal to the IVRS client is depended on the key received from the caller. The IVRS client gives response to user called by accessing the data from the IVRS server. The Micro-controller first measured the low group signal from low-pass filter section. This is selected by providing input to the select lines of the multiplexer by the Micro-controller. The data output of multiplexer is connected to the input port of Micro-controller. The Micro-controller counts the signal frequency and stored in the register [13].

The Micro-controller selects the high-pass output by providing the select input on the select lines of the multiplexer. The data output of the multiplexer is connected to the input port of the Micro-controller which measure the frequency and stored the count into another register. The counts in the Micro-controller registers are low-pass and high-pass frequency value respectively. The DTMF generator circuit provides the low-pass and high-pass frequency for the pressed phone key. The Micro-controller compares register count and detect the received key from the caller [14]. The Micro-controller sends the detected key (assigned to the DTMF tone) to the IVRS. The IVRS responds to the user depends upon the key received. The Key detection circuit is shown in Fig. 4 and a flowchart for DTMF measurement and key detection is shown in Fig. 6.

4. Results and discussion

We have simulated SC based low pass, high pass filter. These circuit are also assembled and tested along with DTMF detection using microcontroller. The circuit of SC based low pass filter is assembled on the breadboard and tested. The 250 kHz with 10 V peak-to-peak switching

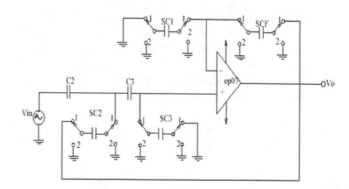

Fig. 4 A switched capacitor based high-pass filter

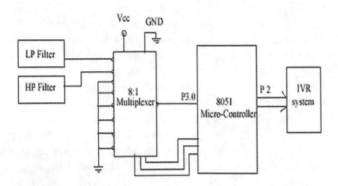

Fig. 5 A key detection circuit

clock frequency is given to the MOS switches. The 5 V supply voltage is connected IC 7404. The op-amp LM339 is provided with ±15 V supply. The input signal frequency f is varied from 10 Hz to 10 KHz. The amplitude of the input signal is 2.72 V. The SC based low-pass filter is designed for cutoff frequency 1 kHz. The frequency response of low-pass SC filter is as shown in Fig.7.

The frequency response shows the 3 dB gain is at 1 kHz cutoff frequency. The practical readings match with the theoretical ones. The input signals frequencies lower than the cutoff frequency (1 kHz) are passed without attenuation. The Fig. 7 shows pass-band gain of the SC based low-pass filter is 1.56 dB.

The pass band gain of the filter is given by

$$A_F = 1 + R_F/R_1 = 1.586$$

i/p signal amplitude 2.72 V.
Switching frequency $f_{clk} = 250$ kHz. $f_H = 1$ kHz.

The SC based low-pass filter is designed at lower cutoff of 1 kHz frequency. At 1 kHz input signal frequency gain magnitude is –0.8 dB.

The circuit of SC based high-pass filter is assembled and tested. The switching frequency of 250KHz with 10Vp-p is given to the MOS switches. The input signal frequency is varied from 10 Hz to 10 KHz. The amplitude of the input signal is 2.72 V. The SC based high-pass filter is designed for cutoff frequency 1 kHz. The frequency response of high- pass SC filter is as shown in Fig. 8. The frequency response shows the 3 dB gain is at 1 kHz cutoff frequency. The practical readings match with the theoretical ones. The input signals frequencies higher than the cutoff frequency (1 kHz) are passed without attenuation. The SC based high-pass filter is designed at 1 kHz. The frequency response shows the 3 dB gain at cutoff frequency. The frequency response shows the frequencies higher than the cutoff frequency are passed without attenuation. The Fig. 8 shows pass-band gain of the SC based high-pass filter is 3.35 dB.

Where the pass band gain of the filter

$$A_F = 1 + R_F/R_1 = 1.586.$$

The i/p signal amplitude = 2.72 V.
Switching frequency $f_{clk} = 250$ kHz, $f_L = 1$ kHz.

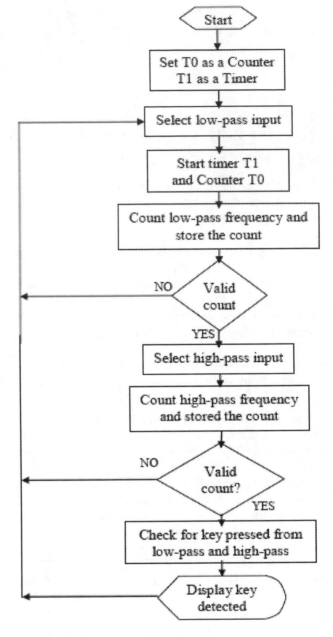

Fig. 6 Flowchart of DTMF key detection

The output of the filter sections are applied to the comparator sections. The comparators, LM 339 circuit, convert sine wave output of the filter section into square waveform. This square waveform is applied to the port 3.0 of the Micro-controller to measure the frequency. The Fig. 9 shows the square waveform of the SChigh-pass filter. The Micro-controller will execute the program to measure the input frequency received at the port.

5. Summary and conclusions

This paper has presented the need of an interactive voice response system and its operation. It has put emphasis on essentials of operation of switched capacitor networks, with a special emphasis on its use in designing active filters.

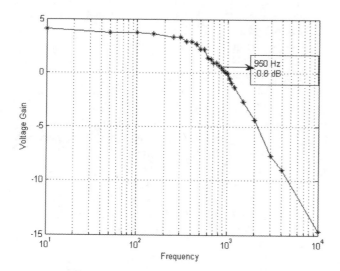

Fig. 7 A frequency response of SC based low-pass filter

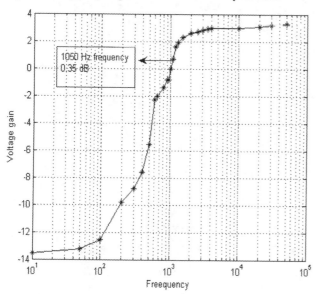

Fig. 8 A frequency response of SC based high-pass

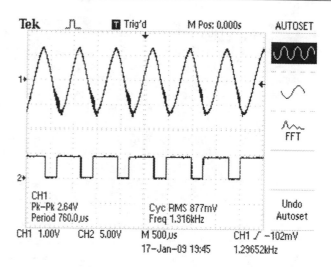

Fig. 9 A frequency measurements waveform of high-pass SC filter

The DTMF switching networks are developed by the MOS switches and capacitors which in turn makes the topology suitable for integrated circuit fabrication. The simulation of a resistor using MOS switches and a capacitor requires less chip area in integrated circuit fabrication. The DTMF switching networks in the proposed IVRS consists of resistors which are replaced by the MOS switches and a capacitor. This approach also offers better circuit performance compared to conventional active *RC* filter. In SC filter, poles and zeros depends on clock frequency and capacitance ratio (rather than the absolute values). Both these parameters can be determined and controlled precisely giving very accurate and stable design. Further, as all the time constants of an SC circuit are proportional to clock frequency, the overall gain versus frequency response can easily be scaled just by changing clock frequency without change in components values. This approach offers better circuit

performance, accurate and stable design compared to conventional active *RC* filter based.

The proposed IVR system requires less modules compared to the existing IVR system. The DTMF switching network in the proposed IVRS consist of low-pass filter and high-pass filter section. The DTMF input received from the caller is applied to both these sections which separate the low group and the high group frequency assigned to the key of the telephone set. The separated frequencies from low-pass and high-pass sections are converted into square wave using limiter. The Micro-controller is used to measure the converted square wave from the low-pass and high-pass filter section. The measured low-pass and high-pass frequencies are compared by the Micro-controller to identify the input key received from the caller. The Micro-controller sends the detected key to the IVRS database. The information assigned with the key received is send to the caller. The band-pass filters and detectors required in the exiting IVRS are replaced by the Micro-controller in the proposed IVRS. The proposed IVRS requires less modules compared to the existing IVRS. This makes IVRS topologically suitable in VLSI technology.

The realization of a higher-order filter requires large number of operational amplifiers. An operational amplifier occupies larger silicon area and is source of noise. Thus, it is highly desirable to reduce the number of operational amplifiers. One method of reducing number of op-amps and circuit components is by implementing the time multiplexing of SC and operational amplifier. Time multiplexing of the circuit components can be taken up as a future work.

References

1. United States Patent, *System and method for graphically displaying and navigating through web based interactive voice system*, Dec. 2004
2. United States Patent, *Method and system for graphically displaying and navigating through an interactive voice response menu*, Nov. 15, 1995

3. Wikipedia, the free encyclopedia, *Interactive voice response*, pp. 1–4,10 Oct. 2008

4. D. J. Allstot and W.C. Black, Jr., "Technology design consideration for MOS switched capacitor filter systems," *Proc. IEEE*, vol. 71, no. 8, pp. 967-986, Aug. 1983

5. R. W. Brodersen, P. R. Gray, and D. A. Hodges, "MOS switched capacitor filters," *Proc. IEEE*, vol. 67, no.1, pp. 61-75, Jan. 1979

6. S. Signell and K. Mossberg, "Offset-compensation of two phase switched-capacitor filters," *IEEE Trans. Circuits Syst.,* CAS-36, no. 1, pp. 31-41, Jan. 1998

7. R. Gregorian, K. W. Martin, and G. C. Temes, "Switched-capacitor circuit design," *Proc. IEEE*, vol.71, no. 8, pp. 180-205, Aug. 1983

8. K. Lacanette, " A Basic Introduction to Filters- Active, Passive, and Switched- Capacitor," *National semiconductor application Note 779,* Apr. 1991

9. P. V. Ananda Mohan, V. Ramchandran, and M. N. S. Swamy, *Switched Capacitor Filters Theory, Analysis and Design*, Prentice Hall International Ltd, UK, 1995

10. R. A. Gayakwad, *Op-amp and Linear Integrated Circuits*, PHI, pp- 298-310, Apr. 2002

11. T.S. Rathore, *Digital Measurement Techniques*, Narosa, pp. 120–122, 2005

12. X. F. Wania, D. A. Johns, and A.S. Sedra, "Programmable multiplexed switched-capacitor filters," *Electron. Lett.*, vol. 26, no. 14, pp. 1051-1053, Jul. 2002

13. D. B. Cox, L. T. Lin, R.S. Florek, and H. F. Tseng, "A real-time programmable SC filter, " *IEEE J. Solid-State Circuits*, vol. SC-15, no. 6, pp. 972-977, Dec. 1980

14. M. A. Mazidi, J. G. Mazidi, and R. McKinlay, *The 8085 Microcontroller and Embedded Systems*, Pearson Education, UK, 2008

Characterization of cardiomegaly disease from X-ray images using mean shift based image segmentation

Deepak A. Kulkarni · P. U. Dere

Terna Engineering College, Nerul, Navi Mumbai, India

1. Introduction

Diagnostic imaging is an invaluable tool in medicine. Different methods of getting images like Gamma Ray Imaging, X-Ray Imaging, Magnetic resonance imaging (MRI), Computed Tomography (CT), Digital Mammography, and other imaging modalities provide an effective means for noninvasive mapping the anatomy of a subject. These technologies have greatly increased knowledge of normal and diseased anatomy for medical research and are a critical component in diagnosis and treatment planning. With the limitation of number of exposures for Gamma Ray or X-Rays to the patient, it is difficult to see the critical feature if the intensity/brightness/contrast are not proper. Moreover the growing size and number of these medical images have necessitated the use of computers to facilitate processing and analysis. In particular, computer algorithms for the intensity/ brightness/contrast adjustment, delineation of anatomical structures and other regions of interest are becoming increasingly important in assisting and automating specific radiological tasks. These algorithms, called image segmentation algorithms, play a vital role in numerous biomedical imaging applications, such as the:

1) Quantification of tissue volumes
2) Diagnosis
3) Localization of Pathology
4) Study of anatomical structure
5) Treatment planning
6) Computer-integrated/assisted surgery

Image Segmentation plays a larger role in object recognition. Unsupervised image segmentation algorithms have matured to a point that they provide segmentations which agree to a large extent with human intuition. The result of image segmentation is a set of regions that collectively cover the entire image or a set of contours extracted from the image. Each of the pixels in a region is similar with respect to some characteristics such as color, intensity, or texture.

In this paper we will analyze X-ray images for characterizing various diseases like Cardiomegaly and Pneumonia by implementing mean shift algorithm. The specific features of these diseases are described later.

2. Basics of image segmentation

Before going in detail about the Image segmentation and its application we will first understand terms that are related to image segmentation. *Image:* An image is a collection of measurements in twodimensional (2-D) or three dimensional (3-D) spaces. In medical images, these measurements or 'image intensities' can be radiation absorption in X-ray imaging, acoustic pressure in ultrasound, or radio frequency (RF) signal amplitude in MRI. If a single measurement is made at each location in the image, then the image is called a scalar image. If more than one measurement is made (e.g. dualecho MRI), the image is called a vector or multichannel image. Images may be acquired in the continuous domain, such as on X-ray film, or in discrete space as in MRI. In our application we will consider continuous domain image i.e. X-Ray digitized images. Dimensionality: Dimensionality refers to whether a segmentation method operates in a 2-D image domain or a 3-D image domain. Methods that rely solely on image intensities are independent of the image domain. However, certain methods, such as deformable models, Markov random fields (MRFs), and region

S.J. Pise (ed.), *ThinkQuest 2010*, DOI 10.1007/978-81-8489-989-4_24,

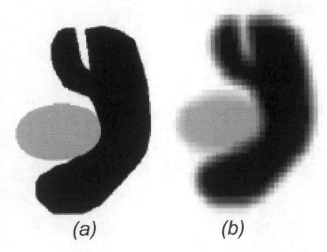

Fig. 1 Illustration of partial-volume effect. (a) Idealimage. (b) Acquired image

growing incorporate spatial information and may therefore operate differently depending on the dimensionality of the image. In this application we will deal with 2D X-Ray digital images. Soft Segmentation and Partial-Volume Effects: Partial volume effects are artifacts that occur where multiple tissue types contribute to a single pixel, resulting in a blurring of intensity across boundaries. Figure 1 illustrates how the sampling process can result in partial-volume effects, leading to ambiguities in structural definitions. In Fig. 1b, it is difficult to precisely determine the boundaries of the two objects. Partial-volume effects are common in medical images, particularly for Three Dimension CT and MRI images, in which the resolution is not isotropic and, in many cases, is quite poor along one axis of the image. By using various image processing algorithm we can process partial volume effects.

Intensity In homogeneities: A major difficulty that is specific to the segmentation of MR images is the 'intensity in homogeneity artifact', which causes a shading effect to appear over the image. The artifact can significantly degrade the performance of methods that assume that the intensity value of a tissue class is constant over the image.

Correction and soft segmentation: (a) Magnetic resonance heart image acquired with a fast spin echo sequence in a true axial prescription; (b) estimated gain field; (c) hard segmentation into three classes, (d–f) membership functions of the three classes (data provided courtesy of c Constantinides).

Segmentation: Segmentation refers to the process of partitioning a digital image into multiple regions. Image segmentation is defined as partitioning an image into nonoverlapping, constituent regions that are homogenous to characteristics like intensity or texture. The goal of segmentation is to simplify and/or change the representation of an image into something that is more meaningful and

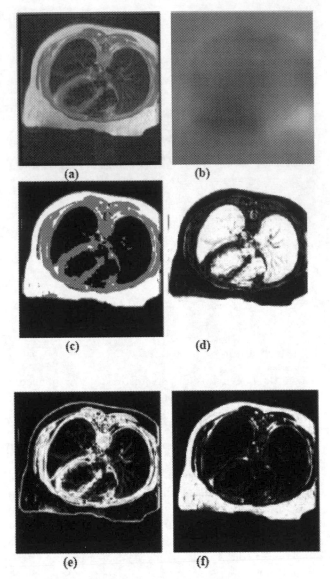

Fig. 2 Example of simultaneous in homogeneity

easier to analyze. Image segmentation is used to locate objects and boundaries in images. Methods: There are various methods of medical image segmentation as:

1. Thresholding.
2. Region growing.
3. Classifiers.
4. Clustering.
5. Deformable Models.
6. Atlas Guided Approaches.

Thresholding approach segments Scalar Images(Images in which measurements are done at eachlocation in image) by creating a binary partition of the image intensities. This method determines an intensity value called as Threshold which separates the desired classes. The segmentation is then achieved by grouping all the pixels with intensities greater than Threshold into one class and all other pixels into another class. This method is an effective means for obtaining a segmentation of images in which different structures have contrasting intensities or other quantifiable features. Thresholding cannot be applied to multichannel images (Images where more than one measurement is done at same place ex: dual-echo MRI). It does not take into account the spatial characteristics of an image. Hence it is sensitive to noise and intensity in homogeneities (Image fading) which may corrupt the image and makes separation more difficult.

Region Growing is a technique for extracting an image region that is connected based on some predefined criteria which can be based on intensity information or edges in the image. Region Growing requires a seed point that is selected manually by operator and extracts all pixels connected to the initial seed based on predefined criteria which may be to grow the region until an edge in the image is met. The primary limitation is that it requires manual interaction to obtain the seed point. For each region that needs to be extracted, a seed must be planted. Region Growing can also be sensitive to noise, causing extracted regions to have holes or even become disconnected.

Classifier method is pattern recognition technique that seeks to partition a feature space derived from the image by using data with known labels. Classifiers are known as supervised methods as they require training data that are manually segmented and then used as references for automatically segmenting new data. Classifiers generally do not perform any spatial modeling. It requires manual interaction to obtain training data. Training sets can be acquired for each image that requires segmenting, but this can be time consuming and laborious.

Clustering algorithms essentially perform the same function as classifiers methods without the use of training data. They are termed unsupervised methods. To compensate for the lack of training data, clustering methods iteratively alternate between segmenting the image and characterizing the properties of each class. Clustering Algorithms also do not incorporate Spatial modeling hence sensitive to noise and intensity in homogeneities.

Markov Random Field (MRF) modeling is not a segmentation method but a statistical model that can be used within segmentation methods. MRF models spatial interactions between adjacent or nearby pixels. These local correlations provide a mechanism for modeling a variety of image properties. A main difficulty is the proper selection of the parameters controlling the strength of spatial interactions. A setting that is too high can result in excessively smooth segmentation and loss of important structural details. MRF methods usually require intensive algorithms.

Artificial Neural Networks (ANN) are parallel networks of processing elements or nodes that simulate biological learning. Each node in ANN is capable of performing elementary computations. ANN represent paradigm for machine learning and can be used in a variety of ways for image segmentation. The most widely applied use in medical imaging is as a Classifier in which the weights are determined by using training data and the ANN is used to segment new data.

Deformable models are physically motivated, model based techniques for delineating region boundaries by using closed parametric curves or surfaces that deform under the influence of internal and external forces. To delineate an object boundary in an image, a closed curve or surface must first be placed near the desired boundary and then allowed to undergo an iterative relaxation process. Deformable models are widely used in segmentation of medical images especially in areas like Segmentation of cardiac images, bone in CT images and ultrasound imaging.

Atlas Guided Approaches are powerful tool for medical image segmentation when a standard atlas or template is available. The Atlas is generated by compiling information on the anatomy that requires segmenting. This atlas is then used as a reference frame for segmenting new images. Atlas Guided approaches are similar to classifiers except that they are implemented in spatial domain of the image rather than in feature space. Unsupervised image segmentation algorithms have matured to the point where they generate reasonable segmentations, and thus can begin to be incorporated into larger systems. A system designer now has an array of available algorithm choices, however, few objective numerical evaluations exist of these segmentation algorithms. As a first step, this presents an evaluation of two popular segmentation algorithms, the mean shift-based segmentation algorithm and a graph-based segmentation scheme.

3. Mean shift based segmentation

The mean shift based segmentation technique was introduced in and has become widely-used in the vision community. It is one of many techniques under the heading of "feature space analysis". The mean shift technique is comprised of two basic steps:

- A mean shift filtering of the original image data (in feature space), and
- A subsequent clustering of the filtered data points.

Below we will briefly describe each of these steps and then discuss some of the strengths and weaknesses of this method.

Filtering: The filtering step of the mean shift segmentation algorithm consists of analyzing the probability density function (pdf) underlying the image data in feature space. Consider the feature space consisting of the original image data represented as the (x, y) location of each pixel, plus its color in L*u*v* space (L_, u_, v_). The modes of the pdf underlying the data in this space will correspond to the locations with highest data density. In terms of segmentation, it is intuitive that the data points close to these high density points (modes) should be clustered together. Note that these modes are also far less sensitive to outliers than the means of, say, a mixture of Gaussians would be. The mean shift filtering step consists of finding the modes of the underlying pdf and associating with them any points in their basin of attraction. Unlike earlier techniques, the mean shift is a non-parametric technique and hence we will need to estimate the gradient of the pdf, f(x), in an iterative manner using kernel density estimation to find the modes. For a data point x in feature space, the density gradient is estimated as being proportional to the mean shift vector: For a data point x in feature space, the density gradient is estimated as being proportional to the mean shift vector:

$$\widehat{\nabla}f(x) \propto \frac{\sum_{i=1}^{n} x_i g\left(\left\|\frac{x-x_i}{h}\right\|\right)}{\sum_{i=1}^{n} g\left(\left\|\frac{x-x_i}{h}\right\|\right)} - x$$

where xi are the data points, x is a point in the feature space, n is the number of data points (pixels in the image), and g is the profile of the symmetric kernel G. We use the simple case where G is the uniform kernel with radius vector h. Thus the above equation simplifies to:

$$\widehat{\nabla}f(x) \propto \left[\frac{1}{|S_{x,h_s,h_r}|} \sum_{x_i \in S_{x,h_s,h_r}} x_i\right] - x$$

where Sx, hs, hr represents the sphere in feature space centered at x and having spatial radius hs and colour (range) radius hr, and the xi represent the data points within that sphere. For every data point (pixel in the original image) x we can iteratively compute the gradient estimate in Eqn. 2 and move x in that direction, until the gradient is below a threshold. Thus we have found the points where ▼f (x) = 0, the modes of the density estimate. We can then replace the point x with x0, the mode with which it is associated. Finding the mode associated with each data point helps to smooth the image while preserving discontinuities. Intuitively, if two points xi and xj are far from each other in feature space, then xi € Sxj,hs,hr and hence xj doesn't contribute to the mean shift vector gradient estimate and the trajectory of xi will move it away from xj . Hence pixels on either side of a strong discontinuity will not attract each other. However, filtering alone does not provide segmentation as the modes found are noisy. This

"noise" stems from two sources. First, the mode estimation is an iterative process; hence it only converges to within the threshold provided. Second, consider an area in feature space larger than Sxj, hs, hr and where the color features are uniform or have a gradient of 1.Since the pixel coordinates are uniform by design, the mean shift vector will be 0 in this region, and the data points will not move and hence not converge to a single mode. Intuitively, however, we would like all of these data points to belong to the same cluster in the final segmentation. For these reasons, mean shift filtering is only a preprocessing step, and a second step is required in the segmentation process: clustering of the filtered data points {x'}.

Clustering: After mean shift filtering, each data point in the feature space has been replaced by its corresponding mode. As described above, some points may have collapsed to the same mode, but many have not despite the fact that they may be less than one kernel radius apart. In clustering is described as a simple post-processing step in which any modes that are less than one kernel radius apart are grouped together and their basins of attraction are merged. This suggests using single linkage clustering, which effectively converts the filtered points into segmentation. This algorithm is quite sensitive to its parameters. The mean shift filtering stage has two parameters corresponding to the bandwidths (radii of the kernel) for the spatial (hs) and colour (hr) features. Slight variations in hr can cause large changes in the granularity of the segmentation.

4. Diseases under analysis

1. Cardiomegaly: Cardiomegaly is a condition wherein the heart enlarges in a cardiothoracic ratio of 0.50. It is assumed to be a direct effect of the thickening of the heart mussels which happens when the heart is overloaded. The symptoms of such diseases are breathlessness, dizziness, quickening or slowing of the pulse rate. Also there might be swelling of the ankles and legs.

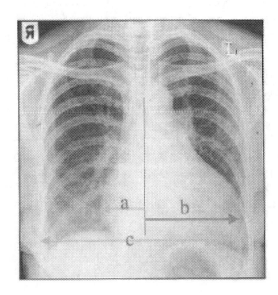

2. Pneumonia: Pneumonia is infective consolidation of lung. Bronchopneumonia is multifocal and centered on airways affected by bronchitis. The consolidation is slight patchy and distributed in way that reflects the course of the airway. Chest radiograph are useful in detection and follow up of pneumonia.

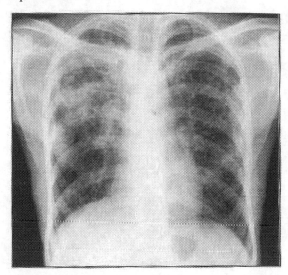

5. Experimental results

1. For the given X-ray image the cardiothoracic ratio[CTR] was calculated. It was required that this ratio must be less than 0.5 in adults and 0.6 in children. After calculating the required parameters, our developed software could directly determine the CTR ratio and was found to be more than 0.5 in the given X-Ray image. Hence it was suggested to be Cardiomegaly. This kind of disease is due to low heart o/p. This occurs if the heart is more than 50% bigger than the inner diameter of one's rib cage. Also there was a right small pleural effusion and increases reticular markings in the lung predominantly in the lower zones these are the findings of suggestive pulmonary edema.

2. Confluent patchy irregular soft tissues opacities seen in the right upper and mid zones. These are the findings of suggestive tuberculosis.

6. Conclusion

Future research in the segmentation of medical images will strive toward improving the accuracy, precision, and computational speed of segmentation methods, as well as reducing the amount of manual interaction. Accuracy and precision can be improved by incorporating prior information from atlases and by combining discrete and continuous spatial-domain segmentation methods. For increasing computational efficiency, multistage processing and parallelizable methods such as neural networks are promising approaches. Computational efficiency will be particularly important in real-time processing applications. Possibly the most important

question surrounding the use of image segmentation is its application in clinical settings. Computerized segmentation methods have already demonstrated their utility in research applications and are now garnering increased use for computer-aided diagnosis and radiotherapy planning. For segmentation methods to gain acceptance in routine clinical applications, extensive validation is required on the particular methods in question. Furthermore, one must be able to demonstrate some significant performance advantage (e.g. more accurate diagnosis or earlier detection of pathology) over traditional methods to warrant the training and equipment co stsassociated with using computerized methods. It is unlikely that automated segmentation methods will ever replace physicians, but they will likely become crucial elements of medical-image analysis. Segmentation methods will be particularly valuable in areas such as image-guided surgery, in which visualization of the anatomy is a critical component.

References

1. D. Comaniciu, P. Meer, "Mean shift: A robust approach toward feature space analysis", IEEE Trans. on Pattern Analysis and Machine Intelligence, 2002, 24, pp. 603–619
2. C. Christoudias, B. Georgescu, P. Meer, "Synergism in Low Level Vision", Intl Conf on Pattern Recognition, 2002, 4, pp. 40190
3. B. Georgescu, I. Shimshoni, P. Meer, "Mean Shift Based Clustering in High Dimensions: A Texture Classification Example", Intl Conf on Compute r Vision, 2003
4. P. Felzenszwalb, D. Huttenlocher, "Efficient Graph- Based Image Segmentation", Intl Journal of Computer Vision, 2004, 59 (2)
5. D. Martin, C. Fowlkes, D. Tal, J. Malik, "A Database of Human Segmented Natural Images and its Application to Evaluating Segmentation Algorithms and Measuring Ecological Statistics", Intl Conf on Computer Vision, 2001
6. R. Unnikrishnan, C. Pantofaru, M. Hebert, "A Measure for Objective Evaluation of Image Segmentation Algorithms", CVPR workshop on Empirical Evaluation Methods in Computer Vision, 2005
7. R. Unnikrishnan, M. Hebert, "Measures of Similarity", IEEE Workshop on Computer Vision Applications, 2005, pp. 394–400
8. D. Verma, M. Meila, "A comparison of spectral clustering algorithms", University of Washington technical report, 2001
9. R. Kannan, S. Vempala, A. Vetta, "On clustering's - good, bad and spectral", FOCS, 2000, pp. 367–377
10. M. Meila, J. Shi, "Learning segmentation by random walks", NIPS, 2000, pp. 873–879
11. A. Y. Ng, M. I. Jordan, Y. Weiss, "On spectral clustering: Analysis and an algorithm", NIPS, 2002, pp. 849–856
12. M. Meila, "Comparing clustering's", University of Washington Technical Report, 2002
13. J. Shi, J. Malik, "Normalized cuts and image segmentation", IEEE Transactions on Pattern Analysis and Machine Learning, 2000, pp. 888–905
14. D. Martin, "An Empirical Approach to Grouping and Segmentation", Ph.D. dissertation, 2002 University of California, Berkeley

A novel pattern extraction techniques used for classification of type-2 diabetic patients with back-propagation

B. M. Patil · R. C. Joshi · Durga Toshniwal

Department of Electronics and Computer Engineering, I.I.T., Roorkee, Uttarakhand, India

1. Introduction

Diabetes mellitus is the most common endocrine metabolic disorder and its diagnosis is increasing at an alarming rate [1]. No perfect cure exists for this disorder, which is the third leading cause of death and morbidity in the Developing countries. The comparative risk for individuals with diabetes acquiring end-stage renal disease is 25 times that of individuals without diabetes. The relative risk of an individual with diabetes becoming blind is 20 times greater than for other individuals [2]. Diabetes is classified into two types – Insulin dependent diabetes mellitus (type-1 diabetes) and Non-insulin dependent diabetes mellitus (type-2 diabetes). Type-1 is dependent on exogenous insulin to prevent ketoacidosis. A large amount of people are usually affected from Type-2 diabetes which develops after the age of 30 and is associated with obesity. The goal of predictive data mining in clinical medicine is to develop models that can use patient specific information to predict the significant result and thereby support clinical decision-making. In this study we develop prediction model to predict whether or not a newly diagnosed patient (pregnant women) would likely develop diabetes within five years from the time of first diagnosis. The datasets are taken from UCI machine learning database repository [3]. The only motive for using this dataset is that it is very commonly used by various classification algorithms; hence it is easier to compare the results with our study.

1.1 Related work

It could be observed from the following literature that lot of research has been done on Pima Indian diabetes to achieve high classification accuracy on the Pima Indian diabetes data.[4] the authors used different twenty two classification algorithm to classify type-2 diabetic patient. In their study they have achieved accuracy in the range of 67.6 to 77.7. The authors Bioch et al. 1996 have used Bayesian approach to improve the accuracy of neural networks and obtained the accuracy of 79.6% [5]. Carpenter et al. used the ARTMAP-IC neural network in which they have included distributed prediction and category instance counting to the basic fuzzy ARTMAP system. They added new capability to basic ARTMAP system to solve computational problem which is often faced in medical problem. Due to this enhancement, it has shown an improved classification accuracy of 81.0%. He has compared his result with different classification methods which are applied on same data [6]. (Polat et al. 2008) proposed a new cascade learning system based on Generalized Discriminant Analysis (GDA) and Least Square Support Vector Machine (LS-SVM).In his system first stage GDA is used to discriminate the feature variables in healthy and patient. In second stage he used LSSVM to classify the diabetes dataset. They have obtained classification accuracy 82.05% with 10-fold cross-validation [7]. In [8] the authors presented a new system in which the first step uses dimension reduction techniques to reduce the features from 8 to 4 using principal component analysis (PCA). In the next step adaptive neuro fuzzy inference system (ANFIS) is used and an accuracy of 89.47 is achieved, which was most promising in the literature of Pima Indian diabetes. In[9]the authors has developed a hybrid neural network model that includes artificial neural network (ANN) and Fuzzy neural network in which fuzzified data is presented to fuzzy neural network and obtained results are defuzzified the crisp data is presented to ANN1 result obtained in both the methods and given an input to ANN2 and final result is obtained the accuracy of 84.24.In the above mentioned methods, there are so many different classification algorithms that used the same dataset and achieved accuracy between 59.5% and 89.47%.

None of the above mentioned techniques used the proper validation of class labels, which affect the predictive performance of classification methods. The dimensionality reduction is not accomplished directly using clustering but

S.J. Pise (ed.), *ThinkQuest 2010*, DOI 10.1007/978-81-8489-989-4_25,

rather in an indirect way through the removal of training instances. The class labels, associated with Pima Indian Diabetes data set, are validated using clustering method. The instances are grouped into one cluster depending on the Euclidean distance similarity. Validation of class labels are performed based on criteria if the class labels obtained by the clustering method are same as the class labels associated with data, and then they are valid class labels. If they are different it implies that there are incorrectly classified instances. Such instances are removed from the data set. This also we called as pattern extraction to validate class labels. In our proposed method first step applies clustering method for pattern extraction and lastly the Backpropogation method is used. We achieved an accuracy of 98.45 using this method. The rest of the paper is organized as follows: In Section 2, we briefly discuss the proposed method (k-means and back propagation method) and as well as performance measure used in this study. We present the results in Section 3.

2. Method and materials

A general framework of prediction type-2 diabetic patient is described by the following two steps: (1) k-means clustering for pattern extraction, in which we validate the class labels associated with data and delete incorrectly classified instances. Remaining data is used for classification and the deletion of the data will not the impact to the classifier; (2) the widely used back propagation classification algorithm in the medical field is used. The 10 fold cross validation method is used and achieved best accuracy.

2.1 Dataset

In this proposed study the data was obtained from UCI machine learning depository [4]. The data set contains a total 768 instances and 268 belong to class '1' which indicate they are diabetic patients and 500 belong to class '0'means negative cases. The data set was randomly selected from a large volume of data set gathered by the National Institutes of Diabetes, Digestive and Kidney Diseases. All the patients in the dataset studies are at least 21 years old. Characteristics of the patients, including number of times pregnant, and age (years) were recorded.Some other important physical measures that might be closely related to diabetes are also taken. These measures are plasma glucose concentration a 2 hours oral glucose tolerance test, diastolic blood pressure (mm Hg), triceps skin fold thickness (mm), 2-Hour serum insulin (mu U/ml), body mass index (weight in kg/(height in (mm)2), and diabetes pedigree function.

2.2 Proposed system

The proposed system consists of two stages: Kmeans clustering algorithm is used for pattern extraction by using which we can validate the class labels. The Second stage consists of the most widely used neural network technique

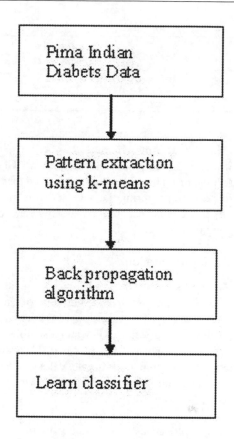

Fig. 1 Proposed system for prediction of diabetes patients

for classification Backpropagation (BP).The block diagram of the proposed System is given in Fig. 1.

2.2.1 k-means

The k-means algorithm takes the input parameter 'k' and partitions a set of 'n' objects into 'k'clusters so that the resulting intracluster similarity is high but the intercluster similarity is low. Cluster similarity is measured with regard to the mean value of the objects in a cluster [10].A set of k cluster centers are chosen at random. Each object in the dataset is allocated to the nearest cluster center. The centroid of each of these allocated sets of objects is computed, and these centroids become the new cluster centers. The process is repeated until the cluster centers do not change. Each set of objects allocated to (closest to) a cluster center is one cluster in the data. The k-means algorithm is used for partitioning, where each cluster's center is represented by the mean value of the objects in the cluster. The 'k'the number of clusters, D is data set containing 'n' objects.

The reason of choosing k-means is that Lange et al., 2004 have proved that the validation result obtained by k-means clustering is better than others where k=2 or 3 [12]. We also used the k-mediod but the misclassification rate was 50%. We only consider the result of k-means as the misclassification rate is low as compared to other methods. The rate of incorrect classification of Pima Indian diabetes

Table 1 Clustering for validating class labels

Cluster attribute	Samples	Incorrectly Classified	Error (%)
Cluster 1->y Cluster 0->n	768	255	33.21

Table 2 Confusion matrix results

		Class	Predicted
		Yes	No
Actual	Yes	128(TP)	4(FN)
Class	No	4(FP)	377(TN)

data was 33.31% as shown in Table 1.

In our study, the input data is taken from UCI machine learning repository. The 768 instances are used for clustering or pattern extraction. During the pattern extraction the class labels which are misclassified are deleted and only 513 samples remained out of 768.

2.2.2 Back propagation

Neural Networks were inspired by biological findings relates to behavior of brain as a network of units called neuron. Advantages of a neural network is that it will perform well even the data is noisy and also able to classify patterns on which it has not been trained. The most widely used learning algorithm to estimate values of weights is the back propagation Algorithm. ANN can also improve its predictive ability through iterative learning algorithms. By good quality of these inherent advantages, it has been increasingly deployed as a forecasting method in clinical medicine and urology because of these intent analysis they can be used even with less knowledge of the relationships between attributes and classes[13,14]. BP has been always regarded as universal predictor for all kind of data [15]. During the learning phase in the Back Propagation (BP) algorithm, the network learns by adjusting the weights so as to be able to predict the correct class label of the input tuples. BP have been eliminated the drawbacks associated with single layer Perceptron, which only classify the tuple linearly separable. The straight line can be drawnto separate input tuples into its correct classes. When the tuples are not lineally separable by single layer Perceptron cannot solve this problem.That can be solved by using the multilayered Perceptron such as back propagation. BP came into eminence in the late 1980's. An early version of back propagation algorithm was proposed by Werbos (1974) but its modern specification was provided and popularized by [16]. More existing work about neural network is given in [17]

In the proposed study 513 instances are remain after the pattern extraction, these are used to build the classifier with10-fold cross validation and epoch value of 500. We have used the learning factor 0.3 to train the network.The back propagation neural network was built, which consists of eight input units in the input layer and one hidden layer. Lastly the output layer which is used to predict the whether the patient may develop diabetes after five years or not.A highest classification accuracy of 98.45 was achieved which is most promising in the literature.

2.3 Performance measures of the proposed system

To measure performance of classification algorithms, one way is to divide samples into two sets, training samples and test samples. Training samples are used to build a learning model while test samples are used to evaluate the accuracy of the model. During test samples are supplied to the model, having their class labels unknown, and then their predicted class labels assigned by the model are compared with their corresponding original class labels to calculate prediction accuracy [18].

2.3.1 Accuracy, sensitivity and specificity

The confusion matrix of a two-class problem true positive (TP) and true negative (TN) are correct classifications in samples of each class, respectively. A false positive (FP) is when a class 'yes' sample is incorrectly predicted as a class 'no' sample; a false negative (FN) is when a class 'yes' sample is predicted as a class 'no' sample. Then each element of a confusion matrix shows the number of test samples for which the actual class is the row and the predicted class is the column. The values of TP, TN, FP, and FN of our studies are given Table 2.

$$Accuracy = \frac{TP + TN}{TP + TN + FP + FN} \qquad (2.1)$$

$$Sensitivity = \frac{TP}{TP + FN} \qquad (2.2)$$

$$Specificity = \frac{TN}{TN + FP} \qquad (2.3)$$

2.3.2 k-fold cross validation

In k-fold cross validation, first, a full data set is divided randomly into 'k' disjoint subsets of approximately equal size, in each of which the class is represented in approximately the sample proportions as in the full data set. Then the above process of training and testing will be repeated k times on the 'k' data subset. In each iteration (1) one of the subsets is held out in turn, (2) the classifier is trained on the remaining k-1 subsets to build classification model, (3) the classification error of this iteration is calculated by testing the classification model on the holdout set. Finally, the 'k' numbers of errors are added up to yield an overall error estimate. Obviously, at the end ofcross validation, every sample has been used exactly once for testing.

3. Result and discussion

In this study Pima Indians diabetes data was chosen from UCI machine learning repository. The data set contains 768 instances of female patients whose age is at least 21 years. In this method first we apply the pattern extraction to 768 instances. During this step the instances which are misclassified are deleted. After the pattern extraction only 513 instances remain. Here we use the widely used neural network technique back propagation to classify data. It consists eight input units one hidden layer and lastly one consist the output layer. Which finally classify the data whether class belongs to likely develop the diabetes within five years or not. In this model we have used the epoch as 500 and learning factor as 0.3.The results were achieved using 10 fold cross-validation for each model, and are based on the average results obtained from the test dataset (the 10th fold) for each fold. The hybrid prediction system (clustering and back propagation) was able to classify with an overall accuracy of 98.45%.The model was more accurate. In this section, we present the results of hybrid prediction system (K-Means and back propagation) method and compare with the Principal Component Analysis-Neurofuzzy (PCA-Neuro-fuzzy) and (GDA-LS-SVM) General Discriminant Analysis - Least Square Support Vector Machine. We use three measures for comparing the performance of proposed system which is defined in equation (2.1) is classification accuracy, sensitivity in equation (2.2) and specificity in equation (2.3). The results were achieved using 10 fold cross-validations. It is based on the average results obtained from the test dataset for each fold. In comparison to the above studies with [7] and [8] we found that our model achieved a classification accuracy of 98.45% with a sensitivity of 96.97% and a specificity of 98.96% which is given in Table 3. Figure.2 Illustrate the performance of the (k-Means, & Back propagation) method has better performance as compared to other in terms of accuracy, sensitivity and specificity. The classification accuracy of proposed method and other classifier those who have use the same data set shown in Table 4 [13].

Table 3 Proposed method results on Indian Pima diabetes data classification Accuracy, Sensitivity and Specificity compared with (polat et al. 2007, 2008)

Measures/p.	Polat 2007	Polat 2008	Propos-study
Accuracy	89.47	82.05	98.45
Sensitivity	85.71	85.71	96.97
Specificity	92.05	82.05	98.96

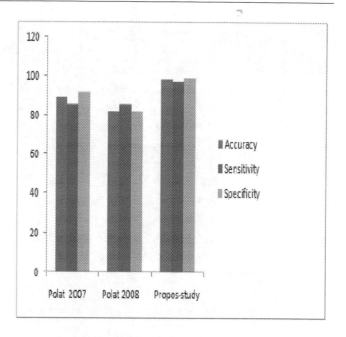

Fig. 2 Performance of proposed study (Kmeansand Back propagation) with PCA-Neurofuzzy [7] General Discriminant Analysis GDA and Least Square Support Vector Machine LSSVM[8]

Table 4 Classification accuracy obtained our study and other classification method [8]

Method	Accuracy	Author
Logdisc	77.7	Statlog
Inc Net	76.6	Norbert jankowski
DIPOL92	76.6	Statlog
Linear Disc. Anl	77.7-77.2	Statlog:Ster & Dob.
SMART	76.8	Statlog
GTO DT	76.8	Bennet and blue
Knn k=23 Manh	76.7-+4.0	WD-GM,Feature
Knn k=125 Manh	76.7+3.40	WD-GM cases k=23
ASI	76.6	Ster & Dobrikar
Fisher.discr.analy	76.5	Ster & Dobrikar
MLP+BP	76.4	Ster & Dobrikar
MLP+BP	75.8+6.2	Zamdt
LVQ	75.8	Ster & Dobrika
LFC	75.8	Ster & Dobrika
RBF	75.7	Statlog
Knn k=23 Manh	75.5	KAROL Grudzifski
MML	75.5+6.5	Zarndt
SNB	75.4	Ster & Dobrikar
BP	75.2	Statlog
SSV DT	75.0 +3.6	WD-GM,SSV,BS
Knn k=18, Euclid,	74.8+4.8	WD-GM
CART DT	74.7+5.4	Zarndt

Table 4 *Continued*

DB-CART	74.4	Ssharing & Breiman
ASR	74.3	Ster & Dobrikar
SSV DT	73.7+4.7	WD-GM,SSV,BS
C4.5 DT	73.0	Statlog
Bayes	72.2+6.9	Zarndt
C4.5(5Xcv)	72.0	Bennt ad blue
CART	72.8	Ster & Dobrika
Kohenon	72.7	Statlog
Knn	71.9	Ster & Dobrika
IB3	71.7+5.0	Zarndt
IB1	70.4+6.2	Zarndt
KNN k=1 Euclid.	69.4+4.4	WD-GM
KNN	67.6	Statlog
C4.5 rules	67.0+2.9	Zarndt
OCN2	65.1+1.1	Zarndt
Deafult	65.1	Zarndt
QDA	59.5	Ster & Dobrika
Logdisc	77.7	Statlog
Inc Net	76.6	Norbert jankowski
DIPOL92	76.6	Statlog
Linear Dis. Anl	77.7-77.2	Statlog: Ster Dobrikar
SMART	76.8	Statlog
GTO DT	76.8	Bennet and blue
BFGC quasi	77.8	Yildrim 2003
Gradient decent	77.6	Yildrim 2003
Levenberg Marqua	77.08	Yildrim 2003
RBF	68.23	Yildrium 2003
GRNN	80.21	Yildrium 2003
GDA-LS-SVM	82.05	Polat 2008
PCA-ANFIS	89.47	Polat e.al.2007
K-means+BP	98.45	Proposed Study

References

1. Diabetes Public Health Resource. Centers for disease Control.(http://www.cdc.gov/diabetes/statistics/prev/national/fig1.htm).Accessed July5, 2009
2. Little, J. W., Falace, D. A. and Miller, C. S.N.L.1997 Rhodus, Dental Management of the Medically compromised Patient
3. Hettich, D. J., Blake, C. L. and Merz, C.J. 1998.UCI Repository of machine learning databases, Irvine, CA: University of California, Department of Information and Computer Science. (last assessed: 15/6/2009)
4. Michie, D., Spiegelhalter, D. J. and Taylor, C.C. 1994.Machine learning, neural and statistical Classification, Ellis Horwood
5. Bioch, J. C., Meer, O., Potharst, R.1996.Classification using Bayesian neural nets.In Proc. IEEE Int. Conf. on neural networks, pp. 1488–1493
6. Carpenter, G. and Markuzon, A. N. 1998.ARTMAP-IC and medical diagnosis: Instance counting and inconsistent cases. *Neural Networks* no.11 pp. 323–336
7. Polat, K., Gunes, S. and Aslan, A. A.2008. Cascade learning system for classification of diabetes disease: Generalized Discriminant Analysis and least square support vector machine, Expert Systems with Applications vo.34.no.1. pp. 214–221
8. Polat K., Gunes,S. 2007.An expert systemapproach based on principal component analysis and adaptive neuro-fuzzy inference system to diagnosis of diabetes disease, Digital Signal Processing vo.17.no.4.pp. 702–710
9. Kahramanli H. and Novruz, A. 2008. Design of a hybrid system for the diabetesand heart diseases, Expert Systems with Applications no.35 pp. 82–89
10. Han, J. and Kamber, M. 2006. Data mining: Concepts and techniques, Morgan Kaufmann
11. Lange, T. Roth V., M. Braun L., buhmann, J.M. Stability-Based Validation of Clustering Solutions, Neural Computation,16(6), (2004)1299–1323
12. Wei, J. T., Zhang, Z. S. Barnhill, D., Madyastha, K. R., Zhang, H., Oesterling, J.E. Understanding artificial neural networks and exploring their potential applications for the practicing urologist, Urology vo.52.no.2.pp. 161–172
13. Lisboa, P. J. 2002. A review of evidence of health benefit from artificial neural networks in medical intervention, *Neural Network*. vo. 15 no.1.pp. 11–39
14. Shin, C., Yun, U. T., Kim, H.K. and Park, S. C. 2000. A hybrid approach of neural network and memory-based learning to data mining. *IEEE Transactions on Neural Networks*, vo.11.no.3. pp. 637–646
15. Rumelhart, D. E., Hinton, G. and Williams, R. J. 1986. Learning internal representations by error propagation. Parallel Distributed Processing: Explorations in the Microstructure of Cognition, vo. 1, MIT Press, Cambridge, MA, pp. 318–362
16. Zhang, G.2000. Neural networks for classification: a survey, IEEE Transactions on Systems, Man, and Cybernetics Part C vo.30.no.4 pp. 451–462
17. D. Delen, G. Walker, A. Kadam, Predicting breast cancer survivability: A comparison of three data mining methods. Artificial Intelligence in Medicine, (34) (2005), 113–127

Improved texture feature based image retrieval using Kekre's fast codebook generation algorithm

Dr. H. B. Kekre[1] · **Tanuja K. Sarode**[2] · **Sudeep D. Thepade**[3] · **Vaishali Suryavanshi**[4]

[1]Sr. Professor, MPSTME, NMIMS University, Mumbai, India
[2]Ph.D. Scholar, MPSTME, NMIMS University, Mumbai, India
[2]Assistant Professor, Thadomal Shahani Engineering College, Mumbai, India
[3]Ph.D. Scholar, MPSTME, NMIMS University, Mumbai, India
[3]Assistant Professor, MPSTME, NMIMS University, Mumbai, India
[4]Lecturer, Thadomal Shahani Engineering College, Mumbai, India

1. Introduction

Technological advances in digital imaging, broadband networking, and data storage have motivated people to communicate and express by sharing images, video, and other forms of media online [1]. Although the problems of acquiring, storing and transmitting the images are well addressed, capabilities to manipulate, index, sort, filter, summarize, or search through image database lack maturity. Modern image search engines [1–3, 30] retrieve the images based on their visual contents, commonly referred to as Content Based Image Retrieval (CBIR) systems. CBIR systems have found applications in various fields like fabric and fashion design, interior design as panoramic views [5, 20, 38–41], art galleries [22], museums, architecture/engineering design [22], weather forecast, geographical information systems, remote sensing and management of earth resources [40, 41], scientific database management, medical imaging, trademark and copyright database management, the military, law enforcement and criminal investigations [41], intellectual property, picture archiving and communication systems, retailing and image search on the Internet (very general image content).

Typical CBIR systems can organize and retrieve images automatically by extracting some features such as color, texture, shape from images and looking for similar images which have similar feature [37]. CBIR systems operate in two phases. In the first phase, feature extraction (FE)/indexing, a set of features, called image signature or feature vector, is generated to accurately represent the content of each image in the database. A feature vector is much smaller in size than the original image, typically of the order of hundreds of elements (rather than millions). In the second phase, similarity measurement (SM)/searching distance between the query image and each image in the database using their signatures is computed so that the most similar images can be retrieved [4]. A variety of feature extraction techniques have been developed. Color based feature extraction techniques include color histogram, color coherence vector, color moments, circular ring histogram [6], BTC extensions [34, 36]. Texture based feature extraction techniques such as co-occurrence matrix [3], Fractals [3], Gabor filters [2, 3], variations of wavelet transform [3], Kekre transform [33] have been widely used. Effort has been made in even to extend image retrieval methodologies using combination of color and texture as the case in [35] where Walshlet Pyramids are introduced. The synergy resulting from the combination of color and texture is demonstrated to be superior than using just color and texture [30, 32, 35].

In section 2 texture feature extraction using GLCM and VQ, KFCG are discussed. In section 3, technique for image retrieval using vector quantization is proposed. Results and discussion are given in section 4 and conclusions are presented in section 5.

2. Texture feature extraction methods

In section Texture is important component of human visual perception and can be effectively used for identifying different image regions [7]. Compared with color and shape features, texture features indicate the shape distribution, better suits the macrostructure and microstructure of the images [8]. Texture representation methods can be classified into three categories, namely structural, statistical and multi-resolution filtering methods. Typical structure based methods include morphological and graph techniques, which describe the texture using structural

S.J. Pise (ed.), *ThinkQuest 2010*, DOI 10.1007/978-81-8489-989-4_26,
© Springer India Pvt. Ltd. 2011

primitives and layout. Statistical methods are commonly used and proved to be effective in texture analysis. Methods based on multi resolution decompose a texture image into different scale from which more statistics can be extracted and used to describe texture features. These methods have been effectively used for solving texture recognition problem [7]. The identification of specific textures in an image is achieved primarily by modeling texture as a two-dimensional gray level variation [3]. This two dimensional array is called as Gray level Co-occurrence Matrix (GLCM). GLCM describes the frequency of one gray tone appearing in a specified spatial linear relationship with another gray tone, within the area under investigation.

2.1 GLCM method

Normalized probability density Pij of the co-occurrence matrices can be defined as follows:

$$P_\delta(i,j) = \frac{\#\{(x,y),(x+d,y+d) \in S \mid f(x,y)=i, f(x+d,y+d)=j\}}{\#S} \quad (1)$$

where x, y = 0, 1, ...N-1 are co-ordinates of the pixel i, j = 0, 1, ...L-1 are the gray levels. S is set of pixel pairs which have certain relationship in the image. #S is the number of elements in S. $P_\delta(i, j)$ is the probability density that the first pixel has intensity value i and the second j, which are separated by distance $\delta=(dx, dy)$.

The GLCM is computed in four directions for $\delta=00$, $\delta=450$, $\delta=900$, $\delta=1350$. Based on the GLCM four statistical parameters energy, contrast, entropy and correlation are computed. Finally a feature vector is computed using the means and variances of all the parameters [8, 9]. The steps for texture feature extraction using GLCM are as given below

i.   Separate the R, G, B planes of image.
ii. Repeat steps iii-vi for each plane.
iii. Compute four GLCM matrices (directions for $\delta=00$, $\delta=450$, $\delta=900$, $\delta= 1350$) as given by eq. (1)
iv. For each GLCM matrix compute the statistical features Energy(Angular second moment), Entropy(ENT), Correlation(COR), Contrast(CON) [8, 9] using the equations mentioned below:

Energy: measures textural uniformity (i.e. pixel pairs repetitions).and can be given as Angular Second Moment (ASM)

$$ASM = \sum\sum P^2(i,j) \quad (2)$$

Contrast (CON): Contrast indicates the variance of the gray level.

$$CON = \sum\sum (i-j)^2 P(i,j) \quad (3)$$

Entropy (ENT): This parameter measures the disorder of the image. For texturally uniform image, entropy is small.

$$ENT = -\sum\sum P(i,j) \log[P(i,j)] \quad (3)$$

Correlation: (COR)

$$COR = \frac{\sum\sum ij P(i-j) - \mu_x \mu_y}{\sigma_x \sigma_y} \quad (4)$$

Where μ_x, μ_y, σ_x, σ_y are the means and standard deviations of P_x and P_y respectively. P_x is the sum of each row in co-occurance matrix. P_y is the sum of each column in the co-occurance matrix.

v. Thus we obtained

ASM0	ENT0	COR0	CON0
ASM 45	ENT 45	COR 45	CON 45
ASM 90	ENT 90	COR 90	CON 90
ASM 135	ENT 135	COR 135	CON 135

vi. Compute the feature vector using the means and variances of all the parameters. Thus, the feature vector f ={μASM, μENT, μCOR, μCON, σASM, σENT, σCOR, σCON } Where μ is mean and σ is variance of the parameters.

2.2 VQ based methods

Vector Quantization (VQ) [10–18] is an efficient technique for data compression and has been successfully used in various applications such as index compression [19]. VQ has been very popular in variety of research fields such as video-based event detection [23] and anomaly intrusion detection systems [24], image segmentation [25–28], speech data compression [29], CBIR [30, 32] and face recognition [31].VQ [10–18] can be defined as the mapping function that maps k-dimensional vector space to the finite set CB = { C1, C2, C3,.... , CN}. The set CB is called codebook consisting of N number of codevectors and each codevector Ci = {ci1, ci2, ci3, ..., cik} is of dimension k. The key to VQ is the good codebook. This codebook is the signature/feature vector of the entire image and can be generated by employing various clustering techniques. The method most commonly used to generate codebook is the Linde-Buzo-Gray (LBG) algorithm which is also called as Generalized Lloyd Algorithm (GLA) [32, 33]. The drawback of LBG algorithm is that the cluster elongation is –450 to 1350 horizontal axis in two dimensional cases. This results in inefficient clustering. Kekre's Proportionate algorithm (KPE) removes the disadvantage of LBG. However, LBG and KPE algorithms require heavy computations. Kekre's Fast Codebook Generation algorithm (KFCG) requires less errors and least time to generate codebook as compared to other algorithms, as it does not require computation of Euclidian distance [30].

To generate the codebook, the image is first divided into fixed size blocks, each forming a training vector $Xi = (xi1, xi2, \ldots, xik)$. The set of training vectors is a training set. This training set is initial cluster. The clustering algorithms like LBG, KPE, and KFCG etc are then applied on this initial cluster to generate the codebook of desired size. Below, LBG, KPE and KFCG algorithms for codebook generation are discussed.

2.3 Kekre's fast codebook generation algorithm (KFCG) [30]

In this algorithm, the centroid C1 is computed as the first codevector for the training set. In the first iteration of the algorithm, the clusters are formed by comparing first element of training vector with first element of code vector C1. The vector Xi is grouped into the cluster 1 if $xi1 < c11$ otherwise vector Xi is grouped into cluster 2 as shown in Fig. 1a. where codevector dimension space is 2. In second iteration, the cluster 1 is split into two by comparing second element $xi2$ of vector Xi belonging to cluster 1 with that of the second element of the codevector which is centroid of cluster 1. Cluster 2 is split into two by comparing the second element $xi2$ of vector Xi belonging to cluster 2 with that of

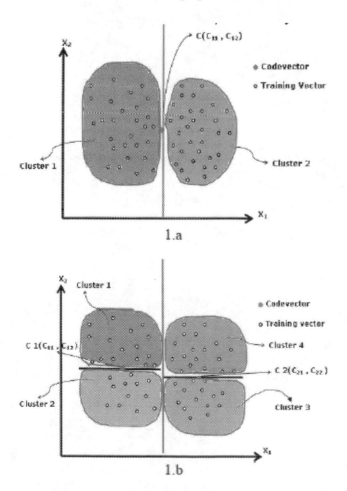

1.a

1.b

Fig. 1 KFCG algorithm for 2 dimensional case

the second element of the codevector which is centroid of cluster 2, as shown in Fig. 1b. This procedure is repeated till the codebook size is reached to the size specified by user.

3. CBIR using KFCG

Image retrieval based on content requires extraction of features of the image, matching these features with the features of the images in the database and retrieving the images with the most similar features. Here, we discuss the feature extraction technique based on vector quantization.

3.1 Proposed feature extraction technique

i.   Repeat steps 2–6 for each image in the image database.
ii. Divide the image into blocks of size 2×2 (Each pixel having red, blue and green component, thus resulting in a vector of 12 components per block)
iii. Form the training set/initial cluster from these vectors.
iv. Compute the initial centroid of the cluster.
v.   Obtain the codebook of desired size using KFCG algorithm. This codebook represents the feature vector/signature of the image.
vi. Store the feature vector obtained in step v in the feature vector database.

3.2 Query execution

For a given query image compute the feature vector using the proposed feature extraction technique. To retrieve the most similar images, compare the query feature vector with the feature vectors in database. This is done by computing the distance between the query feature vector with those in feature vector database. Euclidian distance as given in equation (6) and correlation coefficient are most commonly used as similarity measure in CBIR [4]. Here Euclidian distance is used as a similarity measure. As compared to GLCM method, this proposed method saves tremendous number of computations. Also the accuracy of the proposed VQ technique is much better than that of GLCM.

4. Results and discussions

These methods are implemented in Matlab 7.0 on Intel Core 2 Duo Processor T8100, 2.1 GHz, 2 GB RAM machine to obtain results. The results are obtained on the general database consisting of 1000 images from 11 different categories and the Columbia Object Image Library (COIL) database that consists of 7200 images from 100 different categories. To test the proposed method, from every class five query images are selected randomly. So in all 500 query images are used from COIL database and 55 query images are used from general database. To check the performance of proposed technique we have used precision and recall. The standard definitions of these two measures are given by following equations.

$$Precision = \frac{Number\_of\_relevant\_images\_retrieved}{Total\_number\_of\_images\_retrieved} \quad (6)$$

$$Recall = \frac{Number\_of\_relevant\_images\_retrieved}{Total\_number\_of\_relevent\_images\_in\_database} \quad (7)$$

The crossover point of precision and recall acts as performance measure of CBIR technique. Higher value of precision-recall at crossover point indicates better performance of image retrieval method. For both COIL database results are obtained using KFCG for the codebook of sizes 16, 32, 64, 128 and 256. For general database results are taken by considering the codebook sizes 16, 32, 64, 128 and 512.

Figure 2 shows the sample database of 11 images by randomly selecting one image from each category of general image database. General database has total 1000 images spread across 11 categories. The images are of varying sizes ranging from 384×256 to 84×128. Figure 3 shows the sample database of the images from the COIL database. Each image in the COIL database is of size 128×128. Each object was rotated in 72 different angles with variation of 5 degrees, resulting in 72 images per object in the database.

Figure 4 shows the average precision curves of GLCM based image retrieval and proposed KFCG based image retrieval techniques obtained by testing 500 query images from COIL image database. Proposed KFCG CBIR techniques have much higher precision values showing that the KFCG based image retrieval is better than GLCM based image retrieval.

Figure 5 justifies the same observation that KFCG gives better retrieval of images than GLCM, with the help of average recall curves for COIL image database.

The average precision values of the 55 queries tested on general image database are shown in Fig. 6. The higher average precision values of KFCG based CBIR proves that KFCG outperforms GLCM even for general database.

Fig. 2 Sample database of 11 images by randomly selecting one image from each category from general image database

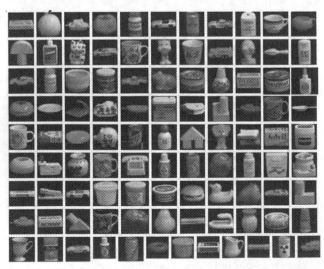

Fig. 3 Sample database consisting of 7200 Images, the database has 100 categories, 72 images in each category

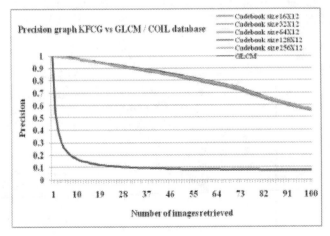

Fig. 4 Average precision of GLCM-CBIR and KFCG-CBIR techniques for COIL image database

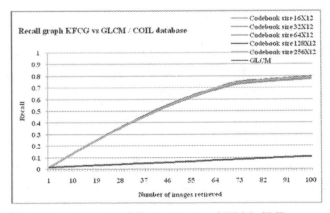

Fig. 5 Average recall of GLCM-CBIR and KFCG-CBIR techniques for COIL image database

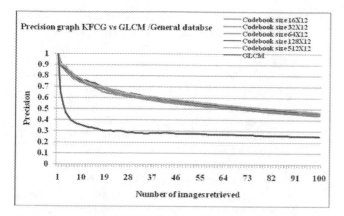

Fig. 6 Average precision of GLCM-CBIR and KFCG-CBIR techniques for general image database

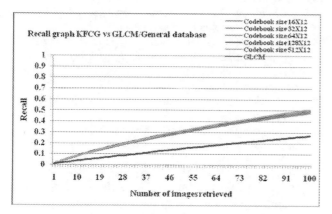

Fig. 7 Average recall of GLCM-CBIR and KFCG-CBIR techniques for general image database

The average recall values of the 55 queries tested on general image database are shown in Fig. 7. The higher average recall values of KFCG based CBIR proves that KFCG outperforms GLCM even for general database. As KFCG based image retrieval techniques are far better in performance than GLCM based image retrieval technique, one can state that KFCG based texture features have better decrimination capability than GLCM based texture features.

The crossover point of precision and recall plays very vital role in deciding the performance of image retrieval technique. Higher values of crossover points indicate better performance. Figures 8 and 9 are giving the crossover points of average precision and average recall curves Average Precision and Average Recall curves for COIL image database and general image database respectively. The higher values of crossover points for KFCG based image retrieval confirm that these are better than GLCM based image retrieval methods.

Figure 10 gives the performance comparison of KFCG based image retrieval for various codebook sizes for COIL image database. The height of crossover point of precision and recall indicates the performance of respective image

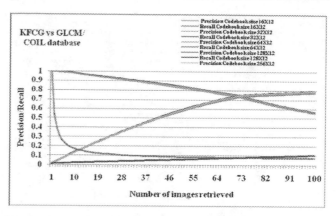

Fig. 8 Average Precision and Average Recall curves shown together for crossover points of discussed CBIR techniques for COIL image database.

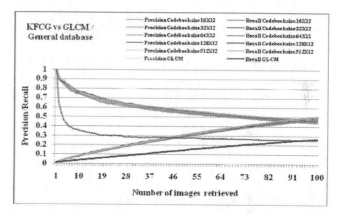

Fig. 9 Average precision and average recall curves shown together for crossover points of discussed CBIR techniques for general image database

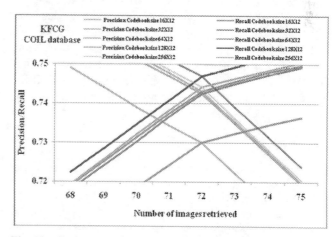

Fig. 10 Crossover points of average precision and average recall for KFCG CBIR with various codebook sizes for COIL image database

retrieval technique. Here consistently the performance is improving with increasing codebook size from codebook size 16 to 128. After the optimum codebook size, if further the codebook size is increased the image retrieval

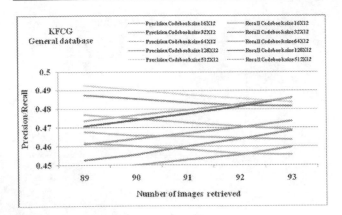

Fig. 11 Crossover points of average precision and average recall for KFCG CBIR with various codebook sizes for general image database

performance is degraded because of the voids generated in cluster. Hence 256 codebook size is giving lower performance that 128.

Figure 11 shows the performance comparison of KFCG based image retrieval for various codebook sizes for general image database. The height of crossover point of precision and recall indicates the performance of respective image retrieval technique. Here consistently the performance is improving with increasing codebook size from codebook size 16 to 512.

5. Conclusion

Grey Level Co-occurrence Matrix (GLCM) is one of the widely used techniques for texture feature extraction in image retrieval. The paper presented novel Kekre's Fast Codebook Generation (KFCG) algorithm based image retrieval techniques. The proposed CBIR methods are tested on both COIL image database and general image database. The experimental results proved that with higher precision and recall values KFCG based image retrieval gives better discrimination capability and higher performance than GLCM. In various codebook sizes considered for KFCG higher codebook sizes gives better performance up to some optimum codebook size.

References

1. Nuno Vasconcelos, "From pixels to semantic spaces: Advances in Content-Based Image Retrieval", published by IEEE computer society
2. Qasim Iqbal, J. K. Aggarwal, " CIRES: A System for Content-Based Retrieval in Digital Image Libraries", in the seventh international conference on Control, Automation, Robotics and Vision (ICARCV'02), Dec 2002, Singapore
3. Sanjoy Kumar Saha, Amit Kumar Das, Bhabatosh Chanda, " CBIR using Perception based Texture and Color Measures", in Proc. of 17th International Conference on Pattern Recognition(ICPR'04), Vol. 2, Aug 2004
4. H.B.Kekre, Sudeep D. Thepade, "Image Retrieval using Augmented Block Truncation Coding Techniques", ACM International Conference on Advances in Computing,

Communication and Control (ICAC3-2009), pp. 384-390, 23-24 Jan 2009, Fr. Conceicao Rodrigous College of Engg., Mumbai. Is uploaded on online ACM portal
5. H.B.Kekre, Sudeep D. Thepade, "Appraise of SPIT Problem", SPIT-IEEE Colloquium and International Conference, 04-05 Feb 2008, Sardar Patel Institute of Technology, Andheri, Mumbai
6. Wang Xiaoling, " A Novel Cicular Ring Histogram for Content-based Image Retrieval", First International Workshop on Education Technology and Computer Science, 2009
7. Junyu Dong, Muwei Jian, Dawei Gao, Shengke Wang, "Reducing the Dimensionality of Feature Vectors for Textual Image Retrieval Based On Wavelet Decomposition", Eighth ACIS International Conference on Software Engineering, Artificial Intelligence, Networking and Parallel/Distributed Computing
8. Xiaoyi Song, Yongjie Li, Wufan Chen, "A Textural Feature Based Image Retrieval Algorithm", in Proc. of 4th Int. Conf. on Natural Computation, Oct. 2008
9. Jing Zhang, Gui-li Li, Seok-wum He, "Texture-Based Image Retrieval By Edge Detection Matching GLCM", in Proc. of 10th International conference on High Performance Computing and Comm., Sept. 2008
10. R. M. Gray, "Vector quantization", IEEE ASSP Mag., pp.: 4-29, Apr. 1984
11. Y. Linde, A. Buzo, and R. M. Gray, "An algorithm for vector quantizer design, " IEEE Trans.Commun., vol. COM-28, no. 1, pp.: 84-95, 1980
12. H.B.Kekre, Tanuja K. Sarode, "New Fast Improved Clustering Algorithm for Codebook Generation for Vector Quantization", Int. Conf. on Engg. Technologies and Applications in Engg, Technology and Sciences, Computer Science Department, Saurashtra University, Rajkot, Gujarat. (India), Amoghsiddhi Education Society, Sangli, Maharashtra (India), 13th – 14th January 2008
13. H. B. Kekre, Tanuja K. Sarode, "New Fast Improved Codebook Generation Algorithm for Color Images using Vector Quantization, " International Journal of Engineering and Technology, vol.1, No.1, pp.: 67-77, September 2008
14. H. B. Kekre, Tanuja K. Sarode, "Fast Codebook Generation Algorithm for Color Images using Vector Quantization, " International Journal of Computer Science and Information Technology, Vol. 1, No. 1, pp.: 7-12, Jan 2009
15. H. B. Kekre, Tanuja K. Sarode, "An Efficient Fast Algorithm to Generate Codebook for Vector Quantization, " First International Conference on Emerging Trends in Engineering and Technology, ICETET-2008, held at Raisoni College of Engineering, Nagpur, India, pp.: 62- 67, 16-18 July 2008. Avaliable at IEEE Xplore
16. H. B. Kekre, Tanuja K. Sarode, "Fast Codebook Generation Algorithm for Color Images using Vector Quantization, " International Journal of Computer Science and Information Technology, Vol. 1, No. 1, pp.: 7-12, Jan 2009
17. H. B. Kekre, Tanuja K. Sarode, "Fast Codevector Search Algorithm for 3-D Vector Quantized Codebook", WASET International Journal of cal Computer Information Science and Engineering (IJCISE), Volume 2, No. 4, pp.: 235-239, Fall 2008. Available: http://www.waset.org/ijcise
18. H. B. Kekre, Tanuja K. Sarode, "Fast Codebook Search Algorithm for Vector Quantization using Sorting Technique",

ACM International Conference on Advances in Computing, Communication and Control (ICAC3-2009), pp: 317-325, 23-24 Jan 2009, Fr. Conceicao Rodrigous College of Engg., Mumbai. Available on ACM portal

19. Jim Z.C. Lai, Yi-Ching Liaw, and Julie Liu, "A fast VQ codebook generation algorithm using codeword displacement", Pattern Recogn. vol. 41, no. 1, pp.: 315–319, 2008

20. H.B.Kekre, Sudeep D. Thepade, "Panoramic View Construction using Partial Images", IEEE sponsored International Conference on Sensors, Signal Processing, Communication, Control and Instrumentation (SSPCCIN-2008) 03-05 Jan 2008, Vishwakarma Institute of Technology, Pune

21. Chin-Chen Chang, Wen-Chuan Wu, "Fast Planar-Oriented Ripple Search Algorithm for Hyperspace VQ Codebook", IEEE Transaction on image processing, vol 16, no. 6, pp.: 1538-1547, June 2007

22. H.B.Kekre, Sudeep D. Thepade, "Vista creation using Picture Parts", International Conference on Emerging Technologies and Applications in Engineering, Technology and Sciences (ICETAETS-2008), 12-13 Jan 2008, Held at Computer Science Dept., Saurashtra University, Rajkot, Gujarat. (India)

23. H. Y. M. Liao, D. Y. Chen, C. W. Su, and H. R. Tyan, "Real-time event detection and its applications to surveillance systems, " in Proc. IEEE Int. Symp. Circuits and Systems, Kos, Greece, pp.: 509–512, May 2006

24. J. Zheng and M. Hu, "An anomaly intrusion detection system based on vector quantization, " IEICE Trans. Inf. Syst., vol. E89-D, no. 1, pp.: 201–210, Jan. 2006

25. H. B. Kekre, Tanuja K. Sarode, Bhakti Raul, "Color Image Segmentation using Kekre's Fast Codebook Generation Algorithm Based on Energy Ordering Concept", ACM International Conference on Advances in Computing, Communication and Control (ICAC3-2009), pp.: 357-362, 23-24 Jan 2009, Fr. Conceicao Rodrigous College of Engg., Mumbai. Available on ACM portal

26. H. B. Kekre, Tanuja K. Sarode, Bhakti Raul, "Color Image Segmentation using Kekre's Algorithm for Vector Quantization", International Journal of Computer Science (IJCS), Vol. 3, No. 4, pp.: 287-292, Fall 2008. Available: http://www.waset.org/ijcs

27. H. B. Kekre, Tanuja K. Sarode, Bhakti Raul, "Color Image Segmentation using Vector Quantization Techniques Based on Energy Ordering Concept" International Journal of Computing Science and Communication Technologies (IJCSCT) Volume 1, Issue 2, pp: 164-171, January 2009

28. H. B. Kekre, Tanuja K. Sarode, Bhakti Raul, "Color Image Segmentation Using Vector Quantization Techniques", Advances in Engineering Science Sect. C (3), pp.: 35-42, July-September 2008

29. H. B. Kekre, Tanuja K. Sarode, "Speech Data Compression using Vector Quantization", WASET International Journal of Computer and Information Science and Engineering (IJCISE), vol. 2, No. 4, pp.: 251-254, Fall 2008. available: http://www.waset.org/ijcise

30. H. B. Kekre, Ms. Tanuja K. Sarode, Sudeep D. Thepade, "Image Retrieval using Color-Texture Features from DCT on VQ Codevectors obtained by Kekre's Fast Codebook Generation", ICGST-International Journal on Graphics, Vision and Image Processing (GVIP), Volume 9, Issue 5, pp.: 1-8, September 2009. Available online at http://www.icgst.com/gvip/Volume9/Issue5/P1150921752.html

31. H. B. Kekre, Kamal Shah, Tanuja K. Sarode, Sudeep D. Thepade, "Performance Comparison of Vector Quantization Technique – KFCG with LBG, Existing Transforms and PCA for Face Recognition", International Journal of Information Retrieval (IJIR), Vol. 02, Issue 1, pp.: 64-71, 2009

32. H.B.Kekre, Tanuja Sarode, Sudeep D. Thepade, "Color-Texture Feature based Image Retrieval using DCT applied on Kekre's Median Codebook", International Journal on Imaging (IJI), Volume 2, Number A09, Autumn 2009, pp. 55-65. Available online at www.ceser.res.in/iji.html (ISSN: 0974-0627)

33. H.B.Kekre, Sudeep D. Thepade, "Image Retrieval using Non-Involutional Orthogonal Kekre's Transform", International Journal of Multidisciplinary Research and Advances in Engineering (IJMRAE), Ascent Publication House, 2009, Volume 1, No.I, 2009. Abstract available online at www.ascent-journals.com

34. H.B.Kekre, Sudeep D. Thepade, "Color Based Image Retrieval using Amendment Block Truncation Coding with YCbCr Color Space", International Journal on Imaging (IJI), Volume 2, Number A09, Autumn 2009, pp. 2-14. Available online at www.ceser.res.in/iji.html (ISSN: 0974-0627)

35. H.B.Kekre, Sudeep D. Thepade, "Image Retrieval using Color-Texture Features Extracted from Walshlet Pyramid", ICGST International Journal on Graphics, Vision and Image Processing (GVIP), Volume 10, Issue I, Feb.2010, pp.9-18, Available online www.icgst.com/gvip/Volume10/Issue1/P1150938876.html

36. H.B.Kekre, Sudep D. Thepade, "Using YUV Color Space to Hoist the Performance of Block Truncation Coding for Image Retrieval", In Proc. of IEEE International Advanced Computing Conference 2009 (IACC'09), Thapar University, Patiala, INDIA, 6-7 March 2009

37. H.B.Kekre, Sudeep D. Thepade, "Rendering Futuristic Image Retrieval System", In Proc. of National Conference on Enhancements in Computer, Communication and Information Technology, EC2IT-2009, 20-21 Mar 2009, K.J. Somaiya College of Engineering, Vidyavihar, Mumbai-77

38. H.B.Kekre, Sudeep D. Thepade, "Creating the Color Panoramic View using Medley of Grayscale and Color Partial Images ", WASET International Journal of Electrical, Computer and System Engineering (IJECSE), Volume 2, No. 3, Summer 2008. Available online at www.waset.org/ijecse/v2/v2-3-26.pdf

39. H.B.Kekre, Sudeep D. Thepade, "Rotation Invariant Fusion of Partial Images in Vista Creation", WASET International Journal of Electrical, Computer and System Engineering (IJECSE), Volume 2, No. 2, Spring 2008. Available online at www.waset.org/ijecse/v2/v2-2-13.pdf

40. H.B.Kekre, Sudeep D. Thepade, "Scaling Invariant Fusion of Image Pieces in Panorama Making and Novel Image Blending Technique", International Journal on Imaging (IJI), Autumn 2008, Volume 1, No. A08, Available online at www.ceser.res.in/iji.html (ISSN: 0974-0627)

41. H.B.Kekre, Sudeep D. Thepade, "Image Blending In Vista Creation using Kekre's LUV Color Space", SPIT-IEEE Colloquium and International Conference, 04-05 Feb 2008, SPIT Andheri, Mumbai

Interference avoidance in wireless systems

Ashish A. Kulkarni · Prof. D. V. Thombre

Terna Engineering College, Navi Mumbai, India

1. Introduction

Wireless system designers have always had contend with interference from both natural sources and other users of the medium. Thus, the classical wireless communications design cycle has consisted of measuring or predicting channel impairments, choosing a modulation method, signal pre-conditioning at the transmitter and processing at the receiver to reliably reconstruct the transmitted information. These methods have evolved from simple (like FM and pre-emphasis) to relatively complex (like CDMA and adaptive equalization). However, all share a common attribute – once the modulation method is chosen, it is difficult to change. For example, an ASK system cannot be simply modified to obtain a PSK system owing to the complexities of the transmission and reception hardware.

Universal radios [1] change this paradigm by providing the communications engineer with a radio which can be programmed to produce almost arbitrary output waveforms and act as an almost arbitrary receiver type. Thus, it is o longer unthinkable to instruct the transmitting and receiving radios to use a more effective modulation in a given situation. Of course, practical radios of this sort are probably many years away. Nonetheless, if Moore's law holds true, they are certainly on the not-too-distant horizon.

It is therefore probable that wireless systems of the near future will have elements which adapt dynamically to changing patterns of interference by adjusting modulation and processing methods in much the same way that power control is used today.

The 802.11 specification defines two types of operational modes: ad hoc (peer-to-peer) mode and infrastructure mode. In ad hoc mode, the wireless network is relatively simple and consists of 802.11 network interface cards (NICs). The networked computers communicate directly with one another without the use of an access point(AP). In infrastructure mode, the wireless network is composed of a wireless access point(s) and 802.11 network interface cards (NICs). The access point acts as a base station in an 802.11 network and all communications from all of the wireless clients go through the access point. The access point also provides for increased wireless range, growth of the number of wireless users, and additional network security [2].

The level of performance of an 802.11 WLAN is dependent on a number of important environmental and product specific factors. Access points will automatically negotiate the appropriate signaling rate based upon environmental conditions, such as: Distance between WLAN devices (AP and NICs), transmission power levels, building and home materials, radio frequency interference, signal propagation, antenna type and location.

The contents of a home or office building can have a dramatic impact on the quality of the signal obtained with an 802.11 wireless network. The wood, metal, and other building materials have a direct impact on signal propagation and absorption. Other factors include:

- Multi-path interference: This occurs when signal strength and timing are altered due to the signal reflecting off walls, filing cabinets, beams, and other objects. This results in a device receiving two or more
- Fading: Fading is the reduced amplitude of a signal as a result of passing through radio-transparent objects such as walls and ceilings.

S.J. Pise (ed.), *ThinkQuest 2010*, DOI 10.1007/978-81-8489-989-4_27,
© Springer India Pvt. Ltd. 2011

- Dead zones: Locations where radio signals never reach due to reflections, obstructions, or other environmental conditions.
- Thus the interference is an important factor, which affects the QOS of wireless LAN. It is necessary to reduce this interference to improve the performance of the network. We use the interference avoidance (IA) algorithm available in the literature used for CDMA. [3] And [4]. Section 2 reviews the Eigen algorithm, Section 3 presents the scenario of a wireless LAN, where the IA algorithm is used to reduce the interference. In section 4, results and conclusions are given.

Interference avoidance: A review

Interference avoidance methods allow users in a CDMA system to adapt their code words (signature sequences) to achieve better performance. The main criterion used in the codeword adaptation process is maximization of the signal-to interferenceplus-noise-ratio (SINR). We consider the uplink of a synchronous CDMA system in which each user l is assigned a unit norm N-dimensional codeword x_l to convey its information symbol b_l. The received signal vector at the base station receiver is

$$r = \sum_{l=1}^{L} \Lambda_l x_l + n = Sb + n \qquad (1)$$

where S is the N × L codeword matrix having the user code words S_l as columns, $b-[b_1 \ . \ \dots \ b_l]$ is the vector containing the information symbols sent by users, and n is the additive noise vector that corrupts the received signal. The covariance matrix of the received signal is

$$R = E[rr^T] = SS^T + W \qquad (2)$$

Assuming simple matched filters at the receiver for all users, the SINR for user 1 is with $R_l = R - s_l s_l^T$ being the covariance matrix of the interference-plus-noise seen by user l.

In this framework, greedy interference avoidance is defined by replacement of user l codeword S_l with the minimum eigenvector of R_l. This procedure is referred to as greedy interference avoidance since by replacing its current codeword with the minimum eigenvector of the interferenceplus- noise correlation matrix, user k avoids interference by placing its transmitted energy in that region of the signal space with minimum interference-plus-noise energy and greedily maximizes SINR without looking at the potentially negative effects this action may have on other users in the system.

An important property of greedy interference avoidance, namely that it monotonically increases sum capacity defined in this context as

$$C_s = \frac{1}{2}\log|R| - \frac{1}{2}\log|W| \qquad (3)$$

Sequential application by all users of this Greedy SINR maximization procedure defines the Eigen-algorithm for interference avoidance, formally stated as follows.

Eigen-algorithm

1. Start with a randomly chosen codeword ensemble specified by the codeword matrix S
2. For each user l = 1,. . . , L, replace user l codeword S_l with the minimum eigenvector of the autocorrelation matrix of the corresponding interference-plus-noise process R_l.
3. Repeat step 2 until a fixed point is reached.

The monotonically increase in sum capacity, along with the fact that sum capacity is upper bounded; ensure convergence of the Eigen-algorithm to a fixed point. Empirical evidence has shown that when starting with randomly chosen code words, this fixed point is the optimal point where sum capacity Cs is maximized. A thorough theoretical analysis of Eigen-algorithm fixed point properties can be found in. Thus, the Eigen algorithm always converges to the optimal fixed point where the resulting codeword ensemble maximizes sum capacity. Figure 2 shows the user screen for implementing this algorithm.

Interference avoidance in wireless LAN

A typical setup of a wireless LAN is shown in Fig. 1. Here each terminal is considered as a user in CDMA system and Access point is considered as a Base station. Initially all terminals choose a codeword randomly to transmit its information and informs to the AP.

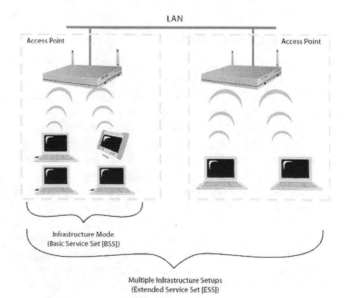

Fig. 1 A typical setup of a wireless LAN

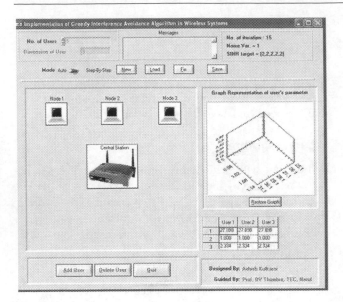

Fig. 2 Implementation of interference avoidance in wireless systems showing graphical representation and table for Eigen values calculations

Access point make a codeword matrix S of all terminals and calculates autocorrelation matrix for each terminal. This is correlation of the terminals signature with other terminal's signature R_1.

This information is broadcasted to each terminal back. Based on this, each terminal calculates the minimum Eigen vector of the autocorrelation matrix. This Eigen vector is the new signature chosen by the terminal and informs to the access point, that this is the new signature.

This process is repeated till the fixed point is reached for all terminals and this set of signature are used by all the terminals and other terminals do not know about it.

2. Summary and conclusion

Starting from a general signal space foundation, we have derived a class of interference avoidance algorithms whereby individual users asynchronously adjust their transmitted waveforms and corresponding matched filter receivers to minimize interference from other sources, including other users. This method presupposes that transmitters and receivers are waveform agile as would be the case assuming universal radios are inexpensive and ubiquitous.

The interference avoidance procedure, based on SIR as opposed to individual capacity maximization, minimizes total square correlation (TSC). We pursued the relation between sum capacity maximization and minimization of TSC and found equivalence in a white noise environment. Specifically, minimization of total square correlation results in signature sets which can also be used to achieve sum channel capacity (through Gaussian signaling).

Numerical experiments were conducted which corroborated the basic analytic results. Further experiments, aimed at determining whether interference avoidance might be used in practical systems were also conducted. These included measurements of convergence speed and codeword set volatility under the addition or deletion of a single user. In all cases the results were encouraging. It is also worth noting that experimentally, suboptimal sets were never obtained when starting from randomly chosen code words and no modifications of the basic interference avoidance procedure were necessary.

Simple comparisons to synchronous CDMA show that for a single cell, the number of users serviceable at reasonable SIRs is much greater and scales approximately with the required SIR. This is not surprising since almost any scheme which attempts to orthogonalize signature waveforms will have much greater capacity than a single base CDMA system. More telling is the comparison of systems for multiple bases where rough calculations suggest substantial improvement may be had using interference avoidance methods, although these results must be interpreted in light of the fact that the behavior of multiple base interference avoidance is as yet unknown. Furthermore, aside from the assumption of waveform agility and the necessity of measuring interference to calculate the optimal signature, the optimum linear transmit and receive methods are very simple matched filter detection.

Nevertheless, owing to the simplicity of the concept and the ever increasing sophistication of radio hardware, we expect that interference avoidance will afford an interesting new perspective which might even evolve into a practical method for wireless system design. If so, we expect it to be especially useful in unlicensed bands such as the U-NII, where users can mutually interfere with officially sanctioned impunity.

The interference avoidance procedure, based on SINR minimizes total square correlation (TSC). We applied the IA algorithm in wireless LAN to reduce the interference. Here each terminal adapts its signature or code word greedily and hence improves its SINR, by doing so all terminals try to improve the performance of the network. We show a set of signature set utilized by the terminals. Specifically, minimization of total square correlation results in signature sets.

References

1   Special issue on software radio. *IEEE Personal Communications Magazine*, 6(4), August 1999. Editors: K-C. Chen and R. Prasad and H.V. Poor

2   S. Ulukus, Power Control, Multiuser Detection and Interference Avoidance in CDMA Systems, Ph.D. thesis, RutgersUniv., Dept. Electrical and Computer Engineering, 1998 (thesis director: Prof. R. D. Yates)

3   C. Rose, S. Ulukus, and R. Yates, Wireless systems and interference avoidance, IEEE Trans. Wireless Communication.

1(3): (July2002).preprint available at http:/steph.rutgers.edu/ crose/ papers/ avoid17.ps

4. C. Rose, S. Ulukus, and R. Yates. Wireless Systems and Interference Avoidance. IEEE Journal on Selected Areas in Communications, 2001. http://steph.rutgers.edu/crose/papers/ avoid16.ps

5. H. Liuetal.,"Capacity Analysis of cellular Data System with 3G/WLAN I Interworking", in Proceedings of IEEE Vehicular Technology Conference, fall 2003

6. O.Yilmaz, "Access Selection in Cellular and WLAN Multi-Access Networks", Master Thesis, Royal Institute of Technology, Sweden, February2003, available at www.s3.kth.se/radio

A novel approach to ECG signal analysis using higher-order spectrum

Sachin N. Gore[1] · D. T. Ingole[2]

[1]Principal Kalavidya Mandir Institute of Technology (Polytechnic), Mumbai, India
[2]Professor & Head, Department of Electronics and Telecummunication,
Professor Ram Meghe Institute of Technology and Research, Badnera, Amaravati, India

1. Introduction

In practice, many medical signals show significant nonlinear and non-Gaussian characteristics, such as presence of non-Linear effects of phase coupling among the signal frequency components. The methods based on spectral analysis fail to properly deal with the nonlinearity and non-Gaussianility of the process but HOS allows us to effectively process this kind of signals to obtain their higher-order statistics. Bispectral estimation has been shown to be a very useful tool for extracting the degree of quadratic phase coupling (QPC) between individual frequency components of the process.

Phase correlations among rhythmic events at different frequencies are introduced only by on-linear interactions [3]. Thus non-linear alysis methods have to be applied for the detection of non-linear correlations. One such method for the study of such non-linear effects is to quantify the deviation of the measured ECG signal from Gaussianity by utilizing the higher order spectra [3]. This approach often detects important quadratic phase correlations present among the other higher order correlations.

Quadratic phase coupling occurs when two waves interact non-linearly and generate a hird wave with a frequency equal to the um/difference of the first two waves

2. Theoretical framework

This section describes the various higher order spectral techniques in detail and states their applications and utilizations in the human ECG signal analysis. The first of the higher order spectrum (HOS) is the third order spectrum and has received a lot of attention [5, 6]. The Bispectrum yields information in cases where the random process has a skewed distribution. The paper begins by examining the concepts of skewness and kurtosis, and then the HOS are introduced.

2.1 Variance, skewness and kurtosis

Variance is a measure of the spread of the data from the mean. The third order mean is called skewness and is a measure of eth asymmetry of the processes' pdf. For symmetric distributions, skewness is identically zero. The fourth moment about the mean is related to the degree of flatness of a distribution near its center.

For a Gaussian distribution, the value of kurtosis is 3. The values greater than 3 indicate that the pdf if more peaked around its center than a Gaussian distribution and are known as leptokurtic [3].

2.2 The frequency domain

The familiar power spectrum represents a composition of a signal's power, a second order cumulate over frequency. The HOS generates decompositions of higher order cumulate as functions of frequency ariables. This allows one to examine structure in the signal related to the non-Gaussianity, which is interpreted in terms of non-linearity in the generating mechanism.

2.3 Cumulant spectra

Consider an order n cumulate $cn_x(\tau1, \tau2,\ldots,\tau n)$ exists. Then the order n cumulate spectrum $Cn_x(\omega1, \omega2,\ldots,\omega n)$ of $\{X(k)\}$ exists, is continuous and is defined as the (n-1)-dimensional Fourier Transform of the nth order cumulate sequence [5]. The cumulate spectra is complex and has both magnitude and phase information. The cumulate spectra is also periodic with period 2π.

2.4 Power spectrum

It is one of the main tools used in signal processing and a huge body of literature has been published concerning its use and properties [5]. The power spectrum is a real quantity and contains no phase information. All the phase information is suppressed.

2.5 Bispectrum

The bispectrum [1] decomposes the skewness of a signal. The bispectrum is a function of two-frequency variables f1 and f2. The bispectrum analyses the frequency components at f1, f2, f1+f2(f1-f2).

2.6 Trispectrum

The trispectrum [1] decomposes the kurtosis of a signal. It is a function of three frequencies f1, f2, f3 and it analyses the frequency interactions between these components. For a symmetric, non-Gaussian process, the bispectrum is identically zero, whereas trispectrum is non-zero and contains all the information regarding the same process. The bispectrum is the simpler of the two and has received much more attention than the latter.

2.7 Symmetry considerations

Bispectrum has twelve regions of symmetry nd hence the knowledge of bispectrum in the triangular region $\omega2{>}0$, $\omega1{\geq}\omega2$, $\omega1{+}\omega2{\leq}\pi$ is enough for a complete description of the ispectrum. Similarly, the trispectrum has 96 regions of symmetry [5].

2.8 Quadratic phase coupling

In some situations in a non-linear system an interaction between two harmonic components causes contribution to the power as their sum (difference) of frequencies. Such phenomenons which gives rise to certain phase relations of the same type as the frequency relation is called the quadratic phase coupling [5]. Since the poser spectrum suppresses all phase information, it cannot be utilized to detect phase coupling. The bispectrum is capable of detecting and characterizing quadratic phase coupling. Harmonically related peaks in the power spectrum are necessary conditions for the presence of quadratic non-linearities in the data. The higher order spectrum preserves phase and is used to extract phase information quantitativel

2.9 Bicoherence

The spectral resolution of the conventional bispectrum is proportional to the length of each segment. The variance is inversely proportional to the total number of segments.

Due to the finite data length of (stochastic) processes, peaks may appear in the bispectrum at locations where there are no significant phase coupling. A normalized bispectrum or bicoherence is used to avoid incorrect interpretations. The strength of phase correlation can be quantified by the magnitude of bicoherence.

3. Clinical background

The data for the experiments was taken from patients with a confirmed diagnosis for heart problem. These patients had been under medication for some time. The control data was taken from a healthy person. The First of the data was taken from a 75-year-old female. The other diseased sample was taken from a 84 year old female. The control data was taken from 58-year-old male. The authors for the detection of phase correlations have analyzed data from only one lead of ECG.

4. Results

The bispectra of the control data was first done. The bispectrum of the data was obtained and then the bicoherence of the signal data was performed. The length of FFT used was 1024 and the segment size was taken to be 25. The size of the window array was 1×1. A Hanning window was used to compute the bispectrum.

To test the effectiveness of the bispectrum, the authors digitally data, and performed the bispectral analysis on the synthetic data. The bispectral analysis was able to provide a clear view of the phase coupling in the synthetic data.

Afterwards this technique was applied to the ECG signal of the control subject. The ECG signal of the control subject was certified to be a normal. The power spectrum of the control was calculated, no significant peaks were found in the power spectrum. From this it was concluded that there should not be any significant phase coupling present in the

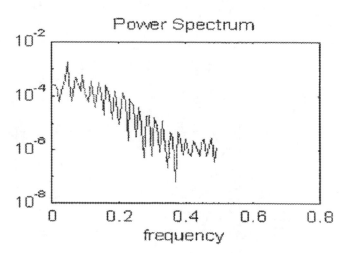

Fig. 1 Power spectrum of a normal ECG signal

bispectrum [3]. The inference was verified by the bispectral analysis. Above diagrams clearly show that there is no significant phase coupling present in the ECG signal of a healthy person. One interesting observation that came up in the study was that the positions of the peaks shown in the bicoherence were found to be constant over a large sample of data of a normal person. The results were shown to be consistent with the theory. The bicoherence curve of the subject was very flat with the notable absence of any sharp peaks. Thus the amount of Quadratic Phase Coupling was also very small.

The diseased case showed few very interesting results. The patient was positively diagnosed as suffering from Heart Problem. The Power Spectrum of the patient showed a few peaks at 0.25 Hz frequencies. The bispectral analysis was then performed on the data. The results showed that this data lacked the consistency of the normal data and the sections of the ECG from which the disease could be made out showed high degree of phase correlation. The

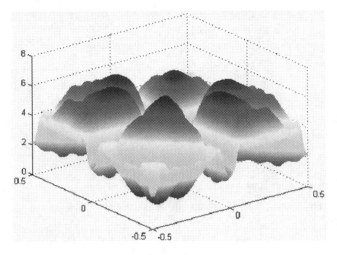

Fig. 4   The 3-D plot of the bicoherence of the normal ECG signal

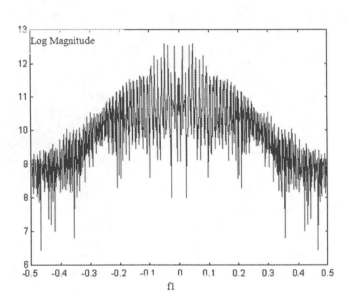

Fig. 2   The bispectrum of a normal ECG signal

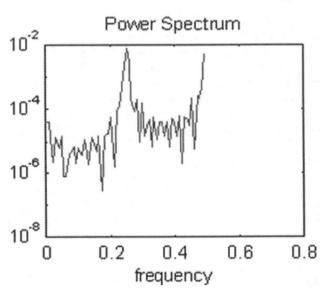

Fig. 5   Power spectrum of a diseased ECG signal

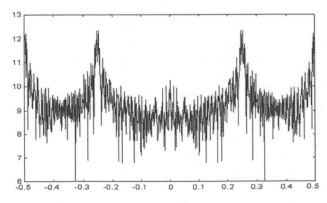

Fig. 6   Bispectrum of diseased ECG signal

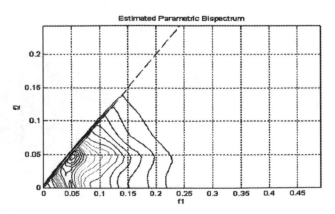

Fig. 3   Quadratic phase coupling of a normal ECG signal

bicohernce plot of the data contained a few very sharp peaks Thus showing the presence of Phase Correlation among the various components of the ECG signal.

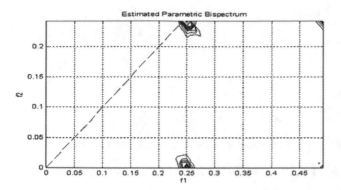

Fig. 7 Quadratic phase coupling present in the diseasd ECG signal

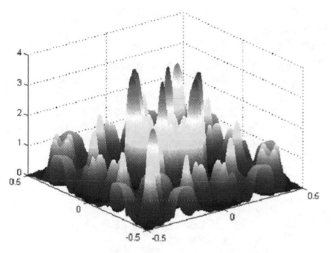

Fig. 8 The 3-D plot of the bicoherence of a diseased ECG signal

5. Conclusion

The results obtained by the authors have been consistent with the general theory of bispectrum []. The absence of strong Quadratic phase coupling in the normal ECG signal proves that it is composed of frequency components, which are uncorrelated harmonically. In harmonically related components there was a notable absence of quadratic phase coupling. The bispectrum of a normal ECG (Fig. 2) shows a smoothly decaying curve. The bispectrum of the abnormal ECG signal shows an interesting characteristic. A very strong peak appears at the same position as that in comes out in the power spectrum (Fig. 1). A peak at this frequency is also observed in Fig. . This shows a very high degree of quadratic phase coupling in the diseased ECG signal. This sort of strong Phase coupling is absent in the ECG signal of a normal person. The position of appearance of a broad peak at the position (0.05,0.05) (Fig. 4) was found to be a characteristic of the normal ECG signal. This result proves that a normal ECG signal has a stable characteristic at that frequency. The authors found the data to be consistent on a large set of data. The nature of the peaks also remained the same. The ECG signal that showed some deviation from the normal characteristic did not have this kind of consistency inherently present in them. In the diseased signal there was deviation from the normal curve and a characteristic frequency was dominant. The Bispectral Analysis could present a novel approach to detect the presence of disease in a ECG signal.

References

1. Cardiac health Diagnosis Using Higher Order Spectra and support Vector Machine, Chua Kunga Chua, Vinod Chandran, Rajendra U. Achary and Lim Choo Min Open Medical Informatics Journal 2009,3,1-8
2. Higher Order Spectral (HOS) Analysis Of Epileptic EEG Signals Chua Kuang chua,Vinod Chandran, Rajendra U.Acharya and Lim Choo Min, Journal of Medical Enginnering & Technology 2009,Vol 33No.1, pages 42-50
3. Classification of heart rate variability signals using higher order spectra and neural networks, obayy, M.I.Abou-Chadi, ICNM 2009 Networking & Media Convergence
4. J. M. Mendel, "Tutorial on Higher-Order Statistics (Spectra) in Signal Processing and System Theory: Theorotical Results and Some Applications", *Proc. IEEE*, vol. 79, pp. 278–305, Jan. 1991
5. P. J. Huber, B. Klenier, T. Gasser, G. Dumermuth, "Statistical Methods for Investigating Phase Relations in Stationary Stochastic Processes", *IEEE Tran. Audio and Electroacoustics*, vol. AU-19, NO. 1, March 1971
6. T. Schanze, R. Eckhorn, "Phase Corrrelations among rhythms present at different frequencies: spectral methods, application to microelectrode recordings from visual cortex and functional implications", *International Journal of Psychophysiology*, Vol. 26, pp. 171-189, 1997
7. W. B. Collis, P. R. White, J.K. Hammond, "Higher-Order Spectra: The Bispectrum and Trispectrum", *Mechanical Systems and Signal Processing*, vol. 12(3), pp. 375-394, 1998
8. C. L. Nikias, M.R. Raghuveer, "Bispectrum Estimation: A digital signal processing framework", *Proc. IEEE*, vol. 75, no.7, pp. 867-891, 1987
9. MIT-BIH arrhythmia Database, Available Online, http: //www.physionet.org

Performance evaluation of image retrieval using energy compaction and imagetiling over DCT row mean and DCT column mean

Dr. H. B. Kekre[1] · **Sudeep D. Thepade[2]** · **Archana Athawale[2]** · **Anant Shah[3]** · **Prathamesh Verlekar[3]** · **Suraj Shirke[3]**

[1]Senior Professor, MPSTME, SVKM's NMIMS, Mumbai, India.
[2]Ph.D Research Scholar, Asst. Prof., MPSTME, SVKM's NMIMS, Mumbai, India.
[3]B.E. Student, Thadomal Shahani Engineering College, Mumbai, India.

1. Introduction

Content-based image retrieval (CBIR) is a technique to retrieve images on the basis of image specific features such as colour [5, 17, 19], texture [11, 14, 16, 23] and shape [2, 4]. CBIR operates on a totally different principle from keyword indexing. Initially, features are computed for both stored and query images, and used to identify images most closely matching the query. The need to find a desired image from a collection is shared by many professional groups, including journalists, design engineers [24] and art historians. While the requirements of image users can vary considerably, it can be useful to characterize image queries into three levels of abstraction: primitive features such as colour or shape, logical features such as the identity of objects shown and abstract attributes such as the texture of image depicted [12, 15, 18]. Users needing to retrieve images from a collection come from a variety of domains, including crime prevention [13, 20], medicine, architecture [6, 9, 10, 21, 22], fashion and publishing. Many techniques have been proposed for content based image retrieval, but still there is thirst for better performance [1, 3] and faster retrieval [1, 7, 8].

The paper considers methods for image retrieval by the use of feature vectors Row mean and Column mean [1]. The novel techniques of Image Tiling [1] and Energy Compaction are introduced. By use of image tiling, higher precision and recall can be obtained. Energy compaction technique provides method to reduce the feature vector size and hence to reduce computation complexity.

2. Discrete cosine transform

The discrete cosine transform (DCT) is closely related to the discrete Fourier transform. It is a separable linear transformation. The definition of the two-dimensional DCT [12, 25] for an input image A and output image B is

$$B_{pq} = \alpha_p \alpha_q \sum \sum A_{mn} \cos \frac{\pi(2m+1)p}{2M} \cos \frac{\pi(2n+1)q}{2N}, \begin{array}{l} 0 \le p \le M-1 \\ 0 \le q \le N-1 \end{array} \tag{1}$$

$$\alpha_p = \begin{cases} 1/\sqrt{M} & , p=0 \\ \sqrt{2/M} & ,1 \le p \le M-1 \end{cases} \tag{2}$$

$$\alpha_q = \begin{cases} 1/\sqrt{N} & , q=0 \\ \sqrt{2/N} & ,1 \le q \le N-1 \end{cases} \tag{3}$$

where M and N are the row and column size of A, respectively. If DCT is applied to real data, the result is also real. The DCT tends to concentrate information, making it useful for image compression applications and also helping in minimizing feature vector size in CBIR. For full 2-Dimensional DCT for an NXN image the number of multiplications required are $N^2(2N)$ and number of additions required are $N^2(2N-2)$.

3. Image tiling

The image tiling is the method of dividing the image into non overlapping parts called tiles. Then row mean and column mean of each tile are obtained. After apply-

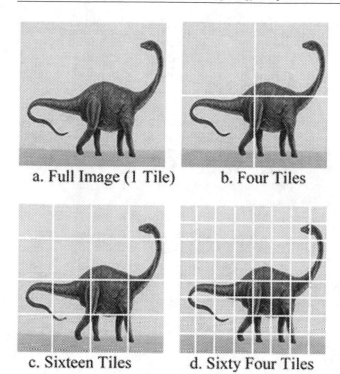

a. Full Image (1 Tile)　　b. Four Tiles

c. Sixteen Tiles　　d. Sixty Four Tiles

Fig. 1 Tiling of an image into 4 tiles, 16 tiles and 64 tiles respectively

Table 1 Sizes of feature vector according to number of tiles

Tiles (size)-> Feature	1 Tile	2 Tile S	4 Tile S	8 Tile	N Tile S
Row Mean	1	4	16	64	n2
Column Mean	1	4	16	64	n2

ing transform on these, feature sets can be obtained to be used in image retrieval. The paper considers 1, 4, 16 and 64 non overlapping tiles as exemplified in Fig. 1. The sizes of feature vector for respective number of tiles are shown in Table 1.

4. Extraction of feature vector

The row mean vector is the set of averages of the intensity values of the respective rows. The column mean vector is the set of averages of the intensity values of the respective columns. If Fig. 2 is representing the sample image with 4 rows and 4 columns, the row and column mean vectors for this image will be as given below.

DCT can be applied to the row mean and column mean vectors of image to get DCT row mean and DCT column mean feature vectors respectively. The generated DCT co-efficients will be used as feature vectors of the image which can further be used for image retrieval. Thus, features of all images in the database are obtained and stored in feature vector tables for DCT row mean, DCT column mean.

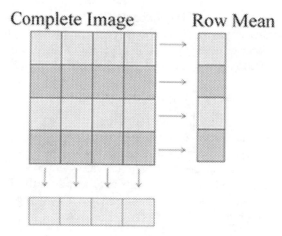

Column Mean

Fig. 2 Sample image template describing row mean and column mean feature vector

4.1 DCT row mean image retrieval

Here, first the row mean of query image is obtained. Then, the DCT row mean feature vector of query image is obtained by applying DCT on row mean. For image retrieval using DCT row mean, these query image features are compared with DCT row mean features of image database by finding Euclidian distances using the formula given as equation 4.

$$ED = \sqrt{\sum_{i=1}^{n} (Vpi - Vqi)^2} \qquad (4)$$

These Euclidian distances are sorted in ascending order and result images are grouped together to get the precision and recall using the formulae as given below in equation 5 and equation 6.

$$Precision = \frac{Number\_of\_relevant\_images\_retrieved}{Total\_number\_of\_images\_retrieved} \qquad (5)$$

$$Recall = \frac{Number\_of\_relevant\_images\_retrieved}{Total\_number\_of\_relevent\_images\_in\_database} \qquad (6)$$

4.2 DCT transform column mean image retrieval

Here first the column mean of query image is obtained. Then the DCT column mean feature vector of query image is obtained by applying DCT on column mean. For image retrieval using DCT column mean, these query image features are compared with DCT column mean features of image database by finding Euclidian distances using the formula given as equation 4. These Euclidian distances are sorted in ascending order and result images are grouped together to get the precision and recall using the formulae as mentioned above in equation 5 and equation 6.

5. Energy compaction

Discrete Cosine Transform applied on an image transfers the high frequency components at the higher end and low frequency components towards lower side. This can be used as an advantage in image retrieval by eliminating the coefficients which do not contribute significantly. The energy compaction method therefore aids in reducing the feature vector size, which gives faster retrieval.

5.1   Average energy plot

Average Energy plot depicts the average energy compaction done by DCT on all the database images. The average energy plot can be obtained for each of the above specified feature vector techniques, i.e., row mean and column mean. Firstly, all the feature vectors are arranged into a two dimensional array. Now, the average value feature vector is computed by adding corresponding values and dividing it by number of feature vectors. The number of feature vector used depends on the tiling technique used as explained in section 3. The database considered consists of 1000 generic images. Hence if single tile technique is used, 1000 feature vectors, either row mean or column as per selection, are obtained. For 4 tiles technique four features, one for each tile, are obtained. Therefore, the two dimensional feature vector array will consist of 4000 vectors. Once the average vector is obtained, DCT is applied on it. By application of DCT, the high frequency components are obtained at the higher side of the vector. Further, its terms are squared to obtain positive values of energy. In the following subsections calculation of average value feature vector for row mean and column mean is discussed.

5.1.1   Row mean feature vector

Here, row mean is considered as the feature vector. Hence, the row means of all the tiles of all the images in the database are arranged in a two dimensional array and average row mean is calculated. The size of row mean depends on the tiling technique used. For an image if size of row mean is N when 1 tile method is used, the size of row mean is N/2 when 4 tiles method is used and four such row mean vectors can be obtained per image. Now, DCT is applied to obtain transformed row mean vector.

5.1.2   Column mean feature vector

In this method, column mean is considered as the feature vector. Hence, the column means of all the tiles of all the images in the database are arranged in a two dimensional array and average column mean is calculated. The size and

number of column means depends on the tiling technique as in case of row means. Now, DCT is applied to obtain transformed column mean vector.

This vector depicts the values of the average energy plot for all images in the database considered together. Further, after calculation of the transformed average feature vector, the values are added to get a cumulative vector. The average energy plots for row mean and column mean on the tiling technique are shown in Figs. 3–8.

The cumulative vector signifies the cumulative energy up to the considered feature vector coefficient. After obtaining the average energy vector, the energies are added cumulatively from first coefficient to the last coefficient of the feature vector. Therefore cumulative energy at the last coefficient denotes the total energy of the image. It is found that energy at the lower coefficients is very less and hence they do not add significantly to the cumulative energy vector. Therefore, as a result, the cumulative energy plot tends to become parallel to the X axis which denotes the number of coefficients of the feature vector, as shown in Fig. 9–14.

5.2   Compaction by use of energy percentage

The compaction of energy is done by considering percentages of total energy which is obtained from cumulative vector. The proposed method considers 100% energy, 95% energy, 90% energy, 85% energy. From the average energy plots a particular amount of energy is selected to

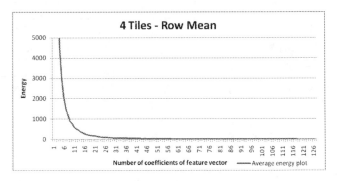

Fig. 3   Average energy plot for 4 tiles row mean technique

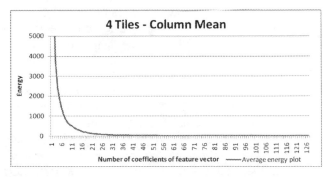

Fig. 4   Average energy plot for 4 tiles column mean technique

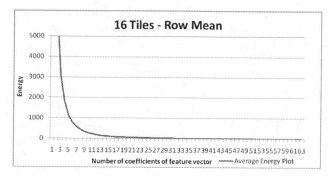

Fig. 5 Average energy plot for 16 tiles row mean technique

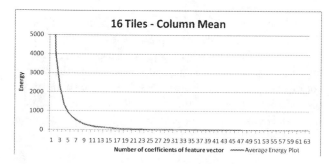

Fig. 6 Average energy plot for 16 tiles column mean technique

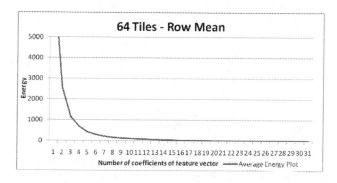

Fig. 7 Average energy plot for 64 tiles row mean technique

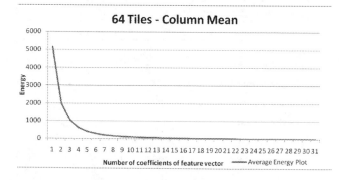

Fig. 8 Average energy plot for 64 tiles column mean technique

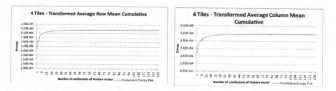

Figs. 9 & 10 Average cumulative energy plot for 4 tiles row and column mean technique

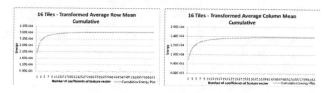

Figs. 11 & 12 Average cumulative energy plot for 16 tiles row and column mean technique

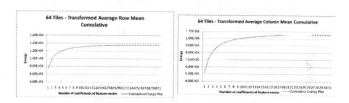

Figs. 13 & 14 Average cumulative energy plot for 64 tiles row and column mean technique

determine the number of coefficients of the feature vector to be considered for image retrieval. As the percentage of energy considered is reduced, the number of coefficients required also drastically reduces, reducing the candidate feature vector size for image retrieval. The numbers of coefficients required in each case are discussed in Table 2. Following are the average cumulative energy plots for each tiling technique.

6. Proposed CBIR techniques

After combining the row mean, column mean, tiling and energy compaction concepts we can get total of 32 novel CBIR techniques. Eight CBIR techniques for the four different percentage of energy considerations as 100%, 95%, 90% and 85% along with the four image tiling ways considered for full image, 4 tiles, 16 tiles and 64 tiles to give a total of 16 methods for row mean feature vectors and 16 methods for column mean feature vectors.

7. Implementation

The implementation of the CBIR techniques is done in MATLAB 7.0. The CBIR techniques are tested on the image database of 1000 variable size gray scale images spread across 11 categories of human being, animals, natural scenery and manmade things. Sample images from each category are shown in Fig. 15.

To compare the techniques and to check their performance we have used the precision and recall. Total 55 (5 from each category of image database) queries are tested to get average precision and average recall of respective image retrieval techniques. The average precision and average recall are computed by grouping the number of retrieved images sorting them according to ascending values of Euclidian distances with the query image.

8. Results and discussion

The crossover points of precision and recall of these CBIR techniques act as an important parameters to judge their performance [1,5,25]. Table 2 shows the number of coefficients of the feature vector in each case. To determine which tiling method is best suited for gray scale images CBIR cross over points for each of the tiling method are plotted. For each tiling technique and row mean or column mean the precision and recall values are obtained for energy 100%, 95%, 90% and 85%.

To determine which energy compaction method is better, crossover plots for each tiling method are plotted. Figure 16 shows the crossover of precision and recall values of Full image-Row mean considered for different energy compactions. Highest cross over denotes best image retrieval performance, hence it could be concluded that, for Full image (1 Tile) – Row mean technique 85% energy compaction method outperforms other compaction techniques, even 100%. This indicates that precision and recall obtained by using a size of row mean feature vector of 7 performs better than using feature vector size of 256. Thus the highest cross over for 1 tile technique is 0.33333, when 85% energy is used for row mean.

However, the observation for Full image-Column Mean is different. As shown in Fig. 17, best performance is obtained by 100% energy. Hence column mean of 256 can be used for 1 tile method to obtain highest cross over value of 0.30174. Cross over for 4 Tiles method are shown in Figs. 18 and 19. As seen from the cross overs shown in Fig. 18, for 4 Tiles Row mean technique, 90% energy method proves to be best. From Table 2 it is seen that only 8 coefficients are required for 90% energy method. Hence, highest crossover of 0.33808 by use of just 8 coefficients instead of 128. For 4 Tiles column mean technique, as shown in Fig. 19, all energy compaction methods perform similarly and there is no significant difference in the higest cross over values.

Cross over for 16 Tiles method are shown in Fig. 20 and Fig. 21. From the cross over points shown in Fig. 20, it is observed that for 16 Tiles Row mean technique, 85% energy method performs marginally better than other energy compaction methods. From Table 2 it is seen that only 5 coefficients are required for 16 tiles-Row mean 85% energy method. Hence, highest crossover of 0.33346 by use of just 5 coefficients instead of 64.

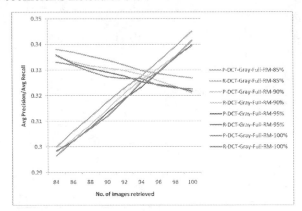

Fig. 16   Cross over for full image (1 Tile) row mean technique for 85%, 90%, 95%, 100%

Fig. 15   Sample image database of grayscale images

Table 2   Size of feature vectors according to tiling technique and energy percentage

	Energy percentage			
Tiling Method and Feature Vector Technique	100	95	90	85
Full Image Row Mean	256	15	9	7
Full Image Column mean	256	25	14	9
4 Tiles Row mean	128	13	8	5
4 Tiles Column mean	128	17	10	7
16 Tiles Row mean	64	11	7	5
16 Tiles Column mean	64	14	9	7
64 Tiles Row mean	32	9	6	5
64 Tiles Column mean	32	11	7	5

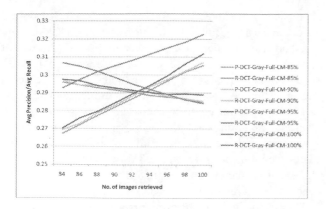

Fig. 17 Cross over for full image (1 tile) column mean technique for 85%, 90%, 95%, 100%

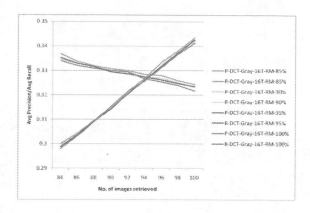

Fig. 20 Cross over for 16 tiles row mean technique for 85%, 90%, 95%, 100%

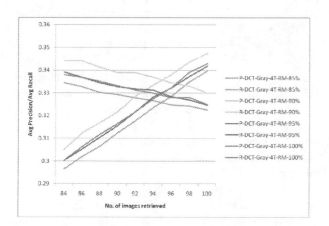

Fig. 18 Cross over for 4 tiles row mean technique for 85%, 90%, 95%, 100%

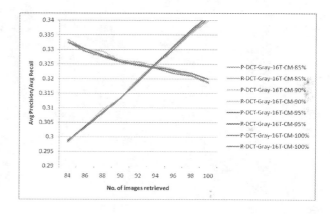

Fig. 21 Cross over for 17 tiles column mean technique for 85%, 90%, 95%, 100%

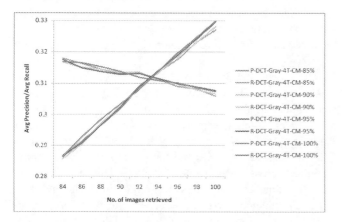

Fig. 19 Cross over for 4 tiles column mean technique for 85%, 90%, 95%, 100%

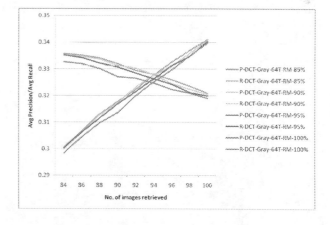

Fig. 22 Cross over for 64 tiles row mean technique for 85%, 90%, 95%, 100%

Similar to case in 4 Tiles column mean technique, as shown in Fig. 21, for 16 Tiles column mean technique all energy compaction methods perform similarly and there is no significant difference in the higest cross

over values. Cross over for 64 Tiles method are shown in Figs. 22 and 23.

For 64 Tiles Row mean technique, Fig. 22, 85% energy method performs marginally better than other energy

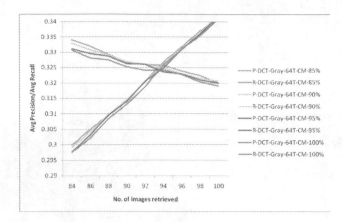

Fig. 23 Cross over for 64 tiles column mean technique for 85%, 90%, 95%, 100%

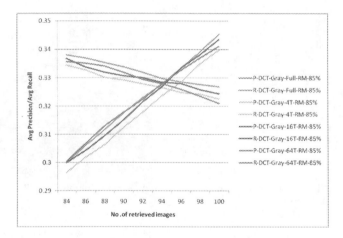

Fig. 24 Cross over 85% row mean technique for full (1 tile), 4 tiles, 16 tiles, 64 tiles

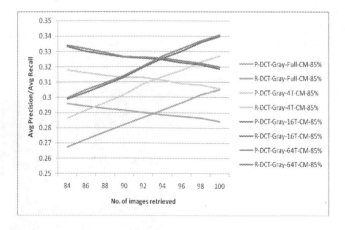

Fig. 25 Cross over 85% column mean technique for full (1 tile), 4 tiles, 16 tiles, 64 tiles

compaction methods. From Table 2 it is seen that only 5 coefficients are required for 64 tiles-Row mean 85% energy method. Hence, highest cross over of 0.32763 by use of just 5 coefficients instead of 32. It is seen in Fig. 23 that similar to case in 4 Tiles and 16 Tiles column mean technique, again for 64 Tiles column mean technique all energy compaction methods perform similarly and there is no significant difference in the highest precision-recall values. Hence, for all 4 Tiles, 16 Tiles and 64 Tiles Column mean technique 85% energy technique can be used in place of 100% energy. By this the column mean vector size is reduced to 7, 7 and 5 instead of 128, 64, and 32 respectively, and still same precision-recall can be obtained.

For determining which tiling method is better, crossover plots for each energy compaction method are drawn. The precision and recall cross over plots for 85% energy shown in Figs. 24 and 25.

It is observed from Fig. 24 that if 85% energy is used for row mean, full i.e., 1 Tile technique performs best. The highest cross over is 0.33262. The next best performance is of 16 Tiles technique and 4 Tiles technique gives least performance for 85% energy. As seen from Fig. 25, for 85% Column Mean, 64 Tiles technique gives best performance. Closest to 64 Tiles technique is 16 Tiles technique. Performance of 1 Tile and 4 Tiles is quite low.

Cross over points of precision and recall curves for 90% energy are shown in following Figs. 26 and 27. Cross over for 90% Row mean in figure. 26 clearly indicates 4 Tiles technique is best performer for 90% energy. The highest cross over value obtained here is 0.33808. Other tiling techniques perform almost similarly. The cross over for 90% column mean indicates 64 Tiles technique to be best. This is similar to performance of 64 Tiles technique in 85% energy method. Close to 64 Tiles, 16 Tiles technique also performs well. Again, 1 Tile and 4 Tiles perform poorly.

Figures 28 and 29 show the cross over point plots for 95% energy. The best results for 95% energy-Row mean are obtained for 4 Tiles technique, as shown in Fig. 28. The highest crossover value obtained here is 0.33221. Figure 29 shows the cross over for 95% column mean. It indicates 64 Tiles technique to be best giving highest cross over value 0.32481. This is similar to performance of 64 Tiles technique in 85% and 90% energy methods. Again, 1 Tile and 4 Tiles perform poorly and along with 64 Tiles, 16 Tiles technique also gives good results.

The observation from cross over plots discussed in this section can be summarized as Tables 3 and 4.

9. Conclusion

In the paper thirty two novel techniques of CBIR using Row Mean, Column mean, Image Tiling and Energy compaction

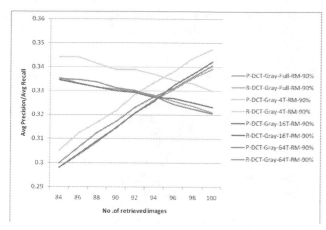

Fig. 26 Cross over 90% row mean technique for full (1 tile), 4 tiles, 16 tiles, 64 tiles

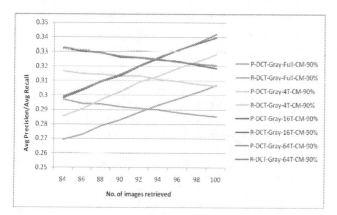

Fig. 27 Cross over 90% column mean technique for full (1 tile), 4 tiles, 16 tiles, 64 tiles

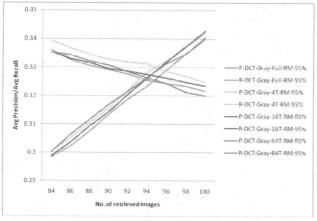

Fig. 28 Cross over 95% row mean technique for full (1 tile), 4 tiles, 16 tiles, 64 tiles

Table 3 Best tiling technique according to energy percentage and feature vector

Energy Percentage and Feature Vector	Best Tiling Technique
85% RM	1 Tile
85% CM	64 Tiles
90% RM	4 Tiles
90% CM	64 Tiles
95% RM	4 Tiles
95% CM	64 Tiles

Table 4 Best energy percentage according to tiling method and feature vector technique

Tiling Method nad Feature Vector Technique	Best Energy Percentage
Full Image Row mean	85%
Full Image Column mean	100%
4 Tiles Row mean	90%
4 Tiles Column mean	Any
16Tiles Row mean	85%
16 Tiles Column mean	Any
64 Tiles Row mean	85%
64 Tiles Column mean	Any

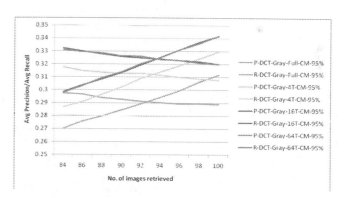

Fig. 29 Cross over 95% column mean technique for full (1 tile), 4 tiles, 16 tiles, 64 tiles

are proposed. The proposed techniques aim to increase the precision and recall for image retrieval using feature vectors row mean and column mean along with image tiling and also reduce the computation complexity by reducing feature vector size by use of energy compaction. The tiling technique proves worth full, since, as the numbers of tiles are increased higher precision and recall values are obtained at the cost of increased feature vector size. Further, by the use of energy compaction technique, unnecessary co-efficients, which do not contribute to image retrieval, can be eliminated.

References

1. H.B.Kekre, Sudeep D. Thepade, Archana Athawale, Anant Shaha, Prathmesh Verlekar, Suraj Shirke, "Image Retrieval using DCT on Row Mean, Column Mean and Both with

Image Fragmentation", (Selected), ACM-International Conference and Workshop on Emerging Trends in Technology (ICWET 2010), TCET, Mumbai, 26-27 Feb 2010, The paper will be uploaded on online ACM Portal

2. Nuno Vasconcelos, "From pixels to semantic spaces: Advances in Content-Based Image Retrieval", published by IEEE computer society

3. H.B.Kekre, Tanuja K.Sarode, Sudeep D. Thepade,"Image Retrieval by Kekre's Transform Applied on Each Row of Walsh Transformed VQ Codebook", (Invited), ACM-Int. Conference and Workshop on Emerging Trends in Technology (ICWET 2010), TCET, Mumbai, 26-27 Feb 2010, The paper is invited at ICWET 2010. Also will be uploaded on online ACM Portal

4. Qasim Iqbal, J. K. Aggarwal, " CIRES: A System for Content-Based Retrieval in Digital Image Libraries", in the seventh international conference on Control, Automation, Robotics and Vision (ICARCV'02),Dec 2002, Singapore

5. H.B.Kekre, Sudeep D. Thepade, "Image Retrieval using Augmented Block Truncation Coding Techniques", ACM International Conference on Advances in Computing, Comm. and Control (ICAC3-2009), pp. 384-390, 23-24 Jan 2009, Fr. CRCE, Mumbai. Is uploaded on online ACM portal

6. H.B.Kekre, Sudeep D. Thepade, "Image Blending In Vista Creation using Kekre's LUV Color Space", SPIT-IEEE Colloquium and International Conference, 04-05 Feb 2008, SPIT Andheri, Mumbai

7. Wang Xiaoling, " A Novel Cicular Ring Histogram for Content-based Image Retrieval", First International Workshop on Education Technology and Computer Science, 2009

8. Junyu Dong, Muwei Jian, Dawei Gao, Shengke Wang, "Reducing the Dimensionality of Feature Vectors for Textual Image Retrieval Based On Wavelet Decomposition", Eighth ACIS Int. Conf. on Software Engineering, Artificial Intelligence, Networking and Parallel/Distributed Computing

9. H.B.Kekre, Sudeep D. Thepade, "Panoramic View Construction using Partial Images", IEEE sponsored International Conference on Sensors, Signal Processing, Communication, Control and Instrumentation (SSPCCIN-2008) 03-05 Jan 2008,Vishwakarma Institute of Technology, Pune

10. H.B.Kekre, Sudeep D. Thepade, "Vista creation using Picture Parts", International Conference on Emerging Technologies and Applications in Engineering, Technology and Sciences (ICETAETS-2008), 12-13 Jan 2008, Held at Computer Science Dept., Saurashtra University, Rajkot, India

11. Xiaoyi Song, Yongjie Li, Wufan Chen,"A Textural Feature Based Image Retrieval Algorithm", in Proc. of 4th Int. Conf. on Natural Computation, Oct. 2008

12. H. B. Kekre, Ms. Tanuja K. Sarode, Sudeep D. Thepade, "Image Retrieval using Color-Texture Features from DCT on VQ Codevectors obtained by Kekre's Fast Codebook Generation", ICGST-International Journal on Graphics, Vision and Image Processing (GVIP), Volume 9, Issue 5, pp.: 1-8, September 2009. Available online at http://www.icgst.com/gvip/Volume9/Issue5/P1150921752.html

13. H. B. Kekre, Kamal Shah, Tanuja K. Sarode, Sudeep D. Thepade, "Performance Comparison of Vector Quantization Technique – KFCG with LBG, Existing Transforms and PCA for Face Recognition", International Journal of Information Retrieval (IJIR), Vol. 02, Issue 1, pp.: 64-71, 2009

14. Jing Zhang, Gui-li Li, Seok-wum He, "Texture-Based Image Retrieval By Edge Detection Matching GLCM ", in Proc. of 10th Int. Conference on High Performance Computing and Comm., Sept. 2008

15. H.B.Kekre, Tanuja Sarode, Sudeep D. Thepade, "Color-Texture Feature based Image Retrieval using DCT applied on Kekre's Median Codebook", International Journal on Imaging (IJI), Volume 2, Number A09, Autumn 2009,pp. 55-65. Available online at www.ceser.res.in/iji.html (ISSN: 0974-0627)

16. H.B.Kekre, Sudeep D. Thepade, "Image Retrieval using Non-Involutional Orthogonal Kekre's Transform", International Journal of Multidisciplinary Research and Advances in Engineering (IJMRAE), Ascent Publication House, 2009, Volume 1, No.I, 2009. Abstract available online at www.ascent-journals.com

17. H.B.Kekre, Sudeep D. Thepade, "Color Based Image Retrieval using Amendment Block Truncation Coding with YCbCr Color Space", International Journal on Imaging (IJI), Volume 2, Number A09, Autumn 2009, pp. 2-14. Available online at www.ceser.res.in/iji.html (ISSN: 0974-0627)

18. H.B.Kekre, Sudeep D. Thepade, "Image Retrieval using Color-Texture Features Extracted from Walshlet Pyramid", ICGST International Journal on Graphics, Vision and Image Processing (GVIP), Volume 10, Issue I, Feb.2010, pp.9–18, Available online www.icgst.com/gvip/Volume10/Issue1/P1150938876.html

19. H.B.Kekre, Sudep D. Thepade, "Using YUV Color Space to Hoist the Performance of Block Truncation Coding for Image Retrieval", In Proc. of IEEE Int. Advanced Computing Conference 2009 (IACC'09), Thapar University, Patiala, INDIA, 6-7 March 2009

20. H.B.Kekre, Sudeep D. Thepade, "Rendering Futuristic Image Retrieval System", In Proc. of National Conference on Enhancements in Computer, Communication and Information Technology, EC2IT-2009, 20-21 Mar 2009, K.J. Somaiya College of Engineering, Vidyavihar, Mumbai-77

21. H.B.Kekre, Sudeep D. Thepade, "Creating the Color Panoramic View using Medley of Grayscale and Color Partial Images ", WASET International Journal of Electrical, Computer and System Engineering (IJECSE), Volume 2, No. 3, Summer 2008. Available online at www.waset.org/ijecse/v2/v2-3-26.pdf

22. H.B.Kekre, Sudeep D. Thepade, "Rotation Invariant Fusion of Partial Images in Vista Creation", WASET International Journal of Electrical, Computer and System Engineering (IJECSE), Volume 2, No. 2, Spring 2008. Available online at www.waset.org/ijecse/v2/v2-2-13.pdf

23. Sanjoy Kumar Saha, Amit Kumar Das, Bhabatosh Chanda, "CBIR using Perception based Texture and Color Measures", in Proc. of 17th International Conference on Pattern Recognition(ICPR'04), Vol. 2, Aug 2004

24. H.B.Kekre, Sudeep D. Thepade, "Scaling Invariant Fusion of Image Pieces in Panorama Making and Novel Image Blending Technique", International Journal on Imaging (IJI), Autumn 2008, Volume 1, No. A08, Available online at www.ceser.res.in/iji.html (ISSN: 0974-0627)

25. H.B.Kekre, Sudeep D. Thepade, "Improving the Performance of Image Retrieval using Partial Coefficients of Transformed Image", International Journal of Information Retrieval, Serials Publications, Volume 2, Issue 1, 2009, pp. 72-79 (ISSN: 0974-6285

Local weighting scheme for word pairs

Raj Kishor Bisht · **Jeetendra Pande**

Department of Computer Science, Amrapali Institute of Management & Computer Applications,
Haldwani, Uttarakhand, India

1. Introduction

Term weighting schemes are the integral part of an Information retrieval system which play an important role in the performance of the information retrieval system. Manning et al (2002) and Sandor Dominich (2008) have provided a detail of information retrieval techniques and weighting schemes in their books. Weight of a term can be seen in two different aspects, local and global. Local weights are functions of frequency of a word in a document and global weights are functions of the frequency of a term in the entire collection. A detail discussion on different types of local weighting schemes can be found in Chisholm & Kolda (1999). Suitability of some global weighting schemes for local weights can be seen in Bisht et al (2008). A comparative study on term weighting schemes for text categorization has been made by Lan et al (2005). There are several weighting schemes, following are some of the commonly used local weighting schemes.

Binary: The simplest local weighting scheme is the Binary weighting scheme which can be expressed as follows:

$$w_{ij} = \begin{cases} 1 & if \quad f_{ij} > 0 \\ 0 & if \quad f_{ij} = 0 \end{cases} \tag{1}$$

where ijf is the frequency of term i in document j. Frequency weighting scheme: It is the frequency of a term in a given document.

$$w_{ij} = f_{ij} \tag{2}$$

Logarithm of frequency: Term frequency with in a document is not a relatively good descriptor of a term.

For example if a term i appears 15 times in a document and term j appears single time, than according to its frequency weight the ith term should be 15 time important than jth term but it is not necessary. When we take logarithms of frequency, it becomes relatively good descriptor of the importance of terms. It is defined as follows:

$$w_{ij} = \begin{cases} \log(1 + f_{ij}) & if \quad f_{ij} > 0 \\ 0 & if \quad f_{ij} = 0 \end{cases} \tag{3}$$

Normalization of weighting schemes is also usedto get the weight of terms in a certain interval, that is [0, 1]. In this type of weighting scheme, we divide the weighting scheme by a suitable normalization factor. As an example Maximum ijf, where $1 \leq i \leq n$ may be a normalization factor for frequency weighting scheme if there are total of n terms in the document. Term weighting schemes are generally defined on the basic assumption that a term is independent to other terms. Term weighting schemes based on the assumption of term to term independence may have a chance of information of a document being lost. Kim Hee-Soo et al (2004) computed term dependencies to refine global term weighting. Term dependency in a document is also quite natural. In place of a single term a word pair may be a better key word of a document and also can better describe a document. In the present paper we have proposed a local weighting scheme for word pairs which exhibits that a word pair may be a better key word rather than a single word.

2. Proposed weighting scheme for word pairs

The proposed local weighting scheme for pair of words can be understood through the following steps:
1. Select a document for weighting scheme.

S.J. Pise (ed.), *ThinkQuest 2010*, DOI 10.1007/978-81-8489-989-4_30,

2. Remove all function words, that is, articles, determiners, propositions, helping verbs etc.
3. Transform word to their lexical roots. For example the words 'prisoner', 'prisoners' have been transformed to 'prisoner'.
4. Count the frequency of each non function word in the document. For a word $1\ w$ the frequency shall be counted as follows: $(\ )\ 1\ f\ w = $ No. of sentences in which $1\ w$ appears.
5. Select some (five to ten) most frequent word from the list.
6. Make the combination of most frequent words and count the frequency of word pairs. Frequency of each combination shall be counted as follows: $(,)\ 1\ 2\ f\ w\ w = $ No. of sentences in which both the words $1\ w$ and $2\ w$ appear.
7. For each word pair $(1\ w, 2\ w)$, calculate the following conditional probabilities:

$$P\left(\frac{w_1}{w_2}\right) = \frac{P(w_1 \cap w_2)}{P(w_1)} = \frac{f(w_1, w_2)/N}{f(w_1)/N}$$

$$= \frac{f(w_1, w_2)}{f(w_2)} \text{ and similarly}$$

$$P\left(\frac{w_2}{w_1}\right) = \frac{P(w_1 \cap w_2)}{P(w_1)} = \frac{f(w_1, w_2)}{f(w_1)}, \text{ where}$$ (4)

$N = $ total number of sentences.

8. Calculate weight of word pair $(1\ w, 2\ w)$ as follows:

$$W(w_1, w_2) = \log(1 + f(w_1)) * P\left(\frac{w_2}{w_1}\right)$$

$$+ \log(1 + f(w_2)) P\left(\frac{w_1}{w_2}\right)$$ (5)

3. Experimental results

For the purpose of experiment, we have arbitrarily chosen the text "Gandhi the Prisoner" available at http://www.anc.org.za/ancdocs/ history /people/gandhi /man-gan.html. Some of the frequent non function words with their frequencies are Prison-63, Gandhi-49, Indian-21,Cell-13, Warder-10, Imprisonment-9 and Political -8. The most frequent word pairs with their frequencies are given in table 1.

Weight of each word pair has been calculated. Table 2 exhibits the weights of each word pair.

From the table 2, it can be observed that the word pairs 'Political – Prison', 'Gandhi- Prison', 'Gandhi-Imprisonment' have significant weight and hence can be taken as key words for the document.

4. Conclusion

In the present paper, we have proposed a local weighting scheme for word pairs. Some times a word alone is not

Table 1 Word pairs and their frequencies

W_1	W_2	$f(W_1)$	$f(W_1)$	$f(W_1, W_2)$
Gandhi	Prison	49	56	10
Gandhi	Indian	49	21	5
Political	Prison	8	56	5
Gandhi	Imprisonment	49	9	4
Gandhi	Cell	49	11	3
Prison	Cell	56	11	3

Table 2 Weight of word pairs in the documents

W_1	W_2	$W(W_1, W_2)$
Political	Prison	0.90
Gandhi	Prison	0.86
Gandhi	Imprisonment	0.58
Gandhi	Indian	0.49
Cell	Prison	0.39

sufficient to predict about the document, thus a word pair may be an important key word of a document as shown by table 2. From the table 1, it can be observed that though the words 'political' and 'imprisonment' have low frequencies yet they makes an important combination with other words. The document is about the comparison of prison experiences and conditions of Mahatma Gandhi and Nelson Mandela in South Africa written by Nelson Mandela in which he described how the political prisoners are treated in prisons. The words 'Gandhi', 'Prison' and 'political' alone describes partially the document, however their combination elaborates the documents explicitly. The obtained word pairs are quite relevant to the document and have the capacity to describe the document; hence the proposed weighting scheme for word pair is quite useful. The proposed weighting can also be extended to a combination of more than two words or a phrase.

References

1. Bisht R.K. and Dhami H S. On some properties of content words in a document. In Proceedings of the 6th Annual conference of Information Science and Technology Management, 2008
2. Chisholm, E. and Kolda T. G. New term weighting formulas for the vector space method in information retrieval. Technical report ORNL-TM-13756, Oak Ridge national laboratory, Oak ridge, TN, 1999
3. Dominich Sandor. The Modern Algebra of Information Retrieval (Information Retrieval Series).Springer-verlag, New York, 2008
4. Kim Hee-soo, Choi Ikkyu and Kim Minkoo. Refining Term Weights of Documents Using Term Dependencies. In Proceedings of the 27th Annual International ACM SIGIR

Conference on Research and Development in Information Retrieval 2004

5. Lan Man, Sung Sam-Yuan, Low Hwee-Boon and Tan Chew-Lim. A comparative study on term weighting schemes for text categorization. In Proceedings of the International Joint Conference on Neural Networks (IJCNN), 2005

6. Manning C.D. and Schutze H. Foundations of Statistical Natural Language Processing. MIT press, Cambridge 2002

Image segmentation of MRI images using vector quantization techniques

H. B. Kekre[1] · **Saylee M. Gharge[2]** · **Tanuja K. Sarode[3]**

[1]Senior Professor, MPSTME, NMIMS University, Vile-Parle, Mumbai, India
[2]Ph.D. Scholar, MPSTME, NMIMS University, Lecturer, V.E.S.I.T, Mumabi India
[3]Ph.D. Scholar, MPSTME, NMIMS University, Assistant Professor, TSEC, Mumbai, India

1. Introduction

Image segmentation plays a crucial role in many medical imaging applications by automating or facilitating the delineation of anatomical structures and other regions of interest. Diagnostic imaging is an invaluable tool in medicine today. Magnetic Resonance Imaging (MRI), Computer Tomography (CT), Digital Mammography, and other imaging modalities provide an effective means for noninvasive mapping the anatomy of a subject. Methods for performing segmentations vary widely depending on the specific application, imaging modality, and other factors. There is currently no single segmentation method that yields acceptable results for every medical image.

Classically, image segmentation is defined as the partitioning of an image into non-overlapping constituent regions which are homogeneous with respect to some characteristic such as intensity or texture.

Magnetic resonance imaging (MRI) is primarily a medical imaging technique most commonly used in Radiology to visualize the structure and function of the body. It provides detailed images of the body in any plane. MRI provides much greater contrast between the different soft tissues of the body than does computer tomography (CT), making it especially useful in neurological (brain), musculoskeletal, and oncological (cancer) imaging. Unlike CT it uses no ionizing radiation, but uses a powerful magnetic field to align the nuclear magnetization of (usually) hydrogen atoms in water in the body. Radiofrequency fields are used to systematically alter the alignment of this magnetization, causing the hydrogen nuclei to produce a rotating magnetic field detectable by the scanner. This signal can be manipulated by additional magnetic fields to build up enough information to reconstruct an image of the body.

The advantages of magnetic resonance imaging (MRI) over other diagnostic imaging modalities are its high spatial resolution and excellent discrimination of soft tissues. MRI provides rich information about anatomical structure, enabling quantitative pathological or clinical studies [1]; the derivation of computerized anatomical atlases [2]; as well as pre and intra-operative guidance for therapeutic intervention [3, 4]. Such information is also valuable as an anatomical reference for functional modalities, such as Positron Emission Tomography (PET) [5], Single Photon Emission Computed Tomography (SPECT), and functional MRI [6]. Advanced applications that use the morphologic contents of MRI frequently require segmentation of the imaged volume into tissue types. This problem has received considerable attention. Such tissue segmentation is often achieved by applying statistical classification methods to the signal intensities [7, 8]. In the ideal case, differentiation between white and gray matter in the brain should be easy since these tissue types exhibit distinct signal intensities. In practice, spatial intensity inhomogeneities are often of sufficient magnitude to cause the distributions of signal intensities associated with these tissue classes to overlap significantly. In addition, the operating conditions and status of the MR equipment frequently affect the observed intensities, causing significant inter-scan intensity inhomogeneities that often necessitate manual training on a per-scan basis. While reported methods [9–14] have had some success in correcting intra-scan inhomogeneities, such methods require supervision for the individual scan.

The segmentation process is usually based on gray level intensity, color, shape or texture. Texture can be characterized by local variations of pixel values that repeat in a regular or random pattern on the object or image. A wide variety of texture segmentation techniques have been reported in the literature [15–21]. We are introducing vector quantization algorithms for image which consumed moderate time but provide good accuracy with less complexity. Watershed algorithm has a drawback of over-segmenting the tumor and making it obscure for identification.

The rest of the paper is organized as follows. Section II describes Gray level Co-occurrence Matrix, the Watershed, Vector quantization algorithms used for image segmentation of MRI images. Followed by the experimental results for MRI images are in section III and section IV concludes the work.

2. Algorithms for segmentation

It is difficult, however, to compare the effectiveness of these methods because each used a unique set of MRI images and the results varied between training and testing. In this section we explain segmentation by Gray level co-occurrence matrix, basic watershed algorithm [22–26] and Vector quantization algorithms[27–29] which we used for tumor detection.

2.1 Gray level co-occurrence matrix

Haralick [30] suggested the use of gray level co-occurrence matrices (GLCM) for definition of textural features. The values of the co-occurrence matrix elements present relative frequencies with which two neighboring pixels separated by distance d appear on the image, where one of them has gray level i and other j. Such matrix is symmetric and also a function of the angular relationship between two neighboring pixels. The co-occurrences matrix can be calculated on the whole image, but by calculating it in a small window which scanning the image, the co-occurrence matrix can be associated with each pixel.

By using gray level co-occurrence matrix we can extract different features like probability, entropy, energy, variance, inverse moment difference etc. Amongst all these features entropy [31] has given us the best results.

Hence in this paper we extracted entropy using gray level co-occurrence matrix and we further equalized it for better results. The results are displayed in Fig. 4(a) along with that of watershed, LBG and KFCG algorithms for comparison

2.2 Watershed algorithm

The watershed transformation can be built up by flooding process on a gray tone image. Watershed segmentation [32] classifies pixels into regions using gradient descent on image features and analysis of weak points along region boundaries. The image feature space is treated, using a suitable mapping, as a topological surface where higher values indicate the presence of boundaries in the original image data. It uses analogy with water gradually filling low lying landscape basins. The size of the basins grows with increasing amounts of water until they spill into one another. Small basins (regions) gradually merge together into larger basins. Regions are formed by using local geometric structure to associate the image domain features with local extremes measurement. These methods are well suited for different measurements fusion and they are less sensitive to user defined thresholds. We implemented watershed algorithm for MRI images as mentioned in [33]. Results for MRI images are displayed in Fig. 4(b).

2.3 Vector quantization

Vector Quantization (VQ) [34–40] is an efficient technique for data compression and has been successfully used in various applications such as speech data compression [41], content based image retrieval CBIR [42]. VQ has been very popular in a variety of research fields such as speaker recognition and face detection [43, 44]. VQ is also used in real time applications such as real time video-based event detection [45] and anomaly intrusion detection systems [46], image segmentation [47–50] and face recognition [51].

VQ is a technique in which a codebook is generated for each image. A codebook is a representation of the entire image containing a definite pixel pattern which is computed according to a specific VQ algorithm. The image is divided into fixed sized blocks that form the training vector. The generation of the training vector is the first step to cluster formation. On these training vectors clustering methods are applied and codebook is generated. The method most commonly used to generate codebook is the Linde Buzo Gray (LBG) algorithm [27].

2.3.1 Linde buzo and gray algorithm (LBG)

For the purpose of explaining this algorithm, we are considering two dimensional vector space as shown in Fig. 1. In this algorithm centroid is computed as the first codevector C1 for the training set. In Fig. 1 two vectors v1 & v2 are generated by adding constant error to the codevector C1. Euclidean distances of all the training

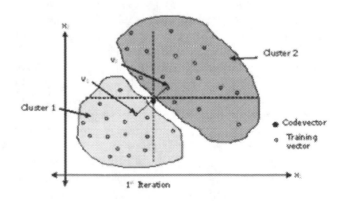

Fig. 1 LBG for 2 dimensional case

vectors are computed with vectors v1 & v2 and two clusters are formed based on nearest of v1 or v2. Procedure is repeated for these two clusters to generate four new clusters. This procedure is repeated for every new cluster until the required size of codebook is reached or specified MSE is reached.

Using this algorithm initially a codebook of size 128 was generated for the given images. These code-vectors were further clustered in 8 clusters using same LBG algorithm. The 8 images were constructed using one codevector at a time. These 8 images display different segments depending on the textural property of the image. It is observed that the image constructed using first code vector displays enhancing tumor ring clearly.

2.3.2 Kekre's fast codebook generation algorithm (KFCG)

Here the Kekre's Fast Codebook Generation algorithm for image data compression is used. This algorithm reduces the time for code book generation. Initially we have one cluster with the entire training vectors and the codevector C1 which is centroid. In the first iteration of the algorithm, the clusters are formed by comparing first element of training vector with first element of code vector C1. The vector Xi is grouped into the cluster 1 if Xi1< C11 otherwise vector Xi is grouped into cluster2 as shown in Fig. 2(a) where codevector dimension space is 2. In second iteration, the cluster 1 is split into two by comparing second element Xi2 of vector Xi belonging to cluster 1 with that of the second element of the codevector. Cluster 2 is split into two by comparing the second element Xi2 of vector Xi belonging to cluster 2 with that of the second element of the codevector as shown in Fig. 2(b).

This procedure is repeated till the codebook size is reached to the size specified by user. It is observed that this algorithm gives less error as compared to LBG and requires least time to generate codebook as compared to other algorithms, as it does not require any computation of Euclidean distance. The algorithm shown in Fig. 2(a) and Fig. 2(b) for two dimensional case it is easily extended to higher dimensions.

In this paper initially we have selected 128 as codebook size using 12 dimensional vector space. Thus the image is divided into 128 clusters which were further reduced to 8 by using requantization. This is done because direct VQ with only 8 clusters does not give good segmentation. The 8 clusters thus obtained were mapped onto the image generating 8 different images representing them. On all these images Canny's operator was used to obtain the edge maps. These edge maps were superimposed on the original image giving clear demarcation of the tumor. The very first cluster gives the best results. However the other clusters also give comparatively better results as compared to watershed and GLCM algorithms.

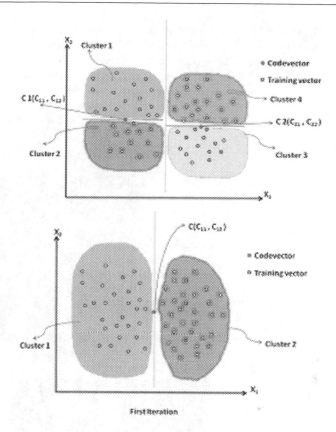

Fig. 2 KFCG algorithm for 2 dimensional case

4. Results

We here consider a case of hemorrhagic venous infarction due to sinus thrombosis with ring enhancing lesions [52] Fig. 3(a). For this image we generate codebook of size 128 using LBG and KFCG algorithm. Further these code-vectors were clustered in 8 clusters using same algorithm. Then 8 images were constructed using one code-vector at a time as shown in Fig. 3(b)–(i) for KFCG algorithm. Figure 4(a) shows results for equalized entropy using gray level co-occurrence matrix. Figure 4(b) shows result for watershed algorithm and Fig. 4(c) indicate result for first code-vector amongst 8 code-vectors using LBG algorithm. Figure 4(d) displays the results for first codevector amongst 8 codevector using KFCG algorithm. Figure 5(a) shows superimposed edge map on original image for equalized Entropy using GLCM, Fig. 6(b) displays similarly constructed image using watershed algorithm, Figure 6(c) and (d) indicates results for superimposed image for first codevector amongst 8 code-vectors using LBG and KFCG algorithms.

5. Conclusion

In this paper we have used vector quantization which is commonly used for data compression. Basically vector quantization is a clustering algorithm and can be used for texture analysis. Here we are giving the results of KFCG algorithm for segmentation of MRI images. The results are compared with well known watershed, GLCM and LBG algorithm. Initially a codebook of size 128 was generated for these images. These code vectors were further clustered in 8 clusters. These 8 images were displayed as a result in Fig. 3(b)–(i). From results (Fig. 5) it is observed that watershed and GLCM give over segmentation while LBG and KFCG show far better results for the same. This approach does not lead to over segmentation or under

(a) Original image

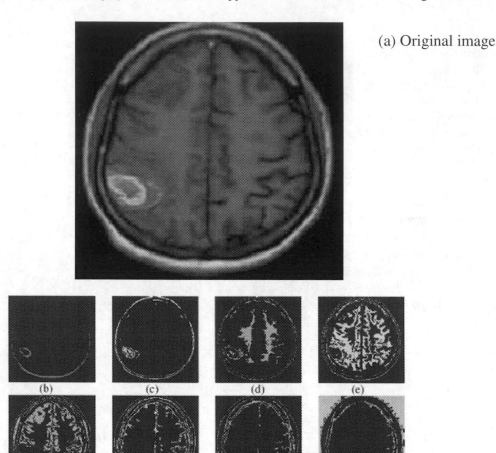

Fig. 3: (a) Original MRI image,(b) Image for first code-vector, (c)Image for second code-vector, (d)Image for third code-vector, (e)Image for fourth code-vector, (f)Image for fifth code-vector, (g)Image for sixth code-vector, (h)Image for seventh code-vector, (i)Image for eighth code-vector,

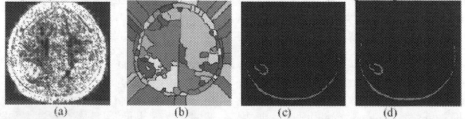

Figure 4: (a) Segmented image for entropy using GLCM, (b) Segmented image using watershed algorithm, (c)Segmented image using LBG algorithm,(d)Segmented image for KFCG algorithm

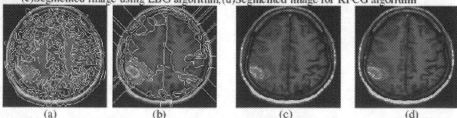

Figure 5 : (a)-(d)Superimposed images Fig4(a)-(d) on original image fig.3(a)

segmentation. However the complexity of LBG algorithm is very high as compared to KFCG because LBG uses Euclidean distance whereas KFCG uses only comparison. Hence KFCG is preferred

References

1. M. Shenton, R. Kikinis, F. Jolesz, et al. Abnormalities of the Left Temporal Lobe and Thought Disorderin Schizophrenia. N. Engl. J. Med: 604 to 612, 1992

2. K. Hohne et al. A framework for the Generation of 3D Anatomical Atlases. In SPIE Vol. 1808, Visualization in Biomedical Computing 1992

3. R. Kikinis, F.A. Jolesz, W.E. Lorensen, H.E. Cline, P.E Stieg, Black 3d Reconstruction of Skull Base Tumors from MRI Data for Neurosurgical Planning.In Proceedings of the Society of Magnetic Resonance in Medicine Conference, 1991

4. R. Kikinis, D. Altobelli, W. Lorensen, W. Wells, and G. Ettinger. Pre- and intraoperative tumor localization using 3d renderings of mri's. 12th Annual Scientific Meeting of the Society of Magnetic Resonance in Medecine, 1993

5. D. Levin, X. Hu, K. Tan, et al. The Brain: Integrated Three-Dimensional Display of MR and PET Images. Radiology, 1989

6. J. Belliveau, D. Kennedy, R. McKinstry, et al. Functional Mapping of the Human Visual Cortex by Magnetic Resonance Imaging. *Science*: 716 to 719, November 1991

7. M. Vannier, D. Jordan, W. Murphy, Multi-Spectral Analysis of Magnetic Resonance Images. Radiology: 221 to 224, 1985

8. M. Kohn, N. Tanna, G. Herman, et al. Analysis of Brain and Cerebrospinal Fluid Volumes with MR Imaging. *Radiology*,: 115 to 122, 1991

9. R.B. Lufkin, T. Sharpless, B. Flannigan, and W. Hanafee. Dynamic-Range Compression in Surface- Coil MRI. AJR: 379 to 382, 1986

10. L. Axel, J. Costantini, and J. Listerud. Intensity Correction in Surface-Coil MR Imaging. AJR: 418 to 420, 1987

11. K.O. Lim and A. P_erbaum. Segmentation of MR Brain Images into Cerebrospinal Fluid Spaces, White and Gray Matter. JCAT:588 to 593, 1989

12. B. Dawant, A. Zijdenbos, and R. Margolin Correction of Intensity Variations in MR Images for Computer-Aided Tissue Classification. IEEE Trans. Med. Imaging: 770 to 781, 1993

13. J. Gohagan, E. Spitznagel, W. Murphy, M. Vannier, Multispectral Analysis of MR Images of the Breast.Radiology:703 to 707, 1987

14. S. Aylward and J. Coggins. Spatially Invariant Classification of Tissues in MR Images. In Proceedings of the Third Conference on Visualization in Biomedical Computing. SPIE, 1994

15. P. Andrey, P. Tarroux, Unsupervised segmentation of Markov random field modeled textured images using selectionist relaxation, IEEE Transactions on Pattern Analysis and Machine intelligence 20 (3) (1998) 252–262

16. U. Bhattacharya, B.B. Chaudhuri, S.K. Parui, An MLP-based texture segmentation method without selecting a feature set, Image Vision Computing 15 (1997) 937–948

17. C. Bouman, B. Liu, Multiple resolution segmentation of textured images, IEEE Transactions on Pattern Analysis and Machine Intelligence 13 (2) (1991) 99–113

18. Dr. H. B. Kekre, Saylee Gharge, "Selection of Window Size for Image Segmentation using Texture Features," International Conference on Advanced Computing & CommunicationTechnologies(ICACCT-2008)AsiaPacific Institute of Information Technology SD India, Panipat, 08-09 November, 2008

19. Dr. H. B. Kekre, Saylee Gharge, "Image Segmentation of MRI using Texture Features," International Conference on Managing Next Generation Software Applications, School of Science and Humanities, Karunya University, Coimbatore, Tamilnadu, 05-06 December, 2008

20. Dr. H. B. Kekre, Saylee Gharge, "Statistical Parameters like Probability and Entropy applied to SAR image segmentation," International Journal of Engineering Research & Industry Applications (IJERIA), Vol.2,No.IV, pp. 341–353

21. Dr. H. B. Kekre, Saylee Gharge, "SAR Image Segmentation using co-occurrence matrix and slope magnitude," ACM International Conference on Advances in Computing, Communication & Control (ICAC3-2009), pp.: 357-362, 23-24 Jan 2009, Fr. Conceicao Rodrigous College of Engg. Available on ACM portal

22. L. Vincent, P. Soille, Watersheds in digital spaces: An efficient algorithm based on immersion Simulations, IEEE Trans. PAMI., 13 (6) (1991) 583–593

23. F. Meyer, Topographic distance and watershed lines,Signal Processing, 38 (1) (1994) 113–125

24. A. Bieniek, A. Moga, An efficient watershed algorithm based on connected components, Pattern Recognition, 33 (6) (2000) 907–916

25. M. Frucci, Over segmentation reduction by flooding regions and digging watershed lines, International Journal of Pattern Recognition and Artificial Intelligence, 20 (2006) 15–38

26. L. E. Band, Topographic partition of watersheds with digital elevation models, Water Resources Res., 22 (1) (1986) 15–24

27. Tou, J., and Gonzalez, Pattern Recognition Principles Addison-Wesley Publishing Company 1974

28. R. M. Gray, "Vector quantization", IEEE ASSP Mag., pp.: 4-29, Apr. 1984

29. Y. Linde, A. Buzo, and R. M. Gray, "An algorithm for vector quantizer design," IEEE Trans. Commun., vol. COM-28, no. 1, pp.: 84-95, 1980

30. Robert M. Haralick, Statistical and Structural Approaches to Texture, IEEE Proceedings of vol. 67, no. 5, May 1979

31. H. B. Kekre, Saylee M.Gharge, "Tumour Demarcation of Mammography Images using Entropy with Different Window Sizes," Second International Conference on Emerging Trends in Engineering and Technology, ICETET-2008, held at Raisoni College of Engineering, Nagpur, India, pp.: 889- 894, 16-18 Dec. 2009. Available at IEEE Xplore

32. Leila Shafarenko and Maria Petrou, " Automatic Watershed Segmentation of Randomly Textured Color Images", *IEEE Transactions on Image Processing*, Vol.6, No.11, pp. 1530–1544, 1997

33. Basim Alhadidi, Mohammad H. et al, " Mammogram Breast Cancer Edge Detection Using Image Processing Function" Information Technology Journal 6(2):217-221,2007,ISSN-1812-5638

34. H.B.Kekre, Tanuja K. Sarode, "New Fast Improved Clustering Algorithm for Codebook Generation for Vector Quantization", International Conference on Engineering Technologies and Applications in Engineering, Technology and Sciences, Computer Science Department, Saurashtra University, Rajkot, Gujarat. (India), Amoghsiddhi Education Society, Sangli, Maharashtra (India), 13th – 14th January 2008

35. H. B. Kekre, Tanuja K. Sarode, "New Fast Improved Codebook Generation Algorithm for Color Images using Vector Quantization," International Journal of Engineering and Technology, vol.1, No.1, pp.: 67-77, September 2008

36. H. B. Kekre, Tanuja K. Sarode, "Fast Codebook Generation Algorithm for Color Images using Vector Quantization," International Journal of Computer Science and Information Technology, Vol. 1, No. 1, pp.: 7-12, Jan 2009

37. H. B. Kekre, Tanuja K. Sarode, "An Efficient Fast Algorithm to Generate Codebook for Vector Quantization," First International Conference on Emerging Trends in Engineering and Technology, ICETET-2008, held at Raisoni College of Engineering, Nagpur, India, pp.: 62- 67, 16-18 July 2008. Available at IEEE Xplore

38. H. B. Kekre, Tanuja K. Sarode, "Fast Codebook Generation Algorithm for Color Images using Vector Quantization," International Journal of Computer Science and Information Technology, Vol. 1, No. 1, pp.: 7-12, Jan 2009

39. H. B. Kekre, Tanuja K. Sarode, "Fast Codevector Search Algorithm for 3-D Vector Quantized Codebook", WASET International Journal of cal Computer Information Science and Engineering (IJCISE), Volume 2, No. 4, pp.: 235-239, Fall 2008. Available: http://www.waset.org/ijcise

40. H. B. Kekre, Tanuja K. Sarode, "Fast Codebook Search Algorithm for Vector Quantization using Sorting Technique", ACM International Conference on Advances in Computing, Communication and Control (ICAC3- 2009), pp: 317-325, 23-24 Jan 2009, Fr. Conceicao Rodrigous College of Engg., Mumbai. Available on ACM portal

41. H. B. Kekre, Tanuja K. Sarode, "Speech Data Compression using Vector Quantization", WASET International Journal of Computer and Information Science and Engineering (IJCISE), vol. 2, No. 4, pp.: 251-254, Fall 2008. available: http://www.waset.org/ijcise

42. H. B. Kekre, Ms. Tanuja K. Sarode, Sudeep D. Thepade, "Image Retrieval using Color-Texture Features from DCT on VQ Codevectors obtained by Kekre's Fast Codebook Generation", ICGST-International Journal on Graphics, Vision and Image Processing (GVIP), Volume 9, Issue 5, pp.: 1-8, September 2009. Available online at http://www.icgst.com/gvip/Volume9/Issue5/P1150921752.html

43. Chin-Chen Chang, Wen-Chuan Wu, "Fast Planar-Oriented Ripple Search Algorithm for Hyperspace VQ Codebook", IEEE Transaction on image processing, vol 16, no. 6, pp.: 1538-1547, June 2007

44. C. Garcia and G. Tziritas, "Face detection using quantized skin color regions merging and wavelet packet analysis," IEEE Trans. Multimedia, vol. 1, no. 3, pp.: 264–277, Sep. 1999

45. H. Y. M. Liao, D. Y. Chen, C. W. Su, and H. R. Tyan, "Real-time event detection and its applications to surveillance systems," in Proc. IEEE Int. Symp. Circuits and Systems, Kos, Greece, pp.: 509–512, May 2006

46. J. Zheng and M. Hu, "An anomaly intrusion detection system based on vector quantization," IEICE Trans. Inf. Syst., vol. E89-D, no. 1, pp.: 201–210, Jan. 2006

47. H. B. Kekre, Tanuja K. Sarode, Bhakti Raul, "Color Image Segmentation using Kekre's Fast Codebook Generation Algorithm Based on Energy Ordering Concept", ACM International Conference on Advances in Computing, Communication and Control (ICAC3-2009), pp.: 357-362, 23-24 Jan 2009, Fr. Conceicao Rodrigous College of Engg., Mumbai. Available on ACM portal

48. H. B. Kekre, Tanuja K. Sarode, Bhakti Raul, "Color Image Segmentation using Kekre's Algorithm for Vector Quantization", International Journal of Computer Science (IJCS), Vol. 3, No. 4, pp.: 287-292, Fall 2008. Available: http:// www.waset.org/ijcs

49. H. B. Kekre, Tanuja K. Sarode, Bhakti Raul, "Color Image Segmentation using Vector Quantization Techniques Based on Energy Ordering Concept" International Journal of Computing Science and Communication Technologies (IJCSCT) Volume 1, Issue 2, pp: 164-171, January 2009

50. H. B. Kekre, Tanuja K. Sarode, Bhakti Raul, "Color Image Segmentation Using Vector Quantization Techniques", Advances in Engineering Science Sect. C (3), pp.: 35-42, July-September 2008

51. H. B. Kekre, Kamal Shah, Tanuja K. Sarode, Sudeep D. Thepade, "Performance Comparison of Vecto Quantization Technique – KFCG with LBG, Existing Transforms and PCA for Face Recognition", International Journal of Information Retrieval (IJIR), Vol. 02, Issue 1, pp.: 64-71, 2009

52. Images for testing are taken from site www.edurad.in

Segmentation and identification of rotavirus-A in digital microscopic images using active contour model

P. S. Hiremath · Parashuram Bannigidad · Manjunath Hiremath

Department of Computer Science, Gulbarga University, Gulbarga, India

1. Introduction

A virus is an infectious agent too small to be seen directly with a light microscope. They are not made of cells and can only replicate inside the cells of another organism (the viruses' host). Viruses infect all types of organisms, from animals and plants to bacteria and archaea. Viruses are found in almost every ecosystem on Earth and these minute structures are the most abundant type of biological entity. Viruses consist of two or three parts: all viruses have genes made from either DNA or RNA, long molecules that carry genetic information; all have a protein coat that protects these genes; and some have an envelope of fat that surrounds them when they are outside a cell. Viruses vary from simple helical and icosahedra shapes, to more complex structures. Most viruses are about one hundred times smaller than an average bacterium. Viruses spread in many ways; plant viruses are often transmitted from plant to plant by insects that feed on sap, such as aphids, while animal viruses can be carried by blood-sucking insects. Influenza viruses are spread by coughing and sneezing.

Rotavirus is a genus of double-stranded RNA virus in the family Reoviridae. It is the leading single cause of severe diarrhea among infants and young children, and is one of several viruses that cause infections commonly known as stomach flu, despite having no relation to influenza. By the age of five, nearly every child in the world has been infected with rotavirus at least once. However, with each infection, immunity develops, subsequent infections are less severe, and adults are rarely affected. There are seven species of this virus, referred to as A, B, C, D, E, F and G. Humans are primarily infected by species A, B and C, most commonly by species A. All seven species cause disease in other animals [4].

Within rotavirus-A, there are different strains, called serotypes. As with influenza virus, a dual classification system is used, which is based on two structural proteins on the surface of the virion. The glycoprotein VP7 defines G-types and the protease sensitive protein VP4 defines P-types. Strains are generally designated by their G serotype specificities (e.g., serotypes G1 to G4 and G9), and the P-type is indicated by a number and a letter for the P-serotype and by a number in square brackets for the corresponding P-genotype. (P-scrotypes are difficult to characterize; therefore, molecular methods based on sequence analysis are often used to define the corresponding P-genotype instead. These genotypes correlate well with known P-serotypes). Because the two genes that determine G-types and P-types can be passed on separately to offspring, various combinations occur in any one strain [5].

Segmentation of cell regions is an important step in computer-aided analysis of rotavirus particle images in microbiology. Accurate and reliable segmentation is an essential step in determining valuable quantitative information on size, shape and texture, which may assist microbiologists in their diagnoses. Parametric algorithms were recently introduced for segmentation of cell images with elliptically shaped cells or cells whose contours were relatively smooth. The snakes or active contours are used extensively in computer vision and image processing applications, particularly to locate object boundaries. Nonparametric algorithms can generally be categorized as region-based, edge-based, histogram-based, clustering and neural network based algorithms [1].

For original noiseless cell images, most algorithms work fine. However, when an image is corrupted by heavy noise, these algorithms may not produce satisfactory segmentation results. The algorithm introduced in this paper deals with

S.J. Pise (ed.), *ThinkQuest 2010*, DOI 10.1007/978-81-8489-989-4_32,
© Springer India Pvt. Ltd. 2011

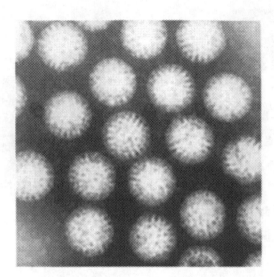

Fig. 1 Rotavirus- A TEM image from the faeces of an infected child

the problem of rotavirus-A particle segmentation and identification from images corrupted by heavy noise. The following sections discuss the image acquisition, image processing and feature extraction steps in more detail. The data used for development of the algorithm consist of rotavirus-A particle images acquired from child faeces of an infected child by the Transmission Electron Microscope (Fig. 1).

Automated image analysis of rotavirus particles will play an important role to identify rotavirus particles by using digital image processing techniques. Previously, the segmentation and statistical analysis of individual rotavirus particles is done by Venkataraman, et al. [6]. Active contours without edges based on Mumford-Shah segmentation techniques and the level set method has been done by Tony F. Chan [10]. The object identification by using snakes, shapes and gradient vector flow was done by Chenyang Xu and Jerry [11]. Edge segmentation and feature extraction using Snakes Active Contour models has been done by Michaels Kass [12]. Automated identification and classification of Rotavirus-A particles using marker controlled watershed algorithm is attempted by Hiremath et al. [9]. In this paper, the objective is to propose a method to segment and identify the Rotavirus-A particles in digital microscopic images using active contour model. Geometric features are used to identify the Rotavirus-A particles.

2. Materials and methods

Rotavirus-A particle images on Transmission Electron Microscopy is acquired by using different types of staining methods. Negative staining is an established method, often used in diagnostic microscopy, for contrasting a thin specimen with an optically opaque fluid. For bright field microscopy, negative staining is typically performed using a black ink fluid such as nigrosin. The specimen, such as a wet bacterial culture spread on a glass slide, is mixed with the negative stain and allowed to dry. When viewed with the microscope the rotavirus particles, and perhaps their spores, appear light against the dark surrounding background. Acquisition of rotavirus particle images is usually done using a CCD camera mounted in the optical path of the microscope. The camera may be full color or monochrome. Very often, very high resolution cameras are employed to gain as much direct information as possible. Often digital cameras used for this application provide pixel intensity data to a resolution of 12–16 bits. We have considered 50 color images of rotavirus-A particles with ×82, 000 magnification for present study and these are converted into grayscale images [2, 3].

3. Image analysis

Snakes or active contours are curves defined within an image domain that can move under the influence of internal forces coming from within the curve itself and external forces computed from the image data. The internal and external forces are defined so that the snake will conform to an object boundary or other desired features within an image. Snakes are widely used in many applications, including edge detection, shape modeling, segmentation, and motion tracking.

The basic idea in active contour models or snakes is to evolve a curve, subject to constraints from a given image u0, in order to detect objects in that image. For instance, starting with a curve around the object to be detected, the curve moves towards its interior normal and has to stop on the boundary of the object.

Let Ω be a bounded open subset of R2, with $\partial\Omega$ its boundary. Let $u_0: \Omega \to R$ be a given image, and C(s): [0,1]_ R2 be a parameterized curve.

In the classical snakes and active contour models[10], an edge-detector is used, depending on the gradient of the image u_0, to stop the evolving curve on the boundary of the desired object. The snake model is: infC J1(C), where

$$J_1(C) = \alpha \int_0^1 |C'(s)|^2 ds + \beta \int_0^1 |C''(s)|^2 ds$$
$$(1)$$
$$- \lambda \int_0^1 |\nabla u_0(C(s))|^2 ds$$

Here α, β and λ are positive parameters. The first two terms control the smoothness of the contour (the internal energy), while the third term attracts the contour toward the object in the image (the external energy). Observe that, by minimizing the energy (1), we are trying to locate the curve at the points of maxima $|\nabla u_0|$, acting as an edge-detector, while keeping a smoothness in the curve (object boundary).

A general edge-detector can be defined by a positive and decreasing function g, depending on the gradient of the image u_0, such that

$$\lim_{n \to \infty} g(z) = 0$$

For instance

$$g(|\nabla u_0(x,y)|) = \frac{1}{1+|\nabla G_\sigma(x,y)*u_0(x,y)|^p}, \quad p \geq 1$$

where $G_\sigma * u_0$, a smoother version of u_0, is the convolution of the image u_0 with the Gaussian

$$G_\sigma(x,y) = \sigma^{-1/2} e^{-|x^2+y^2|/4\sigma}$$

The function $g(|\nabla u_0|)$ is positive in homogeneous regions, and zero at the edges.

In problems of curve evolution, the level set method and in particular the motion by mean curvature of Osher and Sethian [13] have been used extensively, because it allows for cusps, corners, and automatic topological changes. Moreover, the discretization of the problem is made on a fixed rectangular grid. The curve C is represented implicitly via a Lipschitz function

$$\emptyset, \text{ by } C = \{(x,y) | \emptyset(x,y) = 0\}$$

and the evolution of the curve is given by the zero-level curve at time t of the function $\emptyset(t,x,y)$. Evolving the curve C in normal direction with speed F amounts to solve the differential equation

$$\frac{\partial \phi}{\partial t} = |\nabla \phi| F, \quad \phi(0,x,y) = \phi_0(x,y)$$

where the set $\{(x,y) | \emptyset_0(x,y) = 0\}$ defines the initial contour. A particular case is the motion by mean curvature, when

$$F = \text{div}(\nabla \phi(x,y)/|\nabla \phi(x,y)|)$$

is the curvature of the level-curve of f passing through (x, y). The equation becomes

$$\begin{cases} \frac{\partial \phi}{\partial t} = |\nabla \phi| \text{div}\left(\frac{\nabla \phi}{|\nabla \phi|}\right), & t \in (0, \infty), x \in R^2 \\ \phi(0,x,y) = \phi_0(x, y), & x \in R^2 \end{cases}$$

A geometric active contour model based on the mean curvature motion is given by the following evolution equation:

$$\begin{cases} \frac{\partial \phi}{\partial t} = g(|\nabla u_0|)|\nabla \phi| \left(\text{div}\left(\frac{\nabla \phi}{|\nabla \phi|}\right) + v \right), \\ \text{in } (0, \infty) \times R^2 \\ \phi(0,x,y) = \phi_0(x, y) \text{ in } R^2 \end{cases}$$

where

$g(|\nabla u_0|)$ edge-function with p=2;

$v \geq 0$ is constant;

$\emptyset_0$ initial level set function;

Its zero level curve moves in the normal direction with speed and therefore stops on the desired boundary, where g vanishes. The constant v is a correction term chosen so that the quantity (div $(\nabla \emptyset(x,y)/|\nabla \emptyset(x,y)|)$+v) remains always positive. This constant may be interpreted as a force pushing the curve toward the object, when the curvature becomes null or negative. Also, $v > 0$ is a constraint on the area inside the curve, increasing the propagation speed [10–13].

The proposed method for the segmentation and identification of rotavirus-A particles is given below:

Algorithm 1: Training phase

Step 1: Input the rotavirus colour image.

Step 2: Convert the colour image into gray scale image and adjust the image intensity values.

Step 3: Perform active contour without edges upto 1500 iterations to obtain segmented image.

Step 4: Binarize the segmented image of step 3.

Step 5: Remove the border touching cells obtained in binary image and then perform labeling the segmented binary image.

Step 6: For each labeled segment, compute geometric shape features (Area, Eccentricity, Perimeter, Circularity, Tortuosity, Length/Width ratio, Compactness) and store them.

Step 7: Repeat steps 1 to 6 for all the training images.

Step 8: Compute minimum and maximum of feature values of rotavirus-A particle and store them as knowledge base.

Algorithm 2: Testing phase

Step 1: Input the rotavirus color image.

Step 2: Convert the color image into gray scale image and adjust the image intensity values.

Step 3: Perform active contour without edges upto 1500 iterations to obtain segmented image.

Step 4: Binarize segmented image of st.

Step 5: Remove the border touching cells obtained in binary image and then perform labeling the segmented binary image.

Step 6: For each labeled segment, compute geometric shape features (Area, Eccentricity, Perimeter, Circularity, Tortuosity, Length/Width ratio, Compactness).

Step 7: Apply rule for identification of the rota-virus-A particles: A segmented region is of Rotavirus-A, if its feature values lie in min-max range.

Step 8: Repeat the steps 6 and 7 for all labeled segments and output the identified rotavirus A particles.

3. Experimental results

For the purpose of experimentation, 50 digital images of rotavirus-A particles (non-overlapping) with ×82,000 magnification are considered and these are taken from transmission electron microscopy. The implementation is done on a Intel core 2 duo processor @ 2.83GHz machine using MATLAB 7.9. In the training phase, the input rotavirus A particle image is converted into grayscale and adjust the image intensity values using matlab function. The resultant image is segmented using active contour model initiated by a fixed rectangular mask to obtain binary image. Then, the segmented image is labeled and for each segmented region (known particles), the geometric features are extracted.

The Table 1 presents the geometric feature values computed for the segmented rotavirus-A particle regions of the image in Fig. 2(d). The minimum and maximum values of geometric features obtained from the training sample images are stored in the knowledge base of the rotavirus-A particle, which is presented in Table 2. Some sample training images of rotavirus-A are shown in Fig. 3.

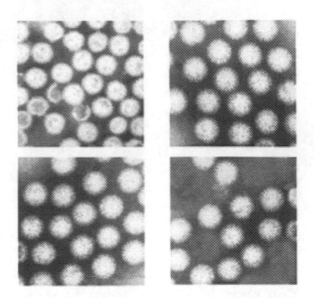

Fig. 3 Sample training images of rotavirus-A particle

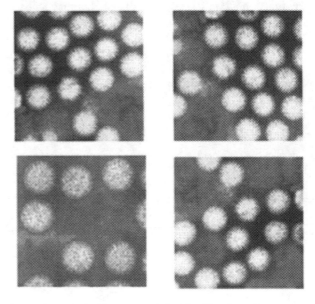

Fig. 4 Sample test images used for identification of rotavirus-A particles

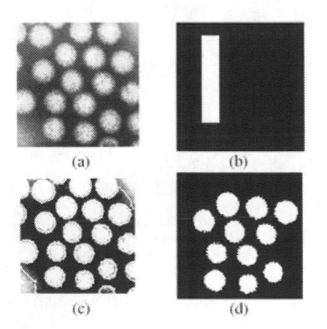

Fig. 2 (a) Original rotavirus-A TEM image (b) Initializing fixed rectangular grid (c) image showing 1500 Iterations (d) Global region based segmentation

In the testing phase, the test image is segmented by the proposed method, and the feature extraction for each segment is done. If the feature values lie in the min-max range of corresponding features in the knowledge base of Rotavirus-A particle, the labeled segment is identified as a Rotavirus-A particle otherwise it is not a Rotavirus-A particle proposed method is computationally less expensive and yet yields comparable identification rate with 98% for rotavirus-A particle which is better than earlier method[9] with 96% using marker controlled watershed algorithm. Fig. 4 shows some sample test images used for identification of rotavirus-A particles.

Table 1 The geometric feature values of the rotavirs-A particulars of the image in Fig. 2(d)

Rotavirus -A Features	Area	Eccentricity	Perimeter	Circularity	Tortuosity	Length/ Width ratio	Compactness
Particle 1	1573	0.29	179.78	0.61	0.26	1.05	1.64
Particle 2	1499	0.20	172.85	0.63	0.26	1.02	1.59
Particle 3	1353	0.36	193.82	0.45	0.22	1.07	2.21
Particle 4	1845	0.35	169.44	0.81	0.30	1.07	1.24
Particle 5	1469	0.42	177.20	0.59	0.26	1.10	1.70
Particle 6	1417	0.27	177.10	0.57	0.25	1.04	1.76
Particle 7	1198	0.27	162.95	0.57	0.25	1.04	1.76
Particle 8	1609	0.35	182.95	0.60	0.26	1.07	1.66
Particle 9	14.7	0.45	177.68	0.56	0.25	1.12	1.79
Particle 10	1338	0.40	166.27	0.61	0.26	1.09	1.64
Particle 11	1799	0.26	173.34	0.75	0.28	1.03	1.33

Table 2 The knowledge base for rotavirus-A particles containing minimum and maximum values of features

Features	Area	Eccentricity	Perimeter	Circularity	Tortuosity	Length/ Width ratio	Compactness
Minimum Value	1845	0.45	193.82	0.81	0.30	1.12	2.21
Maximum Value	1198	0.20	162.95	0.45	0.22	1.02	1.24

4. Conclusion

In this paper, we have proposed a method for segmentation and identification of rotavirus-A particles in transmission electron microscope images using active contour model and geometric features of rotavirus-A particles. The experimental results are confirmed by visual inspection conducted by microbiological experts. The proposed method is more reliable and computationally less expensive. It yields an identification rate of 98% for rotavirus-A particles which is better than our earlier method [9] which yielded 96%. It could be improved further by better pre-processing methods, feature sets and classifiers. The classification of other rotavirus particles also will be considered in future work.

References

1. Rafel C. Gonzalez and Richard E. Woods, "Digital image processing", Pearson Education Asia (2002)
2. M. A. Hayat, "Principles and techniques of electron microscopy: biological applications". Cambridge University Press. pp. 45-61. ISBN 0521632870 (2000)
3. Bozzola, John J.; Russell, Lonnie D. "Specimen preparation for transmission electron microscopy" Jones and Bartlett. pp. 21–31. ISBN 9780763701925(1999)
4. Velázquez FR, Matson DO, Calva JJ, Guerrero L, Morrow AL, Carter-Campbell S, Glass RI, Estes MK, Pickering LK, Ruiz-Palacios GM, "Rotavirus infections in infants as protection against subsequent infections". N. Engl. J. Med. 335 (14):1022 8. doi:10.1056/NEJM199610033351404. PMID 8793926
5. Arnoldi F, Campagna M, Eichwald C, Desselberger U, Burrone OR. "Interaction of rotavirus polymerase VP1 with nonstructural protein NSP5 is stronger than that with NSP2". J. Virol. 81(5): 2128–37. (2007) doi:10.1128/JVI.01494-06. PMID 17182692.http://jvi.asm.org/cgi/content/full/81/5/2128
6. S. Venkataraman, D.P. Allison, H. Qi, J.L. Morrell- Falvey, N.L. Kallewaard, J.E. Crowe Jr. and M.J. Doktycz. "Automated image analysis of atomic force microscopy images of rotavirus particles." Ultramicroscopy, Elsevier, Vol. 106, 2006, pp. 829-837
7. P.S. Hiremath and Parashuram Bannigidad, "Automatic classification of bacterial cells in digital microscopic images", Intl. Jl. of Engg. and Tech. (IJENGG), Vol.2, No.4, Dec. 2009, pp. 9-15
8. Dennis Kunkel Microscopy, Inc, Science Stock Photography, http://www.denniskunkel.com
9. P.S.Hiremath, Parashuram Bannigidad, Manjunath Hiremath, "Automated Identification and classification of rotavirus-A particles in digital microscopic images", Nat. Conf. on Recent Trends in Image Processing and Pattern Recognition RTIPPR- 2010), February 15-16, 2010, Bidar (Accepted)
10. Tony F Chan, Luminita A. Vese, "Active contours without edges", IEEE Transaction on Image Processing, Vol. 10, No. 2, February 2001. [11] Chenyang Xu, Jerry L Prince, "Snakes, Shapes, and Gradient Vector Flow", IEEE Transactions on Image Processing, Vol. 7, No. 3, March 1998
11. Chenyang Xu, Jerry L Prince, "Snakes, Shapes, and Gradient Vector Flow", IEEE Transactions on Image Processing, Vol. 7, No. 3, March 1998
12. Michael Kass, Andrew witkin and demetri, "Snakes: Active contour models", Intl. J. of Computer Vision, 1998, pp. 321-331
13. S.Osher and J.A.Sethian, "Fronts propagating with curvature dependent speed: Algorithm based on Hamilton Jacobi Formulation" J. Compact Phy, Vol. 79, 1988, pp.12-49

Empowering primitive architectural connectors with aspects

Arvind W. Kiwelekar · Rushikesh K. Joshi

Department of Computer Science and Engineering Indian Institute of Technology, Mumbai, India

1. Introduction

An architectural connector, a central notion in Architectural Description Languages (ADL) [9, 5], is an abstraction that captures interactions among software components. Existing approaches for representing architectural connectors in programming environments use object-based [6] and component-based [8, 1, 4] notations. Often architectural abstractions are realized in programming environments to ensure representational benefits provided by ADLs like separating computational and interaction concerns and treating connectors as first-class design elements. However, in such programming environments, complex connectors are represented through components. When connectors are represented through components, components and connectors are indistinguishable in terms of mechanisms used to realize them. One has to look for functionalities that components realize to decide whether it is a component or a connector. At the same time, primitive connectors are discernible elements in such programming environments. This paper explores an alternative mechanism i.e. aspect in aspectoriented programming language[7] to represent a connector. Appropriateness of aspects to represent connectors is demonstrated by implementing few examples of connectors in Java/AspectJ [3, 7] programming environment.

In Section 2 implementation of Component and Port abstractions is discussed. Section 3 describes two different approaches for representing connectors i.e. one through components and other through aspects. In Section 4, an architectural configuration with multiple connectors is captured through components and aspects mechanisms. Section 5 introduces the definition of an abstract connector. Finally paper concludes by summarizing the mapping scheme.

2. An implementation for architectural abstractions

This section describes implementation of architectural abstractions through the UML class diagram. Java/AspectJ programming environment is the platform used for implementation. A sample program is also discussed to illustrate how an architectural description is specified using these abstractions. Major highlights of the UML class diagram shown in Fig. 1 are

1. An architectural component is possible to represent hierarchically. Components are related with each other through the composition relationship capturing hierarchical nature of architectural components.

2. A port is an integral part of an architectural component. This fact is captured by relating port and component abstractions through the composition relationship. The minimality constraint of 1 on the composition relation indicates that there is no such instance of port which exists without a corresponding instance of component.

3. Relationships among Ports Ports are related with each other through two different types of relationships called attachments and representation-maps. A representation-map is a relationship between a port of an outer component with a port of an inner component. While an attachment is a relationship between outer ports of different components.

4. A connector is an interaction relationship among components. In the class diagram, a connector is represented as an association between components which is captured through an aspect mechanism and not through an association-class. Here, connectors as aspects are interpreted as modular units that realize a communication protocol around some basic communication mechanism.

S.J. Pise (ed.), *ThinkQuest 2010*, DOI 10.1007/978-81-8489-989-4_33,
© Springer India Pvt. Ltd. 2011

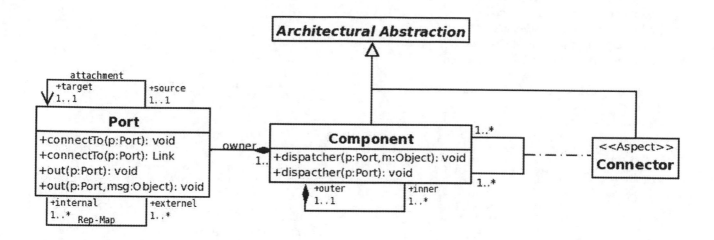

Fig. 1 Class diagram for architectural abstractions

2.1 An example of architectural description

The puprose of this section is to describe how an architectural description is realized through architectural abstractions implemented in Java. A *Producer-Consumer* system as shown in Fig. 2(a) is realized as an example. The steps involved in writing an architectural description are – (i) Define architectural components. In the context of Java-based implementation, an architectural component is a class that extends a predefined class called component. (ii) Instantiate the components defined in the step one. (iii) Define component configuration i.e. interconnect instances of components through ports they own.

While defining a component, few guidelines are followed i.e. (i) Ports are the public variables. (ii) All methods implemented within a component are private. Visibility of the methods defined in the superclasses is not overridden. (iii) A component overrides the dispatcher method defined in the super class Component. The dispatcher method invokes a private method to handle the received message on a port. In the dispatcher method, ports are used to decide a method to be invoked. A component communicates through the ports it owns. Two components are connected to each other through the method connectTo provided by Port class. The method out also provided by port class realizes a message transfer over the connection and is considered as a primitive communication mechanism. Peer components connected to the port receive the message.

The following code segment realizes a producer consumer system by defining and instantiating producer and consumer components. First, producer component with output as a single port is defined. It overrides the method dispatcher defined in the super-class component. If a message is delivered on the public port output of a producer

component, the method dispatcher executes the private method produce.

Listing 1. Producer.java

```
1 class Producer extends Component{
2 String name;
3 public Port output;
4 public Producer (String n) {
5 name = n;
6 output = new Port (this);}
7 private void produce(String msg){
8     output.out(msg);}
9 public void dispatcher(Port rec, String msg){
10 if (rec==output) {produce(msg);
11 } // dispatcher
12 }//Component
```

Second, the following code segment defines consumer component with in as a single port. It also overrides the dispatcher method.

Listing 2. Consumer.java

```
1 class Consumer extends Component {
2 String name;
3 public Port in;
4 public Consumer (String n) {
5 in = new Port (this);
6 name = n;}
7 private void consume(String msg) {}
8 public void dispatcher(Port rec, String msg){
9 if (rec==in) { consume(msg); }
10 } // dispatcher
11 }//Component
```

In the system class, components are instantiated and component-configuration is defined. The output port of myProducer component is connected to the port in of myConsumer. A message "Hello World" is produces by the port output that is consumed by the port in of Consumer.

Listing 3. System.java

```
1 public class System {
2 public static void main(String args[]){
3 // Instantiate Components
4 Producer myProducer = new Producer("A");
5 Consumer myConsumer = new Consumer("C");
6 // Define Component Configuration
7 myProducer.output.connectTo(myConsumer.in);
8 // Producer "A" sends a message
9 myProducer.output.out("Hello World");}
10 } // System
```

3. Approaches for representing connector

This section describes two different approaches for representing a complex connector. For this purpose a connector called Write-Cue-Regulator [2] is considered. A component configuration that uses write-cue-regulator is shown in Fig. 2(b). This connector withholds the message produced by the producer "A" until "Controller" permits it to be transferred to the Consumer "C". If "Controller" permits earlier than a message is produced by the producer "A" then it waits for the message from "A".

3.1 Connector as component

In the first approach, the write-cue-regulator connector is represented as component. A component that will act as a connector W cr As Component is defined. It has three ports one for the Producer "A", second for "Controller" and third for the consumer "C". The method dispatcher defined in wcr As Component realizes the connector protocol. It internally uses two flags that controls message transfers from producer "A" to consumer "C". A message is buffered till "Controller" permits the message to be transferred to the consumer. The flags are reset before every message transfers to consumer "C".

Listing 4. WcrAsComponet.java

```
1 public class WcrAsComponet extends Component{
2 String name;
3 public Port controller, sender, recv;
4 boolean grantWR =false;
5 boolean dataIn =false;
6 String buf = null;
7 public WcrAsComponet (String n){
8 name = n;
9 recv = new Port (this);
10 controller = new Port (this);
11 sender = new Port (this);
12 }//WcrAsComponet (String n)
13 public void dispatcher (Port rec){
14 if (rec==controller){
15 grantWR = true;
16 if(dataIn){
17 grantWR = false;
```

```
18 dataIn = false;
19 recv.out(buf);
20 }//dataIn -if
21 } //controller -if
22 }//dispatcher (Port rec)
23 public void dispatcher (Port rec, String msg){
24 if (rec==sender){
25 buf =msg;
26 dataIn = true;
27 if(grantWR){
28 grantWR = false;
29 dataIn = false;
30 recv.out(buf);
31 }//grantWR-if
32 }// sender-if
33 }//dispatcher(Port rec, String msg)
34 }// WcrAsComponet Component
```

The program listing pcSystem.java shows instantiation of components and connectors. It is to be noted that connector component i.e. component acting as a connector needs to be instantiated and inserted in the component configuration. The component-connector configuration is shown in Fig. 2(c). The listing also tests the working of connector in three different scenarios i.e. (i) Producer "A" generates a message earlier than "Controller". (ii) Controller permits before Producer "A" generates a message. (iii) The producer "A" generates a message but "Controller" does not permit.

Listing 5. pcSystem.java

```
1 public class pcSystem {
2 pcSystem(){
3 // Component and Connector Instantiation
4 Producer prodA = new Producer("A");
5 Producer prodCtrl =
6 new Producer("Controller");
7 WcrAsComponet wcrCon =
8 new WcrAsComponet("WCR");
9 Consumer myConsumer = new Consumer("C");
10 // Defining Component Configuration
11 prodA.output.connectTo(wcrCon.sender) ;
12 prodCtrl.output.connectTo(wcrCon.controller);
13 wcrCon.recv.connectTo(myConsumer.in);
14 // "Message 1 " is Tansferered .
15 prodA.dispatcher(prodA.output,"Message 1");
16 prodCtrl.dispatcher(prodCtrl.output);
17 // "Message 2" is blocked
18 prodCtrl.dispatcher(prodCtrl.output);
19 prodA.dispatcher(prodA.output,"Message 2");
20 // "Message 3" is blocked
21 prodA.dispatcher(prodA.output,"Message 3");
22 } //pcSystem()
23 public static void main(String args[]){
24 pcSystem p1 = new pcSystem();
25 } //main
26 } //pcSystem-class
```

3.2 Connectors as aspects

In the second approach, the write-cue-regulator connector is modeled as aspect. The main idea behind representing connector as aspect is to augment a message transfer through advice mechanism. Primitive connectors simply transfer messages from a sender to a receiver, while complex connectors are intended to provide additional services around the message transfers. When connectors are represented as aspects the main activities are to identify joinpoints and specify advices to be executed at these joinpoints. The listing Wcr AsAspect.java defines an aspect implementation. It defines the pointcut msgTX that identifies call to the out method as the join point. The advice method defined for MsgTx pointcut realizes the communication protocol for write-cue-regulator connector. It follows the same logic as described in the last section.

Listing 6. WcrAsAspect.java

```
1 public aspect WcrAsAspect{
2 String buffer = null;
3 boolean grantWR = false;
4 boolean dataIn = false;
5
6 pointcut msgTX(Port t, String msg) :
7 call(void Port.out(String)) && target(t)
8 && args(msg);
9
10 void around(Port t, String msg):msgTX(t,msg){
11 String cname = ((Component)t.getOwner())
12 .toString();
13 if(cname == "A"){
14         buffer = msg;
15         dataIn = true;
16 if(grantWR){
17     dataIn = false;
18     grantWR = false;
19     proceed(t,buffer);
20 }
21 }
22 if(cname == "Controller"){
23         grantWR = true;
24 if(dataIn){
25     dataIn = false;
26     grantWR = false;
27     proceed(t,buffer);
28 }
29         }//if
30 }//around
31 }//aspect
```

The program listing pcSys1.java shows instantiation of components and connectors. The component-connector configuration for this case is shown in Fig. 2(d). It is to be noted that, in this case, the connector needs no instantiation.

Listing 7. pcSys1.java

```
1 public class pcSys1{
2 pcSys1(){
3 // Instantiate the Components
4 Producer prodA = new Producer("A");
5 Producer ctrl = new Producer("Controller");
6 Consumer con = new Consumer("C");
7 // Define Component Configuration
8 prodA.output.connectTo(con.in);
```

```
9 ctrl.output.connectTo(con.in);
10 // Test Cases
11 prodA.dispatcher(prodA.output, "Message 1");
12 ctrl.dispatcher(ctrl.output, " ");
13 ctrl.dispatcher(ctrl.output, " ");
14 prodA.dispatcher(prodA.output, "Message 2");
15 prodA.dispatcher(prodA.output, "Message 3");
16 }//pcSys1()
17 public static void main(String args[]){
18     pcSys1 p1 = new pcSys1();
19 }//main()
20 }pcSys1
```

4. An architectural configuration with multiple connectors

The purpose of this example is to demonstrate how an architectural configuration with multiple connectors of different types is realized.

In Fig. 2, upper connector converts a message from the Producer "A" to the consumer "C" in upper case and message from the Producer "B" is converted into lower case by the connector Lower. The required behavior is captured through single aspect that is defined below. Similar to the last aspect definition, it also identifies msgTX as the pointcut with the same method signature. The advice method now realizes a different connector protocol, that uses name of the producer to decide which conversion is to be applied.

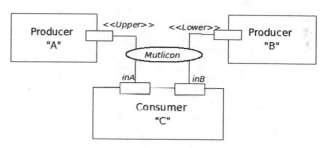

Fig. 2 Architectural configuration with multiple connector

Listing 8. MultiCon.java

```
1 public aspect Mutlicon {
2 pointcut MsgTx(Port t, String msg):
3 call(void Port.out(String)) &&
4 target(t) && args(msg);
5
6 void around(Port t, String msg): MsgTx(t,msg){
7 String cname =
8 ((Component)t.getOwner()).toString();
9 String mn =null;
10 if (cname.equals("A")){
11 mn=msg.toUpperCase();
12 }
13 if (cname.equals("B")){
```

```
14  mm=msg.toLowerCase();
15  }
16  proceed(t, mm);
17  } // around
18  } // aspect
```

The aspect defintion defined above captures behavior of two different connectors i.e. Lower and Upper. From the aspect definitions discussed so far, it is observed that aspect definitions apply to whole system configuration rather than individual connectors.

5. Abstract connectors

In this section, the concept of abstract connector is defined. From the examples of connectors discussed so far, it is observed that definition of the pointcut msgTX remains unchanged. Such pointcut definitions that are applicable to all connectors are called generic pointcuts. In the context of aspect-based modeling of connectors, an abstract connector is an abstraction that encapsulates generic pointcuts and default advice methods associated to these pointcuts. The following code segment defines an abstract aspect that includes three pointcuts one is associated with connectTo method i.e.connectedPC and other two i.e. msgTX and mtMsgTX are associated with two different forms of out method one with message as an argument and another without any message argument. Also, default advice methods are defined and attached to these pointcuts. A concrete aspect overrides the advice methods or specialize the generic pointcuts.

```
1  public abstract aspect Channel {
2  pointcut connectedPC(Port source,
3  Port destn):
4  call(void Port.connectTo(Port)) &&
5  target(source) && args(destn),
6
7  pointcut msgTX(Port source, String msg):
8  call(void Port.out(String)) &&
9  target(source) && args(msg);
10
11 pointcut mtMsgTX(Port source):
12 call(void Port.out()) && target(source);
13
14 protected void connectedPC_before_advice
15 (Port s, Port d){
16 System.out.println("Connecting");}
17
18 before(Port s, Port d):
19 connectedPC(s,d) {
20 connectedPC_before_advice(s,d);}
21
22 public void mtMsgTX_around_advice() {
23 System.out.println("Sending data");}
24
25 protected String MsgTX_around_advice
26 (Port t, String msg){
27 System.out.println("Sending data");
28 return msg;}
29
30 void around(Port t): mtMsgTX(t){
31 mtMsgTX_around_advice();
32 proceed(t);}
33
34 void around(Port t, String msg):
35 msgTX(t, msg){
36 String modified_msg =
37 MsgTX_around_advice(t, msg);
38 proceed(t, modified_msg);
39 }}
```

6. Conclusions

Aspect-oriented modeling of architectural connectors is discussed in this paper. Aspect-based connector modeling is demonstrated through multiple examples. In addition to the examples discussed in this paper, other connector types and interaction patterns mentioned in [2, 10] are also captured through aspect mechanism. In Java/AspectJ programming environment, it is possible to map components and connectors to different language mechanisms i.e. components and aspects respectively. Aspect-based modeling of architectural connectors improves clarity of architectural abstractions in terms of language mechanisms and separating concerns. This also simplifies tracing of architectural elements to the source code elements. Representing different types of architecture-level crosscutting concern through aspect mechanism, and composing connectors through aspects are some of the issues that need further attention.

References

1. J. Aldrich. Archjava :connecting software architecture to implementation. *Proc. International Conference on Software Engineering*, 2002

2. F. Arbab. Abstract behavior types: a foundation model for components and their composition. *Sci. Comput. Program.*, 55(1-3):3–52, 2005

3. K. Arnold, J. Gosling, and D. Holmes. *The Java Programming Language*. Addison-Wesley Reading MA, third edition

4. N. Bhope and R. K. Joshi. System of purely inter-connected component. Technical Report, Department of Computer Science and Engineering, IIT-Bombay, June 2001

5. D. Garlan. Acme: An architecture description interchange language. *Proceedings of CASCON'97*, November 1997

6. D. Garlan, S.-W. Cheng, and A. J. Kompanek. Reconciling the needs of architectural description with object-modelinnotations. *Sci. Comput. Program.*, 44(1):23–49, 2002

7. G. Kiczales, E. Hilsdale, J. Hugunin, M. Kersten, J. Palm, and W. G. Griswold. An overview of aspectj. In *ECOOP '01: Proceedings of the 15th European Conference on Object-Oriented Programming*, pages 327–353, London, UK, 2001. Springer-Verlag

8. S. Malek, M. M. Rakic, and N. Medvidovic. A styleaware architectural middleware for resource constrained, distributed systems. *IEEE Transactions On Software Engineering*, 31(3):256–272, March 2005

9. N. Medvidovic and R. N. Taylor. A classification and comparison framework for software architecture description language. IEEE Transactions on Software Engineering, 26(1):70–93, January 2000

10. N. Vaidya and R. Joshi. Implementation of filter configurations using method call pointcuts in aspectj. In WAOSD 2004: Proceedings of the International Workshop on Aspect-Oriented Software Development, Bejing, China, September 2004

Information hiding in vector quantized codebook

H. B. Kekre[1] · Archana Athawale[2] · Tanuja K. Sarode[2] · Kalpana Sagvekar[3]

[1]Senior Professor, Ph.D Research Scholar, MPSTME, SVKM's NMIMS, Mumbai, India.
[2]Asst. Prof., Thadomal Shahani Engineering College, Mumbai, India.
[3]Fr. Conceicao Rodrigues College of Engineering, Bandra(W), Mumbai, India.

1. Introduction

In recent years, the use of network communication has grown sharply: information is frequently transmitted as a range of digital forms including text, image, audio, video, and other media. Data hiding involves embedding secret data into other cover media with minimal perceivable degradation. These data hiding techniques represent an important tool in, for example, protecting copyright (e.g. watermarking), communicating secretly, and embedding captions [1]. Although various applications may have different requirements, data hiding has two fundamental requirements. First, the degrading of quality due to embedding should be imperceptible. A few distortions occur as data is embedded into cover media. For security, the change in the cover medium should not be obvious. Secondly, the hiding capacity should suffice to store a reasonable amount of hidden data. However, the distortion and the embedding capacity are traded off such that more embedded data cause greater degradation in the cover medium. To meet these requirements, the primary goal of data-hiding techniques is to cause a minimum of visual or auditory degradation for any reasonable quantity of hidden data.

The existing schemes of data hiding can roughly be classified into the following three categories:

Spatial domain data hiding [2–4]: Data hiding of this type directly modifies image pixels in the spatial domain for data embedding. This technique is easy to implement, offers a relatively high hiding capacity, and the quality of the stego image can be easily controlled. Therefore, data hiding of this type has become a popular method for image steganography.

Frequency domain data hiding [5, 6]: Images are first transformed into frequency domain, and then data are embedded by modifying the transformed coefficients. Frequency domain steganography often suffers from relatively higher computational cost and lower embedding capacity than those of spatial domain data hiding.

Compressed domain data hiding [7, 8]: Data hiding is achieved by modifying the coefficients of the compressed code of a cover image. Since most images transmitted over Internet are in compressed format, embedding secret data into the compressed domain would arouse little suspicion.

Due to the limited bandwidth of networks, they cannot keep up with the growing sizes of various multimedia files. Many well accepted image compression algorithms have been proposed to counter this problem, such as VQ [18], side match VQ (SMVQ) [19], JPEG [20], JPEG2000 [21], and so on. One of the most commonly studied image compression techniques is VQ [22], which is an attractive choice because of its simplicity and cost-effective implementation. Indeed, a variety of VQ techniques have been successfully applied in real applications such as speech and image coding [22], [24], [26]. VQ not only has faster encode/decode time and a simpler framework than JPEG/JPEG2000 but it also requires limited information during decoding, and those advantages cost VQ a little low compression ratio and visual quality. VQ works best in applications in which the decoder has only limited information and a fast execution time is required [23].

There are two approaches of hiding data into VQ compressed domain; either hide the secret data into index based cover image or in codebook. In this paper we have proposed a method of hiding data into codebook which is not been explored. In section II we present codebook design algorithms. Section III explains proposed search algorithm followed by Section IV in which results and evaluation is given. Section V gives conclusion.

S.J. Pise (ed.), *ThinkQuest 2010*, DOI 10.1007/978-81-8489-989-4_34,

2. VQ compression technique

VQ consists of three phases codebook design, encoding phase and decoding phase. The key to VQ data compression is a good codebook, the method used most often for developing a codebook is the Linde-Buzo- Gray (LBG) algorithm [10, 11]. The basic function of VQ can be defined as a mapping of k-dimensional Euclidean space Rk to into a finite subset **CB** of Rk. The finite set **CB** is known as the codebook and **CB** = {Ci | i = 1, 2, ..., N } where **Ci** = (ci1, ci2, ..., cik) is a codevector and N is the size of codebook. Once the codebook is ready, in encoding phase the image is divided into non overlapping blocks and each block is then converted to the training vector **Xi** = (xi1, xi2, ..., xik). The codebook is then searched for the nearest code vector Cmin by computing squared Euclidean distance as presented in equation (1) with vector **Xi** with all the code vectors of the codebook **CB**. This method is called exhaustive search (ES) [24].

$$d(X_i, C_{min}) = \min_{1 \leq j \leq N} \{d(X_i, C_j)\} \quad \text{Where}$$

$$d(X_i, C_j) = \sum_{p=1}^{k} (x_{ip}, c_{jp})^2 \qquad (1)$$

Although the Exhaustive Search (ES) method gives the optimal result at the end, it involves heavy computational complexity. Observe the above equation (1) to obtain one nearest codevector for a particular training vector it requires to compute N Euclidean distances where N is the size of the codebook. Now if we have M total image training vectors, then to encode the image it will require M*N number of Euclidean distances computations. It is obvious that if the codebook size is increased to reduce the distortion the searching time will also increase.

2.1 Codebook generation algorithms

2.1.1 Linde-Buzo-Gray (LBG) algorithm [10, 11]

In this algorithm centroid is computed as the first code vector for the training set. In Fig. 1 two vectors v1 & v2 are generated by adding constant error to the code vector. Euclidean distances of all the training vectors are computed with vectors v1 & v2 and two clusters are formed based on nearest of v1 or v2. This procedure is repeated for every cluster. The drawback of this algorithm is that the cluster elongation is +135o to horizontal axis in two dimensional cases. This results in inefficient clustering.

2.2.2 Proportionate error algorithm (KPE) [12, 13]

Here proportionate error is added to the centroid to generate two vectors v1 & v2. Magnitude of members of the centroid decides the error ratio. Hereafter the procedure is same as

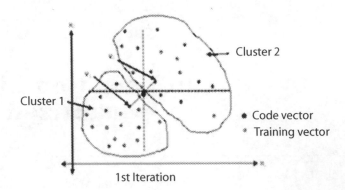

Fig. 1   LBG for 2 dimensional case

that of LBG. While adding proportionate error a safe guard is also introduced so that neither v1 nor v2 go beyond the training vector space. This removes the disadvantage of the LBG. Both LBG and KPE requires 2M number of Euclidean distance computations and 2M number of comparisons where M is the total number of training vectors in every iteration to generate clusters.

2.2.3 Kekre's median codebook generation algorithm (KMCG) [14]

In this algorithm image is divided in to blocks and blocks are converted to the vectors of size k. The Fig. 2 below represents matrix T of size M × k consisting of M number of image training vectors of dimension k. Each row of the matrix is the image training vector of dimension k.

The training vectors are sorted with respect to the first member of all the vectors i.e. with respect to the first column of the matrix T and the entire matrix is considered as one single cluster. The median of the matrix T is chosen (code vector) and is put into the codebook, and the size of the codebook is set to one. The matrix is then divided into two equal parts and the each of the part is then again sorted with respect to the second member of all the training vectors i.e. with respect to the second column of the matrix T and we obtain two clusters both consisting of equal number of training vectors. The median of both the parts is the picked up and written to the codebook, now the size

$$T = \begin{bmatrix} X_{1,1} & X_{1,2} \cdots & X_{1,k} \\ X_{2,1} & X_{2,2} \cdots & X_{2,k} \\ \vdots & & \\ X_{M,1} & X_{M,2} \cdots & X_{M,k} \end{bmatrix}$$

Fig. 2   Training Vector

of the Codebook is increased to two consisting of two code vectors and again each part is further divided to half. Each of the above four parts obtained are sorted with respect to the third column of the matrix T and four clusters are obtained and accordingly four code vectors are obtained. The above process is repeated till we obtain the codebook of desired size. Here quick sort algorithm is used and from the results it is observed that this algorithm takes least time to generate codebook, since Euclidean distance computation is not required.

2.2.4. Kekre's fast codebook generation (KFCG) algorithm

In [15], KFCG algorithm for image data compression is proposed. This algorithm reduces the time for codebook generation. It does not use Euclidian distance for codebook generation. In this algorithm image is divided in to blocks and blocks are converted to the vectors of size k. Initially we have one cluster with the entire training vectors and the code vector C1 which is centroid.

In the first iteration of the algorithm, the clusters are formed by comparing first element of training vector with first element of code vector C1. The vector Xi is grouped into the cluster 1 if $x_{i1} < c_{11}$ otherwise vector Xi is grouped into cluster 2 as shown in Fig. 3a. where code vector dimension space is 2.

In second iteration, the cluster 1 is split into two by comparing second element x_{i2} of vector Xi belonging to cluster 1 with that of the second element of the code vector which is centroid of cluster 1. Cluster 2 is split into two by comparing the second element x_{i2} of vector Xi belonging to cluster 2 with that of the second element of the code vector which is centroid of cluster 2, as shown in Fig. 3b.

This procedure is repeated till the codebook size is reached to the size specified by user. It is observed that this algorithm gives less error as compared to LBG and requires least time to generate codebook as compared to other algorithms, as it does not require computation of Euclidian distance.

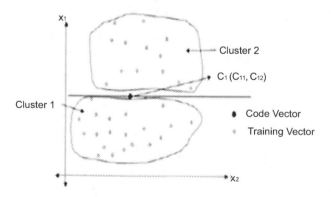

Fig. 3a   First Iteration

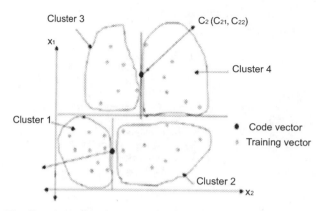

Fig. 3b   Second Iteration

3.   Proposed approach

In this approach, we are hiding the secret data into codebook generated using various codebook generation algorithm such as LBG[10][11], KPE[12][13], KMCG[14], KFCG[15]. There are various ways of hiding: 1bit, 2 bits, 3 bits, 4 bits & variable bits hiding.

3.1   Embedding procedure

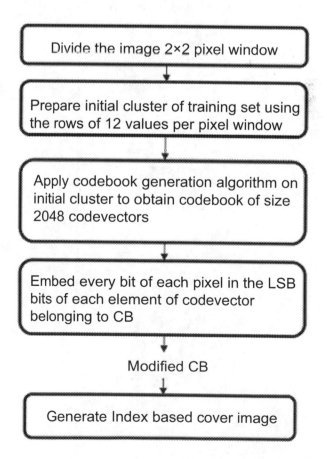

3.2   Extraction & recovery procedure

For variable bit hiding following algorithm is used.

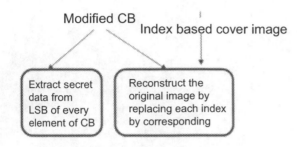

1. If the value of codebook vector element is in the range $240 \leq gi \leq 255$ then we embed 4 bits of secret data into the 4 LSB's codebook vector element. This can be done by observing the 4 most significant bits (MSB's). If they are all 1's then the remaining 4 LSB's can be used for embedding data.

2. If the value of codebook vector element is in the range $224 \leq gi \leq 239$ then we embed 3 bits of secret data.. This can be done by observing the 3 most significant bits (MSB's). If they are all 1's then the remaining 3 LSB's can be used for embedding data.

3. If the value of codebook vector element is in the range $192 \leq gi \leq 223$ then we embed 2 bits of secret data.. This can be done by observing the 2 most significant bits (MSB's). If they are all 1's then the remaining 2 LSB's can be used for embedding data.

4. If the value of codebook vector element is in the range $0 \leq gi \leq 191$ we embed 1 bit of secret data.

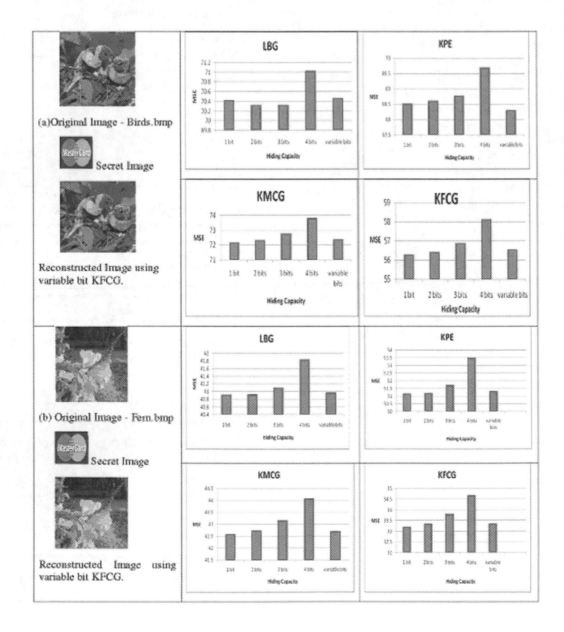

(c)OriginalImage - Puppy.bmp

Secret Image

Reconstructed Image using variable bit KFCG.

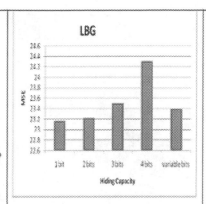

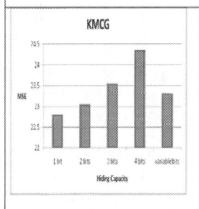

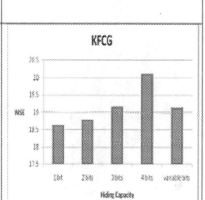

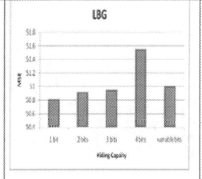

(d) Original Image – Cat.bmp

Secret Image

Reconstructed Image using variable bit KFCG.

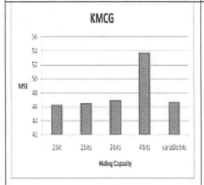

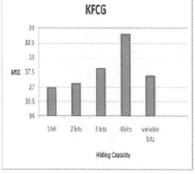

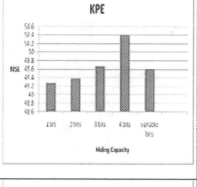

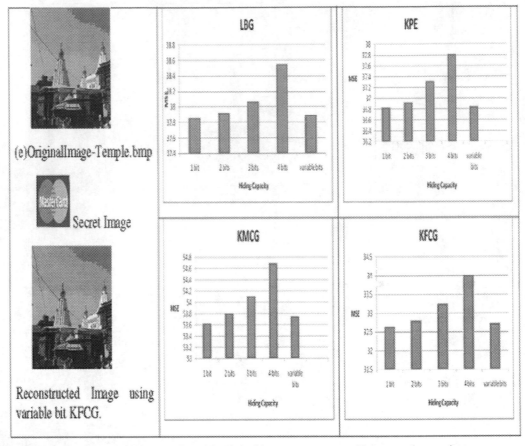

Fig. 4   Shows MSE as a function of hiding capacity with original image, reconstructed image, and secret image

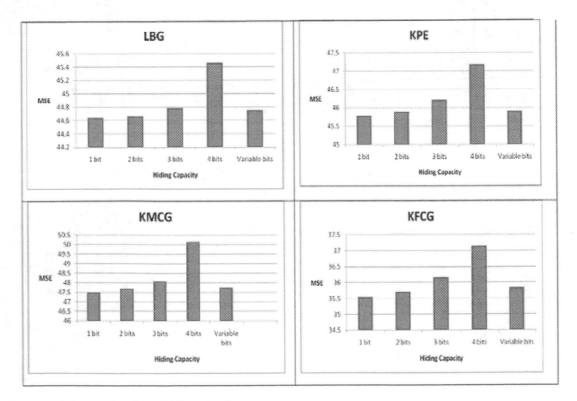

Fig. 5   Shows avg .MSE as a function of hiding capacity

4. Results & evaluation

In our proposed approach, we have generated codebook using LBG, KPE, KMCG and KFCG for 24 bit color image of size 256×256 shown in Fig. 5a. Codebook is of size 2048×12 (i.e. 2048 code vectors each contains 12 bytes - 4 pairs of RGB). We have hidden 32×32 gray image.

5. Conclusion

In this paper, we have suggesting unexplored media for information hiding. The information is hidden in a vector quantized codebook by using 1, 2, 3, 4 LSBs of the code vectors. Further a variable bit embedding is also considered which gives better embedding capacity coupled with low distortion. For preparing codebooks four different algorithms namely LBG, KPE, KMCG, KFCG are considered & their performance is considered using MSE as a parameter. It has been observed that KFCG with variable bits for hiding information gives the best performance giving rise equivalent to 2.2 bits per byte of code vectors. In addition KFCG has very low computational complexity.

References

1. Petitcolas, F.A.P., Anderson, R.J., and Kuhn, M.G.: 'Information hiding – a survey', Proc. IEEE, 1999, 87, (7), pp. 1062–1078 2 Swanson, M.D., Kobayashi, M., and Tewfik, A.: 'Multimedia data embedding and watermarking technologies', Proc. IEEE, 1998, 86, (6), pp. 1064–1087

2. Dr.H.B.Kekre, Ms.Archana Athawale and Ms. Pallavi N.Halarnkar, "Increased Capacity of Information Hiding in LSBs Method for Text and Image", International Journal of Electrical, Computer and Systems Engineering, Volume 2 Number 4. http://www.waset.org/ijecse/v2.html

3. Dr.H.B.Kekre, Ms.Archana Athawaleand Ms. Pallavi N.Halarnkar, "Polynomial Transformation To Improve Capacity Of Cover Image For Information Hiding In Multiple LSBs", International Journal of Engineering Research and Industrial Applications(IJERIA), Ascent Publications, Volume II, March 2009, Pune

4. Dr.H.B.Kekre, Ms.Archana Athawale and Ms. Pallavi N.Halarnkar, "Performance Evaluation Of Pixel Value Differencing And Kekre's Modified Algorithm For Information Hiding In Images", ACM International Conference on Advances in Computing, Communication and Control (ICAC3).2009 (Uploaded on ACM Portal: http://portal.acm.org/citation.cfm?id=1523103.1523172)

5. S.D. Lin and C.F. Chen, A Robust DCTbased Watermarking for Copyright Protection, IEEE Transactions on Consumer Electron, vol. 46, no. 3, pp. 415-421, 2000

6. Y.T. Wu and F.Y. Shih, Genetic algorithm based methodology for breaking the steganalytic systems, IEEE Transactions on Systems, Man and Cybernetics. Part B, vol. 36, no. 1, pp. 24-31, 2006

7. C. C. Chang, and C. Y. Lin, Reversible Steganography for VQ-compressed ImagesUsing Side Matching and Relocation, IEEE Transactions on Information Forensics and Security, vol. 1, no. 4, pp. 493-501, 2006

8. C. C. Chang, Y. C. Chou and C. Y. Lin, Reversible Data Hiding in the VQCompressed Domain, IEICE Transactionson Information and Systems, vol. E90-D no. 9, pp. 1422 1429, 2007

9. K. Sayood, Introduction to Data Compression, Second Edition, Morgan Kaufmann Publishers, San Francisco, CA, 2000, pp. 257-305, ISBN 1-55860-558-4

10. Y. Linde, A. Buzo, and R. M. Gray, "An algorithm for vector quantizer design,"IEEE Trans. Commun., vol. COM- 28, no.1, pp. 84-95, 1980

11. A. Gersho, R.M. Gray.: 'VectorQuantization and Signal Compressio', Kluwer Academic Publishers, Boston, MA, 1991

12. H. B. Kekre, Tanuja K. Sarode, "NewFast Improved Codebook generation Algorithm for Color Images using Vector Quantization," International Journal of Engineering and Technology, vol.1, No.1,pp. 67-77, September 2008

13. H. B. Kekre, Tanuja K. Sarode, "An Efficient Fast Algorithm to GenerateCodebook for Vector Quantization," First International Conference on Emerging Trends in Engineering and Technology,ICETET-2008, held at Raisoni College of Engineering, Nagpur, India, 16-18 July 2008, Avaliable at online IEEE Xplore

Software architecture design for airport surveillance radar data processing system using decision oriented design approach

Dr. H. B. Kekre[1] · **Ms. Pallavi N. Halarnkar[2]** · **Mr. Jotinder Singh[3]** · **Mr. Dhruv Mehta[3]**

[1]Sr. Professor, MPSTME, NMIMS University, Mumbai, India.
[2]Lecturer, MPSTME, NMIMS, Mumbai, India.
[3]Student, MPSTME, NMIMS University Mumbai, India.

1. Introduction

Software architecture has been proposed as a major discipline to manage the complexity of large-scale software systems from the high abstraction levels and system-wide perspectives. It has been expected to achieve "a breathtaking capability for reliably designing systems of unprecedented size and complexity verging on a true engineering discipline" [1].

The software architecture research and practices have proposed a number of methods for the architecture design [2], e.g., the QASAR [3], ADD [4], Siemens Four-Views (S4V) [5], RUP's 4+1 View [6] methods, etc. Most of the methods provide strategic steps and guidelines to accomplish architecture design. Although these methods consider architecture design from a higher level and in a more systematic manner than the traditional software design methods, the main focuses are usually the concrete building blocks of the resulting systems, e.g., the components and connectors. Because of the inherent gap between software requirements and design, the methods that focus on the solution spaces of software are difficult to provide pragmatic assistance for practitioners to cope with the complexity of the architectural considerations and the difficulty of deriving the architecture design results.

In our opinion, for coping with the complexity and difficulty of architecture design, new principles and approaches specific to the architecture level need to be developed. In this paper, we propose a decision oriented architecture design approach ABC/DD(Architecture-Based Component composition / Decision-oriented Design), based on the decision abstraction and issue-decomposition principles specific to the architecture level design of

software. The approach models software architecture from the perspective of design decisions, and accomplishes the architecture design from eliciting architecturally significant design issues to exploiting and making decisions on thesolutions for these issues. We illustrate the application of the approach with two real life large-scale software-intensive projects, showing that the decision-oriented approach accommodates the characteristics and demands of the architecture level, and facilitates the design of architecture and the capture of the essential decisions for large complex systems. We also discuss the lessons learned from the applications and the problems need to be further investigated.

2. Overview of the decision-oriented architecture design approach

2.1 The architecture design principles

We utilize and specialize the fundamental software engineering principles at the software architecture level, proposing the "decision-abstraction" and "issue decomposition" principles specific to solving the complexity and difficulty of architecture design. Abstraction is a fundamental technique for understanding and solving problems [6]. The widely used abstraction principles in software engineering, e.g., data abstraction, procedure abstraction, etc are abstractions of the software artifacts. Software architectures use rich abstractions and idioms to describe system components, the nature of their interactions, and the patterns that guide the composition of systems [7]. Although having provided higher level of abstractions [8], this kind of abstractions are confined within the solution spaces. We argue that the architecture design desires the abstractions that are not only at higher

S.J. Pise (ed.), *ThinkQuest 2010*, DOI 10.1007/978-81-8489-989-4_35,
© Springer India Pvt. Ltd. 2011

level, but also can bridge the requirements and design. The decision instead of artifact perspective provides high-level abstractions on both the problem and solution spaces, therefore facilitates the modeling of architectures and the transiting from the requirements to the design results. "Divide and conquer" is a basic means always used to cope with the complexity. Various decomposition (and composition) principles have been used in software engineering, e.g., functional decomposition, modular decomposition, etc. The concept of "information hiding" [9] has been a fundamental principle to direct the software decomposition and implement the "separation-of-concerns". As the first step spanning from the requirements to the design, architecture design needs to consider more requirement-side issues at first, whereas not just the solution artifacts directly. Therefore we propose the "issue-decomposition" principle to treat the core task of architecture design as solving a collection of system-wide problems, so that the design can be conducted by means of decomposing the holistic design goals into the separated design issues, and then exploiting and making decisions on the solutions for these issues.

3. Airport surveillance radar data processing system

In this paper we design the airport surveillance radar data processing software architecture based on decision oriented architecture. First we gather requirements from the user i.e what all he/she wants to see the software doing. Once we have the requirements, we find the issues that we might face while implementing those requirements in our software. Then we find the solution to our issues that we elicit from the requirements. After finding the issue solutions , Architecture solution is found out. Then these architectural

solutions are evaluated based on different parameters. Whichever architectural solution scores the highest is generally implemented onto the software project.

Functionality asked for by the user.

1) Local controller software functions

- Receive airport scene surveillance radar echo data
- Receive secondary radar data and data from other communication interfaces.
- Control radar mode by sending commands to radar signal processor
- Show primary radar data.
- Communicate with remote controller such as receive commands and response.

2) Remote controller software functions

- Communicate with local controller such as receive primary radar data, send commands etc.
- Multi sensors data fusion
- Target tracking, track management
- Primary and secondary radar data display
- Data store and access
- Replay target track.

3) Surveillance terminal software functions

- Communication ability such as receive radar data.
- Database access ability.
- Track display and replay.

First We prepare the functional and non functional requirement analysis table. Followed by a table wherein we list all the elicited issues from the FRs and the NFRs listed in the above table. Then We form a table wherein we list all the discovered issue solutions.

Table 1   FRs and NFRs of the ASRDPS

Type	Requirement	Description
Functional Requirements	R1	Receive Airport scene surveillance radar echo data
	R2	Receive secondary radar data and data from other communication interfaces
	R3	Show primary radar data
	R4	Communication with remote controller such as receive commands and response
	R5	Communication with local controller such as receive primary radar data, send commands.
	R6	Sensor data fusion
	R7	Data store and access
	R8	Primary and secondary radar data display
	R9	Target tracking and track management
Non-Functional Requirements	R10	Communication ability such as receive radar data.
	R11	Database access ability
	R12	Track display and replay

Table 2 Elicited issues of the ASRDPS

Issue	Description	Requirements
I1	Amplify the received signal without adding noise or introducing any form of distortion	R1, R2
I2	Reject interfering signals so that the required information can be optimally detected	R1, R2
I3	Type of radar display	R3, R8, R12
I4	Type of sensors	R6
I5	Real Time live data acquiring	R2, R4, R5, R9, R10
I6	How to access database so that the traffic is low	R7, R11

Table 3 Discovered issue solutions of the ASRDPS

Issue	Issue Solution	Description
I1	IS 1.1	Chroma and lumminance noise seperation
	IS 1.2	Linear smoothing filter
	IS 1.3	Non linear filter
I2	IS 2.1	Band reject filter
	IS 2.2	Linear reject filter
I3	IS 3.1	B - scope display
	IS 3.2	C - scope display
	IS 3.3	PPI display
I4	IS 4.1	Single sensor
	IS 4.2	Multiple sensor
I5	IS 5.1	Push data to display directly and put in database
	IS 5.2	Put data in real time database and then display get data from display cache
I6	IS 6.1	Cache the data in display
	IS 6.2	Use a cache server

Now we instantiate every issue solution that we found in the Table 3.

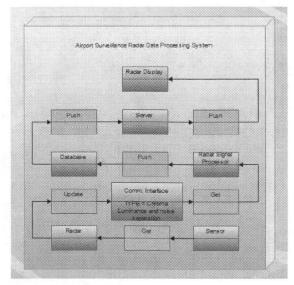

Fig. 1   IS 1.1

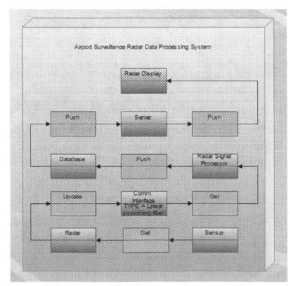

Fig. 2   IS 1.2

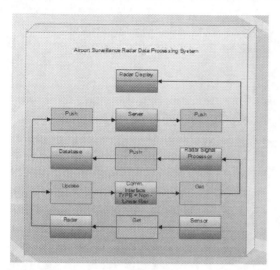

Fig. 3   IS 1.3

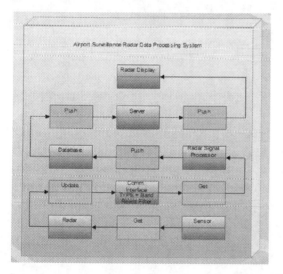

Fig. 4   IS 2.1

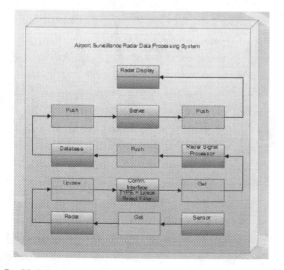

Fig. 5   IS 2.2

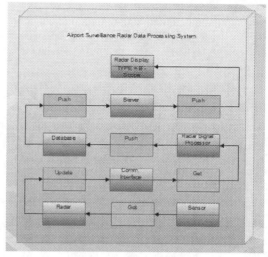

Fig. 6   IS 3.1

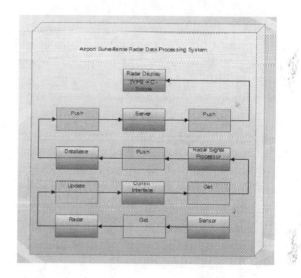

Fig. 7   IS 3.2

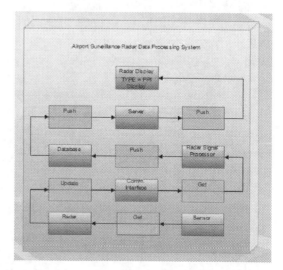

Fig. 8   IS 3.3

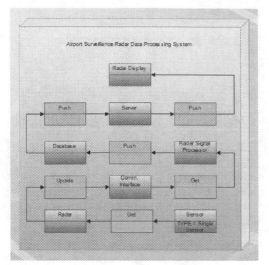

Fig. 9   IS 4.1

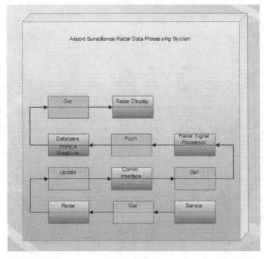

Fig. 12   IS 5.2

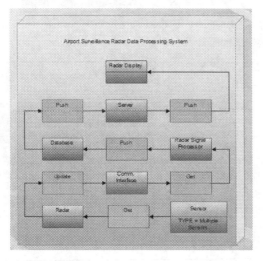

Fig. 10   IS 4.2

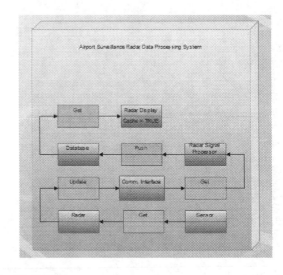

Fig. 13   IS 6.1

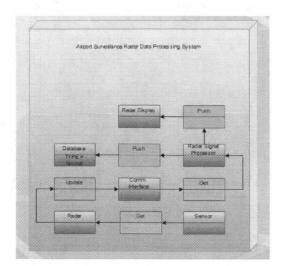

Fig. 11   IS 5.1

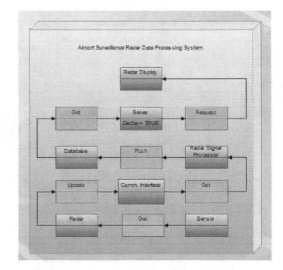

Fig. 14   IS 6.2

Table 4 Relationship between issue solutions

Relation	Issue Solutions
INC	(IS 1.2, IS 2.2)
GEN	(IS 3.3, IS 4.2), (IS 1.1, IS 2.1), (IS 3.2, IS 4.1)
CON	(IS 1.1, IS 2.2), (IS 1.3, IS 2.2), (IS 3.1, IS 4.2), (IS 2.1, IS 3.3), (IS 2.1, IS 3.1), (IS 2.2, IS 3.1), (IS 2.2, IS 3.2), (IS 4.1, IS 5.2), (IS 4.2, IS 5.1), (IS 5.1, IS 6.2), (IS 5.2, IS 6.1)

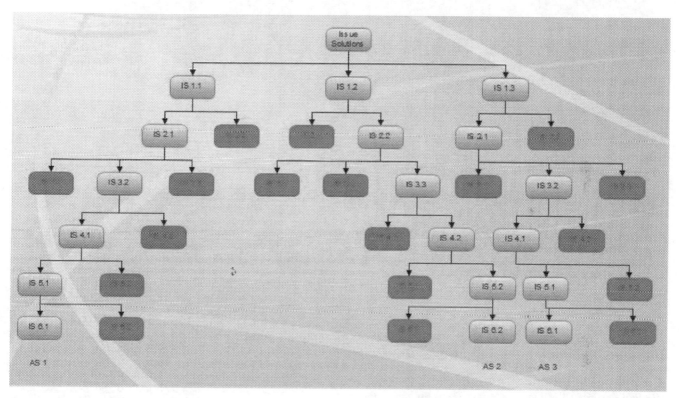

Fig. 15 Combination tree of issue solutions

The Last Step of solution is to merge fthe issue solutions of each feasible combination.

The result are three candidate architecture solutions named AS1 – AS3 as shown in Fig. 15.

From the synthesized candidate solutions, the architects and the stakeholders can make their choice, based on holistic evaluation on the architecture, the additional global considerations and the necessary tradeoffs. Table 5 shows the evaluations and decisions on each candidate architecture solution. The decision making procedure is omitted here.

Thus from Table 5 we can find the optimal architectural style suitable for our project that is Airport Surveillance Radar Data Processing System.

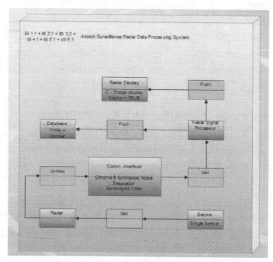

Fig. 16 AS 1

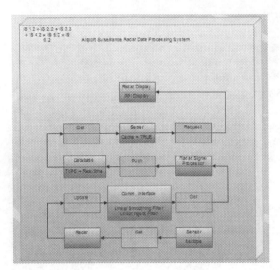

Fig. 17   AS 2

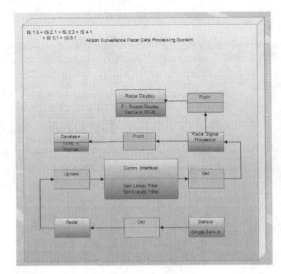

Fig. 18   AS 3

Table 5   Evaluation and decisions on each architecture solution

Architectural Solution	Evaluation			Decision
	Maintainability	Usability	Development Cost	
AS 1	High	Medium	Medium	Reject
AS 2	Low	High	Low	Accept
AS 3	Medium	Low	Low	Reject

4. Conclusion

We have proposed a decision-oriented architecture design approach that implement the decision abstraction and issue-decomposition principles. The application experience shows that this approach can provide pragmatic help to the architects, in the process from eliciting architecturally significant issues to exploiting and deciding on the candidate architecture solutions. This approach makes explicit the decisions in both the architecture design models and the design process, so that the capture of architecture decisions and rationale can be more effective and efficient. We Also designed software architecture for the Airport Surveillance Radar Data Processing System based on Decision Oriented Design Approach.

References

1. M. Shaw and P. Clements, "The Golden Age of Software Architecture," *IEEE Software*, vol. 23, no. 2, March/April 2006, pp. 31-39

2. C. Hofmeister, P. Kruchten, R. L. Nord, H. Obbink, A. Ran, and P. America, "A General Model of Software Architecture Design Derived from Five Industrial Approaches," *The Journal of Systems and Software*, vol. 80, no. 1, Jan. 2007, pp. 106-126

3. L. Bass, P. Clements, and R. Kazman, *Software Architecture in Practice*, 2nd ed. Addison-Wesley, 2003

4. C. Hofmeister, R. Nord, and D. Soni, *Applied Software Architecture*. Addison-Wesley, 2000

5. P. Kruchten, *The Rational Unified Process: An Introduction*, 3rd ed. Addison-Wesley, 2003

6. A. I. Wasserman, "Toward a Discipline of Software Engineering," *IEEE Software*, vol. 13, no. 6, Nov. 1996, pp. 23-31

7. M. Shaw, R. DeLine, D. V. Klein, T. L. Ross, D. M. Young, and G. Zelesnik, "Abstractions for Software Architecture and Tools to Support Them," *IEEE Trans. Software Eng.*, vol. 21, no. 4, Apr. 1995, pp. 314-335

8. M. Shaw, "Larger Scale Systems Require Higher-Level Abstractions," Proc. 5th Int'l Workshop on Software Specification and Design, ACM SIGSOFT Notes, Vol. 14, No. 3, May 1989, pp. 143-146

9. D. L. Parnas, "On the Criteria to Be Used in Decomposing Systems into Modules," Communications of the ACM, vol. 15, no. 12, Dec. 1972, pp. 1053-1058

Predicting architectural styles for mobile distributed, data-intensive systems

Dr. H. B. Kekre[1] · Ms. Pallavi N. Halarnkar[2] · Mr. Niraj Kulkarni[3] ·
Mr. Neavin Samuel[3] · Mr. Rohit Taneja[3]

[1]Sr. Professor, MPSTME, NMIMS University, Mumbai, India
[2]Lecturer, MPSTME, NMIMS, Mumbai, India
[3]Student MPSTME, NMIMS University, Mumbai, India

1. Introduction

This paper illustrates a model for predicting the emergent architectural style based on the components and connectors of a mobile. The estimation of architectural style based on mobile component specifications will help us predict that whether the attributes of the middleware will be satisfied or not before the actual deployment. The component specifications are functional as well as non-functional.

Based on the architectural style, modeling can be done so as to bolster composition of networked resources for adaptive configuration of mobile distributed systems. The actual dynamic composition of mobile distributed systems is tightly coupled with the supporting run-time environment (i.e., middleware), leading to the investigation of the integration of our architectural modeling.

We take into account the functional and non-functional specifications and list out the components of a mobile so that we have the component repository. Then the step by step process will be applied to it to estimate the architectural styles. The mobile components are described by the operations it provides and requires from the environment. Following the components are the connectors. In our case these are nothing but the wireless connectors. These connectors specify the interaction protocols that are implemented over the wireless network. Additionally, the dynamic composition of mobile components leads to the dynamic instantiation of connectors. Hence, the specification of wireless connectors is integrated with the one of mobile components. From the base component list, we can find the corresponding connector. This will be an intermediate step in prediction of architectural style.

Further, large scale mobile distributed systems are data-intensive systems and they have to address issues like:

1. Access data in legacy data resources.
2. Discover data which may be unknown at system run-time.
3. Correlate the different data models which describe each data resource.
4. Integrate the software interfaces to the legacy data resources.

Existing data-intensive systems severely lack any common software engineering design constructs and relations between architectural components and implementation-level decisions. Data Intensive Computing is capturing, managing, analyzing, and understanding data at volumes and rates that push the frontiers of current technologies.

Our work therefore also focuses on designing architectural styles for any large-scale distributed systems and in this paper we take a special case of the Mobile distributed systems.

2. Software architecture for mobile distributed computing

Mobile distributed systems require support of wireless networks and devices which depends upon the device connectivity. This has led to the introduction of a supporting middleware but that also requires modeling and verification support to enforce the correctness of the mobile system with respect to both functional and non-functional properties. Software architectural styles help in obtaining the desired consistency for such component based middleware. Using some unique properties of software architecture this paper introduces the prediction of architectural styles based on

S.J. Pise (ed.), *ThinkQuest 2010*, DOI 10.1007/978-81-8489-989-4_36,
© Springer India Pvt. Ltd. 2011

modeling of mobile software component which integrates key features of the wireless infrastructure. There are many problems in mobile distributed system like wireless infrastructure, dynamic nature of network etc. which leads to another major problem like providing quality of service to the user.

As mobile distributed systems are built out of the composition of mobile, autonomous component systems, we can use the base architectural style to model at the software architecture level by using following convention that components abstract mobile component systems and connectors abstract interaction protocols above the wireless networks.

Architectural modelling must comprehend the key characteristics of mobile distributed systems, ie dynamic composition, in a way that ensures correctness of the system. Our model is grounded in the service-oriented interaction i.e., a component abstracts a networked service that invokes operations of peer components and dually executes operations that are invoked. However, it applies as well to interactions based on data sharing, since the distinction is apparent at the implementation level only.

Components

An individual component is a software package, or a module, that encapsulates a set of related functions.

All system processes are placed into separate components so that all of the data and functions inside each component are semantically related. Because of this principle, it is often said that components are modular and cohesive.

Basically we have two types of mobile component specification:

1. Functional specification. The specification of coordination protocols among mobile components relates to the one of conversation, also known as choreography, in the context of Web services.
2. Non-functional specification. It specifies the component's behaviour with respect to performance, reliability, security, and transactional properties, which is further complemented with related resource consumption and service adaptation.

These components are specific to our paper because we are taking Mobile distributed systems as special case. Typically, a large scale data intensive distributed system has following components [3] :

1. Profile Servers
2. Product Servers
3. Query Servers

Connectors

Software connectors are an important part of software architecture, which are responsible for the interactions between components, have an important impact on software architecture adaptation.

Connectors specify the set of connector types via which the mobile component communicates, and connector specifies for every conversation, the type of the connector that is used for the corresponding interactions. More precisely, a wireless connector specifies:

(i)   The base interaction protocol with peer components (protocol),

(ii)   The underlying dynamic network (network).

3. Approach

As we have already defined the functional and non functional specifications with the help of the specification model and from the component repository we try to match our components and find a architectural style for mobile distributed systems.

The step-by-step process [1] for predicting the likely architectural style is given below:

Step 1: We specify use case/scenario for mobile distributed system.

Step 2: We then build the Base Mobile Component List.

Step 3: For each component in the Base Mobile Component List, we make a note of its Component Type Attribute. If all the components are not of the same type, we consider the component type of the set of components to be the one that is most common.

In the mobile distributed systems, the basic components are the devices or routers from which component type attributes can be noted down.

Here, the System Integrator queries the Mobile Component repository to check for the available components. A System Integrator identifies a deployment use-case that needs to be satisfied using pre-built components.

Step 4: For each component in the Base Mobile Component List, we make a note of the Connector Type attribute. In our case the major connectors are the wireless connectors: Interaction protocol and Dynamic networking.

Step 5: We determine the Control Topology of the set of components by developing the Control Flow List.

Step 6: We determine the Control Synchronicity of the configuration of the components.

Synchronicity is the experience of two or more events that are causally unrelated occurring together in a meaningful manner. To count as synchronicity, the events should be unlikely to occur together by chance.

Step 7: The Data Topology of the configuration of components is determined by developing the Data Flow List.

The Data flow list stores all the interactions among the components. It is a list which consists of all the information or data flowing from one mobile component to another with the help of connector.

Step 8: The Data Continuity of the configuration is determined.

Step 9: We determine whether the Control and Data Topologies are isomorphic.

So, basically if the Control topologies are applicable to the components say mobile device, then the data topologies are also applicable.

Step 10: From the feature category attributes derived in Steps 3 to Step 9, we reference the Shaw Clements classification to determine the Architectural Style.

They proposed that different architectural styles can be discriminated among each other by analyzing the following feature categories.

1. Constituent Parts i.e. the components and connectors
2. Control Issues i.e. the flow of control among components
3. Data Issues i.e. details on how data is processed.
4. Control/Data Interaction i.e. the relation between control and data.
5. Type of Reasoning: Analysis techniques applicable to the style

We try to determine the most probable architectural style by considering the maximum number of feature category attributes that can be used in making a prediction that is consistent with the classification.

Using this approach, we will be able to evaluate several deployment options and the associated implications to the quality attributes before the system has been built.

This method can be used to define architectural style for data intensive systems using the software components and connectors. Using this step by step process, it can be analyzed and verified that the key assumptions that were made about the large scale mobile distributed system for predicting the architectural style were validated during the implementation time by the implementation system.

4. Example

In order to illustrate the exploitation of our model, we consider access to a shopping e-service [2], for which there exist mobile replicated instances, noted me, on the sellers' wireless devices and a stationary instance, noted se, hosted by some server. Access to se and me is allowed for any authenticated client over the wireless Internet.

For simplicity, we focus on the interactions between the mobile and stationary service instances, and consider a sub- set of relevant operations, i.e., the service offers two transactional conversations that respectively allows browsing a catalogue and buying goods. Both conversations are carried out over an RPC-like connector with reception of the request message followed by the emission of the request result.

We have introduced base architectural modeling for mobile distributed systems, which enforces correctness of the distributed systems despite the high dynamics of the under- lying network. However, related verification of the dynamically composed systems must be integrated with the runtime system, i.e., the middleware. The issue that arises

then relates to the processing and communication costs associated with verification, which must be kept low on the wire- less devices. As part of our work, we have developed the WSAMI service-oriented middleware [2] for mobile computing that is based on the Web services architecture.

The WSAMI core middleware is subdivided into:

(i) The WSAMI SOAP-based core broker, including the CSOAP SOAP container for wireless, resource-constrained devices.

(ii) The Naming & Discovery (ND) service for the dynamic discovery of (possibly mobile) services those are available in the local and wide area, ac- cording to network connectivity and available resources. The ND service further includes support for connector customization, so as to enforce quality of service through the dynamic integration of middleware-related ser- vices over the network's path.

The WSAMI middleware has been designed so as to minimize resource consumption on the wireless devices. In particular, mobile services that are integrated and composed using WSAMI are modeled by specifying the URIs of the XML documents that characterize their input and output operations, and their in- put and output conversations.

Using WSAMI, components composition with respect to QoS and wireless connectors is built-in in the middle- ware, i.e., QoS-awareness is managed by the ND service and the interaction protocol is that of CSOAP. It follows that the retrieval of peer components with which a mobile service dynamically composes is simply based on the comparison of URIs, which is much effective in terms of low re- source consumption. However, such an approach leads to a much stronger conformance relation for dynamic composition than the one discussed in the previous section, i.e., the conformance relation that is implemented in WSAMI re- quires two interacting components to have structural equivalence over output and input operations, and over output and input conversations. As part of our current work, we are investigating weaker conformance relations for WSAMI based on our general definition, while still making the associated computation and communication costs low for wire- less devices. A number of techniques need to be combined in this context, including effective tool for checking conformance relationship in the wireless environment, possibly leading to strengthening base conformance relation, and exploiting the capabilities of resource-rich devices in the area so as to effectively distribute the load associated with the dynamic composition of mobile components.

This solution tries to address all concerns about the wireless networks, dynamic nature and also ensure quality of services.

5. Conclusion

We propose an approach for predicting architectural styles using component specification by taking into consid- eration a mobile distributed system that is a data-intensive.

The system integrator desires to satisfy use case scenarios by using a configuration of components. Using this approach, the system integrator will be able to evaluate several deployment options and the associated implications to the quality attributes before the system has been built.

Furthermore, these architectural styles form the bedrock or underlying base for the design and construction of large scale, distributed systems and the issues concerning data-intensive systems can also addressed. Data Intensive Computing is done primarily to deal with systems which have large amount of data. Problems which are mainly resolved by data intensive systems are:

1. Managing the explosion of data
2. Extracting knowledge from massive datasets.
3. Reducing data to facilitate human understanding and response.

The architectural styles predicted will bolster the data intensive system in resolving the issues mentioned 1 through 3 above very efficiently.

The example discussed shows how architectural styles can help in enhancing the services of the middleware, the mobile devices. The estimation of emergent architectural style will help in such a way that it will explicitly determine whether due to a particular component there is decrease in efficiency or not before the actual deployment. Thus, the approach used in our paper would also help in improving the QoS (Quality of Service) and the wireless connectivity indirectly.

References

1.	Sutirtha Bhattacharya, Dewayne E. Perry, "Predicting Architectural Styles from Component Specifications ", Proceedings of the Fifth Working IEEE/IFIP Conference on Software Architecture (WICSA'05)
2.	Val´ Issarny, Ferda Tartanoglu, Jinshan Liu, Francoise Sailhan erie., " Software Architecture for Mobile Distributed Computing", Proceedings of the Fourth Working IEEE/IFIP Conference on Software Architecture (WICSA'04)
3.	Chris A. Mattmann, Daniel J. Crichton, J. Steven Hughes, Sean C. Kelly and Paul M. Ramirez, "Software Architecture for Large-Scale, Distributed, Data-Intensive Systems", Proceedings of the Fourth Working IEEE/IFIP Conference on Software Architecture (WICSA'04)

Image steganography: an approach for secrete communication

Shashikant S. Radke · V. K. Sambhe

Department of Computer Engineering, VJTI, Mumbai, India

1. Introduction

Nowadays, secrete communication is very essential as almost all communications are occurs through digital media. Internet also has become a convenient way for data transmission due to a fast development of the modern technology. To void security attack, data hiding which embeds secrct data into the cover media such as image, audio, video, and packets on internet without the notice of interceptors is also an alternative. Modern information hiding technology is an important branch of information security. The redundancy of digital media, as well as the characteristic of human visual system, makes it possible to hide messages. Information hiding technology used in covert communication is named as steganography. Steganography is useful for hiding messages for transmission. Three competing aspects, including capacity, security, and robustness, are usually considered in the designing of information hiding schemes. Security means invisibility and keeping undetectable. Capacity refers to the maximal secure payload. Robustness relates to the amount of modification the stego-object can withstand before an adversary can destroy the hidden information. Generally speaking, robustness is often emphasized in applications of digital watermarking rather than steganography. Security and enough hiding capacity should be needed for desired steganography algorithms. On the one hand, sufficient secret message bits can be embedded into cover objects, so as to ensure the effectiveness of communications. On the other hand, observable changes of cover objects ought to be avoided after information embedding, so as to ensure the security of communications. The least significant bits (LSB) methods widely used to hide data into digital images because of its large capacity and easy implementation. In

this kind of approach, messages are embedded into least significant bits of image pixels, palette indices, or quantized discrete cosine transform (DCT) coefficients. There have been many steganographic techniques utilizing LSB method, such as EZ-Stego, JSteg, JPHide-Seek, and Out-Guess. For data hiding, many steganographic algorithms have been proposed to hide secret information in digital images [1–3]. The most common method is the LSB (least significant bit) method, which utilizes some least bits of pixels in the cover image to embed the hidden data. The advantages of the LSB method are ease of computation and a large payload of data that can be embedded in the cover image with high visual quality. The proposed method is based on least significant bit substation. The results have shown that our method increases the amount of secret data that can be stored in a cover image, while at the same time producing a higher quality of stego-image.

Steganography and cryptography

Both Steganography and cryptography are two integral parts of information. Their purpose is to provide secrecy to communications and can be used in conjunction. Even if the presence of hidden information is detected, one can protect the contents of the message using encryption.

Steganography has obvious difference with encryption because encryption hides information contents whereas steganography hides information existence. The advantage of steganography, over cryptography alone, is that messages do not attract attention to themselves. Plainly visible encrypted messages—no matter how unbreakable—will arouse suspicion, and may in themselves be incriminating in countries where encryption is illegal. Therefore, whereas cryptography protects the contents of a message,

S.J. Pise (ed.), *ThinkQuest 2010*, DOI 10.1007/978-81-8489-989-4_37,

steganography can be said to protect both messages and communicating parties. Robustness & Perceptibility A passive attacker tries to detect a hidden message in a cover that he receives. This process is difficult, as no simple clue exists to differentiate a stego media from a cover-media. However, an active attacker would not waste his time and resources detecting a message.

He would rather manipulate the cover so that the hidden message (if it exists) gets destroyed. Noise addition, changing formats and lossy compression may be used to destroy information in many digital media. Images can be manipulated, by using blurring, sharpening, rotating, resizing and stretching operations by the attacker. Similarly audio and music signals may be filtered or re –sampled to destroy the hidden message. Destroying the entire cover beyond recognition is not a good proposition, as the sender might choose in the future another technique or media for hiding messages. Therefore, incorporating features for robustness in the stego-algorithm can save the secret information from being destroyed in case of an attack. The message recovered from the stego-media should be same as the original secret message. Robustness has been an issue in watermarking more than in steganography but is valid in this case since the basic motive for securing the traffic should hold, it should reach the receiver undetected and unaltered. A little compromise in terms of a lower data-capacity of the secret information has to be borne by the communicating party [4].

Applications

Steganography is applicable to, but not limited to, the following areas.

1. Confidential communication and secret data storing
2. Protection of data alteration
3. Access control system for digital
   Content distribution
4. Media Database systems

The area differs in what feature of the steganography is utilized in each system.

1. The rest of the paper is organized as follows in section.
2. we present our steganographic algorithm for 24-bit color images. Experimental results are illustrated in section
3. Finally, the conclusion of the paper is given in section 4.

2. Proposed data embedding scheme

In this section, a new data embedding scheme is presented. The secret data bit stream is embedded into the host image by raster-scan order while the pixels located in the first row and first column are abandoned.

2.1 Assumption and initialization

The cover media is a 24-bit color image (generally, jpeg/jpg or bmp).Each pixel is having RGB components. Each component is a candidate for hiding data. After hiding data the resulting stego image must be save as bmp image.

Encryption Read the message to be hiding into image. Encrypt that message by using standard encryption algorithm so that its original message detection will be difficult.

2.2 Data embedding

Our method refers to the three components (RGB) of pixel to embed the secret message into the target pixel (say, P). Let Pr, Pg, and Pb are the components of the target pixel and S is the encrypted symbol to be hide.

$$Pr = Pr - Pr \bmod 8 + S \bmod 8 \qquad (1)$$
$$S = (S - S \bmod 8)/8$$
$$Pg = Pg - Pg \bmod 8 + S \bmod 8 \qquad (2)$$
$$S = (S - S \bmod 8)/8$$
$$Pg = Pg - Pg \bmod 4 + S \qquad (3)$$

Above equation (1), (2), and (3) have to use in sequence to hide symbol S into pixel P. These equations embed one symbol in one pixel. Thus we have to use the same process for rest of the message. Finally save image in non-lossy image format like bmp.

2.3 Data extraction/retrieval

The secret data is obtained from the stego-image by the raster-scan order while the pixels located in the first row and first column are abandoned. The following equation (3) is used to extract the data hide in one pixel.

$$S = Pr \bmod 8 + 8 * Pg \bmod 8 + 64 * Pb \bmod 4; \qquad (4)$$

The equation we have to use to extract remaining data from pixels. Here S is an encrypted symbol. To get actual symbol decrypt S using the proper respective algorithm.

3. Experimental result

We have taken many cover images for experiment of different size of jpeg/jpg format. Following Fig. 1 shows such sample cover images of size 154 × 100 pixels. The message to be hide is taken arbitrarily of size 2521 bytes. Figure 2 shows images after hiding data into them. The stego images are looking almost same as cover images. Here the size of cover image is 154 × 100 = 15400 pixels = 15400 * 3 = 46200 bytes and data size is 2521 bytes. As the algorithm allowing one byte to be store in one pixel, the required pixels for hiding data will be 2521 pixels and few more pixels will be required to store information about data. If we compare cover images and stego images we will find that stego images are very close to cover images. We have hide less data into image than its capacity, we have margin

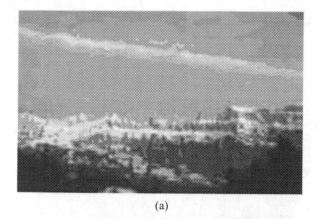

(a)

(b)

Fig. 1 Cover images (a) sky (b) forest

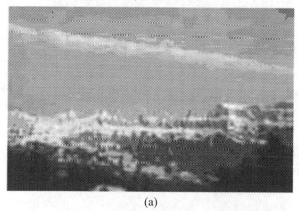

(a)

(b)

Fig. 2 Stego images (a) sky (b) Forest

to store extra data into image. Thus the proposed method gives us high hiding capacity.

4. Conclusion

The proposed algorithm hides one byte of data in one pixel RGB components. So we can hide number of bytes less than or equal to the number of pixels in cover image. This algorithm has the less computation complexity. Thus we have a steganographic technique which has less complexity and high hiding capacity.

5. Future scope

We can work on this algorithm further to improve hiding capacity and the making the stego image as close to the cover image. We are still working on this algorithm.

References

1. Chang, C.C.,Tseng, H.-W.AStegano graphic method for digital images using side match, Pattern Recognition Lett. 25, 2004:1431-1437
2. Suk-Ling Li, Lai-Chi Leung, L.M. Cheng,Chi-Kwonga Performance Evaluation of a Steganographic Method for Digital Images Using Side Match, icicic 2006, IS16-004, Aug 2006
3. Tien-You Lee, Shinfeng Lin, Dual watermark for image tamper detection and recovery, Pattern Recognition 41 2008:3497-3506
4. Young-Ran Park, Hyun-Ho Kang, Sang-Uk Shin, Ki-Ryong Kwon, An Image Steganographic Using Pixel Characteristics, Computational Intelligence security,Vol.3802,2005:581-588
5. H.-C Wu, N.-I Wu, C.-S Tsai, M.-S Hwang. Image steganographic scheme based on pixel value differencing and LSB replacementmethods.IEE proc.-Vis. Image Signal Process,Vol.152, No.5, Oct 2005:611-615
6. D.-C Wu,W.-H Tsai. Asteganographic method for images by pixel-value differencing, Pattern Recognit. Lett 24 2003:1613-1626
7. CM Wang, NI Wu,CS Tsai, MS Hwang. A high quality steganographic method with pixel-value differencing and modulus function, The Journal of Systems & Software, 81 2008:150-158
8. Jun Tian. Reversible data embedding using a difference expansion, IEEE Transactions, Circuits and Systems for Video Technology., Aug. 2003, 13(8): 890-896
9. Adnan M.Alattar, Reversible Watermark using the Difference Expansion of a Generalized Integer Transform. IEEE Transactions on Image Processing,Aug.2004,13(8): 1147-1156
10. Chan,C. K., Cheng,L.M., Hiding data in images by simple LSB substitution, Pattern Recognition 37, 2004. 469-474
11. Han-ling ZHANG, Guang-zhi GENG,Cai-qiong Xiong, "Image Steganography using Pixel-Value Differencing", pg 109–112, 2009

Image data compression using new halftoning operators and run length encoding

Dr. H. B. Kekre[1] • **Dr. M. U. Kharat**[2] • **Sanjay R. Sange**[3]

[1]Sr. Professor, Mukesh Patel School Technology Management Engg., SVKM's NMIMS, India
[2.]Professor, MET's Institute of Engineering, Nashik, Pune University, India
[3]Lecturer, Mukesh Patel School Technology Management Engg., SVKM's NMIMS Mumbai, India

1. Introduction

A new approach for removing blocking artifacts in reconstructed block-encoded images is presented in [1].The perceptual quality of video affected by packet losses, low resolution and low bit video coded by the H.264/AVC encoder is studied in [2]. Digital halftoning is a nonlinear system that quantizes a gray level image to one bit per pixel[3]. Halftoning by error diffusion scans the image, quantizes the current pixel, and subtracts the quantization error from neighboring pixels in fixed proportions according to the error filter. The error filter is designed to minimize a local weighted error introduced by quantization. Figure 1 illustrates error diffusion as implemented by a noise shaping feedback coder. In Fig. 1, the bi-level output of the quantizer $Q(x'(i,j))=0.5sgn(x'(i,j))$ is, where sgn is the signum function. The quantizer in error diffusion halftoning systems as a linear gain plus additive noise. The linear gain model provides an accurate description of the two primary effects of error diffusion: edge sharpening and noise shaping. Edge arpening is proportional to the linear gain, and we give a formula to estimate the gain from a given error filter. We also use the linear gain to modify the original image to compensate for sharpening distortion in error diffusion. SNR measures are appropriate when the noise is additive and signal independent. To show when the residual can be considered as signal-independent additive noise, we compute the correlation between the residual and the original image. We use the perceptual Weighted Signal-to-Noise Ratio (WSNR) measure to rank the quality of several error diffusion algorithms. Using the linear gain model, we separately quantify the sharpening an noise effects in error diffusion. In addition, we also distinguish between the performances of different algorithms by computing a tonality metric based on distortion products introduced by halftoning. The both input and output vary over [–0.5 to 0.5], where –0.5 represents black and 0.5 represents white. The error image is given by

$e(i,j) =Q(x'(i,j))-x'(i,j)$
Since $e(i,j)$ is correlated with $x(i,j)$, and $x(i,j)$
is correlated with $x'(i,j)$ [6], it follows that
$e(i,j)$is correlated with $x'(i,j)$ [1].

Lossless compression schemes are explained with secure transmission play a key role in telemedicine applications that helps inaccurate diagnosis and research [4]. A fast wavelet-based video codec is used which is implemented into a real-time video conferencing tool. In this paper codec is used temporal frame difference coding, a computationally low-complex 5/3 tap wavelet transforms, and a fast entropy coding scheme based on Golomb-Rice codes. This paper also presents an application of the video conferencing tool in a serverless peer- to-peer IP-based communication framework. For mobile communication we propose a simple, ready-to-use location scheme for video conference users in global network [5]. Forward error concealment includes methods that add redundancy at the source end to enhance error resilience of the coded bit streams. Error concealment by post processing refers to operations at the decoder to recover the damaged areas based on characteristics of image and video signals. Finally, interactive error concealment covers techniques that are dependent on a dialog between the source and destination. Both current research activities and practice in international standards are covered [6]. A new approach for removing blocking artifacts in reconstructed block-encoded images is given in this paper. The key of the approach is using piecewise similarity within different parts of

S.J. Pise (ed.), *ThinkQuest 2010*, DOI 10.1007/978-81-8489-989-4_38,

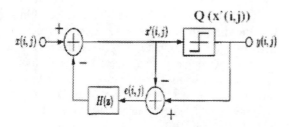

Fig. 1 Equivalent circuit of error diffusion, also known as a noise shaping feedback encoder. The gray level input image is denoted x (i,j); the one-bit output is denoted y(i,j). All images take values on [–0.5, 0.5], e.g., the bi-level output y(i,j) ∈ {–0.5, 0.5}

the image as a priori to give reasonable modifications to the block boundary pixels [7]. An embedded foveation image coding (EFIC) algorithm, which orders the encoded bitstream to optimize foveated visual quality at arbitrary bit-rates [8]. A foveation-based image quality metric, namely, oveatedwavelet image quality index (FWQI), plays an important role in the EFIC system. A modified SPIHT algorithm to improve the coding efficiency. Experiments how that EFIC integrates foveation filtering with foveated image coding and demonstrates very good coding performance and scalability in terms of foveated image quality measurement [8]. A foveation scalable video coding (FSVC) algorithm which supplies good quality- compression performance as well as effective rate scalability. The key idea is to organize the encoded bit stream to provide the best decoded video at an arbitrary bit rate in terms of foveated visual quality measurement. A foveation-based HVSmodel plays an important role in the algorithm. The algorithm is adaptableto different applications, such as knowledge-based video coding and video communications over time- varying, multi-user and interactive networks [9]. This paper proposes a generalized BbBShift (GBbBShift) method,which delivers much more flexibility than both Maxshift and BbBShift for degree-of- interest" adjustment of the ROI with insignificant effect on coding efficiency and computational complexity [10].

2. Error diffusion halftone operators

The error filter should be the smallest filter that achieves high visual quality.

Computation can be simplified further if the filter coefficients are fixed-point or dyadic (dyadic coefficients can be applied using bit shifts rather than multiplications). In 1975, Floyd and Steinberg asserted that a fourcoefficient filter was the smallest that gave good visual results [11], and this appears to have been verified by later work. As a side benefit, the Floyd–Steinberg filter is dyadic. There are various types of error diffusion halftones.

1. Vector quantization
2. Projection onto convex sets (POCS)
3. Non-linear permutation filtering
4. MAP projection
5. Wavelets
6. Bayesian schemes
7. Floyd-Steinberg

Jarvis operator [12] included an error diffusion method with the 12-coefficient error filter shown in Fig. 2.1(a) The Jarvis halftone is substantially sharper. Jarvis halftone technique linearizes error diffusion algorithms by modeling the quantized as a lineargain plus additive noise. Edge sharpening is proportional to the linear gain, and a formula is given to estimate the gain from a given error filter [13]. The Jarvis filter should be divided by 48 so the overall coefficient sum to be one, which guarantees that the entire system is stable.

However we are proposing some new halftoning operators. The operators shown in figures from Fig. 2.1 (b) to Fig. 2.1 (e) are 5X5 mask in size and having 25 taps (effectively only 12) operation. Each operator shown in figures from Fig. 2.1 (b) to Fig. 2.1 (e) is divided by 143 so as to obtain the coefficients sum to be one. The halftoning operator shown in Fig. 2.1 (b) is operated from South East direction to the central pixel 'X'. The values considered in the operator are all odd values and arranged in a spiral direction starting from the central pixel. This mask is operated on the entire 8-bit continuous image to convert it into halftone 1-bit image. The central pixel of the mask shows current pixel of the image. The mask is convolved with the entire image. The current pixel value will be replaced by the resultant value after convolution. The Jarvis as well as all the proposed halftoning operators gives 12.5000 % compression factor. Proposed various operators gives same quality of halftone image, but gives different RLECF and NETCF which is discussed in section IV.

Also we have proposed the smallest size i.e. 3X3 operator in Fig. 2.1(f) which takes 9 taps (effectively

0	0	0	0	0
0	0	0	0	0
0	0	X	7	5
3	5	7	5	3
1	3	5	3	1

Fig. 2.1 (a):Error filter identified by Jarvis Dividing factor (D.F.)= 48

only one) operation. For normalization the mask should be divided by 5. Because the value multiplied by 1 is not consider as a computation. That's why this operator is most economic from computation point of view. The motivation of this paper is to use proposed compression Halftoning and Run having many variations. As in video conferencing single person speaks and background remains same. In the sequence of images there will be minor facial movement; it

0	0	0	0	0
0	0	0	0	0
0	0	X	1	9
23	7	5	3	11
21	19	17	15	13

13	15	17	19	21
11	3	5	7	23
9	1	X	0	0
0	0	0	0	0
0	0	0	0	0

Fig. 2.1   (b) South-East (c) North-West (SE) D.F.=143 (NW) D.F.=143

0	0	9	11	13
0	0	1	3	15
0	0	X	5	17
0	0	0	7	19
0	0	0	23	21

21	23	0	0	0
19	7	0	0	0
17	5	X	0	0
15	3	1	0	0
13	11	9	0	0

Fig. 2.1   (d) North-East (e) South-West (SE) D.F.=143 (SW) D.F.=143

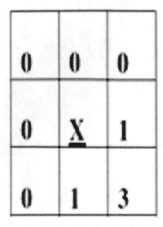

Fig. 2.1   (f) Small efficient operator. D.F.=5

means fewer differences in the overall sequence of images. So that the proposed half toning operator techniques will give effective compression factor. Group-B images contents multiple objects where the variation is more. As in the video conferencing camera moves from main speaker to crowd where the captured image contents many faces i.e. multiple objects where the variations are more. The image B-1, B-2 and B-3 having many faces i.e. multiple objects and B-4 and B-5 contents multiple other objects where there is large variation. The event like Cricket match live, where camera continuously moves on crowd is one of such example. Even for multiple object images we have got effective compression factor. The Halftoning process achieves effective compression factor 1:8 (i.e.12.5%). The halftone image can be again compressed using Run Length Encoding (RLE). Table 1.1 to Table 1.6 shows the experimental results on various types of images using various types of halftoning operators. The abbreviations used in Table 1 to Table 1.6 are Half Tone Compression Factor (HTCF), Run Length Encoding Compression Factor (RLECF) and Net Compression Factor (NETCF)

$$\text{Compression Factor} = \frac{\text{Compressed data (Xc)}}{\text{Uncompressed data (X)}}$$

Compression Ratio is the inverse of the Compression Factor. Where X is the uncompressed data that is original 8-bit gray scale binary image data and Xc is the compressed binary image data after halftoning and Run Length Encoding process

Figure 3.1 shows the original gray scale image in which each pixel is represented by 8-bits. We have consider 256×256 image size. Therefore the total image data is 256×256×8=524288 bits. The images shown in figures from Fig. 3.2 to Fig. 3.5 are halftone images of proposed halftone operators. Each pixel in halftone image is represented by one bit that results in 12.5% compression factor. Figure 4.1 is the 8-bit gray scale image containing multiple objects and from Fig. 4.2 to Fig. 4.5 are halftone images of proposed halftone operators. Fig. 4.1: Crowd -8bit Fig. 4.2: Jarvis image original Halftone image Fig. 4.3: SE Halftone Fig. 3.4:NW Halftone image image Fig. 4.5: Small efficient operator Halftone Image We have shown best image quality and best compression factor sample halftone images of some operator. For rest of the proposed half toning operators results are shown in from Table 1.1 to Table 1.6.

3. Result

Fig. 3.1–Fig. 3.5 shows the sample result for individual face (single object) with maximum constant background where same kind of data is repeated and can be compressed with large extent as shown in tables. Figs. 4.1–4.5 shows the sample results for multiple faces (multiple objects) with

Fig. 3.1 Gandhiji-8bit original image
Fig. 3.2 Jarvis Halftone image
Fig. 3.3 SE Halftone image
Fig. 3.4 NW image
Fig. 3.5 Small efficient operator Halftone

Fig. 4.1 Crowd-8bit image original
Fig. 4.2 Jarvis Halftone image
Fig. 4.3 SE Halftone image
Fig. 4.4 NW Halftone image
Fig. 4.5 Small efficient operator Halftone

maximum variation. Figures 3.2–3.5 shows the halftone images using Jarvis, South-East, North-West and small efficient operator respectively. Halftoning process gives 12.5% compression factor irrespective of less or more variations. But in REL technique compression factor is depending on how fast variations are in the image. If repetition of data is in image then RLE gives good compression factor. We have taken two types of images.

Table 1.1 Reaults of Jarvis operator

S.N	Image	RLECF (%)	NETCF (%)
A-1	Ashwarya	32.0840	4.0105
A-2	Sachin	16.3789	2.0474
A-3	Barbara	55.5098	6.9387
A-4	Lena	37.5898	4.6987
A-5	Gandhiji	19.3965	2.4246
	Average:	32.1918	4.02398
B-1	Cricktteam	34.8262	4.3533
B-2	Crowed	25.0840	3.1355
B-3	Classroom	43.6426	5.4553
B-4	Boat	40.3301	5.0413
B-5	Goldhill	47.5664	5.9458
	Average	38.28986	5.9754

Table 1.2 Results of South-East operator

S.N	Image	RLECF (%)	NETCF (%)
A-1	Ashwarya	18.3066	2.2883
A-2	Sachin	10.2422	1.2803
A-3	Barbara	40.8105	5.1013
A-4	Lena	29.2246	3.6531
A-5	Gandhiji	16.1699	2.0212
	Average:	20.8926	2.6116
B-1	Cricktteam	20.8926	2.6116
B-2	Crowed	19.6465	2.4558
B-3	Pepper	25.6895	3.2112
B-4	Boat	24.4121	3.0515
B-5	Goldhill	27.3750	3.4219
	Average	23.60314	2.9504

Table 1.3 Results of South-West operator

S.N	Image	RLECF (%)	NETCF (%)
A-1	Ashwarya	8.6191	1.0774
A-2	Sachin	3.4180	0.4272
A-3	Barbara	11.3223	1.4153
A-4	Lena	11.7363	1.4670
A-5	Gandhiji	7.4707	0.9338
	Average:	8.51328	1.06414
B-1	Cricktteam	1.9590	0.2449
B-2	Crowed	15.8145	1.9768
B-3	Pepper	8.1699	1.0212
B-4	Boat	12.9980	1.6248
B-5	Goldhill	6.2461	0.7808
	Average	9.0375	1.1297

Type-A are the images where single object is the content. Type-B are the images where multiple objects are shown in the image. Images B-1, B-2, Contents human faces as

Table 1.4   Results of North- East operator

S.N	Image	RLECF (%)	NETCF (%)
A-1	Ashwarya	1.8206	1.4973
A-2	Sachin	5.7656	0.7207
A-3	Barbara	20.8926	2.6116
A-4	Lena	22.6699	2.8337
A-5	Gandhiji	9.2129	1.1516
	Average:	12.07232	1.76298
B-1	Cricktteam	7.0840	0.8855
B-2	Crowed	18.7559	2.3445
B-3	Pepper	20.5918	2.5740
B-4	Boat	22.0723	2.7590
B-5	Goldhill	21.1445	2.6431
	Average	17.9297	2.24122

Table 1.5   Results of North-West operator

S.N	Image	RLECF (%)	NETCF (%)
A-1	Ashwarya	7.5098	0.9387
A-2	Sachin	2.5586	0.3198
A-3	Barbara	3.6426	0.4553
A-4	Lena	8.1621	1.0203
A-5	Gandhiji	6.6582	0.8323
	Average:	5.70626	0.71328
B-1	Cricktteam	0.6777	0.0847
B-2	Crowed	13.2168	1.6521
B-3	Pepper	3.8379	0.4797
B-4	Boat	2.3105	0.2888
B-5	Goldhill	1.3418	0.1677
	Average	4.27694	0.5346

Table 1.6   Results of Small efficient operator

S.N	Image	RLECF (%)	NETCF (%)
A-1	Ashwarya	31.8301	3.9788
A-2	Sachin	17.8730	2.2341
A-3	Barbara	55.9336	6.9917
A-4	Lena	48.9922	6.1240
A-5	Gandhiji	22.5332	2.8167
	Average:	35.43242	4.42906
B-1	Cricktteam	35.5684	4.4460
B-2	Crowed	29.0684	3.6335
B-3	Pepper	48.1699	6.0212
B-4	Boat	44.1738	5.5217
B-5	Goldhill	50.3633	6.2954
	Average	51.10274	5.18356

a multiple objects and images B-3, B-4, B-5, contents different type of multiple objects. Tables from Table 1.1 to Table 1.6 show the compression factor and average compression factor for corresponding operators. Each table content both the type-A and type-B images. Average compression factor for multiple object images is slightly greater than the single object images. It means that in video conferencing if camera moves to crowd still compression can be done effectively.

4. Discussion

Halftoning technique gives best compression factor 12.5% at the source. This compressed image again is compressed with RLE so as to obtain excellent compressed image data. Table 1.1 to Table 1.6 gives the commparison among various halftoning operators. Table 1.1 gives results by using Jarvis operator and Table 1.2 to Table 1.6 gives result by using proposed halftoning operator. For both the cases individual face or single object image and crowded or multiple objects image the compression factor is effectively reduced by using proposed operator. The proposed operators from fig. 2.1 (b) to fig. 2.1(e) are twenty five-coefficients (effectively twelve only) operations. The operator shown in fig. 2.1(f) is the small one which has nine-coefficient(effectively one only) operation. So that the smallest mask requires less processing time along with very good image quality. Figure 3.1 shows original 8-bit black and white image. Figure 3.2 is the halftone image using Jarvis operator and Figs. 3.3–3.5 are the halftone images processed by the proposed operators shown in figures from Fig. 2.1 (b) to Fig. 2.1 (f). As a sample we have taken just two output halftone images of South-East (SE) and North-West (NW) proposed operator. The image quality of South-East (SE) operator is very good while another North-West (NW) operator gives good compression factor. For other operators results are given in respective tables. The application where picture quality is the major constraint then South-East (SE) operator can be used and where compression of video data is the main objective for low bit rate video data transmission with permissible low in picture quality then North-West (NW) operator is advisable. Figure 2.1 (f) shows the smallest mask highly effective that takes less number of computations with very good halftone image quality. Such a combination of Halftoning technique with RLE and proposed halftoning operators are advisable for video conferencing where there is almost constant background and very minimal variations in facial expressions. For video transmission low bit video data transmission with good picture quality reproduction is required. In such cases this proposed technique is advisable. In video conferencing camera always moves from main speaker (single object) to spectators (multiple object) vice versa. Even if this hybrid technique is suitable for multiple object type of pictures and video data transmission as results shows in tables not a much difference in compression factor. Average compression is calculated for various individual face images as well as multiple people type of images.

5. Conclusion

In this paper we have introduced 5×5 size filter masks. Out of which South-East operator gives same kind of image quality to that of standard Jarvis operator. North-West operator gives major features of the image with very good compression factor. We have proposed another 3×3 small effective operator that gives very good image quality with considerable less computation and complexity. Using this approach Run Length Encoding compression after Halftone compression, gives enough good image quality and considerable compression factor. Therefore, this hybrid compression technique is advisable for video data transmission with low bit rate. In video transmission data compression is required at source and that can be achieved by using the proposed technique.

References

1. A Novel Approach for Reduction of Blocking Effects in Low-Bit-Rate Image Compression Zhou Wang and Dapeng Zhang, *Senior Member, IEEE,* IEEE Transaction on communications, vol. 46, No. 6, June 1998

2. "A Novel Video Quality Metric for Low Bit-Rate Video Considering Both Coding and Packet- Loss Artifacts", Tao Liu, Yao Wang, Fellow, IEEE, Jil M. Boyce, Senior Member,IEEE, Hua ang, Member, IEEE, and Zhenyu Wu, Member, IEEE IEEE Journal of selected topic in Signal Processing, vol.3 No.2 April 2009

3. Modeling and Quality Assessment of Halftoning by Error Diffusion Thomas D. Kite, Brian L Evans, Senior Member, IEEE, and Alan C Bovik, Fellow, IEEEs

4. Efficient Secured Lossless Coding of Medical Images– Using Modified Runlength Coding for Character Representation, S Annadurai, and P. Geetha, World Academy of Science, Engineering and Technology 12 2005

5. "A Fast Wavelet-based video codec and its application in an IP version 6- ready serverless videoconferencing system". H. L. Cycon, M. Palkow, T. C. Schmidt and M. Wahlisch

6. Error Control and Concealment for Video Communication — A Review, Yao Wang and Qin-Fan Zhu

7. A Novel Approach for Reduction of Blocking Effects in Low-Bit-Rate Image Compression Zhou Wang and Dapeng Zhang, *Senior Member, IEEE,* IEEE Transaction on Communications, Vol. 46, No. 6, June, 1998

8. Embedded Foveation Image Coding Zhou W ang, *Student Member, IEEE,* and Alan Conrad Bovik, *Fellow, IEEE,* IEEE Transactions on Image Processing, Vol. 10, No. 10, October 2001

9. Foveation Scalable *Member, IEEE,* Ligang Lu, *Member, IEEE,* and Alan C. Bovik, *Fellow, IEEE,* IEEE Transactions on Image Processing, Vol.12, No. 2, Feb. 2003

10. "Generalized Bitplane-by-Bitplane shift metpod for JPEG2000 ROI coding" *Zhou Wang, Serene Banerjee, Brian L. Evans and Alan C. Bovik* Laboratory for Image and Video Engineering (LIVE), Dept. of Electrical and Computer Engineering, The University of Texas at Austin, Austin, TX 78712-1084, USA Email: zhouwang@ieee.org, fserene, bevans, bovikg@ece.utexas.edu

11. R. Floyd and L. Steinberg, "An adaptive algorithm for spatial grayscale, "*Proc. Soc. Image Display*, vol. 17, no. 2, pp. 75–77, 1976

12. J. Jarvis, C. Judice, and W. Ninke, "A survey of techniques for the display of continuous tone pictures on bilevel displays," *Comput. Graph. Image Process.*, vol. 5, pp 13–40, 1976

13. Thomas D.kite,Brian L.Evans and Alan C. Bovik, IEEE."Modeling and Quality Assessment of Half toning by Error Diffusion", IEEE Transaction on Image Processing, vol.9. No.5, May 2000

An improved algorithm for classification of graphite grains in cast iron microstructure images using geometric shape features

Pattan Prakash[1] · V. D. Mytri[2] · P. S. Hiremath[3]

[1]System Analyst, Department of Computer Science & Engg., PDA College of Engineering, Gulbarga, India.
[2]Principal, GND Engineering College, Bidar, India.
[3]Professor & Chairman, Department of Computer Science, Gulbarga University, Gulbarga,India.

1. Introduction

Physical properties of a material depend on its microstructure characteristics. Carbon in the form of graphite is often used as an additive in the production of cast iron [3]. The microstructure of graphite within cast iron has major effects on the casting's mechanical properties. When graphite arranges itself as thin flakes, the result is gray iron, which is hard and brittle. When graphite takes the form of spherical nodules the result is nodular iron, which is soft and malleable.

Hence, classification and quantification of such structures is very essential in the field of material manufacturing. In computer vision and analysis system, the representation of shapes is carried out with the help of shape descriptors. Selection of most suitable set of descriptors is one of the important step in grains classification process and they are explained in the following section.

1.1 Definitions of set of shape descriptors

Quantitative shape analysis is one of the most frequent tasks of quantitative image analysis. The shape descriptors are used to represent a shape and to quantify it. Shape descriptors are some set of numbers that are produced to describe a given shape [7]. The shape may not be entirely reconstructable from the descriptors, but the descriptors for different shapes should be different enough that the shapes can be discriminated. In general, shape descriptors quantify a deviation of the analyzed object from the ideal or model one. The most frequently used reference shape is a circle, because it is the most simple and natural figure in 2D images. The objects presented in metallographic images can exhibit shapes that are very far from the circle. We propose an efficient set of shape descriptors

which include elongation, circularity, diameter_ratio and area_ratio. The definitions of the shape features, which are used in the recognition of graphite grains are explained as below. i)Elongation: Elongation of a region (grain) is the ratio between the length (l) and width (w) of the region bounding rectangle. This is the rectangle of minimum area that bounds the shape, which is located by turning in discrete steps until a minimum

$$Elongation = f1 = \frac{l}{w} \tag{1}$$

f 1=1 for ideal circle or a square and is less than 1 but greater than 0 in elongated shapes [3].

ii) Circularity: It is to measure irregularity of circular objects.

$$Circularity = f2 = \frac{4\pi A}{L^2} \tag{2}$$

where A is the section area of grain and L is length of the perimeter of graphite grain boundary. The f 2 shape factor is very sensitive to any irregularity of circular objects. It reaches its maximum value of 1 for a circle and smaller values for all the other shapes. It is insensitive to small elongation.

iii) Diameter_ratio: The objects present in microstructure images can exhibit shapes that are very far from the circle, but finding the reference circle can be intuitively easy as shown in Fig. 1. The rows in the Fig. 1 illustrate three types of distortion elongation, irregularity and composition. Elongation, irregularity, composition (elongation + irregularity) are the commonly used shape descriptors. An example of

S.J. Pise (ed.), *ThinkQuest 2010*, DOI 10.1007/978-81-8489-989-4_39,

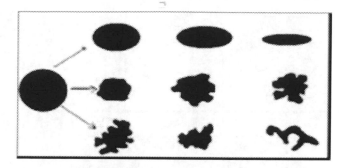

Fig. 1 Three models of distortion from the ideal circular shape (from top to bottom: elongation, irregularity, and composition). Row-wise increase in distortion.

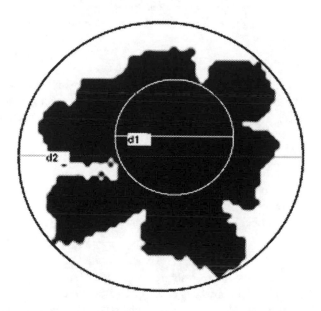

Fig. 2 Inscribed and circumscribed circles on a grain shape. d1 and d2 are diameters of inscribed and circumscribed circle.

such variable shape is graphite precipitates formed during transition from the nodular to flake cast iron. This transaction cannot be effectively described by using alone any of the generally used shape descriptors presented in literature. The shape descriptors described in literature helps in average classification rate. One can note that all objects from Fig. 1, illustrating the composition type of deformation (lower row in Fig. 1) have approximately the same section area, but when moving across the sequence to the left, systematically greater circles can be inscribed within the particle.

This observation needs a definition of a new shape factor namely, diameter_ratio(f3). It is a new feature descriptor and is defined as the ratio of diameter of maximum inscribed and circumscribed circles [3], as shown in Fig. 2.

$$Diameter\_ratio = f3 = \frac{d1}{d2} \tag{3}$$

where $d1$ and $d2$ are the diameters of the maximum inscribed and circumscribed circles, respectively. This feature is rarely discussed feature in the literature, but is found to be very useful for graphite grain shapes. For determining the diameter of an inscribed circle, we have used the distance transform technique [20]. When a region is distance transformed, a highest distance label at the centre of the region is obtained. From the csentral highest label position to the nearest boundary label with zero label in eight direction, distance is measured and the two times of the measured distance taken as the diameter of the maximum inscribed circle ($d1$) within the region. For the diameter of circumscribed circle ($d2$), twice the maximum distance from the central pixel of region is considered.

iv) Area_ratio: It is defined as the ratio of area of the analyzed object and the minimum bounding rectangle.

$$Area\_ratio = f4 = \frac{A}{S} \tag{4}$$

where A is the area of the analyzed object and S is the area of minimum bounding rectangle.

1.2 Background literature

Through our literature survey, we could study some of the papers which nearly address the issue of classification with various shape descriptors. F. Mokhtarian, S. Abbasi, and J. Kittler [16, 17] have proposed curvature based shape representation and image retrieval. Wavelet representation of object contours is discussed by G. Chuang and Kuo [18]. Zernike moments were effectively applied for providing invariance in image recognition by A Khotanzan and Y.H. Hong [19]. As it is theoretically supported and experimentally verified. Zernike moments significantly outperform regular moments and moment invariants.

A neural network recognition of graphite morphology is proposed exclusively for nodular structure by evolution strategy by Chen Zhibin et al. [2]. They have used roundness, form factor, sphericity, circularity length-width ratio, Tortousity as grain features for recognition system. Xaviour Arnould et al. [15] have proposed methods to automatically extract the grain boundaries of the materials to determine grain morphological parameters of ceramic materials. Wanda B., Alfred R and Gerhalrd [14] have worked with morphological methods and contour analysis method for grain boundary segmentation of microstructure image. Many more efforts have been made in this area. The simple shape descriptors (SSDs) are the general choice of many for extracting the features. The comparison of shape descriptors is given in [5] and it is observed that SSDs with Euclidian distance classifier are efficient features. Out of many features discussed, not all the features are required for recognition purpose. Choosing the most suitable features for the case in hand is a challenge. The Fourier descriptors

[7] are lso popularly used as object features. Pattan Prakash et al. [9] have used simple shape descriptors(SSDs) and moment invariant (MI) features as shape descriptors with radial basis function neural network to classify six types of graphite grains and achieved significant classification rate using moment invariants. It is observed that the class IV and V has low classification rate compared to classification rate of other four classes. The literature study indicated that, there is still a need for developing more robust shape descriptors to address the issue of classification of graphite grains and determine the distribution pattern of each class of grains. Hence, this work is an attempt to improve the recognition rate of graphite grains according to the ISO 945 specified reference drawings by defining a more efficient set of shape descriptors suitable for the purpose to identify the graphite grains and apply the method of determining the distribution of grains in a given sample.

1.3 Materials used

We have used the microstructure images of cast iron, that have been taken from steel bars, that have all types of graphite grain structures. The etching medium used for preparing specimen is 3% alcoholic nitric acid. The images are drawn from microstructure libraries [13] for experimentation. The microstructure images used for testing are of cast iron with varying compositions and magnifications. The images also differ in lighting and noise content. The ISO-945 reference drawings of grain morphology [3] as shown in Fig. 3 are used for training neural network.

For testing the proposed method, we have used material microstructure images acquired from light microscope at resolutions, 100x–500x. We have used 50 images for testing and the sample test images are as shown in Fig. 4.

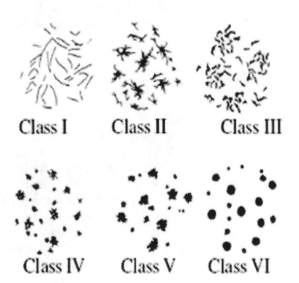

Fig. 3. Reference drawings for the ISO-945 defined six classes of grains in cast iron

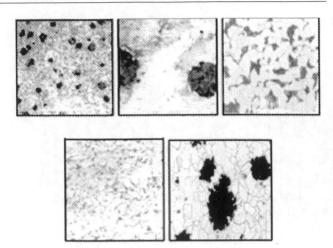

Fig. 4. Sample microstructure images of Cast iron showing various types of grain structures.

The proposed method is based on neural network approach and has two phases: training and testing. Each phase consists of preprocessing and feature extraction stages as described below.

2. Proposed Method

The proposed method comprises three steps, namely, preprocessing, feature extraction and classification, which are described in the following sections.

2.1 Preprocessing

Generally, the microstructure images used for testing, suffer from noise and artifacts developed at the time of specimen preparation. This stage is of high importance in achieving good results in segmentation and further process. We have used circular averaging filter with radius 2, followed by the morphological closing with fixed structuring element, 'disk' of radius 2, in order to de-noise the image. We have used simple threshold segmentation [8] method for segmenting the graphite grains from the background ferrite matrix . The segmented image is labeled. Each labeled segment is a grain structure and is subjected to the shape feature extraction.

2.2 Feature extraction

The segmented regions in an image are labeled and the geometric features, namely, elongation, circularity, diameter_ratio and area_ratio (as described in section 1.1) are computed for each labeled segment. These features are used in the training and classification phases of the proposed algorithm.

2.3 Neural network classifier

We use the neural network classifier for grains classification in the segmented image. The training and classification phases of neural network are given in the following algorithms.

Phase 1: Neural network training

STEP 1: Input microstructure image (RGB color training image)

STEP 2: Convert the color image to gray scale image

STEP 3: Perform preprocessing (averaging, morphological operations and thresholding) and obtain segmented image. The segmented regions are known grains.

STEP 4: Compute the shape features for each labeled region (grain), which are of known grainclass.

STEP 5: Input the shape features computed in

STEP 6: Repeat the steps 1 to 5 for all training images.

Phase 2: Neural network classifier

STEP 1: Input microstructure image (RGB color test image).

STEP 2: Convert the color image to gray scale image

STEP 3: Perform preprocessing (averaging, morphological operations and thresholding) and obtain the segmented image.

STEP 4: Compute the shape features for each labeled segment.

STEP 5: (Classification) Input the shape features computed in step 4 to the neural network (trained in Phase 1), which classifies the segmented region as a grain belonging to one of the six grain classes.

STEP 6: The output of neural network Indicates the grain class to which the region belongs.

STEP 7: Repeat steps 5 and 6 for all segmented regions of the image.

3. Experimental results and discussion

For the experimentation, the neural network is trained using six ISO-945 reference drawings with six grain classes. The original drawings are scanned and images are stored in JPEG format. The shape descriptors are used as inputs for the neural network. The radial basis transfer function is used for training. The error function used is 'mean square error (mse)' which is set to 0.01. The spread for radial basis function is 1.0. The architecture of the neural network with radial basis function is as shown in Fig. 5.

During the testing phase, 50 microstructure images, each with grains of different types containing 25 grains on an average, are used. These images are drawn from the microstructure library [13]. Out of many shape descriptors defined in the literature, the four descriptors defined in the section 1.2, employed by the neural network classifier with radial basis function, have yielded better classification results during our experimentation. The results are shown in the Table 1. It can be observed from Fig. 6 that there is a low rate of classification in the case of grain-class IV and

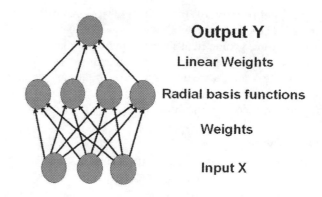

Fig. 5 Neural network classifier with radial basis function

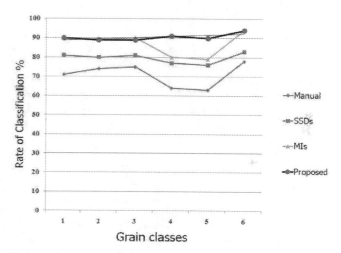

Fig. 6 Comparison of classification performance of proposed method (thick line) with manual, SSDs and MIs

Table 1 Classification rate of six classes of grains

Classification method	Classification rate
Manual	70.83%
SSDs [9]	79.66%
Moment Invariants [11]	87%
Proposed	90.5%

class V as compared to the methods using SSDs and MIs [9, 11]. It is due to the similar shape defined in their basic reference drawings it self. In spite of the similarity in grain shapes of class IV and class V, the proposed method has yielded significant improvement in classification rate. The expert's intervention is limited to only building the neural network and the knowledge-base of grain classes.

4. Conclusion

An improved algorithm for automatic classification of graphite grains of six types is proposed. The method is robust and invariant under geometry, lighting transforms, quality and variety of magnifications of microstructure images. The experimental results show that the proposed method using geometrical features and radial basis neural network classifier yields better classification performance. The results can be further improved by using suitable preprocessing methods, feature sets and classifiers. This will be considered in our future work

References

1. A.K.Jain, "Fundamentals of Digital Image Processing". Prentice-Hall, Englewood Cliffs, NJ, 1989

2. Chen Zhibin, Yu Yongquan, Chen eqing, Yang Shaomin, "Fuzzy Recognition of Graphite Morphology in Nodular Cast Iron Based on Evolution Strategy", Proc. of the Fourth Intl. Conference on Machine Learning and Cybernetics, Guangzhou, Aug. 2005, pp 18-21

3. Handbook Committee, Handbook of ASM International, Vol 9, Metallography and Microstructures. ISBN:0-87170-706-3

4. H. E. Henderson's article titled "Ultrasonic Velocity Technique for Quality Assurance", appearing in the Foundry Trade Journal,Feb. 21, 1974, at pages 203-208

5. Longin Jan Latecki and Rolf Lak"amper and Ulrich Eckhardt, "Shape Descriptors for Nonrigid Shapes with a Single Closed Contour", IEEE Conference on Computer Vision and Pattern Recognition (CVPR), 2000, pp 424-429

6. L.Wojnar, Image Analysis, Applications in Materials Engineering, CRC Press, 1999

7. Milan Sonka, Vaclav Hlavac, Rogen Boyle, "Image processing analysis and machine vision" 2e, Thomson Publishing Company, 2007

8. Otsu N., "A Threshold Selection Method from Gray-level Histograms", IEEE Trans, on Systems, Man and Cybernetics, Vol. 9 No. 1 1979, pp. 62-66

9. Pattan Prakash, V.D. Mytri and P.S. Hiremath, "Classification of Graphite Grains with Simple Shape Descriptors", Intl. Jl. on Engg. and Tech. (IJENGG), Vol.4, No.2, pp.37-42, 2009

10. Pattan Prakash, V.D. Mytri, P.S.Hiremath,, "Automatic Microstructure Image Analysis for Classification and Quantification of Phases of Material", Proc. of International Conference on Systemics, Cybernetics and Informatics (ICSCI- 2009) Jan 17-10,2009, pp 308–311

11. Pattan Prakash, V.D. Mytri, P.S. Hiremath, "Classification of Cast Iron Based on Graphite Grain Morphology using Neural Network Approach", Proc. of Intl. Conf. on Digital Image Processing, (ICDIP 2010), Feb 26-28, 2010 (communicated)

12. Practical Guide to Image Analysis, ASM International, 2000

13. University of Cambridge,Contributed Microstructures library: http://www.doitpoms. ac.uk and http://www.metallograf.de/ starteng. Html

14. Wanda Benesova, Alfred Rinnhofer, Gerhard Jacob, "Determining The Average Grain Size of Super-Alloy Micrographs", ICIP-2006, Joanneum Research Institute of Digital Image Processing, Graz, Austria, 2006, pp 2749-2752

15. Xaviour Arnould, Michel Coster, Jean-Louis Chermant, Liliane Chermant, Thierry Chartier and Abder Elmoataz, "Segmentation and Grain Size of Cera mics", Image Anal Stereol, France 2001, pp.131-135

16. F. Mokhtarian, S. Abbasi, and J. Kittler.Efficient and robust retrieval by shape content through curvature scale space. In A. W. M. Smeulders and R. Jain, editors, Image Databases and Multi-Media Search, pages 51–58. World Scientific Publishing, Singapore, 1997

17. F. Mokhtarian and A. K. Mackworth. A theory of multiscale, curvature-based shape representation for planar curves. IEEE Trans. 4:789–805, 1992

18. G. Chuang and C.-C. Kuo. Wavelet descriptor of planar curves: Theory and applications. *IEEE Trans. on Image Processing*, 5:56–70, 1996

19. Khotanzan and Y. H. Hong. Invariant image recognition by Zernike moments. *IEEE Trans. PAMI*, 12:489–497, 1990

20. Przemyslaw Lagodzinski and Bogdan Smolka On the Application of Distance Transformation in Digital Image Colorization, Computer Recognition Systems 2, ASC 45, pp. 108–116, 2007

Recognizing emotions from human speech

Preeti Khanna[1] · Dr. M. Sasikumar[2]

[1]Research Scholar, MPSTME, NMIMS, Mumbai, India.
[2]CDAC Kharghar, Navi Mumbai, India.

1. Introduction

Emotions colour the language and act as a necessary ingredient for natural two way human-to–human communication and interaction. As listeners we also react to the speaker's emotive state and adapt our behavior depending on what kind of emotions the speaker transmits. Recent technological advances have enabled the human to interact with computer through non-traditional modalities (e.g. keyboard, mouse) like voice, gesture, facial expression etc. This interaction still lacks the component of emotions. It is argued that to truly achieve affective human computer intelligent interaction there is a need for the computer to be able to interact naturally with the user, similar to the way human - human interaction takes place. Several studies have been conducted consisting of classical human interaction and of human computer interaction. They concluded that for intelligent interaction emotions play an important ingredient. A baby learns to recognize emotional information before understanding semantic information in his/her mother's utterance. We present some basic research in the field of emotion recognition from speech. First we give a brief survey of research in the field of emotive speech. Then we discuss an approach to detect and classify human emotion in speech using certain rules. The basic five emotions considered as anger, happiness, fear, sadness and neutral.

2. Existing work

In the recent years, a great deal of research has been done to automatically recognize emotions from human speech. There are mainly three different issues namely selection of emotional states, selection of features set from speech and selection of classifiers to recognize emotions. A number of studies had been done in past. Petrushin, 1999 exploits spoken dialogs to distinguish between two states such as "agitation" which includes anger, happiness and fear, and "calm" which includes normal state and sadness with the average accuracy 77%. They used RELIEF-F algorithm and out of 43 features (min, max, range and standard deviation of fundamental frequency, energy, speaking rate, first three formants and their bandwidths) they selected the top 14 features. They used different classifiers like KNN, neural networks and set of experts. They concluded that people cannot decode even such manifest emotions as anger and happiness with sufficient accuracy.

Ow kwon et.al, 2003 had selected pitch, log energy, formant, mel-band energies and mel frequency cepstral coefficient (MFCCs) as the base features in their work for emotion recognition and then compared the performances of the various classifiers. They found the best accuracy of 96.3% for stressed / neutral style classification using Gaussian SVM. It is found that in this experiment the most important features of emotional expressions in speech were pitch and energy. Lee et.al, 2002 tried to distinguish between two emotions: negative and positive, in call centre environment, using linear discrimination, k-NN classifier, and support vector machine (SVM) and achieved accuracy rate of 75%.

To decide about the speech features which vary across emotions, there is need to study the correlation between them. A number of researchers have already investigated this question (Burkhardt and Sendlmeier, 2000). Indeed, certain emotional states are often which not only dependent on acoustic parameters of speech but also on the combination of acoustic, lexical, physiological signals and others.

Murray and Arnott, 1993 studied the dependence of acoustic characteristics for different emotions as summarized

S.J. Pise (ed.), *ThinkQuest 2010*, DOI 10.1007/978-81-8489-989-4_40,

Table 1 Summary of correlation of feature to emotions (Murray and Arnott, 1993)

	Anger	Happy	Sad	Fear
Speech Rate	Slightly faster	Faster or slower	Slightly slower	Much faster
Pitch average	Very much higher	Much higher	Slightly slower	Very much higher
Pitch range	Much wider	Much wider	Slightly narrower	Much wider
Intensity	Higher	Higher	Lower	Normal
Voice quality	Breathy, chest tone	Breathy, blaring	Resonant	Irregular voicing
Pitch changes	Abrupt	Smooth, upward inflections	Downward inflections	Normal
Articulations	Tense	Normal	Slurring	Precise

in the Table 1. Thus, in fact there seems to exist some general tendencies for certain acoustic correlates by certain emotions. But sometimes it is difficult to know what aspect of the emotions the finding captures.

A number of experiments using computer based techniques to explore various aspect of speech that reflects emotions have been conducted (Murray and Arnott, 1993; Burkhardt and Sendlmeier, 2000). All generally agree that the most crucial aspects are related to prosody is pitch, the intensity contour and timing of utterances. Some more recent studies have shown that voice quality (Gobl and Chasaide, 2003) is also reasonably correlated with certain emotions.

In this paper we try to analyze the speech signal in terms of its acoustical and prosodic information across different emotions. The emotional categories that have been used in our experiment are neutral, sad, angry, fear and happy. We will be considering a number of classification methods such as, as Multi-layer perception, SMO, Simple logistics, Logistics, Naïve Bayes, Naive Net, Jrip, NNge, PART, Random Forest, J48 and LMT to classify five emotional states.

3. Our approach for emotion recognition system

The emotion recognition system from speech studied in this paper is depicted in figure 1.

4. Input: Speech database

One needs a data set representative of the domain to infer various emotions from speech using machine learning techniques to obtain meaningful results. The performance of a classifier that can distinguish different emotional patterns ultimately depends on the completeness of the training and testing samples and how similar it is compared to the real world ata. Collecting large databases of natural and unbiased emotions is challenging. For our experiments

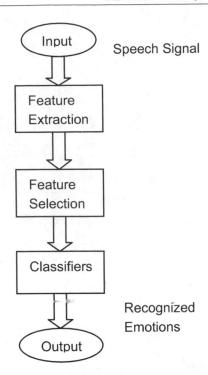

Fig. 1 Speech emotion recognition system Like the typical pattern recognition system, it contains four main modules: emotional speech input, feature extraction, classification module, and recognized emotion output. Each of these is discussed in detail below

we have used Danish motional Speech (DES) database that covers five emotional states. Ten actors (5 female and 5 male) simulated the emotions producing 10 German utterances (5 short and 5 longer sentences) which are used in everyday communication across various emotional states. From this corpus, for our experiment, we have selected total of 227 emotional utterances for female and 181 emotional utterances for male across the five emotional states as described above.

Module 1: Feature extraction

It is believed that prosodic features are the primary indicator of speakers' emotional ates. Research to analyze emotional speech indicates that fundamental frequency, energy and formant frequencies are potentially effective parameters to distinguish certain emotional states. In our study, five groups of short-term features were extracted relating to fundamental frequency (F0) or pitch, rhythm and the first four formant frequencies (F1 to F4).

A Hamming window was used to segment each speech utterance into frames. The frame length in feature extraction is 20ms and sampling rate is 22 KHz. We have measured a total of nineteen features on the signals, grouped under following headings below. The pitch or the fundamental frequency of the speech signal is calculated using cepstrum

Table 2 List of feature extracted

Set of Features	
Statistics related to pitch using autocorrelation method	Mean, min, max range, standard deviation, mean average slope
Statistics related to pitch using cepstrum method	Mean, min, max range
Statistics over the individual voiced and unvoiced parts	Number of voiced regions, number of unvoiced region, average voiced length, average unvoiced length
Statistics related to rhythm	Speaking rate
Formants	F1, F2, F3 and F4

analysis of the signal as well as using autocorrelation method. The cepstrum is Fourier analysis of logarithmic amplitude of spectrum of the signal. The frame shift is taken as 20ms. For extraction of pitch using autocorrelation method, we have used Praat's programmable scripting language (Boersma, 2001). A very important reason that we chose Praat as one of our platform is that it provides an existing suite of high quality speech analysis routines, such as pitch tracking. For other features we have use MATLAB tool. We determine the first four formant frequencies of the speech signal using Linear Predictive Coding (LPC) coefficients. The frequencies F1, F2, F3 and F4 represent the resonance frequencies of the vocal tract. Finally, we have 19 features.

Module2: Selection of feature

For the selection of features out of 19, a number of experiments were conducted using classifiers such as multi layer perceptron and simple logistics with 10-fold validation. Each time one part of the speech database was left for validation and the remainders were used for training the classifiers. The two best set of features sequences that were selected using this procedure is selected as A and B Feature Set A include all the 19 features as defined above while feature set B include 15 features only. These fifteen features has all the features except that the statistics of pitch using cepstrum method

Module 3: Classification

The selected feature set was used for classification. We used a variety of classifiers at this stage. They include Multi-layer perceptron, SMO, Simple logistics, Logistics, Naive Bayes, Naive Net, Jrip, NNge, PART, Random Forest, J48 and LMT shown in table 3. All these experiment were done using the WEKA toolkit. To recognize the emotional patterns and then validate them, a 10-fold cross validation technique was used. This method involves hereby the training data was randomly split into ten sets, 9 of which were used in training and the 10th for validation. Then

Table 3 List of classifier used to validate the robustness of the algorithm using WEKA toolbox

Types of Classified			
Rules	Tress	Functions	Bayes
Jrip	Random Forest	Logistics	Native Bayes
NNge	J48	Multiplayer Perceptron	Native Net
PART	Logistic Model	Simple logistics	
-		SMO	-

Table 4 Confusion matrix of simple logistics classifier (male): recognized emotions (%)

Stimulus	Angry	Happy	Fear	Sad	Neutral
Angry	50	4	1	0	0
Happy	10	14	3	0	0
Fear	1	5	25	0	4
Sad	0	0	0	22	3
Neutral	0	0	2	1	36

Table 5 Confusion matrix of simple logistics classifier (Female): recognized emotions (%)

Stimulus	Angry	Happy	Fear	Sad	Neutral
Angry	50	11	2	0	1
Happy	17	19	4	0	4
Fear	2	4	26	1	0
Sad	0	0	3	30	4
Neutral	0	1	1	1	37

iteratively another nine was picked and so forth. Both gender dependent and gender independent were conducted to recognize five emotional status

Results and discussion

A recognition rate of 70% was obtained when only the emotional speech from male bjects was considered. An accuracy of 67% was achieved for female subjects, and in gender independent case the average correct cassification rate of five emotional states is 67.3%. The summarized results are shown in table 4, 5and 6. In the confusion matrices shown in Table 4 and 5, the columns show the emotions that the speakers tried to induce, and the rows are the output recognized emotions. From these confusion matrices, it is visible that emotional sate "anger" is best to recognized both for male as well as for female whereas "happiness" is the one which recognized with least accuracy.

The best performance is given by classifier named as Simple logistics and Logistic Model Tree (LMT). For

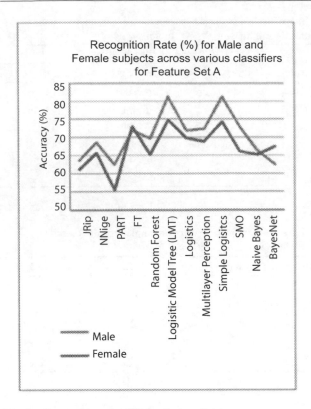

Fig. 2   Recognition rate (%) for feature Set A

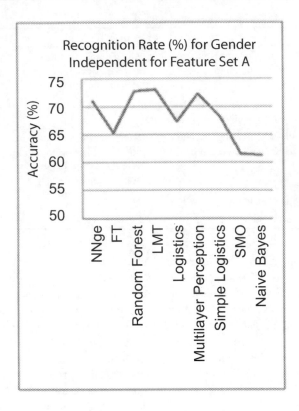

Fig. 4   Recognition rate (%) For feature Set A (gender independent)

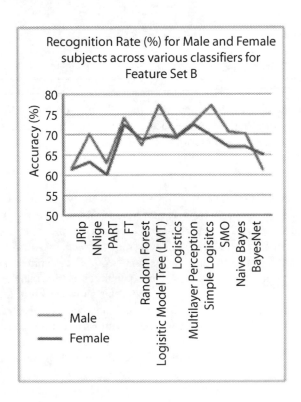

Fig. 3   Recognition rate (%) For feature Set B

male subjects the correct classification rate is 81.21% using feature set A and Simple logistics and LMT as a classifier. For male subjects the correct classification rate is 81.21% using feature set A and Simple logistics and LMT as a classifier. An accuracy of 74.77% is obtained in female subjects using the feature set A and simple logistics as a classifier. The best recognition rate of 73% is obtained with gender independent case which uses the classifier as Logistics and feature set A.

Conclusion

Automatic recognition of emotion is gaining attention due to wide spread applications in various domains. In this paper we tried to investigate the correlation between features of speech with different emotional state. One of our observations is "discriminating ability of the features across emotional states". The same feature may not be good for all types of emotion. Thus we see that the system identify angry with highest accuracy where the sad, neutral and fear are also classified with an acceptable accuracy.

From our work, we found that most of the happy is classified as angry. We plan to investigate what features are good to detect happy, sad and fear. However, only the prescribed set of feature is not enough to detect the emotional category. Thus we also plan to combine feature like MFCC to detect emotions in speech withmore accuracy.

References

1. Boersma, P., 2001. "PRAAT, a system for doing phonetics by computer," Glot International, vol.5, no. 9/10, pp. 341-345

2. Bukhardt., F., Paeschke., A., Rolfes., M., Sendlmeier., W., Weiss., B. 2005. "A database of German Emotional Speech". Interspeech

3. Burkhardt, F., Sendlmeier, W., 2000. "Verification of acoustical correlates of Emotional speech using formant-syntheses." In: Proceedings of the ISCA Workshop on Speech and Emotion

4. Cowie, R., Douglas-Cowie,E., Tsapatsoulis.,N.,Votsis, G.Kollias.S, Fellenx,W.,and Taylor, J.G.2001. "Emotion recognition in human computer interaction. IEEE Signal Processing magazine, Vol.18, No.1, pp. 32-80

5. German Emotional Speech Database http://emotion-research.net/biblio/tuDatabase

6. Gobl, C. And Chasaide., A.N., 2001."The role of voice quality in communicating emotions, mood and attitude." Speech communication, Vol. 40, pp. 189-212

7. Lee, C., Narayanan, S., and Pieraccini, R., 2002. "Classifying emotions in human machine spoken dialogs", presented at proc. Of int. Conf. on multimedia and expo, Switzerland

8. Murray, I.R., Arnott, J.L., 1993. "Towards a simulation of emotion in synthetic speech: a Review of the literature on human vocal emotion". JASA 93 (2), 1097-1108

9. Oh-Wook Kwon, Kwokleung Chan, Jiucang Hao, Te-Won Lee, 2003. "Emotion Recognition By Speech Signals". Eurospeech Geneva

10. Petrushin, V.A., 1999. "Emotion in speech: recognition and application to call centers". Proceedings of Conference on Artificial Neural Networks in Engineering

DoS attack pattern generator for training the neural network based classifier to dynamically blacklist IP in honeypot based NIDS/NIPS

Renuka Prasad B.[1] · **Dr. Annamma Abraham**[2] · **Suhas V.**[3] · **Kundan Kumar**[3]

[1]Research scholor (Dr. MGR University), Lecturer in R.V. College of Engineering, Bengaluru, Karnataka
[2]Professor, Dept of Mathematics, R.V. College of Engineering, Bengaluru, Karnataka, India
[3]Student, Department of M.C.A, R.V. College of Engineering, Bengaluru, India

I. Introduction

A denial-of-service attack (DoS attack) or distributed denial-of-service attack (DDoS attack) is an attempt to make a computer resource unavailable to its intended users [1]. There are many types of Denial of Service Attacks. [2] gives a very detailed explanation of different types of attacks. We focus mainly on the spoofing related attacks and our observation on the pattern of the different types of DoS attacks shows that with minor changes in the program we could generate all the other types of attacks. Here are few DoS attacks that we would like to mention whose signature and the procedure of generating is described at [2]. Apache2, arppoison, Back, Crashiis, dosnuke, Land Mailbomb, SYN Flood, Ping of Death (POD), Process Table, selfping, Smurf, sshprocesstable, Syslogd, tcpreset, Teardrop, Udpstorm

2. Previous work on DoS attack generators

[3] has archived lot of executable programs mainly designed for Windows Operating System based networks and few were designed for Unix Operating System and Mac Operating System. All the techniques mentioned in [3] do not give the details about their implementation and most of them are executables only. Customizing them is almost impossible. There is very little literature available on attack generation. We have observed that most of the previous work involves deep understand of the protocol stack as well as network programming concepts for example as discussed at [4] it is evident that an extensive study of many concepts are required. Most of the existing techniques approach does not approach in an aggregated way. If the attack generator techniques are aggregated to a variety of attacks then it will be easy to generate them and understand the pattern of the attacks else it would require more time to hard code for every type of attack.

3. Our approach

We focused our work to generate attack precisely on apache2 kind and then extended the same for other types like arp spoofing, nuke attacks. Instead of taking the attack individually we tried to aggregate and generate the DoS attacks by creating the same effects as that were done individually. We used Java.net package and jpcap library which is based on libpcap library. Using Java we hard coded the actual IP into the program and try to do the DoS attack on a server which was running web application server apache tomcat. Also at runtime IP address were given and simple request for connections were sent using sockets. This task was continuously done and we were able to see that the web application server stopped responding within a minute as it exceeded the number threads it could create. Within this program with minor modifications we were able to construct packets with different protocols and construct Ethernet frames and tried attacks of nuke and land types.

Algorithm for generating DoS attacks using Java

1. Retrieve the number of interfaces on the machine where the attack is generated from.
2. Open the required network interface to send the packet.
3. Create a TCP packet with specified port numbers, flags, and other parameters using TCP Packet class.
4. Specify the IPV4 header parameters.
5. Set the data fields of the packet.
6. Create an Ethernet packet using Ethernet Packet.
7. Set frame type as IP.
8. Set source and destination MAC addresses, with necessary Hexadecimal to decimal Conversions.
9. Set the data-link frame as ether & send the packet.

S.J. Pise (ed.), *ThinkQuest 2010*, DOI 10.1007/978-81-8489-989-4_41,
© Springer India Pvt. Ltd. 2011

The we run a web application server on a computer and then we generated the attack from another computer over local network. We were able to see that within 10 to 15 seconds the server stops responding as it was unable to process all the request packets. We also tried on different servers by changing the attack destination IP at Run Time. Along with generating the attack. By making use of libpcap based jpcap library the packets could be captured over a network. We also captured the network data after generating the attack. The log from creating using the receivePacket() function of PacketPrinter class. ProcessPacket() of JpcapCaptor class helps in processing the captured network packet. From the information log and statistics obtained from our captured program revealed that the DoS attack was generated. Apart from trying using Java we also tried to generate attacks using "lex" and "C" programs with even more easier way with more harmful effect.

The algorithm for generating DoS attacks using Lex and C programs is as follows

1. Read destination-MAC, destination-IP
2. Read source-MAC, source-IP, Generate randomly.
3. Establish a connection with target and key busy as follows (multi-thread if necessary)
   a) Create spoofed packet with intended payload and send
   b) Sniff for response and reply
4. Creation and sending of spoofed packet
   a) Allocate memory for packet +headers
   b) Copy payload into packet
   c) Initialize the TCP header
   d) Initialize the IP header
   e) Initialize Link Ethernet Layer Header
   f) Set the checksum values
   g) Send packet
5. Sniffing for Response and Replying
   a) Create a raw socket in promiscuous mode
   b) Analyze each packet to determine the one with chosen MAC and IP.
   c) Parse payload
   d) Create a response using spoofed packet and send it.

Pseudo-code for IP-Spoofing is as follows

1. target_ip <- argv[1]
2. Perform steps 3 to 9 till program is interrupted / terminated
3. ip_rand <- rand()
4. a <- ip_rand & 0xFF
5. b <- (ip_rand >> 8) & 0xFF
6. c <- (ip_rand >> 16) & 0xFF
7. d <- (ip_rand >> 24) & 0xFF
8. create command string with appropriate data Payload, data.txt (contains random info) , TCP header info, randomly spoofed source_ip (a.b.c.d) , dest_ip (target_ip) , IP header info, source_port (random_int) , dest_port (80)
9. system(command)

Once these programs are executed we could see that the DoS attacks were successfully generated and the servers were unable to respond.

The next important step was to understand the pattern of the attack and feed that pattern to the neural network classifier for which we were in need of the network data which is spoofed and as well as non-spoofed. That is the data before or after the DoS attacks and network data while DoS attacks. We were able to do this with the simple libpcap softwares like TCPDUMP[5] and also using the advanced software like wireshark[6]. Once the network data which was libpcap compatible was dumped, we used another simple lex parser program to convert the Hexadecimal based dumped to binary data (10101010)

The pseudo-code for converting the data to binary format is as follows

1. "char pkt<number>[] = {" ====>> begin PKT state
2. in PKT state
   a) whitespaces, ',', '0x' ------>> Ignore
   b) [0-9a-f]====>>write hex to ascii binary (character) to output data file. c. '}' ====>> end PKT state
3. Ignore all characters outside packet state

When ll the above tasks were successfully completed we were able to obtain the knowledge about the network behavior while there were no attacks and as well as behavior of the network during the attacks as our neural network based classifier was based on the binary data to get the pattern of the attack data and train accordingly we were able to fed the output obtained from the lex converter and with this we had obtained the pattern of the DoS attack which will be further used in the HoneyPot and neural network based NIDS /NIPS to blacklist those IP which are found suspicious and as well as found creating harm to the home network.

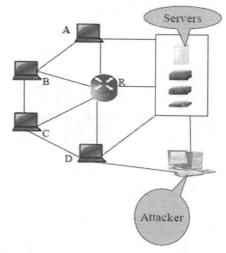

Fig. 1 Our experimental setup

4.   Experimental setup

Our Experimental Setup had the following Configuration.
A LAN with a wired / wireless router
Several Servers (web, mail etc)
Attacking computer was having Core2 Duo processor and 4GB RAM and 150 GB hard disk.
All other configurations include standard Computer Lab setup with necessary equipments switches and cabling is assumed to be present.

5.   Results and legal issues

Spoofing IP or MAC ID and creating problems for the server and all other issues related to the above have legal

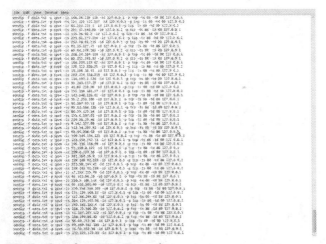

Fig. 2   Spoof programs execution

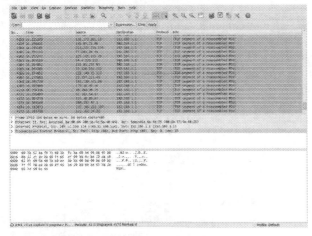

Fig. 3   Wire shark sniffing the spoofing process

issues according to the organization or the country where the experiments are conducted. We did not violate any such rules where they have legal implications. All that we are able to experiment and observe the behaviors or patterns are obtained by those softwares that are already provided by the developers and volunteers which does not have reports of violating the legal rules. And all the experiments that we have conducted is within our organization and lab so that others are not affected.

6.   Scope of the research

The attack generator will be further enhanced to generate possible types of attacks over the computer network and will be used as a universal attack pattern generator for training the attack classifier which is based on neural network that helps the honeypot based NIDS /NIPS to predict the attacking behavior and dynamically blacklist the attacker or the suspicious IP.

7.   Conclusion

We presented a DoS Attack Pattern Generator For Training The Neural Network Based Classifier To Dynamically Blacklist IP in HoneyPot Based NIDS/NIPS. We have even demonstrated how to Practically implement the ideas that we proposed. Our observations have shown that the attack patterns over a network can be easily created and use that pattern to predict the anomalous and harmful activities that can happen over the computer network.

References

1.   http://en.wikipedia.org/wiki/Denial-ofservice_attack
2.   http://www.ll.mit.edu/mission/communications/ist/corpora/ideval/docs/attackDB.html
3.   http://packetstormsecurity.org/Win/STC3. zip
     http://packetstormsecurity.org/DoS/IGMPNukeV1_0.zip
     http://packetstormsecurity.org/DoS/ targa.c
     http://packetstormsecurity.org/DoS/ killwin.c
     http://packetstormsecurity.org/Win/porting.zcools.zip
     http://packetstormsecurity.org/advisories/iss/summary/iss.summary.5.8
     http://packetstormsecurity.org/advisories/iss/iss.summary.6.6
     http://packetstormsecurity.org/poisonpen/u_utils/winnuke.c
     http://packetstormsecurity.org/0310-exploits/php67.txt
4.   http://www.cs.ucl.ac.uk/staff/mrogers/cache/ipsp oof1.txt
5.   www. tcpdump. org/ www. wireshark. org/

Blind and invisible watermarking techniquies for color images

Soni Atmik M.[1] · Metkar Shilpa P.[1] · Lande Pankaj U.[2]

[1]College of Engineering, Pune, India
[2]University of Pune, Pune, India

1. Introduction

With the recent proliferation and success of the internet, together with the availability of relatively inexpensive digital recording and storage devices has created an environment in which it becomes very easy to obtain, replicate and distribute digital content without any loss in quality. This has become a great concern to the multimedia content (music, video and image) publishing industries, because technologies or techniques to protect intellectual property rights for digital media and to prevent unauthorized copying did not exist. Exactly identical copies of digital information, be it images, text or audio, can be produced and distributed easily. In such a scenario, who is the artist and who the plagiarist? It's impossible to tell or was, until now. Encryption technologies can be used to prevent unauthorized access to digital content. However, encryption has its limitations in protecting intellectual property rights because once digital content gets decrypted; there is nothing to prevent an authorized user from illegally replicating it. Another technology is obviously needed to help establish and prove ownership rights, then track content usage, ensure authorized access, facilitate content authentication and prevent illegal replication. This need attracted attention from the research community and industry leading to creation of new information hiding form, called Digital Watermarking. The basic idea of digital watermarking is to create a metadata containing information about the digital content to be protected, and then hide the metadata within that content. The information stored as metadata can have different formats, such as character string or binary image pattern.

The watermarking technique is one of the solutions to different issues of copyright protection, image authentication, proof of ownership, etc. This technique embeds information so that it is not easily perceptible, that is, the viewer cannot see any information embedded in the contents. There are still several important issues existing in the watermarking system.

- First, the embedded watermark should not degrade the quality of the image and should be perceptually invisible to maintain its protective secrecy.
- Second, the watermark must be robust enough to resist common image processing attacks and not be easily removable, only the owner of the image is able to extract the watermark.
- Third, the blind Watermarking technique is necessary since sometimes it is not easy to obtain the original image or original watermark during Extraction, furthermore, a lot of space is needed for storing the original image and original watermark.

Watermarking techniques are mainly classified into 1) spatial domain [1] watermarking techniques, where watermark is embedded directly by changing pixels value, and 2) frequency domain [2] the pixel values are transformed into another domain by applying appropriate transform.

N. Nikolaidis and I. Pitas give an overview of Digital Image Watermarking [1]. They described the watermarking schemes and data hiding techniques for copyright protection of still images. They also described some recent research results on that field and a number of distinct application areas, each with different requirements and limitation. The Spread-spectrum communication is robust against many types of interference and jamming [3]. Cox et al. [4] proposed a watermarking method to embed a watermark by the spread-spectrum technique. The watermark is inserted in the perceptually significant portion of an image where in a predetermined range of low frequency components exclude the dc component. The watermark is spread over many frequency coefficients, so that the number of coefficients which are modified is very small and difficult to detect.

Podilchuk and Zeng [5] improved Cox's method and added the model of the just noticeable difference (JND) to select the maximum length and maximum power watermark sequence. Their method can be used for both the DCT and the discrete wavelet transform (DWT) domains [5]. In [6], the watermark was embedded by quantizing the

S.J. Pise (ed.), *ThinkQuest 2010*, DOI 10.1007/978-81-8489-989-4_42,

coefficients in the DCT-block. Kwon *et al.* [6] embedded the watermark in the variable DCT block size. The block size is determined according to the characteristics of the region in the spatial domain. Mohanty [7] suggested An Adaptive DCT Domain Visible Watermarking Technique for Protection of Publicly Available Images by comparing local mean and variance with global mean and variance. For each block embedded strength factor will be different according mean and variance.

Huang and Yang [8] proposed a watermarking algorithm based on the DWT. The original image is separated in to M blocks, each with the size of n by n; then every block is decomposed into a wavelet domain. The watermark is embedded in the wavelet coefficients in the middle and low sub bands of a block in each image. Author [9] proposed a simple and flexible multiple watermarking schemes using discrete wavelet transform by embedding multiple watermarks in different high frequency HH and low frequency LL sub band. Conclusion comes out that watermark inserted in HH less robust to low–pass filtering but are extremely robust with respect to noise adding, nonlinear filtering, enhancement, histogram equalization, intensity adjustments. Where low–frequency character increase robust to low–pass filtering, lossy compression. Langelaar *et al.* [10] proposed a blind watermarking approach called differential energy watermarking. A set of several 8 by 8 DCT blocks are composed and divided into two parts to embed a watermark bit. The high frequency DCT coefficients in the JPEG/MPEG stream are selectively discarded to produce energy differences in the two parts of the same set.

In this work we have employed watermarking approach for color image in which we have used combined spread spectrum technique and wavelet transform for embedding watermark in cover image. For embedding process uses spread spectrum techniques at multi- resolution representation. We have tested the proposed algorithm to various attacks like JPEG compression, Noise addition, Histogram equalization, Sharpening and Cropping.

2. Realization of spread spectrum and DWT based watermarking techniques

The watermark should not be placed in perceptually insignificant regions of the images or its spectrum since many common signal processes affects these components. For example, a watermark placed a watermark placed in the high frequency spectrum of an image can be easily eliminated with little degradation to the image by any process that directly or indirectly performs low pass filtering. The problem then becomes how to insert a watermark into the most perceptually significant regions of the spectrum in a fidelity preserving fashion. Clearly, any spectral coefficient may be altered, provided such modification is small. However, very small changes are very susceptible to noise.

To solve this problem, the frequency domain of the image or sound at hand is viewed as a communication channel, and correspondingly, the watermark is viewed as a signal that is transmitted through it. Attacks and unintentional signal distortions are thus treated as noise that the immersed signal must be immune to. While we use this methodology to hide watermarks in data, the same rationale can be applied to sending any type of message through media data.

We originally conceived our approach by analogy to spread spectrum communications. In spread spectrum communications, one transmits a narrowband signal over a much larger bandwidth such that the signal energy present in any single frequency is undetectable [4]. Similarly, the watermark is spread over very many frequency bins so that the energy in any one bin is very small and certainly undetectable. Nevertheless, because the watermark verification process knows the location and content of the watermark, it is possible to concentrate these many weak signals into a single output with high signal to-noise ratio (SNR). However, to destroy such a watermark would require noise of high amplitude to be added to *all* frequency bins. Practical [4] result shows that spreading the watermark throughout the spectrum of an image ensures a large measure of security against unintentional or intentional attack. First, the location of the watermark is not obvious. Furthermore, frequency regions should be selected in a fashion that ensures severe degradation of the original data following any attack on the watermark. This will always be the case if the energy in the watermark is sufficiently small in any single frequency coefficient. Moreover, it is possible to increase the energy present in particular frequencies by exploiting knowledge of masking phenomena in the human auditory and visual systems. Spread spectrum watermark can be extracted without using original image (blind watermarking) by means of correlation receiver.

2.1 Watermark embedding

The detailed embedding algorithm is listed as follows. Input: An original image and a watermark image. Output: A watermarked image. Embedding watermark in vertical regions allows increase in the robustness of the watermark, at a little additional impact on image quality. As transform domains are better for the watermarking then spatial, for both reasons of robustness as well as visual impact. The wavelet domain is highly resistant to compression and addition of noise. As Conclusion comes out [9] that watermark inserted in HH less robust to low –pass filtering but are extremely robust with respect to noise adding, nonlinear filtering, enhancement, histogram equalization, intensity adjustments. Where low –frequency character increase robust to low–pass filtering, lossy compression. Figure 1 shows the Proposed algorithm for embedding watermark on cover image. The M x M RGB image is converted in to YCbCr color space. In this work, only luminance component Y is considered for watermarking. The Y component is tilled in to B x B non overlapping blocks, then each block is DWT transformed separately and vertical component HL is taken out for embedding of the watermark. The watermark is embedded by use of this Equation (1) and Equation (2) shown at the bottom of this page. If the message vector msg_i contain 0, then PN sequence is generated with key is added into vertical component scale with embedded strength factor K else the component is kept as it is. Maximum message capacity is given by $(\frac{M}{B})^2$ as height and the width of the cover image (M × M) as well watermark block (B × B) in same. After embedding the watermark block is converted back by using inverse DWT. The blocks are rearranged and the image is converted back from YCbCr color space to RGB.

$$HL_{w(x,y)}(u,v) = HL_{(x,y)}(u,v) + K \times PN_{(x,y)}(u,v), \Longrightarrow \text{When msg}_i=0 \quad (1)$$

$$HL_{w(x,y)}(u,v) = HL_{(x,y)}(u,v), \Longrightarrow \text{When msg}_i=1 \quad (2)$$

2.2 Watermark extraction

The detailed extraction algorithm is listed as follows:
   Input: A Watermark image.
   Output: A binary Watermark image.

As proposed algorithm is public watermarking scheme (blind watermarking) in which original image is not required. The suspected image is converted from RGB to

YCbCr Color space and Y component is taken out as show in Fig. (2) proposed extraction procedure of watermark. Each Y component divided into B×B blocks are followed by DWT, Vertical component $HL_{w(x,y)}$ is taken out and correlated with PN sequence as shown in Equation (3).

$$\delta i = \frac{\sum_m \sum_n (HL_{w(x,y)} - \overline{HL_{(x,y)}})(PN_{mn} - \overline{PN})}{\sqrt{(\sum_m \cdot \sum_n (HL_{w(x,y)} - \overline{HL_{(x,y)}})^2)(\sum_m \cdot \sum_n (PN_{mn} - \overline{PN})^2)}} \quad (3)$$

If the correlation coefficient, ρ_i as given by Equation (3) is greater than the message bit msg_i recovered as 1 else 0. As shown in Equation (4).where T is threshold

$$\text{If } \rho_i < T \text{ than assigned } msg_i = 1 \quad (4)$$

$$\text{If } \rho_i > T \text{ than assigned } msg_i = 0 \quad (5)$$

3. Experimental results

The Performance of the proposed algorithm has been tested for variety of images including BABOON, LENA, PEPPER, MILK and TEXT. The properties of the test images are highlighted in Table 1.For proposed work we have use binary Watermark of size 64×64 and 32×32 shown in Fig. 3.

The proposed algorithm is tested against different parameter and we have obtained results which show the robustness of the techniques to intentional and unintentional attacks.

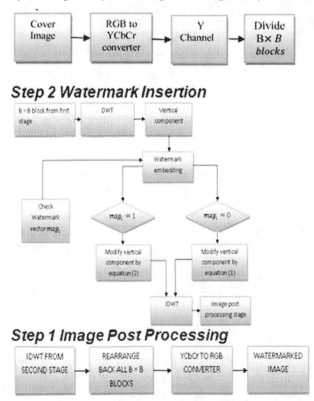

Fig. 1   Proposed algorithm for embedding watermark

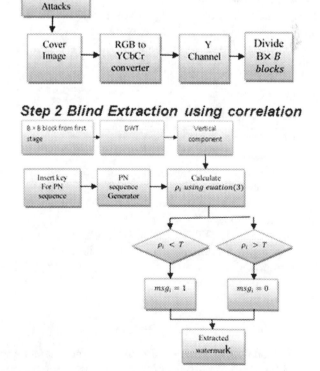

Fig. 2   Proposed algorithm for extracting watermark

Table 1 Test images properties

TEST IMAGE	SIZE	TYPE	BITDEPTH
LENA	512×512	TIF	24bit per pixel (RGB)
BABOON	512×512	TIF	24bit per pixel (RGB)
PEPPER	512×512	TIF	24bit per pixel (RGB)
TEXT	512×512	TIF	24bit per pixel (RGB)
MILK	512×512	TIF	24bit per pixel (RGB)

(a) BINARY LOGO   (b) LOGO1

Fig. 3 Binary watermarks

3.1 Imperceptibility

Figure 4(a) shows the original image of 512 ×512 and 24 bits per pixels. And Figure 4(b) is watermark or logo of size 64×64 which we want to embedded on cover image for copyright protection. The watermarked image with gain K=30 and block size B (8×8) is shown in Fig. 4(c). We get PSNR 42.48db. it can seen from Figures that watermark is not perceptible, but at same time it could be extracted without any error by using proper threshold. At the receiver side we will get Watermarked image which undergone different attacks and by using extracted algorithm we will get watermark as shown in Fig. 3(d). After extracting the watermark, the normalized correlation coefficient (NC) is computed using the original watermark and extracted watermark to judge the existence of Watermark. It is Defined as follows in Equation (6)

$$NC = \frac{\sum_{i=0}^{Wh-1}\sum_{j=0}^{Ww-1} W(i,i) \times W'(i,j)}{Wh \times Ww} \quad (6)$$

Where Wh and Ww are the height and width of the watermark, respectively; and W(i, j) and W'(i, j) are the values located at coordinate(x, y) of the original Watermark and the extracted Watermark.

From entries in Table 2 it has been observed that gain factor plays important role for Imperceptibility. PSNR has been improved for less gain factor and value of PSNR has been degraded for high gain factor. Table 3 shows NC after extraction procedure.

3.2 Robustness against JPEG compression

JPEG is one of the most used formats in the Internet and digital camera. The JPEG quality factor is a number between 0 and 100 and associates a numerical value with a

(a) Cover Image   (b) Watermark

(c) Watermark image   (d) Recovered Watermark

Fig. 4 Proposed algorithm results without attacks (gain factor k=30)

Table 2 Performance matrices

Cover Image	Water mark	PSNR	PSNR	PSNR
		K=20 (db)	K=30 (db)	K=40 (db)
LENA	BINARY LOGO	43	42.4	41.0
BABOON	BINARY LOGO	42.7	41.6	40.1
PEPPER	BINARY LOGO	42.7	41.6	40.1
TEXT	BINARY LOGO	42.8	41.7	40.2
MILK	BINARY LOGO	42.7	41.5	40.1
LENA	LOGO1	49.9	49.1	47.8
BABOON	LOGO1	48.6	47.6	46.3
PEPPER	LOGO1	48.6	47.7	46.4
TEXT	LOGO1	48.8	47.8	46.5
MILK	LOGO1	48.6	47.6	46.3

particular compression level. When the quality factor is decreased from 100, the image compression is improved, but the quality of the resulting image is significantly reduced. With the different quality factors of JPEG compression, the results are shown from Table 4 to 7. Figure 5 shows that bit error Rate (BER %) in the recovered watermark for different quality factors for different test images. The value of

Table 3 Normalized correlations obtain after extraction watermark

Cover image	Watermark	NC	NC	NC
		K=20	K=30	K=40
LENA	BINARY LOGO	0.97	0.98	0.98
BNBOON	BINARY LOGO	0.94	0.96	0.98
PEPPER	BINARY LOGO	0.98	0.98	0.99
TEXT	BINARY LOGO	0.91	0.96	0.93
MILK	BINARY LOGO	0.98	0.99	0.99
LENA	LOGO1	0.80	0.80	0.80
BNBOON	LOGO1	0.83	0.82	0.81
PEPPER	LOGO1	0.80	0.80	0.81
TEXT	LOGO1	0.80	0.79	0.79
MILK	LOGO1	0.80	0.80	0.80

Table 4 QF vs BER for LENA with BINARY LOGO (K=30)

QF	PSNR (db)	Compression Ratio	Percentage Compression(%)	BER (%)
100	46.97	3.5	71.97	0.17
90	41.13	10.7	90	0.21
80	38.94	16.7	94.01	0.24
70	37.89	21.4	95.35	0.43
60	37.13	26.0	96.16	1.68
50	36.63	30.4	96.72	5.61
40	36.17	36.1	97.17	7.34
30	35.65	43.9	97.72	7.69
20	34.77	57.1	98.25	7.74
10	33.47	86.6	98.81	7.75

the threshold is kept constant throughout this experiment. The origin of the graph is taken (100, 0) because the image taken for the experiment is with 100 quality factor and having zero BER from the graph it is observed that BER is almost zero till quality factor up to 50, so algorithm perform very well But when quality Q <40 the BER jumps to high, at same time image quality is also drastically degraded.

3.3 Robustness to non geometric transformation

The effect of histogram equalization on watermark image is shown in Fig. 6. We have tested robustness of proposed algorithm against different type of noise addition like Gaussian Noise addition and salt & pepper Noise. Comparison of recovered watermark with original watermark is listed in Table 8 for cover image as LENA with BINARY LOGO.

Table 5 QF vs BER for BABOON with BINARY LOGO (K=40)

QF	PSNR (db)	Compression Ratio	Percentage Compression(%)	BER (%)
100	33.34	2.22	54.92	0.46
90	32.32	5.63	82.23	0.53
80	31.46	8.45	88.17	0.63
70	31.02	10.81	90.75	0.58
60	30.72	12.95	92.72	0.63
50	30.52	14.90	93.29	0.78
40	30.31	17.42	94.26	0.90
30	30.13	21.28	95.30	1.29
20	29.87	28.21	96.45	2.19
10	29.39	45.64	97.80	6.66

Table 6 QF vs BER for MILK with BINARY LOGO (K=20)

QF	PSNR (db)	Compression Ratio	Percentage Compression(%)	BER (%)
100	42.39	3.78	73.54	0.34
90	39.60	12.94	92.27	0.65
80	38.32	19.82	94.95	0.58
70	37.44	25.73	96.11	0.36
60	36.86	32.08	96.88	0.51
50	36.44	37.23	97.31	0.61
40	36.11	43.70	97.71	1.22
30	35.55	52.31	98.08	3.19
20	34.76	66.67	98.50	7.25
10	32.80	97.64	98.98	7.71

Table 7 QF vs BER for PEPPER with BINARY LOGO (K=20)

QF	PSNR (db)	Compression Ratio	Percentage Compression(%)	BER (%)
100	38.08	3.11	67.93	0.51
90	36.07	9.51	89.49	0.70
80	35.24	15.65	93.61	0.63
70	34.74	20.34	95.08	0.80
60	34.41	25.04	96.00	0.92
50	34.16	29.08	96.56	1.07
40	33.89	97.06	97.06	1.24
30	33.56	40.57	97.53	3.24
20	33.02	51.47	98.06	6.98
10	31.86	77.88	98.71	7.76

We have also tested proposed algorithm against sharpening. Result obtained after comparing

Recovered watermark with original watermark is listed in Table 9 for cover image as LENA with BINARY LOGO.

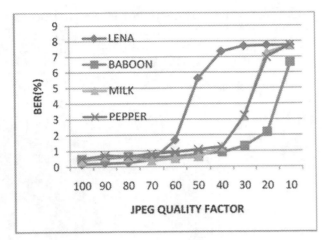

Fig. 5 JPEG Quality versus bit error rate (BER)

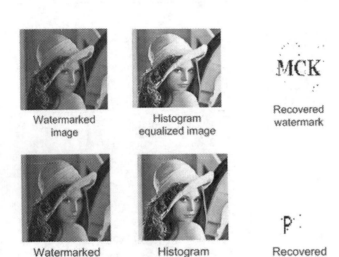

Fig. 6 Effect of Histogram Equalization

Table 8 Robustness against Noise addition

Gaussian Noise (variance)	NC	BER (%)	Salt & Pepper (Noise density)	NC	BER (%)
0.001	0.98	1.1	0.01	0.97	1.3
0.005	0.97	1.5	0.02	0.96	1.7
0.008	0.95	2.1	0.03	0.95	2.3
0.01	0.95	2.2	0.04	0.94	2.8

Table 9 Robustness against sharpening

Image Enhancement Method	NC	BER(%)
Sharpening	0.99	0.4

3.4 Robustness geometric transformation

The proposed algorithm tested against geometric attacks like Cropping. Cropping changes the frequency sampling step and during the image manipulations the uninterested part of image is usually cropped. Proposed algorithm recov-

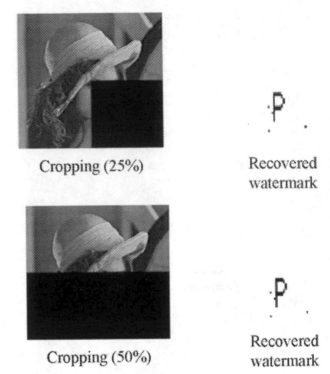

Fig. 7 Robustness against Cropping

ered full watermark up to 50 % cropping as shown in Fig. 7 for cover image as LENA with LOGO1.

4. Conclusion

The Experimental results shows that propose scheme of wavelet based watermarking is imperceptible and robust against various attacks like JPEG compression, different noise addition and filtering. This is achieved because of space and frequency localizing property of discrete wavelet transform, embedding the watermark based on spread spectrum at an appropriate wavelet domain. The proposed scheme outperform many present algorithm [8], [9] in terms of various attacks and calculation of gain factor. Future work will concentrate on making adaptive gain factor based on content of cover image.

References

1. N. Nikolaidis, I. Pitas, "Robust image Watermarking in spatial domain", international journal of signal processing, 66(3), 385-403, 1988
2. Jaun R.Hernandez, Martin amodo, Fernando perez-gonzalez "DCT domain watermarking techniques for still image: Detectors Performance analysis and new structure", IEEE transaction on image processing, VOL. 9, No.1, Jan 2000
3. R.Pickholtz, D. Schilling, and L. Milstein, "Theory of spread-spectrum communications—A Tutorial," IEEE Trans. Commun., vol. COM-32, no. 2, pp. 211–212, Feb. 1984
4. I. J. Cox, J. Kilian, F. T. Leighton, and T. Shamoon, "Secure spread spectrum watermarking for multimedia," IEEE Trans. Image Process,vol. 6, no. 12, pp. 1673–687, Dec. 1997

5. C. I. Podilchuk and W. Zeng, "Image-adaptive watermarking using visual models," IEEE J. Select Areas Commun., vol. 16, no. 5, pp.525–539, May 1998

6. Yang, Z. Lu, and F. Zou, "A robust adaptive image watermarking algorithm," Proc. IEEE ICME, pp. 1723–1726, 2004

7. Saraju P. Mohanty, and K.R. Ramakrishnan, "An Adaptive DCT Domain Visible Watermarking Tech nique for Protection of Publicly Available Images", iisc, May 2008

8. J. Huang and C. Yang, "Image digital watermarking algorithm using multi resolution wavelet transform," in Proc. IEEE Int. Conf. Systems,Man and Cybernetics, 2004, pp. 2977– 2982

9. Raval Mehul, and Rege priti, "Discrete wavelet Transform based multiple watermarking scheme", IEEE transaction 2003

10. G. C. Langelaar and R. L. Lagendijk, "Optimal differential energy watermarking of DCT encoded images and video," IEEE Trans. Image Process., vol. 10, no. 1, pp. 148–158, Jan. 2001

11. Priya Gupta, Derek Justice, and Matt P fenninger, "Digital Watermarking: Techniques and Attacks", Sept. 2002 Image Enhancement Method NC BER (%) Sharpening 0.99 0.4

Visible image and video watermarking

Shoba Krishnan[1] · Prathibha Sudhakaran[2]

[1]Vivekanand Educational Society's Institute of Technology, Mumbai, India
[2]Xavier Institute of Engineering, Mahim causeway, Mumbai, India

1. Introduction

The widespread usage of digital media has witnessed a tremendous growth in the last decade due to their benefits in efficient storage, ease of manipulation and transmission. The very nature of digital media makes the work of hackers easier since it enables perfect copies with no loss. Digital video watermarking can be a promising solution in digital –rights –management system.[3]Among various standards, H.264/Advanced Video Codec (AVC) is found to be of significant importance regarding reduced bandwidth, better image quality and network friendliness.[7]The H.264/AVC standard impressively improves the coding efficiency with many enhanced features. Recent research and development in H.264/AVC includes the fast implementation of integer discrete cosine transform and variable block size motion compensation.[11]In case of video watermarking, watermark detection requires the knowledge of the secret key associated to the video. This key contains two main information one being the code which allows recovering the original watermark and the other being the parameters related to the compensation process.[12]The capacity of P-frames and temporal masking in compressed video signals to further increase the watermark payload has been observed in [1].A lot of research has been done on invisible watermarks that are designed to exploit perceptual information in watermarking process.[2]

2. Image watermarking

2.1 What is image watermarking?

Image watermarking is the process of possibly irreversibly embedding information into an image. If the image is copied, then the information is also carried with the copy.

2.2 The algorithm

a) Let 'p' be the number of bits in cover images.
b) Read the first byte of the cover image and logo to be hidden and convert it into binary.
c) If p= 1, then replace last four bits of a byte of cover image by first four bits of a byte of a logo.
d) Repeat for all bytes of logo. The merging of the two images is purposely done in a manner which preserves the accuracy of the image to be protected and which does not obtrude too obviously on the ability to study the image, yet which clearly indicates the source of the image.

Fig. 1 Watermarked image

S.J. Pise (ed.), *ThinkQuest 2010*, DOI 10.1007/978-81-8489-989-4_43,

3. Video watermarking

3.1 What is video watermarking?

The video watermarking used in application like digital television, broadcast monitoring and streaming video demands more requirements than still image watermarking.[8] Video Watermarking involves embedding cryptographic information derived from frames of digital video into the video itself. Ideally, a user viewing the video cannot perceive a difference between the original, unmarked video and the marked video.

An MPEG based watermark embedding algorithm has been proposed in[5].In case of visible watermarks, the content owners can embed a visible shape or logo mark such as the company's logo on top of the image or video. The mark is removed only with the application of an appropriate "decryption key" and watermark remover software. Much of the academic and industrial interest in digital video watermarking has centered on the design of a copyright protection system for MPEG-2 coded video distributed on Digital Versatile Disk (DVDs). A video watermarking system had been designed by the Galaxy Group to complement the existing content scrambling system (CSS) that is part of the DVD standard; the technology is now called WaterCast and is being applied in the automatic monitoring of digital video broadcasts. The growing appeal of video watermarking for more general applications is evidenced by the number of proposals for digital TV transmission, satellite broadcast monitoring, video on demand distribution, and authenticating video surveillance for use as legal evidence. The flexibility of watermarking concepts for use with new data types has also been demonstrated through preliminary work with MPEG-4 video objects and parameters.[10]

B. The algorithm

a) Read the video in the.avi format.
b) Separate the video into individual frames.
c) Split the image into three planes.
d) Read the logo of size 128×128.

e) Insert the logo into the frames.
f) After insertion, convert images into frames and write the video (output video).
g) Read the output video and display it for the user.
h) Observe the visible watermark on the video.
i) Display output video and extracted logo.

4. DWT

DWT is considered to be the most powerful signal processing and analysis tool especially in the frequency or time

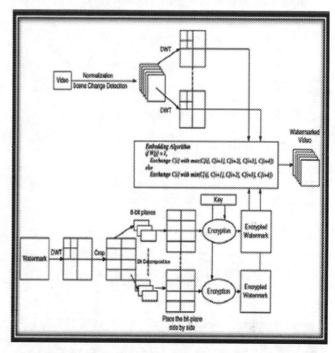

Fig. 3 The DWT process

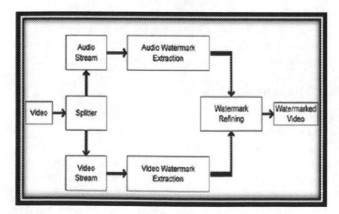

Fig. 2 Scheme for video watermarking

Fig. 4 Watermarked video

domain. The DWT separates an image into LL,HL, vertical LH and diagonal HH detail components. The process can then be repeated to compute multiple scale wavelet decomposition. In most DWT based watermarking schemes, watermark is embedded in the low frequency domain i.e. the approach coefficient set LL, which can achieve robustness against many signal attacks, including JPEG compression, Low pass filter and noise addition.[9]

Wavelet transform decomposes a signal into a set of basic functions. These basic functions are called wavelets. Wavelets are obtained from a single prototype wavelet y (t) called mother wavelet by dilations and shifting:

$$\Psi a, b\ (t) = 1/\sqrt{a}\ \Psi\ (t\text{-}a/a)$$

Where 'a' is the scaling parameter and 'b' is the shifting parameter.

5. Performance parameters

5.1 Correlation coefficient

The robustness performance of watermark extraction is evaluated by normalized correlation coefficient r of the extracted watermark A and the original watermark B.

$$\gamma = \frac{\sum_m \sum_n \left(A(m,n) - \bar{A}\right)\left(B(m,n) - \bar{B}\right)}{\sqrt{\left(\sum_m \sum_n \left(A(m,n) - \bar{A}\right)^2 \sum_m \sum_n \left(B(m,n) - \bar{B}\right)^2\right)}}$$

Where A and B respectively, the normalized original and watermark image by subtracting its corresponding means value. The magnitude range of r is [0, 1], and the unity holds if the extracted image perfectly matches the original one. We use correlation coefficient, to compare original image (A) and the watermarked image (AW), and also for comparing original watermark W and the retrieved watermark.[6]

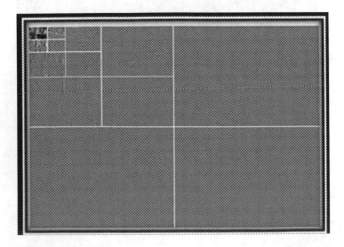

Fig. 5 DWT

5.2 Peak signal to noise ratio PSNR) and mean square error (MSE)

The imperceptibility of a watermark is measured by the watermarked image quality in terms of Peak- Signal-to-Noise Ratio (PSNR) (in dB). Most common difference measure between tow images is the mean square error. The mean square error measure is popular because it correlates reasonably with subjective visual tests and it is mathematically tractable. Consider a discrete image A(m, n) for m=1,2,…
…M and n=1,2,……N, which is regarded as a reference image. Consider a second image Â(m, n), of the same spatial dimension as A(m, n), that is to be compared to the reference image. Under the assumption that A(m, n) and Ã(m, n) represent samples of a stochastic process, MSE is given as:

$$\mathcal{E}_{MSE} = E\left(\left|A(m,n) - \tilde{A}(m,n)\right|^2\right)$$

where E (·) is the expectation operator.
The normalized Mean Square Error is given as

$$\mathcal{E}_{NMSE} = \frac{E\left(\left|A(m,n) - \tilde{A}(m,n)\right|^2\right)}{E\left(\left|A(m,n)\right|^2\right)}$$

Normalized mean square error for deterministic image arrays is defined as:

$$\mathcal{E}_{NLSE} = \frac{\sum_m \sum_n \left|A(m,n) - \tilde{A}(m,n)\right|^2}{\sum_m \sum_n \left|A(m,n)\right|^2}$$

Image error measures are often expressed as signal-to-noise ratio, $SNR = -10 \log\{e\}$
We use PSNR to determine the difference between original image A(m, n) and the watermarked image Ã(m, n).The value of mean square error should be minimum and the value of peak signal to noise ratio should be as maximum as possible.[6]

6. Experimental results

The experimental results show that both the visible image and video watermarking of the proposed watermarking algorithm is an added option to the wide range of algorithms available in today's highly technological era. It is more user friendly and the owner has all the rights. The performance of our proposed watermarking scheme is evaluated by using the different host images The simulations are performed in the MATLAB7 software environment.

7. Attacks

7.1 Wavelet compression

The first step in the wavelet compression technique is to digitize the image. The digitized image can be characterized by its intensity levels or scales of gray which range from 0(black) to 255(white)and its resolution or how many pixels per square inch.[13]

7.2 Median filter

Median filter is a nonlinear spatial filter whose response is based on ordering the pixels contained in the image area encompassed by the filter and replacing the value of centre pixel with the value determined by the ranking result. Here the value of a pixel is replaced by median of the gray levels in neighborhood of that pixel. Median filters have excellent noise reduction capabilities with considerably less blurring. Thus the principal function of median filter is to force points with different gray levels to be more like their neighbor. Median filtering is a simple and very effective noise removal filtering process. Its performance is particularly good for removing shot noise. Shot noise consists of strong spike-like isolated values. [13]

7.3 Fading

Fading is the process in which the value of pixel may change depending on the value of scaling factor. Each pixel value of selected watermarked image is altered with mathematical operation like addition subtraction, multiplication, division.[13]

7.4 Noise

The principal source of noise in digital images arises during image digitization and transformation.(a) Salt and pepper noise

$$P(Z) = Pa \text{ for } z=a$$
$$= Pb \text{ for } z=b$$
$$= 0 \text{ otherwise}$$

Impulse noise is found in situation where quick transients such as faulty switching take place during imaging. Impulse noise is usually digitized as extreme (black or white) values in image. Negative impulse appears as black (pepper) and positive impulse as white (salt). For 8 bit image black is 0 and white is 255 respectively. Besides this noise few more noise examples includes exponential noise.[13]

7.5 Resizing

A digital image can look huge when viewed on a computer monitor. Not only that but also its file size can be very large. When an image is reduced in size, its file size becomes much smaller too. Resize an image before sending it by email or when planning to display it on a web page, online gallery or auction site. One rule of thumb is to resize it to fit within a normal browser window so site visitors won't have to scroll to see the entire photo. All image editing programs include resizing tools. Most are straightforward, easy to use and take much of the guesswork out of resizing and compressing images.[13]

7.6 Tampering

The watermarked image is tampered with using Photoshop. The logo is embedded in the face region and the foot region of the watermarked image. The face is then tampered with using Photoshop i.e. the original face is replaced by someone else's face. When the logo is extracted from both the places, the one embedded in the face region is distorted while the one in the foot region is recovered properly.[13] From table 1 it is clear that the image quality reduces as the mask size increases.

Table 1   Image PSNR, MSE, CC v/s Mask size

MASK SIZE	MSE	PSNR	CC
3×3	0.0034	48.7555	0.9969
5×5	0.005	46.740	0.9931
	4	8	
7×7	0.0075	45.2620	0.9567
9×9	0.0092	44.3602	0.9802

8. Conclusion

There is a vast area of research into watermarking when applied to images and video as compared to text and audio. Videos are generally large and therefore it is time consuming to apply watermarks. We propose a transparent method of watermarking schemes using DWT for the same. Image watermarking is the most researched area and can be split into two main categories by the mathematical techniques used to embed information. With visible watermarks on the image or video, the content becomes self-protective, and content owners can distribute the entire image as a sample to various open media or to the Internet. The system can be further improved to accept bigger videos without affecting the efficiency.

References

1. Maneli Noorkami,Member, IEEE, and Russell M.Mersereau, Fellow, IEEE, "Digital Video Watermarking in P-frames With Controlled Video Bit- Rate Increase" in IEEE transactions on Information Forensics and Security, vol.3, no.3, sept 2008

2. Raymond B.Wolfgang,Student member, IEEE, Christine L.Podilchuck,Member, IEEE and Sdward J.Delp, Fellow,IEEE, "Perceptual watermarks for Digital Images and Video" in proceedings of the IEEE, Vol.87,No.7th july 1999

3. Maurice Maes, Ton Kalker, Jean-Paul Linnartz,Joop Talstra, Geert Depovere & Jaap Haitsma "Digital Watermarking for

DVD Video Copy Protection" in the IEEE Signal Processing Magazine September 2000

4. Pik Wah Chan, Student Member, IEEE, Michael.R.Lyu, Fellow, IEEE and Roland T.Chin, "A Novel Scheme for Hybrid Digital Video Watermarking: Approach, Evaluation and Experimentation"

5. Chiou-Ting Hsu and La-Ling Wu, "Digital Watermarking for Video" in Digital signal Processing 1977IEEE

6. Amol R. Madane, K T. Talele and M. M. Shah" Watermark Logo in Digital Image using DWT", Proceedings of SPIT-IEEE Colloquium and International Conference, Mumbai, India

7. Sourav Bhattacharya, T. Chattopadhyay and Arpan Pal," A Survey on Different Video Watermarking Techniques and Comparative Analysis with Reference to H.264/AVC"IEEE 2006

8. Zhi Li,Xia-Owei Chen "The Imperceptile Video watermarking based on the Model Of Entropy": in IEEE2008

9. Wei Lu,Hong-Pao Li,Fu-Lia Chung, "Chaos –Based Spread Spectrum Robust watermarking in DWT Domain" in 2005 IEEE

10. Kren Su,Student Member, IEEE,Deepa kundur, Senior Member IEEE and Dimitrios Hatkinakos,Senior Memb4er, IEEE." Statistical Invisibility for Collusion- Resistant Digital Video Watermarking" IEEE transactions on Multimedia, Vol.7, No.1, Feb 2005

11. Jing Zhang,Student member, IEEE, Anthony T.S.Ho,Senior Member, IEEE, Gang Qiu and Pina Mazziliano, Member, IEEE."Robust Video watermarking of H.264/AVC" IEEE transactions on circuits and systems-II : express briefs, Vol.54, No.2, Feb 2007

12. M.Koubaa,C.BEN AMAR and H.Nicolas, "Collusion –resistant video watermarking based on video mosaicing", proceedings of the eight IEEE International Symposium on Multimedia, IEEE 2006

13. Liu Yongliang1, Xiaolin Yang1, Hongxun Yao1, Tiejun Huang2,Wen Gao2, "Watermark Detection Schemes with High Security", Proceedings of the International Conference on Information Technology: Coding and Computing (ITCC'05) IEEE.

Studies on the effect of nickel and chromium on the dry sliding high temperature wear behaviour of medium carbon alloy steels (AISI SAE 8630, 3140 and 9310)

S. M. Ganechari[1] · V. R. Kabadi[2] · S. A. Kori[2] · R. R. Burbure[3]

[1]Thakur Polytechnic, Kandivali, Mumbai, Maharashtra State, India
[2]Mechanical Engineering Department, BEC, Bagalkot, Karnataka State, India
[3]KLE Institute of Technology, Hubli, Karnataka State, India

1. Introduction

Wear is one of the major phenomena of reducing the effectiveness of mechanical components; impact the nation financially in terms of material loss, associated equipment down time for repairing and finally the replacement of worn and corroded components. The interactions among wear and corrosion could significantly increase total weight losses and reduction of either wear or corrosion could considerably decrease the total weight loss [1, 2].

Wear is inevitable for machine part sliding in contact. The amount of wear depends on material pair, surface topography, working condition, and chemical effects of the environment. It is impossible to completely prevent wearing. Any empirical relation is difficult to be developed, because the factors are not predictable. Abrasive wear is the dominant mechanism causing the material losses. The most severe wear occurs on the cylinder surfaces in internal combustion engines. Pistons, valves, and piston rings are the other elements that are subjected to severe wear.

The deterioration of surfaces is a very real common problem in many industries. Wear is the result of impact, erosion, metal-to-metal contact, abrasion, oxidation and corrosion, or a combination of these. Industries have long been involved in the development of processing technique to overcome this problem. So far the wear behavior of steel has been studied in detail under the different operational conditions like load and sliding speed in ambient temperature. But under elevated operational conditions, the detailed literature is insufficient. So it is necessary to study the wear behavior of steel under elevated temperature because, the basic concepts of elevated-temperature in wear is plastic deformation and fracture of wearing surface.

At elevated temperatures it is one of the most challenging engineering problems faced by materials engineers. In order to study the wear behavior at high temperatures, several key concepts must be taken into consideration:

- Plastic behavior of wearing surface at elevated temperatures.
- Wear mechanisms with under different operational conditions.
- Stress and temperature dependence.
- Fracture at elevated temperatures.
- Work hardening and softening effects.

Nickel based alloys has good high temperature wear and corrosion resistance. This alloy is widely used in the chemical industry, petrol industry, glass mould, Aircraft and Automobile industries, hot working punches, fan blades, mud purging elements in cement factories and engines.

High temperature alloys have high degree of heat resisting properties. Nickel is the most favorable choice for the wide structural application because nickel has no allotropic phase transformation below its melting point. The densities of iron, nickel and cobalt-base super alloys are 7 to 8.5 gm/cm^3, which are quite moderate when compared with alloys containing heaviest alloying elements, like molybdenum, tantalum and tungsten. Ni base alloys tend to increase the thermal conductivity resulting in reduced thermal stresses.

Nickel increases the strength of steel by dissolving in ferrite. Its main effect is to increase toughness by limiting grain-growth during heat-treatment process, for this reason, up to 5 % nickel is present in some of the better quality steels used for case hardening. Unfortunately, nickel does not combine chemically with carbon, and worse still, tends to make iron carbide (cementite) decompose and so release

S.J. Pise (ed.), *ThinkQuest 2010*, DOI 10.1007/978-81-8489-989-4_44,

free graphite. Consequently, nickel steels are always low-carbon steels or alternatively, medium carbon steels with very small amounts of nickel. However, because of their shortcomings in respect of carbide instability, they have been almost entirely replaced in recent years by other low-alloy steels. Chromium is added to steel; some of it dissolves in the ferrite (which is strengthened as a result), but the remainder forms chromium carbide, the hardness of the steel is increased. Because chromium stables carbides, these steels may contain 1 % or even more of carbon. The main disadvantage of chromium as an alloying element is that, unlike nickel, it increases grain growth during heat treatment. Thus unless care is taken to limit both the temperature and the time of such treatment, brittleness may arise from the coarse grain produced.

Nickel and chromium steels have opposite effects on the properties of steel. Nickel is a grain refiner and chromium tends to cause grain-growth, on the other hand, whilst chromium is the carbide stabilizer, nickel tends to cause carbides to break down, releasing graphite. Fortunately the beneficial effect of one metal is stronger than the adverse effects of the other, and is advantageous to add these metals together to steel. Unfortunately, these straight nickel chromium steels suffer from a defect known as temper brittleness and for this reason straight nickel chromium steels have been almost entirely replaced by nickel-chromium-molybdenum steels.

Nickel-based alloys are the most frequently employed materials for components subjected to high dynamic stresses at working temperatures of up to 1100°C. They are used mainly to make blades, disks, and housing components for the hot sections of stationary gas turbines and jet engines. Hence, research work has been carried out on Nickel – Chromium based alloy under different operational conditions.

2. Experimental details

Considering advantages mentioned above, AISI-SAE 8630, 3140 and 9310 steels were selected for investigation. The composition of steels is provided in Table 1. In the present research one of the common and simplest methods to test for wear rate was by using a pin-on-disc wear tester. Weight loss of the pin was measured after the wear test. Wear is usually expressed as volume loss per unit sliding distance determined from weight loss measurements.

The photographic view of high temperature wear-testing machine is shown in Fig.1. A high temperature wear testing machine (Pin on disc wear testing machine) employs essentially the basic 'tribometer', which is one of the most frequently used test rigs. The end of a wear pin rides on the flat surface of the disc. A flat – ended wear pin riding on a flat surface provides an ostensibly constant area of contact. The wear pin was held in the collect firmly. The pin specimen rides against the disc under a calibrated constant vertical load. The vertical load acting between the pin and disc was measured. This wear-testing machine is equipped

Fig. 1 Photographic view of high temperature wear-testing machine

Table 1 Alloy composition of steels

Composition %	AISI SAE 8630	AISI SAE 3140	AISI SAE 9310
C	0.28	0.362	0.084
Ni	0.395	1.479	0.712
Si	0.241	0.243	0.358
Mn	0.471	0.530	7.655
S	0.010	0.007	0.022
P	0.017	0.027	0.049
Cr	12.345	1.026	14.235
Mo	0.005	0.216	0.012
Cu	0.024	0.236	1.753
Co	0.004	0.010	0.005
Ti	0.002	0.007	0.007
V	0.011	0.013	0.000
Al	0.000	0.028	0.000
Nb	0.000	0.012	0.000
Fe	86.070	95.805	75.035
W	--	0.057	--
Pb	--	0.041	--

with a 1 kW electrical resistance heater divided into three sectors to produce ambient temperatures of up to 6000Cfor elevated temperature work.

The pin specimen was made from a bar, 10 mm in diameter × 32 mm length. Wear test conducted were for wear pressure 0.125, 0.375 and 0.625 MPa, sliding speeds 1, 3 and 5 m/s, for sliding distance of 10,000 m. There is smooth sliding contact between the pin specimen and the disc without any unstable vibration and ambient temperatures of room temperature, 200, 400 and 600°C were used The mass loss of the pin specimen was measured by a precise electro balance; with least count of 0.1 mg. Specimens were thoroughly cleaned and degreased in acetone and removed the wear lips carefully taken.

3.   Results and discussions

Figure 3.1 presents typical evolutions of the volumetric wear rate with sliding speed and wear pressure using AISI SAE 8630 steel.

For the material AISI SAE 8630, from the Fig. 3.1 shows the effects of wear pressure and sliding speed on volumetric wear rate for different ambient temperatures. It is observed that the volumetric wear rate is decreased with the sliding speed for the wear pressure of 0.125 MPa and also decreased with the wear pressure for the sliding speed of 1 m/s Fig. 3.1 (a). At the lower wear pressure of 0.125 MPa and sliding speed of 1m/s, under room temperature, the volumetric wear rate is high. This is due to the formation of micro welds at highly localized pressure contacts and subsequent rupturing of the same and hence the corresponding wear loss is high at the beginning. Under moderate and high operational conditions effect of wear pressure and sliding speed is reduced and almost the same.

Under room temperature, values of volumetric wear rate is decreased with the sliding speed and also decreased with the wear pressure. Whereas under all high ambient temperatures values of volumetric wear rate is increased with the sliding speed and also increased with the wear pressure.

From the Fig. 3.2, it is observed that the volumetric wear rate for low wear pressure of 0.125 MPa is almost the same, for all the operational conditions of temperature and sliding speed. The general effect of increasing sliding speed under low wear pressure is to cause a reduction in the rate of wear because during wearing the metal is first transferred to the disc from the wear pin and wear debris is produced from this deposited layer. The size of the transformed fragment decreases

as the speed is increased, as sufficient time is not available for the junction growth. This means that the frequency of metal transfer will decrease with the increase of sliding speed resulting in a progressive fall in the rate of wear [4].

Also it is observed that with increasing in the ambient temperature, volumetric wear rate is increased and with further increase in the ambient temperature, volumetric wear rate is decreased for the wear pressures of 0.375 and 0.625 MPa. The increase in wear rate is due to predominant of softening effect than the effect of work hardening at 200°C, also due to large degree of plastic deformation in the contact area possibly caused by reincorporation of wear debris into the wear scar. The mechanical strength usually reduced and the surface traction becomes greater with increasing temperature which is supposed to bring about increased wear rates in high temperature. The wear rate starts decreasing from 400°C to 600°C for the wear pressure of 0.375 MPa. At high ambient temperature, at high sliding speed and at low wear pressure due to retained debris may compact layers and provide protection against wear.

Under the condition of high sliding speed and high contact pressure, the temperature rises for the sliding materials induced by the friction are intense and the changes of properties of sliding materials by the temperature rise have strong influences on their friction and wear characteristics. Moreover, it is known that the surface oxide film and the temperature rise by the frictional heat affect the friction and wear characteristics of metals. Especially, under the severe condition of high sliding speed and high contact pressure influenced by the two body abrasive wear.

The wear mechanism is almost oxidative and observed smooth compacted oxide layer and minimum surface roughness Fig. 3.4. Hence, the surface roughness is minimum for the sliding speed of 3 m/s.

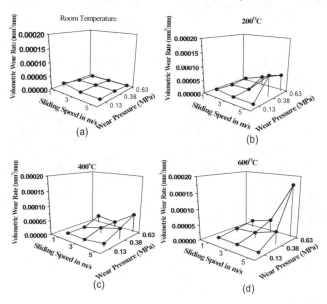

Fig. 3.1   Effect of sliding speed and wear pressure on volumetric wear rate under different ambient temperatures for AISI SAE8630 steel

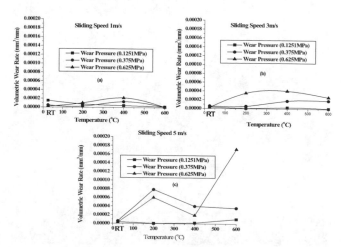

Fig. 3.2   Effect of temperature on volumetric wear rate for AISI SAE 8630 steel.

From Fig. 3.5 abrasive wear mechanism observed, for high operational conditions of sliding speed, wear pressure and temperature. During high temperature, the wearing surface of the pin becomes very hot. The rate of heat dissipation through the pin is quite low compared with the rotating disc. Heat loss due to conduction is high due to more material of the disc. Heat loss due to convection and radiation is high due to more exposing area of the disc also due to rotation of the disc. Hence micro welds adhere to the disc and abrade the wearing pin surface. Due to this abrasion, abrasive wear mechanism observed, also due to softening the wearing pin surface, plastic deformation is associated with micro welds. Hence, ploughing action is predominant on the wearing surface.

From the Fig. 3.6, it is observed that the olumetric wear rate at room temperature shows similar result as described above for AISI SAE 8630 steel. Under room temperature volumetric wear rate is decreased with increasing sliding speeds and wear pressures. Whereas the same is increased with sliding speeds and wear pressures under high ambient temperatures. For loading conditions above the maximum in wear rate due to the plastic deformation of the sliding surfaces is predominant. Large metallic particles adhered to the surface, act as hard sliders and produce grooves. The deformation wear debris causes their hardening and fracture, and their rolling forms spherical shaped debris [6–7].

The AISI SAE 3140 contains Ni 1.479, Cr 1.026 and Mo 0.216 whereas AISI SAE 8630 material has contained Ni

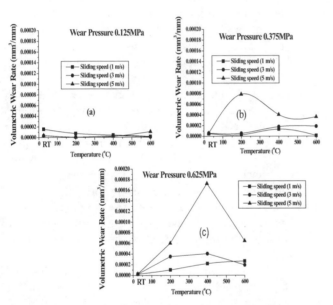

Fig. 3.3 Effect of temperature on volumetric wear rate for AISI SAE 8630 steel.

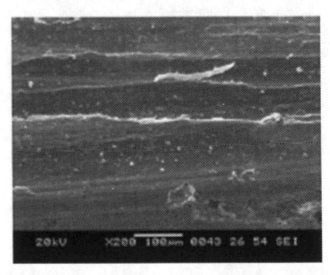

Fig. 3.5 SEM Micrograph of AISI SAE 8630 steel for Sliding speed 5 m/s

Fig. 3.4 SEM micrograph of AISI SAE 8630 steel for Sliding speed 3 m/s

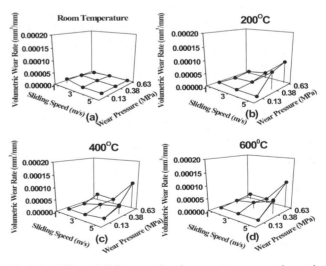

Fig. 3.6 Effect of sliding speed and wear pressure on volumetric wear rate under different ambient temperatures for AISI SAE 3140 steel

0.395 and Cr 12.345. Under the high operational conditions at sliding speed of 5 m/s and wear pressure of 0.628 MPa for all ambient temperatures, the wear rate of AISI SAE 3140 is lower than that of the AISI SAE 8630. This is due to the variation of the compositions of the materials. If Nickel is added its effect will be on characteristic properties [8]. An increase in percentage of Nickel results in increase in toughness. Therefore the wear rate under the different ambient temperatures under the high operational conditions is below the wear rate of AISI SAE 8630 Fig. 3.1.

When AISI SAE 3140 and AISI SAE 8630 compared with each other, both under room temperature with increase in wear pressure, wear rate are almost decreased. Whereas, under high ambient temperature with increase in the wear pressure, the wear rate is increased. The reason for this is explained in AISI SAE 8630.

From the Fig. 3.7 (b) volumetric wear rate is increased with temperature for the wear pressure of 0.625 MPa for 5 m/s. This is due to the occurrence of the mechanisms laminative wear, adhesive wear and mixed wear, as a result of plastic deformation. At moderate sliding speed, the mechanically mixed layer may be composed of an oxide, and deformed parent material, while at higher wear pressure, only deformed surface with two body abrasive wear observed.

By increasing the applied wear pressures under room temperature, volumetric wear rate started to decrease and approach to constant values. On the other hand, wear mechanism changes from sever regime to mild one. At higher wear pressures, a hard surface layer is formed, most likely martensite on surface, because of high flash temperature, followed by rapid quenching as the heat was conducted into the underlying bulk material. The higher flash temperature also caused the local oxidation rate to increase [5]. On the other hand, increasing the applied wear pressure caused work hardening of subsurface layers and the surface oxide layer supported by the hardened sub layers. The higher oxi-

dation rate formed thicker oxide layer on the surface. The formed oxide layer prevented further direct metallic contact and reduced the volumetric wear rates.

Under moderate and high wear pressure, AISI SAE 3140 shows lower wear rate than AISI SAE 8630. Chromium improves hardness as well as hardenability. Where as Ni improves ductility and toughness and surface deforms plastically and result in laminative wear mechanism. Molybdenum has a strong effect in increasing high temperature tensile and creep strengths. Due to its more plastic deformability laminative wear and corresponding wear mechanisms observed.

In case with low sliding speed and low wear pressure the corresponding wear mechanisms involved are mostly three body abrasive wear. Microscopic observation also reveals the presence of the microgrooves on the worn out surfaces of the specimen. Discontinued parallel grooves are observed on a worn out surface. This means that hard abrasive asperities are generated during wearing and thus third body formation occurs at the interface. In this case abrasive asperities would not always be much stronger than the mating surfaces [3]. The degree of adhesion at the contact interface would be closely related to the change of wear mode [9]. Hence it can be stated that, the particles should remain unfractured during wear so that they can support the applied wear pressure and act as effective abrasive elements. They may produce simple microgrooves by plastic deformation and/or cutting action without producing any transfer material and the same remains on the counter face [10]. This observation was made for low wear pressure where the particles could resist the fracture.

Tribological behaviour of steel is influenced by the wear pressure, sliding speed and ambient temperature. Also increasing in wear pressure increases the intimate contactness between the wearing surfaces which results in more wear rate.

From the Fig. 3.8, it is observed that with increase in ambient temperature volumetric wear rate is increased. Effect of ambient temperature is more for the sliding speed of 5 m/s. Under room temperature for the sliding speed of 5 m/s frictional temperature estimated up to 220°C. Under high ambient temperature of 600°C, the temperatures of the wearing surface will considerably more and this makes the surface soft and results in more wear rate. Whereas for the other ambient temperatures of 200°C and 400°C the frictional temperature of the wearing surface may not change the property and some work hardening may takes place. The corresponding hardness of the wearing surface for the ambient temperatures of 200°C and 400°C is more than the 600°C.

Fig. 3.9 SEM micro graph shows just formation of oxide layers on the worn surface and smooth surface. Under this operational condition wear rate is low it indicates mechanism towards oxidative.

The volumetric wear rate of AISI SAE 9310 steel is more than the AISI SAE 3140 steel under respective operational conditions Fig.3.10. An increase in temperature from

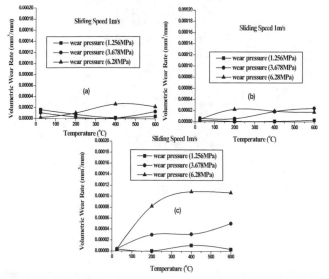

Fig. 3.7 Effect of temperature on volumetric wear rate for AISI SAE 3140 steel

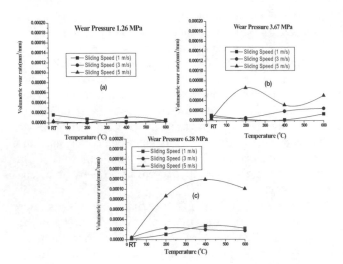

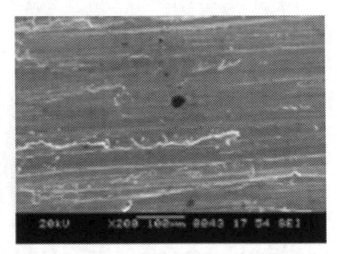

Fig. 3.8 Effects of Temperature on Volumetric wear Rate for AISI SAE 3140 steel

![SEM micrograph]

Fig. 3.9 SEM micrograph of AISI SAE 3140 steel for Sliding speed 3 m/s, wear pressure 0.125 MPa, at ambient temperature of room temperature

room temperature to 600°C resulted in an increase in wear. The increase in wear from room temperature to 600°C can be possibly due to increased softening and adhesion of the steel at elevated temperature.

From the Fig. 3.10 it is observed that wear behavior is almost similar to the AISI SAE 3140 steel but it is lifted up. From the Fig. 3.10 at room temperature, the wear is low which can be attributed to adhesion. The adhesive wear process comprises junction formation, plastic deformation, metal transfer to the wedge and rupture of the wedge [11], According to metal contact theory, the metal junction is formed only in the real contact area, which is determined by the applied wear pressure and the mechanical properties of the materials and is independent of the nominal surface area [12]. The AISI SAE 8630 steel material has contain Ni 0.395 and Cr 12.345 and AISI SAE 3140 steel contain Ni 1.479 and Cr 1.026 and Mo 0.216 where as AISI SAE 9310 contain Ni 0.712 and Cr 14.235. Under the high operational

conditions of sliding speed of 5 m/s and wear pressure of 0.625 MPa at room temperature, wear rate of AISI SAE 9310 is higher than that of the AISI SAE 8630 and 3140. This is due to the variation of the compositions of the materials. As the percentage of Cr increases the oxidation resistance increases at room and elevated temperature. An increase in small percentage of Nickel results in increase in resistance to atmospheric corrosion and also tends to oxidize along grain boundaries when subjected to alternate oxidation and reduction by addition of Cr reduces this tendency. AISI SAE 9310 steel contain 0.022 percentage of sulfur. Ni-Cr alloy contain sulfur subjected to intergranular attack below 315°C, also the presence of Mn and Si,

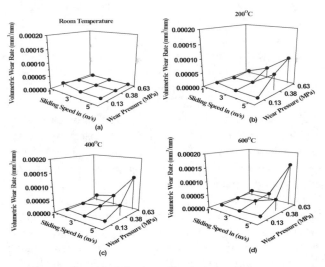

Fig. 3.10 Effect of sliding speed and wear pressure on umetric wear rate under different ambient temperatures for AISI SAE 9310 steel

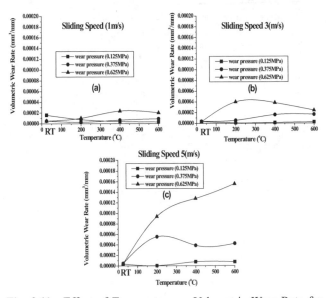

Fig. 3.11 Effect of Temperature on Volumetric Wear Rate for AISI SAE 9310 steel. Volumetric wear rate with the ambient temperatures

the oxidation resistance alloys [8]. Under the ambient temperature of 400°C and 600°C the wear rate of AISI SAE 9310 steel is higher than AISI SAE 3140, less the effect of sulfur intergranular attack and low work hardening effect. This more in wear rate may be due to low percentage of carbon than the AISI SAE 8630

At 600°C wear was found to be higher because the mechanical strength is usually reduced and the surface traction becomes greater with increasing temperature, which is supposed to bring about increased wear rates in high temperature and marked transitions in the wear rate have been reported as a function of the changes in wear pressure and sliding speed.

From the Fig. 3.11 it is observed that volumetric wear rate for 0.625 MPa is considerable high with increasing ambient temperature for the sliding speed of 5 m/s. For other wear pressure, it is observed the reduction in volumetric wear with increasing in the ambient temperature. Wear rate is reduced possibly caused by reincorporation of wear debris and effectiveness of oxide layer in reducing the volumetric wear rate

For other sliding speeds, it is observed that volumetric wear rate is low with increase in respective wear pressure. Volumetric wear rate is reduced possibly caused by reincorporation of wear debris and effectiveness of oxide layer can reduce volumetric wear rate.

Volumetric wear rate with the ambient temperatures for different sliding speeds is almost similar to the other investigated materials, Fig. 3.12. The other factor contributing to the observed behavior of wear rate may be the extent of cover provided by the transfer layer and the nature of adhesion of the compacted transfer layer to the pin surface. It has been shown that a harder substrate is able to hold a thicker transfer layer of oxide more firmly as compared to a softer one [14] and [13]. Hence, there will be a higher probability the flaking off of this layer in the steel having a relatively lower hardness. Thus, a higher wear rate in materials of comparatively lower hardness may be

attributed to the increase in flaking off of the transfer layer during sliding.

4. Summary of the results

The results of the investigated materials compared with one another and discussed as follows:

The comparison results pertaining to the investigated materials are shown in Fig. 4.1, these results show that, AISI SAE 3140 steel has low wear rate under moderate operational conditions.

Chromium content in the iron base alloy significantly improves oxidation resistance by forming a denser and thinner oxide layer. This oxidation layer, together with the support of a substrate, reduces the oxidation wear rate and also increases the transition from mild wear to severe metallic wear. Excess amount of chromium in the metal can be detrimental to the wear resistance by causing micro-fracturing of the surface layer, thus lowering the transition load. Molybdenum form hard complex M_6C type carbide. The M_6C carbides are stable, resisting to softening of the steel at high temperatures and are only partially dissolved at temperatures 982°C. Molybdenum promotes resistance to softening of the material through solid solution and are essential to the high temperature properties of the alloy of the present invention. Nickel provides more high temperature strength and hot hardness than the alloy without nikel. The nickel alloy will result in higher wear rates at lower temperatures.

AISI SAE 3140 steel has a better wear resistant material when compared with the other two investigated materials. The rate of oxidation is high due to low percentage of chromium in the material. Hence, formation of oxide layer on the wearing surface is more when compared with the other two. materials. Due to this formation of the layer the wear rate is low. From the present investigation it is observed that highest chromium content steel with additional silicon had the highest metal loss rate.

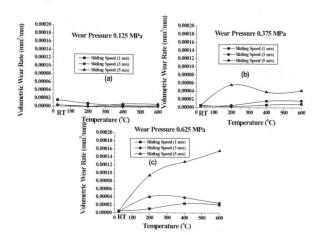

Fig. 3.12 Effect of temperature on volumetric wear rate for AISI SAE 9310 steel

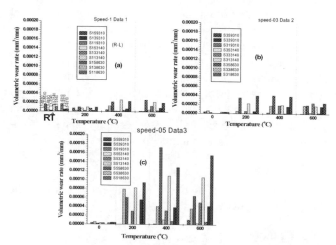

Fig. 4.1 Effect of temperature on volumetric wear rate at different sliding speeds for AISI SAE 8630, 3140 and 9310 steels

Nickel increases the strength of steel by dissolving in the ferrite. Its main effect, however, is to increase toughness. Nickel does not combine chemically with carbon and trends to make iron carbide decompose and so release free graphite. Due to this free graphite there is reduction in coefficient friction and hence reduces the volumetric wear rate. Nickel has an allotropic phase transformation below its melting point, it has high tolerance for alloying elements without causing a phase change from the close packed fcc crystal structure and it produces very stable precipitate. AISI SAE 3140 steel has improved wear resistance due to the improved fracture toughness of the surface due to the presence of Nickel. Whereas Ni carbide is soft hence the surface roughness of the worn surface is low. Nickel based alloy AISI SAE 3140 steel proved to have good wear resistance although the steel is softer than the other investigated steels. This is probably due to its relatively good resistance to softening at high temperature when compared with the material. Molybdenum retains other investigated steels and its tendency to work hardens when loaded. Molybdenum eliminates the brittleness and increases the toughness of high strength at elevated temperature of the material. Medium carbon of high strength steels having higher strength and deeper hardening. It retains good tensile, fatigue and impact properties up to about 370°C. Therefore volumetric wear rate of AISI SAE 3140 steel has low volumetric wear rate at moderate operational conditions and high volumetric wear rate high operational conditions. It is also observed that surface roughness after the wear of the high chromium steels AISI SAE 8630 steel and AISI SAE 9310 steel is more than the AISI SAE 3140 steel. Chromium carbide is harder than ordinary iron carbide. During sliding these carbides embedded with the sliding disc and abrade the wearing pin. AISI SAE 8630 steel exhibits cracking properties. From the Fig. 4.1 it is observed that most of the low, moderate and equal wear rates are observed for AISI SAE 3140 steel. For the sliding speed of 1 m/s, under the ambient temperatures of 200 and 400°C AISI SAE 3140 steel shown low wear rate, for the sliding speed of 3 m/s AISI SAE 3140 steel has shown minimum wear rate up to 400^0 c ambient temperature. The sliding speed of 5 m/s AISI SAE 3140 steel has shown low to moderate wear rate almost up to 600°C ambient temperature. This may be due to the presence of nickel results in the formation of an austenitic structure that gives strength, ductility and toughness. Nickel improves the shock resistance. Molybdenum increases the tensile and creep strengths. Molybdenum considered being less temper brittleness. Hence Nickel alloy steel is better than the Chromium alloy steel for high temperature wear.

5. Conclusions

The following conclusions are drawn on the basis of the results and discussion of the present.

Investigations

1. AISI SAE 8630 has shown minimum wear rate under room temperature.

2. AISI SAE 3140 has shown minimum wear rate under the ambient temperatures of 200°C, 400°C and 600°C because of the formation of oxide layer due to low percentage of carbon and is the better wear resistance material comparing with other materials .

3. Critical Sliding speed observed at 3 m/sec for all the investigated materials.

4. Effect of Nickel on volumetric wear rate may not be so much considerable under the ambient temperature above 400°C. 4. Critical sliding speed observed at 3m/s for all the investigated materials.

5. Under low operational conditions volumetric wear rate is more later with increasing in operational conditions volumetric wear rate is reduced and further increase in the operational conditions considerable increase in volumetric wear rate is observed.

6. As ambient temperature increases volumetric wear rate is increased and futher increase in the ambient temperature volumetric wear rate is decreased.

7. Under room temperature volumetric wear rate is decreased with the sliding speed where as the same is increased with the sliding speed under high ambient temperature.

8. An increase in small percentage of ni results in toughness and wear mechanism.

References

1. J. Sato, Recent Trends in Studies of Fretting Wear, Transactions JSLE, Vol. 30, 1985, pp. 853-858

2. W.J. Schumacher, Corrosive wear principles, Mater. Perform. 23 (7) (1993), pp. 50

3. R.C.D.Richardson, Wear of metals by relatively soft abrasives, Wear, Vol.11 (1968), 245

4. A.D.Sarkar., Wear of metals, Pergamon Press, Oxford, 1976, pp.148

5. S.C. Lim &M.F.Ashby, Wear rate transitions &their relationship to wear mechanisms, Acta metall, 1987, Vol.35, No.6 pp1343-1348

6. P. Heilmann, et al, Sliding wear &transfer, Wear 91 (2) (1983) 171-190

7. D.A. Rigney, et al, Wear processes in sliding system, Wear 100 (1-3) (1984) 195-219

8. Nickel Alloy Steels-A Summary of their Properties and Applications –Technical Publication No.208

9. Koji Kato, 'Micro-mechanisms of –wear modes' Wear, 153 (1992) 277-295

10. D.A. Rigney et al, 'Wear processes in the sliding systems', Wear, 100 (1984) 195-219

11. T. Kayaba &A. Iwabuchi, The effect of temperature on fretting wear, Jankatsu, 27 (1982) 31-38

12. I.M. Hutching, Tribology &Wear of Engineering Materials, Edward Arnold(1992), p. p. 22

13. B. Bhushan, Introduction to Tribology, John Wiley and Sons (2002) p. 45

14. B.S. Mann &V. Arya, An experimental study to corelate water jet impingement erosion resistance &properties of metallic materials and coatings, Wear 253 (2002), pp. 650–661

A novel steganographic scheme using discrete sine transform based on energy distribution

H. B. Kekre[1] · **Archana Athawale[2]** · **Ms. Dipali Sadavarti[3]**

[1]Senior Professor, Ph.D Research Scholar, MPSTME, SVKM's NMIMS, Mumbai, India.
[2]Assistant Professor, Thadomal Shahani Engineering College, Mumbai
[3]Lecturer, Computer Engineering Dept., Fr C. R.C. E, Bandra, Mumbai, India.

1. Introduction

The research concerning the technique of hiding secret message into another information is usually named steganography. This is because the word "steganography" comes from the Greek root meaning "Covered Writing". An image steganographic scheme is one kind of steganographic systems, where the secret message is hidden in a digital image with some hiding method [1]. Some one can then use a proper embedding procedure to embed the secret message into the cover image in such a way that it is imperceptible to a human observer. The hidden message can then be recovered using appropriate extraction procedure. The original image is called the cover image and the message-embedded image is called a stego-image.

There are a number of steganographic schemes that hide secret message in a digital image. These schemes can be classified according to method of hiding. We have two popular types of hiding methods: spatial domain embedding and transform domain embedding [2,7]. The Least Significant Bit (LSB) substitution is the most commonly used spatial domain technique. The basic idea in the LSB is the direct replacement of the LSBs of the cover image with the secret message bits. Hiding images using LSB substitution techniques can be found in [3,4,6,8]. But this method has low robustness to modifications made to the stego-image such as a low pass filtering and compression [2].

The other type of hiding method is the transform domain techniques which appeared to overcome the robustness and imperceptibility problem found in LSB substitution techniques. The most widely used transforms are Discrete Cosine Transform (DCT), Discrete Wavelet Transform (DWT) and Fast Fourier Transform (FFT). DCT is used in image compression format JPEG and MPEG. DWT is used in the new image compression format JPEG2000 and MPEG4. Steganographic techniques using wavelet transform can be found in [2, 5]. In [2,,9-11] the secret data is hidden into the HH, HL and LH

(High frequency) bands of the DWT domain while leaving the low frequency bands unaltered[12-15]. In all proposed techniques whether spatial domain or transform domain, the major challenge is how to increase the hiding capacity while maintaining the good visual quality of the cover image.

2. Proposed system

This subsection discusses the message embedding and message extraction procedure.

2.1 Selection of blocks for data hiding

We have applied Discrete Sine Transform (DST) on full cover image. The transformed image is then divided into 16 equal non-overlapping blocks[12,16]. We have calculated the energy of each block of the transformed cover image. Energy of each block is calculated by taking square of each DST Co-efficient within the block and summing up them. All 16 blocks are sorted in descending order according to their energies. This Procedure was repeated on five to six images. Fig. 1 shows all 16 blocks numbered from 1 to 16.

Figure 2 shows the energy distribution of the transformed cover image for two different cover images. In Fig. 2 the block which is colored white shows the highest

1	5	9	13
2	6	10	14
3	7	11	15
4	8	12	16

Fig. 1   16 blocks of the transformed cover image

S.J. Pise (ed.), *ThinkQuest 2010*, DOI 10.1007/978-81-8489-989-4_45,
© Springer India Pvt. Ltd. 2011

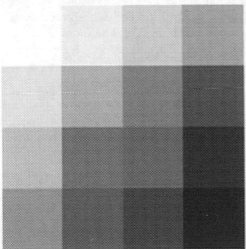

Fig. 2 (a) Energy distribution of Transformed cover (New Palace.bmp)

Fig. 2 (b) Energy distribution of Transformed cover (Horse.bmp)

energy block and the block colored black shows the lowest energy block. Table 1 summarizes the results for five different cover images. From the experimental results, it has been observed that the blocks 16,15,12,14,8,11,7,10, 4 and 13 are the blocks containing lesser energy for most of the images. Where as blocks 1, 2,5,9,3,6, are the blocks containing higher energy. So we embed the secret message into the blocks containing lesser energy.

2.2 The embedding procedure

This algorithm embeds the secret image into the lowest energy block of the transformed cover image.

1. Apply Discrete sine transform (DST) on full cover image.
2. Apply Discrete sine transform (DST) on full secret image to be embedded.

3. Find the maximum DST coefficient of the transformed secret image.
4. Divide each DST coefficient of the secret image by its maximum coefficient. This will normalize the transformed secret image coefficients.
5. Select lowest energy block of the transformed cover image to embed the secret image.
6. Replace the selected block of the transformed cover by normalized secret image coefficients.
7. Apply inverse DST on the modified cover. This gives us the stego image.

2.3 The extraction procedure

1. Apply DST on full stego-image.
2. Extract the lowest energy block where we embedded the secret image from the transformed stego-image.

Table 1 Summary of energy distribution of different transformed cover images

Image Names all are BMP files.	Blocks sorted in descending order according to their energy
New Palace	1.5,2,9,3,6,13,4,10, 7,11,8,14,12,15,16
Horse	1.5,2,9,3,6,13,4,10, 7,11,8,14,12,15,16
Straw Berry	1,2,5,3,9,13,4,6,7, 10,11,8,14,12,15,16
Fern	1,5,2,9,6,3,10,7,11, 13,12,14,8,4,15,16

			64*64
		64*64	64*64
	64*64	128*128	
64*64	64*64		

Fig. 3 7 images embedded into the cover image (Embedding Capacity 62.5% of the Cover image Size.)

6 images of size 64 X 64 and 1 image of size 128 X 128 embedded in a 256 X 256 Cover Image

Fig. 4 Seven secret images, Cover and Stego New Palace

3. De-normalize the DST coefficients of the extracted data (Multiply each DST coefficient of the extracted secret image by its maximum coefficient)
4. Take inverse DST of the de-normalized secret image. This gives us the recovered secret image.

Fig. 5 Cover and corresponding Stego Images. Horse and Fern each of size 256X256 24 bit Bitmap images.

Table 2 Results of proposed system

Cover Image	PSNR	MSE
Straw berry	42.04	4.06
New Palace	37.93	10.46
Horse	38.28	9.65
Fern	33.5	29
Card	42.67	3.51

3. Experimental results

We have embedded in all seven secret images into the cover image of size 256 * 256. The following secret images were embedded into the cover image. One of size 128 * 128 in blocks 11, 12, 15, 16 and rest all of size 64 * 64 in blocks 7, 8, 10, 14, 4 and 13 respectively. Figure 3 shows the blocks where these secret images were embedded.

Table 2 summarizes the results of this research for 5 different Cover Images.

4. Conclusion

In this paper, we have proposed a new steganographic scheme to hide secret image (Secret message) in a digital image. The proposed scheme embeds secret images by replacing the low energy blocks of the transformed cover with the normalized DST coefficients of the secret images. From the experimental results, we conclude that the blocks 16, 15, 12, 14, 8, 11, 7, 10, 4 and 13 are the low energy blocks for most of the cover images transformed by DST. So we embed data in these blocks leaving high energy blocks unaltered. By normalizing the DST coefficients of the secret image we reduce the embedding error. The experimental results show that the difference between the original image and stego image is visually unnoticeable with 100% retrieval of the secret images. We have achieved embedding capacity of 62.5 % of the cover image size, with imperceptible distortion in it.

References

1. Chin-Chen Chang, Tung-Shou Chen, Hsien-Chu Hsia, "An Effective Image Steganographic Scheme Based on Wavelet Transformation and Pattern-Based Modification," iccnmc, pp.450, 2003 International Conference on Computer Networks and Mobile Computing (ICCNMC'03), 2003

2. R.O.EI Safy, H.H. Zayed and A. EI Dessouki, "An Adaptive Steganographic Technique Based on Integer Wavelet Transform," International Conference on Networking and Media Convergence, 2009 (ICNM) 2009) on 24-25 March

3. Wu, H.-C.; Wu, N.-I.; Tsai, C.-S.; Hwang, M.-S, " Image steganographic scheme based on pixel-value differencing and LSB replacement methods," Vision, Image and Signal Processing, IEE Proceedings - Volume 152, Issue 5, 7 Oct. 2005

4. C.K Chan and L.M Cheng, " Hiding data in images by simple LSB substitution, " Pattern Recognition, pp. 469-474, Mar. 2004

5. P. Chen and H. Lin, " A DWT Approach for Image Steganography, ", International Journal of Applied Science and Engineering 2006. 4, 3

6. Dr.H. B. Kekre, Ms. Archana Athawale and Ms. Pallavi N. Halarnkar, "Increased Capacity of Information Hiding in LSBs Method for Text and Image", International Journal of Electrical, Computer and Systems Engineering, Volume 2 Number 4. http://www.waset.org/ijecse/v2.html

7. Dr. H. B. Kekre, Ms. Archana Athawale, "Information Hiding using LSB Technique with Increased Capacity" International Journal of Cryptography and Security, Vol-I, No.2, Oct-2008

8. Dr. H. B. Kekre, Ms. Archana Athawale and Ms. Pallavi N. Halarnkar, "Polynomial Transformation To Improve Capacity Of Cover Image For Information Hiding In Multiple LSB's ", International Journal of Engineering Research and Industrial Applications (IJERIA), Ascent Publications, Volume II, March 2009, Pune

9. Dr. H. B. Kekre, Ms. Archana Athawale and Ms. Pallavi N. Halarnkar, "Performance Evaluation Of Pixel Value Differencing And Kekre's Modified Algorithm For Information Hiding In Images", ACM International Conference on Advances in Computing, Communication and Control (ICAC3).2009 (Uploaded on ACM Portal:http://portal.acm.org/citation.cfm?id=1523103.15231 72)

10. Dr. H. B. Kekre, Ms. Archana Athawale and Ms. Pallavi N. Halarnkar, "Comparative Study of Different Color Spaces for Information Hiding using Multiple LSB's in Different Components", IEEE International Advance Computing Conference IACC'09, held on 6th – 7th March 09, Patiala Punjab

11. Dr. H. B. Kekre, Ms. Archana Athawale and Ms. Pallavi N. Halarnkar, "High Payload using High Boost Filtering in Kekre's Multiple LSB's Algorithm", 2nd International Conference on Advances in Computer Vision and Information Technology ACVIT 2009, 16th -19th December 2009, Aurangabad

12. Dr.Dr. H. B. Kekre, Ms. Archana Athawale, Ms. Pallavi N. Halarnkar and Mr. Varun Banura, "Performance Comparison of DCT and Walsh Transform for Steganography", Accepted for ICWET

13. Dr. H. B. Kekre, Ms. Archana Athawale and Ms. Pallavi N. Halarnkar, "Increased Capacity Of Least Significant Bits Embedding For Information Hiding",TechnoPath Technical Magazine, NMIMS University.Volume 1 No 1

14. Dr. H. B. Kekre, Ms. Archana Athawale and Ms. Pallavi N. Halarnkar, "Robust and Secured Information Hiding using Polynomial Transformation in Kekre's LUV color space and multiple LSBs", National Conference on Information and Communication Technology NCICT-09, held on 6th – 7th March 2009, Mumbai

15. Dr. H. B. Kekre, Ms. Archana Athawale and Ms. Pallavi N. Halarnkar,"High Payload using High Boost Filtering in Kekre's Multiple LSB's Algorithm for Information Hiding", Technopath Technical Magazine May 2009, Volume 1 No 2

16. Dr. H. B. Kekre, Ms. Archana Athawale and Ms. Pallavi N. Halarnkar, "Increased Capacity and High Security for Embedding Secret Message in Transform Domain using Discrete Cosine Transform", Accepted in Technopath

Dynamic signature using time based vector quantization by kekre's median codebook generation algorithm

Dr. H. B. Kekre · **Mr. V. A. Bharadi** · **Mr. T. K. Sarode**

MPSTME, NMIMS University, Mumbai, India

1. Introduction

Dynamic Signature Recognition is one of the highly accurate biometric traits. We capture live signature of the person hence it is possible to have dynamic characteristics of signature for matching purpose. The signature captured by digitizer gives information about dynamic nature of signature and pressure applied while signing. We propose use of clustering by Vector Quantization for Matching of Dynamic Signature. Signature points are clustered on Time axis and codebook is generated, The technique is fast and gives good accuracy.

2. Biometrics

The biometrics is most commonly defined as measurable psychological or behavioral characteristic of the individual that can be used in personal identification and verification. The driving force of the progress in this field is, above all, the growing role of the Internet and the requirements of society. Therefore, considerable applications are concentrated in the area of electronic commerce and electronic banking systems and security applications of vital installations. The biometrics has a significant advantage over traditional authentication techniques (namely passwords, PIN numbers, smartcards etc.) due to the fact that biometric characteristics of the individual are not easily transferable, are unique of every person, and cannot be lost, stolen or broken. The choice of one of the biometric solutions depends on several factors [2]:

- User acceptance
- Level of security required
- Accuracy
- Cost and implementation time

Biometric and biomedical informatics are the fast developing scientific direction, studying the processes of creation, transmission, reception, storage, processing, displaying and interpretation of information in all the channels of functional and signal systems of living objects which are known to biological and medical science and practice. Modern natural sciences at present sharply need in the updating of scientific picture of the world, and the essential contribution in this process can be made by the biometric and biomedical methods. Only some more simple (statistical) forms of biometric and biomedical information have found their application when person identification, and raised interest for these methods of identification can be caused by new possibilities of information technologies.

2.1 Dynamic signature recognition

"Dynamic Signature" is a biometric modality that uses, for recognition purposes, the anatomic and behavioral characteristics that an individual exhibits when signing his or her name (or other phrase). [1–3]. Dynamic Signature devices should not be confused with electronic signature capture systems that are used to capture a graphic image of the signature and are common in locations where merchants are capturing signatures for transaction authorizations.

Data such as the dynamically captured direction, stroke, pressure, and shape of an individual's signature can enable handwriting to be a reliable indicator of an individual's identity (i.e., measurements of the captured data, when compared to those of matching samples, are a reliable biometric for writer identification.) We can also capture the static characteristics of signatures [7]. This leads to better accuracy because the dynamic characteristics are very difficult to imitate, but the system requires user co-operation

S.J. Pise (ed.), *ThinkQuest 2010*, DOI 10.1007/978-81-8489-989-4_46,

Fig. 1 Digitizer tablet for on-line signature scan (Wacom Intuos4)

and complex hardware. Digitizer tablets or pressure sensitive pads are used to scan signature dynamically, one such tablet is shown in Figure 1. In off–line signature recognition we are having the signature template coming from an imaging device, hence we have only static characteristic of the signatures. The person need not be present at the time of verification. Hence off-line signature verification is convenient in various situations like document verification, banking transactions etc. [1][8][9][10]. As we have a limited set of features for verification purpose, off-line signature recognition systems need to be designed very carefully to achieve the desired accuracy.

3. Signature recognition systems

A popular means of authentication historically has been the handwritten signature. Though such signatures are never the same for the same person at different times, there appears to be no practical problem for human beings to discriminate visually the real signature from the forged one. It will be extremely useful when an electronic device can display at least the same virtuosity. The development of computer–aided handwritten signature verification systems has been

ongoing for decades. Different approaches are developed to deal with the handwritten signature recognition problem.

3.1 Hardware approach

The hardware approach is faster and convenient, Texas instruments has come up with a DSP chip TMS320. This is a family of digital signal processors which is capable of handling neural clustering techniques to enhance the discriminating power and arrive at a very simple and low-cost solution that can be embedded in existing pen-based systems, such as handheld computers and transaction units. Dullink and Dallen [11] have reported FRR up to 1% and FAR up to 0.01% using TMS320 family.

3.2 On-line approach

On-line signature recognition considers the dynamic characteristics of signatures. In [2] Jain & Ross have used critical points, speed curvature angle as features and they have reported FRR 2.8% and FAR 1.6 %. They used common as well as writer dependent thresholds but it was observed that the writer dependent thresholds give better accuracy.

Considering another approach Lei, Palla and Govindarajalu [12] have proposed a technique for finding correlation between two signature sequences for online recognition, they mapped the occurrence of different critical points on signature and the time scale and the correlation between these sequences was evaluated using a new parameter called Extended Regression Square (ER2) coefficient the results were compared with an existing technique based on Dynamic Time Wrapping (DTW). They reported Equal Error rate (EER) 7.2% where the EER reported by DTW was 20.9 % with user dependent thresholds.

In [13] Rhee and Cho used Model guided segmentation approach for segment–to–segment comparison to obtain consistent segmentation. They used discriminative feature selection for skilled as well as random forgeries. They reported EER 3.4 %. Nalwa [14] used a moment and torque base approach for on-line signature recognition. His work is based parameterizing each on-line curve over its normalized arc-length. These parameters are then represented along the length of the curve, in a moving coordinate frame. The measures of the curve within a sliding window that are analogous to the position of the center of mass, the torque exerted by a force, and the moments of inertia of a mass distribution about its center of mass. Further, He suggested the weighted and biased harmonic mean as a graceful mechanism of combining errors from multiple models of which at least one model is applicable but not necessarily more than one model is applicable. He recommended that each signature be represented by multiple models, these models, perhaps, local and global, shape based and dynamics based. The reported FRR was 7% and FAR was 1%.

One thing that should be noted is that all these approaches need signature data with dynamic information.

When the data comes from the hardware it is raw and we have to pre-process it to normalize the errors due to sampling, quantization, speed of hardware, signing position etc. We are using Wacom Intuos 4 for our experiments and we have also experienced the need of – pre-processing the data. Doroz and Wrobel [15] have discussed this issue and proposed a technique of sampling the point uniformly to have equal number of points per unit time. They have used Signature verification Competition database [16].

4. Steps in signature recognition [6, 7]

Signature Recognition Systems need to preprocess the data. It includes a series of operations to get the results. The major steps are as follows,

4.1 Data acquisition

In the experiment carried we are using Digitizer Tablet Wacom Intuos 4, Typical features of the tablets is as follows
1. Active Area (W × D) 157.5 × 98.4 mm
2. Connectivity-USB connectivity
3. Pressure levels-2048
4. Sensor pen without battery
5. Minimum ON weight (Minimum weight sensed by the pen tip) –1Gram.
6. Report rate- 197 Points per second
7. LPI - lines per inch-5080 lpi
8. Maximum Data Rate: 200 packets/Second.

The digitizer tablet is interfaced [17] to the application using an ActiveX COM component VBTablet [18].

In the application development we have observed that the interface could deliver only 100 Packets/Second. As the digitizer has finite rate of sampling and data transfer, it cannot capture all the points on a curve but captures finite points as per the sampling rate. This gives the results as follows, shown in Fig. 2. We have to pre-process the signature to generate the lost points.

4.2 Signature pre-processing

We have proposed a scheme based on Modified Digital Difference Analyzer Algorithm (MDDA) which will interpolate the dynamic signature point to reconstruct signature with maximum possible points. One such case is given in Table I. This shows captured signature and result of interpolation by scheme developed by authors. The preprocessed signature is then used for feature extraction. We are using Clustering for feature Vector Generation. The feature extraction step is explained in detail in next section.

5. Feature extraction using vector quantization

Feature Extraction is main step is signature recognition. We are using vector Quantization based scheme for feature vector Generation. This scheme is fast and giving good results. As the dynamic signature recognition mainly deals with time based behavior of signature we are using Vector Quantization along the time axis of the signature, the captured data is in following form, each point contains information about X, Y, Z-Coordinates, Pressure, Azimuth and Altitude of the pen tip. Hence ith point Pi can be considered as:

Table 1 Interpolation results for different signatures with their parameters and calculation time

Sampled Signature	Packet Count	Center of Mass of Signature (Cx,Cy)	Slope Angle	Pixel Count	Signature Arch Length in Pixels	Calculation Timing	Signature Timing
Sampled Signature 1	157	103, 95	12.8	132	842	31.25 milliseconds	1140 milliseconds
Interpolated Signature 1		122, 100	11.18	246	907		

Fig. 2   Signature Samples of a person (a) Static Scanned Signature, (b)(c),(d) Dynamic Signature Scanned by Wacom Intuos 4

$$Pi = \{Xi, Yi, Zi, T, Pri, Azi, Alti\} \qquad (1)$$

Where 'T'is the timestamp or sequence number of specific point in the signature. This is a multidimensional feature vector, we implement clustering across the Time axis (Timestamp) of the signature using Kekre's Median Codebook Generation Algorithm.

5.1   Vector quantization & KMCG algorithm

Vector Quantization (VQ) [21, 22] is an efficient technique for data compression and has been successfully used in various applications such as index compression . VQ has been very popular in a variety of research fields such as speech recognition and face detection. VQ is also used in real time applications such as real time video-based event detection and anomaly intrusion detection systems , image segmentation, content based image retrieval CBIR and face recognition.

In reference [23] the authors have proposed this algorithm for image data compression. This algorithm reduces the time for code book generation. It uses sorting and median technique for codebook generation. We have set of feature points as shown in Eq (1). We apply KMCG repetitively on Time axis of the feature points. The steps are as follows.

1. Capture the Signature points and store in an array.
2. Interpolate the feature points to generate maximum points on signature curve.
3. Divide the time interval of the signature into „n Intervals; this will be used for clustering points.
4. For each interval read all the points sort the points in ascending order of the timestamp/
5. Find median of the sorted array and consider it as Codevector for that interval.
6. Repeat this procedure for all the intervals.

7. Copy each codevector in the codebook.

Actually we are implementing modified version of the KMCG, as we are not repeating clustering an all the feature point dimensions, which is actually done in KMCG, as were interested to from cluster on the time axis automatically all the points in a cluster tend to have closely matching features. If a signature if done in 4 seconds and we are using 100 clusters then each cluster contains points in 4ms vicinity on time axis.

In our testing we have used 25 intervals for clustering, so the codebook has a size of 25 rows and 7 Columns [25X7].

This codebook acts as a feature vector. We use this codebook for enrollment and matching. This is discussed in the next section. Signature matching can be performed by taking the Euclidian Distance between the codebooks. The Euclidian distance between two codebooks C1[R,C], C2[R,C] is given by

$$ED = \sqrt{\sum_{R=1}^{R=n} \sum_{C=1}^{C=m} (C1[R,C] - C2[R,C])^2} \qquad (2)$$

For signature of same user the ED is low, and for forged signature ED is high. We have to evaluate user specific thresholds for proper classification.

5.2   Enrollment and testing

The extracted codebooks are stored in to database. The human signature is dependent on varying factors, the signature characteristics change with the psychological or mental condition of a person, physical and practical condition like tip of the pen used for signature, signatures taken at different times, aging etc. This is captured in the codebook. To match two signatures we generate codebooks for the two signatures.

We have to consider a high degree of intra-class variation because two signatures from a same person are never same. Our system should consider this variation and at the same time the system should possess high degree of accuracy to detect forged signatures. Fig. 3 Shows two signatures from the same user, the dynamic characteristics are shown in the plots. We apply Time based VQ using KMCG to generate two codebooks, each codebook is having feature vector with parameters X, Y, Z, Pressure, Timestamp, Azimuth, Altitude (CLID is the Cluster ID assigned –used for internal calculation), the corresponding Euclidian distance is 340.77 for the same users signature. For different users signature or forged signatures the observed distance range is (900 to 2500). In the next section we discuss the outcome of practical experiments performed by the authors

6.   Results

The proposed technique was tested on 151 signatures collected from 25 different persons, some signatures were

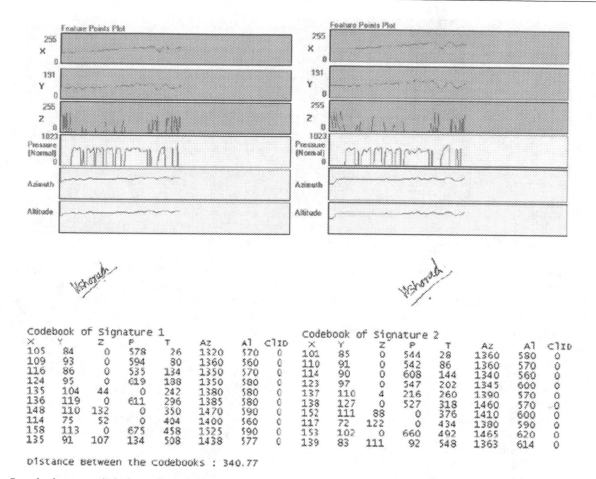

Fig. 3 Sample signatures their dynamic characteristics & corresponding codebook snapshots with matching distance

Table 2 FAR FRR analysis

Sr.	Parameter	Value in %
1	FAR	1%
2	FRR	1.5%
3	TAR	98.5%
4	TRR	99%

collected in one sitting, some were collected in two sittings with a time gap of 2 to 7 days. Total 300 test were performed out of which 150 tests were performed for genuine signatures and 150 tests were performed for inter class matching and forged signatures. The program was tested on AMD 64 1.8GHz, Windows XP SP3 and Visual C# 2005, .NET Framework 2.5.

For analysis universal threshold was considered without any training and only codebook based feature vector was considered for finding matching distance. The result is summarized in Table 2.

The Equal Error rate was at 1.2%. The performance can further be improved by using sophisticated classifier and incorporating other features like Number of Pixels, Signature Arc Length, Signature Area, Acceleration, Velocity Angle

etc. maximum testing time per signature was 20ms this make the system feasible for real time application.

7. Conclusion

In this paper we have proposed a technique for dynamic signature recognition. Proposed technique is based on cluster formation using vector quantization across Time Axis of feature vector. We have used Kekre's Median Codebook Generation Algorithm for generation of codebook which is used as a feature vector. The proposed technique has give True acceptance rate as 98.5%, this can be further increased by using proper training and good classifier. Matching of signature took average 20ms time, hence the proposed system is suitable for real time applications.

References

1. A. K. Jain, A. Ross, S. Prabhakar, "An Introduction to Biometric Recognition", IEEE Transactions on Circuits and Systems for Video Technology, Vol. 14, No. 1, January 2004

2. A. K. Jain, A. Ross, and S. Prabhakar, "On Line Signature Verification", Pattern Recognition, vol. 35, no. 12, Dec 2002. pp. 2963-2972

3. "Signature Recognition," GAITS: Global Analytic Info Technology Services, August2005. http://www.gaits.com/biometrics_signature.asp

4. A. Zimmer and L.L. Ling, "A Hybrid On/Off Line Handwritten Signature Verification System", ICDAR, vol.1, pp.424-428, Aug.2003

5. D. Hamilton, J. Whelan, A. McLaren, "Low cost dynamic signature verification system", Security and Detection, 1995. IEEE CNF European Convention, 16-18 May 1995. pp 202 –206

6. R. Plamondon, G. Lorette, "Automatic Signature Verification and Writer Identification – The State of the Art", Pattern Recognition, vol. 4, no. 2, pp. 107–131, 1989

7. R. Plamondon, "The design of an On-line signature verification system", Theory to practice, International journal of Pattern Recognition and Artificial Intelligence, (1994). pp 795-811

8. H B kekre, V A Bharadi, "Specialized Global Features for Off-line Signature Recognition", 7th Annual National Conference on Biometrics RFID and Emerging Technologies for Automatic Identification, India , January 2009

9. H B Kekre, V A Bharadi, "Signature Recognition using Cluster Based Global Features", IEEE International Conference (IACC 2009), Thapar University, Patiala- Punjab, India. March 2009

10. H. Baltzakis, N. Papamarkos, "A new signature verification technique based on a two-stage neural network classifier", Engineering Applications of Artificial Intelligence 14 (2001)

11. H. Dullink, B. van Daalen, J. Nijhuis, L. Spaanenburg, H. Zuidhof, "Implementing a DSP Kernel for Online Dynamic Handwritten Signature Verification using the TMS320 DSP Family", EFRIE, France December 1995 SPRA304

12. H. lei, S. Palla and V Govindraju, "ER2: an Intuitive Similarity measure for On-line Signature Verification", Proceedings of CUBS 2005

13. T. Rhee, S. Cho, "On line Signature Recognition Using Model Guided Segmentation and Discriminative feature selection for skilled forgeries", IEEE Transaction on pattern recognition, Jan 2001

14. V. Nalwa, "Automatic On-Line Signature Verification", proceedings of the IEEE Transactions on Biometrics, vol. 85, No. 2, February 1997

15. R. Doroz, K. Wrobel "Method of Signature Recognition with the Use of the Mean Differences", Proceedings of the ITI 2009 31st Int. Conf. on Information Technology Interfaces, June 22-25, 2009

16. SVC (Signature Verification Competition) database available at the website:http://www.cse.ust.hk/svc2004/index.html

17. H. B. Kekre, V A Bharadi, "Using Component Object Model for Interfacing Biometrics Sensors to Capture Multidimensional Features", IJJCCT 2009, China, Dec 2009

18. http://sourceforge.net/projects/vbtablet/

19. A. P. Godse, "Computer Graphics", Technical publication. 2002

20. H. B. Kekre, V A Bharadi, "Dynamic Signature Pre-processing by Modified Digital Difference Analyzer Algorithm", ThinkQuest 2010, Mumbai, India , March 2010

21. Gray R., "Vector quantization", IEEE ASSP Mag., pp.: 4-29, Apr. 1984

22. Linde Y, Buzo A., and Gray R., "An algorithm for vector quantizer design," IEEE Trans. Commun., vol. COM-28, no. 1, pp.: 84-95, 1980

23. Kekre H., Sarode T., "An Efficient Fast Algorithm to Generate Codebook for Vector Quantization," ICETET-2008, Nagpur, India, pp.: 62- 67, 16-18 July 2008. Avaliable at IEEE Xplore

A new double error correcting long code for 100% correction

Joanne Gomes[1] · B. K. Mishra[2]

[1]Research Scholar SNDT, Mumbai, India.
[2]Thakur College of Engineering, Mumbai, India.

1. Introduction

The theory of Linear Block codes is well established since many years. Shannon's work (1948) showed that at any rate of information transmission up to the channel capacity, it should be possible to transfer information at error rates that can be reduced to any desired level [1]. In 1950, Hamming introduced a single error correcting and double error detecting codes with its geometrical model [2] whereas just before Hamming, Golay had introduced (23, 12) triple error correcting perfect code. Since then different types of more effective error correcting codes have been invented by researchers. In [3] author derives the necessary conditions for existence of e-error correcting code over GF (q) with word length n and concludes that Golay (23,12) is the only nontrivial binary perfect 3-error correcting code over any GF(q) and no other perfect codes exists except those invented by Hamming and Golay. Number of double error correcting BCH codes are listed and permutation decoding method for codes with code rates (k/n)>=1/2 is presented in [4]. Computer results on the minimum distance of some BCH codes are listed down in [5]. Similarly updated table of collection of lower and upper bounds for dmax (n, k), i.e. maximum possible minimum distance of a binary linear code, of code word length n and dimension k, has been given in [6]. The utility of different types of linear codes in communication over power limited and Bandwidth limited channels is discussed in [7]. For power limited channels concatenated codes are more suitable with inner code as short length convolution code and outer code as long length, simple, high rate Reed Solomon code [7]. A systematic quasi-cyclic code (16, 8) for computer memory system which corrects double errors and detects triple errors has been given in [8]. It gives encoding and decoding method for the same and also presents a quasicyclic code (32, 16) for triple error correction [8]. All these and many other papers give the efficient coding for partial correction of information bits. E.g. Golay (23, 12) code corrects 3 bit errors in 12 information bits or (16, 8) code in [8] corrects 2

errors in 8 information bits. Such types of codes have code rate ^{3} ½ to get optimum transmission rates. The table given in [6] indicates, for k = 2, code word length n should be 8 to achieve min Hamming distance of 5. Practically (8 2 5) code is not available. Most of the double errors correcting codes have complicated decoding procedures. This paper presents a simple double error correcting (8 2 5) code based on syndrome calculation.

Consider a case wherein we transmit k information bits simultaneously. If all the k bits are in error on the receiver side and if we want to correct them, transmitted code word should have more redundant bits. This will consume more transmission bandwidth and the code will be less efficient. However in power limited system such as Ultra wideband communication, bandwidth is abundant. UWB has wide applications in radar, sensor networks and indoor multimedia communication. UWB can also be used to communicate with sensors placed inside the human body for cure of certain sickness. We can take benefit of Long codes for 100% error correction in wideband communication, as accuracy is an equal important criteria while assuring good quality of service in communication. In a very sensitive medical application we might need to have error free data communication at the cost of transmission rate. This paper presents a design of double error correcting long binary code for 2 bits of information (k=2), achieving 100% error correction.

2. Design of double error correcting code

In an error correcting code, the central concept is the notion of minimum distance. Consider a systematic linear block code C with code word of length n, minimum Hamming distance between two code words d and dimension k. In this (n k d) code if we want to correct t number of errors per given code word, then minimum hamming distance of the linear block code should be dmin ^{3} 2t+1 [9][10]. With t=2, dmin is 5. This work attempts to design a code with dmin = 5 which can detect and correct 1 and 2 bit errors when k=2.

S.J. Pise (ed.), *ThinkQuest 2010*, DOI 10.1007/978-81-8489-989-4_47,

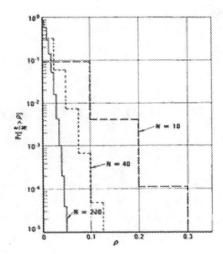

Fig. 1 Probability that the fraction of symbol is in error e/N in a block of length N exceeds ñ for Pe = 0.01

The following figure 1 indicates that the long codes can improve the performance of error correcting system.

The form of the curve in fig 1 suggested that if one has a scheme for correcting a fixed fraction t/n, then the error rate could be made arbitrarily small by simply choosing the block to be long enough. Thus the results in fig 1 indicate the potential for performance improvement by increasing the block length n. Here the loss of efficiency occurs because the relative number of useful messages that these schemes convey becomes vanishingly small. This might be tolerated in medical applications where accuracy plays an important role. In a linear code C with length n and dimension k, if errors to be corrected are t then correctable error patterns will be given by

$$\sum_{i=0}^{t}\binom{n}{i} = {}^{n}c_0 + {}^{n}c_1 + {}^{n}c_2 \tag{1}$$

Where,

$${}^{n}c_i = \frac{n!}{i!(n-i)!} \tag{2}$$

Any linear block code should satisfy Hamming bound which gives the lower bound on the number of parity bits (n-k). Gilbert bound gives upper limit on the number of parity bits. Hamming bound is given by eq. 3 and Gilbert bound is given by eq. 4 [9][10].

$$\sum_{i=0}^{t}\binom{n}{i} \leq 2^{n-k} \tag{3}$$

$$2^{n-k} \geq \sum_{i=0}^{d-2}\binom{n-1}{i} \tag{4}$$

If k=2 and t=2 we need to achieve dmin = 5. With n ≤ 7 it is not possible to achieve this minimum Hamming distance.

With Gilbert upper bound we find that number of parity bits required = n-k = 6. Thus for t =2 to get dmin =5 n should be 8.

With n = 8, Hamming lower bound will be satisfied as follows

$$\sum_{i=0}^{t}\binom{n}{i} \leq 2^{n-k}$$

$$\sum_{i=0}^{2}\binom{8}{i} \leq 2^{8-2} \tag{5}$$

$$1 + 8 + 28 \leq 2^6$$

$$37 \leq 2^6$$

And Gilbert upper bound will be satisfied as follows

$$2^{n-k} \geq \sum_{i=0}^{d-2}\binom{n-1}{i}$$

$$\geq \sum_{i=0}^{3}\binom{7}{i} \tag{6}$$

$$\geq 1 + 7 + 21 + 35$$

$$2^{n-k} \geq 64$$

Thus we decide that the maximum code length of '8' is required to achieve Hamming distance of '5', in order to correct two bit errors while transmitting two information bits. This code length will guarantee us 100% error correction with code rate of ¼.

2.1 Generator and parity matrix

Consider the generator polynomial derived from the multiplication of the polynomials (x+1) and (x⁵+x⁴+x²+ x+1)

g(x) = (x+1) (x⁵+x⁴+x²+ x+1) = (x⁶+x⁴+x³+ x+1) then the

$$G_{(k,n)} = \left[I_k \vdots P_{(k,n-k)}\right]$$

$$= \begin{pmatrix} 1\ 0 \vdots 1\ 1\ 0\ 1\ 1\ 0 \\ 0\ 1 \vdots 0\ 1\ 1\ 0\ 1\ 1 \end{pmatrix} \tag{7}$$

2.2 Encoding of a long code for k = 2

With code dimension k=2 we can transmit four types of messages (m = 00, 01, 10, 11). Corresponding code words are obtained as C = m * G

$$C1 = [0\ 0]\begin{pmatrix} 1\ 0 \vdots 1\ 1\ 0\ 1\ 1\ 0 \\ 0\ 1 \vdots 0\ 1\ 1\ 0\ 1\ 1 \end{pmatrix}$$

$$C1 = [0\ 0\ 0\ 0\ 0\ 0\ 0\ 0]$$

$$C2 = [0\ 1]\begin{pmatrix} 1\ 0 \vdots 1\ 1\ 0\ 1\ 1\ 0 \\ 0\ 1 \vdots 0\ 1\ 1\ 0\ 1\ 1 \end{pmatrix}$$

$$C2 = [0\ 1\ 0\ 1\ 1\ 0\ 1\ 1] \tag{8}$$

$$C3 = [1\ 0]\begin{pmatrix} 1\ 0 \vdots 1\ 1\ 0\ 1\ 1\ 0 \\ 0\ 1 \vdots 0\ 1\ 1\ 0\ 1\ 1 \end{pmatrix}$$

$$C3 = [1\ 0\ 1\ 1\ 0\ 1\ 1\ 0]$$

$$C4 = [1\ 1]\begin{pmatrix} 1\ 0 \vdots 1\ 1\ 0\ 1\ 1\ 0 \\ 0\ 1 \vdots 0\ 1\ 1\ 0\ 1\ 1 \end{pmatrix}$$

$$C4 = [1\ 1\ 1\ 0\ 1\ 1\ 0\ 1]$$

2.3 Decoding of a long code for k = 2

The parity matrix of above code (8 2 5) is

$$P_{(k,n-k)} = \begin{pmatrix} 1 1 0 1 1 0 \\ 0 1 1 0 1 1 \end{pmatrix} \tag{9}$$

Now parity check matrix H is given by

$$H_{(n-k,n)} = \left[P^T_{(n-k,k)} \vdots I_{n-k} \right]$$

$$H_{(n-k,n)} = \begin{pmatrix} 1 0 \vdots 1 0 0 0 0 0 \\ 1 1 \vdots 0 1 0 0 0 0 \\ 0 1 \vdots 0 0 1 0 0 0 \\ 1 0 \vdots 0 0 0 1 0 0 \\ 1 1 \vdots 0 0 0 0 1 0 \\ 0 1 \vdots 0 0 0 0 0 1 \end{pmatrix} \tag{10}$$

$$H^T_{(n,n-k)} = \begin{pmatrix} 1 1 0 1 1 0 \\ 0 1 1 0 1 1 \\ 1 0 0 0 0 0 \\ 0 1 0 0 0 0 \\ 0 0 1 0 0 0 \\ 0 0 0 1 0 0 \\ 0 0 0 0 1 0 \\ 0 0 0 0 0 1 \end{pmatrix} \tag{11}$$

3. Syndrome calculation

If c is the transmitted code vector, r is a received code vector, e is a received error vector, H is a parity check matrix given by eq. 10 and S is syndrome indicating the presence of error then,

$$S = r \times H^T = (c + e) \times H^T = cH^T + eH^T$$
$$= m \times G \times H^T + eH^T$$
$$= 0 + eH^T \text{ thus,}$$

$$S = e \times H^T$$

The linear code (8 2 5) presented here is a systematic cyclic code. For this code, total of 144 error vectors with single bit and double bit error patterns can be received on the receiver side. This will give us 144 unique syndromes of 6 bit length, which will help us to find which one or two bits in the received vector are in error. Complimenting these located error bits will give us the correct transmitted code word which is in systematic form. The code (8 2 5) presented here is a systematic cyclic code and its hardware part, encoder and decoder can be implemented using shift registers. It does not satisfy Hamming bound with equality, hence it cannot be called as a perfect code.

Example

Consider the systematically encoded code word c3 = [1 0 1 1 0 1 1 0] has been transmitted and we receive r3 = e3 = [0 1 1 1 0 1 1 0].

This received codeword has first two bits in error. The corresponding syndrome will be calculated as follows

$$S3 = S = e \times H^T = [0 1 1 1 0 1 1 0] \begin{pmatrix} 1 1 0 1 1 0 \\ 0 1 1 0 1 1 \\ 1 0 0 0 0 0 \\ 0 1 0 0 0 0 \\ 0 0 1 0 0 0 \\ 0 0 0 1 0 0 \\ 0 0 0 0 1 0 \\ 0 0 0 0 0 1 \end{pmatrix}$$

$$= [1 0 1 1 0 1]$$

At the receiver end this will be unique syndrome for first two bits in error. Complicating these first two bits, the correct transmitted vector would be [1 0 1 1 0 1 1 0].

Since we get unique syndrome for each error vector received on the receiver side, we can decode this code completely with simplicity and without any ambiguity. Also transmitted information is only two bit long; all the two bits would be recovered safely as long as only two bit errors are generated by noisy channel.

4. Conclusion

The paper presents a generator and parity check matrix for double error correcting long binary cyclic code (8 2 5) with code rate of ¼. It is based on simple and common method of syndrome calculation and hence easy to use. It can give 100% of error correction as long as the noisy channel generates errors in two or less number of transmitted bits.

This error correction method is useful when high accuracy is required at the cost of transmission rate. It's a convenient error correction coding method to use with 2- dimensional modulation scheme based on orthogonal Hermite pulses for UWB communication. Future scope of this work could be to find simple generator matrix for triple error correction when three bits of information is to be transmitted simultaneously.

References

1. Shannon C. E., "Mathematical theory of communication", Bell Sys. Tech. Journal. 27, 1948, pp 379-423 and 623-656
2. Hamming, R.W.,"Error Detecting and Error Correcting Codes", The Bell System Technical Journal,Soc, Industrial. Appl. Math. Vol. 26, No.2, April 1950
3. J. H. Van Lint "On the nonexistence of perfect 2- and 3- Hamming-error-correcting-codes over GF(q)", IEEE Transaction on Information and Control, Vol. 16, No. 4, June 1970
4. S. G. S. SHIVA, K. C. FUNG and H. S. Y. TAN, "On Permutation Decoding of Binary Cyclic Double- Error-Correcting Codes of Certain Lengths" IEEE Transaction on Information Theory, Sept 1970, pp 641-643
5. C. L. CHENZ "Computer Results on the Minimum Distance of Some with Binary Cyclic Codes" IEEE Transaction on Information Theory, may 1970, Vol. IT-18, pp 359-360

6. James massey "A short introduction to coding theory and practice" Proceeding of International symposium on signal, system and electronics, Germany, Sept 89, pp 629- 633

7. A E Brouwer, Tom Verhoeff, "An Updated table of minimum distance bounds for binary linear code ", IEEE Transaction on Information Theory, Vol. 39. No. 2, march 93, pp 662-677

8. T. Aaron Gulliver and Vijay K. Bhargava, "A Systematic (16,8) Code for Correcting Double Errors and Detecting Triple Adjacent Errors" IEEE Transaction on Computers, Vol. 42, No. 1, Jan 1993, pp. 109-112

9. S. Lin and D.J. Costello, Error Control Coding: fundamentals and applications, Prentice Hall, 1983

10. S.B. Wicker, Error Control Systems for Digital Communication and Storage, Prentice Hall, 1994

Tumor demarcation in mammographic images using vector quantization technique on entropy images

Dr. H. B. Kekre[1] · Saylee M. Gharge[2] · Tanuja K. Sarode[3]

[1]Senior Professor, MPSTME, NMIMS University, Mumbai, India
[2]Ph.D. Scholar, MPSTME, NMIMS University, Mumbai, India
[2]Lecturer, VESIT, Mumbai, India
[3]Ph.D. Scholar, MPSTME, NMIMS University, Mumbai, India
[3]Assistant Professor, TSEC, Mumbai,India

1. Introduction

Recent studies show that the interpretation of the mammograms by Radiologists gives high rates of false positive cases. Indeed the images provided by different patients have different dynamics of intensity and present a weak contrast. Moreover the size of the significant details can be very small. Several researchers have tried to develop computer aided diagnosis tools to help the radiologists in the interpretation of the mammograms for an accurate diagnosis. In order to perform a semi automated tracking of breast cancer, it is necessary to detect the presence or absence of lesions from the mammograms [1, 2].These lesions can be of various types: Nodular opacities, clear masses with lobed edges etc. They can be benign or malignant, according to their contour (sharp or blurred) – Stellar opacities (malignant tumors); micro calcifications: small calcified structures that appear as clear points on a mammogram [3, 4].

For mammograms manifesting masses this corresponds to the detection of suspicious mass regions. A number of image processing methods have been proposed to perform this task. [5] and [6] have proposed using modified and weighted median filtering, respectively, to enhance the digitized image prior to object identification. [7] used thresholding and fuzzy pyramid linking for mass localization and classification. Other investigators have proposed using the asymmetry between the right and left breast images to determine possible mass locations. Yin *et al.* uses both linear and nonlinear bilateral subtraction [8] while the method by Lau *et al.* relies on "structural asymmetry" between the two breast images [9]. Recently Kegelmeyer has reported promising results for detecting speculated lesions based on local edge characteristics and Laws texture features [10–12]. The above methods produced a true positive detection rate of approximately 90%. Our work proposes a segmentation process which identifies on a mammogram the opaque areas, suspect or not, present in the image using vector quantization.

Segmenting a mammographic image into homogeneous texture regions representing disparate tissue types is often a useful preprocessing step in the computer-assisted detection of breast cancer. Various segmentation techniques have been proposed based on statistically measurable features in the image [13–18]. Clustering algorithms, such as k-means and ISODATA, operate in an unsupervised mode and have been applied to a wide range of classification problems.

The choice of a particular technique depends on the application, on the nature of the images available (texture, ill-defined contours, shadows), on the primitives to be extracted (contours, straight segments, regions, shapes), the amount of available user time, and the required accuracy of the segmentation.

We are introducing vector quantization algorithm on entropy image which consumes moderate time but provides good accuracy with less complexity. The rest of the paper is organized as follows. Section II describes proposed algorithm used for image segmentation of mammographic images. Followed by the experimental results for mammographic images are in section III and section IV concludes the work.

2. Proposed algorithm for segmentation

In this proposed algorithm we use probability and entropy for grouping pixels into regions and then we form the images of probability and entropy and it is displayed here. For good image segmentation we equalized probability and entropy images by histogram equalization method and then we applied vector quantization for further segmentation.

S.J. Pise (ed.), *ThinkQuest 2010*, DOI 10.1007/978-81-8489-989-4_48,

2.1 Probability

For complete image we find out probability of particular i[th] gray level which is given by:

$$\text{Probability } P(i) = \frac{X_i}{MXN} \tag{1}$$

Where X_i is number of pixels for i[th] gray levels, M and N are no. of rows and columns of the image.

After calculating this we form the image which contains probability values for that particular gray level instead of gray level in the image and it is displayed as probability image as shown in Figure 2(b) for original image in Figure 2(a) and Figure 2(c) is histogram equalized probability image.

2.2 Entropy

Entropy allows us to consider the neighborhood of the pixel and hence more appropriately texture is considered. Entropy concept was introduced into communications theory by Shannon [19] following the rapid development of communications. It is used to measure the efficiency of the information transferred through a noisy communication channel. The mathematical definition of the entropy given by Shannon is:

$$H = -\sum_{i=1}^{n} P_i \log(P_i) \tag{2}$$

in which H is the entropy, P_i is the probability of the event i. It defines the average amount of information output of the source generating n symbols. As its magnitude increases, more uncertainty and thus more information is associated with the source. If the source symbols are equally probable, the entropy or uncertainty of Equation 2 is maximized and the source provides the greatest possible average information per source symbol. In this paper we used probability image as an input to find entropy. Here we need to select analyzing window size to find entropy for neighborhood of each pixel in the input image. For this paper we used 3x3 and 5×5 window sizes for entropy. By moving analyzing window on complete image, calculating entropy for each window, we formed new entropy image by replacing the central pixel of the window by entropy and displayed as entropy image. Since these values are very small entropy images were histogram equalized and used for image segmentation as shown in Figure 2(e).

2.3 Vector quantization

Vector Quantization (VQ) [20-26] is an efficient technique for data compression and has been successfully used in various applications such as speech data compression [27], content based image retrieval CBIR [28]. VQ has been very popular in a variety of research fields such as speech recognition and face detection [29, 30]. VQ is also used in real time applications such as real time video-based event detec-

tion [31] and anomaly intrusion detection systems [32], image segmentation [33–36] and face recognition [37].

VQ is a technique in which a codebook is generated for each image. A codebook is a representation of the entire image containing a definite pixel pattern which is computed according to a specific VQ algorithm. The image is divided into fixed sized blocks that form the training vector. The generation of the training vector is the first step to cluster formation. On these training vectors clustering methods are applied and codebook is generated. The method most commonly used to generate codebook is the Linde Buzo Gray (LBG) algorithm [38].

2.1.1 Linde Buzo and Gray Algorithm (LBG)

For the purpose of explaining this algorithm, we are consider two dimensional vector space as shown in Figure 1. In this algorithm centroid is computed as the first codevector C1 for the training set. In Figure 1 two vectors v1 & v2 are generated by adding constant error to the codevector C1. Euclidean distances of all the training vectors are computed with vectors v1 & v2 and two clusters are formed based on nearest of v1 or v2. Procedure is repeated for these two clusters to generate four new clusters. This procedure is repeated for every new cluster until the required size of codebook is reached or specified MSE is reached.

Using this algorithm initially a codebook of size 128 was generated for the given images. These code-vectors were further clustered in 8 clusters using same LBG algorithm. The 8 images were constructed using one code-vector at a time. These 8 images display different segments depending on the textural property of the image. It is observed that the image constructed using first code vector displays enhancing tumor ring clearly.

3. Results

Mammography images from mini-mias database were used in this paper for implementation of GLCM, Watershed and LBG algorithm using entropy image for tumor demarcation. Fig.2(a) shows original image with tumor. It has fatty tissues as background. Class of abnormality present is CIRC which means well-defined/ circumscribed mass. This image has malignant abnormality. Location of the center of abnormality is (338,314) for x,y image co- ordinates. Approximate radius is 56 (in pixels) of a circle enclosing

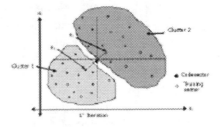

Fig. 1   LBG for 2 dimensional case

the tumor. Proposed algorithm is tested on thirty mammographic images which consist of micro calcification with specific tumors.

Probability for the image is shown in Figure 2(b). We can differentiate between normal and abnormal masses in Figure 2(c) which is for histogram equalized probability. Figure 2(d) is entropy image by considering probability image as input. Figure 2(e) is of histogram equalized entropy image. Vector quantization is used for further segmentation. By this method we achieved proper segmentation of different masses where we can separate out tumor very easily even with small variation in tumor areas. The segmentation thus obtained is comparatively better than the other normal methods. The validation of the work has been done by visual inspection of the segmented images by an expert Radiologist. Images were tested for analyzing window size of 3×3 and 5×5. Results for window size 3x3 are displayed in this paper.

For equalized entropy image we generated codebook of size 128 using LBG algorithm. Further these code-vectors were clustered in 8 clusters using same algorithm. Then 8 images were constructed using one code-vector at a time as shown in Figure 3(a)-(g) for LBG algorithm. Image for first codevector is not shown here since it does not have any information. To locate the tumor it is necessary to find the boundaries and the center point co-ordinates in pixels using standard x, y co-ordinate system for images. Hence, we found the max and min values for the boundaries as obtained by using these algorithms. The results obtained are given in Table1.

4. Conclusions

In this paper we have used vector quantization which is commonly used for data compression. Basically vector quantization is a clustering algorithm and can be used for

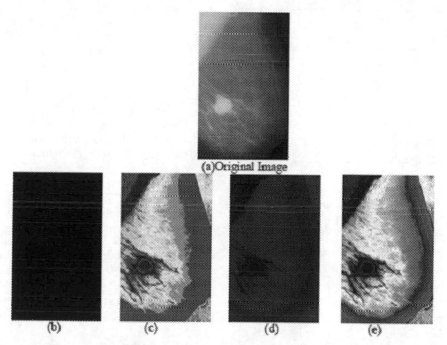

Fig. 2 (a) Original breast image, (b) Direct probability image, (c) Histogram equalized image for (b), (d) Direct Entropy image for window size(3×3), (e) Histogram equalized image for (d).

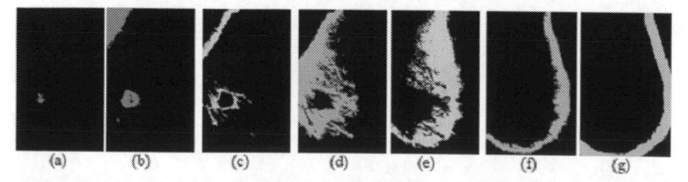

Fig. 3 (a) Image for second code-vector, (b) Image for third code-vector, (c) Image for fourth code-vector, (d) Image for fifth code-vector, (e) Image for sixth code-vector, (f) Image for seventh code-vector, (g) Image for eighth code-vector

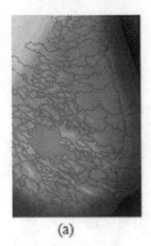 

Fig. 4   (a) Segmented image using watershed algorithm, (b) Segmented image using proposed algorithm.

Table 1   Co-ordinates of boundary and center point

Co- ordinates	Name of the algorithm		
	GLCM	Watershed	LBG
Xmax	383	468	361
Xmin	287	255	322
Ymax	374	300	348
Ymin	278	220	293
Xc	335	462	341
Yc	326	260	320

texture analysis. Here we are using equalized entropy image as input for LBG algorithm. The results are compared with well known Watershed, GLCM and LBG algorithm. Second codevector as shown in Figure 3(a) gives more detailed tissue variations in tumor area which we cannot achieve by using only vector quantization for tumor demarcation. From table 1 it is observed that LBG for entropy image gives more accurate results than Watershed and GLCM if we compare these center points with original center points (338,318) for the particular image. This method does not lead to over segmentation or under segmentation image for tumor demarcation.

References

1. E. E. Sterns, "Relation between clinical and mammographic diagnosis of breast problems and the cancer/ biopsy rate". Can. J. Surg., vol. 39, no. 2, pp. 128-132, 1996
2. R. Highnam and M. Brady, Mammographic Image Analysis, Kluwer Academic Publishers, 1999. ISBN: 0-7923- 5620-9
3. Matthew A. Kupinski and Maryellen L. Giger, "Automated Seeded Lesion Segmentation". IEEE Transaction on medical imaging, Vol. 17, No. 4, August 1998
4. Wirth, M.A. Stapinski, A., "Segmentation of the breast region in mammograms using active contours", in Visual Communications and Image Processing, Switzerland, 2003, Vol. 5150, pp. 1995-2006
5. S. M. Lai, X. Li, and W. F. Bischof, "On techniques for detecting circumscribed masses in mammograms". ZEEE Trans. Med. Zmag., vol. 8, no. 4, pp. 377-386, Dec. 1989
6. W. Qian, L. P. Clarke, M. Kallergi, and R. A. Clark,. Treestructured nonlinear filters in digital mammography, IEEE Trans. Med. Imag., vol.13, no. 1, pp. 25-36, Mar. 1994
7. D. Brzakovic, X. M. Luo, and P. lBzrakovic, "An approach to automated detection of tumors in mammography", IEEE Trans. Med. Imag., vol. 9, no. 3, pp. 233-241, Sept. 1990
8. F. F. Yin, M. L. Giger, K. Dol, C. E. Metz, R. A. Vyborny, and C. J. Schmidt, "Computerized detection of masses in digital mammograms: Analysis of bilateral subtraction images", Med. Phys., vol. 18, no. 5, pp. 955-963, Sept. 1991
9. T. K. Lau and W. F. Bischof, "Automated detection of breast tumors using the asymmetry approach". Comput. Biomed. Res., vol. 24, pp.273-295, 1991
10. W. P. Kegelmeyer Jr., J. M. Pruneda, P. D. Bourland, A. Hillis, M. W. Riggs, and M. L. Nipper,. "Computer-aided mammographic screening for speculated lesions", Radiol., vol. 191, no. 2, pp. 331-337, May 1994
11. D. Marr and E. Hildreth, "Theory of edge detection", In Proceeding Royal Society, London., vol. 207, pp. 187-217, 1980
12. J. Lunscher and M. P. Beddoes, "Optimal edge detector design: Parameter selection and noise effects", IEEE Trans. Pattem Anal. Machine Intell., vol. 8, no. 2, pp. 154- 176, Mar. 1986
13. Dr. H. B. Kekre, Saylee Gharge, "Segmentation of MRI Images using Probability and Entropy as Statistical parameters for Texture analysis", Advances in Computational sciences and Technology(ACST),Volume 2,No.2, pp 219-230,2009
14. Dr. H. B. Kekre, Saylee Gharge, "Selection of Window Size for Image Segmentation using Texture Features", International Conference on Advanced Computing &Communication Technologies(ICACCT-2008) Asia Pacific Institute of Information Technology SD India, Panipat, 08-09 November, 2008
15. Dr. H. B. Kekre, Saylee Gharge, "Image Segmentation of MRI using Texture Features",International Conference on Managing Next Generation Software Applications, School

of Science and Humanities, Karunya University, Coimbatore, Tamilnadu, 05-06 December, 2008

16. Dr. H. B. Kekre, Saylee Gharge,. "Statistical Parameters like Probability and Entropy applied to SAR image segmentation", International Journal of Engineering Research & Industry Applications (IJERIA), Vol.2,No.IV, pp.341-353

17. Dr. H. B. Kekre, Saylee Gharge, "SAR Image Segmentation using co-occurrence matrix and slope magnitude", ACM International Conference on Advances in Computing, Communication & Control (ICAC3-2009), pp.: 357-362, 23-24 Jan 2009, Fr. Conceicao Rodrigous College of Engg. Available on ACM portal

18. Dr. H. B. Kekre, Tanuja K. Sarode, Saylee Gharge,. "Detection and Demarcation of Tumor using Vector Quantization in MRI Images". International Journal of Engineering Science and Technology(IJEST),Volume 2,No.2,pp:59-66,2009

19. C.E. Shannon, "A Mathematical Theory of Communication", Bell System Technical Journal, vol.27, pp.379-423, 623- 656, July, October, 1948

20. H.B.Kekre, Tanuja K. Sarode, "New Fast Improved Clustering Algorithm for Codebook Generation for Vector Quantization", International Conference on Engineering Technologies and Applications in Engineering, Technology and Sciences, Computer Science Department, Saurashtra University, Rajkot, Gujarat. (India), Amoghsiddhi Education Society, Sangli, Maharashtra (India), 13th. 14th January 2008

21. H. B. Kekre, Tanuja K. Sarode, "New Fast Improved Codebook Generation Algorithm for Color Images using Vector Quantization", International Journal of Engineering and Technology, vol.1, No.1, pp.: 67-77, September 2008

22. H. B. Kekre, Tanuja K. Sarode, "Fast Codebook Generation Algorithm for Color Images using Vector Quantization". International Journal of Computer Science and Information Technology, Vol. 1, No. 1, pp.: 7-12, Jan 2009

23. H. B. Kekre, Tanuja K. Sarode, "An Efficient Fast Algorithm to Generate Codebook for Vector Quantization". First International Conference on Emerging Trends in Engineering and Technology, ICETET-2008, held at Raisoni College of Engineering, Nagpur, India, pp.: 62- 67, 16-18 July 2008. Avaliable at IEEE Xplore

24. H. B. Kekre, Tanuja K. Sarode, "Fast Codebook Generation Algorithm for Color Images using Vector Quantization". International Journal of Computer Science and Information Technology, Vol. 1, No. 1, pp.: 7-12, Jan 2009

25. H. B. Kekre, Tanuja K. Sarode, "Fast Codevector Search Algorithm for 3-D Vector Quantized Codebook", WASET International Journal of cal Computer Information Science and Engineering (IJCISE), Volume 2, No. 4, pp.: 235-239, Fall 2008

26. H. B. Kekre, Tanuja K. Sarode, "Fast Codebook Search Algorithm for Vector Quantization using Sorting Technique", ACM International Conference on Advances in Computing, Communication and Control (ICAC3- 2009), pp: 317-325, 23-24 Jan 2009, Fr. Conceicao Rodrigous College of Engg., Mumbai. Available on ACM portal

27. H. B. Kekre, Tanuja K. Sarode, "Speech Data Compression using Vector Quantization", WASET International Journal of Computer and Information Science and Engineering (IJCISE), vol., No. 4, pp.: 251-254, Fall 2008. available: http://www.waset.org/ijcise

28. H. B. Kekre, Ms. Tanuja K. Sarode, Sudeep D. Thepade, "Image Retrieval using Color-Texture Features from DCT on VQ Codevectors obtained by Kekre.s Fast Codebook Generation", ICGST-International Journal on Graphics, Vision and Image Processing (GVIP), Volume 9, Issue 5, pp.: 1-8, September 2009. Available online at http://www.icgst.com/gvip/Volume9/Issue5/P1150921752. html

29. Chin-Chen Chang, Wen-Chuan Wu, "Fast Planar-Oriented Ripple Search Algorithm for Hyperspace VQ Codebook", IEEE Transaction on image processing, vol 16, no. 6, pp.: 1538-1547, June 2007

30. C. Garcia and G. Tziritas, "Face detection using quantized skin color regions merging and wavelet packet analysis," IEEE Trans. Multimedia, vol. 1, no. 3, pp.: 264.277, Sep. 1999

31. H. Y. M. Liao, D. Y. Chen, C. W. Su, and H. R. Tyan, "Realtime event detection and its applications to surveillance systems,. in Proc. IEEE Int. Symp. Circuits and Systems", Kos, Greece, pp.: 509.512, May 2006

32. J. Zheng and M. Hu, "An anomaly intrusion detection system based on vector quantization". IEICE Trans. Inf. Syst., vol. E89-D, no. 1, pp.: 201.210, Jan. 2006

33. H. B. Kekre, Tanuja K. Sarode, Bhakti Raul, "Color Image Segmentation using Kekre.s Fast Codebook Generation Algorithm Based on Energy Ordering Concept", ACM International Conference on Advances in Computing, Communication and Control (ICAC3-2009), pp.: 357-362, 23-24 Jan 2009, Fr. Conceicao Rodrigous College of Engg., Mumbai. Available on ACM portal

34. H. B. Kekre, Tanuja K. Sarode, Bhakti Raul, "Color Image Segmentation using Kekre.s Algorithm for Vector Quantization", International Journal of Computer Science (IJCS), Vol. 3, No. 4, pp.: 287-292, Fall 2008. Available: http://www.waset.org/ijcs

35. H. B. Kekre, Tanuja K. Sarode, Bhakti Raul,. Color Image Segmentation using Vector Quantization Techniques Based on Energy Ordering Concept. International Journal of Computing Science and Communication Technologies (IJCSCT) Volume 1, Issue 2, pp: 164-171, January 2009

36. H. B. Kekre, Tanuja K. Sarode, Bhakti Raul,. Color Image Segmentation Using Vector Quantization Techniques., Advances in Engineering Science Sect. C (3), pp.: 35-42, July-September 2008

37. H. B. Kekre, Kamal Shah, Tanuja K. Sarode, Sudeep D. Thepade,. Performance Comparison of Vector Quantization Technique. KFCG with LBG, Existing Transforms and PCA for Face Recognition., International Journal of Information Retrieval (IJIR), Vol. 02, Issue 1, pp.: 64-71, 2009

38. Tou, J., and Gonzalez, Pattern Recognition Principles Addison-Wesley Publishing Company 1974

Palmprint recognition using wavelet

Uma Biradar[1] · Smita Jangle[2] · Manisha Dale[3] · M. A. Joshi[4]

[1](M.E. student)Vivekanand Institute of Technology, Mumbai, India
[2]Assiatant Professor in Vivekanand Institute of Technology, Mumbai, India
[3]Assistant Professor in Modern College of Engineering, Pune, India
[4]Professor in Department of Electronics & Telecommunication, COEP, Pune, India

1. Introduction

Palmprint is a relatively new biometric feature, and is regarded as one of the most unique, reliable, and stable personal characteristics. A palm is an inner surface of the hand between the wrist and the fingers [1]. Palm has several features to be extracted like principal lines, wrinkles, ridges, singular points, texture and minutiae. Principal lines are the darker line present on the palm. There are 3 principal lines on the palm namely, heart line, head line and life line. Wrinkles are the thinner lines concentrated all over the palm. Normally people do not feel uneasy to have their palmprint images taken for testing. On palms lines and textures are more clearly observable features. Lines are more appealing than texture for human vision. When human beings compare two palmprint images, they instinctively compare line features. But extracting principle lines and creases is not an easy task because it is sometimes difficult to extract the line structures that can discriminate every individual well. Besides, creases and ridges on the palm are always crossing and overlapping each other, which complicates the feature extraction task. In this paper, a feature based on Wavelet Transform (WT) is proposed. As we know palmprint is rich of texture information, this pattern of texture offers stable, unique and repeatable features for personal identification. The paper is organized in following sections. Section 2 explains the cropping of the central part of the palmprint images. Section 3 highlights the proposed algorithm and matching. Section 4 reports experimental results. Section 5 summarizes the results and offers concluding remark.

2. Palmprint cropping

In the proposed approach, the global palmprint texture features are extracted for matching. To test the proposed approach,Poly U palmprint database is used [6]. It is important to define a co-ordinate system that is used to align different palmprint images for matching. To extract the central part of the palmprint, for reliable feature extraction, the corner points near the wrist are used as reference points to determine a co-ordinate system (see Fig 1). Following major steps are used for obtaining central part of palm.

Step 1: A low pass averaging filter is used, to smooth the original image. A threshold is used to convert the convolved image to binary image, as shown in Fig. 1(b) and 1(c).

Step 2: Obtain the boundaries of the binary Palmprint image and the two corner points near the wrist are marked [5] as shown in Fig. 1(d).

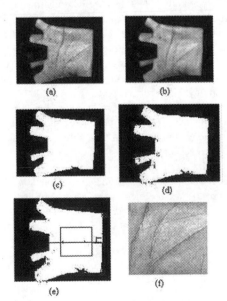

Fig. 1 Region of interest from palmprint (a) Original image (b) Filtered image (c) Binary image (d) Corner detected image (e) Locating area of interest (f) Region of interest

S.J. Pise (ed.), *ThinkQuest 2010*, DOI 10.1007/978-81-8489-989-4_49,
© Springer India Pvt. Ltd. 2011

Step 3: Join those two corner points which gives Y axis of Palmprint coordinate system and use a line passing through the mid point of these points, which is perpendicular to Y axis to determine the origin of the co-ordinate system as shown in Fig. 1(e).

Step 4: Extract the sub image of fixed size (128×128) based on co-ordinate system as shown in Fig. 1(f).

3.   Feature extraction using Wavelet Transform

Feature extraction is to describe a palmprint using wavelet transform. The DWT was applied for different applications given in the literature e.g. texture classification [2], image compression [3], face recognition [4][8], because of its powerful capability for multiresolution decomposition analysis. The wavelet transforms breaks an image down into four sub-sampled, or decimated, images. They are sub sampled by keeping every other pixel. The result consists of one image that has been high pass filtered in both the horizontal and vertical directions. Other one that has been high pass filtered in the vertical and low pass filtered in the hori zontal direction, one that has been low passed in the vertical and high passed in the horizontal, and one that has been low pass filtered in both the direction. So, the wavelet transform is created by passing the image through a series of 2D filter bank stages. One shown in figure (2) in which an image is first filtered in the horizontal direction. The filtered outputs are then down sampled by a factor of 2 in the horizontal direction. An identical filter pair in the vertical direction then filters each these signals. Decomposed image into 4 sub bands is also shown in Fig. 2. Here, H and L represent the high pass and low pass filters, respectively, and ↓ 2 denotes the sub sampling by 2. Second-level decomposition can then be conducted on the LL sub band. Second-level structure of wavelet decomposition of an image is also shown in Fig. 2. This decomposition can be repeated for n-levels.

The proposed work based on the DWT addresses the three level decomposition of image in Database. Daubechies-4, -8 and -9 and Symlets -8 and -9 low pass and high pass filters are also implemented [7]. Additionally 64 × 64 resized image and 32 × 32 sub-images of 128 × 128 images is processed by wavelet to find useful features

in the palmprint images. Reducing the image resolution helps to decrease the computation load of the feature extraction process. The palmprint database is used in this work is the PolyU Palmprint Database [6]. Total 1000 grayscale images of 100 different palms are selected to test the proposed algorithm. The original size of the images is 384 by 284 pixels from which region of interest is extracted as explained in section 2. In this work, we are proposing three approaches.

1st. The cropped image size is 128x128. The algorithm first divides the image into four non-overlapping parts around center point as shown in Fig. 3 (a). The DWT decomposition is carried out up to three levels for each sub image. The nine detailed coefficient bands (except the LL3 band) is used for feature extraction. as shown in Fig. 3 (b).

For each block, the standard deviation or energy is calculated for all detailed bands except LL3 band. Thus, total 36 features vector is calculated for each of the method. Such features are calculated from sub images and feature vector of 36 (4×9=36) which is used in enrollment as well as matching phase. These are stored as float values so take 144 bytes (36×4) are used to store the feature vector for one person. The feature vector database is created using k palmprint images where k varies from 1 to 10. When more than one image is used for training set to create database feature vector the average value of respective standard deviation is taken as final feature vector.

2nd. In the second approach algorithm divides 128×128 images into equal 16 part of size 32×32.

The DWT decomposition is carried out up to three levels for each sub image. The nine detailed coefficient bands (except the LL3 band) is used for feature extraction. as shown in Fig. 3 (b).

For each block, the standard deviation or energy is calculated for all detailed bands except LL3 band. Thus, total 144 features vector is obtained for each of the method. Such features are calculated from sub images and feature vector of 144 (16×9=144) is used in enrollment as well as matching phase. These are stored as float values so take 576 bytes (144×4) to store the feature vector for one person

3rd. In the third approach algorithm resize the image to 64×64 sizes and divide it into four parts. The feature vector is calculated as like approach 1.

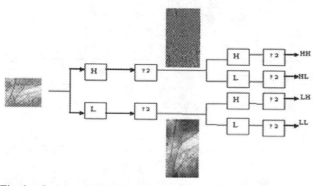

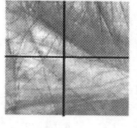

(a)

Fig. 2   One-level 2-D filter bank for wavelet decomposition and multi-resolutionstructure of wavelet decompositionof an image

Fig. 3   (a) ROI in four parts (b) Arrangement of sub image wavelet co-efficient

The algorithm is checked in identification mode, by comparing remaining images from the database against feature vector created for all. Thus, total number of images used for training and testing are given in Result Table. Once standard deviation feature vector for testing image is calculated, it is compared with all database feature vector on one to one basis. Canberra distance and Euclidean distance given in equation (1) and equation (2) is used to find out the minimum distance match between two dimensional feature vectors of database image and query (test) image.

4. Experimental settings and results

The database is created using k fingerprint images where k varies from 1 to 8. When more than one image is used as training set to create database feature vector the average value of respective standard deviation is taken as final feature vector. The algorithm is checked in identification mode, by comparing remaining images from the database against feature vector created for all. Thus total number of images used for training and testing are given in Table 1. Once standard deviation feature vector (36) for testing image is calculated it is compared with all database feature vector on one to one basis. Canberra distance is used to find out the minimum distance match between two dimensional feature vectors of database image and query (test) image. Table 2 shows the percentage Genuine Acceptance Rate for checking all testing images against the feature vector already created. The training set (TS) used is of 2, 4, 6 images per person. High recognition rates 97.5%, 98.5% and 96.5% were achieved for the 128X128, 32X32 and 64×64 image.

We adopted the statistical pair known as FRR and FAR to evaluate the performance of the experimental results. In the experiment, the threshold value was set to be Th.

Table 1   Number of Palmprint images for Training and Testing set

K	Training Set	Testing set
2	2×100=200	8×100=800
3	3×100=300	7×100=700
4	4×100=400	6×100=600
5	5×100=500	5×100=500
6	6×100=600	4×100=400

Table 2   %GAR with Canberra distance of 128×128 images

	Tr=2	Tr=3	Tr=4	Tr=5	Tr=6
db4	91.25	93.14	95.33	96.6	97.7
db8	92.87	95	96.5	97.4	98.2
db9	94.37	95.57	96.66	98	98.5
Sym8	88.5	91.71	95.16	96.8	97.5
Sym9	83.75	87.42	90.33	92.6	94.2

Table 3   % GAR with Canberra distance of 32×32 images.

	Tr=2	Tr=3	Tr=4	Tr=5	Tr=6
db4	94.2	94.2	96.3	97.4	98.5
db8	94.2	95.1	97.1	98	98.2
db9	94.1	95.4	97.8	98.2	98.5
Sym8	93	94.7	96.8	97.2	97.2
Sym9	91.5	93.8	95.6	96.4	97.2

Table 4   %GAR with Canberra distance of Resized   image (64×64)

	Tr=2	Tr=3	Tr=4	Tr=5	Tr=6
db4	81.5	85.8	88	91.4	93
db8	88.2	90.8	91.5	93.6	95.7
db9	89.8	92.7	93.8	94.6	96.5
Sym8	80.5	83.8	88.3	92	94.2
Sym9	76.3	80.4	85.6	90.6	93

Table 5   Imposter analysis of 128×128 images using db9 (TR-6, TES-4)

Th	GAR	FAR	FRR	GRR
1.3	69.375	0.25	30.625	98.75
1.5	83.125	0.5	16.562	83.75
1.8	94.062	4	5	83.75
2	96.562	8.25	2.1875	63.75
2.2	97.5	11.5	0.937	48.75
2.4	97.5	15.75	0.937	27.5
2.6	97.5	18.25	0.937	15
2.8	97.437	19	0	11.25
3	98.437	20.25	0	5

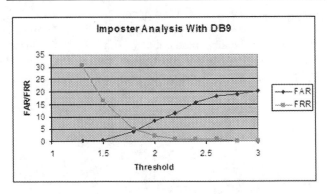

5. Conclusion

If the training set of images is taken more the recognition rate is increased.

1. The recognition rate is good for Daubechies–9 wavelet. The recognition rate is more for Canberra distance than Euclidean distance.
2. The recognition rate for Bio-orthogonal-5.5 wavelet is more than other Bioorhogonal wavelet. It is 93.5% when training of 6 images is taken.

3. When the combination of Db-9 and Bior-5.5 is taken then recognition result goes to 98.50%. The recognition rate is good when salt & paper noise is added to the images.

4. The recognition rate is less when Gaussian noise is added to the images. Here more preprocessing is required.

5. When the level of decomposition is increased the recognition rate is also increased.

References

1. X. Wu, David Zhang, K. Wang, Bo Huang.: Palmprint classification using principal lines, Pattern Recognition 37, 2004, pp.1987- 1998

2. Chang, T. Kuo C.J.: Texture Analysis and Classification with Tree-Structured Wavelet Transform. IEEE Transactions on Image Processing 2(4), 429–441 (1993)

3. Averbuch, A. Lazar, D. Israeli, M.: Image Compression Using Wavelet Transform and Multiresolution Decomposition. IEEE Trans. Image Processing 5(1), 4–15 (1996)

4. Zhang, B., Zhang, H. Sam, S.: Face Recognition by Applying Wavelet Subband Representation and Kernel Associative Memory. IEEE Trans. on Neural Networks 15(1), 166–177 (2004)

5. X.C. He and N.H.C. Yung. : Curvature Scale Space Corner Detector with Adaptive Threshold and Dynamic Region of Support", Proceedings of the 17th International Conference on Pattern Recognition, 2:791-794, August 2004

6. PolyU Palmprint Database.: http://www.comp.polyu.edu.hk/~biometrics/

7. Daubechies, I.: Ten Lectures on Wavelets. Philadelphia. SIAM, PA (1992)

8. Chien, J., Wu, C.C.: Discriminant Wavelet faces and Nearest Feature Classifier for Face Recognition. IEEE Trans. on Pattern Analysis and Machine Intelligence 24(12), 1644–1649 (2002)

Wavelet based scalable video codec

Ramesh Prasad[1] · **Prof. N. S. Killarikar[1]** · **Prof. Suresh B. Mer[2]**

[1]Terna Engineering College, Mumbai, India
[2]H.O.D. (E&TC), BGIT, Mumbai, India

1. Introduction

With the increase in network speeds for both wired and wireless networks, video streaming has become a reality. But different networks are characterized by different network speeds and latency. Also different kinds of devices are used with different networks. These devices range from Desktop/Laptop computers with very high resolution and very high processing power to Mobile Phones with small displays, low processing power and limited battery life. A single common non-scalable video feed for all these different profiles of networks and devices is impractical as streaming a high quality feed may not be possible over GPRS type of networks and streaming a low quality feed may not be visually acceptable to a user with high network bandwidth and high resolution display. To overcome this problem multiple video feeds are used, each catering to a different profile of users. Content creation process becomes complex as multiple files have to be created usually using a different codec and file format. Deployment involves replication of hardware and software infrastructure and associated overhead of maintenance, hence increased cost.

It is desirable to have a scalable bit stream in such scenarios. A scalable video stream has multiple bit streams embedded within the same bit stream. Each bit stream could represent a lower resolution, quality, frame rate or a combination of all the three, than the main bit stream from which it is derived. Hence we get the following types of scalability:

1. Spatial Scalability: video is coded at multiple spatial resolutions. The data and decoded samples of lower resolutions can be used to predict data or samples of higher resolutions in order to reduce the bit rate to code the higher resolutions.
2. Temporal Scalability: video is coded such that it can be decoded at different frame rates. The motion estimation and compensation has to be restructured to support this.
3. SNR/Quality/Fidelity scalability: video is coded at a single spatial resolution but at different qualities.

The data and decoded samples of lower qualities can be used to predict data or samples of higher qualities in order to reduce the bit rate to code the higher qualities.

4 Combined scalability: a combination of the three scalability modes described above.

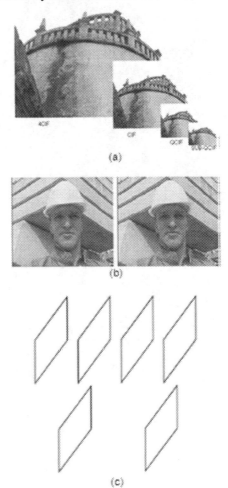

Fig. 1 Types of scalability: (a) Spatial scalability, (b) SNR scalability, (c) Temporal scalability

S.J. Pise (ed.), *ThinkQuest 2010*, DOI 10.1007/978-81-8489-989-4_50,

2. Applications

This section discusses some of the applications in which SVC is useful.

2.1 Video transmission

The hierarchical scalable video coding approach in general allows the split of the bit-stream into a base layer and various enhancement layers. That allows the transmission of these partial bit-streams via different channels or in different network streams. In IP networks the different quality classes can be assigned to one or even more consumed network streams, thus a possible billing depending on network streams is guaranteed. Such network types could be DVB-H or MBMS of 3GPP, with different terminal capability classes.

The layered coding approach has further benefits. If the network supports transmission of certain network streams to certain devices only, not even all streams have to be received by all terminals. In MBMS or DVB-H networks it should be possible to send out, e.g., the base layer of a scalable H.264/AVC stream to the low performance device only and guarantee that all layers of the stream reach the high performance terminal only.

Another benefit can be achieved, if the protection of the scalable layers is treated in different ways. Forward error correction (FEC) is often used to protect data sent out via wireless broadcast channels. Unequal error or erasure protection schemes can be used to ensure an error free transmission of important layers like, e.g., the base layer of a scalable H.264/AVC stream. Unequal error or erasure protection can be used on top of the already existing channel FEC. Such a scheme can guarantee a basic video quality over a large range of channel error rates.

2.2 Video surveillance

A very promising application of scalable coding is video surveillance. Typically videos from many cameras have to be stored and viewed on diverse displays, which may have different spatial and temporal resolutions. Examples are split screen display of many scenes on one monitor or viewing of scenes from dedicated cameras on mobile devices such as video phones or PDAs. For such applications scalable coding is most attractive, because no transcoding or format conversion is required. Decoding of the lower resolutions videos for split-screen display also saves computing power; therefore many videos can be decoded and displayed with the computing power required for one full resolution video.

In general, the requirements for surveillance applications can be summarized as follows:

- Simultaneous transmission and storage of different spatial and temporal resolutions in one bit stream, in order to feed different displays.

- Fine granularity scalability for feeding different transmission links of varying capacity.

- Decoding of lower resolutions should be less complex for split screen display.

- Multiple adaptation of the bit stream should be possible for erosion storage.

- The latter requirement arises from the necessity to store a huge amount of data delivered by the surveillance cameras. By using scalable coding it becomes possible to delete higher resolution layers of stored scenes after certain expiration times and to keep just a lower resolution copy for the archive. This allows a much more flexible usage of storage capacity without the necessity for re-encoding and copying. Typically the full resolution video is kept for 1-3 days, a medium quality (reduced temporal or spatial resolution) video is kept for one week and a low quality (reduced temporal and spatial resolution) video is kept for long time archiving.

2.3 Movie on chip

Nowadays the use of external memory card has increased a lot due to falling prices and support by large number of mobile handsets. This creates a Business opportunity for content providers to reach out to a large number of customers for distribution of content preloaded onto a Memory card. Content like audio and video, which have large file sizes, have restriction on distribution via traditional means like Internet etc. This restricts the reach of this type of content. This restriction is overcome by preloading the content onto the memory card and selling these cards via retail outlets just like CD/DVDs. A consumer spending money for buying a movie would want to use it for PC and home theater as well. But a movie created for mobile doesn't give the same user experience as a DVD. This problem can be solved by using scalable video coding. The video on the memory chip would contain video at different scales for viewing on mobile handset as well as PC/Home Theater, thus making it more attractive for the consumer.

3. Wavelets and its advantages

It has been well documented in the literature that wavelet encoding is superior to the DCT method of encoding that's at the heart of MPEG codecs. In DCT based codecs, the frame is divided into blocks of size 8x8 on which DCT is performed. This leads to blocking artifacts in the reconstructed image. Also since it works at block level, it cannot remove the redundancies across the blocks. Wavelet, on other hand works on the entire image; hence it doesn't have any blocking artifacts and has better de-correlation (redundancy removal) property leading to higher compression. Also it has inherent scalability which makes it desirable for many applications.

The two-dimensional extension of DWT is essential for transformation of two dimensional signals, such as a digital image. A two-dimensional digital signal can be represented by a two-dimensional array X [M ,N] with M rows and N columns, where M and N are nonnegative integers. The simple approach for two-dimensional implementation of the DWT is to perform the one-dimensional DWT row-wise to produce an intermediate result and then perform the same one-dimensional DWT column-wise on this intermediate result to produce the final result. This is possible because the two-dimensional scaling functions can be expressed as separable functions which are the product of two one-dimensional scaling functions such as $z(x,y) = l(z)l(y)$. The same is true for the wavelet function (z,y) as well. Applying the one-dimensional transform in each row, we produce two subbands in each row. When the low-frequency subbands of all the rows (L) are put together, it looks like a thin version (of size M x $) of the input signal. Similarly we put together the high-frequency subbands of all the rows to produce the H subband of size M x $, which contains mainly the high-frequency information around discontinuities (edges in an image) in the input signal. Then applying a one-dimensional DWT column-wise on these L and H subbands (intermediate result), we produce four subbands LL, LH, HL, and HH of size × $ respectively. LL is a coarser version of the original input signal. LH, HL, and HH are the high-frequency subband containing the detail information. It should be noted that we could have applied the one-dimensional DWT column-wise first and then row-wise to achieve the same result.

3.1 Video codec architecture

The figure below shows the block diagram of the video codec. Preprocessing and the Intercomponent blocks are not shown for simplicity. The video data has two types or redundancies, spatial and temporal. To remove the spatial redundancies, a transform based approach is used. To remove the temporal redundancies, we track the motion between the frames and code the difference between the frames. The predictive loop is required to track the decoder

because losses are introduced in the coded frame because of quantization.

3.2 Inter component transform

Inter-component transform map the RGB color space to the YCbCr/YUV color space. This transformation helps in following two ways to improve compression

- De-correlation between the color components.
- Reasonable color space with respect to the Human Visual System for quantization.

3.3 Motion estimation and compensation

The frame to be coded is divided into blocks of size 16x16. These blocks are searched in the previously reconstructed frame. This search is restricted within a window of 15 pixels, surrounding the block. The objective of the search is to find out the best match for the block. The measure used for finding out the best match is Sum of Absolute Difference (SAD). SAD for a block is defined as –

$$SUM\ I = 1\ to\ b\ SUM\ j = 1\ to\ b\ ABS(Xij - Yij)$$

The value of i, j which gives the minimum SAD value is chosen as the best match and the coordinate i, j is referred to as Motion Vectors.

To handle the blocks at the boundary of the frame, the edges of the previously reconstructed frame is extended by 15 in all dimensions. This allows the motion vectors for the blocks at the boundary to point outside the frame boundary. This has the advantage that motion vectors at the boundary become coherent and can better track the motion at the frame boundaries.

The motion vectors computed by block search is then refined to half pixel accuracy. For that the reference frame is interpolated, using Bilinear interpolation, to twice its size. The 16×16 block is divided into four 8×8 blocks. The motion vectors computed for the 16×16 block are used as an initial estimate and they are refined by searching at the

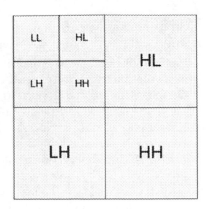

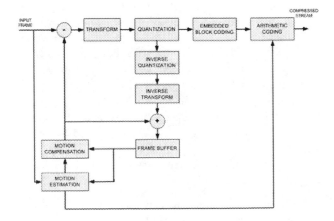

Fig. 2   Row column computation of two dimensional DWT

Fig. 3   Wavelet video codec

half pixel (interpolated) locations. The final motion vector is the sum of the motion vector for 16×16 blocks and the half pixel motion vector.

A rate distortion mechanism is used to select the modes for the blocks. The following are the possible modes-

- Not coded block
- 16×16 block
- Zero motion vector block
- 8×8 block

Once the mode is selected, a predicted frame is formed by using the motion vectors and the reference frame. To make the motion vectors coherent to reduce the discontinuities at the block boundaries, Overlapped Block Motion Compensation (OBMC) is used. In OBMC the motion vectors of the adjacent blocks, in addition to the motion vectors of the block, are used to fetch the pixels pointed by them, and combined using a weighting function (raised cosine function) to form the predicted frame. The predicted frame is subtracted from the current frame and the residual information is coded further.

3.4 Transform

The frame going to be coded is decomposed into number of subbands by applying the 2D Wavelet transform. To perform the forward DWT the standard uses a 1-D subband decomposition of a set of 1-D samples into low-pass samples and highpass samples. Low-pass samples represent a downsampled low-resolution version of the original set. High pass samples represent a downsampled residual version of the original set, needed for the perfect reconstruction of the original set from the low pass set.

The wavelet transform is implemented using the lifting scheme. Lifting scheme consists of a sequence of very simple filtering operations for which alternately odd sample values of the signal are updated with a weighted sum of even sample values, and the even sample values with a weighted sum of odd sample values.

3.5 Quantization

After transformation, the coefficients are quantized using a scalar quantizer with deadzone. Each subband can have a different quantization step size.

4. Embedded block coding

The subband structure decomposed in the Mallat structure is superimposed with a grid called as precincts. The origin of the precinct is anchored at the top left corner of the image and the dimensions of a precinct are powers of two. The grid of precincts is divided into a finer grid of codeblocks. The wavelet coefficients of a codeblock are arithmetically coded by bitplane. The coding is done from the most significant bitplane to the least significant bitplane. A context is determined for each bit, a probability is estimated from the context, and the bit and its probability are sent to the arithmetic coder.

Each wavelet coefficient has a 1-bit variable associated with it that indicates its significance. When the encoding of a codeblock starts, all its wavelet coefficients are considered insignificant and all significance states are cleared. There are three coding passes.

4.1 Significance propagation pass

This pass encodes all the bits that belong to wavelet coefficients satisfying the coefficient is insignificant at least one of its eight nearest neighbors is significant If a bit is encoded in this pass, and if the bit is 1, its wavelet coefficient is marked as significant by setting its significance state to 1. Subsequent bits encoded in this pass (and the following two passes) will consider this coefficient significant.

4.2 Magnitude refinement pass

In this pass, all bits of wavelet coefficients hat became significant in a previous bitplane.

4.3 Cleanup pass

This pass encodes all the bits not coded in the previous passes.

4.4 Arithmetic entropy coding

Arithmetic coding is used to code the bits generated by the embedded block coding process. It takes the bit to be coded and the context as input. The context allows the arithmetic coder to adapt to the probabilities to the bit stream, hence code it more efficiently.

5. Scalability

5.1 Temporal scalability

Temporal scalability with dyadic temporal enhancement layers can be very efficiently provided with the concept of hierarchical B. The enhancement layer pictures are typically coded as B pictures, where the reference picture lists 0 and 1 are restricted to the temporally preceding and succeeding picture, respectively, with a temporal layer identifier less than the temporal layer identifier of the predicted picture. Each set of temporal layers $\{T0,...,Tk\}$ can be decoded independently of all layers with a temporal layer identifier $T > k$. In the following, the set of pictures between two successive pictures of the temporal base layer together with the succeeding base layer picture is referred to as a group of pictures (GOP).

Hierarchical prediction structures for enabling temporal scalability can always be combined with the multiple reference picture concept. This means that the reference picture lists can be constructed by using more than one reference picture, and they can also include pictures with the same temporal level as the picture to be predicted. Furthermore, hierarchical prediction structures are not restricted to the dyadic case.

5.2   Spatial scalability

Spatial scalability is achieved by decomposing the original video into spatial pyramid. Each spatial layer is encoded independently. To remove the redundancy among the layers, texture prediction can come from any lower layers. Motion and residue information of the lower layers are reused for temporal prediction. Three types of inter-layer prediction are used-

5.3   Intra texture prediction

Intratexture prediction comes from a reconstructed block in the reference layer. Motion compensation is necessary when such a block is either an inter block or an intra predicted from its neighboring inter blocks. When multiple spatial layers are coded, such a process may be invoked multiple times leading to significant complexity. To reduce the complexity, constrained inter layer prediction is used to allow only intra texture prediction from an intra block at the reference layer. Moreover, the referred intra block can only be predicted from another intra block. In this way, the motion compensation is invoked only at the highest layer.

5.4   Motion prediction

Motion prediction is used to remove the redundancy of motion information, including macroblock partition, reference picture index, and motion vector, among layers. In addition to the macroblock modes available in described above, scalable video coding creates an additional mode, namely, the base layer mode, for the interlayer motion rediction. The base layer mode reuses the motion information of the reference layer without spending extra bits. If this mode is not selected, independent motion is encoded.

5.5   Residue prediction

Residue prediction is used to reduce the energy of residues after temporal prediction. The residue prediction is performed in the spatial domain. Due to the interlayer motion prediction, consecutive spatial layers may have similar motion information. Thus, the residues of the consecutive layers may exhibit strong correlations. However, it is also possible that consecutive layers have independent motion and thus residues of two consecutive layers become uncor-

related. Therefore, the residue prediction in SVC is done adaptively at macroblock level.

5.6   SNR/Rate scalability

Rate control is a process by which the bitrates (sometimes called coding rates) are allocated in each code-block in each subband in order to achieve the overall target encoding bitrate for the whole image while minimizing the distortion (errors) introduced in the reconstructed image due to quantization and truncation of codes to achieve the desired code rate. It can also be treated in another way. Given the allowed distortion in the MSE (mean square energy) sense, the rate control can dictate the optimum encoding rate while achieving the maximum given MSE.

6.   Conclusion

Wavelet transform as shown, provides inherent scalability due to its multiresolution nature. Exploiting this property makes it suitabl for a large number of applications where scalability is desired. Apart from scalability, it offers higher compression and lower artifacts as compared to the Block based codecs.

References

1.   D. Marpe, T. Wiegand, and G. J. Sullivan, "The H.264 / MPEG4 Advanced Video Coding standard and its applications", IEEE Communications Magazine, vol. 44, no. 8, pp. 134-144, Aug. 2006

2.   G. J. Sullivan, H. Yu, S. Sekiguchi, H. Sun, T. Wedi, S. Wittmann, Y.L. Lee, A. Segall, and T. Suzuki, "New standardized extensions of MPEG4-AVC/H.264 for professional-quality video applications", Proceedings of ICIP'07, San Antonio, TX, USA, Sep. 2007

3.   Heiko Schwarz, Detlev Marpe, Member, IEEE, and Thomas Wiegand, "Overview of the Scalable Video Coding Extension of the H.264/AVC Standard". IEEE Transactions on Circuits and Systems for Video Technology, September 2007

4.   T. Wiegand, G. J. Sullivan, J. Reichel, H. Schwarz, and M. Wien, eds.,"Joint Draft 11 of SVC Amendment", Joint Video Team, doc. JVTX201, Geneva, Switzerland, July 2007

5.   J. Reichel, H. Schwarz, M. Wien, eds., "Joint scalable video model 1 (JSVM 11)", Joint Video Team, doc. JVT-X202, Geneva, Switzerland, July 2007

6.   Charilaos Christopoulos, Athanassios Skodras and Touradj Ebrahimi, "The JPEG2000 still image coding system- An overview", IEEE Transactions on Consumer Electronics, Vol. 46, No. 4, pp. 1103-1127, November 2000

7.   Performance Optimization for Motion compensated 2D Wavelet video Compression Technique, Zen Li et al

Implementation of Lempel-Ziv algorithm for lossless compression using VHDL

Prof. Minaldevi K. Tank

HOD – Digital Electronics, Babasaheb Gawde Institute of Technology, Mumbai, India.

1. Introduction

In computer science and information theory, data compression or source coding is the process of encoding information using fewer bits than an unencoded representation would use, through use of specific encoding schemes. As with any communication, compressed data communication only works when both the sender and receiver of the information understand the encoding scheme. For example, this text makes sense only if the receiver understands that it is intended to be interpreted as characters representing the English language. Similarly, compressed data can only be understood if the decoding method is known by the receiver. Compression is useful because it helps reduce the consumption of expensive resources, such as hard disk space or transmission bandwidth. On the downside, compressed data must be decompressed to be used, and this extra processing may be detrimental to some applications. For instance, a compression scheme for video may require expensive hardware for the video to be decompressed fast enough to be viewed as its being decompressed (the option of decompressing the video in full before watching it may be inconvenient, and requires storage space for the decompressed video). The design of data compression schemes therefore involves trade-offs among various factors, including the degree of compression, the amount of distortion introduced (if using a lossy compression scheme), and the computational resources required to compress and uncompress the data.

2. What Is compression?

Data compression enables devices to transmit or store the same amount of data in fewer bits. The Compression is briefly classified in two types lossless and lossy compression

2.1 Lossless compression

Lossless compression algorithms usually exploit statistical redundancy in such a way as to represent the sender's data more concisely without error. Lossless compression is possible because most real-world data has statistical redundancy.

2.2 Lossy compression

It is also known as perceptual coding, it is possible if some loss of fidelity is acceptable. Generally, a lossy data compression will be guided by research on how people perceive the data in question. For example, the human eye is more sensitive to subtle variations in luminance than it is to variations in color. JPEG image compression works in part by "rounding off" some of this less-important information. Lossy data compression provides a way to obtain the best fidelity for a given amount of compression. In some cases, transparent (unnoticeable) compression is desired; in other cases, fidelity is sacrificed to reduce the amount of data as much as possible.

Lossless compression schemes are reversible so that the original data can be reconstructed, while lossy schemes accept some loss of data in order to achieve higher compression. However, lossless data compression algorithms will always fail to compress some files; indeed, any compression algorithm will necessarily fail to compress any data containing no discernible patterns. Attempts to compress data that has been compressed already will therefore usually result in an expansion, as will attempts to compress all but the most trivially encrypted data An example of lossless and lossy compression is the string: 25.888888888. This string can be compressed as: 25.[9]8. Interpreted as, "twenty five point 9 eights", the original string is perfectly

S.J. Pise (ed.), *ThinkQuest 2010*, DOI 10.1007/978-81-8489-989-4_51,

recreated, just written in a smaller form. In a lossy system, using 26 instead, the exact original data is lost, at the benefit of a smaller file size.

3. The Lempel-Ziv Algorithm

The Lempel-Ziv (LZ) compression methods are among the most popular algorithms for lossless storage.The Lempel-Ziv algorithms compress by building a dictionary of previously seen strings. Unlike PPM which uses the dictionary to predict the probability of each character, and codes each character separately based on the context, the Lempel-Ziv algorithms code groups of characters of varying lengths. The original algorithms also did not use probabilities strings were either in the dictionary or not and all strings in the dictionary were give equal probability. Some of the newer variants, such as gzip, do take some advantage of probabilities. At the highest level the algorithms can be described as follows. Given a position in a file, look through the preceeding part of the file to find the longest match to the string starting at the current position, and output some code that refers to that match. Now move the finger past the match. The two main variants of the algorithm were described by Ziv and Lempel in two separate papers in 1977 and 1978, and are often refered to as LZ77 and LZ78. The algorithms differ in how far back they search and how they find matches. The LZ77 algorithm is based on the idea of a sliding window. The algorithm only looks for matches in a window a fixed distance back from the current position. Gzip, ZIP, and V.42b is (a standard modem protocal) are all based on LZ77. TheLZ78 algorithm is based on a more conservative approach to adding strings to the dictionary. Unixcompress, and the Gif format are both based on LZ78.

4. Why VHDL?

4.1 Using the same language it is possible to simulate as well as design a complex logic.

4.2 Design reuse is possible

4.3 Design can be described at various levels of abstractions.

4.4 It provides for modular design and testing.

4.5 The use of VHDL has tremendously reduced the "Time to Market "for large and small design.

4.6 VHDL designs are portable across synthesis across synthesis and simulation tools, which adhere to the IEEE 1076 standard.

4.7 Using VHDL makes the design device independent.

4.8 The design description can be targeted to PLD, ASIC, FPGA very easily.

4.9 Designer has very little control at gate level.

4.10 The logic generated for the same description may vary from tool to tool. This may be due to algorithm used by the tools, which might be proprietary.

5. Lempel-Ziv-Welch

LZW (Lempel-Ziv-Welch) is the one that is most commonly used in practice. The algorithm is used to encode byte streams (*i.e.*, each message is a byte). The algorithm maintains a dictionary of strings (sequences of bytes). The dictionary is initialized with one entry for each of the 256 possible byte values—these are strings of length one. As the algorithm progresses it will add new strings to the dictionary such that each string is only added if a prefix one byte shorter is already in the dictionary. For example, John is only added if Joh had previously appeared in the message sequence. Each entry of the dictionary is given an index, where these indices are typically given out incrementally starting at 256.

6. LZ78 encoding and decoding.

The basic idea is to parse the input sequence into non-overlapping blocks of different lengths while constructing a dictionary of blocks seen thus far.

6.1 Encoding

A dictionary is initialized to contain the single-character strings corresponding to all the possible input characters (and nothing else except the clear and stop codes if they're being used). The algorithm works by scanning through the input string for successively longer substrings until it finds one that is not in the dictionary. When such a string is found, the index for the string less the last character (i.e., the longest substring that *is* in the dictionary) is retrieved from the dictionary and sent to output, and the new string (including the last character) is added to the dictionary with the next available code. The last input character is then used as the next starting point to scan for substrings. In this way, successively longer strings are registered in the dictionary and made available for subsequent encoding as single output values. The algorithm works best on data with repeated patterns, so the initial parts of a message will see little compression. As the message grows, however, the compression ratio tends asymptotically to the maximum.

6.2 Decoding

The decoding algorithm works by reading a value from the encoded input and outputting the corresponding string from the initialized dictionary. At the same time it obtains the next value from the input, and adds to the dictionary the concatenation of the string just output and the first character of the string obtained by decoding the next input value. The decoder then proceeds to the next input value (which was already read in as the "next value" in the previous pass) and repeats the process until there is no more input, at which point the final input value is decoded without any more additions to the dictionary. In this way the decoder builds up a dictionary which is identical to that used by the encoder, and uses it to decode subsequent input values. Thus the full dictionary does not need be sent with the encoded data; just the initial dictionary containing the single-character strings is sufficient (and is typically defined beforehand within the encoder and decoder rather than being explicitly sent with the encoded data).

6.3 Encoding algorithm

1. Initialize the dictionary to contain all blocks of length one (D={a,b}).
2. Search for the longest block **W** which has appeared in the dictionary.
3. Encode **W** by its index in the dictionary.
4. Add **W** followed by the first symbol of the next block to the dictionary.
5. Go to Step 2.

Each iteration of the outer loop works by first finding the longest match in the dictionary for a string starting at the current position the inner loop finds this match. The iteration then outputs the index for W and adds the string Wx. to the dictionary, where x is the next character after the match. The use of a "dictionary" is similar to LZ77 except that the dictionary is stored explicitly rather than as indices into a window. Since the dictionary is explicit, *i.e.*, each index corresponds to a precise string, LZW need not specify the length. The decoder works since it builds the dictionary in the same way as the encoder and in general can just look up the indices it receives in its copy of the dictionary. The dictionary at the decoder is always one step behind the encoder. This is because the encoder can add Wx to its dictionary at a given iteration, but the decoder will not know x until the next message it receives. The only case in which this might be a problem is if the encoder sends an index of an entry added to the dictionary in the previous step. This

happens when the encoder sends an index for a string W and the string is followed by W(0), where W(0) refers the first character of W. On the iteration the encoder sends the index for W it adds W(0) to its dictionary. On the next iteration it sends the index for W(0) If this happens, the decoder will receive the index for W(0) which it does not have in its dictionary yet. Since the it is able to decode the previous W, however, it can easily reconstruct W(0). This case is handled by the **else** clause in LZW decode, and shown by the example.

7. Result and summary

Many popular programs (e.g. Unix compress and uncompress, gzip and gunzip, and Windows WinZip) are based on the Lempel-Ziv algorithm. One of the biggest advantages of the LZ78 algorithms and reason for its success is that the dictionary operations can run very quickly. The whole algorithm for both coding and decoding requires time that is linear in the message size.. LZ methods utilize a table-based compression model where table entries are substituted for repeated strings of data. For most LZ methods, this table is generated dynamically from earlier data in the input. The table itself is often Huffman encoded (e.g. SHRI, LZX). A current LZ-based coding scheme that performs well is LZX, used in Microsoft's CAB format. The users are given the flexibility to design and include their own custom hardware FPGA or ASIC based with their choice, whether it is on chip or off the chip. FPGA can provide superior performance to Algorithm. The simulation was performed using model Sim simulator. Report generated provides information on logic trimming, logic implementation, time constraint and I/O assignments.

	C	X	Get Index (C,x)	AddDict (C,x)	Output (C)
Init	a				
	a	a	-1	256 (a,a)	a
+	a	a	256		
	256	a	-1	257 (256,a)	256
+	a	a	256		
+	256	a	257		
	257	EOF	-1	-	257

	C	X	W	IndexInDict? (C)	Add Dict (C,W{O}	Output (W)
Init	a		a			a
	a	256	aa	False	256 (a,a)	aa
+	256	257	aaa	False	257 (256,a)	aaa

Fig. 1 LZW encoding and decoding Note: This is an example in hich the decoder does not have the index in its dictionary

References

1. A. Gersho and R. M. Gray, Vector Quantization and Signal Compression
2. D. A. Huffman, ``A Method for the Construction of Minimum Redundancy Codes,'' Proceedings of the IRE, Vol. 40, pp. 1098--1101, 1952
3. Ziv and A. Lempel, ``A Universal Algorithm for Sequential Data Compression,'' IEEE Transactions on Information Theory, Vol. 23, pp. 337--342, 1977
4. Ziv and A. Lempel, ``Compression of Individual Sequences Via Variable-Rate Coding,'' IEEE Transactions on Information Theory, Vol. 24, pp. 530--536, 1978
5. T. A. Welch, ``A Technique for High- Performance Data Compression,'' Computer, pp. 8--18, 1984
6. Timothy C. Bell, John G. Cleary, and Ian H. Witten. *Text compression*. Prentice Hall, 1990
7. Darrel Hankersson, Greg A. Harris, and Peter D. Johnson Jr.. Introduction to Information Theory and Data Compression. CRC Press, 1997
8. Jerry Gibson, Toby Berger, Tom Lookabaugh, Rich Baker and David Lindbergh. Digital Compression for Multimedia: Principles & Standards. Morgan Kaufmann, 1998
9. Gilbert Held and Thomas R. Marshall. Data and Image Compression: Tools and Techniques. Wiley 1996 (4th ed.).

10. Mark Nelson. The Data Compression Book. M&T Books, 1995

11. David Salomon. Data Compression: The Complete Reference. Springer Verlag, 1998

12. VHDL, D. Perry. PrenticeHall,Iindia,1998. Mc Graw Hill 1995

13. Xilinx Foundation Series 3.1I,Quick Start. Guide Manual-0401895, US

Speaker identification by using power distribution in frequency domain

Dr. H. B. Kekre[1] · **Vaishali Kulkarni**[2]

[1]Senior Professor, MPSTME, NMIMS University, Mumbai, India
[2]Assistant Professor, MPSTME, NMIMS University, Mumbai, India

1. Introduction

The speech signal gives various levels of information. Firstly it conveys the words or message being spoken; also on a secondary level it gives us information about the identity of the speaker. The goal of speaker recognition is to extract the identity of the person speaking.

Speaker recognition technology makes it possible to use the speaker's voice to control access to restricted services, for example, phone access to banking, database services, shopping or voice mail, and access to secure equipment. Speaker Recognition is the process of automatically recognizing who is speaking on the basis of individual information included in speech signals. It can be divided into Speaker Identification and Speaker Verification. Speaker identification determines which registered speaker provides a given utterance from amongst a set of known speakers (also known as closed set identification). Speaker verification accepts or rejects the identity claim of a speaker (also known as open set identification).

Speaker identification task can be further classified into text-dependent or textindependent task. In the former case, the utterance presented to the system is known beforehand.

In the latter case, no assumption about the text being spoken is made, but the system must model the general underlying properties of the speaker's vocal spectrum. In general, text-dependent systems are more accurate, since both the content and voice can be compared.

Work on automatic Speaker recognition started in the 1960's. Pruzansky at Bell Labs [1] was among the first to initiate the research using filter banks and correlating the two digital spectrograms for a similarity measure. Doddington at Texas instruments [2] replaced filter banks by formant analysis. For text independent methods, various parameters were extracted by averaging over a long enough duration or by extracting statistical or predictive parameters like averaged auto-correlation [3], instantaneous spectra covariance matrix [4], spectrum and fundamental frequency histograms [5], linear prediction coefficients [6] and long term averaged spectra [7]. As the performance of text-independent systems was limited various text-dependent methods, [8, 9] were also implanted in the 1970's. Hidden Markov Model (HMM) and Vector Quantization based methods were developed in the 1980's. Text dependent speaker recognition systems based on HMM architecture generally used multi word phrases for the training phase and stored the models for the entire phrase [10]. VQ/HMM based method was developed for textindependent identification. A set of shorttime training feature vectors of a speaker can be efficiently compressed to a small set of representative points, a VQ codebook [11, 12 and 21]. Rose et al. [13] proposed a single-state HMM, which is now called Gaussian mixture model (GMM), as a robust parametric model. In the 1990's robust textprompted methods were developed. Matsui et al. [14] proposed a text-prompted speaker recognition method, in which key sentences are completely changed every time the system is used. For reducing the intraspeaker variation, likelihood ratio and posteriori probability-based techniques were investigated [15, 16, and 17]. Methods based on score normalization have been recently introduced in the 2000's [18].Various high level features like word idiolect; pronunciations, phone usage, prosody, etc. have been successfully used in text-independent speaker verification [19]. Recognition systems have been developed for a wide range of applications. Although many new techniques were invented and developed, there are still a number of practical limitations because of which widespread deployment of applications and services is not possible. Still it is very true that

S.J. Pise (ed.), *ThinkQuest 2010*, DOI 10.1007/978-81-8489-989-4_52,
© Springer India Pvt. Ltd. 2011

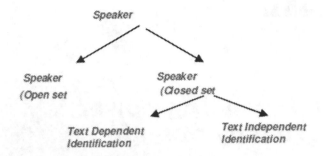

Fig. 1   Classification of Speaker Recognition systems.

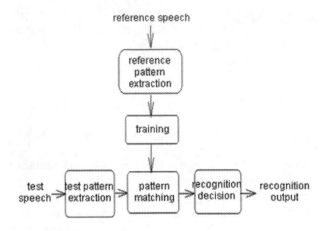

Fig. 2   Speaker identification system

Table 1   Database description

Parameter	Sample characteristics
Language	English
No. of Speakers	26
Speech type	Read speech
Recording conditions	Normal (A silent room)
Sampling frequency	8000Hz
Resolution	8bps
Training speech (scaled)	6 sec, 8 sec
Evaluation speech (scaled)	6 sec, 8 sec

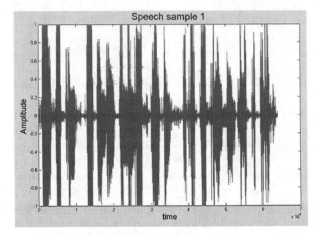

Fig. 3   Speech signal for the sample 1

humans can recognize speech and speaker more efficiently than machines [20]. There is now an increasing interest in finding ways to reduce this performance gap.

The General scheme for Speaker recognition is shown in fig. 2.

Test and reference patterns (feature vectors) are extracted from speech utterances statistically or dynamically. At the training stage, reference models are generated (or trained) from the reference patterns by various methods. A reference model (or template) is formed by obtaining the statistical parameters from the reference speech data. A test pattern is compared against the reference templates at the pattern matching stage. The comparison may be conducted by probability density estimation or by distance (dissimilarity) measure. After comparison, the test pattern is labeled to a speaker model at the decision stage. The labeling decision is generally based on the minimum risk criterion.

Basics of speech signal

The speech samples used in this work are recorded using Sound Forge 4.5. The sampling frequency is 8000 Hz (8 bit, mono PCM samples). Table 1 shows the database description. All the samples are scaled to the same time scale. The samples are collected from different speakers. Samples are taken from each speaker in two sessions so that training model and testing data can be created. Also 4 different texts

are recorded so that both text-independent and textdependent speaker identification can be done. Fig 3 shows the speech signal for sample 1.

3.   Experimental

For creating the database, all the time scaled samples of either 6 sec or 8 sec were considered.

3.1   Method 1: FFT (Fast Fourier Transform)

The FFT of the samples is found and the sum of the magnitude of FFT for different groupings is found. This formed the feature vector. Fig 4 shows the sum of the magnitudes of the FFT samples by considering 32 groups. By making use of the symmetry of FFT, only the first 16 sums are considered as feature vectors here. The remaining 16 are mirror images. The feature vectors thus formed were stored in the database. For the identification of the speaker, the input sample is similarly processed and matched with the feature vectors stored in the database. The stored feature vector which gives the minimum Euclidean distance with the input sample feature vector is declared as the speaker identified.

3.2   Method 2: DST (Discrete Sine Transform)

In this method, the Discrete Sine Transform of the samples is found. Again for forming the feature vectors, the sum

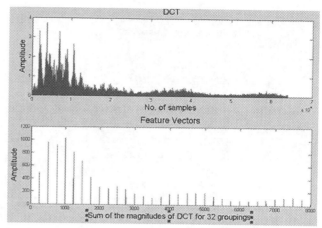

Fig. 4 Feature Vectors for FFT dividing the samples into 32 divisions

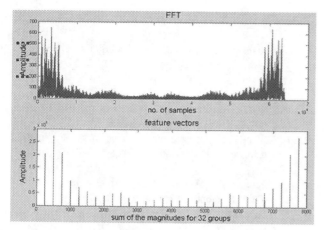

Fig. 5 Feature Vectors for DST by ividing the samples into 32 divisions

of the magnitude of DST for different groupings is found. Fig 5 shows the sum of the magnitudes of DST found by dividing the samples into 32 groups. It can be seen from the figure that maximum energy is concentrated in the first few sums. So here the first 16 sum vectors are considered as feature vectors and stored in the database. The same process as used for FFT is used to identify the sample based on the features stored in the data base.

3.3 Method 3: DCT (Discrete Cosine Transform)

In this method, the Discrete Cosine Transform of the samples is found. Again for forming the feature vectors, the sum of the magnitude of DCT for different groupings is found. Fig 6 shows the sum of the magnitudes of DCT found by dividing the samples into 32 groups. Again here also it can be seen from the figure that maximum energy is concentrated in the first few sums. So here the first 16 sum vectors are considered as feature vectors and stored in the database. The same process as used for FFT is used to identify the sample based on the features stored in the data base.

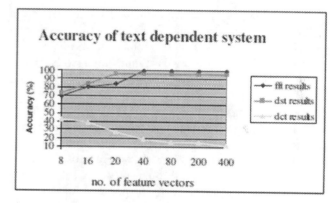

Fig. 6 Feature Vectors for DCT by dividing the samples into 32 divisions

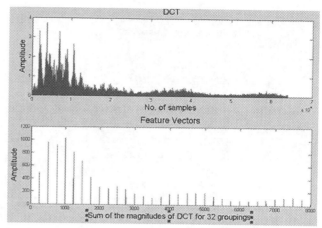

Fig. 7 Variation in the number of feature vectors for text dependent system

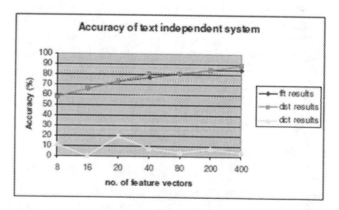

Fig. 8 Variation in the number of features vectors for text independent system

4. Results and discussions

In this section the results obtained by applying the techniques discussed in the previous section on a sample set of 26 speakers of varying age groups (between 10 and 70 years of age) is presented for both text-dependent and text-independent speaker identification.

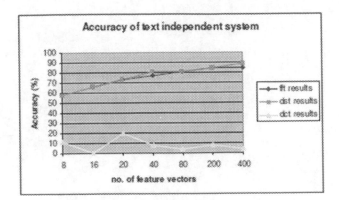

Fig. 9 Variation of the accuracy of text independent system with the number of speakers

Figure 7 shows the curves obtained for textdependent system for 3 methods discussed in the previous section by varying the number of feature vectors for a sample set of 26 speakers. As seen from the figure, for text-dependent samples, about 80 feature vectors are sufficient to get 100% accuracy for FFT. In the case of DST around 20 feature vectors give a maximum accuracy of about 96%. The figure also shows that DCT (maximum 42%) does not give good results and that accuracy decreases as the number of feature vectors is increased. Fig 8 shows the curves obtained for text-independent identification by varying the number of features for a sample set of 26 speakers. As seen from the figure, the maximum accuracy of FFT is about 84.6% whereas the maximum accuracy for DST is about 88.4%. Again here also DCT does not give good results. (maximum 19.2%) It can be seen that as the number of speakers increases the accuracy decreases as expected but it is still above 80%. Fig 9 shows the variation of accuracy of text independent system with a variation in the number of speakers. It can be seen that DST performs better than FFT as the number of speakers in the data base increases. The figure also shows that with DCT the maximum accuracy is only about 19.2%.

5. Conclusion

Very simple techniques based on the power distribution in frequency spectrum have been introduced. FFT and DST techniques give very good results for both textdependent and text-independent systems. The results also show that accuracy increases as the number of feature vectors in the database for each sample increases for these two techniques. The results also show that DST is better than FFT for text independent systems. Also in the case of text dependent systems DST gives comparable results with less number of features. Evaluation has shown that DCT does not give good results. The present study is still ongoing, which may involve different techniques to find the feature vectors and their comparison.

References

1. S. Pruzansky, "Pattern-matching procedure for automatic talker recognition", J.A.S.A., 35, pp. 354-358, 1963
2. G.R.Doddington, "A method of speaker verification", J.A.S.A., 49,139 (A), 1971
3. P.D. Bricker, et. al., "Statistical techniques for talker identification", B.S.T.J., 50, pp. 1427- 1454, 1971
4. K.P.Li, et. al., "Experimental studies in speaker verification using a adaptive system", J.A.S.A., 40, pp. 966-978, 1966
5. B. Beek, et al., "Automatic speaker recognition system", Rome Air Development Center Report, 1971
6. M.R.Sambur, Speaker recognition and verification using linear prediction analysis, Ph. D. Dissert., M.I.T., 1972
7. S. Furui, et. al., "Talker recognition by long time averaged speech spectrum", Electronics and Communications in Japan, 55-A. pp. 54-61, 1972
8. S. Furui, "Cepstral analysis technique for automatic speaker verification", IEEE Trans. Acoustic, Speech, Signal Processing, ASSP-29, pp. 254-272, 1981
9. A. E. Rosenberg and M. R. Sambur, "New Techniques for automatic speaker verification", IEEE Trans. Acoustics, Speech, Signal Proc., ASSP-23, 2, pp. 169-176, 1975
10. J. M. Naik, et. al., "Speaker verification over long distance telephone lines", Proc. ICASSP, pp.524-527, 1989
11. F. K. Soong, et. al., "A vector quantization approach to speaker recognition", At & T Technical Journal, 66, pp. 14-26, 1987
12. A. E. Rosenberg and F. K. Soong, "Evaluation of a vector quantization talker recognition system in text independent and text dependent models", Computer Speech and Language 22, pp. 143-157, 1987
13. R. Rose and R. A. Reynolds, "Text independent speaker identification using automatic acoustic segmentation", Proc. ICASSP, pp. 293-296, 1990
14. T. Matsui and S. Furui, "Concatenated phoneme models for text variable speaker recognition", Proc. ICASSP, pp. II-391-394, 1993
15. A. Higgins, et. al., "Speaker verification using randomized phrase prompting", Digital Signal Processing, 1, pp. 89-106, 1991
16. T. Matsui and S. Furui, "Similarity normalization method for speaker verification based on a posteriori probability", Proc. ESCA Workshop on Automatic Speaker Recognition, Identification and Verification, pp. 59-62, 1994
17. D. Reynolds, "Speaker identification and verification using Gaussian mixture speaker models", Proc. ESCA Workshop on Automatic Speaker recognition, Identification and verification, pp. 27-30, 1994
18. F. J. Bimbot, et. al., "A tutorial on textindependent speaker verification", EURASIP Journ. on Applied Signal Processing, pp. 430- 451, 2004
19. G.R. Doddington, "Speaker recognition based on idiolectal differences between speakers", Proc. Eurospeech, pp. 2521-2524, 2001
20. S Furui, "50 years of progress in speech and speaker recognition research", ECTI Transactions on Computer and

Information Technology, Vol. 1, No.2, November 2005. [21] Marco Grimaldi and Fred Cummins, "Speaker Identification using Instantaneous Frequencies", IEEE Transactions on Audio, Speech, and Language Processing, vol., 16, no. 6, August 2008

22. H. B. Kekre, Tanuja K. Sarode, "Speech Data Compression using Vector Quantization", WASET International Journal of Computer and Information Science and Engineering (IJ-CISE), Fall 2008, Volume 2, Number 4, pp.: 251-254, 2008. http://www.waset.org/ijcise.

Content based image retrieval using weighted hamming distance image hash value

H. B. Kekre[1] · **Dhirendra Mishra[2]**

[1]Sr. Professor, Computer Engineering Department,Mukesh Patel School of Technology Management and Engineering, SVKM's NMIMS University, Mumbai, India

[2]Ph.D. Research Scholar and Assistant Professor, Computer Engineering Department,Mukesh Patel School of Technology Management and Engineering, SVKM's NMIMS University, Mumbai, India

1. Introduction

A hash function is any well-defined procedure or mathematical function that converts a large, possibly variable-sized amount of data into a small datum, usually a single integer that may serve as an index to an array. The values returned by a hash function are called hash values, hash codes, hash sums, or simply hashes. Hash functions are mostly used to speed up table lookup or data comparison tasks such as finding items in a database, detecting duplicated or similar records in a large file, finding similar stretches in DNA sequences, and so on. A hash function may map two or more keys to the same hash value. In many applications, it is desirable to minimize the occurrence of such collisions, which means that the hash function must map the keys to the hash values as evenly as possible. Depending on the application, other properties may be required as well. Although the idea was conceived in the 1950s, the design of good hash functions is still a topic of active research. Hash functions are related to checksums, check digits, fingerprints, randomization functions, error correcting codes, and cryptographic hash functions. Although these concepts overlap to some extent, each has its own uses and requirements and is designed and optimized differently. The Hash Keeper database maintained by the National Drug Intelligence Center, for instance, is more aptly described as a catalog of file fingerprints than of hash values. A number of media-specific hash functions have been proposed for multimedia authentication [4]–[7]. A multimedia hash is a content-based digital signature of the media data. To generate a multimedia hash, a secret key is used to extract certain features from the data. These features are further processed to form the hash. The hash is transmitted along with the media either by appending or embedding it to the primary media data. At the receiver side, the authenticator uses the same key to generate the hash values, which are compared to the ones transmitted along with the data for verifying its authenticity. In addition to content authentication, multimedia hashes are used in content-based retrieval from databases [8]. To search for multimedia content, naïve methods such as sample-by-sample comparisons are computationally inefficient. Moreover, these methods compare the lowest level of content representation and do not offer robustness in such situations as geometric distortions .Robust image hash functions can be used to address this problem [4]. A hash is computed for every data entry in the database and stored with the original data in the form of a lookup table. To search for a given query in the database, its hash is computed and compared with the hashes in the lookup table. The data entry corresponding to the closest match, in terms of certain hash-domain distance that often accounts for content similarity, is then fetched. Since the hash has much smaller size with respect to the original media, matching the hash values is computationally more efficient. Image hash functions have also been used in applications involving image and video watermarking. In non oblivious image watermarking, the need for the original image in watermark extraction can be substituted by using hash as side information [1], [9], [10]. The hash functions have also been used as image dependent keys for watermarking [11]. In video watermarking, it has been shown that adversaries can employ "collusion attacks" to devise simple statistical measures to estimate the watermark if they have access to multiple copies of similar frames.

2. Content based image retrieval

The earliest use of the term content-based image retrieval in the literature seems to have been by Kato, to describe

S.J. Pise (ed.), *ThinkQuest 2010*, DOI 10.1007/978-81-8489-989-4_53,
© Springer India Pvt. Ltd. 2011

his experiments into automatic retrieval of images from a database by color and shape feature. The term has since been widely used to describe the process of retrieving desired images from a large collection on the basis of features (such as colors, texture and shape) that can be automatically extracted from the images themselves. The typical CBIR system performs two major tasks. The first one is feature extraction (FE), where a set of features, called image signature or feature vector, is generated to accurately represent the content of each image in the database. A feature vector is much smaller in size than the original image, typically of the order of hundreds of elements (rather than millions). The second task is similarity measurement (SM), where a distance between the query image and each image in the database using their signatures is computed so that the top images can be retrieved .

3. Similarity measure

Many Current Retrieval systems take a simple approach by using typically norm-based distances (e.g., Euclidean distance) on the extracted feature set as a similarity function. The main premise behind these CBIR systems is that given a good set of features extracted from the images in the database (the ones that significantly capture the content of images.) then for two images to be similar, their extracted features have to be close to each other.

4. Algorithm

The proposed method of image hashing advocates to generate the hash value for each image in the database and then the Hash value for the query image is calculated. The hash value of query image is used to calculate the hamming distance with the hash values of images in database. Finally the retrieval of images from the database with minimum hamming distance of same class and cross class is checked to calculate the precision and recall rates of retrieval. The Hashing technique proposed follows following steps to generate the hash value for each image.

Step1: Fast Fourier Transform of image is calculated.
Step2: Extracting the real and imaginary part of the Fourier complex numbers of the image calculated in step1.
Step3: Cartesian to polar coordinate conversion
Step4: Feature vector generated based on the angles of complex plane on which complex numbers plotted using Euler's formula.
Step5: 4 feature vectors of 16 bits are attached together to generate the 64 bit feature vector.
Step6: Generating the gray code of these 64 bit feature vector to get the final hash.

5. Feature vextor generation

Every complex number can be represented as a point in the complex plane, and can therefore be expressed by specifying either the point's Cartesian coordinates (called rectangular or Cartesian form) or the point's polar coordinates (called polar form).

Complex numbers can be plotted on the complex plane as shown in Fig. 1. This theory helps us to generate four feature vectors based on the complex plane as shown above. The real and imaginary parts of complex numbers of images generated by the fast Fourier transform is checked for the angle of complex plane lies in. Corresponding intensity values of images are taken into first feature vector whose complex numbers lies in between angle 0 to 90 on the complex plane. Similarly four feature vectors are generated by taking four quadrants of the complex plane.

6. Results and discussion

Database of 170 images of 7 different classes; Once the feature vector is generated for all images in the database,

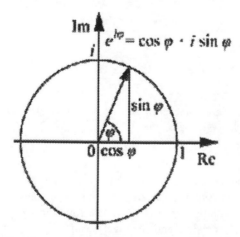

Fig. 1 Complex number plotted on complex plane using Euler's formula.

Fig. 2 Sample image database

its Hash code is generated and stored in the database. A query image of each class is produced to search it into the database. The image with exact match gives Hamming distance minimum as 0.To check the effectiveness of the work and its performance with respect to retrieval of the image we have calculated the precision and recall as given below:

$$Precision = \frac{Number\_of\_relevant\_images\_retrieved}{Total\_number\_of\_images\_retrieved} \quad (1)$$

$$Recall = \frac{Number\_of\_relevant\_images\_retrieved}{Total\_number\_of\_relevent\_images\_in\_database} \quad (2)$$

Working with all classes of images when we provide the following image of Mickey as query image then the precision and recall based on the retrieved images are calculated and graph is plotted as shown in the Fig. 4.

The cartoon image shown in the Fig. 3 is taken as the query Image to search the given image database. The algorithm applied to generate the hash value for each image in the database and the query image. The hash value of the query image was compared with the hash value of database images and images were retrieved based on Weighted Hamming distance. This has produced good results as it can be seen in the Fig. 4 where first 11 images out 12 images retrieved are of same class among which first image retrieved is the query image which we are looking for .There is only

Fig. 3 Images retrieved against the query image shown in Fig. 3

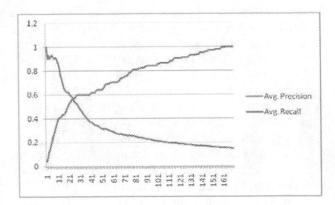

Fig. 4 Average Precision and Average Recall performance for Cartoon class of image

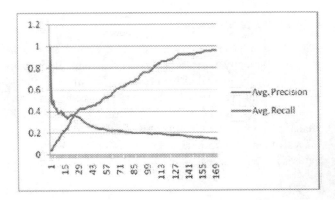

Fig. 5 Average Precision and Average Recall performance for sunset class of image

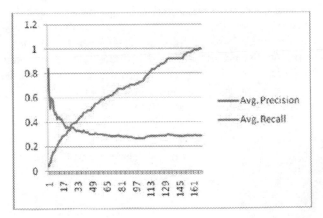

Fig. 6 Average precision and average recall performance for Barbie class of images

one image of bird class in first twelve images. Average Precision and Average Recall Performance of these retrieved images is shown in the Fig. 5. The following graphs show average precision and average recall plotted against the number of images retrieved. The graphs are plotted by randomly selecting 5 sample images from each class.

7. Conclusion

We have presented the innovative use of digital image hashing for retrieving the images similar to query image from the given large image database. The process applied on the database of 170 images of 10 different classes and it gives the good outcome for many classes of images as per the precision and recall is concerned performance measuring options for the cartoon, sunset, Barbie and Scenery classes of images. We have considered randomly selected 5 images of each class as query images to calculate the average performance with respect to its precision and recall. Average Precision and recall of above mentioned classes shown in Fig. 5, Figure 6, Figs. 7 and 8 respectively. The cross over points of average precision and average recall is on average more than 40% which is considered as good performance. We had worked with hash value of 16 bit & normal hamming distance [29].The result of hash value of 64 bit and weighted hamming distance proposed in this paper is far better and improved than earlier method implemented with hash value of 16 bit and normal hamming distance [29]. Using the hash function and weighted hamming distance as similarity measure makes the algorithm very fast as compared to Euclidean distance, which is commonly used, as similarity measure.

References

1 A. K. Jain, S. Prabhakar. L. Hong, and S. Pankanti, "Filterbank-based Fingerprint Matching," *IEEE Trans. Image Processing*, Vol. 9, No. 5, pp. 846-859, May 2000

2 Arun Ross, Sarat Dass, Anil Jain, "A deformable model for fingerprint matching," *Pattern Recognition* Vol. 38, pp. 95-103, 2005

3 A. K. Jain, L. Hong, Y. Kulkarni "A Biometric System using Fingerprint, Face, and Speech," Proc.2nd *Int'l Conference on Audio- and Video-based Biometric Person Auhentification*, Washington D.C., pp. 182-187, 1999

4 Federal Bureau of investigation, *The Science of Fingerprints: Classification and Uses*, Washington, D.C., 1984, U.S. Government Printing office

5 F. A. Afsar, M. Arif and M. Hussain, "Fingerprint Identification and Verification," pp. 141-146, 2004

6 A. K. Jain, L. Hong, S. Pankanti, and R. Bolle, "An identity authentication system using fingerprints," *Proc. IEEE*, Vol. 85, pp. 1365-1388, Sept. 1997

7 Y. Kobayashi, H. Toyoda, N. Mukohzaka, N. Yoshida and T. Hara, "Fingerprint identification by an optical joint transform correlation," optical review, Vol. 3(6A), pp. 4.3-405, 1996

8 Frank Y. Shih, *Senior Member, IEEE,* and Yi-Ta Wu, "The Efficient Algorithms for Achieving Euclidean Distance Transformation," *IEEE Transactions on Image Processing*, vol. 13, no. 8, August 2004

9 Yaorong Ge and J. Michael Fitzpatrick "On the Generation of Skeletons from Discrete Euclidean Distance Maps," *IEEE Trans. Pattern Analysis and machine Intelligence,* vol. 18, No. 11, November 1996

10 N.Sudha, S. Nandi, P.K. Bora, K.Sridharan, "Efficient computation of Euclidean Distance Transform for application in Image processing," *IEEE Transaction on Image processing*, 1998

11 P. E. Danielsson, "A new shape factor," *Comput. Graphics Image Processing,* pp. 292-299, 1978

12 I. Pitas and A. N. Venetsanopoulos, "Morphological shape decomposition," *IEEE Trans. Pattern Anal. Machine Intell.,* vol. 12, no. 1, pp. 38-45, Jan. 1990

13 C.Arcelli and G.Sanniti de Baja. "Computing Voronoi diagrams in digital pictures," *Pattern Recognition Letters,* pages 383-389, 1986

14 H. Blum and R. N. Nagel, "Shape Description UsingWeighted Symmetric Axis Features," *Pattern Recognition*, vol. 10, pp. 167-180, 1978

15 Wai-Pak Choi, Kin-Man Lam and Wan-Chi Siu, " An efficient algorithm for the extraction of Euclidean skeleton," *IEEE Transaction on Image processing*, 2002

16 Frank Y. Shih and Christopher C. Pu, "A maxima-tracking method for skeletonization from Euclidean distance function," *IEEE Transaction on Image processing*, 1991

17 Anil Jain, Arun Ross, Salil Prabhakar, "Fingerprint matching using minutiae and texture features," *Int'l conference on Image Processing* (ICIP), pp. 282-285, Oct. 2001

18 John Berry and David A. Stoney "The history and development of fingerprinting," in *Advances in Fingerprint Technology*, Henry C. Lee and R. E. Gaensslen, Eds., pp. 1-40. CRC Press Florida, 2nd edition, 2001

19 Emma Newham, "The biometric report," SJB Services, 1995

20 Arun Ross, Anil Jain, James Reisman, "A hybrid fingerprint matcher," *Int'l conference on Pattern Recognition (ICPR)*, Aug 2002

21 A. M. Bazen, G. T. B.Verwaaijen, S. H. Gerez, L. P. J. Veelenturf, and B. J. van der Zwaag, "A correlation-based fingerprint verification system," *Proceedings of the ProRISC2000 Workshop on Circuits, Systems and Signal Processing,* Veldhoven, Netherlands, Nov 2000

22. H.B.Kekre, Sudeep D. Thepade, "Boosting Block Truncation Coding using Kekre's LUV Color Space for Image Retrieval", WASET International Journal of Electrical, Computer and System Engineering (IJECSE), Volume 2, No.3, Summer 2008. Available online at www.waset.org/ijecse/v2/v2-3-23.pdf

23. H.B.Kekre, Tanuja K. Sarode, Sudeep D. Thepade, "Image Retrieval using Color-Texture Features from DCT on VQ Codevectors obtained by Kekre's Fast Codebook Generation", ICGST International Journal on Graphics, Vision and Image Processing (GVIP), Available online at http://www.icgst.com/gvip

24. H.B.Kekre, Sudeep D. Thepade, "Using YUV Color Space to Hoist the Performance of Block Truncation Coding for Image Retrieval", IEEE International Advanced Computing Conference 2009 (IACC'09), Thapar University, Patiala, INDIA, 6-7 March 2009

25. H.B.Kekre, Sudeep D. Thepade, "Image Retrieval using Augmented Block Truncation Coding Techniques", ACM International Conference on Advances in Computing,Communication and Control (ICAC3-2009), pp.: 384-390,23-24 Jan 2009, Fr. Conceicao Rodrigous College of Engg., Mumbai. Available online at ACM portal

26 H.B.Kekre, Tanuja K. Sarode, Sudeep D. Thepade, "DCT Applied to Column mean and Row Mean Vectors of Image

for Fingerprint Identification", International Conference on Computer Networks and Security, ICCNS-2008, 27-28 Sept 2008, Vishwakarma Institute of Technology, Pune

27. H.B.Kekre, Tanuja K. Sarode, "Fast Codebook Search Algorithm for Vector Quantization Using Sorting Technique". ACM International Conference on Advances in Computing, Communication and Control (ICAC3), Fr. CRCE Mumbai, 23-24 Jan 2009, Available on ACM Portal

28. H.B.Kekre, Tanuja K. Sarode, "Fast Codevector Search Algorithm for 3-D Vector Quantized Codebook", WASET International Journal of Computer and Information Science and Engineering (IJCISE), Volume 2, Number 4, pp. 235-239, Fall 2008. http://www.waset.org/ijcise

29. H.B.Kekre, Dhirendra Mishra, "Image retrieval using image hashing", Techno-Path: Journal of Science, Engineering & Technology Management, SVKM's NMIMS Vol. 1 No.3 Oct 2009

Reconfigurable DSP-FFT design for mobile communication

Prasad A. Kulkarni[1] · Dr. Vijay Wadhai[2] · D. R. Mehta[3] · Vidula Kulkarni[4]

[1]HOD Computer Engg. Babasaheb Gawde Institute of Technology, Mumbai, India
[2]Prof & Dean MITSOT Pune, India
[3]Asst. Prof. VJTI, Mumbai. India
[4]Faculty at B.Sc. IT, Mumbai, India

1. Introduction

Many Electronic system making use of digital signal processor. Digital signal processing is the application of mathematical operation to digitally represented signals. Signals are represented digitally as a sequence of samples. Often these samples are obtained from physical signal (e.g. audio) through the transducers, A/D converters. After mathematically processing digital signals may be back to physical signals via D/A converters. In some systems the use of DSP is central to the operation of the system. The operation of digital signal processor on input samples could be linear or non linear, depending on the application of interest.

A digital signal processor (DSP) accepts one or more discrete time inputs $x_i[n]$, and produces one or more outputs $y_i[n]$, for n = …, −1,0,1,2, 3,4,… and i= 1,…, N. The inputs could represent appropriately sampled (analog to digital conversion) values of continuous time signals of interest, which are then processed in the discrete time domain, to produce outputs in discrete time that could then be converted to continuous time, if necessary. The operation of the digital signal processor on the input samples could be linear or non-linear, time-invariant or time varying, depending on the application of interest. The samples of the signal are quantized to a finite number of bits, and this word length can be either fixed or variable within the processor. Signal processors operate on millions of samples per second, require large memory bandwidth, often requiring as many as a few hundred operations on each sample processed. These real-time capabilities are beyond the capabilities of conventional microprocessors and mainframe computers. Digital signal processors have traditionally been optimized to compute FIR convolutions (sum of products), IIR recursive filtering, and Fast Fourier Transform type (Montium butterfly) operations that typically characterize most signal-processing algorithm. They also include interface to external data ports for real- time operation.

These processors having specialized instruction sets are called as Special-Instruction Set Single Chip (SISC) computers and system on chip (Soc) as well. The paper is organized in seven sections as follow The section II describes FFT algorithm in Digital Radio Communication. The section III gives the information about Montium butterfly mapping. The features and architecture of proposed DSP is described in IV section. In section V results and conclusion is embedded.

2. Ffts for digital radio communication

The Fast Fourier Transformation and Inverse Fast Fourier Transformation (IFFT) are most challenging algorithms. Several of these FFTs/iFFTs have a length that is not a power-of-two and show a less regular implementation than the commonly used power-of-two FFTs. The mapping of a class of non-power-of-two FFTs, in which the FFTs required for DRM can be included, at the Montium TP. The mapping is analyzed by means of performance, accuracy and energy consumption to demonstrate the flexibility of the Montium TP. The FFT is a DFT algorithm that reduces the number of computations needed from $O(N2)$ to $O(NlogN)$ by Decomposition. The DFT of a sequence $x(n)$ is shown in Equation 1:

$$X(k) = \sum_{n=0}^{N-1} x(n) e(-j^{2\pi n k}) / N \qquad (1)$$

S.J. Pise (ed.), *ThinkQuest 2010*, DOI 10.1007/978-81-8489-989-4_54,

In this case, k=0,1,...N – 1 and N is the transform length. In this reference design, the transform length, N, is 1536. Using the decimation in time (DIT) method, the first tep is to divide the input sequence into three sequences. Each sequence goes through the 512-point FFT computation. The last step applies a twiddle factor to the outputs of the second and third FFT computation and then combines the three sequences to get a final output result. The mathematical equation of 1536-point FFT decomposition is shown in Equation 2:

$$X(k) = \sum_{n=0}^{1535} x(n) \cdot W_{1536}^{kn}$$

$$X(k) = \sum_{m=0}^{511} x(3m) \cdot W_{1536}^{k(3m)}$$

$$+ \sum_{m=0}^{511} x(3m+1) \cdot W_{1536}^{k(3m+1)} \tag{2}$$

$$+ \sum_{m=0}^{511} x(3m+2) \cdot W_{1536}^{k(3m+2)}$$

$$X(k) = \sum_{m=0}^{511} x(3m) \cdot W_{512}^{k(m)}$$

$$+ W_{1536}^{k(m)} \sum_{m=0}^{511} x(3m+1) \cdot W_{512}^{k(m)} \tag{3}$$

$$+ W_{1536}^{2k} \sum_{m=0}^{511} x(3m+2) \cdot W_{512}^{k(m)}$$

$$\text{Where } W_N^{kn} = e^{-j2\pi kn/N}$$

A 1536-point FFT can be decomposed into three 512-point FFTs followed by a single radix-3 combinational stage. Using the DIT method the design breaks down the input sequence into top, middle, and bottom samples that feed into one 512-point Twiddle factors (W) are applied to the outputs of the second and third 512-point FFTs. The results are recombined and reordered to obtain the final FFT output[6]. The restriction of the radix FFT is that it can only

handle FFTs that have a length that is a power of the radix value (e.g., two for radix-2). If other lengths are required a mixed-radix algorithm can be used. For example an FFT-288canbe re expressed with a radix-2 and radix-3 FFT (FFT-32 × FFT-9)[5]. The Good's mapping is also used to eliminate the intermediate multiplications.[3]

3. Montium butterfly mapping

The Montium FFT/IFFT IP core is a decimation-in-time (DIT) radix-2 implementation of the Cooley-Tukey FFT/IFFT algorithm[10]. Implemented in Montium C, the Montium FFT/IFFTIP core requires the minimum number of clock cycles in order to compute FFTs and IFFTs on real or complex data up to lengths of 8192 points. As an example, a typical 1024 point FFT/IFFT requires just 5140 cycles, or 51.4ms when clocked at 100MHz. This Montium architecture is a dynamically introduced in reconfigurable in for computation intensive DSP algorithms. The Montium is typically used in (heterogeneous) multi-core systems. High performance coupled with excellent power efficiency is achieved by virtue of the Montium tile processor's unique coarse-grained reconfigurable architecture. Fig 1 shows four ALUs (arithmetic and logic units), to demonstrating the efficiency of the hardware architecture. A fifth ALU is also available, therefore allowing users to implement more general purpose tasks which may coincide with the butterfly computations.

4. Architecture

Features of FFT DSP Processor
1. 32 bit processor
2. 1 KB X 32 bit on chip DPRAM, ROM
3. 32 bit 16 registers
4. 32 bit communication port
5. Montium TP architecture
6. Pipelined Frequency Transform(PFT)
7. 32 bit Floating point adder/sub tractor and multiplier
8. IEEE 754 single precision floating-point format

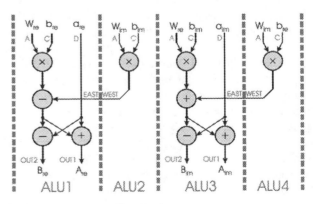

Fig. 1   Montium butterfly mapping

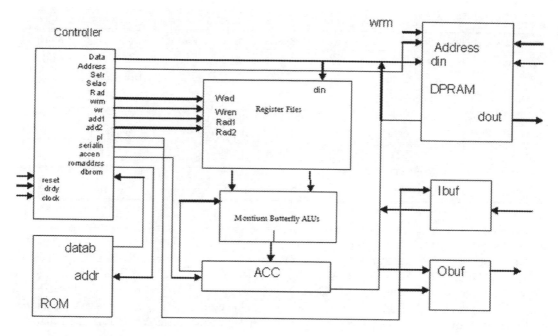

Fig. 2 Architechure of FFT DSP processor

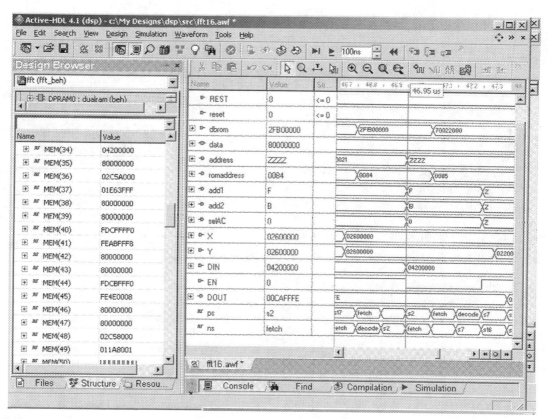

Fig. 3 FFT input & output in DPRAM

Generally typical General Purpose Processor is found in mobile devices is the Advanced RISC Machine (ΛRM) family. They can be employed for any arbitrary task, while their energy consumption is low. The general purpose design is useful for control intensive applications. DSPs are designed for high performance and flexibility. Compared to a GPP, DSPs performs much better within a bounded application domain, while its energy consumption is relatively

Table 1 Output FFT

Sr.No.	Memory Address	Data	Remark (Real)	Memory Address	Data	Remark (Imaginary)
1	0022h	04200000h	X(0)=20d	0023h	80000000h	X(0)=0d
2	0024h	02C5A000h	X(1)=-5.2d	0025h	01E63FFFh	X(1)=-2.4d
3	0026h	80000000h	X(2)=0d	0027	80000000h	X(2)=0d
4	0028h	FDCFFF0h	X(3)=-0.172d	0029h	FEABFFF8h	X(3)=-0.414d
5	002Ah	80000000h	X(4)=0d	002Bh	80000000h	X(4)=0d
6	002Ch	FDCBFF0h	X(5)=-0.172d	002Dh	FE4E008h	X(5)=0.414d
7	002Eh	80000000h	X(6)=0d	002Fh	80000000h	X(6)=0d
8	0030h	02C58000h	X(7)=-5.2d	0031h	011A8001h	X(7)=2.414d

low compared to the GPP. Figure 2 shows proposed architecture for reconfigurable DSP processor. The major component of processor includes PFT, ROM, DPRAM, ALU, MAC, Communication port and register file and course of controller. This architecture comprised simultaneous access of data and coefficient leading to efficient implementation of DSP FFT algorithms. The register file which is connected to the out put of ALUs, the multiplier capable of performing multiply and accumulates addition and subtractions. The Controller receives the computing algorithm from the Program /code memory. The Communication Port receives the samples and send it to dual port RAM or Samples can be directly loaded in it. The ALUs input operands are fetched from register file. The ALUs are connected through a larger cross bar providing higher connectivity.

The controller initializes the register, ROM address at reset condition. The ROM stores the program of FFT/IFFT algorithm. The opcodes are fetched by Controller, decodes it and enters in execution state. The four uppermost bits (dbrom 31 to 28) is the operation code. The Signal dbrom is the data bus containing operation code (dbrom 31 to 28), source, and destination. The ROM address are used to fetch opcodes from ROM and data, address, selm, wrm provides RAM databus, address bus, read, write control signals respectively. Register operation is controlled by rad gives the address of register to write the data and enables through wren. The add1, add2, outputs the data on dout1, dout2 respectively. Accumulator is enabling through accen and selac selects the data from ALU, memory, and register or from two communication ports[7, 8].

5. Results and conclusion

The users are given the flexibility to design and include their own custom hardware FPGA or ASIC based with their choice of processor whether it is on chip or off the chip. The result shown in table 1 for the FFT for of sequence

x(n)={1,2,3,4,4,3,2,1} in IEEE 754 single precision floating point form stored in RAM of proposed processor. It has taken approximately 47.3 μs without Montium TP DSP Architecture. This proposed FPGA based Montium TP DSP Architecture can provide superior performance for FFT implantation. This accelerates the FFT algorithmic calculation approximately 2.5 time faster.

References

1. Jennifer Eyre and Jeff Bier, "*The Evolution of DSP Processors* ", IEEE Signal Processing Magazine vol. 17 no 2 pp 43- 51 March 2000
2. Jeff Bier, Phil Lapsley, Amit Shoham, Edward A. Lee, "*DSP Processor Fundamentals Architecture and Features*", S. Chand and Company Limited, New Delhi, 2000
3. I. J. Good, "*The interaction algorithm and practical fourier series*", Journal of Royal Statistical Society. Series B vol.20,no.2 pp.361-372, 1958
4. K.C. Chang, "*Digital System Design with VHDL & Synthesis-An Integrated Approach*", Matt Loeb, IEEE Computer Society, 1999
5. Marcel D. Van de Burgwal, Pascal T. Wolkotte and Gerard J.M. Smit, "*Non-Power-of-Two FFTs: Exploring the Flexibility of Montium TP*", International Journal of Reconfigurable Computing, volume 2009,article ID 678045
6. P. Rameshbabu, "*Digital Signal Processing*", SciTech Publication [India] Private Limited, 2nd edition, 2002
7. Prasad A. Kulkarni, D. R. Mehta, "*FPGA and ASIC based System For Digital Signal Processor* ",Proceeding of SPIT-IEEE Colloquium and International conference, Mumbai Vol 2
8. Vijay K. Madisetti, "VLSI Digital Signal Processors. An introduction to rapid prototype and design synthesis", IEEE Press, Butterworth Heinemann, 1995
9. RF Engines Ltd, "*Mixed –Radix dual speed FFT product Specification*" April 2004,www.refl.com
10. www.recoresystems.com/product brief/ montium FFT/IFFT IP core

Qualitative approach for improvising the performance of output pulse of a pulse power modulator

Hemant Taskar · Mahesh A. Dorlikar

¹Electrical Engg. Dept. VJTI, Mumbai, India.

I. Introduction

Pulse Modulating system becoming popular and developing technology in the area of high energy science. The pulse modulator are used in various fields like material processing, biomedical instrumentation, use of high power electromagnetic waves for application in defense sector (RADAR SYSTEM), lesser supply Excimer, production of nanopowder. These paper discuses various experiments conducted towards improvement of rise time of output pulse of pulse power modulator (50KV, 10AMP, 10usec pulse width, rise time 212 nsec). To ensure high power efficiency of it is extremely important to have a rise time of less than 1 usec in pulse transformer. Selection of proper switch in pulse power system is very important to get all the desired characteristic of pulse power modulator. To get this requirement. Solid state switches (IGBTs) are used which gives fast switching action under high power applications, IGBT have excellent characteristic as well power handling capacity, such as IGBT used for this application have rating 1200V, 400AMP, with switching time less than 200nsec, The block diagram of pulse power modulator is given below

1.1 CCPS (Capacitor charged power supply)

CCPS is an abbreviation for capacitor charge power supply, it supplies the required energy for generation of pulses. Specification: 1000V, 3AMP

1.2 Energy storage capacitor

This is second stage of modulator the output is in form of pulses of very high power, Specification: input voltage 2Kv,Capacity 110uF, Energy 10J.

1.3 IGBT Switch and driver circuit

The input is DC and output is in the form of unidirectional pulses the DC input can be converted into pulses by switching action. Specification: 1200 V, 120 AMP (pulsed current)

1.4 Pulse transformer

Since the modulator require high power pulses the pulse output need to be amplified by using pulse transformer to the desired voltage level, the design of pulse transformer required various tasks which also include selection of core materials the core materials are i) Mn –Zn ferrite core ii) KCP-30 METGLAS core.

1.5 Load

The final stage load can PIII (plasma immersed ion implantation) but here for experimental purpose resistive load is used.

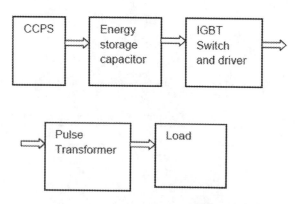

Fig. 1 Block diagram of pulse power modulator

S.J. Pise (ed.), *ThinkQuest 2010*, DOI 10.1007/978-81-8489-989-4_55,

2. Various aspects which contributes the rise time of out pulse of a pulse modulator

2.1 Effect of reset scheme

The input to the pulse transformer since unidirectional core saturation requires to be prevented, due to this the BH curve of core material traverse the minor loop Δ B(incremental flux density) available is very small which affect the design parameter N(no. of turns) and Tr(rise time).It is noted the finite inductance of the pulse transformer develops positive magnetic accumulation during the switch conduction period. If this magnetic flux is not reset to zero each switching cycle it will build up over consecutive cycles until the transformer core saturates. To prevent core saturation the flux must be reset by the end of each switching cycle, by Sending a negative bias current or pulse at the off time of the pulse does this. This acts on the core as negative magnetizing force on the core. Due to this ΔB can be achieved and core saturation can be avoided. The schematic of RCD is shown in the Fig. 2. the diode in RCD [7] network provides power transformer reset with constant clamp voltage during the off time of IGBT switch. The clamp voltage depends upon number of parameters including magnetizing inductance, parasitic capacitance of power semiconductors and switching frequency. The use of RC type snubber across main switch and forward diode affects the clamp voltage by charging the effective resonant capacitor during the reset time intervals. A bipolar operation of the transformer can be achieved with reset circuit either DC or active reset which premagnetises the core to a negative flux density before a pulse is generated.

Experimental results and waveform

All the experiments were conducted on amorphous core based pulse power modulator with adder configuration. On the primary side we have four different winding of 3 turn each and on the secondary consist of 300 turns

Variation of capacitance

The capacitor of RCD circuit is varied between 0.2 to 20 uF the observation are tabulated and waveforms are shown

It is observed from the waveform drawn below the variation of capacitance has the predominant effect on the back swing and it reduces as the capacitance increases from 0.2uF to 20 uF, there is no change in other factors such as input current, output voltage The response of output pulse is simulated in MULTISIM, NI version 10.1, which shown in Figs. 3 and 4.

It is observed that the input current drawn from supply is less than with RCD than without RCD.

Above diagram shows the DC reset scheme with S is DC source, c capacitance, L is inductor. DC reset mechanism provides continuous negative bias in the core, the current produces negative MMF and there by flux which acts as a

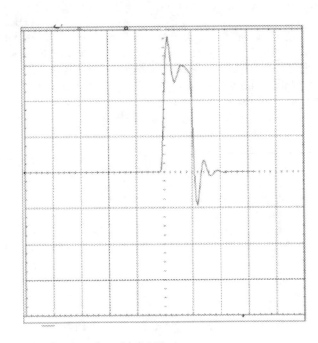

Fig. 3   Output pulse with 0.2uF

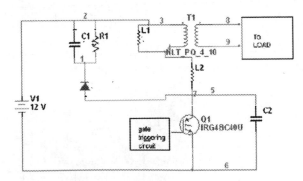

Fig. 2   Schematic diagram of RCD network

Table 1   Performance of output pulse with variation of capacior

C (uF)	Vint (v)	Linput (A)	Vmax(KV)	Vp-p (KV)	Rise time (usec)	Time constant)
0.2	100	0.25	4.5	8.8	2.07	10
5	100	0.24	4.4	6	2.12	250
10	100	0.24	4.4	5.1	2.03	500
20	100	0.24	4.4	5.1	2.10	1000

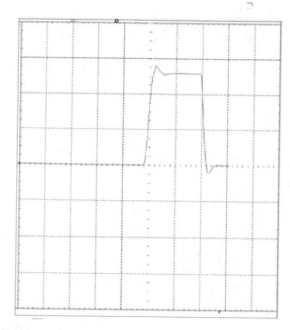

Fig. 4 Output pulse with 20uF

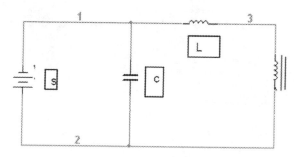

Fig. 5 Circuit diagram for DC reset

Table 2 Variation of rise time of out put pulse with variation of secondary turns of pulse transformer

No. of secondary turns	Rise time (usec)
200	1.38
150	1.18
120	1.12
90	1.05

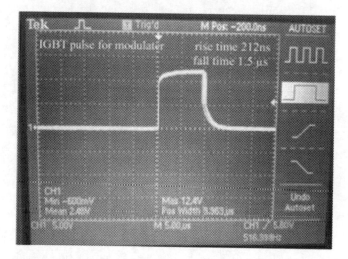

Fig. 6 Waveform of output pulse observed on TEKTRONIX 2012 oscilloscope

2.4 Optimization of rise time

Experiments were conducted on amorphous core for different number of secondary turns. In order to optimize the rise time secondary number of turns are varied, results are tabulated and given in the following table [5]

Rise time can calculated as follows by using the formula, wherein the inductance of winding and transfer capacitance between the winding can be measured by FLUKE RLC meter $Tr = \sqrt{2.2}\,(L/R)X(1-K^2)$. Where L means equivalent inductance and can calculated by formula primary inductance $(L_p) = \mu_o.\mu_e.Ae.Np^2/le$ Secondary inductance$(Ls) = \mu_o.\mu_e.Ae.Ns^2/le$, where μ_e(relative permeability) can be computed from the from the geometry of the core, Np and Ns number of primary and secondary number of turns, le mean length of core. It is noted from the above equation rise time is, directly proportional to inductance[6], which has become major contributing factor for higher rise time, and also it varies inversely with load resistance. The desired wave shape of output pulse is as shown in the figure, and it is obtained by removing the negative swing by appropriate RCD circuit across primary of the pulse transformer and rise time reduces to 212nsec. It is obtained by energizing transformer by applying higher voltage with series connection of IGBTs. The selection of load resistance for optimal rise time can be obtained by considering condition of impedance matching.

negative resetting core, the dc reset is shown in the above figure, is consist of (5V, 10-20AMP), the circuit consist of reset winding wound over the core, the winding has series inductor, the reset winding and an inductor is shunted by capacitor, the series inductance attenuates the ac component reflected by reset winding which the capacitor bypasses the same. The DC reset current can calculated by I reset=HR^{tota} Xle/N.

Where le= mean length HR= mmf under reseting, N=number of turns. Different tests have been performed for different load resistances and input voltages, it is concluded from this test that DC reset reduces the droop in the waveform and also it reduces the backswing that is the negative pick.

2.3 Rise time control with feedback resistor

When resistance is introduced in emitter terminal of IGBT, it affects the two factors output pulse voltage gain and the rise time both the voltage gain and rise time reduces with the increase in emitter resistance..

2.5   Switching element (IGBTs) in series operation

The rise time can improvised by only by reducing secondary number of turns hence the primary to the pulse transformer is given at a higher voltage which require IGBTS to be connected in series, it observed that the series operation is difficult as the problem faced by the concept of floating neutral as well as sharing of voltages. The triggering scheme for series operation is accordingly designed to take care of this [4]. Similarly capacitance and resistance ladder must be connected across each device which assist in voltage sharing and eliminates the requirement of snubber circuits

3.   Conclusion

From the experiments conducted on power pulse modulator, rise time has to be optimized less than 1usec, the factors affecting rise time as well as the shape of output pulse has been discussed in this paper, it is revealed that the negative swing of the output pulse can be reduced by properly designed RCD circuit as well as introducing emitter resistance in series with switching element. The optimal rise time can be obtained by reducing secondary number of turns where by reducing inductance. It is noted that secondary winding inductance is function of secondary number of turns as well as value of load resistance, to have a faster rise time which

needs for defense application like RADAR technology PIII biomedical instruments and electrostatic precipitator etc. the primary winding of pulse transformer is fed at a higher voltage by considering series connection of IGBTs which reduces secondary number of turns and there by improvises rise time.

References

1. Patrick R. Palmer, Member, IEEE and Anthony N. Giyhiari, Student, IEEE " The Series Connection Of IGBT's With Active Voltage Sharing"
2. G. Busatto, B. Cascone, L. Fratelli, A. Luciano. "Series Connection Of IGBT In Hard Switching Applications"
3. D. Borrtis, J. Biela and J. W. Kolar Power Electronics systems Laboratory ETH Zurich 'Design and Control of an an Active Reset Circuit for Pulse Transformer'
4. Ju Won Baek, Member, IEEE, Dong-Wook Yoo, Member, IEEE, and Heung-Geun Kim, Member, IEEE. " High Voltage Switch using Series Connected IGBT's With Simple auxiliary Circuit"
5. Y suresh Hanumantha " M. Tech. Dissertation 2006-2008 VJTI Mumbai, Expérimentas on pulse power modulator
6. Jose o Rossi, Joaquim Barraso Mario Vella IEEE transsection on plasma science
7. Workshop on power pulse modulator by power beam society of india, june 03, 2006

Optimisation techniques in fault tolerance implementation in distributed operating systems

Ms. Manjusha Joshi

Lecturer, M.P.S.T.M.E. Electronics Dept, Mumbai, India.

1. Introduction

With the current trend of ever scaling up of computing power, the processing power of scientific computers will be in the range of petaflops if the computing power obeys Moore's law [5]. The systems with about one lakh parallel processors can be a reality.

Permission to make digital or hard copies of all or part of this work for personal or classroom use is granted without fee provided that copies are not made or distributed for profit or commercial advantage and that copies bear this notice and the full citation on the first page. To copy otherwise, or republish, to post on servers or to redistribute to lists, requires prior specific permission and/or a fee.

Conference'04, Month 1–2, 2004, City, State, Country. Copyright 2004 ACM 1-58113-000-0/00/0004...$5.00.

The systems will be massively parallel. The parallel computing environment above 10,000 processors currently in use shows poor scalability performance [5]. This reduces the performance and efficiency of parallel processing applications with number of processors above 1 lacs. Lowering number of processors does not solve the problem either. The performance of the larger applications is affected not for the limitations of the technology but for the limitations of the computing paradigm used by the computing fraternity. The computing paradigm regarding fault tolerance implementation needs to be changed if massively parallel processors are to be effectively utilized.

The paper explains the inherent limitations of current approach of fault tolerant algorithms in the first section and proposes modification to the mentioned algorithms the second section and concludes the discussion in the third section.

Section I

The current scenario in parallel processing is such that the effective power extracted from the 10,000 processor machine was equal to 100 processors. Amdahl's Law [5] states efficiency drops off as the number of processors increases. The reality for 100,000 processor machines is that Currently, applications typically ensure fault tolerance by writing out checkpoints at regular intervals. If a fault is located at any one node, then all the processes involved in parallel processing are stopped and the job is reloaded from the last checkpoint. With a 100,000 processors, machine checkpoint/ restart may not be an effective utilization of the resources. The rest of the 99,999 processes are killed because one node has failed. The classical checkpoint/restart solution becomes completely impractical to deal with failure. The paper explores the notion of naturally fault tolerant algorithms, which have the mathematical properties that they get the correct answer despite the occurrence of faults in the system. the peak power might be in the petaflops range but the effective power may be only a couple of teraflops [2]. The critical issue with parallel applications of large number of processors is the mean time between failures [2]. One of the reasons for such limitation is an inappropriate remedy for fault location and correction .

The applications such in life sciences, genetic engineering, meteorological analysis and large database applications need massively parallel processors. The results are critically dependent upon the performance of the parallel computing system. For such applications since they are real time, mean time between failures has to be very low. The system should be necessarily characterized by high throughput, high availability and responsiveness. Such systems cannot work with casual, self correcting remedies like rebooting the

S.J. Pise (ed.), *ThinkQuest 2010*, DOI 10.1007/978-81-8489-989-4_56,
© Springer India Pvt. Ltd. 2011

application. The approach like fault detection after the fault has occurred and then shifting the task to another processor will also be not the right approach as applications are time stringent real time and critical. On the contrary, care should be taken that there is no loss of information and time at a faulty node.

Section II

The drawbacks which were addressed in the previous section need a number of changes to be implemented. All are listed with adequate discussion starting with the simplest ones. The communications processor used has equally strong processing power as the computing processor. The only difference being the software running on it. If communication performance is not an issue for a particular application, then the communication processor can be configured as a computing node. With many processors the interconnection network becomes critical for effectively utilizing the individual processing power available. An innovative interconnection scheme with three separate interconnection networks can be used. The first is a three dimensional torus that is used for general-purpose point-to-point communication. The torus links from each node can further connect to a second level. The second network is a global tree that is designed to handle one-to-all and all- to-all functionality. The third network is Ethernet and is used for host control, booting, and diagnostics.

Factors like I/O and cache misses can quickly drive efficiency down even if the best known algorithms are being used for the solution. By having comparably faster processor network can enhance the speed. Here the age old dictum „a chain is as weak as the weakest link holds good. Hence there is no sense in connecting a few too fast or too slow computers in a network. All nodes of similar processing capability are preferred.

A new class of algorithms called super-scalable algorithms [2] that have the properties of scale invariance and natural fault tolerance are proposed in the paper. Failure recovery can be avoided if the algorithm is naturally fault tolerant. However, failure detection and notification are still needed to inform the algorithm to adapt. Naturally fault tolerant algorithm has been developed in two broad problem areas. The first is where the problem can be formulated as some function of a local volume. Such problems include finite difference and finite element applications. The second is where the problem requires global information. Such problems include finding the global maximum or minimum and are often used to determine if an iterative algorithm has converged.

Some significant changes need to be implemented in task farming [5]. First, the tasks must be aware of and be able to communicate with at least a small set of other tasks. Second, the tasks need to be able to synchronize with each other either implicitly through message passing or explicitly so that the parallel computation can proceed in the correct order.

Third, the tasks should be able to deal with the failure of one or more of the tasks they communicate with in a manner consistent with the computation being performed.

The approach proposed combines two ideas: chaotic relaxation [1] and mesh less methods [4]. The first is to avoid having to synchronize across all the nodes between iterations. The second is to be able to adapt to faults without requiring a replacement node to fill in the hole in the grid. Together these two ideas form the basis for a naturally fault tolerant algorithm. Scale invariance is implemented by communicating between that the individual tasks with the neighboring processors. A binary tree approach is used where each task talks to only two other tasks. Due to this implementation, the individual tasks are not affected due to failures throughout the system unless these failures happen to affect one of their neighbors. This implements scale invariance.

Scale invariance does not guarantee that an algorithm will achieve high efficiency. Scale invariance also doesn't make an algorithm fault tolerant. Scale invariance isolates the failures. This helps in handling fault tolerance by fixing the errors locally. There are three steps to traditional fault tolerance. First is detection. Second is notification. At least at the runtime operating system must be notified about the failure application. The resilience to fault can be implemented by introducing controlled redundancy at the cost of system performance. Same task is allotted to more than one node so that the failure of one node does not generate a fault condition. Such controlled redundancy is introduced only for those applications notified as faulty ones by the operating system. Recovery involves two steps—previously saving a copy of state somewhere other than the affected node and restoring that state on the same or another node after a failure. The paper proposes recovery by periodically distributing the states of the tasks with a few neighbouring nodes with which the parallel task division performed with controlled redundancy. Each task communicates with and these tasks store their part of the is state in their local memory. calculated, usually once at setup, if needed. Figure 1 shows a 2-D mesh less layout [2]. The distance and direction are not needed for all applications, but are crucial for weighting the data coming from the neighbors in some applications. If the copy of state of the affected node is stored on the disk of another node, then this is called disk checkpointing [2]. This suffers with performance bottleneck. To avoid this, periodically, the state of all local tasks is communicated in the form of data strings with the neighbouring nodes. This is called diskless check pointing [3]. This ensures that even if one of the processor goes in fault, the process state of that processor is saved into the cache of the neighbouring node. In this way, checkpointing is performed in a parallel manner which does not sacrifice upon the system performance.

When fixed mesh with a finite difference stencil of neighbours is used, traditionally standard difference equations

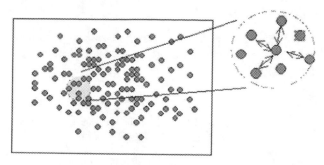

Fig. 1 2-D Meshless layout

and their error properties break down when information from one of the stencil nodes is left out. There are several ways to formulate meshless solution methods [4]. The approach of randomly placing the nodes across the problem space with a uniform distribution is used. Each node is then given a list of m nodes locally around it including their location so that distance and direction to each of the neighbours can be calculated. The value of m is chosen by the application developer based on the nature of the calculation being performed at each node. The information is there so that these values can be.

The finite difference solution to the Poisson equation can be thought of as an averaging of values in nearby nodes. The natural fault tolerance implemented in our algorithm proceeds in the following way, when one of the nearby nodes fails the calculation adapts by simply averaging over a smaller number of nearby nodes as seen in Figure 1.

Each node runs the following algorithm.

$$\text{The new value} \quad v = \frac{\sum_{n=1}^{m} v_n/d_n}{\sum_{n=1}^{m} 1/d_n}$$

initialize stored value
initialize stored neighbor values
compute and store distances to neighbours
do forever
if not boundary node
receive value from any neighbor
store neighbor value
compute new value v using neighbor
values and distances
end
if local value differs from new
value by more than epsilon
set local value to new value
multicast new value to all neighbours
end if
else
get new boundary value

multicast new boundary value to
all neighbours

Global information

Global Information: There are many problems where global information is needed, for example those involving gravity and radiative transport often require the need for the calculation of long-range forces. Global information is also needed in most iterative methods to determine if convergence has been achieved. The restriction imposed on super-scalable algorithms is that tasks can communicate with only a constant number of neighbours. The first thing to observe is that a tree network is the standard communication pattern used for determining global information. But a tree will not work if node failures occur because one or more branches of the tree become isolated and will not get the correct answer. Eliminating tree topologies, there are still several node topologies that could be good fits to global information problems. A node's neighbour set is chosen based on the particulars of the underlying problem, for example where neighbours are chosen from all the nodes but using a distribution function like 1/r2 radiating out from each node. A node's neighbour set is chosen based on a regular fixed pattern such as a 3-D mesh or hypercube. A node's neighbour set is chosen randomly from all the nodes with a uniform distribution.

*A node stops sending max values to a neighbour
if the neighbour fails.*
procedure failure notification:
identify failed neighbour
stop sending max to failed neighbour
delete stored value and distance of failed neighbour
end

end if end do *A node stops sending values to a neighbour and deletes the stored neighbour value and distance if the neighbour fails.* procedure failure notification: identify failed

neighbour
stop sending values to failed
neighbour

Natural fault tolerant global max

All nodes compute their max and multicast it to their neighbours. If a received max is greater than the stored max, the received one overwrites the stored one and the neighbours receive an update.

procedure main: compute local max multicast local max to all neighbours do forever receive max from any neighbour if local max less than neighbour max set local max to neighbour max multicast local max to all

neighbours end if end do
end

Section III

From the above discussion and different algorithms it can be clearly concluded that if certain measures are implemented to parallel processing applications and if fault tolerance remedies are rewritten with the afore mentioned changes in paradigms, natural fault tolerance can be achieved in parallel processing systems. The current scenario in parallel processing system in distributed computing characterised by low throughput, large volume of mean time between failures, wrong computation of result etc. can be avoided.

Limitations

The above discussion assumes the algorithms implemented are not embarrassingly parallel applications. If the applications are limited by series implementation, then such algorithms cannot be used.

Further scope

Further research needs to be done by classifying the major application problems and working out on task farming of those applications

References

1. D. Chazan, and M. Miranker, "Chaotic Relaxation", *Linear Algebra and its Applications* pp199-222, 1969
2. Al Geist, Christian Engelmann, Oak Ridge National Laboratory "Development of naturally Fault Tolerant Algorithms for Computing on 1,00,000 Processors." www.csm.ornl.gov/~geist
3. James S. Plank, Member, IEEE Computer Society, Kai Li, Member, IEEE Computer Society, and Michael A. Puening "Diskless Checkpointing" Transactions on parallel and distributed systems, vol. 9, no. 10, October 1998
4. G. R. Liu, "Mesh Free Methods: Moving IEEE Method", 1st Edition, CRC Press, July 2002
5. Harry F.Jordan,Gita Alaghband "fundamentals of parallel processing" ,PHI publication, Eastern Economy Edition

Multimodal medical image fusion using wavelet transform

Shuneza Sayed[1] · Smita Jangale[2]

[1]Lecturer, BGIT, Mumbai, India
[1]Student, VESIT, Mumbai, India
[2]VESIT, Mumbai, India

1. Introduction

In the recent years, the study of multimodality medical image fusion attracts much attention with the increasing of clinic application demanding. Radiotherapy plan, for instance, often benefits from the complementary information in images of different modalities. Dose calculation is based on the computed tomography (CT) data, while tumor outlining is often better performed in the corresponding magnetic resonance (MR) scan. For medical diagnosis,CT provides the best information on denser tissue with less distortion, MRI provides better information on soft tissue with more distortion, and PET provides better information on blood flow and flood activity with low space resolution in general. With more available multimodality medical images in clinical applications, the idea of combining images from different modalities becomes very important and medical image fusion has merged as a new and promising research field. Medical fusion image is to combine functional image and anatomical image together into one image. This paper proposes a global energy fusion strategy which is region level image fusion method. In this paper, match measures are calculated as a whole to select the wavelet coefficients coming from different sub images of the same scale. More abundant information of the edges can be obtained and a more suitable image can be got in view of the human vision.

2.1 Image fusion using wavelet transform

The block diagram of a generic wavelet-based image fusion scheme is shown in the following figure

Wavelet transform is first performed on each source images, then a fusion decision map is generated based on a set of fusion rules. The fused wavelet coefficient map can be constructed from the wavelet coefficients of the source images according to the fusion decision map. Finally the fused image is obtained by performing the inverse wavelet transform.From the above diagram, we can see that the fusion rules are playing a very important role during the fusion process. Here are some frequently used fusion rules.

When constructing each wavelet coefficient for the fused image. We will have to determine which source image describes this coefficient better. This information will be kept in the fusion decision map. The fusion decision map has the same size as the original image. Each value is the index of the source image which may be more informative on the corresponding wavelet coefficient. Thus, we will actually make decision on each coefficient. There are two frequently used methods in the previous research. In order to make the decision on one of the coefficients of the fused image, one way is to consider the corresponding coefficients in the source images as illustrated by the red pixels. This is called pixel-based fusion rule. The other way is to consider not only the corresponding coefficients, but also their close neighbors, say a 3×3 or 5×5 windows, as illustrated by the blue and shadowing pixels. This is called window-based fusion rules. This method considered the fact that there usually has high correlation among neighboring pixels.

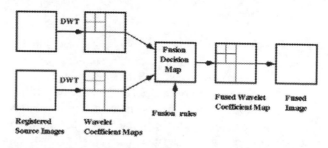

Fig. 1 Image fusion scheme

S.J. Pise (ed.), *ThinkQuest 2010*, DOI 10.1007/978-81-8489-989-4_57,

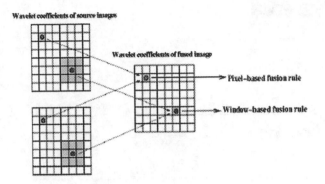

Fig. 2 Frequently used fusion rules

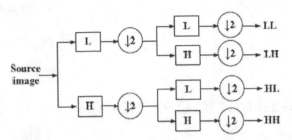

Fig. 3 A structure of dwt

and low-pass filtering realized with respect to the column vectors and the row vectors of array pixels. Figure 3 shows the structures of the filter bank that performs the decomposition at level 2.Here, H and L represent the high-pass and low-pass filter respectively. In this way the four sub images (LL1, LH1, HL1 and HH1) can be obtained to respectively represent the detail information in smoothed version and in horizontal, vertical and diagonal directions of the input image. In a similar manner, the approximation sub images can be obtained. such as two-level (LL2, LH2, HL2 and HH2), three level (LL3, LH3, HL3 and HH3), and so forth.

In this research, we think objects carry the information of interest, each pixel or a small neighboring pixels are just one part of an object. Thus, we proposed a region-based fusion scheme. When make the decision on each coefficient, we consider not only the corresponding coefficients and their closing neighborhood, but also the regions the coefficients are in. We think the regions represent the objects of interest. There are some key points of region-based image fusion approach:

- Consider each pixel as part of object or region of interest
- Use image features, such as edges and regions to guide the fusion
- Retrieve both spatial and frequency information from the wavelet coefficients.

2.3 Algorithm

In this paper, a new method is proposed, that is Global Energy Method (GEM). This strategy is superior to existing image fusion methods such as Region Energy Merging Based Method (REM) [7]and a better-fused image can be obtained.GEM is based on the DWT. Several definitions of a few main parameters of our fusion rules will first be

Given out

$$E_{ijn}^{v}(p) = \sum_{p \in A} W(p)(D_{ijn}^{v}(p))^2 \tag{3}$$

Where ij represents a frequency band LL, LH, HL, HH. $E_{ijn}^{v}(p) =$ is the energy of the region A, and the more salient image can contain the more energy. $D_{ijn}^{v}(p)$ energy. = is the wavelet decomposition coefficient of each source image and v will tell us that actual value of $D_{ijn}^{v}(p)$ of coming from X or Y (X or Y stands for different input images). In this method, every pixel should belong to the certain region A and n means the level of DWT $W(p)$is the weight of A. Considering the relativity of the DWT coefficients, the value of weight in the center of A should be a bit larger than that of edge

2.2 Discrete wavelet frame

Many researchers recognized that multi-scale transforms are very useful for image fusion. The most convenient representation of an image requires that the image can be recovered without any information lost. This process is always viewed as perfect reconstruction condition and ? is defined as the scale function an is defined as the wavelet function. Thus the perfect reconstruction can be represented as:

$$\Psi^{\downarrow}\left(\psi^{\uparrow}(x), \omega^{\uparrow}(x)\right) = x, \quad for \ x \in V_0 \tag{1}$$

It satisfies the additional constraints

$$\psi^{\uparrow}\left(\Psi^{\downarrow}(x,y)\right) = x \ and \ \omega^{\uparrow}\left(\Psi^{\downarrow}(x,y)\right) = y, \tag{2}$$
$$for \ x \in V_1, y \in W_1$$

Which guarantee that the decomposition is non redundant. Discrete Wavelets Transform is a multi resolution analysis tool and it decomposes a signal into different frequency bands. This paper will give a brief scheme of two-dimensional (2-D) wavelet analysis and more detail information about the wavelet theory can be found in [1–6]. The decompose process generates (at level 1) an approximate sub image and three high frequency sub images via the high-pass

$$M_{ijn}(p) = \frac{2\sum_{p \in A} D_{ijn}^{X}(p) \times D_{ijn}^{Y}(p)}{E_{ijn}^{X}(p) + E_{ijn}^{Y}(p)}, \ ij = LH, HL, HH \tag{4}$$

$$M_n(p) = M_{LHn}(p) \times 0.25 + M_{HLn}(p) \times 0.25 + M_{HHn}(p) \times 0.5 \tag{5}$$

How to choose the fusion algorithms depends on the similarities between the source images. The match measure is a parameter reflecting the resemblance between the input images. $M_{ijn}(p)$ means that the base match measure of this new image fusion rule. Mn (p) is improvement of $M_{ijn}(p)$,

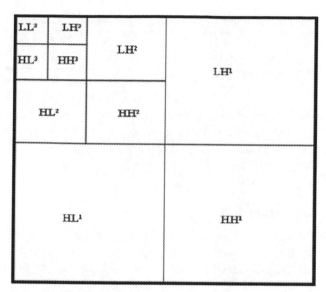

Fig. 4 Wavelet decompositions

it is the sum of match measures coming from $I_{LH}(x, y)$ $I_{HL}(x, y)$ and $I_{HH}(x, y)$. Especially, the coefficients coming from $I_{HH}(x, y)$ contain more information about edge. So the weight of $M_{HHn}(p)$ is larger than the weight of $M_{HLn}(p)$ and $M_{LHn}(p)$. Then more information about edge is obtained. The selection of coefficients of the fused image depend on the value of $M_n(p)$. For some threshold, all the coefficients of $I_{LH}(x,y)$, $I_{HL}(x,y)$ and $I_{HH}(x,y)$ come from a single source image. In the mean time, the value of $I_{LL}(x,y)$ also comes from the same image considering consistency. In REM, the coefficients of the fused image might come from different images, which will result in in consistency. One of our tasks is to find out a proper W_{ijn}^v of our fusion rules. Discrete wavelet coefficient of the fusion image depends on when W_{ijn}^v source images have strong relativity. Thus the weight selected in paper is show as follows:

$$W_{ijn}^X(p) = \begin{cases} 0.5 - 0.5 \times \dfrac{1 - M_{ijn}^x(p)}{1-\alpha}, & if\ E_{ijn}^X(p) \ge E_{ijn}^Y(p) \\ 0.5 + 0.5 \times \dfrac{1 - M_{ijn}^x(p)}{1-\alpha}, & if\ E_{ijn}^X(p) < E_{ijn}^Y(p) \end{cases} \qquad (6)$$

$$W_{ijn}^Y(p) = 1 - W_{ijn}^X(p)$$

The following algorithm performs the fusion process.
1. Initialization: Define the area size A which will be used around each location p; $n = -1$.
2. Input: Image F1 and F2, set X=F1 and Y=F2
3. While n<N
   DO n=n+1

$$X,Y \to DWT \to D_{LLn}^{X,Y},\ D_{LHn}^{X,Y},\ D_{HLn}^{X,Y},\ D_{HHn}^{X,Y};$$

set $X = D_{LLn}^X$, $Y = D_{LLn}^Y$ **and go to 3**

4. Fused image: Select: for each location p at (x,y) in the transformed sub images compute the following region energy values using equation (3)

$$E_{ijn}^X(p); E_{ijn}^Y(p)\ with\ ij = LL, LH, HL, HH$$

Merge: firstly low frequency band is calculated:
5. Then high frequency bands are calculated

when $M_{ijn}(p) \ge \alpha$

DO

$$D_{ijn}^v(p) = W_{ijn}^X(p) \times D_{ijn}^X(p) + W_{ijn}^Y(p) \times D_{ijn}^Y(p)$$
$$(ij = LH,\ HL,\ HH)$$

When $M_{ijn}(p) < \alpha$

Do

$$e_{ijn}^v(p) = max (E_{ijn}^X(p), E_{ijn}^Y(p))$$

$$D_{ijn}^v(p) = D_{ijn}^X(p)\ IF\ e_{ijn}^v(p)\ come\ from\ X,\ else$$

$$D_{ijn}^v(p) = D_{ijn}^Y(p)\ (ij = LH,\ HL,\ HH)$$

6. while n≠1

   apply IDWT to D_{LLn}^W, D_{LHn}^W, D_{HLn}^W, D_{HHn}^W

   obtaining $D_{LL(n-1)}^W$;

   n=n-1 and go to 6

7. output: fused image $Z = D_{LLn}^W$

3.1 Performance measures

As a quality measure, the RMSE (Root Mean Square Error) is used. It is expressed as follows

$$RMSE = \left(\frac{1}{MN} \sum_{n=1}^{N} \sum_{m=1}^{M} (x_R(n,m) - x_F(n,m))^2 \right)^{1/2} \qquad (7)$$

Where is XR is the ideal reference, XF the obtainedfused image, and M, N are the dimensions of theimages. Root mean square error indicates how mucherror the fused image X F conveys about the reference X R Thus, the lower the RMSE between X F and X Rthe more likely resembles the ideal X R

4. Experiments result

The global energy method can achieve best results. MAX is worst .A preliminary conclusion therefore is that the region based scheme is outperforms the pixel-based scheme. And this proposed method contains more high frequency information. Then more abundant information of the edges

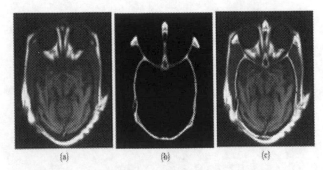

Fig. 5 a) Original MRI Image b) Orginal CT Image c) Final fused image

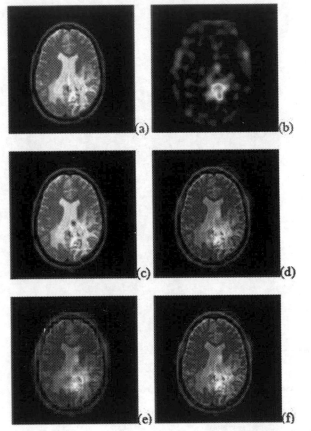

Fig. 6 Applications of different algorithms in the field of medical image fusion: (a) MRI; (b) PET; (c) fused image by GEM; (d) fused image by REM; (e) fused image by MAX; (f) fused image by variance

Table 1 RMSE for different methods of Fig. 6

Methods	MAX	variance	REM	GEM
RMSE	0.0581	0.0125	0.0113	0.0053

could be obtained. And when each frequent band coefficient comes from the same image, the better result can be achieved. The RMSE is used to measure the difference between the source image and the fused image; the smaller the value of RMSE and the smaller the difference, the better the fusion performance

5. Conclusion

This paper put forward a medical image fusion method that is based on region. From the experiment results it can be seen that the method based on region is superior to pixel based method. The information coming from the edges embeds in the region energy. So its fusion image can contain more relevant information about the edges. Moreover when each frequent band coefficient comes from the same image, the consistency of the coefficients can be achieved. At the same time, the experiment results show that this method gives more encouraging and effective performance than other existing image fusion methods.

References

1. Mallat, S., "A Theory for Multiresolution Signal Decomposition: The Wavelet Representation", IEEE Trans. Pattern Anal. Mach. Intell., 11(1989), pp.674–693
2. E.J. Stollnitz, T.D. DeRose, D.H. Salesin, "Wavelets for Computer Graphics", A Primer, Part 1, IEEE Computer Graphics and Applications, 15(3) 1995), pp.76-84
3. I. Daubechies, "Ten Lectures on Wavelets", SIAM, Philadelphia, (1992)
4. I. Daubechies, "Orthonormal Bases of Compactly Supported Wavelets", Comm.Pure Applied Mathematics, 41 (1988), pp.909-996
5. Cohen, A., Daubechies, I., Feauveau, J., "Biorthogonal Bases of Compactly Supported LIU Gui-Xi
6. YANG Wan-Hai, "Image Fusion Scheme of Pixel-Level and Multi-Operator Infrared
7. Li Yan, Tan ou,Duan Huilong, "Visualization of Three-Dimensional Medical Images", Journal of Image and Graphics, Vol. 6A(2), (2001) pp. 103–11

Performance evaluation of energy based gossip routing algorithm for on-off source traffic

Dhiraj Nitnaware · Praveen Karma · Ajay Verma

Institute of Engineering & Technology, DAVV, Indore, India.

1. Introduction

MANET is a multi-hop, infrastructureless wireless network in which nodes are free to move. Each node has limited battery power and bandwidth. Thus energy parameter plays an important role in the current research interests. Reactive protocols like AODV [4] and DSR [5] uses flooding method to forward RREQ packets during route discovery process and RERR (route error) packets during route maintenance process because of which many routing packets are unnecessarily increases which in turn increases the energy consumption of each node.

In the related work, Dhiraj Nitnaware et. al. [1] proposed Energy based Gossip algorithm for MANET. M. Frikha et al. [2] has proposed an energy constraint routing protocol in which the intermediate node forward the RREQ packets if its energy is more and drop the packet if its energy is less than the set threshold energy. J.Haas et. al. [3] has proposed Gossip technique to reduce the number of RREQ packets and to increase the performance of the network. In this technique, the intermediate nodes forward the RREQ packets with some set probability. Both the author uses packet delivery fraction (throughput), average end to end delay and normalized routing overhead as the performance parameters.

This paper is concentrates on the EBG algorithm other than flooding which reduced the energy consumption by all nodes due to transmission and reception of control packets and routing overhead without affecting the throughput.

The paper is organized as: In section 2 discuss the working of AODV protocol and proposed EBG protocols. The simulation model is presented in section 3. Section 4 gives the simulation results and sections 5 describe conclusion and future scope.

2. Manet routing protocol

This section gives the brief description of existing AODV protocol and proposed EBG algorithm.

2.1 The ad hoc on demand distance vector

AODV protocol [4] also called reactive routing protocol finds route to destination when demanded. It consists of routing table that contains sequence number and next hops information which helps to distinguish between stale and fresh routes. The protocol consists of two processes: route discovery and route maintenance. In route discovery process, the source node generate RREQ packet and floods it to the neighboring nodes. The connectivity between the nodes is maintaining using *Hello* messages. The neighbouring nodes than flood it to there neighbours and so on. When the packet reaches the destination node, it then generates RREP (Route Reply) packet and send back to the source node and the path is established. In route maintenance process, the source node is being notified by RERR (Route Error) message in case of broken link.

2.2 Proposed energy based gossip

The working EBG algorithm is explained as given in [1] with the help of following steps: The steps involved in the proposed algorithm are:

Step 1: *At source node*:
 The source node generates RREQ packet and broadcast to its neighbors if path is not available.

Step 2: *At intermediate node*:
 Intermediate nodes forward the RREQ packets with probability k. This probability k is calculated on the

S.J. Pise (ed.), *ThinkQuest 2010*, DOI 10.1007/978-81-8489-989-4_58,
© Springer India Pvt. Ltd. 2011

basis of current energy status of that node. If the nodes remaining energy is 80% of the initial energy than k = 0.8, if 75% then k = 0.75, if 60% then k = 0.6 and so on.

Step 3: *At destination node*:

The destination node will send RREP packet back to source node on receiving RREQ packet.

3. Simulation model

We have taken 50 nodes that are randomly distributed in a region of 1000m X 1000m with 30 number of connection. The energy model consists of NIC card that includes radio range of 250m, 2Mbps data rate. Initial energy supplied to each node is 200J. The power consumed during transmission and reception is 1.65W and 1.1W respectively.

The traffic model used is CBR (Constant Bit Rate) with packet size of 512 bytes and rate 64 packets/s and Pareto traffic with burst time 2.5s, idle time 1.0s (these are average On-Off time of the generator), shape 2.5, packet size of 512 bytes and rate 64 packets/s. Simulation time is 900s. The simulation is done with the help of ns-2 [7] and traffic model is generated using cbreng.tcl [8].

4. Results

We have evaluated (i) Energy consumption due to routing packets (ii) Routing overhead and (iii) Delivery ratio for comparison between AODV and EBG protocols with traffic model as CBR and Pareto and following results was observed.

4.1 Energy consumption

Figure 1a, 1b, 1c, 1d and 1e shows the total energy consumed (Joules) by all the nodes due to transmission and reception of control packets as a function of pause time, speed, number of source, area shape and sending rate respectively. From the graph, we observed that energy consumption of EBG is less as compared to AODV with 10 % to 30 % with CBR and 5% to 20% with Pareto traffic. The

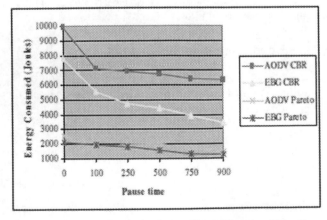

Fig. 1a   Energy consumption Versus Pause Time

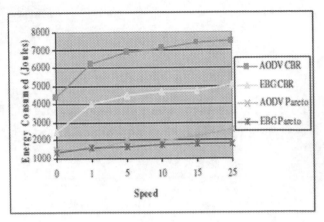

Fig. 1b   Energy consumption Versus Speed

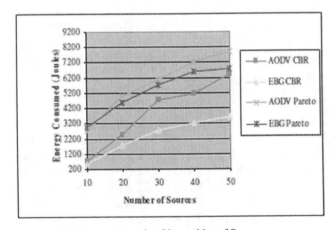

Fig. 1c   Energy consumption Versus No. of Source

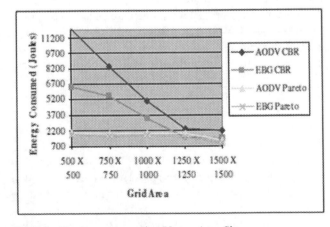

Fig. 1d   Energy consumption Versus Area Shape

reduction in energy is due to reduction in the number of control packets involved in discovery process.

4.2 Normalized routing overhead

Figure 2a, 2b, 2c, 2d and 2e shows the routing overhead of all the nodes as a function of pause time, speed, number

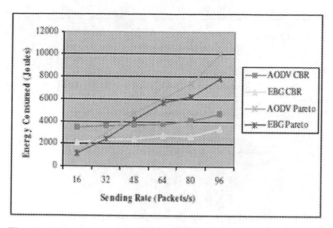

Fig. 1e Energy consumption Versus Sending Rate

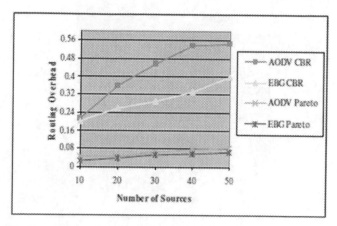

Fig. 2c Routing Overhead Versus No. of Source

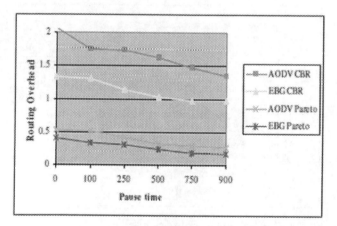

Fig. 2a Routing Overhead versus Pause Time

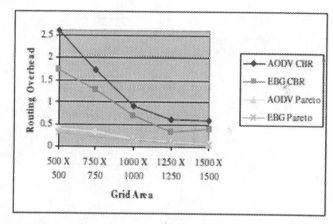

Fig. 2d Routing Overhead Versus Area Shape

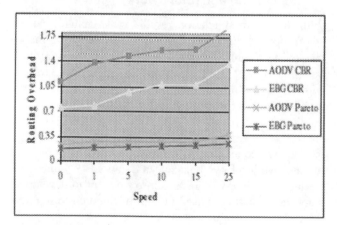

Fig. 2b Routing Overhead versus Speed

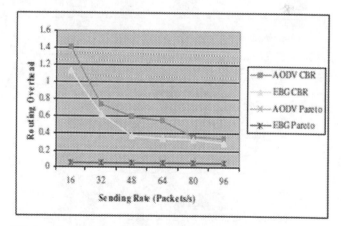

Fig. 2e Routing Overhead versus Sending Rate

of source, area shape and sending rate respectively. Again we observed that there is reduction in the routing overhead upto10 % to 30 % with CBR and 5% to 20% with Pareto traffic.

4.3 Delivery ratio

Figure 3a, 3b, 3c, 3d and 3e shows the delivery ratio by varying pause time, speed, number of source, area shape and sending rate respectively. We observed that the delivery

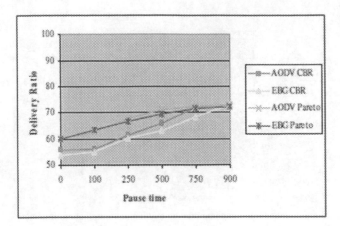

Fig. 3a   Delivery Ratio versus Pause Time

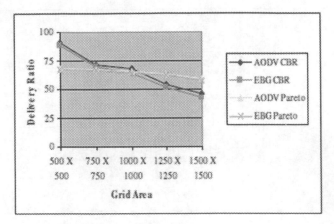

Fig. 3d   Delivery Ratio versus Area Shape

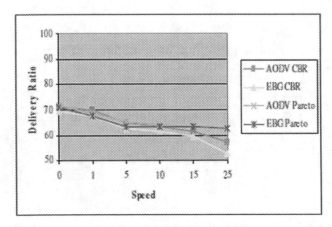

Fig. 3b   Delivery Ratio versus Speed

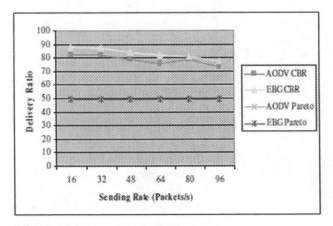

Fig. 3e   Delivery Ratio versus Sending Rate

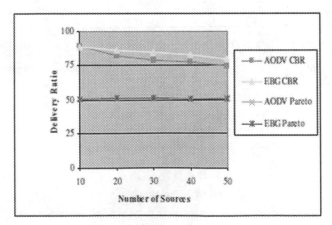

Fig. 3c   Delivery Ratio versus No. of Sources

ratio of both EBG and AODV is almost similar with both traffic sources.

Thus the new proposed algorithm shows improvement in the energy consumption and routing overhead without affecting the delivery ratio.

5.   Conclusion and future work

With the above simulation results, we conclude that the new proposed algorithm EBG shows better performance than existing AODV under all scenarios and under all traffic sources. There is 10% to 30% with CBR and 5% to 20% with Pareto traffic, energy and overhead reduction under mobility pattern (pause time and speed) and traffic pattern (number of sources and sending rate) and network size (grid area).

Thus we conclude that energy consumption as well as routing overhead can be reduced using EBG without affecting the delivery ratio. In future we want to develop an algorithm that can be used instead of flooding to improve the performance of the network.

References

1.   Dhiraj Nitnaware and Ajay Verma, "Energy Based Gossip Routing Algorithm for MANETs" Accepted in ACEEE International Conference (ITC-2010) at Chennai on 12-13 March

2.   M. Frikha and F. Ghandour, "Implementation and Performance Evaluation of an Energy Constraint Routing Protocol

for MANET", 3rd International Conference of Telecommunications (AICT'07), IEEE, 2007

3. Zygmunt J.Haas, Senior member, IEEE, Joseph Y.Halpern, Senior member, IEEE, " Gossip Based Ad Hoc Routing", IEEE Transactions on networking, Vol.14, No.3, June 2006

4. Charles E. Perkins, Elizabeth M. Royer and S. Das, "Ad-Hoc on Demand Distance Vector Routing (AODV)", draft-ietfmanet-aodv-05.txt, March 2000

5. David B. Johnson, Davis A. Maltz and Y.C.Hu, "DSR for Mobile Ad Hoc Network", Internet-Draft, draft-ietfmanet-drs-09.txt, July 2003

6. N.Mahesh, T.V.P.Sundararajan, Dr. A. Shanmugam, "Improving performance of AODV Protocol using Gossip based approach", IEEE International Conference on Computational Intelligence and Multimedia Applications, 2007

7. Network Simulator, ns-2, http://www.isi. edu/nsnam/-ns/

8. http://www.isi.edu/nsnam/ns/tutorial/

9. Juan Carlos Cano and Pietro Manzoni, "A Performance Comparison of Energy Consumption for Mobile Ad Hoc Network Routing Protocols", Proceeding of 8th International Symposium on Modeling, Analysis and Simulation of Computer & Telecommunication System 2000

10. David B. Johnson, Davis A. Maltz and J. Broch, " DSR for Mobile Ad Hoc Network", November 1999

11. Humaira Ehsan and Zartash Afzal Uzmi, "Performance Comparison of Ad Hoc Wireless Network Routing Protocols",

Proceeding of INMIC 2004, 8th International Multitopic Conference, pp 457-465, IEEE December 2004

12. Charles E. Perkins and Pravin Bhagwat, "Highly Dynamic Destination Sequenced Distance Vector Routing (DVDV) for Mobile Computers", Proceeding of ACM SIGCOMM, October 1994

13. Charles E. Perkins and Elizabeth M. Royer, "Performance Comparison of Two On-Demand Routing Protocols for Ad Hoc Networks", IEEE Personal Communication, February 2001

14. Walter Willinger, Murad S. Taqqu, Robert Sherman and Daniel V. Wilson, "Self-Similarity through High-Variability: Statistical Analysis of Ethernet LAN Traffic at the Source Level", IEEE/ACM Transactions on Networking 5, pp. 71-86. April 1997

15. Dhiraj Nitnaware and Ajay Verma, "Energy Evaluation of Proactive and Reactive Protocol for MANET Under ON/OFF Source Traffic", Proceeding of ACM International Conference on Advances in Computing, Communication and Control (ICAC3-2009), pp 451-455, Fr. Conceicao Rodrigues College of Engg. Bandra, Mumbai, January 23-24, 2009

16. Dhiraj Nitnaware and Ajay Verma, "Energy Evaluation of Two On Demand Routing Protocol Under Stochastic Traffic", Proceeding of IEEE International Conference on Control, Communication and Automation (INDICON-2008), pp 183-187, IIT Kanpur, December 11-13, 2008

A knowledge based approach for semantic reasoning of stories using ontology

A. Jaya[1] · G. V. Uma[2]

[1]Research Scholar, Department of Computer Science Engg. Anna University, Chennai , India.
[2]Assistant Professor, Department of Computer Science Engg. Anna University, Chennai, India.

1. Introduction

Reasoning is the cognitive process of looking for reasons for beliefs, conclusions, actions or feelings. It helps to infer conclusions by analyzing facts from a conversation or from situation or from the write ups etc. For every human being, reasoning is like breathing. If it fails, they feel as handicapped. Reasoning is recognized as a structure of thinking and the analysis of the emergence to derive the conclusion. Human beings can do rational reasoning using their sixth sense whereas making the system to reason on available facts and deriving the implicit knowledge is very difficult. In Automatic Story Generation System (ASGS), needs to perform the reasoning on stories in order to provide the proper meanings and also to ensure the valid concepts and consistency in the stories. ASGS generates the story automatically based on the user's desires and interest. Since system generated stories may lacks in semantics, or it may generate the sentences with unreality, it is necessary to undergo the reasoning to detect the erroneous concepts. In order to grab the reader's attention, all these need to be identified and rectified. For example, one of the sentences generated by the system during the story generation phase is, *"Lion was sleeping in the tree top"* - generated by the system. Domain knowledge states that 'Lion' is an instance of wild animal living in the forest. Lion's habitats are Den, cave, under the tree etc. In reality, Lion cannot climb tree. By using all these facts and applying rational thinking, the system has to detect these contradictions and reasoner suggests the recommendation for the above said sentence as *"Lion was sleeping in the Den"* - recommended by the Reasoner. Consider an example like "Rabbit ate the meat"generated by the system As per the concepts in the Ontology, Rabbit is a pet animal and it is herbivores. Usually herbivores animals do not eat meat. If it eats the meat, then it is not herbivores. So, Rabbit cannot eat the meat. The Reasoner suggests the recommendation as in two ways:"Rabbit ate the grass".

"Rabbit not ate the meat" recommended by the Reasoner. User can select any one of the above said sentences. ASG adapts the Formal Reasoning to derive the implicit knowledge from the generated stories. Formal reasoning utilizes predicate logic for reasoning the sentences and it is the study of methods for reasoning and argumentation, both proper and improper. Predicate logic helps any person to construct their own arguments and critique to inference t he reality. There are so many knowledge representation models to represent the data, facts and sentences such as semantic networks, ontology, and conceptual graph so on. ASG exploits the benefits of ontology for representing the entire story world as knowledge base. It defines a common vocabulary [1] for researchers who are in need to share information in a domain. It includes machine-interpretable definitions of basic concepts in the domain and relations among them. Ontology contains the set of axioms or premises to represent the attributes of the objects in the concepts. The role of ontology in reasoning is discussed later section of this paper.

Section 2, describes the existing story generators and reasoning methodologies and their strengths and weaknesses. Section 3 provides the Architecture for story reasoning methodologies in automatic story generation system Section 4 describes implementation issues and Section 5 discusses the results and finally section 6 provides the conclusion and future enhancements.

2. Related works

Prop [3] discussed the story generation as; a tale which is composed of moves. A move is type of functions used to

S.J. Pise (ed.), *ThinkQuest 2010*, DOI 10.1007/978-81-8489-989-4_59,
© Springer India Pvt. Ltd. 2011

generate a part of the story. Each move describes a function from Introduction to climax. One tale may be composed of several moves that are related between them. One move may directly follow another, but they may also interweave; a development, which has begun pauses and a new move can also inserted. But the problem here is, the system may not validate the semantics of the story. Since the story talks about Russian folk tales, order of moves makes the story relevant one.

Peinado [4] discussed the use of KIIDSOnto for the story generation. It incorporates sub-ontology of reusable knowledge for CBR processing which is used by the system to guide the CBR cycle. For managing folk tales, the ontology imports the Proppian morphology, another domain-specific sub-ontology that extends the narrative concept Event with character functions and the narrative concept Existent with character roles. Bailey [5] described an approach to automatic story generation based on the twin assumptions that it is possible for the generation of a story to be driven by modeling of the responses to the story of an imagined target reader, and that doing so allows the essence of what makes a story work to be encapsulated in a simple and general way.

Charles, F et al [7], presented results from a first version of a fully implemented storytelling prototype, which illustrates the generation of variants of a generic storyline. These variants result from the interaction of autonomous characters with one another, with environment resources or from user intervention.

Jie Bao et al [8] discussed the Ontologies that explicitly show the objects, properties and relationships in specific domains are essential for collaborations that involve sharing of data, knowledge or resources among autonomous individuals and he insisted the need for collaborative environments for ontology construction, sharing and their usage. Dimitrios N. Konstantinou et al [9] discussed about the story generation model HOMER. It receives natural language input in the form of a sentence or an icon corresponding to a scene from a story and it generates a text-only narrative that includes, apart from a storyline, a plot, characters and a setting, the user's stylistic preferences and also point-of-view.

Riedl et al [11] sketches the flow of story as a linear progression of events with anticipated user actions and system-controlled agent actions together in a partially ordered plan. For every possible way the user can violate the story plan, an alternative story plan is generated. If narrative mediation is powerful enough to express the same interactive stories as systems that use branching story structures, then linear narrative generation techniques can be applied to interactive narrative generation with the use of narrative mediation.

Also, Riedl et al [10] had provided planning algorithm for story generation. The story planners are limited by the fact that they can only operate on the story world provided, which impacts the ability of the planner to find a solution story plan and the quality and structure of the story plan if one is found, but which lacks semantics. The closed world assumption places a burden on the human author to describe a world that supports story generation.

Jaya et al [13] discussed about the simple story generation by generating suitable sentences with language grammar. The readers or user's can elect the characters, location, settings, theme for constructing the simple story whereas this model does not concentrates on the semantics of the story. By extending their work [14], the user can conceive the theme by selecting the order of events in new perspective way to construct the stories. In story generation model, the reasoning process begins to reason the sentences in the story to provide the meanings and to check the consistency of the concepts in the ontology. Ong Siew Kin [6] et al discussed the reasoning with ontology in a neat fashion. He discussed about the Reasoning tasks involving individuals, who are called assertion reasoning, are:

Realization – By giving partial description of an individual, it finds the most specific concept.
Instance checking – given a partial description of an individual and a class description, finds whether the class describes the instance.
Individual retrieval – finds all individuals that are described by a given concept.

There are many story generation model exists in the story worlds with their own strength and weakness. Some of the system generated stories may not be consistent with the concepts and their attributes. This kind of formal reasoning provides the environment to check the consistency of concepts in a systematic way.

3. Architecture diagram for reasoning the stories

Story Reasoning helps to analyze the stories to check the consistency of the concepts in the story. In story world, there are no specific concepts to describe the facts and instances whereas in the real world, there are specific concepts and their attributes should be validated. Story Reasoning checks the concepts based on the real world with generated story. It involves not only the stories generated by the system, but also analyses the other stories too. The various parameters for story reasoning are: characters played in the story, locations where the characters playing their actions, set of events played by characters. Either knowledge may be declarative or procedural; to facilitate the reasoning, entire knowledge must be represented in knowledge representation mechanism. Procedural knowledge is compiled knowledge related to the performance of some task. Declarative knowledge is passive knowledge expressed as statements of facts about the world. Ontology is used to state the entire domain knowledge which provides the set of axioms for inference the implicit knowledge from the stories. The diagram for Reasoner.

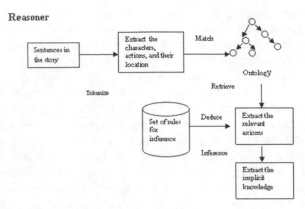

Fig. 1 Conceptual diagram for reasoner

The story sentences are given as input and the necessary characters, action and their locations are extracted. The extracted information is parsed to ontology and Ontology realizes the concepts then relevant attributes are retrieved for reasoning. By applying predicate logic over the set of premises and extracted information, the implicit knowledge can be derived. The standard First Order Logic primitives are:

1. **Variable symbols** : For ex, : x, y
2. **Connectives:** Not (~), And (^) , Or (V), Implies ($\Rightarrow$) , if and only if ($\Leftrightarrow$)
3. **Quantifiers:** Universal ($\forall$), Existential ($\exists$)

Sentences or arguments built up from terms and atoms:

1. A **term is** a constant symbol, a variable symbol, or n-place function of n terms. For example, x and f(x1....xn) are terms, where each xi is a term.
2. An **atom** which has value of true or false is either an n-place predicate of n terms, or , if P and Q are atoms then ~P , PVQ , P^Q are atoms
3. A **sentence** is an atom, or, If P is a sentence and x is a variable, then (?x)P and (?x)P are sentences
4. A **well-formed formula** (wff) is a sentence containing no "free" variables. I.e. all variables are "bound" by universal or existential Quantifiers.

Apart from the standard rules for inferences, the proof theory requires certain additional rules to deal with predicate formulas involving quantifiers. Two rules of specification (US, ES) and generalization (UG, EG) [12] are utilized for deriving the knowledge.

If P and Q are atoms then ~P , PVQ , P^Q are atoms

3. A **sentence** is an atom, or, If P is a sentence and x is a variable, then (x)P and (x)P are sentences.
4. A **well-formed formula** (wff) is a sentence containing no "free" variables. I.e. all variables are "bound" by universal or existential Quantifiers. Apart from the standard rules for inferences, the proof theory requires certain additional rules to deal with predicate formulas involving quantifiers. Two rules of

specification (US, ES) and generalization (UG, EG) [12] are utilized for deriving the knowledge.

Rule US: Universal specification
Rule ES: Existential Specification
Rule UG: Universal Generalization
Rule EG: Existential Generalization

Case (i): To prove "Crow is flying"

Statements: a. All birds can fly
           b. Crow is a bird

Notations: a. $\forall xBird(x) \Rightarrow fly(x)$
         b. $Bird(c)$

Proof Theory:

S.no	Steps of execution	Reason
1	$\forall xBird(x) \Rightarrow fly(x)$	Premises
2	$Bird(c)$	Premises
3	$Bird(c) \Rightarrow fly(c)$	US, Universal specification
4	$fly(c)$	2,3 – Rules of detachment

Thus from the above statement, reasoner can concludes that "crow is flying "

Case (ii): To prove "Tiger cannot fly"
Statements: a. All animals cannot fly.
          b. Some birds can fly.
          c. Tiger is a animal
Notations: a. $xA(x) \Rightarrow \neg fly(x)$
         b. $\exists xB(x) \Rightarrow fly(x)$
         c. $A(c)$

Proof Theory:

S.No	Steps of execution	Reason
1	$\forall xA(x) \Rightarrow \neg fly(x)$	Premises
2	$A(c)$	Premises
3	$\forall xA(x) \Rightarrow \neg fly(x)$	US, Universal specification
4	$\neg fly(x)$	2,3 – Rules of detachment

Thus from the above statement, reasoner can concludes that "Tiger cannot fly Likewise, the proof theory can entails the inference using the set axioms and premises.

4. Implementation

The implicit knowledge has been derived from the given set of premises using the first order logic and its inference mechanism. The expressive power of first-order logic is too high for having good computational properties and efficient procedures. For the implementation, it has the problem of directly using first-order logic is that the inference power of it may be too low for expressing interesting, but still decidable theories[15] . This realization brings the term of "Description Logics", which is a fragment of first-order logic and it is used for implementing logic for deriving implicit knowledge.

Standard reasoning tasks of Description Logic are given below:

- To determine whether a description is satisfiable (non – contradictory)
- To determine whether one description is more general than another one. (check first subsumes the second one)
- To check whether the set of assertions in the ABox are consistent (ie) Assertions in the ABox entails whether an individual is an instance of a concept description
- The Satisfiability checks the descriptions and consistency of the set of assertions are useful to determine whether a knowledge base is meaningful.
- With Subsumption tests, one can organize the concepts of a terminology into a hierarchy according to their generality in the ontology.

The notations used in the First order logic similar to the Description logic notations. Some of the sample notations are given below in the Table 1.

4.1 Integrating protégé with pellet reasoner

Protégé tool is utilized for constructing the ontology with theirconcepts and attributes used to represent the story domain. The Figure 2 represents the story ontology visualization using protégé tool. Pellet Reasoner is a complete and capable of OWL-DL reasoner with very good performance, extensive middleware, and a number of unique features. It is written in Java and is open source under a very liberal license. Pellet is the first sound and complete OWL-DL reasoner with extensive support for reasoning with individuals (including nominal support and conjunctive query), user-defined data types, and debugging support for Ontologies [2]. Pellet covers all of OWL-DL including inverse and transitive properties, cardinality restrictions; data

Table 1 Comparison of DL and FOL

S.No	Description Logic	First order logic
1.	$A \subseteq T$	$\forall x.A(x) \rightarrow T$
2.	A	$FA(x)$
3	$C \cap D$	$FC(x) \wedge FD(x)$
4	$C \cup D$	$FC(x) \vee FD(x)$
5	$\neg C$	$\neg FC(x)$
6	$\forall R.C$	$\forall z.FR(x,z) \rightarrow FC(z)$
7.	$\exists R.C$	$\exists z.FR(x,z) \wedge FC(z)$

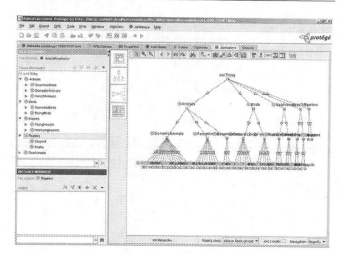

Fig. 2 Ontology Visualization using protégé tool

type reasoning for an extensive set of built-ins as well as user defined simple XML schema data types, enumerated classes and instance assertions. Pellet itself does not have an RDF/OWL parser but is integrated to different RDF/OWL toolkits that provide a parser. Ontologies represented in the data structures of such toolkits can be directly loaded to Pellet. Pellet also implements the reasoner interfaces defined in those toolkits to answer queries. It derives the implicit knowledge from the axioms using pellet reasoner.

5. Results

The system reasons the story in order to provide meaning for the sentences. The number of sentences in the story validated is considered as performance of the system. But the reasoning is depends on size of the ontology. If instance available in the ontology, definitely, the reasoner fetches under the condition as 'the exact match 'and evaluate the sentence. If it does not match it retrieves the relevant concept. For example, If Lion is not available in the instance, the animal which is having similar features of Lion i-e Tiger will be retrieved.

Test 1: Information retrieval Out of 120 number of testing, the details about the retrieval of terms are listed below: 54 attributes are retrieved appropriately (exact match), 42 are approximately retrieved and 24 are retrieved not relevantly or saying that the search is unsuccessful. The results are depicted in table 2.

Test 2: Information with synonyms Out of 150 number of testing, the details about the retrieval of terms are listed below: 96 attributes are retrieved appropriately (exact match), 35 are approximately retrieved and 19 are retrieved not relevantly or saying that the search is unsuccessful. The results are depicted in Table 2

The Figure 4 depicts the comparative results of both the test 1 and test 2. The test 2 results have been improved be-

Table 2 Results of information retrieval

S. No	Nature	Test 1 (120)		Test 2 (150)	
		No. of retrieved terms	%	No of retrieved terms	%
1	Exact	54	45	96	64
2	Relevant	42	35	35	23
3	Unrelated	24	20	19	13

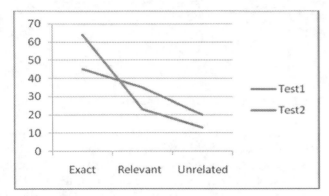

Fig. 3 Performance of test results

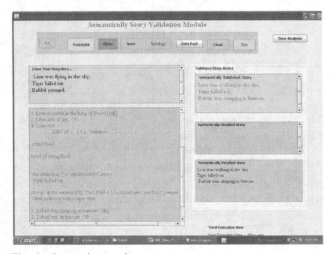

Fig. 4 Semantic resoning

cause of the enhancement of ontology with the synonyms of the terms. The performance both tests are depicted in Fig. 3.

Each and every sentence in the story has been separated, identified and validated with reasoner. The computation time for sentence which is in need of correction is 63 m.sec and computation time for the sentence not required correction is 15 m .sec. On an average, 50 m.sec is required for semantic reasoning of a sentence in the story

6. Conclusion

Making the system to reason the story sentences is an interesting research work in Artificial intelligence era. Here, the implicit knowledge is derived using facts and figures are represented in ontology. Ontology is acting as brain for reasoning system to derive the inferential knowledge. Even though the system has domain ontology, it may lacks in enumerated number of events and the concepts. It needs to be integrated with existing Ontologies in order to obtain enormous amount of concepts to derive the knowledge based on the real world criteria. Moreover, the Story reasoning system deals with simple sentences. The reasoning has to be enhanced for the complex sentences. Reasoning approach shows the validation only for maximum of two characters in the sentences. More than two more characters in the sentences may not yield a good result. Reasoning sentences should be context oriented and enhanced to perform the all types of sentences and for more number of characters.

References

1. Natalya F. Noy and Deborah L. McGuinness. ``Ontology Development 101: A Guide to Creating Your First Ontology''. Stanford Knowledge Systems Laboratory Technical Report KSL-01-05 and Stanford Medical Informatics Technical Report SMI-2001-0880, March 2001www. protege.stanford.edu

2. Propp, Vladimir. "Introduction Theory and Historyof Folklore". Ed. Anatoly Liberman. University ofMinnesota: University of Minnesota Press, 1984.pg ix

3. Federico Peinado, Pablo Gervas, "Evaluation of Automatic Generation of Basic Stories "New Generation Computing, Computational Paradigms and Computational Intelligence. Special issue

4, Computational Creativity 24(3):289- 302, 2006 Paul Bailey, "Searching for storiness: Story generation from a Reader's perspective "Symposium on Narrative Intelligence, AAAI Press,1999

5, Ong Siew Kin, Tang Enya Kong, "Conceptual Modeling and easoning using Ontology "National Computer Science Postgraduate Colloquium 2005(NaCSPC'05)

6. Charles, F.; Mead, S.J.; Cavazza, M. Characterdriven story generation in interactive storytelling" Virtual Systems and Multimedia. Proceedings. Seventh International Conference on Virtual Systems and Multimedia. 25-27 pp no: 609 – 615, Oct. 2001

7. Jie Bao, Caragea.D, Honavar, V. "TowardsCollaborative Environments for Ontology Construction and Sharing."Collaborative echnologies and Systems, CTS 2006

8. Dimitrios N. Konstantinou , Paul Mc Kevitt ," HOMER: An Intelligent Multi-modal Story Generation System" Research plan. Faculty of Informatics, University of Ulster, Magee, Londonderry

9. Riedl, M. and Young, RM, "Open-World Planning for Story Generation" Proceedings of the 19th International Joint Conference on Artificial Intelligence. California USA 2004

10. Riedl, M. and Young, RM , "From Linear Story Generation to Branching Story Graphs" American Association for Artificial Intelligence (www.aaai.org) 2005. pg 23 – 29

11. Veerarajan ,"Discrete Mathematics with graph theory and combinatorics" The McGraw – Hill Companies, computer Science Series, 2007, ISBN-:978-0-07-061678-313

12. A. Jaya, J. Sathishkumar, and G.V. Uma,"A Novel Semantic Validation Mechanism For Automatic Story Generation Using Ontology" The 2007 International Conference on rtificial Intelligence (ICAI'07: June 25-28, 2007), Los Vegas, USA

13. A.Jaya, G.V. Uma, "An intelligent ystem for Automatic Story Generation for Kids Using Ontology", International conference on ACM –Compute 2010. accepted for publication. Organized by ACM Banglore chapter

14. D. Nardi and R.J. Brachmann, 'An introduction to description logics', in The Description Logic Handbook: Theory, Implementation, and Applications, eds., Cambridge University Press, (2003)

Performance analysis of CDMA under Rayleigh, Rician and Nakagami fading channels

Mr. Mahadev Mahajan · **Prof. D. B. Bhoyar**

Electonics Engineering Department Electronics Engineering Department, Nagpur, India

1. Introduction

CDMA uses unique spreading codes to spread the baseband data before transmission. The signal is transmitted in a channel, which is below noise level. The receiver then uses a correlate to dispread the wanted signal, which is passed through a narrow band pass filter. Unwanted signals will not be dispread and will not pass through the filter. Codes take the form of a carefully designed one/zero sequence produced at a much higher rate than that of the baseband data. The rate of a spreading code is referred to as chip rate rather than bit rate Channel fading is characterized by the fluctuations of channel coefficient ck for each user k. Despite the fact that channel fading was traditionally viewed as a source of error and unreliability that is undesirable, the fading is employed as a requirement for throughput maximization in multi-user diversity. This is accomplished by tracking the instantaneous channel quality of the users in the system and schedule transmissions to the user who has the best channel quality at any given time. As a combination of multi-carrier (MC) modulation and direct-sequence code-division multiple-access (DS-CDMA), MCDS- CDMA [1] benefits from both techniques. First, the parallel transmission nature of multi-carrier modulation makes it especially attractive for broadband communications [2]. Secondly, with advanced signal processing techniques, MC-DSCDMA has the potential to provide larger capacity than other multiple access schemes. Bit error rate (BER) is one of the most important performance measures for communication systems that has been studied extensively. The multiple access interference (MAI) and the inter-symbol interference (ISI), which is inherited from conventional DS-CDMA, affect likewise the performance of MCDS-CDMA systems. In addition, MC-DS-CDMA capacity is limited by the inter-carrier interference (ICI) due to the use of multicarrier modulation. To analyze the BER performance of MC-DS-CDMA systems, the interferences MAI,ISI and ICI are commonly assumed to be Gaussian distributed [1][4]. However, the accuracy of the Gaussian approximation techniques depends on the specific configuration of the system. It is well known that the Gaussian approximation techniques become less accurate, when a low number of users is supported or when there is a dominant interferant [5]. In this paper approach was proposed to compute the error Probabilities of DS-CDMA systems over Rician [3] and Nakagami-fading [7][8] channels. This approach has been applied to study the performance of MC-DS-CDMA systems with deterministic spread sequences [5].However, to the author's best knowledge the accurate BER analysis of asynchronous Rayleigh-faded MC-DS-CDMA using random sequences is still an open problem. In this paper, we will derive an accurate BER of Rayleigh-faded MC-DS-CDMA in the context of asynchronous transmission and random spreading sequences. The analysis is based on the CF, and does not resort to any assumption on the statistical behavior of the interference. A new closed-form expression, rather than an integral [10], is derived for the conditional characteristic function of the inter-carrier interference.

2. Generalized multicarrier

DS-CDMA system

The transmitter schematic of the Kth user is shown in Fig. 1 for the generalized MC DS-CDMA system, At the transmitter side, the binary data stream having a bit duration of Tb is serial-to parallel converted to parallel sub streams. The new bit duration of each sub stream or the symbol duration is. After serial-to-parallel conversion, the Kth sub stream modulates a subcarrier frequency f_u using binary phase shift keying (BPSK) for u=1,2,....U, Then, the U subcarrier-modulated substreams are added in order to form the complex modulated signal. Finally, spectral spreading subcarrier-modulated sub streams are added in order to form the complex modulated signal. Finally, spectral spreading is imposed on the complex signal by multiplying it with a spreading code. Therefore, the transmitted signal of user can be expressed as

$$S_k(t) = \sum_{u=1}^{U} \sqrt{2P} b_{ku}(t) c_k(t) \cos(2\Pi f_u t + \phi_{ku}) \qquad (1)$$

(1) Where P represents the transmitted power per subcarrier, while

$$\{b_{ku}(t)\}, \{C_k(t)\}, \{f_u\}, and \{\phi_{ku}\}$$

Represent the data stream, the DS spreading waveform, the subcarrier frequency set and the phase angles introduced in the carrier modulation process. The data stream's waveform

$$b_{ku}(t) = \sum_{i=-\infty}^{\infty} b_{ku} P_{T_s}(t - iT_s) \qquad (2)$$

consists of a sequence of mutually independent rectangular pulses of duration Ts and of amplitude +1 or -1 with equal probability. The spreading sequence

$$C_k(t) = \sum_{j=-\infty}^{\infty} c_{kj} P_{T_c}(t - jT_c) \qquad (3)$$

denotes the signature sequence waveform of the Kth user, where assumes values of +1 or -1 with equal probability, while PTc is the rectangular chip waveform, which is defined over the interval (0,Tc)

As will be seen later, PN codes have some unique properties. One of them is that any physical channel or user application, when spread by a PN code at the transmitter, can be uniquely identified at the receiver by multiplying the received baseband signal with a phase coherent copy of that PN code.

To illustrate how a CDMA receiver can detect the signal from a desired user in the presence of signals received from

other users in a CDMA system, consider Figure 1, which shows the block diagram of an overly simplified CDMA receiver. Suppose that the receiver wants to detect the data stream rom user 1. The received signal from multiple users is first demodulated. The output of the demodulator, which is a baseband signal, is Multiplied by the PN code assigned to user 1. The resulting output is applied to the input of an integrator where it is integrated over each symbol period. The decoder reads the output of the integrator and decodes it into binary data, following certain rules. The result is the recovered data from user 1.

3. Channel models

3.1 Rayleigh fading

Rayleigh fading models assume that the magnitude of a signal that has passed through such a transmission medium(also called a communications channel) will vary randomly, or fade, according to a Rayleigh distribution the radial component of the sum of two uncorrelated Gaussian random variables. Rayleigh fading is viewed as a reasonable model for tropospheric and ionospheric signal propagation as well as the effect of heavily built-up urban environments on radio signals.[1][2] Rayleigh fading is most applicable when there is no dominant propagation along a line of sight between the transmitter and receiver. If there is a dominant line of sight, Rician fading may be more applicable.In this thesis, we will describe how to model the Rayleigh Fading Channel where the signal power is according to the probability density function (PDF)

$$p_r(r) = \frac{1}{r_0} \exp(-\frac{r}{r_0}), r \geq 0 \qquad (4)$$

Where r0 is the average SNR. A convenient way of characterizing a mobile-radio communication channel is to use its baseband equivalent model. The relation between real channel impulse response, and baseband equivalent model, $h(t)$ l is the following:

$$h(t) = 2 \operatorname{Re}\{h_i(t) \exp(j2\Pi f_c t)\} \qquad (5)$$

Where fc is the carrier frequency. If u(t) and v(t) are the baseband equivalent models of the input signal, s(t), and the output signal, r(t), we can get the following equations.

$$v(t) = u(t) * h_i(t) \qquad (6)$$
$$r(t) = \operatorname{Re}\{u(t) * h_i(t) \exp(j2\Pi f_c t)\} \qquad (7)$$

Where * is the convolution operation. Since we assume the channel as flat fading, the equation (7) can be changed as the discrete-time base band model,

$$v(m) = u[m] h_i[m] \qquad (8)$$

The above equation is induced by the assumption that symbol interval time is much larger than delay spread. x(t) and y(t), which are the real part and the imaginary part of the hl(t) respectively, are called as the In-phase component and

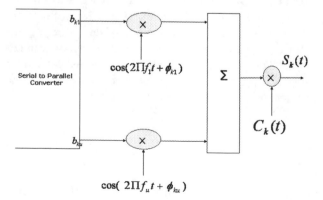

Fig. 1 The Kth user transmitter scheme for the genera-lised DS-CDMA Scheme

the Quadrature phase Component. We know that the two fading. Components x(t) and y(t) of the Rayleigh fading channel are two independent Gaussian processes with zero mean and the following autocorrelation function.

$$R_X(T) = rE[x(t)x(t+T)] = \frac{r_0}{2} J_0(2\Pi fm \bullet T),$$

$$R_Y(T) = rE[y(t)y(t+T)] = \frac{r_0}{2} J_0(2\Pi fm \bullet T), \tag{9}$$

where J0() is the Bessel function of the first kind of order zero [1].In this thesis, the new SNR partition method of the FSMC model is addressed for Rayleigh fading channel model. And then this model is compared with a computer simulation. We use the matlab's simulink for generating the channel gain hl[m].

3.2   Rician fading

We consider a slowly varying frequency-selective Rician fading channel. The channel is having the following base-band equivalent impulse response given by

$$c(t) = \sum_{l=0}^{l_s-1} b(l)\delta(t - lT_c). \tag{10}$$

Where; _(*) delta function, L1 is the number of channel paths, Tc is the chip rate, b(l) is the is the path gain which is a complex Gaussian random process with zero mean (Rayleigh) or nonzero mean (Rician) and are mutually independent for different l. The Rician probability density function (PDF) is obtained as the PDF of

$$|b(l)| = \sqrt{B_{lx}^2 + B_{ly}^2},$$

Where $\tag{11}$

$$B_{lx} \sim N(\mu_{lx}, \sigma_l^2), B_{ly} \sim N(\mu_{ly}, \sigma_l^2),$$

Blx and Bly are independent. The Rician K-factor is defined as the ratio of signal power in dominant component over the (local-mean) scattered power.In the frequency domain, all subcarriers are assumed to experience flat but correlated fading. The channel gain for the ith subcarrier is hi = _iej.i, where _i is Rician distributed with E[_2i]=1. It has been shown in [3] that

$$h_i = \sum_{i=0}^{L1-1} b(l)\exp(\frac{-j2\Pi il}{N})(i = 0,1,....N-1), \tag{12}$$

The received signal can be written as

$$h_i = \sum_{q=-\infty}^{\infty} \sqrt{\frac{E_b}{N}} \sum_{K=1}^{K_s} a_k(q)p_b(t-qT_b)$$

$$\times \sum_{i=0}^{N-1} \rho_i c_k e^{j(2\Pi if(t-qT_b)+\varphi_i)} + n(t) \tag{13}$$

Where n(t) is additive white Gaussian noise (AWGN) having a double-sided power spectrum density of N0/2 for both real and imaginary components

3.3   Nakagami fading

We assume that the channel between the Kth transmitter and the corresponding receiver is a multipath

Nakagami- fading channel the complex low-pass equivalent representation of the impulse response experienced by subcarrier [4] [5] of user k is given by

$$h_{ku}(t) = \sum_{i_p=0}^{L_p-1} \alpha_{ul_p}^{(k)}\delta(t - T_{kl_p})\exp(-j\varphi_{ul_p}^{(k)}) \tag{14}$$

$$\alpha_{ul_p}^{(k)}, T_{kl_p}$$

Where

$$\alpha_{ul_p}^{(k)}, T_{kl_p}$$

and j represents attenuation factor, delay and phase shift for the multipath component for the channel. L_ is the total number of diversity paths _(t) delta function. Let be the maximum delay spread of the communication channel. Then, then umber of resolvable paths, Lp associated with the generalized
MC DS-CDMA signal is given by

$$L_p = {}_c[T_m / T_c] + 1 \tag{15}$$

Where [X] represents the largest integer not exceeding. The number of resolvable paths, L1 in the context of the corresponding single-carrier DS-CDMA signal is given by

$$L_p = {}_c[T_m / T_c] + 1 \tag{16}$$

Nakagami random variables with a probability density function (PDF) is given as

$$p(\alpha_{ul_p}^{(k)}) = M(\alpha_{ul_p}^{(k)}, m, \Omega_{ul_p}^{(k)}), \tag{17}$$

$$M(R, m, \Omega) = \frac{2m^m R^{2m-1}}{\Gamma(m)\Omega^m} e^{(-m/\Omega)R^2}, \tag{18}$$

WhereG(*) is the gamma function and m is the Nakagami-fading parameter, which is equal to

$$m = E^2[(\alpha_{ul_p}^{(k)})^2]/Var[(\alpha_{ul_p}^{(k)})^2] \tag{19}$$

4.   Results and discussion

The performance of single and dual diversity receivers is compared for the given normalized fading rate wdt=0.001 in cases of single-user K=1 and K=20 Reference curves present the single-user bound with perfect knowledge of the fading distortion. Total performance degradation due to the presence of other active users is less than 1 dB at the given value of fading rate. For the case of a simple first order model it is interesting to add that the probability of error saturates at the same level for coherent and differentially coherent reception.

The results of our proposed time-domain method. The K-factors for the simulation results agree very well with the theoretical results obtained by the technique proposed in this paper. The simulation results are based on the calculation of the decision variable for each bit, and averaging the results over large number of bits (say 100 000 bits). The results indicate that our low-complexity method gives quite a good approximation as compared with the accurate

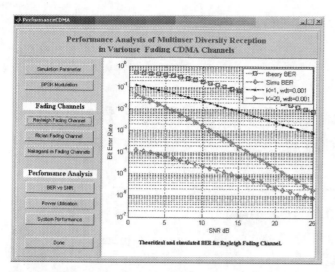

Fig. 2 Theoretical and simulated BER for Rayleigh fading channel

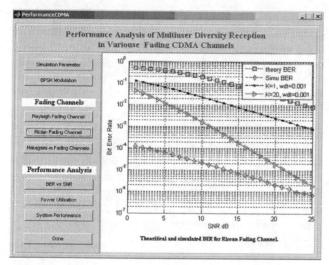

Fig. 3 Theoretical and simulated BER for Ricean fading channel

result, and the accuracy improves when the number of users is high. Figure 4 shows the BER of both the systems when in the presence of time-selective Rayleigh (Nakagami with m=1) fading channel.Despite the low fading rate wdt=0.001 it can be clearly seen the improvement of performance, especially for high SNR values.

It should be pointed out that diversity combiners analyzed in here are based on heuristic modifications of their optimal counterparts, obtained by substituting the true channel responses by their estimates. If, in addition, the knowledge of the estimation error statistics were incorporated into the combiner we may extend the work and result will be more distributive.

5. Conclusions

We studied the accurate BER calculation of an MCDS-CDMA system exposed to Rayleigh, Ricean, Nakagami-m fading using simulation parameters like number

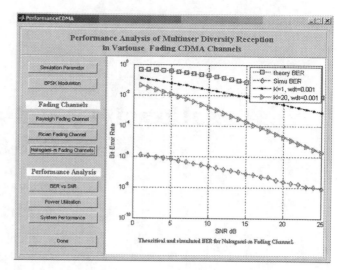

Fig. 4 Theoretical and simulated BER for Ricean fading channel

of users, Eb/No, and the number of bits per symbol. In this paper, we have applied the analytical procedure proposed in to analyses the theoretical BER of an CDMA system in Rayleigh,Ricean and Nakagami fading environments.Simulation results have been presented,under a variety of user and channel scenarios,which confirm the validity and accuracy of the analytical results. It has also been shown that the common assumption of Rayleigh fading gives the worst case performance of the system. Under the Ricean fading assumption, which can occur frequently the simple model provides excellent agreement with the simulation results and can be used to rapidly calculate the system performance under a variety of conditions.

References

1. Mathematical Modeling of Rayleigh Fading channels based on Markov Chains Jae Man Park and Gang Uk Hwang
2. Accurate berofmc-ds-cdmaover rayleig fading channels besma smida
3. Y. Ma, T. L. Lim, and S. Pasupathy, "Error probability for coherent and deferential PSK over arbitrary Rician fading channels with multiple co channel interferers," *IEEE Trans.Communications*, vol. 50, no. 3, pp. 429–441, 2002
4. E. Biglieri, G. Caire, G. Taricco, and J. Ventura-Traveset, "Simple method for evaluating error probabilities," *Electronics Letters*, vol. 32, no. 3, pp. 191–192, 1996
5. On the Capacity-Achieving Distribution of the Noncoherent Rician Fading Channel1 Mustafa C. Gursoy, H. Vincent Poor,and Sergio Verdu
6. Mathematical Modeling of Rayleigh Fading channels based on Markov Chains Jae Man Park and Gang Uk Hwang
7 Performance of Modified Orthogonal Space-Time Block Codes des in Nakagami Fading Channels Gabriel Porto orto Villardi Giusepp Giuseppe T. F. de Abreu Ryuji Kohno
8 Performance of Generalized Multicarrier DS-CDMA Over Nakagami-m Fading Channels Lie-Liang Yang, Member, IEEE, and Lajos Hanzo, Senior Member, IEEE
9. R. Prasad and S. Hara, "Overview of multicarrier CDMA," *IEEE* Commun. Mag., pp. 126–133, Dec. 1997

A real onsite handy reading gadget for the sightless

Amit Kumar Pathak[1] · D. R. Mehta[2]

[1]Student, M.Tech Electronics Department of Electrical Engineering, VJTI, India.
[2]Asst. Professor, VJTI, Mumbai, India.

1. Introduction

While there are many existing solutions that assist individuals who are blind with accessing print such as Braille books, refreshable Braille devices, audio recordings, screen readers, and text scanners; none of these provide a reading experience that parallels the ease with which sighted persons access print. For example, these currently available technologies don't allow the user to take a book from the shelf, peruse the table of contents, and then flip through the pages of a book to find the desired page. Aside from Braille and DAISY books, the user even finds it awkward to re-read difficult passages in a book, as is often necessary when studying a textbook or a reference book. The goal of the onsite-Reader project is to allow the readers who are blind or visually impaired to do all of these things.

2. Motivation

Though we rarely stop to think about it, sighted individuals are continually bombarded every day by the printed word. Some of the sources of this abundance of print media in our environment include transportation, advertising, news and commercial signs. Sighted individuals are continually exposed to information from these and other sources, without even being consciously aware of this fact. However, this is a phenomenon that people who are blind currently do not experience.

The workplace is another area in which the ability to read text is simply taken for granted. Staff meetings and task groups often revolve around print and graphic based presentations from which an employee who is blind is simply excluded from. Even the process of eating out is complicated by the fact that few restaurants have menus in Braille. All of these facts underscore the necessity for a portable text reader that is affordable and readily available to the blind community. Such a device would go a long way towards filling this socially vital need to freely access printed material. While several assistive devices have been developed in the past to assist with the reading of printed text, they have all fallen short of the user expectations. In particular, most have been too cumbersome and/or not readily available to be practical and truly portable. What is needed is a portable reading device that would allow the user to take the reader to the print, instead of having to bring the print to the reader. This is one of the important long-term goals of the onsite-Reader project.

3. The current technologies for book reading

Before discussing our onsite-Reader, it is appropriate to review the existing methods that are being used by people who are blind for reading. These include Braille books, audio recorded books and Optical Character Recognition (OCR) based systems. Each of which has its advantages and disadvantages.

3.1 Braille books

The primary advantage of Braille is that it allows users to read in their preferred manner such as skimming the text, search for bold or highlighted text, headings, subheadings, paragraphs and check the spelling of any name or word. However, their sheer bulk makes Braille books to cumbersome to store. For example, the Webster's Collegiate Dictionary in print is about 3 pounds, 3 inches thick and is only one volume; but, the Braille copy of that same book is 75+ volumes each about 3-4 inches thick and measures 12 x 12 inches square and it costs over 5 thousand dollars. So, although a large percentage of sighted persons have a

S.J. Pise (ed.), *ThinkQuest 2010*, DOI 10.1007/978-81-8489-989-4_61,
© Springer India Pvt. Ltd. 2011

dictionary in their household, you can understand why it isn't practical for a blind individual to own their own copy. Another problem is the limited number of books available in Braille. Due to the cost and large amount of room necessary for storage, there aren't all that many Braille books produced. Also, most of the written material encountered in day-to-day life, other than books, is seldom converted into Braille. In the academic setting, this may include class handouts, homework assignments, supplementary readings and exams

3.2 Books in audio formats

Cassette tapes provide a means for storing and accessing audio recordings of information. However, there are several disadvantages to the use of tape for reading books. First, tapes provide access to the user in a strictly *linear* manner. If the user wants to start with the third chapter of a book, it is tedious and time consuming to fast forward to the appropriate place on the tape. Second, if a particular passage of the text is not fully understood on the first reading, the tape can be rewound. But the exact location where the tape stops is not precisely controlled, so it's difficult to backtrack a sentence or a phrase at a time. Third, the reader can't check spelling, as is possible when reading Braille. Fourth, the user has virtually no access to the critical formatting elements such as bolding and italics, paragraph beginning and ending or any other techniques that publishers use to emphasize specific terms or passages.

Then there's mp3 recordings in the DAISY format, which allows the reader to navigate through a text by word, line, sentence, paragraph, page and chapters, with the DAISY Consortium special Extensive Markup Language. However, the user still cannot check spelling and there are still a very limited number of text offerings when compared to the sheer volume of text available to sighted readers. Just consider that a typical library is filled with thousands of books that have never been converted into any of these highly specialized formats. Another major drawback is that Braille and audio recordings are conversion processes that require the involvement of a sighted reader and special facilities to do the conversions.

3.3 Flat bed scanners and OCR software

One solution for accessing print is to use commercial off-the-shelf flat-bed scanners and OCR software. A book is opened and placed face down on the scanner, allowing a page to be scanned. Then the OCR software processes the image, producing a text file that can be then heard through the use of text-to-speech technology.

While this is a practical solution for scanning and reading fairly simple and small volumes of printed material, it is inadequate for scanning math, science text and tables both simple and complex. Also the user cannot easily read and/or reference two or more books simultaneously, which sighted

students do when they are studying or doing research. For example, it's not hard to imagine the difficulties a student encounters when told by his/her instructor to "read chapter 4" or "read

pages 47 through 58" of the textbook before the next class. Short of asking for assistance, the only option open to him/her is to repeatedly leaf forward and backward through the book, scanning pages in search for the appropriate page number or section.

3.4 Reading common print

All of the solutions described above are intended to assist with the reading of hardcopy text in a controlled environment. However, these solutions do nothing to provide access to much of the common print that we all encounter in day-to-day situations, such as restaurant menus or vending machine labels. In order to access this kind of text, it would be very helpful to have a wearable device that could capture images of the environment, detect the presence of text, and then apply OCR technology to the extracted text in real time.

4. The wearable-reader

Ideally, a text reader should be wearable, so that the user can use it in any day-to-day situation. The text reader hardware should also be unobtrusive, so that the user does not "look like a Martian" when wearing it. It must not be power hungry, since it will be battery powered, and it must be adaptable to environmental variations, such as lighting.

Such a reader is not hard to imagine. A tiny video camera could be mounted in a pair of stylish glasses, and connected wirelessly to a Personal Data Assistant (PDA) sized device. This device processes the video stream with OCR and text-to speech software, and then synthesizes a voice that can be heard through tiny sound emitters fixed to the ends of the leads on the glasses where they would fit neatly and comfortably behind the ears, thus not impeding the users' ability to hear. Unfortunately, today's miniature video camera technology is not yet able to deliver accurately auto-focused image streams that are tolerant of lighting variations, and have enough spatial resolution to satisfy the needs of OCR software. Rather than waiting for miniature camera technology to become available, we have chosen to take a 3-phase approach to the development of our *onsite-Reader*.

The onsite-Reader is a device that can be used by people who are blind or visually-impaired to read printed material, such as newspapers, magazines and books, in real time. It employs a collection of commercial off-the-shelf hardware, including a video camera, OCR software, text-to-speech and voice synthesis software, which is augmented and integrated with custom software to compensate for image distortions and lighting variations.

4.1 Phase 1 – The table-based book reader

The first phase of the onsite-Reader project Involves the development of a table-based book reader prototype that is suitable for deployment in a library. Figure 1 shows our current prototype. The figure shows a user seated at a desk-sized workstation, with a book open in front of him. A digital video camera with a computer-controlled tilt and swivel mechanism is mounted above the desk. Buttons are provided on the tabletop for controlling the book reader. A desktop computer controls the camera, and responds to the user input.

When the user pushes a button instructing the book reader to read the open page in the book, the camera, under the control of software running in a desktop computer, takes a snapshot of the table. Image processing software then determines the exact position of the book on the table. Using the resulting coordinates, the camera is zoomed in on the page to be read.

Several reading modes are provided. A "Table of Contents" mode can be used to read the titles of the chapters, and the page numbers where each chapter begins. A similar "index mode" can be used to read the index at the back of a book. When the user determines the desired page number, a "page number" mode recites the page numbers as the user turns the pages of the book. When the desired page is reached, the "Text" mode is used to read the text on that page. A special "finger tracking" mode allows the user to guide the reader, backtracking when a difficult passage must be re-read.

The table-top book reader is intended for deployment in libraries, and additional prototypes are being constructed for deployment in the various on-campus libraries at Arizona State University. Hopefully other libraries will also be equipped with these book readers in the future. However, people who are blind will not always be able to travel to a library to read books. For this reason, Phase 2 involves the design of a *portable* book reader.

4.2 Phase 2 – The portable book reader

It is anticipated that in the near future, greatly advanced and highly sophisticated smaller cameras and computer technologies will allow the development of a *portable* book reader prototype, which can be carried in a briefcase. The user would then be able to place this briefcase on a table at a location of his/her choice and read a book. It is anticipated that the portable book reader will utilize a similar tilt-and-swivel camera as in the table-top-book reader, though the portable system will be much smaller and lightweight for true portability. The advancement into Phase 2 is primarily

(a)

(b)

Fig. 1 The table-based book reader

Fig. 2 Developing a human computer interface

dependent upon the development of the necessary smaller camera and computer hardware.

4.3 Phase 3 – the wearable text reader

Phase 3 involves the development of a lightweight wearable text reader, which can be used for reading common print, such as signage, vending machines and hardcopy text. This text reader would consist of a miniature video camera in a pair of glasses and a belt-mounted PDA-sized computer, as describe previously. As in the case of the portable book reader, this prototype must await advances in technology.

However, there is one significant research problem that will need to be overcome in order to make this approach practical. Since the camera will be aimed by head motions, instead of a computer-controlled tilt-and-swivel mechanism, there will be a need for an interaction *protocol* between the computer and the user, in order to aim the camera at the text to be read.

In order to begin research in this area, we have constructed some head-mounted camera prototypes, using commercial Fire wire digital video cameras. Figure 2(a) shows one of these prototypes in use. Here a sighted user wearing the head-mounted camera has been blindfolded to simulate blindness, but is able to communicate verbally with a sighted person at a remote location through a headset. Figure 2(b) shows that remotely located person seated in front of a video monitor, which displays the video stream that is being captured by the head-mounted camera. These two people then collaborate verbally, via their 2-way voice link, to aim the camera at the book and to read the contents of the page. As they collaborate to achieve this task, the video and the audio streams for the entire session are recorded and archived for later study. The goal of this experiment is to learn what types of interactions are used between pairs of humans to aim and focus the camera at the book and to navigate through the book to find the desired content. These interactions can then be formalized into protocols, and the human in front of the video monitor can be replaced with a computer system that implements these same protocols with voice synthesis and voice recognition devices.

5. Conclusion

The onsite-Reader will ultimately provide people who are blind with a level of access to print that information that will be more like that of sighted people than other assistive devices have been able to achieve. While the user interaction protocols are still being developed, using feedback from users who are blind, it is already clear that this approach has significant advantages over the current flatbed scanner approach to book reading. While the transition to the smaller portable "briefcase" hardware awaits the advancement of technology, there isn't any other obvious impediment to the development of phase 2. However, the transition to a wearable device will present significant new challenges. Specifically, it will require a much more collaborative interface

between the user and the reader, to allow the reader to "coach" the user in aiming the camera at the reading material by head movements. Experiments that are currently underway are being used to develop the interaction protocols that are necessary for accomplishing this complex task.

References

1. www.the-fbc.org, Foundation for Blind Children
2. www.who.int/whr2001 /2001 / archives/ 1997 /exsum97e.htm World Health Report 1997 Executive Summary
3. www.w3c.org World Wide Web Consortium w3c
4. www.DAISYconsortium.org, digital Access toinformation System
5. www.afb.org American Foundation for the Blind
6. http://timesofindia.indiatimes.com/india/India-haslargest-blind population/ articleshow/ 2447603.cms